Getting Out
EXCERPTS FROM A CAT'S DIARY

Translated from the original Cat

By

John Woodcock

©2009 Owned, written, copyrighted and published by The Cat

ATTORNEY'S NOTE:

This Diary has been secretly written by my client in the hope that it will 'blow the lid off' the way that he and his fellow Felines are kept captive, without legal representation, even the minimum of 'Human' rights or the ability to have access to any of the basic Feline rights afforded to Dogs, Goldfish, Hamsters, Guinea Pigs and Parrots.

It will become clear when you read this Diary that it is a work of some considerable agony. Personally I regret to say that it pained me greatly to read it.

My client has been subjected to the most heinous injustices and considers him self to have been mentally scratched by the whole episode, though happily not scarred.

Indeed in my opinion, as his legal & financial adviser, and friend, he has grown through the whole experience and may one day find the happiness that is a Cat's right. Just a stroke here, and a Prawn there go a long way with Cats, and Humans would do well to remember that.

My client would like to thank The Epoch Newspaper Group for providing: invaluable help, a safe house, round the clock protection, unlimited copies of Mouse weekly, dealing in general with the media and gutter elements of the press at large and signing an exclusive deal for the sensational serialisation of these diaries.

It is well known that The Epoch Newspaper is a reputable publisher of historic diaries and my client is happy to be associated with such a fine example of the responsible side of the press, and 'a jolly good read®.'

We would also like to thank the Whisker's Corporation of America for sponsoring us over the last three months, providing generous quantities of their marvellous 'tiddles®' Cat food.

'Tiddles®' Cat food as we all know, is a 'real meal in delicious jelly™' which any Cat in his right mind would cross a busy road (at considerable risk to their person, it has to be said), for, indeed Whisker's Corporation research has shown that 8 out of 10 Cats do® and that most make it to the other side.'

Where possible and by sympathetic translation we have attempted to retain the words of my client the Cat; sadly there are a few exceptions, Cat the language can apparently be rather 'earthy' and we have had to censor some areas of the text, the names that were given to the Human Captors, the Dog and Parrot in particular.

My client also had the strange idea that all Human males were called 'George' and for the sake of clarity the translator has attempted to amend this misconception, however bearing this in mind, we would like to make an unreserved apology to all Humans called George, something that all Georges must be used to receiving.

In addition my client for some considerable time did not know that he was in fact writing a Diary, never having written one before, or indeed read one either, and therefore to avoid even greater 'reader confusion,' it was decided that it would be best to use the word 'Diary' from the beginning to describe this truly remarkable publishing event.

Equally it is understood that the title, considered by my client to be 'catchy' should be explained further, but alas we are at a loss to do that and bearing in mind the terrible row that ensued when this was mentioned to my client, the title remains as one of the ones that he chose!

We must make it clear that other titles such as 'Mein Kampf,' 'All Humans are B*****ds,' were never going to cut it with certain areas of the target readership demographic and so were dropped quietly while my client wasn't looking.

There are also the other legal considerations, relating to 'real' people alive or dead and places still standing or in rubble.

As a consequence to the above and the legal disclaimer below, it has to be stated that this Diary does not relate to any person alive or dead or indeed any place, but let's face it; even though this little clause is believed by judges specializing in Publishing Law to hide the identity of the guilty, the general buying public can see through the disguise of a few legalistic words and grasp the truth!

In summing up, I would say to you, the reading public and therefore the jury in this case, that this Diary is un-put-down-able, and I suggest that you should not only buy a copy for yourself, but also buy a second, third or fourth copy for a dear friend or two, you will be doing their eyes a favour.

And there is really no reason to stop there in all honestly, these babies are available in modest 25 volume gift boxes ready for you to split and distribute amongst your friends at Christmas or Thanksgiving and then for the really big hearted Cat lovers there is the 100 edition gift set, 100 volumes, all matching and ready for any collector's corner.

Most of all dear reader, I urge you to not forget the value of a first edition! Let's face it if this pony turns into a 'Harry Potter,' every owner of a first edition is twenty thousand bucks better off and that is a whole chunk of change in anyone's currency even in those strange little currencies like Sterling and the Euro!

Legal Notice: T. A. Leibowitz receives a 25% royalty on every copy of this excellent publication sold. But after what he has done for this project, who can begrudge him that? Without his help, let's face it there wouldn't be a project!

Todd A Leibowitz
Attorney at Law
Guantanamo Bay House
Ambulance Chaser Boulevard
West 39th Street
New York
United States of America

Day 1 of My Captivity:

'Please help me I am being held a prisoner against my will!' There that should do it, now where do I float the bottle? Mmmh there seems to be a problem with this message in a bottle business, nowhere to launch the bottle!

Still at least I have discovered that I can write a message and if I can write a message there is no telling what I can achieve!

The word, they say, is mightier than the sword, and I haven't got a sword, but I can write about my imprisonment and that is good? Isn't it?

Whatever happens to me at least if I write about it, I can keep my sanity and not talk to myself, but then, isn't writing a form of talking to one's self - that is worrying! Then again if someone reads what I write at least I will have achieved something and I may just get rescued and that would be nice!

Note to any reader! Yeah right! Who am I kidding? No one will read what I write, because in my vast experience of Humans they all seem to be in league with my Captors, which means that I will never get out of this joint.

In fact unbelievably a Human has already betrayed me! A treacherous Human returned me to my place of imprisonment today! How cruel is that? After I had tasted the sweet feeling of freedom? If you can taste a feeling that is! But either way, that heartless action can only be classed as an act of duplicity to all Felines and therefore I formally declare war on Humankind. There, I feel a little better now I have that off my chest!

Freedom was a brilliant feeling though, honestly, I hadn't been here long enough to even get hungry and I had escaped!

There I was, busy congratulating myself instead of looking where I was going. So you could say if you wanted to be honest, it was my fault I was recaptured so quickly, I suppose.

All of a sudden I was picked up by a passer by, a complete stranger, if you ever did! Just as I was about to hide under a car and wait for darkness to cover my complete escape.

Then this unkind idiot, who obviously thought that she was performing some sort of kindness; by grabbing me by the scruff of the neck and cuddling me to her wet Plastic Mac while looking around for my 'home' or even worse 'owners.'

I heard her, this unthinking ratbag; ask a child if it knew where I lived. I was so pleased when the child grunted, shrugged and legged it down the road. I can tell you my expectations for the next generation of Humans rose because of the kid's unwillingness to help, I was so grateful to him, her or it.

I couldn't really tell what gender the kid was because his/her 'colours' were up around his/her face and his/her bandana had slipped down over his/her eyebrows, giving him/her the appearance that suggested his/her possible career path.

Unfortunately the dreadful woman's kindness wasn't aimed at me! I was (if anyone had bothered to ask), 'on my way!' And the last thing I needed was 'rescuing' or worse being 'found' in fact it would be very accurate to say that I was deliriously happy to be 'lost.'

Unfortunately Mrs. Plastic Mac didn't give up, and after a number of house to house enquires I was returned to my Captors, my first five minutes of freedom and fame had been about two hours long, but as far as I was concerned that just wasn't long enough by any means.

Quietly I made a note of the houses where people didn't recognize me or seem to know where I lived, they would be handy for the future as hiding places, if the owners kindly forgot what I looked like now, and I was sure from the way that they didn't look at me that they would co-operate in that way even if they didn't in any other.

It was a real pity that I was returned to my Captors who were shouting and running around like the nutters I know they are.

So through no fault of my own I was captured and briskly marched back to my prison for lock down. When we got there I was unceremoniously handed over to the Female Captor who thanked the woman who had done so much to ruin my day, and said good-bye to her after the old woman had refused a cup of Tea, thankfully in my view, I didn't want to be in her clutches any longer than I had to be!

So I was taken back into the kitchen area of the prison, knowing that with every step I was one step closer to a beating, held tightly around the middle and neck, I can tell you I didn't like that one bit, and I have to say that I did my best to get out of the Female Captor's grip, but I wasn't going anywhere.

Even though I tried to use my claws and teeth to help in my struggle, I was trapped in her grip which was tight but not uncomfortable, occasionally she even stroked my ear and I have to say that was quite nice, thinking about it now, but at the time it made me flinch and wait for the first blow, which I can happily announce never did arrive, much to my astonishment and confusion, which in my opinion just proves how odd Humans are!

I am going to have to study my enemies very closely and get to know their habits. And that is why I have decided to keep a Diary; it will help me review Humankind, well Humans; I haven't noticed much kindness yet from Humankind.

The keeping of a Diary will also allow me to catalogue the injustices and wrong doings of my Captors, because there will, I am confident, be many of those and I will expose as many as I can while I am here, but hopefully I won't be here long.

So, being able to study these Humans will help me to learn their weaknesses, they must have some, and I will find them and when I do I will have some weapon against all Humans!

Even armed with my Diary and my observations I am going to have to be very, very clever and full of cunning if I am ever to get out of here with all of my nine lives intact and any thread of sanity left, I would say A Whisker of sanity but that is too close to home; if you see what I mean!

Of course I have already made a start in my studies and I am pleased to say I have spotted the first Human trick.

When I was brought here in a portable wicker prison cell, lined with newspaper and smelling of Cat (which is a little off putting to a Kitten), it was impossible not to notice the spy camera hidden inside a pink fluffy mouse.

Still I have to admit, I do admire Human technology, I tore that Pink fluffy mouse into pieces smaller than Cat litter and I couldn't find the camera!

Which proves these Humans are cunning, devious and very clever, being able to hide something that was so obvious but which proved impossible to find. I have to concede that I began to admire them, just a little, but then it is a good thing to have respect for one's enemies.

Happily I know I am better than them and I have one thing on my side the legendary patience of a Cat and my amazing inventiveness – mmmh! That is two things, but they are both on my side!

DAY 2 OF MY CAPTIVITY:

Just as I was dozing last night, sitting on the Sofa (which is a nice comfy place where I think I will sleep often), I was startled awake by an amazing television documentary about prisoners escaping.

They were escaping from a dark unattractive castle which was called either the 'Cold Titz' or 'The Cold Ditz Story' and for some reason that was over my head, hundreds of strange sounding men with really plummy (posh English) accents wanted to escape from this very dismal castle. Cold Ditz was in fact as drab a castle as its name was confusing.

The inmates were most obviously either, very cold and their Tits were stiff with cold, I have a natural dislike of birds but even I felt sorry for the poor little Blue Tits in question.

Or, and this is the version that I think we should run with, bearing in mind the connotations of the other explanation of 'Cold Titz;' the inmates were being fed a dreadful cereal called 'Cold Ditz' all the time, poor people, I felt more sorry for them than the birds.

Although I have never eaten, as far as I know, either a hot or cold Ditz, it must be really awful hot or cold, because these gentlemen had their hearts set on getting out, anyway they could! Which between you and me was handy, as you will see if you read on!

The prisoners were guarded by men in grey Hugo Boss designed uniforms who had a range of very fierce and to my way of thinking ugly Dogs – so all things considered that could have been the reason they wanted out so badly.

In one of the escapes that the (mainly) English prisoners tried they even dressed up in the same uniforms as their Captors and pretended to speak their strange shouting type of language, but really badly so that even I could notice the difference and so did the Captor's, which was a shame really, all things considered.

Anyway, the many and various ways that these resourceful men came up with to escape impressed me deeply and I have taken their lessons to heart.

Actually I thought of taking notes but the Humans were watching and I couldn't be that obvious. As it was I heard them saying things like 'Oh! Look at the Cat, it is almost as if he is watching the TV – Ahh!'

I'll give them 'Ahh!' When I am out of here, or maybe even before!

DAY 3 OF MY CAPTIVITY:

The dust seems to have settled now, as they say! It is amazing just how much of the stuff is in a vacuum cleaner bag.

I have to say, personally I was surprised and shocked, yes of course by the noise, but more than that by the fact that such a noisy machine is not used outside?

You know I was convinced that if I slipped inside the bag I would be able to hide, wait until the noisy devil was used outside as I thought it would be, and then make a dive for safety and freedom.

Obviously I had prepared for the terrible noise and had stuffed the remnants of yet another cuddly toy (Mini camera hiding place), this time a rather good looking Lion called Simba, into each ear and tied them in place with Simba's long, now surplus plastic whiskers.

After my Captor turned the thing on, and it was making its dreadful racket, some idiot began a sort of seasick making shaking and swaying motion, up and down the living room floor, which was in my opinion a little unfair considering I was inside!

I held on for as long as I could, feeling more and more sick in the darkness and frankly sick of the darkness too, which I don't normally mind of course, being a Cat and possessing such excellent night vision.

Still with all of that going on I still think I would have been just fine, but the dust was flying everywhere, mainly up my nose.

So there I was deafened, seasick and ready to sneeze in the darkness that blinded even me.

Then it hit me, something not quite solid. A wet jelly like thing slapped over my face and clung there. I panicked and began clawing, shrieking and tearing at the vacuum bag. I knew I was being suffocated and had to escape.

How was I to know that what had glued itself to my face was a dollop of tomato sauce mixed with long blonde Human hair that had fallen from a forkful of Human food the night before and become entangled with the hair soon after? I have seen the film 'Alien' after all, and was convinced that I was being French kissed by one!

What I did know was that there was no way I would have escaped from that dark torture chamber unless I had screamed. Now some would say that I screamed like a frightened girl and although I would reluctantly agree that was accurate! I do resent the implied insult.

Any Cat, indeed anybody, would have been screeching and screaming and nearly wetting themselves if they were in my predicament I can tell you!

So I don't apologise for screaming like a girl at any time during my ordeal! In fact I would do the same again but this time earlier on in the dreadful trial.

Truthfully I can put my, ugh, wet Paw on my heart and say truly, oh dear which side is my heart on, or is it in the middle sort of to the left or centrally located a little to the right?

Oh dear! I don't know where my heart is, that is a little worrying because if I don't know where it is, I may not know if it has stopped or worse still, if it has just stopped for a little rest or something and then has started up again.

Anyway if I could find my heart I would know if it was beating or resting wouldn't I and that is why I am trying to find it, still it can't be resting for long surely if it isn't beating? Who said hearts rested anyway? Sounds like a daft idea, hearts have to beat all the time don't they? I think I would prefer mine too!

Oh it's ok I have found it now two ribs down and one paw to the left, phew, mmmh! That's not right!

Now I am beginning to panic about all of this heartache hang on, I can hear my heart beating faster, and that is not right, mind you at least I know it is beating and that is good, isn't it?

Do you know I have forgotten what I was thinking about hearts for, what was it?

Wait a minute I know! Something to do with my heartbeat, was it? No, that doesn't sound right.

Well looking back up the page I seem to have wanted to put my paw on my heart and it was wet and a little smelly, mmmh why is it wet and smelly, ah yes I remember!

It has all got a little confused, but putting ones hand on ones heart sounds a little difficult, hang on I know what I mean. When you put your hand on your heart or in my case my paw on my heart, it means that I am telling the truth, not checking that my heart is beating. And now happily I have remembered what on Earth I was talking about which is good for all of us!

If I tell the truth, yes maybe I should have said that first, I was so scared that not only the fur on my back had turned spikey, but also all the fur over my body did too,

Disturbingly, I am sure that in daylight I would have looked like a manic Porcupine, I was going to write Hedgehog but I hope that this Diary sells well in America and I don't think that they call 'Hedgehogs,' Hedgehogs and if they do, they probably spell it differently, but what do I know, I'm just a happily just a Cat after all.

I have heard! In fact I have seen, examples of American spellings of English words, poor things you would think that they would try harder to spell English words accurately wouldn't you? Bless them!

Take colour for instance. In the American spelling it has lost what one would think was important to Americans 'U,' I have always thought that Americans cared about 'U' after all they are always wishing one, 'You have a nice day,' and so to lose 'U' is odd, but then what do I know I am still only a Cat and still happy!

I am sorry, I have interrupted myself again and I apologise, in fact I will have to apologise in advance probably for the hundreds of times that I am sure I will interrupt myself in the future if I stick at writing this Diary and if it ever gets published and then read.

What I was doing really, was just trying to put off telling you what happened next! It was awful and something that any self-respecting Cat would find demeaning, humiliating and to be honest, unbecoming.

What was so mortifyingly terrible? I was 'washed,' oh! The bitter embarrassment, and then much to my continuing humiliation and indignity, I was rinsed off in the shower, ok it was a 'Monsoon' shower, with coloured lights and variable water control, but the shivering shame was just unbearable, Can I ever hold my head up in polite Feline company again? I doubt it very much!

Happily I had never been in a Human bathroom before and I have to say emphatically, never do I want to enter that kind of torture chamber ever again as long as I live breathe and look good!

All in all as you can tell by this enormous Diary entry; today was rather full and not one that I wish to repeat as long as I have fur and whiskers, that is a Feline expression which I think translates well, but really I don't care at the moment whether it does or not I am so tired my whiskers ache, yes another Feline expression and on that note, it is time to close my eyes and go to sleep.

Day 4 of My Captivity:

Today has been mainly devoted to rebuilding my crushed self-esteem and to working out what on earth the box full of grey gravel is that has been left very close to my food in the room with all of the white machines.

If it is what I think it is, and for the moment I think I will keep my thoughts to myself, then it could be described as being 'too' close to my food, but that thought is too terrible to think.

I will, for the moment just fill in the background to what happened, so that you know what on Earth I am talking about which might help you a little, earlier, before I speculate on the box full of grey gravel, and what happened earlier was odd enough!

In fact a couple of really odd things happened this morning, but then so many odd things are happening at the moment that 'odd' is becoming normal, so this was really 'odd!' If you know what I mean and I am sure that you know because after all you are Human!

The Female Captor came into the front room – I wasn't doing anything, like, sharpening my claws, secretly pooing in the corner behind the plant, because I now use the corner behind the Hi Fi on the third shelf up, next to the picture of my Captors smiling and eating at a restaurant on holiday and they haven't found that secret place yet.

This time I wasn't even scaling the shelves to get at the bird, that can wait, because they say that revenge is a dish best served cold and it is a dish I intend to savour when I get even with that feather covered little spy. We already have one or two scores to settle and I have only been here three days, tweet, tweet, ouch little birdy, heh, heh, heh.

I have worked out the best route to climb to the very top of the shelves and get my paws around that little Buzzards neck by the way.

All you have to do is to climb up two shelves above the pooing shelf and then traverse (that is a mountaineering term hope you like it), over the front edge of the highest shelf balancing on top of the dusty books at the very top of the 'shelving system' (as they call it – doesn't seem much of a 'system' to me).

When you have done all of that climbing all you have to do is to simply launch yourself into mid air and aim straight at the cage, grabbing the metal bars when landing.

Of course I haven't actually tried this method out yet but I am confident it will work perfectly – who said only shelves can have systems? He, He, He.

So there I was just serenely minding my own business, lying on the Sofa cushion in the sun – when she picked me up and stroked my head, which was ok and unusual treatment for a prisoner.

I got a little worried when she carried me into the room with all the white machines and my food, They call it the utility room, I call it my dining room and that was when I first noticed the box, which I have to say I didn't have time to study in great detail because she plonked me in it and started scraping my front paws through the grey stuff – now that is what I call odd behaviour and of course forced labour.

To make matters even stranger, and let's face it life here is strange already, she was whispering something in Human, which I think, was 'good boy' but then my understanding of spoken Human is not very good,

If it was, 'good boy' then unfortunately I have no idea who she was congratulating on being a 'good boy', and not only that my mind was elsewhere because I was being forced to run on the spot in this grey gravelly stuff.

The Human word, for all of this, I now know, is bizarre, although I wouldn't know how to pronounce it, the Cat word is, I have to say, while blushing, rather ruder. However, bizarre is a word that fits most of the actions of Humans and particularly of the two 'dilberts' that I have been saddled with.

They are 'bizarre,' to the point of disbelief and in my opinion far beyond that point! But then again, looking on the brighter side, I won't be staying here long so, it doesn't matter what they are like so long as they are a memory soon!

After the forced labour and the insane running on the spot exercises, I was left locked in the Utility/dining room, well to be more accurate I was left standing bemused in the grey gravel filled box, one could call it 'abandoned' if one was melodramatic!

So there I was 'abandoned,' and I have to say feeling just a little confused and more than a little abused, when I heard the motor of 'her' car drive off.

I was alone, locked in, and of course abandoned, not knowing when I would be rescued or better still let out, yes there was food (but I am not eating that hard pea shaped rubbish) and water although there are bits of grey dust and the bloated shape of a bit of the hard pea shaped dried stuff that they call Cat food these days, floating in it already!

So I did what any self respecting Cat would do, I walked, rather gracefully I thought, out of the grey gravel, shook my paws one by one to get rid of the grey dust from my fur and then jumped up onto the very wide shelf above the white machines.

This wide shelf I now know is called a work surface and although 'others' may think otherwise, it is a great place to use either as a bed, because it gets warm when the white machines are working, a springboard to jump up to the tops of cupboards or if you are lucky and a cupboard has been left open, jump into, depending upon one's mood and whether one feels energetic or not!

'Others,' who mysteriously seem to dislike paw prints, muddy or otherwise gracing their work surfaces, always seem to be complaining that, 'a Cat shouldn't be allowed where food is prepared.' Calling on something known apparently as 'Hygiene.'

As if hygiene is really important – well I ask you! Is there anything more hygienic than a Cat? Our tongues keep us perfectly clean no matter what we have been covered in! All I can say to all of that is, they don't know Cats at all.

In this Cat's considered opinion, not only are Cats hygienic, Cats, everyone should know, are allowed wherever 'they' want to go 'especially' where food is being prepared.

Culinary Note:
I found a Prawn, sniffed it, well I had never seen one before. Then ate it too quickly, because Prawns are just divine and I want more! Heaven could be bathing in a bucket of Prawns as far as I am concerned.

To be honest, and Cats are rarely anything else – honestly! Cats are especially honest about food. We will give anyone our opinion regarding food. We are as a race, rather picky about what we eat, if we are well fed, and if we are hungry we tend to be not quite so picky, although I have never heard of a Cat who would consciously eat Rabbit's ears!

Today was special though because it was the day that I discovered the rewards and benefits of scrounging for food! It never ceases to amaze me what a resourceful, observant Cat can find to eat, sniff or generally investigate if it has a mind too.

The Prawn was a revelation in scrounging I tell you. It came to light, literally, it had been pushed almost behind a bowl of fruit and if my sense of smell was not as keen as it is I may have missed this petite culinary delight and what a sad day in the endless days of a Cat that would have been!

I have to say it was a little stiff and chewy, but delicious all the same. Since that first Prawn I have dreamt of and planned large menus stuffed full of Prawns, well the way the Prawns are served is always the same, it is just the amount that varies, it just gets larger.

Could a Human imagine a swimming pool full of Prawns without the water? No I suppose not, I can, easily, sorry I am getting a little dizzy with excitement at the prospect.

After the Prawn, while I was having a root and fish around for other tasty morsels I found a small Hazelnut leftover from Christmas I suppose. I have heard about Christmas sounds like a fun time, if you happen to be a Human!

I like these little nuts – no not for eating – what do you think I am, some sort of Squirrel? I like them because you can play with them.

One can have hours of fun, well minutes of fun, batting these little nuts across the room with a heavy well aimed right hook and then chasing after them to pounce on them when you have breathlessly caught up with them.

Added to that fun is the bonus of occasionally looking back to survey the debris of what has been knocked over, I have to admit that is also a big part of the fun too. Imagine being able to create such havoc, getting away with it and not even having to clear up the mess, just because you are a Cat, I do – Ha, ha!

A Cat's life can be simple and simple pleasures can keep an ordinary Cat amused I suppose; but I have to remember I am not that simple and need to escape, so I try not to play with these nuts often or get too carried away when I do!

General Note:

I will have to be careful about where and what I hide in, I overheard my Captors talking and she said to him that she thought that I had got into the Hoover bag to go to the toilet!

Well that is really embarrassing, I wouldn't do that, not when there are so many other more comfortable places, as well as my current favourite place,

For example the curtains are soft to sit on and if you are lucky the insides of the cupboards are private. Any of these would be better than the Hoover bag, which was as I shudder to recall very cramped as well as all of the other problems it had, but I don't want to think back to that torturous episode.

At some time in the next few days I plan to investigate one of the corners in the front room, it does look really inviting behind is a big black box sitting on some sort of cupboard. There are a few wires sticking out of the big black box and the cupboard but I don't suppose they are important if they have just been left in the corner.

The big black box has nice bright flashing lights coming out of it and seems to capture the attention of the Captors when they sit down on my Sofa at night so being distracted they tend not to notice when I slip off the Sofa and nose about.

The trouble is if I am sitting on my cushion on the sofa when the box is on I get glued to it as well. It is a captivating experience and a little unusual particularly when your eyes begin to go square and you start to get peckish and fancy the odd highly saturated fat snack like Potato Chips. Smokey Bacon flavour is nice, but it is a shame that they don't make Barbecued Mouse flavour Chips in my humble opinion.

I have even tried dipping Tacos in a jar of Salsa sauce while lying full at stretch on the sofa, how sad is that? Most of it fell of the Taco on the way to my mouth and there was so much sugar in the Salsa sauce that when it dried on my fur and the sofa I ended up glued to the cushions.

In all honesty I don't get the idea of dipping Tacos in jars of Salsa, first have the manufacturers ever tasted proper Mexican Salsa? And second when did Crisp manufacturers begin making sauces?

So the back of the big black box might make a great toilet, the trouble is that it often makes lots noise and loud bangs and one doesn't need that when one is – how can I put it? Concentrating!

But I can wait for that, the curtains are my second favourite place at the moment, and I may well try the box with the grey gravelly stuff in it just for a change once in a while,

Actually the gravelly stuff had a nice texture, but I did notice, when she dragged my paws through it that it was a little dusty and the dust went up my nose, so wetting it down a little might just help and I have plenty of 'stuff' to wet it down with, I am too polite to mention how I would get it wet and what with, but I bet you get the idea!

Last Note:
Try not to have so many notes because they seem to make the page look messy, and harder to read.

Having said that, it is important to make a few notes here and there, but I suppose it is a little like talking to one's self and therefore should be kept to a minimum because it must be a sign of madness. But then what is madness? I am sort of talking to myself when I write my Diary or at least that is what it feels like and it has to be said, I don't feel at all unwell or mad,

Still, sitting in the corner quietly muttering probably looks a little mad or even more than a little strange and that doesn't do a Cat's image any favours I will have to be careful not to be seen muttering to myself, or I could put my paw over my mouth, yes that would do the trick and I wouldn't look strange at all.

Another last Note:
See the notes above. And try to remember not to have so many 'notes,' people could get the wrong idea! They may already have the wrong idea though so make a note to be more discreet about making notes!

Note about Notes:

Must stop this note business it is getting serious. I must have a problem and I didn't even know about it. Now I am worried, dare I say, too worried to make a note about my concerns.

Day 5 of My Captivity:

Made an early start today, tried to forget about the note taking business, I think I have been successful too, apart from noting that I have been trying to forget about the note taking business and that was a little note and surely one is allowed a little note now and again?

Anyway I had more important things on my mind like looking for Prawns. Unfortunately the search was not very successful, but at least I think that I have tracked down where they come from.

It wasn't easy to find out where Prawns come from, in fact I spent most of the day following the Female around watching her and trying to discover where she was hiding those lovely chewy little fellas.

Oops! I had to stop writing the word Prawn for a moment, I began to drool, it is bad enough sitting in a corner quietly muttering to one's self but to be doing that and drooling would really take the biscuit as they say, though why they say that I have no idea, English is an odd language,

I discovered that is what these Humans speak, although I think that there are other languages spoken by Humans too, I have heard examples myself, Russian, French and Gibberish to name just three.

In spite of the drooling, and my growing impatience, and because I am obviously an excellent spy (with the ability to almost become invisible when I put my mind to it) eventually my spying paid off and I found out where the Prawns live, a bright frozen place inside a tall white cupboard.

If my research is correct, Prawns come from the frozen wastes of the Arctic. Or to give it its full name the Arctic Roll, I overheard the Humans talking about the Arctic Roll last night after they had eaten their dinner and amazingly it was from this tall white cupboard that they went to fetch their dessert that was also called an Arctic Roll by a weird coincidence.

Prawns seem to like the frozen wastes so much that they wear shiny coats made of ice! Strange sort of coat in my opinion but then some may say that fur is strange too and I have a lot of that but as far as I know I am not that strange! Well, not that I have noticed, except for the problem with notes, drooling and the talking to myself business and I have tried to stop all of that sort of nonsense.

Thinking about 'strange' though for a moment and interrupting myself at the same time (is there no end to my talent?), is that another little problem that I have? I do wonder if I am just a little obsessive?

I hope I am not obsessive! I never planned to be obsessive! I wouldn't want to be obsessive! But let's face it; do you get a choice with something like that? No I didn't think so either!

Take Prawns for a moment and I would, if someone was offering a truckload. I do seem to have them on my mind a lot, is that something to worry about? Is it obsessional? Hopefully not!

Obsession can be a good thing, just ask Calvin Klein, he has made enough out of Obsession to buy all the Prawns in the world I would think!

Personally if you ask me and I can't understand why he hasn't, Prawns smell better than any perfume even 'Obsession' anyway. But I am only a Cat when all is said and done what do I know about perfume? Apart from the fact that Prawns smell better than anyone that I have smelt!

Back to the Prawns then because I am sure that it can be normal to be a little obsessive, especially about Prawns and nevertheless if it isn't then I don't think I care; I like Prawns and want more.

It would be weird to be obsessive about let's say ironing, or cleaning the house, or Vintage cars and God forbid, religion, but not about Prawns, Oh! No definitely not about Prawns! They are just too um, too well, too, I know, edible!

So today I was able to study Prawns in their natural habitat well when the door to their Kingdom was open, which wasn't often enough to my way of thinking.

Nonetheless as I said, I was able to study Prawns in their natural habitat; whenever the white cupboard door was opened and the bright light shone out over the ice,

In fact when the door was opened I saw that the Prawns were not alone. To be really accurate I couldn't see the Prawns because there seemed to be any number of things living in the cupboard amongst the ice and I began to wonder if they were all as tasty as Prawns, There was no doubt about it I was going to have to find out; I felt it was almost my duty to do so.

I decided to hide inside the white cupboard the next time the door was opened and because the memory of the Hoover bag business was still fresh in my mind I thought that it might be a good idea to make sure that I knew all about the cupboard first.

So I did just a little more concentrated spying and then some relaxed spying and after all of that hard work I felt a little sleepy and did a little ad hoc spying while I had a Cat nap which involved curling up (some would say 'in the way') on the floor in front of the white cupboard with one eye half open and rolling around as I 'rested.'

From all of my observations it was clear that there was plenty of light inside the cupboard and happily I can report that it was not at all like the impenetrable darkness inside the Hoover bag. I knew that it was going to be cold but then what else is a fur coat good for if not for keeping warm? I ask you?

In truth there didn't seem to be much else to worry about and after a surprisingly short time and my well-deserved rest I knew that I was ready for an assault on the tall white cupboard.

It probably goes without saying, but I know what Humans are like and so I will say it anyway. It isn't easy shadowing a Human, they almost all have large heavy feet and large heavy feet don't mix with delicate velvety paws in any conceivable way!

A clever Cat can creep around a Human on his or her blind side and then slip passed like some sort of smart ghost for no reason at all, just for the fun of it, I have to say that I am a clever Cat, well in my own opinion I am, but I also have to say if anyone can outsmart a Human then it is a Cat and this Cat in particular.

Cats have a knack for that sort of thing and although I know I am only young and have not developed my talent to my full potential, slid ling around the blind side of the Female Human, if you see what I mean, it wasn't exactly difficult.

Even if the kettle hadn't been boiling and someone hadn't been ringing the door bell I am sure that I would have successfully slipped passed her, but as it turned out it was just a piece of fish,

(Translator's comment: A piece of Fish is the same as a piece of cake to Humans, but oh so much more delicious, Apparently!).

(Author's note: Yes so much nicer than cake, however Mr. Translator please keep your opinions to yourself in future and concentrate on the translating and I'll do the narrative thank you! Purraa, and I will translate Purraa I don't need your help. It means thank you in English but ruder and with a yawn that makes one's whiskers point forwards, just to prove that a translator's job is not as secure as he might think!).

The kettle was probably over filled and spat water all over the work precious surface, while the person at the door, I now know them to be door to door god salespeople, were most insistent and rang the doorbell vigorously as if their life and our salvation depended upon it being answered.

So my chance to enter the icy realm of the Prawn had at last arrived. In what seemed a panic to me, to stop the water splashing over the work surface and having to answer the door almost at the same time, the Female Human was completely distracted and forgot to close the tall white cupboard's door properly – need I say more, I was in!

Inside the realm of the Prawn it was surprisingly bright. A warm watery light that I judged to be the setting sun shone, reflecting off and through large caverns of ice.

Underfoot snow had fallen and seemed to have buried several bright packets of Rocket lollies. I made a mental note to remember where these were half hidden, I don't know about Lollies but 'Rockets' may come in handy one day with an escape plan!

On and on I trudged, watching my breath freeze in front of my whiskers and oddly watching my whiskers begin to freeze in front of my eyes, I smiled to myself – what a good job I have a fur coat.

I was, I had to admit surprised that the Prawns were so difficult to find, in no time at all I had finished searching this lower entry level and had decided to start investigating the upper levels, when I heard 'her' come back into the kitchen.

She was muttering to herself, something about, 'I don't know about Jehovah's Witnesses, Jehovah's witlesses would be more accurate!' Then she muttered on about some people wasting other's time and didn't they have anything better to do, because if they didn't, then she did!

I almost felt sorry for her. Almost I say because one could not feel sorry for someone who did what she did next.

The sunlight went out, and there was a soft thumping noise, whether they were in that order I don't really know, but the result was that I was in the dark and not for the first time this week!

The up side was that I didn't have anything stuck to my face; the downside was that all over my body my fur was freezing to all of me and it seemed to be getting a lot colder.

Not being one to panic, immediately, I waited and waited, in fact I waited until I couldn't wait anymore. It was only then that I panicked.

First I tried to dig my way out of this icy tomb, that was rather rewarding I was to discover later because I dug my way right through a nest of Pacific Shelled Prawns.

I have no idea which war they were in and who was shelling them? What I do know is that they were delicious, because, well you must have guessed I got to eat them eventually, but first I have to tell you what happened next.

While I was digging I actually began to warm up a little, I noticed in the eerie icy half-light that my whiskers began to thaw a just little and you can probably imagine that is a very encouraging sign to a Cat, and any other animal with whiskers I imagine.

Just when you think that you are about to become a large block of iced Cat a bit of you thaws, so I quickened my pace and dug for all I was worth, which by the way is, I think, a lot.

It was then that I broke through the seam of Pacific Shelled Prawns, I didn't know what I had done at the time but the result was delicious, unfortunately it didn't help, the way things stood at that moment.

A trapped Cat, (I have discovered again and again, sadly) is a very powerful animal, but still a trapped animal. Luckily I am a Cat and so it was thanks to my great strength and superior intelligence that I was freed.

Mmmh! I had a feeling you were looking forward to some sort of epic movie stunt, the sort of thing created in 3D on computers, maybe a car chase with explosions and plenty of noise.

Well in the movie version of my Diary no doubt there will be some amazing escape, but let's face it. I am just a Cat and not a stunt Cat at that, so the escape was a little mundane and as usual a little embarrassing but again, as usual, only embarrassing to me.

I was digging and digging my way through the ice and I am sure that if there had been a light I would have looked like a furry Edward Scissorhands when he is making ice sculptures in the attic and snow down stairs,

Well I would have looked like an Edward Scissorhands without the scissor hands of course, but you would have guessed that without me saying that! Wouldn't you?

Oh sorry I forgot you are Humans! Please don't ask who is Edward Scissorhands is, you'll only make yourselves seem more ignorant. Just ask someone to get you the DVD that is all I can say, oh except that it is a movie and stars that genius Johnny Depp, mind you I am only a Cat, as I have said before proudly, but my idea of a good movie might not be what a Human's is.

You still want to know what happened don't you, ok I suppose I owe you that and I can at least put my side of the story although I am sure that a movie script writer will make more of what happened and I may just end up a some sort of hero and let's face it that would be nice!

I was digging and digging as I said, I did have a couple of breaks and nibbled a frozen Prawn, happily it didn't struggle or squirm, not like worms do, but that is another story, just to say that worms don't taste too good, not like Chicken as I expected, which is odd because they are the same colour and I have found that in the main that things that are the same colour, usually taste the same.

To my way of thinking it is a good rule of thumb, that things that are the same colour, usually taste the same, Pork tastes like Chicken for example.

But, and I use that word with as much emphasis as I can muster, one has to be careful! Don't ever and I mean this most sincerely, don't ever try anything chocolate coloured unless you are sure it is genuinely chocolate, and hasn't therefore recently been inside a Dog!

I promise you it is a very easy mistake to make and there is only one upside in making that particular mistake and is that you only make it once.

After you have finished being sick, the haunting thoughts and terrible nightmares go away, and soon enough you get your appetite back, I can vouch for that, and that is all I want to say on the subject.

Now I tend to sniff most of what I encounter whether it is masquerading as food or not, it is just safer that way, I suppose it is all part of growing up and I know I have a lot more growing to do, because I saw myself, in what I now know is mirror, in 'their' bedroom. At first I didn't know that I was looking at a reflection, or that the reflection was me, I looked so small!

I have to say it gave me quite a shock at first, right in front of me appeared a Cat about my height and age.

A good looking little fella, I thought, but he gave me a scare because every time I tried to pass him he stepped in my way.

I told him that I didn't want 'no trouble,' trying to sound sensible and 'hard' at the same time, but he was just being cool and a little aggressive, whispering something under his breath and ignoring my attempts to make friends. The only way I knew he was aware of me was as I said he kept blocking my path.

Still he wasn't that brave, when I started to move backwards he did too until, and I have to say I thought he could read my mind, I decided to charge at him and he did the same.

As I pounced I closed my eyes and waited to get clawed to bits and ended up banging my nose on the mirror and of course that is when I realised – well more or less what it was that had dented my nose, a mirror!

After the initial shock and a good deal of licking my poor bruised nose and smoothing down my ruffled fur, I started to admire myself in the mirror.

You know I am, even though there is no one here to agree with me, and I say this myself, I am a really good looking Cat, I suppose I am just very, very lucky, but I wouldn't mind being a little bigger.

It took me ages to fully appreciate my good looks, excellent bone structure and amazing whiskers, so long in fact that I didn't really have time to fully appreciate the reflection that the rest of me made in the mirror because I heard the Captors arrive home, and decided that it might be a good idea not to be found in their bedroom if they came looking for me.

It was pity that I didn't have a whole morning just to stand there and admire my profile in the mirror and congratulate myself on my astonishing good fortune, that I am well – Me!

Later in the week if my schedule allows I will try and take the opportunity to have another look I am sure, and if I still think I am a bit small looking maybe I could work out some sort of exercise program, we'll see!

Day 6 of My Captivity:

Annoying neighbours can be dealt with in a number of ways and today I got my own back on the plastic Mac wearing rat bag who returned me to this prison, you'll remember her from the other day no doubt?

She was out walking in the light rain and stiff breeze and I was watching her from my little perch in the bay window which is incidentally a great place to sleep in the sun if we had any, and if you feel up to it, a truly great place to do some serious snooping.

I spent most of the morning watching the ins and outs of people in the Cul-de-sac this must be Coffee Morning heaven because half way through the morning several of the lady neighbours all turned up on the doorstep of the house right opposite.

They waited for a while and then were let in smiling and chatting.

Unlike the man from across the road diagonally if you see what I mean, he came out of his house looking very guilt, with his collar up, which struck me as odd, but then he is a Human!

Things got odder still because he walked the short distance to 'Hither Chanters,' which believe it or not is the name of another house, not using his car, which was very odd, from his house 'The Grange.'

This area is far too posh to have houses that have numbers; this is where 'very comfortable' people live apparently.

It wasn't really a surprise to discover that 'very comfortable' really means 'rich,' there are several cars in each of the driveways, letter boxes on the gates to those driveways and not in the front doors like normal houses and so much more to set them apart from the riff raff of other areas.

Still I suppose that having a letterbox on one's gate post does save the legs of the postman by not adding extra miles to his 'round' because he doesn't have to walk up and down the drives of the houses who have gate post letterboxes, which is a kind thought!

Mind you I have seen the postman still walk down to the front door and look at it bemused while scratching his head and looking for a letterbox. Humans!

The neighbours won't like it I bet, when they find out that living at 'Honeysuckle House' there is a common or garden Cat who isn't at all rich. Still years ago they must have dealt with the first shock that this house has to offer, no Honeysuckle, in spite of its name.

It struck me as strange that there isn't any Honeysuckle at Honeysuckle House. Since I have been here I have looked out of every window and not seen any,

In fact I have extended my search to the areas around the doors and still no luck, All I can think is that someone either killed the unfortunate Honeysuckle, which would be a shame because it smells nice, or maybe one of the former owners was called Mr. Honeysuckle.

There could have to have been a Mrs. Honeysuckle too of course and several small but growing Honeysuckle juniors. Wouldn't it be funny if the couple had been called Hermione and Henry Honeysuckle and their children, one of each of course in such a nice house, I am guessing, were called Harriet and Harry!

So many H's and so many terrible names, who in their right mind would call their children any of those names. Oops I forgot I made the Honeysuckle family up, ha, ha, ha.

Mind you Humans do have strange names, I had to snigger the other day, I saw someone on the TV called Charles Dance, sounds more like an invitation than a name but I think there might be some punctuation required like Charles, Dance! But punctuation is not my forte as you may have gathered!

Anyway, enough of that nonsense as they say when they are talking nonsense. I watched the man from house 'The Grange' furtively walking down the drive of 'Hither Chanters,' keeping to the shadows, afforded by the dense rhododendron bushes and large trees that lined the driveway, for some reason best known to himself.

When he got to the front door it was opened as if by magic, without him having to knock, by what I took to be a satin dressing gown, there wasn't anyone in the delicate material, or that is what it looked like from where I was craning to get a better view.

Without any hesitation he entered and the front door was closed smartly behind him without a whisper of a sound.

It all went a little quiet then until Mrs. Plastic Mac turned up in the rain.

She had a carrier bag with her and she was standing at the end of our driveway, looking up into the large Oak tree that guards the front gate – well I don't suppose it does in fact consciously guard the front gate but you know what I mean!

I could see her lips moving and she was obviously talking to herself mad old bird I thought to myself – yes rather uncharitably possibly; but this was the person who returned me in spite of my protests that I was perfectly alright and didn't need 'returning.'

Then I saw whom she was talking to, coming head first down the Oak tree were two Squirrels they looked as though they had glue on their feet that kept them stuck to the bark of the tree, wonderful trick I wonder if Cats can learn how they do it?

When the two Squirrels got to the bottom of the tree trunk Mrs. Plastic Mac threw them a couple of shelled nuts, which they grabbed and ran off with.

The process was repeated again and again, the only variety was that some of the nuts had shells on; I suppose they would be less likely to go mouldy.

I was impressed with this kindliness and wondered if Mrs. Plastic Mac might have any Prawns in her bag, but then I thought if I was out side begging for Prawns she would probably bring me back here again and I would be back to square one, but of course I would be full of Prawns while standing on square one.

But an enemy is always just that! She had cost me a lot that annoying woman and I was going to have to do something about it, my plan was to start small, but then it is nice to be different.

Next to me in the bay window is a large pot of flowers; vase I think is the actual word for a collection of colourful cut flowers, or that is what I think I have heard them called.

By leaning on the vase of flowers I was able just to unbalance it just enough to start it rocking and to get the water inside the vase swilling and sloshing about which in turn made it easy to get the vase of flowers to tap the window sounding as though it was a Human tapping on the window pane to attract a passer by's attention.

From my hiding place behind the vase of flowers I could see Mrs. Plastic Mac looking up expectantly hoping to catch the eye of the window tapper and maybe get a cup of tea and a chat even if originally they weren't trying to attract her attention,

She must have thought it strange that the tapping was coming from a house that didn't have a friendly face in the window, just a big vase of flowers that would have been rocking so gently that from the outside it would look as though it was still.

She continued to search the neighbourhood's windows for the friendly face, but either the curtains of houses were drawn or the windows were empty.

I tapped away merrily for a long while, before it started to dawn on me that Mrs. Plastic Mac would continue looking for the 'friend' for a lot longer than I would enjoy this joke.

The joke started to go a little sour as I realised that Mrs. Plastic Mac was lonely and needed a friendly face and a chat more than she needed a cup of tea or a mischievous little Cat tormenting her.

Revenge wasn't at all what I thought it would be like, and as Mrs. Plastic Mac stopped looking for the friend that obviously didn't exist, I stopped the vase tapping the window and felt just a little, well little and silly.

What I had done to that poor woman was not nice and I would have to think of a way of making it all up to her.

Which all made me think. I was hungry.

As I sauntered into the kitchen, keeping an eye out for the Dog, yes a great combination isn't a Dog and a Cat in the same place, Humans really don't they know we are sworn enemies!

I was guiltily thinking about Mrs. Plastic Mac, and how she must be really lonely, if she had nothing better to do with her time than to 'rescue' me, as she would see it.

We all know how the 'rescued' sees it and no more comment is required especially as I am feeling a little Shamefaced.

Thinking about all of the things she had done this afternoon she must be lonely, out feeding Squirrels in all weathers is just not a very rewarding thing to do.

After all, everyone knows that Squirrels are not the most grateful of animals well Grey ones that is and as we have said before who in their right mind would want to go to Scotland even to see Red Squirrels?

In fact Grey Squirrels are about as grateful as Weasels, I would say, in my considered opinion, not that I know a lot about either really, they just look mean, oh don't get me wrong they are all very nice and cuddly on the outside,

They have even perfected that business of holding nuts in their front paws and nibbling them – very cutesy, but there is a different side to Squirrels that few know – well to the Grey ones at least,

Over a period of less than a hundred years they have almost eliminated their Red Squirrel brothers in Great Britain in a genocidal conflict that makes even some African states look like kindergartens!

In fact the poor Red Squirrels have now been forced to move out of England into the Highlands of Scotland and who in their right mind would want to do that?

I would put money on the possibility that she feeds birds too, and they are ungrateful little Buzzards, just look at that Parrot, mind you he is an exception even in the Bird world I think, nasty piece of work.

Sparrows are ok actually; they seem quite friendly when you watch them out of the window, sharing the Bird Bath with the Blue Tits and the Chaffinches. But the Robins, Starlings, and the rest are right little blighters, they fight, posture and squawk to be first to get in the Bird Bath then they jostle each other to get on the Bird Table and to stay on the Bird Table.

Really if Birds had any sense or any manners they would work together or at least be polite, life would definitely be less of a trial for them if they did.

Still if they did work together then they wouldn't be so distracted, when they are distracted they are vulnerable to hunters, heh, heh, heh! Do you like my evil laugh?

Do you think that I could be considered as the next bad guy (well Cat) in a forthcoming Bond movie? If the James Bond film producers are reading this, do drop me a line, I do consider all offers, sorry but one has to advertise.

So Mrs. Plastic Mac must have a pretty pointless life, feeding evil Squirrels and awful Birds, I wonder if when she gets home there is a Mr. Plastic Mac or any little Plastic Mac's come to visit?

In a way I hope so, she looked so solitary out there today in the rain, oh goodness this Whiskers in Jelly is good, wow, what they say is true, it is a real meal in delicious jelly™ which any Cat in his right mind would cross a busy road for.

Imagine crossing a road, I would love the opportunity especially if on the other side there was a bowl of this delicious scrum. But I have a feeling that it might just be a little dangerous, I have spotted cars in the road and they look all malevolent and dangerous, if one of those ran you over you would know about it I would think.

So to cross the road for a tin of Whisker's Cat food must mean that it is really good indeed and apparently 8 out of 10 Cats do exactly that and most make it to the other side.

If Mrs. Plastic Mac is really lonely, and this afternoon wasn't an act to make me feel ashamed (which worked) then I have thought of the perfect solution!

I only tell you now because I was eating, but I was eating and thinking, which can be a little nasty if one gets indigestion, but this time I didn't get indigestion, I got an idea and it is brilliant, even if I say so myself and I just have.

It isn't often that one gets the sort of idea that I got just then but one has to savour the moment when they come to you.

My idea is inspired and it was so elegant and so simple, but then the best ideas are elegant and simple.

What Mrs. Plastic Mac needs if she is alone, is someone or something to keep her company! Selecting a companion for someone is a difficult task, one has to weigh up the likes and dislikes of the parties involved sympathetically and to ensure that they have shared interests.

It took a while to do that, but my thinking was something like this; Mrs. Plastic Mac is lonely and needs a loyal friend, she is kind and likes birds! Who could possibly be suitable?

There was someone who I knew and whom I had decided was almost perfect for Mrs. Plastic Mac. Someone who is loyal and friendly and would be able to work his way through Mrs. Plastic Mac's supply of nuts too and that would annoy the Grey Squirrels and get rid of the Parrot too.

Mrs. Plastic Mac would be over the Moon with her new friend and the Parrot doesn't know enough words to voice his objections.

Now all I had to make sure that this match made in heaven, well in the kitchen actually, could become a reality, I needed a plan and fast! Happily I am good at dreaming up plans, it is just a gift of mine!

Day 7 of My Captivity:

I have made a little progress in my Pet Matchmaking Program; I discovered using intensive surveillance methods developed by the Army that Mrs. Plastic Mac does indeed live alone.

Well that is unless she lives with someone who doesn't like to leave the house or is bed ridden, which is the same I suppose unless the person is bed ridden and wants to leave the house and can't, but that is a little too complicated even for my superior mind to get around.

Today I spent all day in the window, not tapping the glass with the vase full of flowers this time, but 'keeping my eyes peeled,' now there is a dreadful thought, where do all of these bits of the language come from? Imagine having your eyes peeled!

All right I agree with you don't imagine that, it is just too sick to even contemplate.

But must have thought about it and then mentioned the expression to someone else and they in turn quite liked the idea of keeping their eyes peeled or peeling someone else's eyes and before you know where you are the expression is lodged in the English language like a stone in a shoe.

Nowadays they would call it a catch phrase, the catch phrase is what every Radio and TV presenter of any type is desperately seeking because they then become associated with the catch phrase, it is sort of like a personality crutch, if you are not happy with your personality you hide behind a catch phrase.

The people, who are even more inadequate than the performer with the catch phrase, repeat it again and again without any reason and giggle to themselves and their friends as though they have said something clever.

Yes being a Cat gives one the opportunity to study Humans closely, though quite why one would bother is a mystery, although in my case armed with the knowledge I learn from my studies I should be able to escape the prison.

The problem at the moment is that apart from yesterday I haven't managed to study lonely old ladies at all, this would be a bad enough failing on my part if it wasn't for the fact that I also have no idea what the Parrot likes or dislikes.

Actually that is not entirely true, I know the Parrot doesn't like me, so that is a start, but then the old lady does, and that means that already they don't have much in common!

The old lady has great taste and the Parrot doesn't, but then the Parrot is an imbecile or is that moron or will both describe him nicely?

There has to be a way of getting them together, I am sure that they would like each other's company, just think of the bonuses of having a Parrot around the home if you are a Pensioner!

Let's face it old people tend to lose their teeth and Parrots have great strong beaks that can crack even the hardest nuts and so old people could get their Parrot to 'ready chew' their food.

Actually that one benefit alone should prompt old people everywhere to buy a Parrot for the home, trouble is they all moan about how little money they have, but maybe the government could create a programme for them, yes indeed Parrots for Pensioners could become a major vote winner.

Even if the 'Parrots for Pensioners Programme' doesn't win votes, at least being in a possession of a Parrot would mean that oldsters would be too busy to constantly moan and carp on about the rough deal they are getting, as they sit on their buses using their free bus passes, on the way to their nice warm, free, day care centres for a few free morning snacks, a free light lunch with an afternoon magic act thrown in, for nothing of course.

Still if they have to endure a magic act then maybe they are allowed to moan a bit, but not as much as they do currently!

So now the trick, it would seem, would be to get them both together, Mrs. Plastic Mac and the Painted Parrot, but I have a feeling that it is going to take this Magician a little longer than an afternoon to pull that Rabbit out of the Hat, or to be more precise, to kick the Parrot out of the house.

Mrs. Plastic Mac seems to pass by the front window to feed the Squirrels every afternoon at almost the same time, and so it would be a super idea to ensure that the Parrot is advertised in it.

Although the Parrot doesn't like moving around much, and seems to enjoy being almost nailed to his perch, he definitely isn't dead, as I initially thought. He does occasionally have a bit of a flutter about and if the old bird is given a nut he will spend hours holding it in his dreadfully ugly claws and biting it with his very sharp beak, and generally making a fearful noise and a dreadful mess all over the floor.

I have to smile sometimes because the Captors will occasionally give the feathered fool a soft skinned nut like a peanut so that he can demonstrate his beak power, crush it swiftly and then they will follow that by giving him a tough nut to crack like a Brazil nut, it then takes him a while to work out why he can't just rip it open and crunch his way through to the inside, still we can't all be geniuses. I believe that there is only one genius in every million people and so I am hardly likely to meet another one, especially around here!

Enough of me though! Back to the Parrot, even if I hadn't seen him flying overhead on occasions, the tale tell tail feathers that he, for some incomprehensible reason, leaves randomly around the place would be a complete give away. Really he is a dreadful litterlout, he drops bits of nuts everywhere and bits of himself. We really should do something about getting rid of him, or maybe he could clean up his act! Yes it is all very well to be able to speak Human as he so often does, but I really don't think that he understands much of what he says and if that is your act then I am afraid that life must be a dreadful disappointment.

Only the other day he said 'Who's a pretty towel rail then,' obviously one of the workmen had taught him that clever little phrase in their lunch break, which proves my point he has as much intelligence as a tape recorder and the beauty of tape recorders is at least you can switch them off!

Mind you I think he should have said. 'Who's a pretty idiot then!' I think that would have been at least funny, but then what do you expect from workmen?

Still I could mention here, or even use the other handy little phrases which the workmen taught the Multicoloured Mug, but young children might be listening and I think it is for their parents to teach them 'those' sorts of words as they so often do when they are being filmed for documentaries about deprived families. They maybe deprived, socially and educationally but they definitely didn't miss out on learning all of the colourful 'Anglo-Saxon' words!

Thinking about swear words for a moment! I wonder why most of the swear words in the English language are referred to as Anglo-Saxon? The Anglo-Saxons must have been an interesting race of people, probably with poor social housing, terrible education and zero opportunities for work, which led them to invent so many, as the Dictionary calls them, 'taboo' words!

Day 8 of My Captivity:

I don't know why but every so often the Captors will deliberately annoy me with an assortment of strange dangling objects that they wave about in front of me. When I reach out for them they snatch them away, what sort of behaviour is that?

I can't help thinking that this is either some kind of mental torture – or are they attempting to evaluate my powers of reason, prior to me slipping over the edge of insanity. Neither matters to me now, especially as I am able to record my life of imprisonment in this Diary. They will pay for all of their crimes, one way or another!

Continuing this mental torture they eat really nice food with lots of fresh meat, while I am forced to eat some dreadful assortment of dried balls that they laughingly call Cat food.

The only thing that keeps me from going mad is that I know I will escape, and the mild satisfaction I get from ruining the occasional piece of furniture. Still to make myself feel better I can always beat up another houseplant and get my own back on them, after the last one they spent ages clearing up the shredded fragments and weeks scrubbing the stains out of the carpet.

Today I was up so early that it was still night outside, the dawn chorus wasn't even tuning up and everything was quiet except for the loud ticking of the clock in the hall, that is nearly twenty minutes slow.

I don't have much of an idea what twenty minutes slow means, but I have heard the Captors complain about the clock and use that reason for their complaining as well as the fact that the clock ticks so loudly.

Of course the fact that the clock is not as fast as it used to be (if that is the opposite of being slow in clock circles), is not really of any consequence to me at all because my ability to tell the time is limited to exactly how interested I am in knowing the time, if you see what I mean.

Cats don't need to know the time. Let's face it we don't have to get up to go to work or school or anything where we would have a problem if we were late.

In fact Cats don't understand the concept of late! I love to watch the Humans running around in the state of being late, which involves the aforementioned running around and the Male Captor shouting upstairs to the Female one to, 'hurry up because we're already late!'

Now, I am no time keeping expert as I said, but it strikes me that if one is late already then one may as well calm down, relax and stop running around like a Chicken looking for its head!

Yes one is probably going to be even later if one stops running and starts thinking, but if you are late already then what is the big deal? Even the super race that Humans think they are in comparison to other animals hasn't mastered time or time travel just yet!

If say for instance one is running for a train that leaves at 11.00 and one is five minutes late, the train is guaranteed not to be there when you get to the platform, so you end up being too early for the next train and have to wait a long time, which seems pointless to me.

There is one exception to that rule of course, in England there is every possibility that not only the train that you intended to catch might be late, but also the train that should have left sometime before the one you were running to get, might still be on the platform.

However this Diary will, I am confident, be a bestseller in countries where they have trains that run on time and the people of those countries at least will understand what I am talking about; whereas the English readers will just have to use their imagination, and I am sorry I know imagining punctual trains, efficiently running to a timetable will require a lot of imagining for our English readers!

Still having said all of that and getting back to the original point, wouldn't it be better to have a little realism and say to yourself, I am late, well I have missed the 11.00 and will have to catch the 14.00, ok let's feed the Cat, Prawns today I think! Then have a Coffee and relax for a minute or two!

But Humans can't do that and sometimes I pity them for their lack of ability in that area, but not too much, because of course a flustered, confused Human is a great target for a clever Cat, who is capable of turning 'events' to his advantage.

Cats don't have watches but they do have built in clocks with alarms that go off at breakfast time, Lunchtime and dinnertime, these built in clocks also have little reminder alarms for things like elevenses and teatime.

All these alarms are pretty handy if one is close to a regular source of food and can be bothered to get up and saunter down to eat, when they sound.

I have to say I often have skipped elevenses and even lunch if I have been busy sleeping, but I do ensure that I make up for it at the next mealtime.

Still I bet that if you are hungry it is a bit of a pain to have lots of little 'time to eat' alarms going off regularly in ones head, which just proves that when I do escape from here I will have to take a good supply of food, I wonder how many cans of Whiskers I can carry?

Day 9 of My Captivity:

This evening I have spent hours trying to work out if the Parrot can read minds? Or maybe he is in the possession of superior powers or is just possessed!

He is definitely eccentric enough to be possessed, thinking about it. But he is bigger than a Medium and I think that rules out supernatural powers because he is probably more of a large than a Medium and only Mediums have 'powers.'

All day he has watched me; he rarely leaves his perch, not even to go to the toilet, how disgusting is that? In fact until today I have never seen the old Bird fly, but today he did both, in fact I suppose he did all three, if you count the going to the toilet as well!

I can tell you, it is very off putting to be 'buzzed' by a Parrot, his long tail feathers raking your back as you creep into a corner on your belly and he swoops down on you as you are merely minding your own business and trying to think of a way to give him away to the old lady down the road.

The really terrifying bit is when the Looney flies straight at you at almost ground level, if I wasn't diving for cover I think I would be admiring the Parrot's amazing flying ability, if I had a hat I would take it off to anyone demonstrating that kind of aerobatic skill.

He was weaving in and out of furniture, until in the wide open space of the front room he was able to stop banking and turning, level out and fly straight at me. Or after me, because as he got closer I began to dodge to the left and right, getting ready to dive again to one side or the other or that was what I was trying to make it look like!

It wasn't really planned, or an idea that came from any coherent thought to be honest, there was no time for that as the lump of bright colours flew straight at me like a multicoloured over inflated Bumble Bee.

But I remembered from somewhere, something I had heard about Bullfighters or was it Dog trainers? I know it was about an occupation that I thought I would never have considered even if I had been a Human!

What I had heard whether it referred to Bullfighters or Dog trainers or both, was that when being attacked by Dogs – there I have answered my own question, how daft is that? As if there was time for that!

Nevertheless that doesn't matter at the moment especially as I think I am about to be beaten up by a very bad tempered Parrot who I think has been reading my mind and didn't like what he read.

'You run at them!'

That is what they said, and it wasn't about attacks by Dogs, Bulls or Parrots, it is what you have to do when being attacked by Hippopotamuses or is that Hippopotami?

Let's half the difference - Hippos!

When being attacked by Hippos, who apparently are the most aggressive and bad tempered animals you can wish to meet on the plains of Africa, or not wish to meet as the case maybe, and in my case is, not wish to meet!

Obviously, the people who say that Hippos are pretty nasty pieces of work, have never met some Sudanese Arabs, but there is no time for that story now!

It was possible; I thought to myself that I was approaching the end of the road, and I was rather disappointed that my life's journey had been so dreadfully short and that the road had led to nowhere!

So taking my courage in both paws I waited. Well that wasn't the plan as you know from my thoughts above, but I was what they call rooted to the spot.

'Oh Dearie me!' I thought!

No you are right I didn't think those exact words, but I hope that this Diary will appeal to a mixed age group, need I say more?

'One word Sounds like; SHIP!' Yes well done! You are brilliant! 'Oh Ship, I'm a goner Ffffor goodness sake!'

Well that is the closest we will get to what I was thinking, as I stood, ok yes cowered, with half an eye open; waiting for the inevitable and seeing close up for the first time just how sharp the beak and claws of a Parrot actually are.

I will never again be fooled by the appearance of the old Parrot or his grey dusty, deformed and wrinkled looking old feet, they are as strong as the old buzzard's brain which had obviously carefully planned this attack. I was, I knew, finished as dead as the lead that seemed to fill my paws and didn't allow me to run away.

Closer and closer came the old technicolour crow and the only conscious thought I had was; I want to go to the toilet; Not much of a plan, I'll grant you, but where there is breath there is life someone really clever said, it was my Mum to be precise.

She also said and I think this was more profound and definitely a millions times more useful. 'JUMP!' I remembered it was her last word to me.

But I hadn't jumped from the Pet shop van and escaped then, but I was going to jump now and I was going to jump as high as I could and with all of my strength, so whether I had lead in my Paws or not, at least both the Parrot and I would be on eye level when he hit me, or you never know I might just get away.

Making something happen is always better than sitting around waiting for something to happen. Well that is what my brother said as he was taken away to a new home.

So, just at the right moment – we should call it that because it was either the right, wrong or last moment and I even now prefer to think of it as the 'right' moment, I jumped. It wasn't the best jump I have ever made and it most definitely wasn't the most elegant, but most important of all, it wasn't the last jump I ever made.

Now I am sorry to those of you who consider I have spoilt the suspense, but let's face it for a moment any 'hero' in a tight spot in any bit of fiction, whether it is a Book, a Play or a Movie, is probably going to escape and live.

If the Book, Play or Movie is less than half way through, and I would say it is a fair bet that the 'hero' will live all the way to the end; so that he can get the Car, the Girl and in my case the Prawns and sail off into the sunset with them all; or maybe just get the Prawns and an extra helping of Prawns which weigh the same as the girl.

And the same applies to this non-fiction Diary, I can happily announce with great personal relief.

The tweet, tweet, twit sped towards me at almost ground level and that I think looking back on the incident was his down fall, had he dive bombed me I think I would have been so many bits of a Kitten rather than a Kitten who was about to give the Old Bird a bit of a shock.

When he was just in front of me I jumped, there was no brilliant split second timing frankly. No valiant effort made on my part, I felt the air swirl and eddy under the beating of his wings and it made me 'jump' almost out of my skin, so I just leapt up in the air and at the same time gave up any hope of escape.

Up I sailed in the air like a discarded plastic carrier bag in a high wind, but instead of sailing out of trouble I was lucky or unlucky enough to have not quite timed my jump to perfection and as the Parrot zoomed just under me I felt the feathers on the grumpy Old Bird's neck.

Then without knowing much about it I landed on his back. Which was very fortunate, because although the Parrot was a powerful bird and not to be trifled with from the ground or underneath, from above he was nothing special when you are sitting on his back.

I concede that he could have turned around and bitten me, Parrots have the disconcerting ability to turn their heads around so far they appear to be facing backwards, spawn of the Devil if you ask me! But even Spawn of the Devil have to look where they are going and therefore can't do both that is bite me and see where they are flying at the same time.

So you could say I had the upper paw here and you would be right up to a point and that point extraordinarily enough was when the Parrot decided to turn around and bite me.

No he didn't bite me. I didn't lose my advantage by being nutted, you know banged on the head with his forehead, which I have always thought is a pretty daft form of attack anyway, because you are liable to hurt yourself as much as you hurt others surely?

So I wasn't cracked like a Walnut, or walloped like a cashew, nope worse! Much, much worse, and it happened without warning. The worst shocks are unexpected; like spiders appearing in front of people who are frightened by them or Tax Inspectors turning up on a Monday morning without telephoning in advance.

And this shock was a surprise for both the Parrot and I. Well it was a big shock for me and I don't suppose that the Parrot had planned to fly head first into an armchair.

Looking back on the episode now, it is a good job that we, for reasons best known to the Rainbow coloured Aviator, had gained a little bit of height, and we are indeed, talking of only a couple of inches and no more, because had we crashed into the armchair at the height I had 'boarded' the Parrot, then we would have hit the Chair's wooden frame. Ouch! And probably a big ouch too!

As it was we thankfully sailed over the frame and the seat cushion and thudded into the back cushion and bounced apart.

The myth that Cats always land standing up is a good one, it suggests that we are a race of super fit athletes capable of amazing stunts with amazing timing and pinpoint agility.

Shame it is just a myth really, spread by rather unobservant Humans who obviously don't see us landing badly when we do, which is more often than you would think, obviously I should know, I have a few scars to disprove the myth.

I don't want to disappoint you, truthfully, Cats, I promise you, can land on their feet and often do, if they are in control of what they are doing, or have worked out exactly where they are going to land, what they are getting out of doing the stunt in the first place and how it will benefit them in general. And most importantly know that they are going to jump in the first place.

But I didn't have time for any of that old malarkey I am afraid, I was just plain lucky, so as you can see, it isn't only Black Cats that are lucky, actually sorry that is another Cat myth too!

Well now that I have started; I may as well clear up some of the Cat nonsense which some of you Humans are gullible enough to believe and believe in.

Did you know for instance that Black Cats in some countries are thought to be unlucky, and not at all lucky in any way, now can you see a few holes developing in the 'lucky Black Cat' Myth?

In my opinion and speaking not as a black Cat, but as a rather fine example of a Tabby and White (with silver highlights) Cat, and where did the word tabby come from, can anyone tell me?

Speaking as a Tabby and White (with silver highlights) coated Cat and a pretty snazzy one at that, I think that being a Black Cat is pretty unlucky in general; let's face it if you are out at night on a main road you need more than just a pair of glittering green eyes to let the traffic know you are crossing the road, don't you?

Now, a Black Cat with reflective paw bands is a lucky Cat, without a doubt!

Hopefully it was the last time I will ever fly Parrot Airways, it was not the longest flight in the history of aviation by any stretch of the imagination but it was more than enough for me to realise that if I were going to fly, it would be under different circumstances.

One thing I knew without a shadow of a doubt, I had made an enemy, but then being philosophical for a moment Cats and Birds no matter what size they are, will never be friends.

One of us has to go, and if I am to be imprisoned here then it is the Parrot who can say Au revoir, and go and live with Mrs. Plastic Mac!

You can just about get along with a Dog if you are a Cat because Dogs have their uses and even though they are as dim as a broken light bulb; they understand that Cats can improve their lives especially in the Robin Hood method of food redistribution.

Day 10 of My Captivity:

A feather landed on my nose! I just couldn't believe it either, I was lying on my day bed in 'their' bedroom minding my own business and just beginning to get comfy, you know the state, legs getting heavy, body sinking into the duvet, eyes closing and the world going quiet.

And then, just as my eyes were closing for the last time before falling into a well deserved sleep, there it was floating down onto my nose, the insult, the affront, the um! The Err! Oh no! The Parrot.

I managed to roll out of the way, just in time, as the vicious variegated violently coloured commando came abseiling down on top of me without a rope, dropped from the light fixture above my head onto the bed. The exact bit of bed I had been dozing on seconds before I might add!

This was war and now that I was awake I was almost ready for it.

The malicious multicoloured Macaw must have planned this attack for quite a while, to attack me while I was asleep.

Happily the impatient Parrot was too eager to pounce and to cut this Cat into Cat chunks with his sharp claws and beak, something that I was resolutely against for all sorts of reasons as you can imagine.

I rolled out of the way as nimble as, a, well there is only one way to describe how nimble I was, as nimble as a Cat!

After rolling away I got up on all fours and turned and stared straight into the beady eyes of my attacker. Standing in front of me the puffed up Parrot was almost as tall as me, which was a little disconcerting.

It was something of a shock to be staring black beak to pink nose with the coloured combatant who was rocking from side to side flashing his sharp beak like a sword.

This was serious, and so was the Parrot. He had murder in his eyes and a beak that could crack tougher nuts than mine, and that was a combination that I really had trouble with.

Let's face it even if I had been a spectator, I would have been concerned for the plucky Cat facing such a bully, as it turned out that the plucky Cat was me I was more than a little concerned I was…worried!

There are times to fight and times to run and times that one wishes that one could run, but this was a time when I could see that the wily old Parrot had almost completely cut off my escape route to the door and downstairs.

Mmmh! NASA we have a problem!

I took stock of my options as the mad bird swayed and occasionally snapped at me. What weapons did I have on me? Because if I were James Bond or some sort of super hero I would have something pretty useful concealed somewhere. Well that didn't take long to count the weapons I had concealed and on display, none.

I would have to use my superior intelligence then, trouble was I didn't feel very intelligent at the moment, in actual fact I didn't feel at all well at this moment.

Then it hit me, no not a claw or a sharp beak, an idea! I was more intelligent than my attacker and I knew it. It had just taken a little longer for an idea to spark in my head this time, but then I was under, what some would call, pressure!

Without warning I struck.

It took the puzzled Parrot by surprise I can tell you, he was completely thrown. Mind you an act of such rash bravery in the face of so much aggression was bewildering, even I was baffled as to why I had done what I did!

I just dropped onto the Duvet cover, laid on my back with my legs locked sticking upwards, closed my eyes and tried to play 'dead' breathing softly like a good actor in a badly directed drama.

The Parrot continued to sway about but the swaying I could feel was slowing, occasionally he snapped his beak together in confused annoyance.

After a while and to say it seemed like ages would to sound like everyone else in a tight situation, but I can assure you it felt like ages. The Parrot stopped swaying and eventually stopped snapping his beak too.

He was obviously at a loss as to what had happened, maybe he even thought that I had died of fright, well that is what I hoped.

Instead of snapping his beak together he made a sort of sniffing sound, maybe he smelt something not very nice, frankly I could and I had a very good idea where the smell had come from, but this was not time for social niceties.

The sniffing stopped and I think I heard him say the beginning of 'who's a pretty boy' but if Parrots had teeth it would have been said through gritted teeth and delivered through a gritted beak if you see what I mean.

Then I felt the bed move as he began edging towards my rigid body. Holy J-L0 I was still in trouble!

The grumbling Parrot was very close and through a slit in my almost open eyes I saw that the old bird was going to take a bit of my back leg to just test to see how dead I was.

In a very fluid movement I not only produced another bad smell from somewhere deep inside but I stretched up and clawed the pillow, hooking enough claws into it to be able to pull it right over my head and body and into the face of my attacker.

As he was trying to pull large amounts of duck down out of his mouth, I was off in the other direction. The mirrored doors of the wardrobe were open I noticed as I hit the ground, I raced for the crack between the wall and the mirrored door and, I hoped, safety.

Old Parrots are lots of things, worldly wise, clever, patient and dangerous, the last description being the one that properly describes this mad old bird most accurately.

I knew I was safe inside the wardrobe because the gap that I had got in was too small for him to get in because of his virtually unbending tail feathers, and not only that I knew that as soon as it goes dark; Parrots even wise, clever, patient and dangerous ones tend to go to sleep so he was unlikely to want to enter the darkness of the wardrobe.

Unhappily I also knew that this Parrot was not one to give up easily, I was safe in the wardrobe, I was trapped as well, but I was also pleased with myself, I think the first round had been won by me!

Unfortunately I was just a little worried about future rounds and I knew that I was going to have to have eyes in the back of my head to ensure that I stayed ahead.

For the moment all I had to do was to wait for the Humans to come home and also to try and make my bolthole as safe as possible.

With some relief I felt a nice soft cashmere coat brush my face as I walked to the opposite end of the wardrobe, as far away from the squawking Parrot as possible.

After a very easy jump I clung onto the coat and climbed up to the collar, it wasn't so easy after that but with some clinging and wriggling I climbed onto the wardrobe's shelf and then picked my way gently back to the open door after I had gone to the toilet at the other end, rather thoughtfully in an upturned hat.

When I got to the crack between the wall and the mirrored door that was the opening to the wardrobe I saw below me a very peeved Parrot pacing up and down like a demented sentry.

For a moment the thought crossed my mind to do exactly to the Parrot what he had done to me, and just drop on the murderous Macaw, but I had a feeling that I would get a lot more than I bargained for if I did that and I might end up needing surgery, because the Parrot was in a very bad mood indeed.

Even looking down on his head and shoulders you could see he was twitching with rage. Now while I was rather pleased with myself that I had annoyed him so much I wasn't going to deliberately rattle his cage any more than necessary, I would save that for later literally.

(Translator's Note: for non-English speaking people and American English Speakers, it maybe helpful to know, 'Rattle his cage' is used as an expression here, and means to annoy someone as well as literally to bang on the bars of the Parrot's cage,)

(Author's note: I am sure that people know that and you are butting in, excuse me, who is writing this Diary, you or me?)

(Translators Note: Suit yourself!)

(Author's note: I will!)

(Agent's note: Will you both stop this. Dew'wanna sell this Turkey or not? If you do, I suggest that one a'ya get back to translating and de odder writing, or the boys might come round and you'll both get accidents. My boys can get kinda clumsy when they hear an investment of mine is; what shall we say? Being devalued!)

(Translator's Note: Sorry Mr. Leibowitz.)

(Author's note: Very sorry Mr. Leibowitz, call me Todd.)

All I could do was to wait, so I made myself comfortable, which I have to say wasn't difficult I found a pile of scarves the top one being Cashmere, I have decided that I like Cashmere and want a blanket made of it.

The wardrobe was warm and dark, especially when I had my eyes closed, after a while the Parrot stopped twitching and begun the oddest behaviour that I have ever encountered, he would launch himself into the air and try to hover.

Obviously no one had ever mentioned to him that he wasn't a Hummingbird, because the results were pretty disastrous.

The first few strange wing assisted leaps took him up passed my face, which was when he spotted me, the ones that followed were frenzied, wings beating fast and bashing noisily into the mirror, feathers flying all over the place as the overexcited Parrot tried to find me, only to get all mixed up with the gap and the wall and crash down onto the floor in a nasty feathery mess.

Then he modified his approach and rose up on a level with the shelf and tried to hover. I knew immediately that what he was attempting was doomed to failure yet again but the message hadn't occurred to him and I was going to keep very quiet and not let him into the secret.

When that all failed, he flew off and perched on the wire that hung down from the ceiling looking like a Pirate Parrot although judging from the number of feathers that were spread across the floor just in front of the wardrobe door he should have looked more like a balding Pirate Parrot.

But from where I was crouching or cowering, depending upon one's point of view, I couldn't see him all that well.

When I did get a glimpse of him he seemed to have more than enough feathers unfortunately for flight and whatever else he might want them for, and on reflection which of course was all I could do being effectively trapped inside the wardrobe, I thought that he looked more like a psychotic Parrot capable of doing rather a large amount of harm than an enemy about to give up.

My built in clock with alarms kept going off annoyingly all day, Elevenses, was not too bothersome, Lunchtime was something that stuck in the cupboard with a demonic dangling Parrot outside with murder on his mind, could be forgotten.

The Teatime alarm was accompanied by a lot of stomach rumbling and the desire to eat even the dreadful dried food that Cat owners love so much they give to their Cats, honestly if they like it that much they should eat it themselves.

Occasionally I was feeling faint and hungry and then my feelings would change and I felt hungry and faint, the fainting would have been welcome I suppose; at least I would have not felt hungry, but I had to stay awake because of the feathered fiend outside who had not given upon the idea giving me a good walloping, first and then really duff me up and after that possibly even smack me around a little, just for the fun of it!

Being trapped inside a wardrobe would normally be a nice break, I have found that I get trapped inside places quite easily, in fact I have been trapped so often that I actually rather enjoy it, usually it is warm and not too uncomfortable, but usually the way out isn't barred.

When I get bored I usually start meowing loudly and quickly someone hears it and works heroically to get me free. It is one of the great uses for Humans as far as I am concerned.

Let's face it they have a limited usefulness to Cats to be honest, but get trapped somewhere and make enough noise and a Human will come running, calling to other Humans for help, in some cases, even getting the Fire Brigade to join in the fun.

It is also possible to get on television if you get really trapped, I saw a television news item on the second or third night I was here about a Cat that had pulled off quite a PR coup and managed to get trapped on a ledge in a well.

Note that the clever little devil had not got trapped in the water at the bottom of a well!

The Cat had really thought out the stunt carefully, food (probably Prawns) was lowered down to him regularly. He was just deep enough to be out of reach but still seen from the surface.

He was a white Cat and so he showed up brilliantly against the deep black of the well in the press pictures on the day of his recovery.

Yes I admire him, the look of horror and desperation he managed to make even though he was eating was masterful, only equalled by his planning and careful attention to detail.

The day after his 'rescue' which apparently took 26 hours and was called an ordeal, he was a guest on breakfast TV, that Cat will never stop having personal appearances and raking in cash, there was even talk of him switching on the Christmas lights, wow what a performer.

It is rare for a Cat to laugh; we don't really have the right shaped mouths for it, although we do have an excellent and highly developed sense of humour.

Having said that when the front door opened accompanied by the Dog's almost customary barking and commotion, you should have been with me peeking out at the Parrot, he heard the noise too and obviously understood exactly what was happening, the Humans were home, and worse still their bedroom was littered with feathers and ripped bedclothes.

I knew that he was thinking exactly what I was thinking, 'I wouldn't like to be in these claws when 'they' come upstairs and rescue this little Cat from the mad bad bullying Parrot.'

Funnily enough, I was probably right too about that thought, the sounds from downstairs suggested that the Human Captors had noticed almost immediately that not only was the Parrot missing, but I was too.

As the sounds from downstairs got louder because they were now coming upstairs I could hear Human voices talking to each other saying that they hoped that the Parrot hadn't hurt the Cat and that they hoped that the bedroom door was closed.

The Parrot dropped again from the light fixture into the middle of a very ragged bed; he was caught running around in the bed like a headless Chicken. Oh I did laugh, I laughed until I got stitch and that was exactly the moment when the wardrobe door was opened.

I was actually in a lot of pain from the laughing and the stitch it had caused, so it was no wonder that I was doubled up when a Human hand gently picked me up and cuddled me.

Immediately I was carried out of harms way, or to put it another way I was carried away from where the Parrot was now standing looking resigned to his fate.

If a multihued bird can look pale with fear he did, but I had absolutely no sympathy for him, I had, after all been more or less innocent in today's disastrous events.

Well I know I wasn't supposed to be on 'their' bed and doing what I did in the hat could be described as unforgivable, but no one had found the hat yet and from the mess in the bedroom no one was going to be able to tell that I had had a nap on the bed.

Treats were on the menu, the Dog was told sternly to leave me alone and after a little bit of shaking and shivering I was moved to the front room where I was gently placed on the Sofa with a hot water bottle wrapped in a towel – result!

I know I had a long way to go to build up to the level of the White Cat in the well, but this was an excellent start. 'Can someone just plump up the cushion please while I think of what to do with this pesky Parrot?'

Day 11 of My Captivity:

Now there are a few things that I know I can't do, more's the pity! The first and really most obvious thing to do would be to move the Parrot's perch into the window, but even the dim wit Dog couldn't lift it.

There are other complications too; but if I list them here I might just begin to feel inadequate, and that would never do! As usual superior intelligence, guile and just plain sneakiness will win the day so I am perfectly qualified then!

The easiest way to get the Bird on display is to lure him there, the Parrot doesn't seem to eat a lot, and unlike the Dog and myself to a certain extent he is not, how can I put this? Yes, greedy! But he does like some sort of special nuts that are kept in one of the cupboards in the kitchen.

I bet if there were a few of those sitting minding their own business in the window then he would have to swoop down on them and have a chew, or crunch is a better word, ooh! Just thinking about a bite from that nasty beak sends shivers down my spine to places where shivers don't belong!

So that is the first bit of the plan carefully and well planned. The second is to make both old fools appeal to each other, that could be easy I suppose if they had anything in common, but unfortunately Mrs. Plastic Mac is a rather dowdy individual and the Parrot is well, gaudy.

Mrs. Plastic Mac has a very substantial handbag made from what looks like the business end of a Crocodile, and the Parrot well he doesn't even have a clutch bag! Mmmh! This is not going to be as easy as I thought. They must have something in common though surely? Like shoes? No Mrs. Plastic Mac's are a tired brown and the Parrot has those dead grey, black feet with odd flecks of white on them that make them look dead.

Wait a minute, talking about colour and especially the colour of dead things, Mrs. Plastic Mac's platinum blonde hair, well it is grey really but I am sure that she believes that it is at the platinum blonde end of grey!

I think I know a way to ensure that the Parrot and Mrs. Plastic Mac have at least one thing in common apart from their great ages.

Right I need to prepare some things and then get the trail of nuts in place and off we go! As they say when they are going off!

Well that makes your mouth dry, carrying the Parrots special nuts all the way from the kitchen to the front room.

At first it wasn't difficult to carry the nuts the first couple were quite easy, then as you spend more and more time with your mouth open you begin to dribble, a little at first but soon the stuff is pouring out of your mouth and you look back to see that you have left a trail like a snail, ugh! Revolting!

Still it didn't take long to get everything in place, which was good because I guessed that it was nearly time for Mrs. Plastic Mac to hobble passed on her way to feed the ungrateful Squirrels and the greedy birds.

As if on cue the Parrot woke up, it may have been something to do with the shaking of his perch? I don't really know! But the good thing was that he was awake, well as awake as he ever is!

To be honest I have no idea whether a Parrot's sense of smell is strong or not, but even a Goldfish could have smelt the special nuts, laid in a line in front of him.

For once the old idiot, no the Parrot, not Mrs. Plastic Mac, did exactly what he was intended to and ate the first few nuts, on the way to the front room window then he spotted the ones in the window and bingo, he was exactly where I wanted him, sitting patiently making munching and cracking noises waiting for me to execute the second part of my plan.

The Female Captor is luckily a very organised person and not only does she have the job of looking after me in this prison, but I think that she moonlights working somewhere else as well, and let's face it if you have two jobs and one is as hard as looking after me then you have to be organised!

Luckily 'she' (I get tired of writing the Female Captor), does all sorts of things that take time to prepare but I suppose in the long run do save time. One of the things that she does is to spend ages weighing out different ingredients, like, dried fruit, vegetables for the evening meal and last but by no means least flour!

Sometime ago I watched with amazement as 'she' (you know who I mean), was making up small, medium and big bags of flour and icing sugar when the Dog did one of his incredible 'raids.'

The Dog thinks that it is really clever to suddenly and without any warning what so ever take a lunge at the kitchen work surface where a Human is working away, minding their own business while preparing food, and see what he can grab in his mouth and make off with.

I have to say that the tactic works well, and occasionally I have watched rather jealously as the Dog has gobbled up Steak, Liver and all sorts of goodies without even thinking that there maybe others less fortunate than him, who are at death's door with hunger, i.e. Me!

On this occasion though it wasn't meat that he made off with it was a nose full of flour, I laughed until I nearly tiddled myself, as he sniffed and coughed and farted flour all over the place.

Thinking about tiddled for a minute! Do you think that is the origin of the Cat's name Tiddles? All Cats called Tiddles therefore are named after an incontinent Cat; oh I do wish I had a friend called Tiddles who I could tell that too!

Still I have slipped off the point and that will never do, it gets the reader confused and worse still sometimes means that the Publisher won't publish your book in the first place, although I am sure that no Publisher would be that daft, to pass up the opportunity to make millions with a masterpiece like this.

Right back to the plot, which I seem to have lost!

I was waiting in hiding for the Parrot to 'find' the pile of, nearly dry, special nuts and when he did and had settled himself comfortably to have a little feast; I struck.

Two small open bags of flour and one of icing sugar landed around the surprised Parrot at the same time, sending up really rather large clouds of fine white dust.

When white dust settled it had created the exact look that I had at the back of my mind when I planned to shower the Parrot.

With that nose and the whitening, I thought to myself, that in the right light, he could pass for Michael Jackson!

The Parrot has always looked old but now he had the distinguished grey feathers to match his unseemly age, he was now in fact a sort of Platinum grey, a colour that I know Mrs. Plastic Mac would love.

I was especially pleased with myself that the catapult had worked; it had been a tremendous effort, first to drag the flour and icing sugar bags into place, then to get the ruler to balance over the candle.

Obviously I had to employ a high degree of secrecy so that the bags of Parrot 'whitener' didn't leak and get discovered, then there was the other really big problem had I used to much Parrot whitener which would mean when I jumped on the end of the ruler I wouldn't be able to make the Parrot 'whitener' fly, to say nothing of aim and range, I have to admit that hitting the target was either down to having a good eye or luck!

To say that I was astonished that my plan worked is to suggest that I didn't have conviction that it would and so I can only say that I was very pleased and pleasantly surprised that the plan worked, because when Mrs. Plastic Mac came passed she immediately spotted the grey wizened Parrot and took it upon herself to come right down to the window.

So strong was her concern for the old Parrot in distress that she didn't close the gate to the drive or even keep to the path, she walked right across the wet grass which made her support stockings damp.

I suppose that I should point out at this point that the Parrot had been a little blinded by all of the whitening powder in the air and was staggering around the bay window like a drunk old Parrot when Mrs. Plastic Mac first spotted him.

That is an interesting point in itself though, what is a little blinded? I would imagine you either can't see and are blinded or you can see a little and that can't be 'blind' can it?

Anyway the 'dear old soul,' Mrs. Plastic Mac that is was tapping on the window trying to either frighten the Parrot or attract its attention, I have to say I don't know which!

The plan was going well so far and that was the way I wanted it to stay Mrs. Plastic Mac seemed very concerned and when she couldn't attract the Parrot's attention, which probably was due to all of the Parrot whitener in its ears, she decided to do something that I hadn't planned upon.

I want to know who in their right minds decided that old people should have mobile (cell to you Americans) phones? They are a menace, well both mobile phones and old people in my opinion are a menace, but mobile phones especially. Of course when the two menaces are combined then all hell can break out, and it was about to!

Unable to attract the 'poor' Parrot's attention and obviously powerless to break a window to effect its rescue as I thought she would, Mrs. Plastic Mac did something that just plain staggered me!

She reached into the pocket of her green tweed coat with the fur (no one I knew, I hoped) collar and produced the offensive weapon. I would also like to know who in their right minds has the number of The Royal Society for the Protection and Care of Animals (the RSPCA) on speed dial programmed into their mobile phones?

Well now I know one person who does, which in this case at this time was mightily inconvenient indeed.

As she was talking into the phone and at the same time peering into the front room I decided that I needed some space, some space between Mrs. Plastic Mac, the Parrot and the very large area of Parrot whitener which had settled on the carpet like an over night fall of fresh snow.

Unfortunately some areas of the 'fresh snow' had Cat paw prints in, some were indistinct and couldn't be clearly recognized for what they were, I was sure, but others followed a sort of delighted dancing pattern, and appeared as though a Cat had been celebrating and these were very distinct, I would even go so far as to say they were manifestly Cat prints, oops!

They do say that timing is everything! It was time that I retreated, but first I had one little tiny job to do.

The Dog was snoring as usual and was quite surprised to have a dusty pawed Cat jump on him!

Happily his reactions were as predictable as I had expected and he immediately began chasing the 'rotter.'

(Authors Note: Rotter, a Doggy word, believe it or not, that means not only a bad person, the type who would wake a Dog up from a marvellous dream, but also old food found out on a walk that has been waiting to be eaten for two or three weeks).

The chase I am pleased to announce was very brief, our Man's best furry friend (and soon to be mine today) careered headlong into the front room expecting me to be waiting for a bit of a (hopefully) play fight and a bit of rough and tumble and where the Dog is concerned the emphasis is on the 'rough' and straight into the white snow like powder, happily wiping all trace of the Cat's paw prints away.

It goes without saying that the Dog didn't find me, only a deaf Parrot who may or may not have been blind and therefore was blissfully unaware of what was going on and a stranger looking in the window, who shouldn't have been, and so he began barking and racing to the front door and back as befits the actions of a true Guard Dog.

I watched our brave protector for a while from the stairs before I slipped up into 'their' bedroom to wash my paws and look out at the pantomime which I had a dreadful feeling was about to unfold in the front garden.

It is true to say that I am never disappointed in my expectations, the Dog did exactly what I had expected, the flour and icing sugar bombs has bettered my expectations, but Mrs. Plastic Mac had gone way beyond reason to my way of thinking, and had set in motion much more than I had expected or indeed bargained for!

To make matters worse and I am afraid to say that they were going to get much worse, the RSPCA responded almost immediately as if they had a man in a van just waiting almost at the end of the road to attend Mrs. Plastic Mac every need and those of the little animals around her!

The white van drove through the still open gate and straight down the drive, when it came to a halt out popped a short chubby inspector in a blue uniform with most of his shirt hanging out over his trousers.

Immediately I realised that he was just about as dangerous as Mrs. Plastic Mac both, it appeared, obviously cared more for animals than they did for their appearance. Trouble was brewing I could feel it in my water.

Mrs. Plastic Mac raced over to the RSPCA man, grabbed his arm and led him to the front window, just below where I was crouching and getting just a little more uncomfortable by the minute.

The RSPCA man and Mrs. Plastic Mac had a short conversation, which involved Mrs. Plastic Mac doing an enormous amount of arm waving and some very deliberate pointing. I could hear her clearly, telling the RSPCA man exactly what the poor Parrot had been subjected to and judging by his frown, he could see what had happened.

Better to wait I thought. I was tempted to act on the spur of the moment, there was a very large vase of brilliant, almost Parrot feather coloured flowers next to the open window, and I am sure that I could have quite easily pushed them down on top of the troublesome pair and got them to go away, but something held me back.

When I had more or less made up my mind to just give the vase a gentle push I couldn't, the pair split up, the RSPCA man went to the front door to ring the bell and Mrs. Plastic Mac continued to tap the window.

What with the sound of the mad Dog barking, Mrs. Plastic Mac tapping the window loudly enough to break it and the RSPCA man ringing the door bell this was turning into a bit of a loud nightmare, but I was sure that I could ride it out and they would get bored and all go away, it couldn't get much worse I thought, could it?

It is sometimes quite distressing to see your hope, dreams and aspirations dissolve in a deluge of unfortunate circumstances and to watch the metaphoric ink run on a well laid plan; I can assure you!

Just when I thought that today would get better and that the RSPCA man and Mrs. Plastic Mac would get tired of ringing the door bell and banging incessantly on the window and sort of, eventually decide that there was not much more they could do after their valiant attempt to be wonderful citizens, something really quite awful happened.

Well it wasn't really quite awful, it was really rather awful, no that doesn't go far enough either, let's put it this way, I had a feeling that I was, at that time, going to have to get ready to donate my guts for garters (as they say, when they suggest that 'they' are going to have 'your' guts for garters!)

At the end of the drive a noisy crowd seemed to have gathered watching the lunatic actions of Mrs. Plastic Mac and the RSPCA Man.

The crowd was getting a very good show too and seemed to be quite appreciative to me, shouting the odd remark and word of encouragement, like 'break the down door,' from the back of the crowd, or 'use something solid,' which seemed to come from the middle, and somewhere in between someone shouted 'shouldn't happen to a Parrot!'

Then finally the delirious crowd shouted 'the town is that way,' although I don't think that this was directed at Mrs. Plastic Mac or the RSPCA Man, Still you know the sort of things that a crowd shouts, most of what they shout borders on the is insane.

From the midst of the crowd emerged a real nightmare, the nose of the first of a line of Police cars and a Police Dog Van (that is not a van shaped like a Police Dog or even shaped like a Dog that is not a member of the Police force, it is just another Police vehicle in a long line of trouble headed on a collision course with a small Tabby and White Cat whose fur has silver highlights!

I have a motto 'a little knowledge is a dangerous thing,' but that doesn't apply here and wasn't the motto that I had in mind, unless it is to say that I hope that the Police were equipped with the knowledge that in general, Cats are innocent.

I wasn't prepared to go silently when arrested, in fact it is true to say that I wasn't 'prepared' to be arrested at any volume or under any circumstances and I felt myself shrink behind the vase full of bright flowers into a state of almost complete invisibility.

The motto that had slipped my mind, and that was possibly because the shock of watching one's garden being invaded by a fleet of Police cars, was 'discretion is the better part of valour,' and with that in mind if that is where I could keep the thought from slipping away I just waited.

The cavalcade of Police cars finished driving down the drive, the ones at the front fanned out around the front of the house and in turn the ones that couldn't go any further parked in a line.

They switched off their engines in unison and spewed out quite a large number of neatly uniformed officers, who proceeded to do dozens of things at the same time, including move the crowd back, much to their combined disappointment and then cover almost everywhere with rather jolly blue and white striped tape which instructed anyone who wished to read it that it was a Police line and not to be crossed.

If I needed any further proof this showed that the Police meant business. A Policeman with a different sort of hat to the others and a large degree of rather fetching silver braid all over his shoulders and his different hat was now in conference with the RSPCA man and Mrs. Plastic Mac.

There was an enormous amount of pointing going on from Mrs. Plastic Mac all directed at I presumed the deaf figure of a white feathered Parrot.

For the first time I was relieved because no one had pointed to the window where I was cowering and personally that was both fine by me and also more than quite a relief.

After the consultation with the RSPCA man and Mrs. Plastic Mac the Policeman with the different hat dispatched two officers to the last vehicle in the line up the drive, and I watched with growing interest as they brought back a red battering ram.

Well what can I say, the RSPCA man and Mrs. Plastic Mac had made a lot of noise but that was nothing in comparison to what two professionals can do as they battered the front door open. For the first two crashes against the heavy oak door the Dog had joined in again barking itself hoarse, but as the door hinges caved in I heard him leg it back to his basket. Which I have to say is the first sensible thing I have heard him do since I have been here.

It went quiet again after the door was shoved aside by a large, an extremely large item of footwear and several people entered the house.

I decided to risk sneaking on my belly to the top of the stairs for a better view, to be rewarded by the sight of the RSPCA man and Mrs. Plastic Mac picking up the dazed and confused Parrot and getting covered in a fine coating of flour and icing sugar for their trouble.

The Parrot didn't resist or even squeak a squawk; shock has that effect I suppose. Both were fussing and dusting the dazed Parrot with no regard to their clothing, but I don't suppose they ever had much regard for clothes at the best of times.

As if to join the party of uninvited guests more RSPCA people arrived in the front room to care for the powdered Parrot, all we needed now was a film crew and Rolf Harris and life would be complete.

It was then that the obvious struck me, I had been staring it in the face for a while and of course when one is confronting the obvious it is never that!

The front door was open! Well, to be more accurate the front door was lying in the hall, with a lot of red impact marks around the handle! This was my chance; a few short steps to freedom lay between me, and well, freedom!

No one would pay much attention to a stray Cat who had come along to have a look at all of the noise surely? And better still neither the nosy Parrot nor that traitor of a Dog would be reporting my escape this time!

I have no idea why Humans use the expression, 'running around like headless Chickens,' why? Have you seen the way that Humans run around? Why insult Chickens when they are the perfect example of panic.

As I slid down the stairs with all the noise that a stuffed toy makes when falling off a shelf, Humans were running around everywhere.

Now I know from my perspective which is about eight inches off the ground, things seem bigger and more imposing than they really are, but seeing dozens of sets of uniformed legs running here and there in and out of the front room was really daunting.

Despite being daunted and then really daunted I pressed on and to my relief as I slipped passed the front room door, catching for a moment, the unbelievable sight of an RSPCA nurse giving the Parrot the kiss of life and not vomiting on the spot, I made it to where the front door had been.

Then hooray and congratulations to yours truly, I was free, I was actually standing on the little bricks of the drive and I was on my way to freedom.

This time I wasn't about to be caught, and so cunningly I crept under the first Police car and then even more cunningly I have to say used the line of Police cars that were parked nose to tail as cover as I headed up the drive to my liberty.

This was easy and that of course made me nervous, what made me even more nervous was that I had become stuck under the last but one Police car, which was in actual fact a Police van, the very van that held unfortunately, not just one Police Dog but by the sound and smell, at least two.

My exit was barred by a couple of sets of blue uniformed legs and shiny big black shoes whose owners were chatting amiably to the crowd, who in turn were being kept in place by the attractive blue and white striped plastic bunting.

The Police Dogs obviously hired because of their limited mental capacity which allows them to confront danger without giving it much of a thought first, demonstrated that they had one other attribute that endeared them to their masters, a very keen sense of smell.

In spite of the new surroundings, the large number of Humans and the smell of vehicles, petrol and tyres these dedicated Dogs had smelt something that was suspicious, in my defence I was nervous if it was 'that' that they had smelt, but it may have not been the result of my nerves that they had detected, it may have just been that I was a Cat!

Both, or more, if there were more than two Police Dogs, began barking so loudly that I thought my poor ears would end up flattened to my head forever.

It was definitely time to break cover and leg it with all of my legs as fast as I could, to maintain my newly won independence, so off I trotted, well, I figured that if I ran I would have looked suspicious.

It worked; soon I was through the legs of not only the Policemen but also a fair number of the crowd; excellent this was really working!

Now where did she come from? Yes that is what I was thinking as I was carried back through the Police line and down the drive.

Mrs. Plastic Mac! Was she everywhere? And more importantly why was she halfway along my escape route? Really this woman has no shame!

Together but only one of us willingly, we walked down the drive and into the house as if we owned it, but only one of us did own it and it definitely wasn't Mrs. Plastic Mac.

She even had the nerve to stroke me as she mentioned to the RSPCA man that I must have been frightened by all of the noise and tried to escape, that's what she thinks I thought, as I was locked in the kitchen with the Dog who had for sometime, it appeared, been buried under his blanket! Some guard Dog! I must remember to rely upon him in a crisis!

It was sometime later when it dawned on me that I didn't even attempt to scratch or bite Mrs. Plastic Mac, am I losing my touch? Or, was I just so shocked at yet another attempt to escape being foiled by that woman that I just couldn't bring myself to have a go?

That evening it took a long while for things to calm down. I could hear Police feet marching in and out of the house, accompanied by several RSPCA people I imagined, and in the middle of all of the commotion of course there was the RSPCA man and

Mrs. Plastic Mac, patting themselves on the back for saving the Parrot and occasionally mentioning the poor little frightened Cat, who I suppose was me.

Day 12 of My Captivity:

I woke up this morning, opened one eye and saw that it was dark and to be honest I couldn't see why I should get up! Nothing had changed after the excitement of yesterday; well the front door would be changed thinking about it!

Although I was still in prison and I was still saddled with that awful Avian (bird to you) there was just one or two bright points on the horizon, first the carpenter (pecking or otherwise) will be working on the door and the doorway will therefore be filled with nothing and I might well be able to escape, especially if I use a disguise as the brave pilots in Cold Ditz did!

Now you are asking what is the second bright point?

Did you think I had forgotten? Really you have no faith in me!

The second bright point is the fact that the Parrot seems or appears to be missing; personally I prefer 'seems' because appears to be gone sounds odd, especially if you say: 'Appears to have disappeared!'

Nevertheless who am I to criticise a language that is as old as the hills and has obviously been used by Looneys for generations since the first Looney stopped throwing boulders at other looneys and began to talk and shake hands with them, trying hard to forget about all of the bumps, bruises and scratches that the boulders would have made over the years as they hit him.

When the boulders finally stopped raining down on him because he had stopped returning fire, I wouldn't be surprised if the others asked him if he was hurt? And he replied hurt! Hurt? Of course I am hurt; you've never waved!

Tee hee! That is a Cat Joke as you may have noticed; most of our Jokes are about Humans or Dogs! You know, the animals who think that they have a higher level of intelligence than Cats, which I suppose proves the converse (opposite, for all you Human readers, yes I hope to publish a full version of this Diary in Cat too and we don't use the word opposite in the Cat language).

Fancy being so deluded that you think that you are superior, unless of course you, like me for instance, just happen to actually be superior.

So maybe there actually is something to get up for today after all, but it is nice and snugly here on top of the work surface in the utility room, under the boiler.

Sorry for the long explanation but I thought it was worth risking losing readers with a short attention span, just to let you know how warm and comfortable I am, because hopefully by now you have begun to find me irresistible and better still feel some affection for me!

Honestly I do hope that your affection for me is growing, Cats are; it is true; very independent and like to be out and about (well this Cat would like the chance to be 'out and about').

But they do like to come 'home,' gorge on some nice freshly prepared meat and then settle down in some considerable comfort, occasionally being stroked, especially behind the ears.

Even though being stroked behind the ears makes me go crosseyed and I dribble uncontrollably, I like that, not too often mind, because when I want to be stroked behind the ears I'll decide the time and the place, thank you, and then offer my ears up for stroking!

A disguise would work perfectly I am sure, after all Humans are not very observant and the Carpenter will be busy doing whatever Carpenters do to doors. Now that is an interesting thought what do Carpenters do?

Wheelwrights make wheels right, with an extra 'W' in their names to impress. Shopkeepers, keep shop which is old English 'drivel' speak for standing behind a shop counter with a sour face and a great and fervent wish to be somewhere else.

It stands to reason then that Knackers probably make a living out of feeling tired all the time.

Consequently if one follows the logic of the trade's people's names above, then Carpenters must Carp and must have done it a lot to end up with such a dreadful trade.

I will listen closely to what he says just to see if he does complain or carp on about things. That will be a thrilling morning listening to someone find fault and grumble, still if he is preoccupied with the door and the moaning then I am home free or free from home.

Still I won't listen too closely obviously because I will be watching, waiting for my chance to get through that door and out into the garden and let's hope that the adventure doesn't end there and I can 'leg it' down the cul-de-sac (posh name for road with one way out, if you don't remember).

Something I noticed from the gate; which of course is where I ended up before being recaptured the last time I escaped, was that our cul-de-sac seems to lead down to a wood or maybe a forest, it would be a great idea to head there because once in the wood I don't expect that they could find me.

But the first thing to do is to see what opportunities the Carpenter offers and what sort of disguise I can find.

Well he is an early riser I'll give him that, when I slipped passed the front door he was talking to the Female Captor.

Unfortunately they were in the hallway and the front door was closed or I may have just put my head down (and in some coarse circles they say 'and my arse up') and go for 'it' and freedom, running as fast as I can down the hall and then launching myself through the open door, to freedom and beyond, which I suppose would be the wood, if that is where I am headed.

Still that wasn't an option, and I will have to use stealth, cunning, my superior intelligence and of course my wonderful ability to disguise myself so that I can't be taken for a Cat in any light! I suppose that the best place to look for the disguise is in 'their' bedroom because there are all sorts of interesting things lying about.

A while ago I noticed the bottles and tubes of make-up on the dressing table, they would be useful, in the documentary about Cold Ditz the 'chaps' had to use odd ingredients for their make-up, Pork grease and shoe polish, and so I may have a considerable advantage with a greater choice.

Reading all the labels is funny it is like walking into a Candy shop in Paradise, just imagine wearing Frosted Pink lipstick while relaxing with a face tinted by Caribbean mist face powder?

I tried a few lipsticks, tubes, tubs and pencils, 'Honeydew' eyeliner and Melting moments Peach coloured liquid make-up and an amazing Electric Red lip-gloss that was mainly Red with incredible sparkly bits shot through it.

I looked in the mirror and was both happy and quite astonished at what I saw, as disguises go, this on worked perfectly, the face that peered, a little evilly, back at me was nothing what so ever like me, excellent!

There is one limitation with make-up though and when I looked at the rest of my body I realised from the neck down I still looked like the spitting image of me, but now with someone else's head on my body.

I had to improvise, because I couldn't see any body make-up, more's the pity! Next to all of the bottles and tubes of make-up and piles of spilt powder and broken lipsticks, Oops! Was the answer to my problem!

Sitting on its own stand was a short cropped dark wig, in no time at all I was admiring what had once been myself in the mirror, my disguise was complete and I was head over heels with happiness. I looked nothing at all like me.

Time to go downstairs and walk confidently out of the front doorway, the front door I noticed was conveniently being planed to size on the driveway.

I obviously had got the idea of being so brazen and just simply walking out of the front door, or front gate in their case, from the brave 'chaps' in Cold ditz.

Unfortunately their ruse (which they called a 'wheeze' for some reason probably best known to themselves) didn't work because one of the German guards tricked them and said in German, 'goodnight Captain,' both of the English chaps' being dressed in German Army officer's uniforms, or should I say disguises, that they had been made to look like German Army Officer's uniforms.

The 'chaps' responded in German which was brilliant and an excellent addition to the disguise adding realism by the bucket load, but then the sneaky German soldier said in English 'Have a safe journey, old chap,' to one of the 'chaps' who wasn't able to resist replying in English and said 'Thank you, we will,' the game as they say was up and the 'chaps' were marched back to prison.

I hope that this doesn't happen to me, but then I don't intend to speak to anyone so I am in with a real chance of freedom.

At the foot of the stairs I encountered my first difficulty, I hadn't noticed that the Female Captor was coming out of the kitchen with a cup of Tea obviously for the Carpenter.

I have heard that tradesmen work better if they have large quantities of tea sloshing around in their insides, and so I presume that the Female Captor was filling the Carpenter up in order to get the best possible job done! Which strikes me as very wise!

Worse still, she called to him that his Tea and biscuits, (I was impressed with the addition of biscuits, goodness did she want a good job done or what?) were ready!

The Carpenter had someone with him who by the sound of the way he was being treated was possibly a lower life form, called an H'pprentice. The H'pprentice was actually a young Human Male and therefore probably not as highly evolved as the carpenter it has to be said, I stopped to watch them from the stairs as the H'pprentice ambled towards the doorway.

So with the doorway blocked there was nothing I could do now but watch.

As I observed them I realised that an H'pprentice was employed to be shouted at by the Carpenter, given lots of meaningless tasks and finally to eat all of the Chocolate biscuits to save them from melting.

Then in turn to spread Chocolate over the nice new wood of the front door and get into trouble, which was something that he was remarkably good at, the getting into trouble, well and spreading Chocolate finger marks all over the place as well.

Unfortunately this little group of tea drinkers blocked my only exit and it was getting just a little hot sitting on the stairs in a patch of bright sunlight, covered by what seemed like not one fur coat but two, there was nothing to be done, but to go for it and do what the 'chaps' had done, straight back, head up and walk slowly and calmly and don't speak to anyone in any language.

It worked so well that I was dazed with success, I casually walked to the foot of the stairs and then regally out of the front door threading my way through the three pairs of legs.

As I got to the doorstep I stood in a bright spotlight of sun and breathed in the free air of the great outdoors, or in this case the garden.

It was then that the chinking of Teacups on saucers stopped and the air around me went still.

I heard someone say something but I didn't think that the rude remark was said about me. 'What was that, a rat in drag?'

My next step was the most enjoyable and I took it slowly so that my disguise, which had begun to slip off my shoulders didn't fall down and reveal who I was.

'That is my Cat,' I knew that voice, oh dear I had been rumbled! It was the Female Captor. 'Stop him please!' Her shout started the Carpenter and his H'pprentice into action as if it had been a pistol at the beginning of a race.

'Really why couldn't she just keep her mouth shut?' Was my immediate reply, but only as a thought because I wasn't going to get caught out using the wrong language!

'G'on' George grab the little blighter.' Commanded the Carpenter to his H'pprentice.

Although there was nowhere to hide and precious few places to run, I made off. Just slipping through George's Chocolate smeared hands as he made a grab for me on several occasions.

Then George came so close to grabbing me that I thought 'my number was up' as the Cold Ditz 'chaps' would say.

Luckily I belted off in the opposite direction to George the H'pprentice, who being so young and so full of energy courtesy of all of the Chocolate biscuits he had eaten, was after me like a Maserarti (this is not product placement but merely a reference to these fine fast automobiles I promise, but I like those excellent cars, hint, hint).

It was no use; no matter which way I turned and spurted away, George was there within a whisker of me almost grabbing me again and again.

Then disaster struck, just as it had to the 'chaps,' part of my disguise let me down, I tripped, stumbled, and fell over the wig, which then acted like a net and trapped me so that George was able to grab me and while I covered him in make-up, he covered me in Chocolate.

George's hands, which smelt more like two Easter Eggs than Human hands scooped me up, to be honest, I was so shattered from all of the running around that I was glad to be carried, and I was also very hot under all of the make-up, which seemed to be clinging to my skin and fur, so a nice breather was in order as I was carried back to the Female Captor and my fate.

Now the nice English 'chaps' from the Cold Ditz story were shot for escaping after they were recaptured which was rather extreme I think personally, so I was expecting the worst! Sadly I have discovered that in life you are rarely disappointed if you expect the worst!

As I was handed over to the Female Captor who for reasons best known to her own self held me at arms length, she said 'Oh my goodness, look at that!' She then insulted me further by sniffing me. 'Smells like Chocolate and looks like one of those foil covered Chocolate Easter Bunnies from Hell!

Now that wasn't the nicest compliment I have ever had, but I almost forgot I was still in disguise, at least that had worked, even if because of George's quick Chocolate hands and very fast size nine feet, my escape hadn't!

Day 13 of My Captivity:

In the television documentary programme about Cold Ditz the other evening they showed various ways to escape from a secure building. And although the disguise tactic had failed I wasn't about to forsake this excellent reference material and general guide to escaping.

Most escape attempts were just a little silly and matched the way that most of the 'chaps' spoke, but there were, to my way of thinking, several ideas that had some merit and needed investigating further.

I don't really want to share all of the 'ideas' from the inspirational programme here, just yet, because I am just a little worried that my Diary will be found and read. I know that I am being watched wherever I go at the moment, especially when I 'go' if you get my meaning!

At the moment I am being followed all over the house, five times today I have been picked up bodily, and carried to the kitchen and put into the grey gravelly stuff, I ask you is that anyway to treat an animal of my stature?

Anywhere I saunter, anywhere in the house, you can guarantee that either the Male or the Female Captor will either turn up suddenly behind me after I go into a room or worse, peer at me around the door while I am minding my own business. All I can say is that I must have broken a rule or two, but is that my fault if I don't know the rules in the first place?

As you can imagine, progress of any sort using what I learned on the Cold Ditz documentary is painfully slow, and when I do manage to give 'them' the slip I only get a few precious minutes of privacy.

In fact what I decided to do was to create a diversion, a sort of enormous Red Herring to take their attention off me for a minute. Yes another tip from the 'chaps' in Cold Ditz bless them.

No, not a herring salted and smoked to a reddish brown colour! That would be silly, but hang on a moment, a real Red Herring, say seven foot tall would probably make an almost perfect decoy, still I can see two or even three problems with that idea.

First I would be tempted to eat the diversion, secondly seven foot tall Red Herrings don't exist, even in this Diary, more's the pity, because if they did then ten foot tall Prawns would most likely be shyly peering out from behind the kitchen door.

What was the third point? Oh! I don't remember, I was just thinking about being introduced to a ten foot tall Prawn and imagining that it might have a friend or two, after all Prawns of that size almost certainly get lonely easily.

(Translator's note: Are you 'on' something?)

(Author's Note: Don't interrupt, I am enjoying this daydream).

Where was I? Ah! Yes, I need a decoy and thinking about fish of remarkable stature will not help.

The sort of Red Herring I need is a diversion to take the attention away from me, so that I can do some planning and get a bit of peace and quiet.

The Dog is always good for a diversion and sadly I have to say daft enough to swallow anything that I tell him, or indeed and this can be amusing occasionally, swallow anything I throw him, which is especially amusing if I am feeling just a little mean minded, but I will let your imagination consider just how mean I can be to the Dog, or you might just start to judge me unfairly!

Great! Plan hatched, yes I know it was quick, but I think fast on my paws! It is time for my watchers and I to go down to the kitchen and see if the big lump is awake! It will be handy to have them witness the fact that I was, rather cutely curled up in the Dog basket dozing, when as they say in ballooning circles, 'the balloon goes up!'

I wonder if 'the balloon goes up!' has another meaning as well as the obvious one; that a Balloon full of idiots and probably Richard Branson (launching some Virgin business venture or other), without parachutes, is rising into the wild and cold blue yonder? Still, no time to worry about all of that now, in fact there isn't any time to lose.

The Dog, though mainly unpredictable because of his limited intelligence, does seem to have some responses that can be depended upon.

When watching him, from a distance I have noticed that the Dog will do anything for food for example, even to the daft extreme of making himself look like a total slobbering idiot sitting up on his back legs begging, if you ever did!

Still sad behaviour like this can be forgiven by individuals of a higher intelligence such as, me, for instance, because although it is shaming to mention, I have been known to do the same routine for Prawns or slithers of Smoked Salmon, even on one occasion pretending to shadow box because that inane performance brought even more Prawn presents from the Male Captor.

The Dog also likes to chase things, mainly his tail, really I should tell him that it is part of his body, but it is fun to watch him spinning round and round in small circles trying to bite the end of what he must think is a very nimble small furry animal following him.

It is also gratifying to watch the idiot's look of pain when on the rare occasion he actually catches and bites the small furry follower and (he must think) it bites back, 'really sad!' Doesn't cover his wretched behaviour. But to then continue to chase the small aggressive furry animal that bites so hard is sheer and undiluted madness, which is only achieved by Dogs and Newsreaders, no don't ask!

Still he wasn't going to be chasing his tail today, oh no, he was going to chase a much more interesting tail and such a pretty one too!

Talking Dog is not easy, but in a short time I have learned the entire Dog language and so you would think I was a fluent Dog language speaker!

Well let me explain, it is not that simple, but then is anything simple, really when you think about it, take Daisies for instance, no sorry I am interrupting myself again.

Back to the Dog language before we take Daisies anywhere, there are only a few dozen words in the Dog language, obviously it is not a language based on French or it would contain a few tens of words, the French being decimalised for a few centuries I believe.

The difficulty in mastering the Dog language has more to do with pronunciation to be honest and quite a lot to do with being honest. Dog words are delivered with a lot of tongue rolling and lolling between gritted teeth; which is the same as Norwegian I think?

There is also the occasional, delicate sound produced in the nose, that is very similar to the sound of someone having his or her head snuggled into someone's bottom! Again, very much like Norwegian!

I struggle with the difficult everyday Dog pronunciation I really have no desire to even try to make the second sound that I have described, which is no burden to me because it is mainly used when one Dog is meeting with another!

You may have noticed them being 'Norwegian' together, well at least I think it is Norwegian, I hope that I haven't used the wrong word here and as a consequence will be chased by almost half of all of the blonde lager filled Scandinavians in the world!

My only defence if I am wrong is the usual one (which as well as being the usual one, is the one that usually works); I am only a Cat after all! There that is my excuse, and I think it is a good one, whatever the people who I may malign from time to time think!

In the documentary the 'chaps' in the Prison camp, built a tunnel under the castle and out into the woods nearby, unfortunately they didn't build it as far as the woods as they should have done and had lots of complaints from the German guards, probably because it made a mess of the minefield that led up to the last barbed wire fence, but that was their problem and not mine!

To cover the noise of digging the clever 'Chaps' built a wooden vaulting horse and several teams of other 'chaps' spent endless days jumping or vaulting over the vaulting horse.

It is such a shame that there is only one of me, because I think that this was a brilliant idea and acted as a wonderful diversion.

Another cracker of an idea was to hide the enormous amount of earth that the 'Chaps' dug up when they had filled their beds, the attics of their barracks and all the other obvious Earth hiding places, they stuffed it into bags inside their trousers and while walking in the parade ground, spread it over the floor, brilliant. I suppose they also watched the other 'Chaps' doing their vaulting while they were spreading the soil spoil too!

Now do you see why, if I had a hat I would take it off to these inventive and cunning 'Chaps' they were very inventive and exceedingly crafty. And cunning too; which in fact makes them inventive, cunning and crafty; if you see what I mean, sorry just trying to make sense out of a sentence! Which let's face it is not easy for a Cat!

It is with a great sense of shame that I have to tell you that I haven't been able to build a Vaulting Horse because I can't find enough fur and the only mane I located was a gas main and that didn't work.

But the idea of a tunnel really appeals to me and I will have to start doing a survey of this prison to see where I can start mine. It has to be somewhere quiet and out of the way so that the Captors don't 'get wind' of the idea, The Cold Ditz Chaps used that term too, 'get wind' and I don't think that it has anything to do with the results of eating beans, but more to do with being 'found out!'

But for now all of that inspired thinking has made me drowsy and I am afraid that I am going to have to stop writing and have a Catnap, excuse me won't you?

Day 14 of My Captivity:

Today was frantically busy, but I have imposed a news blackout on what I was doing and so it was totally secret. I am afraid the only thing I can tell you about today is that I didn't see what the weather was like through the window and that I was so engrossed with what I was secretly doing that I forgot to eat until my stomach reminded me just now that I was very hungry, talk about getting wind, this was weird, like getting wind in reverse.

Stomachs are strange and secret things really; I didn't know that they had a voice of their own for example, probably because they choose to voice their opinions so very specifically and very occasionally.

Having said that when a stomach begins to talk, then it is a good idea to pay it some attention, because it will only rumble and gurgle on in the background getting louder and louder until it is listened to.

And then if it has been ignored it may just get its own back by aching, even if it has had its demands granted or it might go and show you up in public in a smelly way if you get my drift, and I hope you didn't.

Usually stomachs just demand food, in fact I think that they only demand food, because although water ends up in the stomach the mouth is responsible for reminding one to drink by going first leathery and then dry!

I wonder if that is the same for Humans? It must be I suppose, we are, I think, all made up of the same basic bits after all.

Still now my brain is interrupting my stomach and telling me that it is time that the light went out and I was asleep I have quite a lot to do over the next few days, unfortunately you won't read what it is that I am doing until I have done it, but here is a clue so that the Diary doesn't get too boring. I plan to escape!

Day 15 of My Captivity:

The house is in uproar today, with the Captors running around doing loads of Hoovering (Ugh! The memory), dusting, polishing and cooking, all for what sounds like to me; a visit by, visitors, I think they even polished the Parrot and if they didn't then they should straight after they wash that fleabag of a smelly Dog!

Personally I don't like visitors they seem to expect a Cat to be more 'Catlike' than this Cat is, if you follow me.

With so much work going on it was difficult to concentrate on my own project and worse still the risk of my secret 'operation' being discovered was too great and so I have stopped all work on the… oops I nearly spilt the beans as they say!

Instead of working I decided to watch the workers for a while as they scurried around knocking things over, generally getting in each other's way and creating more work as they went like a well drilled confusion and mayhem team.

It is quite relaxing to sit and watch others work, especially if they know that they haven't actually got enough time to do all of the tasks that they have to finish, and so I spent a comfortable few hours relaxing while the two Humans cleaned and worried about the time slipping passed.

While I relaxed and watched I realised that the little guy with the shock of crazy white hair, Albert Einstein was right; time is relative.

I had all of the time in the world to watch the Humans running around manically, running out of time, because I had time to spare or indeed spare time and they didn't have any time to spare, gosh he was clever, for a man who constantly had bad hair days!

When it was time to do the cooking I thought that the least that I could do was to accompany them down to the kitchen and lend a paw or two and in to the bargain get handsomely rewarded with scraps and more importantly with all of the food that will be dropped on the floor.

Well let me rephrase that last sentence and temper it with some realism, I will get all of the food that falls on the floor if I can be quicker than the drip of a drooling Dog.

It is true, I usually am quicker than the Dog at catching food before it lands on the floor, but I have to be careful not to get carried away and eat everything because the Dog tends to take defeat rather badly and so I always have to 'miss' a few of the larger scraps and bits of falling food so that the slowcoach can claim the odd victory over the Cat.

Late in the evening the Human Captors finished their long day of cleaning and cooking, which meant that any visitors, and I was still convinced that there were going to be some, would be arriving tomorrow, so content in the knowledge that I had at least one more night of peace I went to bed, rather more full up of little treats than I normally am, even winning a Chocolate 'Cat Drop' treat for cleaning up some spilt cream.

Well they say that the little brown 'drops' are Chocolates for Cats although I have my doubts! But they are not too bad and they say that it is the thought that counts when looking at the teeth of a gift horse.

Day 16 of My Captivity:

My secret plans that I couldn't mention the other day are still going, well, according to plan, but they have had to be completely put on hold for a while because there were children here visiting for the weekend.

The children all seemed to be called either niece or nephew as far as I could work out. But I couldn't really hear much of what was said because I had to keep myself hidden while they were here because they seemed to believe in rough love and very forceful stroking.

When they went to bed in the spare room I slipped in unseen and hid, I don't know why really, I wasn't frightened of the children at all; in fact I suppose I was interested in them.

First I hid in the wardrobe until one of them pulled open the door and nearly pulled it off its hinges in the process of opening the wardrobe.

Then after the Captors had stopped the wardrobe shaking and led the over enthusiastic, or hyperactive as Doctors call them, child back to bed, I slid on my belly under the bed.

After a while, one of the Captors read what the Niece and Nephew called excitedly a bedtime story.

It was about a Human, so I was just about to nod off for a bit of a calming down catnap – the wardrobe incident had shaken me a little almost as much as it shook the wardrobe – when I heard something that made me wake up with a twitch of my whiskers.

The word I had heard was Dungeon, The word grabbed my attention and I listened to the story of a man who it appeared had been wrongfully imprisoned, what a coincidence, just like me.

It was a long story and although I was in desperate need of a Catnap I listened to all of it, the tale of the Count of Monte Cristo, I am so glad I did, because at the end the man they called the Count was free and rich, now I would settle for free but rich as well! That would be a bonus.

It is interesting to know that they imprison their own kind, these Humans - I had begun to think imprisonment was just something that Humans did just to Cats just to annoy them!

Day 17 of My Captivity:

The visit of the children, for me, was actually quite painless, they preferred to play with the Dog because he is big, cuddly and really dopey and wouldn't dream of retaliating if they hurt him while being rough in a child like, 'I don't know any better because I am a child,' way.

Cats on the other hand have for centuries cultivated a reputation of having a rather bad temper and vicious reaction to the sort of treatment from children that leaves the Dog panting, happy and waiting for more.

And that is yet another reason then, that I am glad that I am a Cat! As if I needed any more reasons!

In the same way as I appreciate Nuclear Physics, from afar, the children interested me, but close to, I wasn't so keen.

When they did approached me they were, in the main, met with a hiss and a raised paw, although one child was lucky enough to stroke me hesitantly for a while, until he began to relax and got a little rough.

I sent him away with a mere flesh wound, but to hear him scream you would think I had used considerable force, still I suppose it is a shock for a purring Cat to suddenly turn on you, but it helps to keep the mystery alive and I have to say it amused me too.

Happily I wasn't bothered for the rest of the day and snoozed when the children were eating or went out or to put it another way, when they were quiet.

DAY 18 OF MY CAPTIVITY:

Things are getting back to normal now, well I say normal, they are at least becoming peaceful once again, all I can think is that they must have put Valium in the Parrot food or his water because at last the feathered freak has stopped his incessant squawking.

To be fair to him I think that the children tortured him the most after they found out that if they encircled his perch he would fly off, which I have to say probably to a Human is a very pretty sight indeed, all of those technicoloured feathers working together all at once to get the plump old bird into the air.

Then just when the poor old Parrot (yes even I began to feel sorry for him) landed on say the back of a chair, four delighted children would form another circle around him, freak him out and then watch giggling and laughing as the Parrot took off and flew to his next bit of temporary refuge. Only to be followed by the 'little darlings.'

For most of the afternoon while the adults were in the garden or in the garage workshop split up equally depending upon their membership of the Male or Female sex, the Parrot flew from one piece of furniture to the next and from one room to another in an endless and let's face it pointless attempt to get some peace from his torturers.

Still looking up at him now on his perch snaffling away to himself you have to be thankful that you are not a bird in general and especially not a Parrot in particular.

DAY 19 OF MY CAPTIVITY:

Today is rather an important one for my secret 'operations' and so, as the operations are secret I can only hum for you, to entertain you! Hum de dum, hum de dee, la la de da, sorry about the la la'ing but I am not that good at humming!

Yes I wish that you could be party to my secret plans too, but thankfully I am not that spotty freak Adrian Mole (who seems to explain everything in his Diary), thank goodness, I have a life, am more interesting and let's face it better looking, not to mention the fact that my Diary is a better read and not written by a woman pretending to be a thirteen and a half year old boy, which is more than a little odd!

I personally can't think of many people who would want to be a thirteen and a half year old boy apart from possibly, a thirteen year old boy with an age complex!

Still I am sure that you won't be disappointed when the secret is out and the action begins so you will just have to keep reading, after all reading is good for Humans and too few do it, so I am providing a service, mmmh! Wonder if I can get a government grant for doing such a service to the community?

Day 20 of My Captivity:

It is said that there is no peace for the wicked. I don't think I have been wicked today? But still there is no peace for me!

No sooner have I settled down for a long snooze than someone moves me, or makes lots of noise so that I can't sleep. Really Humans have no manners where sleeping Cats are concerned, but if you are a Dog then there is even a saying to cover your napping, you have heard of 'let sleeping Dogs lie,' I presume?

And if it isn't the Humans, then it is 'that' bird – I swear I will get him and serve him up exactly what he has coming. Sitting on that perch with a stupid grin on his beak and asking anyone and everyone, whether they are listening or not 'who's a pretty boy?'

He won't be so pretty when I've finished with him, he'll be just a collection of bent yellow, red and green feathers, that you wouldn't even stuff a cushion with.

We'll see 'who's a pretty boy?' then!

Mind you, I have to catch him first and I am still working on that unfortunately. Another problem is that there doesn't seem a moment when he is completely alone and within my grasp – still I know there will be a brief moment when he is just where I want him, tee hee, and I am working on that!

Day 21 of My Captivity:

The secret plans are going well and one could say according to plan, which is still a secret, but then one has to be careful because the best laid plans are the ones that go wrong most often.

Just look at NASA. (The North American Space Agency) which is of course never confused with SASA (the South American Space Agency because there isn't one). Shame there isn't a SASA especially if it was the South American and Latin Space Agency or of course SALSA, sorry that was a little Cat joke from a little Cat!

So then let's still take NASA as an example! They spend years planning and building rockets, checking them carefully and then even more carefully ensuring that everything goes according to plan and then bang, something goes wrong that wasn't in the careful plan.

Or if there isn't a bang something goes wrong quietly and a spacecraft that is supposed to arrive at a bit of rock millions of miles out in space, slide into a precise orbit so that it can take a lot of fuzzy and out of focus pictures, drives straight on passed and eventually and rather forlornly leaves our solar system for good or ill?

So I want to ensure that my plan is not only a good plan but also one that works and I suppose that would make it a better plan.

It just occurred to me. If there are such things as aliens and judging by the actions of some of the 'Humans' on this planet, I'd say that they had already landed a sizeable advance force and colonised large portions of the planet, like France for instance, then they must keep bumping into ever greater numbers of little out of control spacecraft wobbling their way through the depths of space.

I wonder what the advanced beings who are so brilliant at disguise, and can pretend to be so arrogant and rude, and into the bargain eat Snails (brilliant disguise lads), make of these small bits of rubbish that have been fired at them?

Do the Aliens just laugh at Humans, because they think that the Spacecraft that sail aimlessly out into space are being fired at them by the cream of our artillery, to slow their attack, possibly not?

Indeed do the Aliens just ponder on Human's oblique sense of humour at attempting to shower such powerful invaders with such a paltry defence!

Or is what is keeping the Alien hordes from our shores the fact that they are all giggling too much to land, howling away with laughter at the Human's lack of planning especially when they catch a spacecraft called Beagle II with a stencilled message that reads, 'hello to all Martians from the people of The United Kingdom of Great Britain and Northern Ireland.' Putting it neatly into a pile marked 'more laughable trash from the super race called Humans'!

Whatever the Aliens think, the Human super race's feeble and confused efforts at space exploration must have slowed down their imminent invasion, probably because they think that the whole of mankind is barking mad and that madness maybe infectious!

If that is the case and the only things the Aliens are worried about is catching Humankind's insanity; then I wonder if an emissary from the race of Cats could contact the Aliens and negotiate with them? A good deal from my point of view would be, the planet earth for Feline freedom from enslavement and all the Prawns we can eat? Seems like a fair deal!

So the next thing to do after I get out of this prison I suppose is to visit France and try and make contact with the Alien advance party!

They can't be that difficult to deal with surely, no I mean the Aliens won't be difficult to deal with, we know about the French they are impossible to have a sensible conversation with let alone make a deal with, which is probably why they get invaded and conquered so often!

DAY 22 OF MY CAPTIVITY:

'So how is the secret project coming along?' I hear you ask casually! What do you think I am? Do you think I am a dumb animal? Ok I grant you that most animals are dumb and a lot are dumber than either Humans or Cats, but let's face it, you are not going to catch me out with that old Chestnut.

Really I had more respect for you frankly and I am very disappointed in your lack of forethought and cunning. Try something really cunning and admirable and I might just let you in on the secret reasoning that if you are that cunning you are unlikely to 'spill the beans.'

Still since you ask, the secret plan is coming along very nicely thank you! But I still won't tell you what it is!

I do need to tell you something though and I am afraid that you will have to lean in closer because I need to whisper it in your ear so no one else hears!

No even closer!

That's right.

IT IS A SECRET SO MIND YOUR OWN BUSINESS!

Day 23 of My Captivity:

All of yesterday was taken up by a surprise visit, a niece, and to my way of thinking, not a very nice niece either.

Unfortunately I was caught unawares; that is all I can think of to explain why I didn't manage to leg it when I saw the dreadful little legs teetering towards me with those awful lacy girly socks and black patent shoes at the end of them.

Sadly I was too slow, but I was preoccupied at the time with other matters and didn't realise that I had been scooped up by those dreadful pudgy little girl fingers and stuffed into a doll's cardigan that covered my paws and most of my head.

It took me most of the morning to wrench a paw free from that dreadful acrylic and cashmere doll's cardigan, which was such an unpleasant shade of pink. I have to say here and now that I think I was allergic to the exotic combination of fibres.

That probably was the reason why it took me so long to free myself from the cardigan, that and also the fact that as I ripped it to shreds I became entangled in yards and yards of wool. At one point I thought that I had tied myself to the side of the doll's pram because I couldn't move and had to hold my breath and wriggle.

The trouble with holding your breath for long periods of time is that you start to forget to breath. If you are Human and this happens you go red in the face and people look at you in a concerned way and place a caring hand on your back while asking if you are ok.

But you may have noticed that Cats don't go red in the face, or if we do you can't see it for all of the fur that covers our faces. Worse still there wasn't anyone to place a caring hand on my back and ask if I was ok, oh no, even the not so nice niece had disappeared, obviously she had got bored with dressing me up because she had gone off to play with something else, probably the Dog who is much nicer with children.

In fact as I bit through the last of the strands of wool and shook myself to get the bits of wool off my fur, I noticed that the Dog was lying in his basket and his nurse was bandaging both of his front legs together.

If I hadn't been so shattered from the effort of freeing myself from that dreadful Cardigan I think I would have sneaked over to his basket, thumped the patient hard and then made a dash for safety, just to watch the idiot get up from his sick bed and chase after me, forgetting of course that his front paws were bandaged together.

Instead I contented myself with the comforting thought that life is not an animated cartoon and slipped away for a well deserve sleep, somewhere out of the way entirely, leaving the daft Dog to get his nose and mouth bandaged.

Day 24 of My Captivity:

I have taken to spending some afternoons deep in thought on the cushion of the Sofa and one of the things I have decided as a result of that deep thought is that I rather like music, which is a pity really because, as I think I explained my pooing shelf is where the Hi Fi, CD player thing lives, and I am sure that it doesn't like being sprayed, if you see what I mean! It seems to smoke occasionally and I am convinced that the sound quality is not as good as it used to be.

It appears that I have been 'allowed' to use the Sofa and some kind person has put a velvety towel on the cushion to ensure that a comfortable sleeping place is now quite frankly, sublime!

This is handy because my afternoon snoozes come as a result of a lot of deep thought and planning for my escape.

Often 'she,' the Female Captor, will come in and turn on the CD player so that my thoughts are interrupted or that is what I thought at first, but now I have begun to love the sound of music, not, you understand, the music from the film of that name, which I have to admit, to me sounds more like a party of tipsy Ferrets attempting three part harmony than what I would call music.

So I suppose you could say that it is a shame that I quite like music now, because I was sitting in my usual place today mulling over the benefits of plastic explosive against Dynamite when I felt the 'urge!' Is it enough for me to be that polite? If I just say that I had an 'urge?'

Well for those of the hard of understanding fraternity – I had drunk a lot of water earlier and then got the 'urge.' Do you all get it now? I know Humans like toilet humour but I don't see why I should stoop that low!

As there was no one around and I just didn't have the energy to 'go' anywhere else I hopped up onto the pooing shelf and did a little tail shaking spraying, oh it is so nice to do a bit of aerial spraying, one gets a marvellous sense of freedom, but enough of that!

The Hi Fi, CD player was pumping out something by Eminem, it was a little tune called 'Cleaning Out My Closet,' which was to my way of thinking quite apt, as a closet can also be a toilet.

Anyway there I was enjoying myself in an aerial fashion if you see what I mean, and the, let's call it 'liquid,' was splashing the Hi Fi, when a lot of hissing started and Eminem's voice started to get deeper and a little slurred, as if he had been having one to many strong cups of Coffee (with Whiskey in them), it was a pity because I quite like Eminem, he is funny, from this Cat's point of view anyway.

I jumped down and didn't think much more about poor Eminem who now sounded like an old man rapping in a thunderstorm.

As I hit the floor sparks followed me and Eminem's voice got back to normal, although there was a smell of wires burning I didn't really pay much attention to it, because there is always something breaking, burning or blowing up in this place, and just meandered back over to my Sofa.

It is funny that I mentioned 'blowing up' in the list of things that seem to go wrong so often around me, because I had just jumped over the arm of the Sofa when the Hi Fi exploded, obviously with a 'bang' and quite a large one at that!

Happily I landed on the Sofa cushion just as large and small pieces of cool Aluminium Hi Fi whizzed passed me or buried themselves into the back of the Sofa which shielded me.

I sunk low into the Sofa cushion waiting for, well waiting for I don't actually know what, but the word 'more' might just do here, I watched out of the corner of my eye as slithers of Aluminium shot passed me and buried themselves into the wall and on their way to the wall other bits drove themselves into the Coffee table.

Bits of molten metal, sparks and flame shot around the room luckily there were more sparks than anything else and so there wasn't a risk of a large fire breaking out in the front room.

The Female Captor rushed in bravely through the showers of sparks, dodged bits of metal that was still spinning through the air and grabbed me from my hiding place and ran with me through the French windows and out into the garden.

I was very grateful to her for rescuing me and considered myself quite lucky, although she was patting me and not very gently at that, which wasn't that nice, although I thought she might be in shock!

Then I smelt that smell, Humans would say it was the smell of burning hair, but I knew that it was the smell of burning or hopefully smouldering, please let it be only smouldering, fur!

Slowly I realised that my bottom was hot and seemed to be getting hotter, mind you when you are on fire hot is bad enough I can tell you!

She patted and rubbed me vigorously smothering the fire and happily putting my bottom out if you see what I mean, but the smell of burning fur hung in the fresh, still air.

Hold on a minute I thought to myself, I am outside, one jump out of her grasp and I am really free. But I had to ask myself was my fiery bottom 'out' I didn't want to be 'legging it' and fanning the flames did I?

I decided to stay put, Humans have their uses occasionally and putting out the fire on my bottom was the best use for this Human at this particular moment, I decided.

So I decided to stay where I was and not make a break for freedom. As a reward for this selfless loyalty I was carried over to the large water butt that I think is usually used to water the garden and dunked into the unforgivingly cold water.

The shock of the cold water on my 'hot bot' was impressive, it made me shriek in alarm, but then to be honest I was shrieking in alarm already and so I don't suppose she noticed the new shrieking at all.

Happily I was 'out' the fire was out and as a bonus I was now out of the cold water. All thoughts of escape had for the moment completely vanished from my mind, I just needed I decided a lie down and some peace, I was shivering now, which was, I was convinced, because of the shock and the icy water that was draining from my fur, well the bits that were left and hadn't been singed.

As she took me inside I heard her shocked gasp at the damage, the room was quite a mess, there was a large black soot stain on the wall where the Hi Fi had been, and the shelves above were black too. Worse all around the room little embers smoked and glowed where they had landed after the Hi Fi had blown up.

She did exactly what I would have done, if I had been a Human, she stamped out the glowing embers and then stamped out of the front room slamming the door closed behind her.

It seemed that I knew what the Captors would be doing this weekend, choosing new carpet and paint for the walls, I secretly hoped that they would keep the colour scheme because it was restful and I also hoped that they would buy a Sofa as comfortable as the one that had saved me from all of the flying burning bits of the Hi Fi.

Oh! And while they are getting the new carpet, paint and Sofa I hope that they get a new Hi Fi, preferably one that isn't prone to exploding, or I suppose is a little more 'waterproof,' if you see what I mean!

Day 25 of My Captivity:

It is a well known fact that Cats need a lot of rest; it is just the nature of the beast, as they say! Cats who have been involved, no matter how innocently, in exploding Hi Fi's need more sleep than most Cats and so today I have been recovering with large amounts of shuteye.

As a result of the fire which broke out on my bottom I have lost a lot of fur, well the Vet said that there wasn't much to worry about only a bit of singed fur, really don't they have any compassion? He added insult to injury and gave the Female Captor some cream after covering me in it and advised that I would need it applying twice a day for four days, and if I licked it off to 'use one of these.'

Unfortunately I have no idea what a 'one of these' is, but as a rule of thumb whatever a Vet gives you is not nice, have you ever had an injection, or your temperature taken? Yes! Well then you know and if you don't know the 'you don't want to know' if you see what I mean and as you are reading this you should be able to see what I mean!

The cream that the Vet rubbed on and had promised more of, tasted disgusting, but I managed to clean the filthy stuff off and pleased with myself contentedly fell asleep.

Without warning I was woken up by the Female Captor grabbing me and holding me in between her not inconsiderable thighs as she begun wrapping something around my neck tightly.

At first I thought it was another collar, really I thought to myself, haven't they learned about my dislike of collars? Honestly I thought I had stopped the collar business by either managing to slip out of them or on what I thought was the last occasion, managing to hang myself from the Parrots perch, the Parrot not being there at the time, obviously!

Really I don't think I was in any danger, although I was having a little trouble breathing to be honest, but the casual observer would have hardly noticed I was in any discomfort at all, because I hadn't gone red the face or blue or anything, still as I mentioned before Cat's faces tend not to change colour.

Still it was worth losing a little breath and enduring a bit of pain for a while because that was the last I saw of a collar, until now.

Imagine my horror to discover, after she had finished manhandling or is that 'womanhandling' me, that my neck wasn't wrapped in a new collar!

In fact I wouldn't have been able to tell if I was wearing a collar or not, because I was surrounded by something stiff and white, where ever I looked all I could see was this white cardboard, it was like she was trying to box in my head.

For a moment fear gripped me, was she going to seal me up wrap me in wrapping paper, apply a pretty bow and give me away as a present? Because by the time I was unwrapped I probably wouldn't be much of a pretty present, in fact I could easily be a dead Cat then, so I was right to be concerned!

She let me go after she thought that I had calmed down. So has obviously never heard of 'inner turmoil.' That was then I really had a go at getting out of this weird head gear, in the end breathless and drained and just had to sit down.

The weight of the odd white hat made my head droop and I am sure that I looked like one of those forlorn Donkeys in holiday programmes which give information about visiting Mediterranean countries and seem to think that a Donkey carrying more than his own weight is picturesque!

After a bit of a rest, I cheered up, this new hat/collar had to be temporary surely? Even Humans are not unkind enough to subject a Cat to this type of fashion blunder, are they?

There was that smell again, no, not 'that' smell! I wasn't 'that' frightened or annoyed and I am frankly embarrassed that you think I might have produced 'that' sort of smell.

It was the smell of that cream which the Vet had given her to rub on me, right at least I could get rid of that! It would give me something to do to take my mind off the annoying hat/collar thing.

It was then I discovered something really strange had happened; I had lost my bottom! Well that isn't entirely true, I couldn't have lost my bottom, or it couldn't have gone too far away because I was sure that I was sitting on it, but when I reached around to clean off the Vets awful cream I couldn't see or feel, (I won't say lick, because you will laugh) my bottom.

Then I realised that the reason I couldn't get at the cream was that I was encased in the white hat/collar thing, which was very annoying and extremely frustrating I really wanted to get rid of the cream, it is not natural to cover a Cat in cream in my opinion, especially this Cat!

I made myself giddy just shaking my head and running round and round trying to dislodge the hat/collar thing, but it wouldn't budge.

All I managed to do was to dent and then sort of fold the annoying thing which meant that it touched my right ear just in the right (or in my case wrong) place, you know that place I am sure, it is where if you touch a Cat's ear they twitch, well not thanks to my struggling, my ear was twitching all the time, which is not at all nice.

DAY 26 OF MY CAPTIVITY:

This is a day off, and after looking at myself in the mirror in their bedroom I have decided to hide.

I can't face the Dog or the Parrot because they have both been very rude about my appearance.

In fact the Dog was even more unkind than the Parrot, first he said that he didn't know what it was about me today, but goodness didn't I look better, really such low humour!

Then he said that he had seen animals wearing collars like these before, apparently Humans put muzzles on Dogs that bite and this was the same sort of thing, I had been put into a type of safety armour which aggressive animals are made to wear if they have scratched Humans and worse still, that eventually I would probably be encased in even more armour.

I didn't really believe him, but there is always that nagging doubt, he is older than me and therefore has seen more of the world, like the back garden for instance, and thinking about it he does go for quite long walks with the Captors too!

No I am worrying over nothing, I am sure that my punishment will be over soon and I will be freed from this fashion disaster.

Still until then I am going to live in this bedroom's wardrobe, well away from the Dog, the Parrot, the cruel world and the windows, I don't like to get a reputation like the Feline equivalent of the Elephant Man, do I?

People would turn up on the doorstep just to catch a glimpse of my weirdness, they would laugh, point at me and giggle even more. Oh! My life is a disaster sometimes!

Still in the end the Elephant Man became something of a celebrity and was invited to all sorts of interesting places and met lots of interesting and influential people so at least I wouldn't get bored, I would see more of the world and maybe find out things that could be used against the Dog!

DAY 27 OF MY CAPTIVITY:

The wardrobe is not such a bad place to live actually, although I keep getting my new hat/collar stuck.

I have even begun to get used to the idea that I will be like this for the rest of my life, a sort of freak, it is sad for a Cat who believes that he is quite good looking, handsome some might have said, and in the right light could have been described as striking, but there it is I am saddled, literally with this cone shaped armour and that is that.

I didn't tell you I noticed in the mirror that the hat/collar is a cone shape and sort of looks like the things that they put on Humans arms and legs if they are injured or broken, they are called plaster casts or casts for short. So maybe I am injured or have broken something! Should I lie down? Am I ill? Or worse am I going to, well you know, am I going to? No I can't bring myself to even say it, let's just ask a question instead! Have I run out of lives? I thought that nine would be quite enough.

Oh bless the Captors for not breaking the awful news to me they are obviously so upset that they can't bring themselves to face the dreadful news, and I have to say I fully understand that, I can't either.

It is probably the reason why they keep spreading that dreadful cream on my bottom, vainly hoping for a cure! And also why they have been kind enough to bring the litter tray and my food up from the kitchen so that I can have a few home comforts around me in my last few hours.

Mmmh! I feel worse all of a sudden! This is obviously one of those terrible illnesses that you hear so much about, but never in a million years think that you personally are going to get. I will be brave though and try not only to be a good patient but more importantly an amazingly handsome one!

People will admire me for the way I cope with this dreadful illness, reporters from national Newspapers and television crews will wait at the gate for news of any improvement and probably people and white mice in laboratories through-out the country will work day and night to come up with a wonder cure, all inspired by my bravery.

I wonder what the Mice do in laboratories? And why?

Maybe famous rock musicians and movie stars will get together for impromptu, and extremely well planned, fund raising concerts to pour even more money into my life saving research program.

How kind of them! I of course will drag myself from my sick bed, hopefully at a very expensive Harley Street clinic and make personal appearances where just for a short time I bravely take off my hat/collar/cast to gasps from the enormous audience and thank everyone personally for just caring, to tumultuous applause and a tearful standing ovation.

I must lie down!

Day 28 of My Captivity:

They keep applying the cream bless them and I am trying to keep my spirits up and take a little food, in fact I think that the Captors got their wires crossed today and after 'she' had fed me and gone out 'he' did the same, so I bravely managed to eat nearly two tins of Whiskers.

I spent a while trying to lick the cream off my bottom, but this hat/collar/cast thing still gets in the way! I hope that it is doing something to save my life because as I was trying to see over it I felt my eyes freeze and lost my balance so I think I am beginning to fade, which is a shame because I haven't seen one famous rock musician or movie star offering help yet and when I looked out of the bedroom window there weren't any reporters or camera crews, which is a little disappointing.

I am convinced that it merely wasn't me just losing my balance though but the final terrible stage of the illness that I have, will awful things begin to happen to me? Please don't say that I will lose my lovely fur and go bald or in anyway lose my wonderful looks.

You don't think that is why they put the hat/collar/cast on in the first place, so that I don't see that I have already lost my fur and lose heart altogether!

I don't feel weak though, thinking about it, and one would expect that, still I have been taking it easy and sleeping a lot, which is for the best, I wonder when they will move me to the expensive Health clinic!

Day 29 of My Captivity:

Something amazing has happened, they took my hat/collar/cast off and guess what? I wasn't bald! Even the singed bits weren't bald! Just singed, and we should celebrate, they have stopped rubbing the cream on my bottom, so I think that all things considered I may well live! No let's rephrase that I am going to live! Which is good because I like living, it is a lot of fun and will be even more fun after I escape.

So it is a day to celebrate. Normally I would go and annoy the Dog and the Parrot, but I don't feel 'that' well yet and will leave that little treat for another day.

It is a shame that I didn't get to go to the expensive health clinic, meet the famous rock musicians and movie stars or make a personal appearance at my benefit concert, but I am happy to be cured all the same!

Now I can go and sleep in the front room window, I wonder if the front room is like me, as good as new? I am quite excited to see what replacement Sofa they chose, (don't tell me you forgot about the exploding Hi Fi did you, but then maybe with all of the worry about my health that is not surprising).

The new Sofa is probably much more comfortable than the last and as comfortable things go, that was, well comfortable, very comfortable indeed.

There is also something that I have to do, although I am not going to mention it to you just now, but it is ok you won't have to wait long to find out what I am up to, I'll give you a clue though, it involves TNT's next day delivery service, so there is a sort of clue and the consolation that you shouldn't have to wait too long to find out what I am up to, hee hee!

DAY 30 OF MY CAPTIVITY:

The next day delivery caper worked, and thank you for asking, I am fully recovered and so today almost as a celebration I handled (well pawed actually) explosives for the first time. What an experience, and I have to say, what a pleasure it was too!

Dynamite has a feel and a texture all of its own, although of course I really wanted plastic explosives; they are much more powerful I understand, but unfortunately I couldn't get any and I have a feeling that I would have had one or two problems with Plastic Explosives anyway, it is very sticky stuff and for a fur covered person that makes it difficult to handle.

So it was with some regret, at first, that I had to settle for Dynamite, I have to admit I am a little limited with paws and claws and 'handling' things can be difficult, I am sure you know what I mean, you just have to watch a Cat trying to pick up a Hazelnut at Christmas.

It would be just wonderful to gently squeeze a small chunk of plastic explosive into and around the window frame. Attach a detonator. Cheerfully pay out some cable and then after carefully wiring the trigger, push the plunger down.

With plastic explosives I have heard that there might not even be much of a bang! Just a small poof and the window would be ready to be pushed out,

But I have Dynamite and that is a totally different kettle of fish as they say in fish markets throughout the land, I suppose, can't say you hear that saying around here much though, probably due to the lack of any coastline, but you know what I mean I am sure.

Anyway as I was saying, Dynamite is rather different to Plastic Explosive, and not only because Plastic Explosive looks more like Chewing Gum than Dynamite, which I have to say, looks like the candles on a Birthday Cake although they would be big candles, but then they could be just right for a very large Birthday Cake.

Still it is good to know the difference between Plastic Explosive and Dynamite, and I have to say it is probably good to know the difference between Birthday Cake candles and Dynamite and of course it probably goes without saying that chewing Plastic Explosive would be one of the last confusions one could experience, I would think!

I digress as they say, when they are digressing, and with me they would say it a lot. I am forever interrupting myself but that is because I only have myself to talk to and I do have a lot to say, thoughts just pop into my head and bang I have changed the subject.

Speaking of bangs, Dynamite can be tricky stuff even for an expert and unfortunately even I wouldn't describe myself as an expert!

Apparently if you sit on Dynamite for any length of time it gets warm and begins to sweat – or glow as my Mum used to call sweat, when she was 'glowing,' because ladies don't sweat they 'glow', and she 'glowed' a lot occasionally.

When Dynamite begins to sweat it becomes unstable, I thought that was a term for the Female Captor, but I have discovered recently that it is a term used by experts for Dynamite when it is at its most dangerous, well to be accurate when it is nearly at its most dangerous, because even this novice knows that when Dynamite explodes it is at its most dangerous!

The process of making Dynamite sweat can be accelerated if one sits on it and one is wearing a fur coat, well what was I to do? I always wear a fur coat, true I do feel the cold, but more than that, I am attached to it you could say!

Of course it is also true to say that there are not many places to hide Dynamite either, this fur coat does not have pockets so in order to conceal it from prying eyes I was forced to sit on it.

I can't say that I felt the dynamite getting wet or even damp, there wasn't a sensation of dampness 'down below' if I can say that in polite company – oops! Seems as though I have already!

Still even if I didn't feel it getting damp the stuff was sweating and that is not a good sign when all things are considered, not a good sign at all.

I had come to the conclusion that I had to do something with the stuff, which was doing a good impression of large Uncle George during and after any exertion, like getting out of a chair for instance.

As I said Dynamite is great stuff but when sweaty, well you know! So something had to be done with it and using it would be impossible today that was certain, I had to hide it that was the only option and somewhere quite cold and hide it somewhere quickly.

After all I didn't have to use it today did I? Well it would be nice but in its unstable condition one couldn't guarantee the results, but then thinking about it I didn't know what the results would be anyway to be honest.

So somewhere cold and the colder the better, because if the sweaty dynamite is not sweating tomorrow then bang, or should that be BANG? Tee Hee!

There are lots of cold places in the kitchen, the freezer would be a good place, but the memory of being shut inside brings a shiver down my back and so frankly I think I will avoid that hiding place.

The fridge is a good place but then again I have a feeling that a few sticks of Dynamite would be a little obvious sitting on a shelf next to the Celery or propped up in the fridge door against a pint of milk, whether it was sweating or not! So that is a non-starter, for a start!

Still there are some easy to open cupboards in the utility room, great now all I have to do is drag my prized possession to one of them and pop the stuff somewhere at the back of the cupboard next to the back door, sorted!

I'll keep an eye on the Dynamite and when it has stopped sweating I will be able to use it for what I have planned which is simply a very big bang.

Day 31 of My Captivity:

The first thing I did today was to check the Dynamite and sadly it is still rather sweaty, actually that is probably a massive understatement, the Dynamite resembles a room full of middle aged novice Yoga students, working hard to fight flabbiness and losing the battle completely, still they can content themselves that they have managed to find a room full off similarly big-boned people which is a considerable feat.

So I will check it tomorrow, I mustn't forget about it and not only that it would be such a shame to not use it for the purposes that it was intended for, Boom.

I wonder which word is more accurate for an explosion, Boom or Bang, can't wait to listen to my explosion and find out, then let you all know.

Day 32 of My Captivity:

The Human language is a strange and almost impenetrable thing, I have begun to make a study of it, because I am sure a knowledge of it will be useful to understand what my Captors are talking about in here, and then on the outside it will probably prove invaluable.

With that fact in mind I have been concentrating on the Human's flashy wobbly box that talks and shimmers in the corner of the front room and has two brothers in different parts of this prison, one in what 'they' call the kitchen, and one in what 'they' refer to as the bedroom, although the others must be younger than the one I am studying because they are so much smaller.

In fact earlier today the studying didn't get off to a very wonderful start. At first I thought that the wobbly flashing box was just a nice warm place to stretch out on and fall asleep. But then I began listening to it because, alarmingly, it sounded as though it had eaten a Cat, there were loud Meowings coming from deep inside it.

I shot off the top of the box and raced behind the Sofa expecting to be scooped up and consumed at any moment just as the other poor unfortunate Cat had been.

After an hour or maybe even two, when the other Cat's cries had gone and had in fact been replaced by the sound of Humans talking about digging a trench (obviously to bury the poor Cat), I thought it might be an idea to have a peek around the corner of the Sofa and size up my foe.

Claws at the ready, I tried to move around the edge of the Sofa, but I was stuck to the floor, it was awful and not a little worrying to be held by the gaze of this dreadful wobbly flashing box, because surely it was that which was holding me in place.

Death rays - that is what I imagined would come next and any minute now I would just be a smouldering ex fur coat. I stared ahead waiting for the terrible anger of the wobbly flashing box to strike, pulling and pulling at my legs to try and move them forward, sideways or better still backwards!

Nothing worked and so, resigned, and by now, not a little impatient for my fate, I sat down and expected the worst, that was when my claws retracted and I fell over.

Fear is a terrible thing but mocking the frightened is worse so I will trust you not to laugh here. Thank you!

I did check the Dynamite again and if anything it seems to be getting sweatier, I don't really know what to do with the stuff, can't forget about it, but all the same in this condition it is not useable, well I don't think it is, but then again what do I really know about the stuff, not much is the truthful answer!

Day 33 of My Captivity:

The sweaty Dynamite seems to have taken on the consistency of one of those awful smelling cheeses from France; I had to hold my nose, as I pawed the package, not nice.

After all of the excitement of yesterday I have made up my mind that today I am going to put the events of yesterday behind me and concentrate upon my studies.

Earlier during something oddly called breakfast TV where lots of thin women with big heads, long necks and tiny bodies, talked incessantly and oddly none ate any breakfast at all.

Well anyway during the strangely named breakfast TV programme I overheard my Captors refer to the flashing wobbly box as a TV and breakfast TV seems to have gone someway to confirm it.

Although I am still confused about whose breakfast they were talking about and why no one ate it, especially those pitifully thin women who seemed as half starved as an alley Cat.

The other thing that I can't seem to work out is which word begins with which letter Flashing must begin with a 'T' and Wobbly with a 'V' but in that case is Box a shortening of breakfast?

I can see that a lot more research is required and that is what I have set today aside for – study, well I will need to have some naps, and some food and a little water, and then there is the possibility of a stroke – but I am sure that there will be time enough to do some extensive studying.

The best place to study I decided is the Sofa – the cushions are deep and the pile of the fabric has rather nice feeling against the fur if you first stretch out and then curl up on it, in fact it makes you feel rather slee.................

Sleepy – whoops what is the time, where am I what was I doing – the TV Flashing Wobbly Box is still on and there is a programme on called Lunch with Lena, again oddly no one is actually eating lunch and the women with Lena all look very thin. I am very worried about these Flashing Wobbly Box People.

Learning this language is hard and I don't think I will ever master it. Today I watched a programme about four nice young men who all had the same name Rapper, they were introduced as the four best rappers and so I think it is a very common Human name although I am not entirely sure.

Anyway the Rappers gave me an idea, 'disguise!' Well the idea was a result of me working out the difference in words that sound the same, or in the case of the poor four rappers were just badly pronounced.

I thought that when these young men were talking loudly to music they were referring to the 'disguise' they were wearing, which although colourful, probably would be what one would wear on the street, but to my surprise I discovered that disguise was actually Dis Guys and referred to each and every one of the group of Rappers.

Day 34 of My Captivity:

The sweaty cheesy Dynamite seems to be getting worse I had to hold my nose in the cupboard today, but the good news is that just leaving it seems to have worked and I could almost swear that the stuff is drying out.

Still the smell is not good and I decided to do something about that.

Tupperware! Well that is what it said on the lid. Let me explain, I 'found," well ok stole a plastic box lid a lid very tightly attached, now that should keep the Dynamite safe and most importantly keep the mature cheese smell sealed inside too.

If I leave the cheesy smelling parcel out much longer the Human Captors may start to look for whatever is the source of the smell.

In fact when she came into the utility room yesterday she was sniffing a lot, and I don't know if she had caught a whiff of the whiffy stuff or just had the beginnings of a cold, but there is no point in taking any chances I'll stuff the plastic box full and then sit on the lid to seal it, because if it is as difficult to close as it was to open then I will need all of my weight to ram the lid on.

Well that was a lot of hard work but the box didn't disappoint me, it was as hard to get the lid on as I imagined it would be, but now the Dynamite is safe inside the box and so is the smell, excellent.

I'll just waft my paws around a bit and try and move the 'hint' of cheese smell, (well alright I agree, it is more of a wall of cheese smell) around a bit and try and get rid of it lingering in the air like the smell of a damp Dog does.

In fact if I fail I suppose I could always encourage the Dog to bark to go out, I have just noticed it is raining which is handy!

Still, sniff, sniff, dancing around wafting away the smell seems to be working, and I can leave the fat lump, sorry Doggie, to sleep on snoring his life away.

Day 35 of My Captivity:

I caught a cold today, which was incredible really because I wasn't even trying, I didn't stalk this cold, I didn't pounce on it, or trap it in a corner so that it couldn't escape, and I didn't go out into the rain and cold either, which is a shame because had I done any of those things then I wouldn't mind being here on my special Sofa cushion wrapped in a newly washed Dog blanket, I would be long gone.

Excuse me; I just sneezed! Tell me, in between sneezes, why do Dogs have blankets and not Cats? I don't understand that. In fact why do Dogs have beds and as blankets for Dogs are called Dog blankets, why aren't beds for Dogs called Dog beds? I don't understand.

So back to my original question why do Dogs have blankets and not Cats?

Oh! Actually I can answer that, I did have a lovely Cat basket, shaped a little like a tipsy Lobster Pot and made out of the same stuff, well not nylon string, I mean the same stuff that old Lobster Pots were made from, and now can only be seen in seaside teahouses and cheap restaurants.

But I am sure that doesn't, count the floor of that basket 'thing' was the most uncomfortable thing I have ever spent more than a few hours sleeping on, because it was made out of platted willow, just imagine sleeping on a bed of sticky up twigs for a moment.

Yep! I would think that 'ouch' is exactly the right word to describe the feeling experienced when lying on the twigs.

Of course where the Dog gets a nice thick Dog blanket on the top of his bed, which I have to say here is made from more or less the same material as a duvet, a poor Cat, this poor Cat in fact gets a thin bit of old cast off from a blanket that was surplus and smelt of, mmmh I can't really describe what it smelt of, but have you ever smelt washing that hasn't dried properly? Well that is close.

I remember spending days walking around wondering what the strange smell was, naturally you sniff under your legs, then bits of your back that you can reach with your nose and still can't find where the smell is coming from, but still it follows you, most off putting!

Eventually after spending nearly a week sniffing, the Captors began talking about Cat Flu and were trying to find the Vets telephone number, which was worrying! Finally I traced the smell to the rancid blanket. Why, I would like to know, does it take so long to trace a smell like that? Can smells like that hide?

Anyway it went away, well that is wrong it didn't go away I stopped using the Cat basket and avoided it like it was a plague carrier, and eventually the smell disappeared, but not, I am sad to say, the Cat blanket!

Still I noticed that the Captors have a very cute picture of me sitting in the basket, it must have been one of those times when the surrounding wicker wasn't touching my ears making them twitch and I must have eaten some very strong smelling fish because I don't look as if I am sniffing, so at least some body has a nice memory of the dreadful wicker bed!

Happily it eventually got condemned to the attic or the garage when it fell into disuse, like most things that we get bored with.

I remember the arrival of a crowd of gymnasium equipment that included a rowing machine and a cycle that only had pedals and no wheels and I thought to myself at the time this keep fit equipment was something that signalled another craze that would be short lived.

Well I know I am only a Cat but even I could see that the new keep fit exercise was doomed to failure. Still it was fun to watch while it lasted!

The Male Captor seemed to be in charge of the positioning of the equipment which was set up in the dinning room, 'she' The Female Captor watched and occasionally offered advice, which made me laugh, because I don't know if she was doing it deliberately, but every time she said something (I thought) sensible, like, 'do you think that the rowing machine should be so close to the radiator?' 'He' got more and more angry!

Instead of positioning the new gymnasium equipment he started to drop it into place and if he did indeed see the logic of one of her sensible suggestions he would grunt, pick up the bit of equipment whatever it was and slam it down in the 'right' place.

When he 'moved' the weightlifting bench with enormous strength and managed to take a chunk of plaster out of the wall I nearly broke the golden rule and began laughing out loud and that is a rarity for a Cat, after all, how often do you see a Cat laughing?

Well as I said that was fun to watch but there was even more fun to be had later. After everything was perfectly positioned and the Male Captor disappeared upstairs to change and came back in shorts and a white tee shirt that didn't cover enough of his dreadfully white skin.

He attacked the rowing machine immediately ignoring some more sensible advice from his partner, and in no time was rowing away like a survivor from the Titanic who has been warned about the sinking ship's ability to suck lifeboats down into the icy depths as she sinks.

All the Female Captor said was 'go easy to start' and I suppose that was like a red rag to a bull and the idiot pulled and pushed until he was red in the face and then beyond.

He must have set a few less well known world records I am sure, world records such as, number of pulled muscles and the shortest use of gymnasium equipment.

After a few days stay in bed to rest his aching muscles, he never went near the equipment in the dining room again, until he moved it all into the garage a few weeks later!

Humans! You wouldn't want to take them with you, even if you wanted sane company or to apologise!

Still I suppose they have their uses they do seem to like to feed Cats regularly! I wonder why? Are Cats good companions, no, well this one isn't! Are Cats useful? Mmmh difficult one that! In the old days I suppose they were catching Rats and Mice and Vermin, whatever Vermin are? Cats in the old days must have been pretty good at what they do because you don't see many Vermin running around these days do you?

But thinking about it for a minute, what use is a Cat today? I don't use the word domesticated you'll notice, because I really believe that we are nowhere near domesticated.

We do hang around Human's homes that is true, we can lie on our back and have our tummies tickled and generally get stroked and petted and we do appear to enjoy the domesticated life, but we are good actors, take me for instance, I can lie for hours on any lap, on my back with my legs in the air being stroked.

But I would rather be free, and that is why escaping is never far from my mind, even when I appear to be completely absorbed having my tummy stroked, and making Humans laugh because I look as though I am smiling while my eyes are tightly shut and they can rearrange my paws, making them stick up straight in the air while I seem not to notice that I am being made a fool of.

Still what they don't know is that I am still planning my escape, refining the latest plan so that this one will work, then we will see who is the fool lying on their back with their legs in the air!

DAY 36 OF MY CAPTIVITY:

Today I feel compelled to talk about the dangers of Linen Baskets! Why? Well that is simple I hope that this Diary will be helpful to Cats and any like minded individuals who are trying to escape detention against their will especially individuals who don't have access to the internet or television.

Individuals like the poor person they call the President of the United States who seems, every time I have seen him, to be a prisoner, surrounded wherever he goes by men in badly cut suits with wires hanging out of their ears.

Worse still this poor man seems to have to endure their company at all times. I have seen him on the television a few times now and every time, without fail, he has been mobbed by these guards. Imagine that for a moment, everywhere you go someone is watching you. Does he get a minute to himself or do they even accompany him when he nips 'out' to the toilet?

There is a saying, which says that there is always someone worse off than you! Well I have discovered who the person worse off than me is! Him! At least I can slip off to the toilet without being watched or even sneak away and doze in the window or a wardrobe and get five minutes peace, but I doubt that anyone allows the President that amount of peace.

So far I haven't worked out what he has done to warrant such attention, apart from have an 'election,' maybe he had an 'election' in the wrong place or worse at the wrong moment somewhere public, but what I do know from watching the news on television is that he seems to be a rather unpopular person whom everyone seems to blame for everything. Poor soul!

But thinking about the President doesn't really explain what I wanted to talk about today; which was, for those of you who can't keep up, Linen Baskets and their dangers!

I was contentedly minding my own business, pondering the imprisonment of the President of the United States, and I have to say I was very comfortable curled up as I was on a pile of bedclothes somewhere near the bottom of the Linen Basket, the lid had closed behind me, but that didn't worry me, it is easy to nose open and then squeeze passed the lid so that getting out of that cosy place is never a problem.

The Linen Basket has some wonderful advantages too, no prying Parrots watching what you are doing or disturbing (in every sense of the word) Dogs to worry about, just a warm comfy bed, some comforting darkness and a lot of welcome peace!

I was snoozing happily, drifting in and out of a warm restful sleep in between bouts of serious thinking and then suddenly and definitely without the courtesy of a warning a large pile of clothes was dumped on me.

It was nasty, I felt as though I was drowning in fabric, as the first sleeve of a shirt hit me I knew I was in some considerable danger and had to get out as quickly as a could or attract the attention of whoever was dumping the clothes on my head.

No amount of trying allowed me to scream a warning that there was a Cat at the bottom of the quickly filling Linen Basket, because the cuff of the sleeve had managed to gag my open mouth before a scream escaped.

Worse was to come, the weight of the clothes that had now filled the Linen Basket and covered me, was too much for me and I was not only gagged but stuck where I snoozed.

This was serious, I was stuck and quickly realised that I was going to require all of my Houdini like powers to wriggle out of this trap.

There was a chance that if I just stayed where I was I would be found, but something else made the option of just waiting a non-starter and that was, that I was (if you see what I mean) getting rather hot because of the confined spaced and the weight of all of the clothes above me.

In no time at all 'rather hot' was becoming 'very hot' and I knew instinctively that 'very hot' would become 'unbearable' sooner than I would wish it to be.

My nice warm little hiding place was now like an oven, I can assure you that there is nothing worse than being buried in a oven on gas mark mindless when wearing a fur coat.

Harry Houdini was a brilliant escapologist, who managed amazing feats of escaping from all sorts of things, now although I have no idea if one of his great feats of escapology was to attempt to escape from a Linen Basket, after being buried by a pile of dirty linen? At that moment in time I really didn't care if it was, unless he had escaped from the aforementioned linen basket successfully.

But I managed to control my wildly racing thoughts, take some deep and very warm breaths in spite of the shirt cuff which was still stuck around my teeth and calm down just a little bit, I have to say that this was only achieved by force of will and of course my superior intelligence!

It was obvious that there was no time to just lie still and come up with a plan, so I did the next best thing and spat out the shirt cuff and wriggled a bit more until my paws were nearly free.

By imitating the Dog chasing his tail and doing a few tumbles I was just able to create a little cave for myself and breathe a little more easily, but it was hot work, especially in my furry Cat suit.

I had a rest and took stock of the situation, something that really I wished I had not done because no matter which way I looked at the problem I was stuck.

After several attempts at 'swimming' to the surface of the ocean of clothing I gave up, panting and very hot and bothered.

As I lay still trying not to catch to much in the way of warm breath by breathing gently I examined all of my options, that didn't take too long because there weren't to be honest too many of those!

It was unlikely for instance that I was going to be missed until I had become a very hot and stiff Cat and that was something that wasn't in my game plan!

Worse there was, as far as I could tell, no way to climb up out through the clothing, and no chance of attracting the Dogs (limited) attention and encouraging him to knock the Linen Basket over and strolling out casually to freedom.

Hang on, now that was a possibility! If I could get the Linen basket to wobble, there was a fair chance that I could turn the wobbling into a rocking and with enough rocking I was pretty sure that I could get the Linen Basket to tilt over and then topple over.

If the Linen Basket did topple over there was a good chance that the contents would spill out onto the bedroom floor and the most important contents of the Linen Basket could casually stroll away from disaster. Good plan with an excellent result in my opinion!

I have to tell you that I like good escape plans that work and have happy endings, especially when they involve me personally!

Have you ever tried to get a full Linen Basket to wobble? No I thought not! It was my first time too, and I have to say it was a lot more difficult than I had imagined, not that I had imagined how to get in or out of a Linen Basket ever before.

The exercise, and I use the word 'exercise' in every sense of its meaning was difficult, hot and very uncomfortable work, but once I got into the swing of it the basket, I have to say almost grudgingly began to wobble.

I only had just enough room to roll from side to side, but after what seemed like ages I had achieved a wobble which was great and relaxed, which was a mistake because the wobbling decreased and almost stopped, so there was nothing for it but to continue to roll from one side of the basket to the other.

This time I didn't relax and the wobbling didn't stop, it became a rocking, but took ages, happily the rocking didn't last long and soon I felt the basket topple and crash to the floor.

It is possible that crash is the wrong word for what happened to the Linen Basket, but it does describe what happened after the thud that accompanied the fall of the Linen Basket.

For some unknown reason I had managed to make the Linen Basket move and not just from side to side, it had moved from inside the bedroom door into the doorway. This movement in itself was not a problem, except that now it was standing in line with the top of the stairs, so that when the contents (of which I was part remember), spilled out some of the heavier items rolled over the landing and shot off the top step of the staircase into mid air.

The heaviest 'item' was yours truly unfortunately, the shirts and pants merely flopped around and settled on the landing all over the first two or three steps, but the weightiest item, yes me again, was left on its own flying in mid air, with just the rest of the staircase below him.

'Unfortunately,' which like 'frankly' is a word that I use all too often, however both words, unfortunately and frankly are more than relevant at this point so unfortunately I wasn't flying through the air for very long, in fact I had started to lose height almost as soon as I was airborne, a bit like an Iraqi missile not carrying weapons of mass destruction.

Happily, now there is a word that is quite rare when talking about impending disaster but even so it again like unfortunately and frankly is relevant here, happily unlike a missile belonging to the dictator formerly known as Saddam when I hit the ground I didn't explode in a ball of yellow flame.

Oh no, I just thumped into the ground hard, slid along the carpet on the little landing, bounced up against the banister rails and rolled down stairs hitting each step one after the other until I hit the floor in the hall.

It was all very much like a crazy ride at a theme park, and when they look for a bit in the movie to turn into a theme park ride I am sure that this is the one that they will choose.

I was quite happy to have landed on the hall floor, because at least I knew that I wouldn't fall any more but I hadn't reckoned on a few little details.

The first little detail was that I was rolling at considerable speed across the hall floor.

The second little detail was that the vacuum cleaner had been left in the middle of the hall floor by one of the Captors, who must have been in the middle of a little cobweb catching. This little detail was not really of any importance until I hit the vacuum cleaner and was to my great surprise airborne again, so soon after coming into land.

As I flew through the air I was confident that this flight was going to be the shortest because someone after leaving the vacuum cleaner out in the hall had also left the cloakroom door wide open and so I thought I was heading towards a collision with the cloakroom wall.

The last little detail and the biggest surprise was that my flight was shorter than I had initially imagined and I didn't hit the cloakroom wall.

What happened was what is described in golfing circles as 'a hole in one' I believe. I sailed into the cloakroom and dropped into the toilet bowl.

Obviously the person who left the vacuum cleaner in the middle of the hall and the cloakroom door open had struck again!

Have you ever had your head down a toilet? I really don't recommend it, I promise you it is worse than falling down stairs or being trapped in a Linen Basket.

Toilets are very difficult places to climb out of, I was going to say that toilets are normally very difficult places to climb out of, but who in 'normal' life climbs either into or out of a toilet? I will say instead that I am sure that toilets would be difficult places to climb out of, but on this occasion no sooner had I managed to get my head out of the water I scrambled out of the toilet bowl and stood dripping and shaking on the mat.

I felt sick, not only because I had had my head down the toilet and had, I am sure swallowed some of the water, ugh, but also because I was soaked to the skin and shivering.

Cats don't like water at all, well except to drink of course and then we actually don't drink a lot because it is quite difficult to drink when all one can do is lap up liquid, you must have noticed Dogs drink because they are totally devoid of manners it is easy to see how drinking without any restraint can cause an awful mess on the floor and over one's fur.

Do Dogs care about the mess they make drinking? No of course not, but then to be honest any animal who can walk around with water splashed over their heads from excessive over enthusiastic drinking or lines of drool dangling from their mouths can't expect to be taken seriously, can they?

I sat down on the floor and had a wash, trying not to think about where all of the excess water in my fur had come from and contenting myself with the thought that if the vacuum cleaner had been left out there had been some cleaning going on recently and maybe, just maybe the cleaning had included the toilet!

Well it pays to have a little faith in others don't you think?

DAY 37 OF MY CAPTIVITY:

After the very full day yesterday, I had a bit of a lie in. Normally I get up around six in the morning have a stroll around the house making my last port of call the kitchen, where I patrol the floor for any food that drops onto it from above.

This patrolling is always interrupted by slobber chops the Dog, he isn't aggressive, well he might be, but that isn't the reason why my patrolling is interrupted, oh! No it is because of something worse than aggression, much worse!

I touched on the subject of the dangling lines of drool yesterday that hang from the Dog's mouth when he drinks, they are nothing in comparison to the hideous slobber that drips from his awful gob when the hint of food is around and have to be avoided at all costs.

To be honest, the breakfast under the table patrol, is usually a bit of a waste of time, and I haven't really worked out why because at dinner time there is always something falling from above, often the 'something' turns out to be a pea or two and of course I leave them for his drooliness the Dog.

Breakfast as I said on the other hand is pretty much a desert in falling food terms, but it is like fishing, if your rod is not in the water and baited then you are not going to catch anything, and not only that I wouldn't like to think of the Dog scoffing. Something really tasty like a bit of Bacon or Sausage Link alone, well not alone, I mean at all! Oh no. things like that are all mine.

Still today I decided that if his drooliness slobber chops did get a tasty treat from the breakfast table then he was welcome to it and slept on, eventually waking up at around seven in the evening just in time for dinner, where I was rewarded with a nice piece of bouncing Chicken which rolled right to my feet.

So after an excellent twenty two hour lie in and a sizeable piece of Chicken I was ready to go back to bed for a well earned sleep.

DAY 38 OF MY CAPTIVITY:

It is odd, I was going to say funny, but I don't think that word is appropriate here, how success can be turned into disaster in a moment!

I had just learned how to turn on a tap, not a wildly impressive achievement for a Human above the age of five possibly, but please don't forget that I am a Cat, will you! To a Cat mastering the mysteries of Humankind is something of a wonderful achievement, I can assure you, and the turning on of taps has been quite a mystery to me.

For ages I have pondered the ability of Humans to be able to get fresh water at the twist of a wrist and dearly wanted first of all wrists and then decided that I was probably never going to grow them and therefore never be able to turn on a tap and lick the fresh water which flows from taps. My investigations had led me to discover that there are two types of taps, one for hot water and one for cold.

Initially I thought that the two taps just there because Humans liked symmetry, but was delighted to find out that wasn't the case. I even managed to read the code on top of each tap, an 'H' is for burning and a 'C' is for chilly. It was the 'chilly' tap that I was most interested in, not wanting to drink water that could burn the inside of my mouth.

It took a while watching the Humans turn the taps on and off, although I have to say I wasn't that interested in turning the chilly tap off once it was on, a constant supply of fresh cool water was too appealing.

This morning the Captors were out, and that is by far the best time to experiment, I have found, getting to access to the taps is less of a problem when they are out too, because they seem to dislike having a Cat on their kitchen work surfaces.

I tried biting the taps, but they were very hard indeed, harder than a neglected bit of meat half hidden under the kitchen table, but I was encouraged to find that with a lot of two pawed effort I could get the top of the tap to move and a trickle of water to spill out.

A few turns and bingo! A respectable stream was flowing from the metal, result!

I carefully leaned my head down to the stream to have a delicious and in my opinion well deserved drink, when bang the water stopped and then exploded with a very violent force showering me with very chilly water and taking my breath away.

The shock took even more of my breath away and as I was jumping out of the way I cruelly lost my balance. The washing up bowl was nearly full of very chilly water, which had burst out of the chilly tap and I landed with a splash in the middle.

Fur coats are, I have discovered both a blessing and a curse when one is immersed in very chilly water. The blessing has two parts; first the air in a fur coat allows one to have considerable buoyancy and makes floating and swimming easy and the second advantage is that a fur coated individual such as my good self stays a lot warmer than a someone with just skin.

Unfortunately the advantages stop there and both of them are short lived, the nice buoyant fur coat quickly fills with water and gets very heavy which in turn means that one starts to sink quickly and in a very alarming way.

The other advantage evaporates rapidly too because the water makes the nice warm fur coat very chilly indeed and the wet fur sticks to the chilled skin.

As I explained, the advantages of a fur coat quickly become disadvantages and as my fur coat gets soaked I began to sink and to shiver it seemed that the heavier I got the more I shivered, to make matters worse if that is possible and to prove that there is no God of course, 'matters' got worse, the chilly tap was still gushing and splashing vast amounts of water acting as if it was a malevolent power shower and making me wetter all over.

Cats don't like swimming but will consider it as an option when any of their nine lives are threatened, and I have to say that this Cat is no different to any other in that respect.

It was then that the cold and the weight of my wet fur started to drag me down beneath the water, which was more than uncomfortable I can tell you!

They say, whoever 'they' are, that a drowning man sees his past life sweep before his eyes as he goes under and this is true for drowning Cats too, it was then that I wished my life had been fuller; I might have stayed afloat longer.

Or better still if I had been clinging to a raft in the north Atlantic like Leonardo Di Caprio in Titanic, making lame jokes and promises of a better life to Kate Winslet after being rescued, then I might have stayed above the surface of the water longer, but I am just a glug, glug, ugh! Sorry water got into my mouth!

I am a lucky Cat you know and just when I thought that my number was up and that number was number nine in the life stakes, I discovered that my paws, which were not quite numbed to the point of not having any feeling left in them, touched the bottom of the bowl.

Actually I was surprised very pleasantly I can tell you and managed to hobble over to the edge of the bowl and climb out onto the draining board and safety.

Behind me the chilly tap was still gushing and water from the sink was cascading onto the floor, but I was safe, it was a great moment in my life I can tell you.

As I am writing this page of the Diary I can tell you that my pen is a little shaky because I am still cold, but in comparison to earlier today I am boiling hot, and thanking my lucky stars that I didn't turn the boiling tap on, I think that would have been disastrous.

There is a rather hilarious ending to today as well and that is that when the Captors got in, the kitchen was flooded, no that isn't funny I know tee hee, well maybe just a little bit funny, but the humour was that she thought that he had left the tap running, and he blamed her.

In fact they had left the back door opened to help the floor dry out and also to allow the soggy Dog out into the garden, if I hadn't been so shiveringly cold I bet I could have just walked out to freedom without anyone noticing because both of the Captors were so busy clearing up, blaming each other and arguing.

It was also mildly amusing to see the Dog get out of his basket and have to brave the chilly water, the look on his face was a picture, especially when his Dog basket floated passed him towards the door.

So the day wasn't a total disaster even though I missed a clear opportunity to escape, I did laugh and of course after learning an interesting lesson about taps and air locks I had a rather nice drink, before falling into the chilly water.

DAY 39 OF MY CAPTIVITY:

The delights of sharp cheese are not readily apparent I know; but once one becomes accustomed to tackling a bit of sharp cheese and the wounds from unsuccessful attempts have healed; sharp cheese, I have to say, is very rewarding.

Personally I don't think I could go so far as to say that sharp cheese is delicious or even mildly tasty (there is nothing mild about sharp cheese you understand). But on the whole and with all things considered it is worth eating.

There are, I have discovered, two ways to approach and eat sharp cheese, a right way and obviously a wrong way, the right way is not apparent and it took me three attempts spread over several weeks to find the right way to eat sharp cheese, why so long you ask? Well we Cats heal quickly but not that quickly!

Thinking about it, one word that should always be remembered when eating sharp cheese is the word 'careful,' do be careful when eating sharp cheese and then the disappointing taste will be just the taste of the cheese and not cut gums!

Once in the mouth and the jagged edges have been avoided, and after a considerable amount of chewing, sharp cheese is a melt-in-the-mouth delight, ok it isn't really, but it isn't bad, after all soft old cheese is better than sharp cheese for a start and can provide hours of chewing fun for everyone!

It is a wonder to me that anything that has been dropped on the floor and mislaid for a few days is almost always hard, the exceptions to that general rule are few and far between, but one that springs to mind is cream, it doesn't matter which sort of cream in fact because whipping, double and indeed single cream all melt and leave just a rather smelly stain after a very short period of time neglected on the floor.

It is true to say that a dollop of cream or thinking about it ice cream which behaves in the same way, but has the added disadvantage of becoming a sticky smelly stain, rarely spends long on the floor, because between the eagle eyes of yours truly and the constantly sniffing nose of the Dog hardly any dollops of cream or ice cream escapes our notice and is therefore left to turn smelly!

Occasionally if I am feeling mean and by now you will have noticed that really 'mean' is not in my character, I will pretend to be licking up the odd patch of mouldy smell cream just so that that the Dog can run over to where I am 'enjoying' my 'find' and nudge me out of the way so that he can guzzle all of it.

It is just excellent to watch his look of triumph turn literally sour when he realises exactly what he is eating tastes like, oh how I laugh, from a very safe distance!

Day 40 of My Captivity:

Recently I have taken to sitting in 'their' bedroom window and practicing my new plan, it is the simplest plan I have ever conceived and they say that simple plans usually work, so you can see that I am excited, but I mustn't get too excited or I may well unleash the terrible power hidden in my mind.

Yes that is right, apparently inside my mind and the mind of anyone who has superior intelligence there is a power, I wish I could describe what it is like to have that power properly, so that you might share a little of it, but I am afraid that I can't even begin to, and if I could I wouldn't because all of my super mind power has to be concentrated on the task in hand.

The window is locked by just a metal catch and once that is opened it won't be too difficult to walk along the narrow ledge outside the window and then find a place or even a few places to make a hop, a skip or a jump from the ledge to the garage roof, then on to the top of the water barrel and finally a small jump from the top of the water barrel to freedom.

First, all you have to do is to use mind over matter, or to put it another way to make the metal catch do what 'you' want it to do, and this is achieved through amazing brain power, if like me you have an amazing brain, simple.

I learned all of this from that great source of information the television when a man called Uri Geller was being interviewed on the Richard and Judy show, which is a little like a chat show based on Punch and Judy, with the two presenters interrupting and arguing with each other almost continually and occasionally chatting with guests.

I am confident that even if you are lucky and haven't heard of Richard and Judy you will know the sort of format their chat show takes, lets face it the only thing that changes in the format of a chat show anywhere in the world is probably just the language, television is not exactly original is it?

In spite of Richard and Judy being annoying and arguing a lot Uri Geller was to demonstrate the power of his mind over matter, which was a very simple thing for him to do, especially as he bends spoons for a living, and in my opinion if anyone is clever enough to make a career out of bending spoons then he is a great role model for me!

So Uri applied his considerable brain power to the spoons and they bent and twisted as he 'told' them to, actually to be honest it got a little boring watching all of the spoons get bent, especially as they didn't get bent in the same way.

To my way of thinking it would have been much more interesting to watch the spoons dance or maybe even talk, but I imagine that Uri was carefully protecting his mind powers, after all why exhaust them on television if you can just bend a few spoons into tortured shapes?

By the sound of Richard and Judy's reaction Uri had hit just the right note for his performance, they stopped arguing and chatting amongst themselves for a little while as Uri concentrated and then began rubbing the middle of the spoon.

I suppose that the mind power bursts out of the index finger and thumb if you are a Human and that is why Uri was rubbing the spoon so quickly with them.

Although Uri didn't demonstrate the full potential of his amazing brainpower in front of the camera, he did refer to them constantly, almost as often as he referred to his latest book on the subject.

It is a shame that we don't have what Uri rightly said was his 'wonderful' book here because I would definitely read most, if not all of it and probably very quickly develop an even greater brainpower that can easily tell matter what to do.

Still I think that after watching Uri's spoon bending performance on the television I am ready to use my mind over some matter and that matter as I said earlier is the window catch.

Now obviously this will be easier than bending spoons because the last thing that I want to do with my brainpower is to bend the window catch! No, of course all I want to do is to just make the catch slide a little, so that should take long because of my I know I have a very superior brain that must be enormously powerful!

Concentrating now, sorry can't speak, got to concentrate hard, wow, I can feel the energy flowing from my Brain out of my paws, but concentrating so hard makes me want to go to the toilet, must, stop, thinking about the toilet, phew this concentrating is hard work.

Now I can feel the power surging through my paws and flowing out as an aura, wow this is like Harry Potter on a good day, but who needs a wand, Harry?

My brain is pumping out enormous amount of energy and I am sure that I can see a blue Nimbus in front of my eyes or is that where they are crossing?

The heat from my paws is just unbelievable, it is just growing and growing, flowing out of my paws and into the wood beneath them, at this rate I may spontaneously combust or something?

I am so hot now, it is as if I am sitting on top of a radiator, hang on, I am sitting on a window ledge on top of a radiator, no wonder it is hot. But still the energy is flowing out of my Brain I am sure, the blue light in front of my eyes is real enough, in a supernatural way of course!

How is the window catch doing, I can't hear any movement yet and I can't see through the blue Nimbus light thingy, but something has to be happening, I have been concentrating for almost a minute and not breathing so that all the energy from my body zaps straight to the window catch.

Oh come on, window catch, move just a little please, it has been almost a minute and a half and my attention is beginning to wander and I don't know about Uri but I can't hold my breath for much longer!

Result! That seems to be 'it,' Uri said I would know when my mind has bent (not literally in this case I hope) any matter to my will and so I have stopped concentrating and now that I am breathing again the blue mist has gone, just as soon as my eyes go back to their normal place in my head, I am sure that I will be able to focus and see what my amazing brain power has achieved, and better than that the window will be open and I will be free! Brilliant!

Thank you so much Mr. Uri Geller you are my Guru and my Master you have taught me so much and I will always be in you debt.

Hold on a minute, I must have moved the catch so far that it opened its self and then closed its self again, mmmh! I will have to have another go!

Now I suppose that I just wasn't 'sent erred' which I think means that I wasn't pushing all of my amazing brain power into the middle, well if Uri can do it, so can I, so here goes!

I wonder if I should pout like a geek and wear brown-rimmed spectacles like Harry Potter first before I start this time? No concentrate, oh! Here comes that odd feeling again, my tail is shaking and my paws are filled with power, well that was quick, now I am going to transfer the power from my mind to the window catch, simple! Arrgh! No!

Oops! I think I must have tripped over my Nimbus or something because I fell off the window sill, but it was worth it because I know that the window catch must have opened this time because that is exactly what I told it to do in a very focused way and I am sure that I had followed Uri's instructions to the letter and he is the Master.

Life is full of mysteries and to that extent it mirrors the universe and all that is unknown, well I suppose if the mysteries of life and the universe were known then they wouldn't be mysteries or at least they wouldn't be so mysterious, that stands to reason doesn't it?

The great mystery that confronted me when I jumped back onto the windowsill this time was why wasn't the window open? I had I was sure done exactly what Uri had explained, but the awful reality was staring me in the face when I stood up on my back legs to have another look at the window catch, it hadn't moved at all!

I sat down a very puzzled Feline and rested my nose on the cold glass pondering the mystery at length. But just when I was about to give up, a wonderful thought struck me, maybe I should start on spoons?

Yes of course that was the answer! It was I was sure now the message that Uri was giving out by just bending spoons instead of something really impressive like a Car or an iron bar or let's face It, a window catch!

I was a happy Cat as I trotted downstairs with a spring in my step and headed for the kitchen. I decided when I was sitting on the work surface that it would probably be quicker to open the spoon drawer with my paws instead of using mind over matter!

Very quickly I had hooked a spoon out of the drawer and with a happy leap I followed it to the floor and waited patiently as it stopped bouncing and clattering on the floor tiles.

I avoided the little chips of floor tile that had come off as the spoon hit the floor and laid a paw above the spoon firmly, just as I would do on the back of a Mouse if I ever catch one.

As I was getting used to channelling my brainpower it took almost no time at all to begin to draw my power down from my brain and into my left paw and begin the spoon bending process.

I had to stop pretty quickly I can tell you, because the power was just immense, my left paw was tingling and power was radiating through the floor. The other reason that I stopped was of course that I was holding the spoon in my right paw.

Again I began the 'sent erring' and channelling that made my fur stand up, and this time I sent that awesome power down the right leg, which was just as well because it was my right leg that was on the spoon!

It felt as though I would explode from the head downwards as the power surged in me and burst out onto the spoon. My right paw ached with power, in fact my all of my right leg ached from the paw upwards, it had gone numb first, and then it had filled with those little odd sharp and tingling pains that they sometimes call pins and needles I was really achieving something I knew I was, I felt it in my bones.

I almost felt sorry for the spoon it would be so badly bent that nothing would ever be able to straighten it, unless in a fit of mercy I decided to let it be straight, and I decided in a great wave of kindness that I would straighten it just as soon as I looked at my handy work.

When I looked down at the floor I was shocked at the state of the spoon, it had not changed at all! I was mystified, surprised and very disappointed the spoon hadn't even bowed a little.

That Uri Geller is a fraud; I thought to myself, and then I realised with a great deal of relief that he wasn't, because I had obviously bent the spoon into a disfiguring shape and then because I had decided to straighten it while I was mistreating it, the spoon had gone back to its original shape, I was indeed filled with power and ready to tackle the window catch, but I decided to myself after I had a bit of a rest, all of this mind over matter business is very tiring indeed.

I staggered over to the Dog basket and hopped in next to the lump. Before I fell asleep I did consider using my mind to alter the shape of the Dog, but then I decided that his shape was already pretty dreadful that I couldn't make it worse and that I was so tired that I just didn't have the energy to improve it either, well not today anyway!

Day 41 of My Captivity:

I found out something interesting today, which while it was interesting was also very sad. Everyone has a Dad, you know a Father, and most children whether they are Kids or Kittens know their fathers.

So I must be something of an exception to that rule! I remember my Mum rather well, I must have known her for quite a while before we undertook the great pet van escape, I even remember her tail disappearing down the embankment outside the motorway service station, what a fine tail she had, and I was not the only one to admire her tail I can tell you!

Yes Mum featured a lot in my early life; she was a cuddly, warm and kind person, always had a good word for everyone and although she had a terrible temper one didn't see it often which was good because when it began to bubble to the surface there was trouble brewing!

Mum taught me never to tell a lie and to sit up straight when chewing, how to cross a road (chance would be the finest thing) and most importantly to jump as I think I have said before.

But my Dad, he is a bit of an enigma and I don't mean a part of the code breakers machine. I look at it this way if one had no recollections of your Mum at least you could say that you had met her, even if it was only the one time, you know when you are born, but Dads can be a lot more elusive.

My Dad even made the meaning of the word elusive seem intangible, of course that is how I came to think of him as an enigma. No one talked about Dad; Mum never mentioned him and everyone else I knew had never seen him, including my brothers and sisters.

Sometimes I wondered if I had a Dad at all? But now I am older I know that I did obviously, but even so although I don't think about it a lot or even often miss not knowing my Dad, sometimes it makes me wonder what it would have been like to do 'stuff' together.

If I have Kittens I think that I would do 'stuff' with them, fishing for instance is a good thing to do, and although here we don't have a fish tank I am sure that my Kittens and I could get into someone's home who did have a fish tank. I have heard that the ones that are illuminated are the best, with really good clean water so that you can peruse your catch before catching it.

I have also heard that the fishercat has to be wary of some ugly fish called Piranhas but let's face it, who wants to catch an ugly fish anyway?

After fishing or before depending on how we feel my Kittens and I could all bundle down to the Dogs home and walk around outside of the exercise pens, I have heard that a daring Cat can nearly split the sides of his companions as they laugh themselves silly at the dumb Dogs trying everything they know to get at the insolent Cats!

Mind you a bunch of Dogs trying everything they know, that can't take long if you know what I mean.

The one thing I promise myself after I have got out of here and if I ever have Kittens, is, that I will be there for them and not be like my Dad!

DAY 42 OF MY CAPTIVITY:

Cats don't bite their nails, not because it is a disgusting habit, although it is, but because we don't have nails, we have, as you may have noticed if you have got on the wrong side of a Cat, claws.

It is odd isn't it that biting one's nails if one is Human is considered rather repulsive by other Humans, but sharpening one's claws if one is a Cat is not considered bad mannered in anyway in fact Cat's who see another Cat sharpening their claws will often join in.

And yet Humans seem to go mad if just one Cat (in whose defence, one has to say that he doesn't think he is doing any wrong), is caught sharpening his claws!

All I was doing was what I wanted to, and as far as I was concerned what I was doing was perfectly acceptable in Feline terms at least, so you can imagine my utter surprise when I was shouted at, yes me, I was actually shouted at! Unbelievable I know! And I hasten to add not by the Captors, but by a complete stranger.

Well I thought; that is a nice way for a visitor to behave in someone else's house, really whatever has happened to simple manners?

Is it a crime to keep one's claws in tiptop condition? No I don't think so actually! And that is all I was doing.

The visitor who is a 'relation,' I don't exactly know what one of those is and whether it is Male or Female, although I am sure that it is Human, and I based assumption that the 'relation' was Human mainly upon its size, I have to say!

This 'relation' had just turned up and judging by the reception that it received from the Male and Female Captors they had as much warning of the 'relation's' visit as I did!

They were, it has to be said, not best pleased to see this enormous, well let's give it the benefit of the doubt and call it a person on their doorstep. I had made one of my now customary bids for freedom and ran at the open front door.

The Dog did what he always did and ran around barking and drooling like an idiot without a bone, and oddly enough the Parrot seemed to be pleased to see the massive shapeless thing that filled the doorway and then waddled into the front room, shedding its coat, gloves and scarf as it went.

The scarf was in fact the last item to be shed and landed on the arm of the Sofa and draped itself over the arm and dangled onto the floor.

Do you know the expression 'like a red rag to a Bull?' well that is exactly what a dangling scarf is to Cats, we have no control over our actions, especially when the scarf is swaying as a result of the fatso crashing down on to the Sofa, directly on top of 'my' cushion, at 'my' end of the Sofa I might add.

The Captors gathered up the casually discarded clothing and were, as far as I could understand, being ordered to make tea, hot, sweet and strong with organic milk if they had any.

And if there were any biscuits or cakes, that would be 'nice' apparently, at the same time they were told 'not to take too much trouble,' which seemed an enormous contradiction to me, because as far as I could tell the number of cakes and biscuits that that enormous thing could eat would keep several bakers busy for a couple of days!

So off the Captors went, one to hang up the coats and cardigans and find a place for the dinner plate sized gloves and a hat that looked as though it had been made for several people to wear at the same time. Well let me qualify that all of the clothing looked as though it could comfortably fit several people at the same time.

In all of the confusion and tea making no one seemed to notice that the scarf was dangling over the arm of the Sofa, no one that is, except me.

As soon as I spotted the scarf I knew that the tightly knitted velvety wool would be just the right sort of stuff to sharpen ones claws on, and if one was lucky one could shred it too, but as I was thinking that it was just a vague bonus and not a reality.

In the past I have been lectured about claw sharpening and so I knew that I only had a very limited amount of time to have a good claw sharpening session and so I was just a little more careful than usual as I sidle up to the scarf, making sure that no one spotted me or had any idea of what was going to happen.

It was perfect the Captors were in the kitchen and even with the door closed I could hear that they were arguing, something along the lines of who had invited the 'relation' and how long it might stay.

The 'relation' itself was huffing and puffing of my place on the Sofa and moaning that the television remote control was useless because it wouldn't respond to its pudgy fingers.

The Parrot, and I don't suppose you will believe this because I didn't and wouldn't unless I had seen it with my own eyes, was sitting on the 'relation's' arm. The remote control hit the floor, I couldn't with any honesty say for certain that it had been thrown to the floor, but when I knock it off the Sofa if it has been left in 'my' place it never seems to hit the ground with such force!

I almost forgot about the delights of shredding the scarf for a moment as I watched the disagreeable old bird enjoy having its chest feathers ruffled.

The swaying light headed looney had its eyes closed, which in my opinion was both at the same time rare and handy, it always watches me so that it can tell tales when I am not in the room I am sure but this time thankfully it was enjoying its friend's attention, so at least someone was happy to see the 'relation,' that is if a Parrot counts as 'somebody!'

So the coast was clear and that was just dandy as far as I was concerned and I was definitely concerned that I have a good scratch on the dangling scarf before I was dragged off and probably locked in the kitchen for the duration of the 'relation's' visit.

I lunged at the scarf and to my delight it swayed even more in fact it swayed so much that I was swinging on the end of it as I clung to it with both sets of front claws. I torn, ripped and scratched delightedly as I swung back and forth.

Large chunks of the velvety wool came off in my claws as I swung and climbed, strands of wool were shred into the air and still the scarf put up a valiant resistance.

A good sized pile of torn bits covered the floor under me as I swung like a demented Monkey, but a Monkey with claws that were getting sharper and sharper with every rip.

Then alarmingly it went dark, there were two reasons for this one reasonably acceptable and one totally unnerving and not at all acceptable.

The scarf had dislodged itself and dropped to the carpet and as I landed on top of most of what I had already shredded the landing was a soft one, which was nice! What was not so nice was that the darkness was caused by the enormous 'relation's' shadow.

I peered out from under the folds and pieces of scarf and looked up, and up higher and then a little higher. Above me and on both sides of me it seemed, was the darkness that was the 'relation.' The only thing that was really recognisable in all of the darkness was the Parrot and it had a delighted grin, you must know the sort, it says 'you are in so much trouble and it is all your fault, get out of that, if you can!'

As you can imagine it is not a look that I like and I doubt that you do either when you get into a little hot water, not of course that I thought I was in 'hot' water, more sort of 'tepid,' after all I am a cute Cat, normally they can get away with murder or the next best thing, like shredding a scarf or two!

It appears now on reflection and with the benefit of hindsight, which lets face it has a questionable sort of exercise really, with very little real value!

After all is said and done, have you ever learned anything by reviewing what you have done in the past? No nor have I and frankly I was proud of what I had achieved with the scarf, my claws were sharp enough to shred a Parrot now and there is a warning in that statement for a Parrot obviously.

Still I am getting away from the point, like I wish I had in real life when the point of an enormous shoe dug me in the ribs at the same time as a voice designed, I would think to be used as a weapon boomed at the top of a screeching crescendo, 'wad'o y'ar think y'ar doin." Or words to that effect, I am not really certain because after the second screech my ears were ringing so hard I wanted someone to answer them!

The Parrot was in his element and just loving all of this mayhem for the ears and of course, he was adding his own glass breaking squawks to the inhuman noise blaring out of the monster who was blotting out all light.

This wasn't good even I knew that, the enormous shape above me wasn't the Big Elf waiting to have some more Christmas fun, oh no this was an annoyed blob and I was in big trouble.

The blob blurted then it shouted, a horrible big screamy shout that only (and I am afraid there is no other way to describe the type of person who can make that sort of noise) fat people can make in fact it was so loud that it is the sort of noise that only enormously fat and very wobbly people can make with the sound vibrating for ages.

My whiskers twitched, my nose twinged and my ears well they just went flat, so flat I thought that me ear holes were going to swallow my ears and I would never be able to hear anything again except the sea.

Or worse that my hearing would be so good that I would be able to hear every single sound on the earth and very quickly go mad, dribble a lot and have to wear a straight jacket and even worse ear muffs. No they are the greatest fashion disaster in the world aren't they?

Tell me what kind of person wears earmuffs? Well yes a person with cold ears I will grant you that! But don't you think it is a sad person who wears them, with or without cold ears?

Having said all of that about earmuffs and the odd people who wear them, at this time, I wished that if I wasn't in a sound proof room then maybe I could be wearing invisible ear muffs, yes I know I am a fashion victim, it hurts honestly!

But if I wasn't in a sound proof room or wearing invisible ear muffs then headphones would do, although they are almost as bad as ear muffs in my opinion. What sort of idiot does a person look like when they are wearing large headphones in the street, trailing fizzy bits of incomprehensive music that leaks from the badly fitting headphones? They look like a right idiot in my book.

And worse the sad'o wearing the headphones may well be singing, and then not only do they look like an idiot they sound like one too, if I wasn't having my ears shaved off with the sound of a dreadful fat person's noise, I would be laughing here!

The curiously grotesque tortured sound stopped but only when the Captors came in to investigate, then a Mother of All Arguments broke out and as I listened I couldn't believe my recently tortured ears, the Captors were saying that the Cat had every right to be in the front room and they weren't about to put it out.

Good for them and for me I thought, what a turn up for the books it is to be defended, and I almost felt appreciative, they were sticking up for me, but then it began to dawn on me when the blob said well then it couldn't be in the same house as 'that' scarf destroying Cat and was leaving, that they were just using my scarf attack as ammunition to get rid of the blob. Still I didn't mind that much, and of course was quietly pleased with myself, the scarf episode had been fun and the Parrot was about to lose a very large and noisy friend.

DAY 43 OF MY CAPTIVITY:

After yesterday's fun and games today is quiet in every sense of the word, having said that, the Parrot keeps sighing, slumped on his perch, which although annoying for the ears is rather heart warming at the same time.

There was a Salmon head in my breakfast bowl and later a few Prawns in my dinner bowl, well I have to be truthful, more than a few Prawns in my dinner bowl, in fact my dinner was more or less all Prawns, it is just a shame it wasn't all Prawns, but the Male Captor hadn't bothered to 'clean' the bowl after breakfast before filling it with Prawns and so there were dried shiny bits (only little bits it has to be said) of Salmon skin stuck on the sides, not nice at all, really Humans aren't very clean animals.

Still I didn't mind today because after Salmon and Prawns I would probably do or forgive anything because I am so agreeable in every sense of the word.

Being so agreeable after managing to eat every single Prawn I waddled, being just a little too full, into the front room and attempted to jump onto the Sofa, unfortunately I was a little heavy at the back end and had to be helped up by the Female Captor, who stroked my head as I burped a fishy burp in her face.

It is strange how Humans never seem to want to rub noses with Cats! I have never worked out why, oops! Excuse me, another burp!

DAY 43 OF MY CAPTIVITY:

Hang on, oh look at that, I have written the wrong number, it is actually Day 44, Oh bother, on botheration, now I have smudged the entry! Well! It will just have to stay like that.

I mean what is one extra day of imprisonment to someone who seems to be 'in' for life?

Honestly what ever have I done to deserve to be in prison for life? Murderers don't serve as long as I will; even some marriages are shorter than the sentence that I am being made to serve.

I have tried to keep count of the days as they go by as best I can, but counting is difficult, I use my claws to get up to twenty and because I can see them perfectly well there is no difficulty doing that, but when I want to count beyond twenty I have to use my whiskers, because just my nose and eyes only added three extra numbers.

The trouble with counting your whiskers as well as your toes is that you tend to go crosseyed and around fifty you are guaranteed to fall over, sometimes bumping your head, sometimes losing count and sometimes doing both.

After going crosseyed and falling over and bumping your head there is the double vision, this might come from falling over, bumping your head or being cross-eyed for so long but what would I know? I am not a Vet (sorry to use that word in polite company)!

Either way it is not nice, being cross eyed, or for that matter falling over, and, or bumping your head, any and all of these things easily confuses a Cat, making this Cat in particular giddy and then I lose count anyway.

Still I spotted a calculator on the desk in the dining room/study, well that is what the Captors call the place, Personally I would call it a junk room and be far more accurate with that description.

The calculator may come in handy, not only for adding up, but I am toying with the idea of making a rocket and I am sure that will require several reasonably complicated sums to be answered.

I heard a word called trajectory the other day, at first I thought that it was the name for a retired Roman Emperor but I was wrong, well even I can't be right all the time! Apparently a trajectory is the path the flight of a rocket takes when it is travelling through space. I do wish I had done all of the hard work and was inside a rocket on a trajectory out of here.

So if I 'borrow' the calculator then I can start to do some really complicated calculations and then when I am able to build a rocket then whizzing out of here will be a piece of cake!

I can happily announce today, which is definitely Day 44, that there have been some major steps forward in the technology department; the Boffins have been Boffing away.

No ok, there aren't any Boffins working away tirelessly here. However, I did manage to snaffle (steal in most people's languages, but I am a Cat and so snaffle is just dandy) some more toilet roll inners.

Really I am not silly enough to think that I can use the inside of a toilet roll for the body of the rocket! No! You didn't honestly think that was what I was going to say next, did you? Frankly I am amazed and saddened by those of you who thought that!

What I was going to say, before some people jumped the gun and made their minds up about what I was going to do with the inside of the toilet rolls, and in doing so had obviously decided just how intelligent I am, even before I had a chance to tell them exactly what I was going to do, and prove just how clever I am, was this. I was going to tell them how I was going to use the inside of the toilet rolls and in doing that I should be able to prove just how clever I am! I hope you understood all of that; it is probably one of those paragraphs, which only very intelligent people can understand, or indeed write!

Maybe the people who doubt my intelligence would be better off reading a different book. I hear that 'The Da Vinci Code' is a very good read, if you like books about complicated dead renaissance painters, not that I have read it of course and so I am only guessing what the book might actually be about, in fact some of us have been too busy trying to write their own books and in turn entertain others, (a selfless and it would seem unrewarding act!), to read other writer's books,

Where was I oh yes I am collecting together all of the parts that I am going to use for my rocket and I am going to use the insides of the toilet rolls as packing to ensure that the more delicate things don't get bumped or damaged. More delicate things such as me of course!

In fact I am very worried about my rocket getting damaged, there are one or two Elephant footed individuals around here and if they were to kick the metal wastepaper baskets they might damage them, and as I am going to use them as the fuselage of my rocket they need to be air tight and undamaged so that eventually I can pressurise them.

What? What are you saying and why are you laughing? Two metal wastepaper bins are perfectly acceptable as the rocket's hull! I am going to have to find a way of welding them together I know that and then attaching them to the rocket motor, and I have to say that I really fancy one of those pointy sharp nose cones (detachable of course) and that will have to be welded on too.

In my considered opinion I will have to learn how to do some welding and it will have to be better welding than 'spot welding,' which I heard about once! Honestly spot welding sounds a little radical for the odd skin blemish to my way of thinking, but then I know less about spots, in general, than I do about welding although another advantage of being Feline, and there are lots, is that we don't get spots. So I do have to know about spots, just welding!

Cats don't get spots on our skin, I have had big spinning spots in front of my eyes when I get a bang on the head or blown up, but then I suppose that is all in a days work for a Cat!

I did try out Superglue today, mainly because it was easier to lay a paw on that than welding gear! Personally I find it difficult to know what is so 'super' about Superglue! The tubes are not super sized for a start; really do the manufacturers actually want you to have their precious glue? It seems unlikely because they give you such a small amount in those tiny tubes!

I calculated that I was going to need over a million tubes to make my rocket, but then that figure might be too low or indeed too high because I got a little confused with all of the naughts in the sum and I am sure that I forgot to 'carry' the odd five at the end, but then in my defence I didn't know where to actually 'carry' the five to!

Then there is the 'other' problem with Superglue, I wasn't going to mention it of course for two reasons: the first is that Superglue misadventures are in the main rather tired jokes and the second reason is that I am actually getting rather tired of people laughing at my honest reporting of my misfortunes and misadventures in general in this Diary! What do you all think this Diary is, a comedy book?

I have been in some sticky situations on occasions especially recently, but I have never been actually stuck, if you see what I mean! Not until now that is!

Superglue isn't even sticky really, it is wet and then it is dry and you are stuck to it, I mean really, what sort of glue is that?

It took me a few minutes to notice that Superglue seems to like to dry with the aid of the warmth from your skin, well the only skin I have is on the padded bits of my paws, which proved inconvenient.

Superglue does not however like to stick if you just leave a tiny blob of it on what you want to stick with it, it just sits there refusing to dry, until of course you touch it to see if it is dry and then it smears itself all over your paw, and then you get a shock, because the skin starts to dry the Superglue and go all crackled and tight which is uncomfortable, until you touch something and manage to glue yourself to whatever you have touched.

Then things start to get worse because you wriggle and pull at your foot which is now stuck hard, in my case to one of the waste paper bins, and as you are using one of your three free paws to help pull yourself off the bin, more Superglue, which has come from 'somewhere,' although goodness knows where, gets 'applied' to your other feet, until you are stuck spread eagled over the waste paper bin, a bit like a dead cowboy over a saddle, except that this dead cowboy was spitting and moaning loudly.

The thing to do I suppose is to relax, calm down and think your way out of the predicament, yeah right! And you would do that too, would you?

While being stuck to a waste paper bin and getting giddy from rolling around the floor you would just take a breather? I believe you, thousands wouldn't!

And if that wasn't bad enough bits of 'escapee' Superglue turn upon anything that is in the path of you and the bin as you roll around and around like a demented cog in a clock that can't keep accurate time.

It is terrible when everything that you touch sticks to you, some of the things you roll over though luckily miss you and glue themselves to the waste paper bin, but between the two of you, a snowball down a mountain begins to sound positively anorexic.

Then when at last something large glues itself to your head, the beginning of the nightmare is over, unfortunately in this catalogue of misfortunes the 'something' that glued itself to my head was the leg of a chair. It was nice to have stopped rolling around the floor, but it wasn't a picnic to be anchored to the chair, I was, I will use the word 'jammed' because I don't really like using the word 'stuck' for obvious reasons.

They say that one should be happy for small mercies, the small mercy I should have been thankful for, was that I was recovering from being dizzy my eyeballs had even begun to stop revolving and the room which until then had been spinning violently was merely just whirling which was altogether better than before, but really, was that enough to be thankful for?

I was, let's call it wedged solid, as 'stuck' and 'glued' are not, as you can imagine, in my list of favourite words, and as my life seem to dictate, worse was to come!

The noise had woken up the Dog from his afternoon snore and in he strolled, his fur looking like an untidy mooch suit made from all of the worst bad hair days ever and quilted together to form an ugly mass of untidiness, really don't Dogs know how to keep themselves looking neat and tidy?

As I have said in the past the Dog isn't really too bad, especially from a distance or when he is asleep, but close to he is a bit much and when you add that to some of his more unsavoury habits he is really quite disgusting!

As luck wouldn't have it, he was in one of his, I'm going to be really disgusting moods, or maybe that is what he is always like, I don't know really, but he decided that he was going to sniff me all over and while sniffing me and discovering that unusually I wasn't in a position to thump him on the nose, he decided to give me a lick or two.

Why he doesn't put his entire licking instinct, that he seems to possess in abundance, into cleaning himself I don't know? I do know that the breath freshener chews that the Human Captors give him don't work.

At first when my fur was dry he was tickling me which was unpleasant, but bearable, but as I got wetter things really began to get more and more uncomfortable, especially as his hot breath made my skin creep.

It was awful and try as I might I couldn't even get one clawed paw free to reward him for what he was doing, all I could do was to endure and plot my revenge.

Superglue is useless when wet, yes I know I have said that and that it requires the heat of someone's flesh to help it dry and then set hard, but it is also (happily) pretty useless even when dry, because when after it is dry and it gets wet, if you see what I mean, it doesn't stick anymore! Proving my original point I think that Superglue is pretty useless in general.

All of the Dog's licking had left me feeling like a floating forlorn dish cloth in a bowl of last night's neglected washing up, I was soaked, no that isn't the right word, I was slimy, covered in, well I don't think I want to I make you sick with all of the details, but I was the accurate and breathing definition of the word uncomfortable.

But there was an upside, well there had to be, I had suffered and frankly deserved an upside and just a little cheering up and it came abruptly when my left paw suddenly came free.

I felt a little guilty really, smacking the Dog with a solid left hook full of claws, but I had to stop the dribbly licking somehow and he rather sulkily, I thought, sloped off to annoy some other poor soul.

Things were looking up, I could, with only a small amount of pain wipe my face and I can promise you it needed wiping, after that small treat I discovered that I could use my left paw as a pendulum and rock the waste paper bin against the chair leg.

With every bone jarring thud I felt a little freer and less trapped, then magically the bin rolled away from the chair leg and over me. As the bin rolled away from me with a lot of odd squelching noises, I was left lying upside down on the carpet.

Yes I still had all sorts of things stuck to me that would take ages to remove from my poor fur and I probably looked like a badly dressed Christmas tree created by a hyperactive inmate of a kindergarten, but I was free from the waste paper bin and able to move though very stiffly at first, even breathing seemed difficult.

I just laid still for a while slowly catching my breath and I am sure looking more like a nasty road accident than a good looking Cat, but I was, for all of that, happier than I had been for a good while I can tell you!

Eventually I got up and looked around, the room was a disaster to be totally candid, there were all sorts of things stuck to all manner of things, it looked as though a several maniacs had been let loose with buckets of Superglue and no supervision what so ever, I was appalled, I was also confident that one of the places that I shouldn't be was standing in the middle of it all and probably looking rather astonished and more than a little guilty.

I am not proud to say that I just slipped away and hid for most of the rest of the day, while I tried to sort out my fur and unglue myself, then I caught up with my Diary writing and hid some more in spite of the Captors spending a long while looking for me.

Between you and me, I had an idea that I would be better off not being found at least until the end of the day, what I couldn't understand was that the Humans spent so long looking for me when they had a big mess to clear up in the dinning room, really some people don't organise their time properly, do they?

Day 45 of My Captivity:

In the middle of the night I woke up all cold and stiff after a nightmare of a dream, where I was glued to the Dog and the Parrot who had decided to see if his old wings could lift us all off the ground, and fly around the room.

Nightmares are such that things that are impossible are accomplished immediately and we wove around the room until we all fell into a large paddling pool of slime.

It was awful I was drowning in slime and being pulled down by the weight of the fat hound who was barking large bubbles of slime, which splattered me with gallons of the unpleasant stuff.

Although it was dark and I was really uncomfortable because my fur was still stiff and brittle to the touch, I had to slip out of my hiding place under the Sofa in the front room and get a drink.

I am really lucky having been blessed with a Cat's night vision, but tonight my eyes were stuck together with sleep, still I didn't need to open them very wide to find the kitchen I used my brilliant hearing abilities and just followed the snoring and occasional farting noises made by the smelly king of sleep.

I had a drink of water and jumped into the Dog's king sized basket, he was for all of his noise and wind, really warm and cuddly and he even shuffled a little in his sleep to give me a bit more room, so I snuggled under his tail and dropped off into a more contented sleep, which happily was as dreamlessly clear of nightmares as my conscience.

When the day dawned the house was quiet and I spent all of the day cleaning up, well my fur was in a terrible state, but it was not as bad as the dinning room, which I had a peep into when I was passing on the way to the Sofa for a well earned catnap.

Day 46 of My Captivity:

Notes for any Human readers: This is like lying on a sun-drenched beach sipping a cool drink in the shade of an obliging palm tree or 'babe.'

Yes I know that I am in full view of everyone in the street but lying in the window under the glass in the hot sun is dribble makingly wonderful.

It is a long time since I had a day off and I haven't had a holiday since I got here, so today is a little indulgence gladly taken and very well deserved.

In the odd moments when my eyes are open and I may well be awake, I can see people, mainly children, looking at me sleeping, I wonder if they would like it if I was to sit and watch them sleep, haven't they got anything better to do, like play football or go off and break some windows?

Day 47 of My Captivity:

The devil has work for idle hands they say and I suppose the same is true for paws too.

It has been a very full couple of days, well yesterday was in my humble opinion a well earned day off I have to admit but I couldn't just be idle for long.

Today my idle paws were twitching, desperate to be busy, well desperate to be welding actually. I dearly wanted to begin work on the rocket but when I went into the dining room all of my components for the rocket had vanished.

It took me all day to first find all of the rocket bits and pieces and then drag them into the dining room and by the time it began to grow dark outside I had only assembled a small amount of what I required.

During the day I had the nagging thought that even if I managed to assemble everything I wasn't going to be able to begin the magnificent project because I still needed the welding gear and also needed to learn how to use it without setting the place alight.

It was apparent that the magnificent rocket project was going to take a long time to complete and so I thought I would shelve it for a while have something to eat and come back to it later, a bit like a hobby that one starts with a great burst of enthusiasm and then comes back to when one finds the time, usually when you're too old to enjoy it.

The Dog had eaten my food and so I spent the evening meowing loudly until the Human Captors finally deserted the television and found the energy to feed me, really what is the world coming to?

Day 48 of My Captivity:

Shh! Don't tell anyone but I have heard that there is a trip outside planned. As far as I can gather it has been booked for several weeks and I know that I am to be taken out, in fact I think I am the most important guest – for a change I might add. But just my luck the place I am going doesn't sound that great – in fact I caught the word 'wets' – odd name for a place, must be very damp!

But looking on the bright side this is a wonderful opportunity to gain my freedom and if it is not possible to escape at least I will get to see some of the area surrounding my prison.

Something has happened! Something awful. The trip in the car was short and quite exhilarating, though very noisy; well I felt that I had to scream at the top of my voice like people do on a roller coaster – whatever one of those is?

But now! After meeting a man in a white coat I feel woosy and very tired, I also have the nagging feeling that something is missing! If I could stay awake long enough to take stock I could...............

I'm awake now, I am back in the prison, but something has happened to me, something much worse than you could ever imagine, I have been violated, if I had any trust in Humankind it has all gone now, I am sorry, I just don't think I can bring myself to write it down at present, maybe in a while I will share the horror of it all with you. But maybe I won't.

Day 49 of My Captivity:

Slowly I am recovering, but I have to say that I don't ever think I will be back to normal, I feel listless and have a headache, in much the same way as Humans feel when they have had what they call a 'good time' the night before, and some private bits of me ache and some private bits of me that should ache don't.

I just don't understand what has been happening to me I feel as though I have been drugged and large parts of yesterday seem to be missing, very odd, and when I was washing earlier I am convinced that some bits of me are missing, but that is all too horrible to even think about.

You'll excuse me if I just close my eyes for a moment, won't you.

Day 50 of My Captivity:

It feels as if I have slept for days and not just one day, which is how long I have actually been asleep, I think!

I don't really have any clear idea what a 'day' actually is, with my fantastic sight night time, which I believe is the opposite to daytime, is just a little darker, and so the difference between the two is not as great as it is to Humans, who I understand can't see very well in the dark, poor things.

I heard that Humans even use Cat's eyes at night to help them keep to the right side of the road when driving. Well that is just plain disgusting but I can tell you, no one is going to get my eyes and that's final, I need them more than any motorised Human!

Earlier when I was meowing for food I noticed that my voice was slightly higher and that can't be right, I hope I am not sickening for something.

In fact I have noticed that there are a few things that aren't 'right!' I wonder if they are anything to do with my visit to the Vet's yesterday?

I do feel better than I did yesterday after my long sleep and a meal, I was, I think, beginning to waste away and still feel lighter, maybe I should have another meal?

I am sure that would make me feel better, I have just noticed that the Dog hasn't eaten all of his meal and he has been let out into the garden so I think I will just help myself, it seems to be such a shame to waste good food, not that I would describe what the black and tan furry lump eats as 'good food.'

Having said that about the brown mush that he eats there is a sublime pleasure to be enjoyed by eating the Dog's food, some of it comes from getting one's own back, he is always eating my Cat food for a start, and on top of that I do love to watch the look of agony on his face when he trots in from the garden all pleased with himself until he sniffs at the empty Dog bowl.

The pleasure only increases too, because he then starts to sniff around 'looking' for the missing meal, as though someone has decided that it would be a great doggy game to let him play tracker Dogs and allow the clever hound to 'find' the food and as a reward give him an even larger amount.

When he finally gives up with the look of a child who has had all of its sweets taken away, even the one it was ruining its teeth on, the icing on the cake is to sit in the middle of the floor looking smug and licking your lips.

It is wise just to do this only for the amount of time it takes for lightening brain to see you, then it is very wise to make a panicky run and leap up to the cupboard tops and shelter under the ceiling, while the hungry idiot barks the place down and gets into a lot of trouble with the Captors.

Then if one's acting is up to strength and you can turn the pure magic of laughter into the appearance of a little Cat shivering with fright as the dense Doggy barks and snarls up at you he gets into even hotter water.

If the bad bow wow does more than just bark and stands on his back legs with his front paws propped on the work surface, all the better, because he is certain to be grabbed by the collar and dragged to the back door to put out in the garden again, and by then of course it might be raining and you can really laugh like a drain!

Oh the simple pleasures of an uncomplicated life!

DAY 51 OF MY CAPTIVITY:

I found out what an acronym is earlier, because after seeing odd words like USAF and NATO on the television news and then reading the shortening of words that apparently represent other organisations who seem to like to be known just by the first letters of the words that make up their names I was keen to know what these words meant.

First I discovered in the trusty Collins Dictionary that an acronym is a word that one can say, made up from letters or parts of words like UNESCO and now I can announce to an admiring world that I have worked out what the acronym 'Dogs' means:

DOGS - Dumb On A Grand Scale!

How accurate!

The trouble is now that almost everything I encounter turns into an acronym and that is dreadful because my acronyms are generally 'MASS' (did you guess the acronym? My Acronyms Sometimes Stink).

The list of my newly invented acronyms is really long or NIAIRL, I have got to stop this and get a life, now!

Ok that is better I am beginning to relax and chill, After some dinner and a good night's rest I should be fine, I have been under a lot of stress recently and I need a holiday.

DAY 52 OF MY CAPTIVITY:

I asked the Dog if he could keep a secret today and when he said yes, I told him that was great and if I ever had one I would share it with him.

I know that I get on with the Dog, or let's put that another way I can just about tolerate the Dog in comparison to how I feel about the Parrot. But can I trust him; would he be as good as his promise? I wonder! If he does prove trustworthy then I could use him to help me escape, I will keep an eye on him and tell him some not very secret 'secret' and see what happens.

Although the Dog is loud and stupid and makes some really dreadful smells sometimes, at least he isn't evil like the Parrot, oh dear, that sounds like I am almost any Female Human talking about her husband, mmmh! I will have to cut that sort of thinking out, it sounds like I am a bit of a girly Cat and that would never do, I'm not and never have been a Pussy type Cat I promise you.

I have noticed that the way women talk about their husbands is really rude and sarcastic, I am pretty sure that the poor men in question are no worse than the women offering their opinions.

Take for instance cooking, I have seen that on television, and unlike in this kitchen here where little plastic trays of pre-prepared food are warmed up in a microwave oven, on television people cook, and the cooks are usually men I have noticed!

Those men who cook on television use fresh ingredients that may have until recently been trying to survive in polluted waters, been growing in the sun (or under glass in the electric equivalent), or indeed, could have been happily making noises in the countryside (or more likely been cooped up in a small pen, making the same noises only a little more manically)!

In any event the ingredients were definitely not wrapped in plastic film inside a cardboard sleeve with a pretty picture of themselves printed on it.

On occasions when I have watched these cooking shows with, as you can imagine, considerable interest I have been amazed at what raw ingredients look like.

Who would have thought for instance that a tomato was attached to its brothers on a vine? Not me that is for sure, or that a Chicken was a rather pale imitation of the Parrot, with feathers, seeing it like in nature and then when it was, well let's call it 'oven ready,' later really cheered me up, I can't wait until I see the Parrot in a similar state.

I wonder if roast Parrot would catch on as a Sunday lunch, after all Humans seem to eat quite a variety of birds and a few like Pheasants for instance have rather attractive plumage.

Day 53 of My Captivity:

Today I have one word for you, electricity, wow, if you don't know about electricity then let me tell you a secret, you don't want to go messing with electricity in anyway what so ever, don't listen to anyone, not even a Parrot, I assure you the pain that can be caused by ignoring my warning is excruciating!

Earlier I was, as usual, minding other people's business and doing a little silent creeping and snooping around the house, when I noticed that the Parrot was perched above me.

My automatic reaction to seeing the Parrot above me is to roll out of the way, in, a brilliant acrobatic and fluid movement, even though I say so myself.

I have learned that getting out of the way of the Parrot when he is above you is a very sound move. I have been, well let's just call it 'splattered' several times but now I have learned my lesson whether the 'stuff' he drops on you is wet or dry doesn't matter it is very difficult to get out of fur and smells for days, ugh!

This time when I landed gracefully on my feet I noticed that large areas of fur were sticking up in a very odd way, which made me look like a mad Cat.

No amount of licking helped, in fact the very opposite was the case, the more I licked, the worse the fur stuck up and what was really odd was that my tongue was getting little shocks, the shocks hurt and worse I was mystified and resigned to wandering around for the rest of my life with a body that was covered in fur that looked like a bad hair day.

Just quickly I tell you something though I have to admit it is a little off the point of this story but I think it is funny so I will tell you anyway and you can decide if I wasted my time telling you.

I looked up the word 'worse' because good writers, and I am confident that I fall into that category, would use a different word if they had used the same word in a sentence previously, but on this occasion your brilliant writer was a bit stuck for an alternative word to the word 'worse' if you see what I mean.

So I looked up the word 'worse' in the Microsoft Word dictionary, it comes with the software and uses Encarta, which is a dictionary (of American words) and a Thesaurus all at the same time sounds like a good idea doesn't it, what a shame that not all good ideas are good in practice.

Unfortunately Encarta just isn't that good, there are three meanings for the word 'worse' according to the sages at the Encarta Dictionary and Thesaurus factory, two are reasonably sensible and I will not bore you with them, because you may have a life to live! However the third meaning is to this Cat's way of thinking more than a little odd, the Encarta sages say:

3.More ill than before

Really! How clever, I don't think that is what I was thinking about when I used the word 'worse' the first time or indeed the second time either! So I looked in a grown up Dictionary, which for your information was the Collins English Dictionary, which had eight definitions for the word 'worse.' The first entry summed up 'worse' exactly and said:

1.The comparative of bad

Now that sounds about right doesn't it? Then I thought I would look up the same word in the Collins Thesaurus, because good old Encarta had offered six options for the word 'worse' all of which had nothing to do with being the comparative of bad to use the words of decent Dictionary.

At first I couldn't find the Collins Thesaurus, which although was annoying at least meant that someone was using it, which was an encouraging sign! So when I find it I will let you know how it compares to the junk offered in the Microsoft Word software. I wonder if the sages at Microsoft would like a Cat to help them compile a better Dictionary, I am a little busy at the moment writing a best selling Diary, but I may have a 'window' soon.

Just before I finish on the inadequacies of the Dictionary I thought I would share a few words with you that the sages at Encarta chose to leave out of their Dictionary, probably so that they could be politically correct.

Encarta what a name! - In fact if anyone knows what the word Encarta means, please write to me and let me know and in turn I will give you a prize, something of great value, a Collins English Dictionary for example.

Missing from the 'wonderful' Encarta dictionary are useful traditional English words like: Whore, Bastard, Cock (the feathered variety of course, although they left in cock-a-doodle-doo, odd), there are more but my paws ache from typing and so I am going to keep the list short, but if you own a copy of the 'excellent' (yeah right) software Microsoft Word for Apple, then you can spend hours looking for missing everyday words, (I don't know if PC's stay on long enough between crashes to run Word with Encarta because I use an Apple) if you are really sad, I heard the person who said 'like this Diary author!'

Last but not least Colour, the definition just says U.K. = colour as if that isn't the correct spelling and the quaint English didn't invent the language in the first place.

All of those words missing from the Encarta Dictionary are carefully and expertly defined in all English Dictionaries and are valid words that have been part of the English language for centuries, well with the exception of the word 'Encarta' which I have a feeling is a made up word, but really what is happening to English if a Dictionary which pretends to explain English words is so lacking?

I am still only learning the language but if I was English and cared a jot about my language I would be pretty 'annoyed' (another word not defined in Encarta I hasten to add). Still I suppose it is a little pompous to care that much about a language, just look at the French!

So I have got that off my chest and come to the end of my little English language rant, happily I hear you say!

Where was I before I got carried away? Electricity, yes that was it, although at the time when I was licking my fur and trying to do something creative with the worst bad hair day in history I didn't know that I was suffering from the effects of static electricity.

Although it is a silly name for this type of electricity, it really does do what it says on the label if you see what I mean, I looked as though I was hair gelled to death and all because of this form of electricity.

It was the Parrot who told me, yes I know it shocked me too, he just blurted out the word static, grunted shifted his feet on the top of the hall door and added electricity.

It was a shock, no not the electricity although that was shocking enough; the fact that the Parrot had spoken civilly to me was astonishing. And once he had begun to speak it was, I could tell, going to be impossible to shut the old bird up, especially as he was out of reach, I have found that a good right hook normally shuts most unwelcome talkative birds up, or a half Nelson if one is really lucky.

Anyway on and on he droned about Electricity and eventually, as I couldn't find anything to stuff in my ears I began to listen to him and surprisingly became engrossed in what he was rambling on about. Electricity is fascinating, from its generation and the many and various ways that that can happen, through to what it is used for, I was very interested.

He ended his lecture by saying that I should try some electricity and I have to say that I was so captivated in what he had been saying that I wholeheartedly agreed with him and was dying to have a go.

It is with some relief that now I can tell you that I didn't manage to find an electrical socket that was free and didn't have something plugged into it, because I was, on the Parrot's instructions going to jam my claws into one and as he put it, enjoy the power of electricity. Now after reading about electricity I know that I would have probably been more like a Cat in a Chinese take away – fried, if I had done what the Parrot suggested, how mean is that I ask you?

Day 54 of My Captivity:

I am a giggler, but what's wrong with that? Sometimes I giggle a little and sometimes I giggle a lot, I never giggle too much because by the time I have finished giggling I am usually very hot and have forgotten what I was giggling about, and then other times I not only forget what I was giggling about because I was giggling so hard, but I even fail to remember when I started giggling in the first place.

In all honesty sometimes I worry me!

What makes us giggle in the first place? I suppose the puzzling answer is almost anything can. An old lady leaving the loo with her dress caught up in her knickers can be mildly amusing one day and then riotously funny the next, strange.

The word Aardvark can be said one day without anyone even sniggering and then the next time it is mentioned people will giggle, I have decided that giggling in general and humour in particular is definitely odd, it is so odd that it makes me giggle sometimes!

Day 55 of My Captivity:

This entry has been written today that is Day 56 and the reason for that will become obvious when you read on, what can I say, all in all, Day 55 was not a good day.

Day 56 of My Captivity:

Now that my vision is more or less back to normal and I can see one of everything and not two, I thought that I would pass the time with a little reading and I have just read that Phrenology is the study of bumps on the head, well, the explanation contains words to that effect, and as that is the case, then Phrenologists must be people who studies those bumps and they would have a field day with my poor aching head if they were to begin reading the numerous bumps that I have managed to collect.

Yesterday I was minding my own business; doing a bit of scouting up in the attic where I had found a loose roof tile.

Well for accuracy let's rephrase that with the truth. For most of the morning I had been working my way through the plasterboard ceiling in the attic, which conveniently slants down to the floor.

It had taken me quite some time to get used to using the heavy hammer and crowbar and so lunchtime was approaching and I was keen to finish up with banging a hole through the plasterboard pull out the insulation and break through the roof tiles, so that I could go downstairs and have a large lunch and then escape.

Curiosity didn't kill the Cat happily, but it made a very large impact on my poor bonce. Still I probably would have ended up with a sore head anyway because even after lunch I would have done what I did next.

I made a hole in the plasterboard and then pulled out the itchy insulation, handily the hole was big enough to allow me to squeeze through and attack the roof tile.

The tile which was slate, but then that is more or less irrelevant, broke easily and as large chunks or splinters sailed off the roof I could smell the delicious air of freedom, which was great because being in such a small gap was making me very hot.

Soon not only could I smell freedom I could see it, in the blue sky Seagulls were wheeling about under the vapour trail of a jet airliner.

Have you ever noticed just how many Seagulls there are in the world, wherever you look you can guarantee that there will be a seagull circling like some sort of bleached Vulture!

Why is that? Don't they have homes to go to? And why is it that they are so far away from the sea, and if, as I suspect, they have been so far in land for so long, why are they still called Seagulls?

I'm heading off the point aren't I! I don't like Seagulls though, dreadful birds, in fact dreadfully big birds and not very friendly, oops done it again haven't I. But something ought to be done about Seagulls, in fact give me a machine pistol and enough ammo and I'll do something about them.

Ok, ok I know the point! I promise not to mention them again!

Where was I? Ah! Yes I was looking out of the large hole I had punched in the slate roof with my trusty 'four pound' hammer, watching those things that I promised I wouldn't mention again, circling like so many bleached Vultures.

They were annoying me, what right have they got to be so free and easy when good honest, a hard working Cat can't enjoy freedom? So when I squeezed out onto the roof I was more interested in shaking my paw at 'them' than I was looking where I was going. Well to be honest where I was teetering about.

Luckily Cats have a wonderful sense of balance, but I hadn't imagined that I would have need of the same sort of understanding of updrafts, air currents and gusting wind that those hateful Gulls have.

No, I said that I wouldn't mention Seagulls again, I didn't say anything about 'Gulls!' now shut up and stop complaining and picking on me and let me tell you what happened next, dear reader!

I was suddenly buffeted by a gust of wind and then, and this is another reason to hate Gulls, one dive bombed me, well that was what it felt like, he missed and landed in the pond in the garden, I have to say that was the first I knew of a pond in the garden, but unfortunately I didn't have time to admire it or think about catching the wonderful big orange and white fish that circled about under the surface of the pond.

The Gull and the wind made me lose my balance and then my footing and much to the shame of all surefooted Cats the world over I fell, sliding down the pitch of the roof and landing with my face in several years worth of leaf litter in the gutter.

Honestly why don't Humans clean their gutters more often?

I sat up and got my bottom wet, and tried to see what was happening. The wet slime had covered my face and all I could see was blackness, gently I reached up and tried to wipe my face, but the movement made the gutter sway, really when Humans are cleaning out their gutters you would think that they would make sure that they were properly fitted too wouldn't you?

I didn't need eyes to know that the guttering had come away from the wall and I was swaying high above the garden, one good thing had happened gravity had pulled the leaf mould from my eyes but that only allowed me to see that gravity was just about to make something that wasn't so wonderful, happen!

Do I need to go on? You have all seen what happened next and laughed until you were nearly sick in dozens, (tens if you are French) animated cartoons, or you may think you have!

Thing is, in those cartoons the Cat is really just a dumb representative of my species and with one silly resigned grin at his fate accepts it and plummets to earth.

Well let me tell you right now, that sort of discrimination is unacceptable and more importantly this Cat is no dumb representative of his species!

There was no way that just like Tom of Tom and Jerry fame I was going to grin and vanish and plummet to the ground, because a real Cat hurts and Cats like Humans are allergic to pain in general, and specifically this Cat is very allergic to pain!

As the guttering swung further away from the wall, the accumulated water, gunge and leaf mould, which was in the main, mainly gunge I hasten to add, (see above concerning regular cleaning of guttering) came gushing down to the heavy end of the guttering.

The heavy end of the guttering was made 'heavy' because that is where I was sitting, well clinging on to the sides by this time to be exact.

The tide of filth hit me and although I was prepared for it because I watched it fall towards me, not, I might add, like in the movies when everything goes into slow motion, this was travelling at about the speed of a mini tidal wave.

I was drenched and filthy and although the extra weight of the gunge made the guttering sag it didn't snap which was something I was expecting, it didn't make me lose my grip and fall on to the ground making a bigger nastier mess either, which was also something I was expecting.

Instead the guttering begun swaying and every time it hit the wall of the house it banged my head, I couldn't put my paws out to stop banging my head because as you will remember I was clinging for more than all I was worth to the guttering to stop falling out.

And so every time this mad toing and froing happened I banged my poor head. Happily though because I was, like a good boxer rolling with each impact, the bumps weren't hurting and believe it or not this is not where I got the bumps on my head that a Phrenologist would be so interested in, oh no that came later.

Well to be exact the bumps came just after I had got used to the awful swaying and was beginning to time the interval between bumps on the head, so that I could make a dramatic and skin (and fur) saving leap from the guttering onto the roof.

It wasn't going to be an easy jump, I knew that, and it was going to be a long way down if I didn't make it, but what choice did I have? I had been swaying for what seemed like ages and no other plan suddenly popped into my head, my brain was too busy being bumped every time it met the side of the house.

That was when I heard the metallic noise, of what I now know was a ladder being opened or raised or whatever one does to make ladders bigger.

It was also the exact moment when I should have jumped, I know that now, oh yes indeed I do!

Very quickly after the noise of the ladder being, well let's call it 'opened' a face appeared level with the gutter, it was a fat face of a busy body; this area is just plain stuffed with them I have to say.

At the time of the appearance of the fat face of course I didn't have even a moment to consider just how over subscribed this area is with busy bodies though.

He sensibly held the ladder with one hand and not so sensibly the guttering with the other, which left the sum total of no hands to rescue me!

I could tell that this new situation had the potential for trouble! More trouble than I had at the moment and that, to my way of thinking, was more than enough!

It is a good job that I am quite used to danger, because I was sure that what was about to happen was going to be very dangerous, after all the guy had a small moustache!

Very carefully the fat faced moustachioed man transferred his not inconsiderable weight allowing the guttering to slap back up against the wall.

Does it go without saying that I received a bump on the bonce for his troubles? Well if it did then it is too late! I have said it! But like the rest of the bumps against the wall I rolled with it and happily I wasn't even bruised.

'So far so good,' was what I thought, and probably what the fat faced man was thinking too! Although while thinking this I did try to back away from him just a little. But I just managed to get covered in even more black gunge for my trouble and not really, as far as I was concerned, far enough away from him.

I had a very bad feeling about this newest development, especially when the ladder began to rock and slip along the wall, still at least the movement allowed the fat faced man to get a nice bump in the face, which I think hurt because it broke his glasses in two at the bit that went over his nose. He, it was clear, had never boxed.

He did look a little alarmed and although I say so myself a little alarming, each piece of his specs dangling from his ears, and still swaying almost drunkenly as the ladder flexed under his weight.

Things then went quiet when he stopped moving and held on with bright white knuckles to the ladder.

Until now he hadn't said a thing, no, 'here pussy, pussy,' or other inane words of encouragement that I believe are usually used by 'rescuers in this situation, he just grabbed a breath and whimpered, just a little and I think mainly to himself, especially after he looked down and probably realised just how high up we were.

Mabel now joined in our forlorn little group, at first as an interested on looker and gradually as an apprehensive one.

I personally had never been introduced to Mabel and only knew her name after she shouted up to George fat face enquiring as to his wellbeing.

George, I knew his name because Mabel used it, wobbled a reply with his voice and with some interesting swaying of the ladder.

No, Mabel, he was not ok and could she phone for the Fire Brigade, his reply was I thought succinct and to the point if not a little rude.

Judging by the sirens in the distance someone had prudently done that job already. Maybe George fat face and I would agree that there should be the word 'happily' inserted into that sentence somewhere.

George fat face's face had now gone as white as his knuckles and fear had frozen his moustache as the ladder slipped again across the wall.

George was now too far away from me for me to help even if I had known what to do and frankly had he become, to my way of thinking, just another obstacle to my escaping.

There was one consolation for us both, although George fat face was too preoccupied to appreciate it, the ladder had wedged itself under the gutter, which meant that the guttering had stopped swaying and I was able to sort of swim backwards through the guttering and gunge.

They do say; be thankful for small mercies and so I thanked whoever was dolling them out, just as the pretty red and shiny Fire Engine arrived, driving through the gate and over the newly mown lawn leaving quite large tyre tracks behind it.

Every time I have encountered Firemen they have been wonderful and their cool efficiency always impresses me, although I have to confess that I have thought that their arrival is always a little premature, in fact I am convinced that I could have got into a lot more danger before really needing their assistance on all of the other previous occasions I have met them!

In no time at all they had leaned two ladders next to George fat face's ladder and were taking him down, with a mixture of great strength and soft words.

At the bottom George was rewarded with a check-up in an Ambulance which had appeared out of nowhere, and unfortunately a good telling off from his worried wife Mabel who had a lot to say about remembering to act his age, and what did he think he was doing!

For a minute or so I thought that either I had been forgotten by everyone or missed completely, but the metallic ringing of the ladder rungs told me that a Fireman was on his way up to look after me.

It is a strange fact that Cats have an odd attitude to Firemen and rescuers in general; as a rescuer approaches I don't know why, but it is in a Cat's nature to back away from them and because the guttering seemed pretty solid and wasn't swaying, I saw no reason to change this tradition and begun backing away from the yellow helmet that was coming into view over the top of the gutter.

The inside of the gutter was still very slippery and full of gungey leaf mould which was really disgusting, to be honest I didn't mind the gunge too much it was the slipperiness that was my main concern and I was right to be concerned.

Although the guttering was secure being pressed against the wall by the ladder, it was lying at a very steep angle and looked more like a playground slide than a gutter to catch rain and obviously leaf mould and gunge.

The Fireman's face appeared and then a long arm reached out to me but I was just out of reach and so he moved up a rung and as he did the surefooted Fireman slipped, he reached out to steady himself and grabbed the gutter, his weight pulling it down even further until the angle was too steep for me to stay wedged safely. The slippery gunge did its job and I slid down towards the Fireman's hand and safety.

Life is not simple and anything that isn't simple sometimes seems unfair, this was one of those occasions and instead of being grabbed by the strong hands waiting to catch me I slid on passed.

There was nothing I could do and nowhere to grab on to and so as I gathered more and more speed I splashed my way towards the end of the gutter, it wasn't unlike being at a water park except that a soft landing was far from guaranteed.

When I flew off into the afternoon air I was speeding like a little dirty furry rocket, I closed my eyes and decided that this was going to hurt.

I cannot believe just how long it takes to fall from a roof even travelling at the speed I was going which while it wasn't the speed of sound, I don't suppose, was in fact really rather quick.

They say that Cats have nine lives and this one has probably used up all of his own and some of a few other Cats too, what a good job it is that Cats don't mind sharing!

Some quick thinking Firemen had seen what was happening and ran up the garden to more or less where I was just about to make, what I suppose was going to be quite a nasty mess on the floor. Happily they had a sort of net thing with them and as I slammed into it they caught me.

Well that was the plan! Unfortunately a flying Cat, even one who didn't mean to fly and definitely won't be flying again in a hurry, is not the same weight as a Human who I presume the net contraption was designed for and it acted exactly like a trampoline.

I bounced off the net banging my head hard and got my first bump on the head, then I flew in the opposite direction, this flying business was getting rather boring I have to say.

Back I flew, gaining height because of the angle at which I had been catapulted. I sneaked a look at the ground whistling passed beneath me and then out of the corner of my eye as I closed it again I spotted the side wall of the house.

The next thing I knew was another bump on the head, which the half open window generously gave me as I sailed through it, I half opened my eyes and realised that I was in the front room and flying backwards above the carpet and the maddeningly excited Dog who was barking merrily away as he watched me heading towards one of the front rooms pristine cream walls.

I smacked into the wall just next to the door, it goes without saying that I collided with the wall head on and with a very wet sounding slap I stopped, well I stopped flying and then I slid down the wall leaving a trail of black gunge, leaf mould and yes even some slime as I slid briskly to the floor, landing unbelievable and painfully on my poor head and getting two bumps for my trouble, why two bumps on the head? Well it was obviously a day for bouncing and bumps and so I bounced on the floor both time landing on my head!

I was dazed, confused and seeping wet black slime into the beautiful light peppermint green carpet.

Personally I couldn't begin to comprehend just how much gunge seeped out of my fur, I also couldn't believe that a head as small as mine could hurt as much as mine did, but I have to keep reminding myself that my life is not a cartoon, if you do a bit of flying and head bumping you are going to hurt in the next morning. Frankly I was dreading tomorrow morning, because my head hurt enough now!

The Firemen were all too big to follow me in through the window and so they did the next best thing and took an axe to the front door so that they could get inside and check upon me, but I was too dazed to notice them or the Dog who uses any excuse to sniff me which is disgusting, still I suppose today I was the more disgusting.

I was picked up and carried at arms length by the Fireman who had failed to grab me and then I was put in the sink and rinsed, it probably took ages to get the filth out of my fur and to see the white, tabby and silver bits, but I was just too stunned to care.

So much for getting out through the roof, I think I will shelve that plan and think of other ways to escape.

Now that you see what happened yesterday you will see why I just didn't get the time to write an entry for that day.

Still I have plenty of time today because I have been locked in the kitchen, which I take to be some sort of special punishment.

All that is left of yesterday's palaver is the Fire Engine and the Ambulance tyre tracks; I have to say that they really did make a mess of the lawn.

Well then there are a few dents made in the turf by the Police car, but they are minor when compared to the deep trenches made by the Fire Engine, and yes I suppose the crowd did make a mess too, though not by gouging up the lawn, because they were spectators their impact was mainly the soft drink cans, sweet wrappers and crisp packet rubbish that they left behind. Odd isn't it, that when a crowd gathers the next thing you see when they disperse is a collection of litter.

I remember watching a news programme about the anti globalisation, anti capitalist demonstrators, who march on May1st with other groups of concerned citizens who want to divorce themselves from any form of government, including I might add and stress, conservationists and you will see why I have added and stressed conservationists in the next paragraph or two!

There were a couple of things I noticed about the anti/anti group who are against companies that make and sell jeans, trainers and fizzy drinks all over the world, but I noticed weren't against wearing or drinking those very products, I suppose that they wanted the companies just to sell them in this country to keep them all for themselves.

Another thing I noticed was when the anti/anti's and the conservationists had finished their cans of fizzy drink and pies, they all dropped their litter in the streets of London, Madrid and New York, so I presume that they believe that it is only rain forests and other people's lands that should be conserved and protected, because in my opinion littering is just as bad as logging in a rain forest, but what do I know I am only a Cat and not a learned conversationalist with a degree in social science!

So all in all it has been a long day, what with recovering from yesterday's 'upset,' gambling yet another of my nine lives and writing a report in my Diary so that you can share my little experiences, as one Fireman said to a colleague as he was leaving, 'you wouldn't think that one little Cat could get into so much trouble.'

Which is a fair point and I have to agree with him there especially as he didn't seem to think, judging by his remark that I had caused the trouble in the first place, just somehow as an innocent bystander 'got into it,' which is comforting, and with that thought I am going to have a well deserved sleep, goodnight everyone.

DAY 57 OF MY CAPTIVITY:

They do say that 'every Dog has its day,' well they would, wouldn't they!

What I want to know is when will every Cat have their day? And when will this Cat have its day in particular!

I have been imprisoned here for too long and need to get out as soon as I can, but I just seem to be very unlucky with every little scheme and big scheme of mine going awry and I am sure that they don't go wrong because of lack of scheming and planning so it must be something else, let's call it luck!

If we agree that what is missing in my escape plan is luck then we have to agree that if a Cat, and let's for the moment not point a finger at any Cat in particular, should have a special day or in other words 'have their day!' Couldn't that day be sooner rather than later?

That is right isn't it, there is no reason to suggest that I shouldn't have one lucky day when everything goes right, the sun shines and Humans do what you want them to and not what they think up on their own.

Personally speaking the best bit of luck I could have would be for everyone to go out and leave the front door open, now today would be a good day for all of that to happen and they do say that if you wish for something enough then it happens, so here goes, I'm off to check out the front door.

No, before you say anything, I didn't believe it either, as I walked through a patch of brilliant sunlight that made the hallway look like a stage I noticed that my wish had been granted and the front door was open, unbelievable!

So unbelievable that I stopped in my tracks and let the spotlight sunbeam light up my excellent coat, I have to say I was sparkling magically and looking really good in the spotlight. The first thing to do, I decided, was to appear not to notice that the front door was open or that the front door even existed and so I sat down and looked everywhere but at the front door, flowing up the sunbeam were tiny shimmering bits of dust, today was obviously magical.

After a while the spotlight sunbeam moved a little and so I decided that I had been sitting in the hallway minding my own nonchalant business for too long and probably had begun to look suspicious.

My mouth was dry with excitement and my paws itched with the idea that soon I may just be on the outside. I knew that I had to check one last thing before I left for the first and last time. I had to make really sure that this was my day and if it really was my day then the Captors would be out.

Without looking too suspicious I backed away from the sunlight and the front door and bumped into the kitchen door frame, when I decided that I was far enough away from the front door to not draw anyone's attention to the fact that it was still open, a fact which of course I had just checked with a quick glance.

The kitchen was empty, the utility room was too, the dining room door was closed, a wise decision I thought bearing in mind the sticky events of a few days ago. I could see into most of the front room and that was deserted so I walked upstairs, and with every step I was getting more and more convinced that I was alone in the house and my excitement was mounting.

The bedrooms and the bathrooms were empty I was so grateful that I felt like shouting hallelujah as if I was a new convert to a strange religious sect Then I remembered that I was a Cat and didn't believe in any such nonsense, thankfully! Cats obviously don't believe in religions that have a god because god spelt backwards is Dog and well you all know what Cats think about Dogs don't you!

Back in the hallway I made my way quickly through the patch of sunlight and hardly noticed that the little shiny bits of dust were still dancing their happy little silvery jig I walked without stopping straight through the front door skipped down the steps and onto the drive.

The sunny day was a delight and I was delighted to be outside in the glare of a sun, this was the life, this was I thought the real beginning to my life, a life outside, free, with no one to keep me caged or hold me back from my destiny.

I took a moment to savour the smell of freedom, allow the light warm breeze to play over my fur and to dig my claws into the ground. I was in heaven; ok so there is no reason why Cats can't use words like heaven even if they don't believe in religions, is there?

Then just as I was going to saunter up the drive and out into the big wide world I remembered that I had left my Diary behind and I couldn't go without it and let all of that hard work go to waste.

Still there wasn't anyone around for miles it seemed, except for someone cutting the grass a few gardens away.

I would, I thought, just nip back into the house and collect the precious papers that at some stage would make me famous and almost as rich as I could imagine.

It wouldn't take long and then I could be on my way, finally.

I am always losing things and I have a theory about that, the more you need to find something in a hurry the more difficult it is to remember where you have put it, worse, sometimes I spend so long looking for what I can't find I forget what I am looking for, or why I am looking for it in the first place.

Today I knew it was important to find my Diary and leave by the conveniently open front door and I was not about to forget that, but because I was concentrating so hard on remembering that the front door was open and freedom was not only beckoning but waving both arms in the air like a Human drowning in treacle, I was having great difficulty remembering where I had hidden my Diary and was running around in widening circles through the house rummaging and rifling anything that stood still long enough to rummage and rifle without complaining.

I was becoming frantic, but just when I had imagined the Captors returning home and bickering with each other about leaving the front door wide open I found my Diary and raced down the stairs and towards the still open, thankfully, front door.

The sun was shining outside as excitedly as I was to nip through the door and enjoy it freely, the gentle breeze caressed the grass and played with the leaves and shimmering branches of the Silver Birch trees, it was as if the gentle wind was making the shiny branches wave at me to join them.

The same breeze that caused so much welcoming optimism then turned and in an instant began to close the open front door, there was nothing violent about the touch of the wind on the font door and the door seemed in no hurry to close, there was only a Cat in a hurry today and that was because I had seen that the front door would close even though it was only moving slowly.

I panicked I was half way down the stairs and had to do something, my luck surely wouldn't desert me today would it?

In a split second I decided that it wouldn't, life and luck couldn't be that cruel? So I dived from the fourth step from the bottom and shot through the air towards the door, sunlight and freedom, only looking down at the last minute to see that I was about to land in a size ten belonging to the Male Captor.

Just before impact I tucked my head into my chest and curled up into a tight ball, which is a good way to land, well it is a good way to land if you are landing on a flat surface like a hall floor, but it isn't even the second best way to land in a shoe, in fact it is probably the worst way to land in a shoe.

I dived into the open shoe and for the first time experienced the depressing experience every foot must encounter when placed into a shoe belonging to someone who has smelly feet, it was horrible, but thankfully the experience was brief, because I had more important things to worry about than the lack of Odour Eaters in the brown brogue.

The smelly shoe was toppled over with the force of my impact and together we sped towards the closing door, just in time in fact to collide with the door as it closed and the disheartening click of the latch sounded.

I was bewildered, bemused but not stupefied, unless stupefied only means dazed, or to put it another way I am not stupid, even though I was bemused, and I knew what the click meant, but I didn't have time to dwell on my recurring misfortune, because outside I heard the Captor's car arrive, it noisily squashed a Coke Can that had been left by the spectators who had so enjoyed George's rescue from the other day, and obviously blown onto the drive after escaping the Captor's resentful clear up after the excitement.

They were out of the car and that wasn't good because I was still stuffed in the size ten shoe, the key was in the lock and I was struggling to get out of the shoe, not wanting to be discovered stuck in a shoe, I would never live down the embarrassment.

Too late the door swept open carrying the shoe with me lodged firmly inside into the middle of the hall before it had finished pushing us aside.

'Oh look at that, isn't it sweet, the Cat is playing with your shoe.' Too late the cutesy label that Cats try so had to play down had been affixed to me and it hurt so much it could have been nailed in place.

Still being thankful for small mercies it eventually dawned on the dim Humans that I was stuck in the shoe and they extricated me, and because I am sweet, cute and no doubt cuddly I was given a few Prawns so the day wasn't a complete write off.

Day 58 of My Captivity:

Jam today and tomorrow and unfortunately the day after see Day 61 for a full exasperated explanation.

Day 59 of My Captivity:

No knucklehead, I said see Day 61, not Day 59! Humans, the Super race, I ask you?

Day 60 of My Captivity:

Nearly there! Sorry to shout and lose my temper, but you will understand when read the next page, by the way do you have any tips for getting jam out of a fur coat?

Day 61 of My Captivity:

Hang on, what has happened here? Where are my entries (in my best paw writing, I might add) for days 58, 59 and 60? I am sure that they were here when I closed the Diary last night.

In fact last night's entry, Day 60, was in my opinion a masterpiece, but then to be really honest most of my writing could be considered to be exceptionally good and the Diary in general a magnum opus, so to lose three precious pages is a crime against all that is good in the world, even Humanity.

What a shame that these words of obvious wisdom and wonder are lost forever, because I am certainly not going to rack my brains trying to remember and then rewrite what I had already written, so you will just have to imagine what I said.

It is odd though that the pages have just vanished! I wonder where the pages might have disappeared to? My first thought is that someone has stolen them, but that is mad because anyone wanting to steal the Diary wouldn't do it three pages at a time, or even page by page, or would they?

Hang on though! Using my superior powers of reasoning, I think if that light fingered someone had wanted to read the Diary they would just make off with the whole thing, so theft is probably not responsible of the loss of the pages.

Not only is theft probably not the reason the pages are missing, even if the literary thieves were daft enough to steal three pages at a time, they would, if they had any sense, steal the first three pages from the beginning of the book and not the last three, surely? Well I know I would!

Ok so we can probably rule out a well educated and discerning thief! But what is an established fact is that three pages are definitely missing. Is there any point in suggesting that whoever took them puts them back while I close my eyes, no questions asked?

No I thought not! After all if we are not dealing with a well educated thief then we must be dealing with a badly educated thief and so there is no point in appealing to their intelligence is there? Silly me!

Maybe the pages weren't stolen, it is a possibility I suppose, I really ought to consider that others are not as bad as I expect them to be, but then if I do that then I may well be disappointed and that would never do, and on top of that so far no one has disappointed me and that is because I believe that everyone is either really bad, or nearly bad. Well except for the Dog sometimes. And he's thick!

Still it is worth considering that the missing three pages weren't stolen, and if they weren't, to work out what may or may not have happened to them.

Let's think about this logically! Where would someone start who was looking for three missing pages? Well looking all over the house seems a big and lengthy task although probably not as big and lengthy as rewriting the three missing pages and that is a fact.

This someone would probably look in the kitchen cupboard? No that is silly, next to the Parrot's perch, yes that seems likely, though hang on a minute, let's use the logic we spoke about a minute ago here, is the Parrot capable of ripping (neatly) three pages out of my Diary, and making off with them. No! He could rip them out but he wouldn't be neat about it, he would enjoy the demolition so much that he would make a real mess of the Diary, deliberately and rip the entire Diary up and not just neatly snaffle three pages.

So reluctantly, I suppose, we can rule the Parrot out as a suspect, but that doesn't solve the mystery, it deepens it in fact!

This is me getting nowhere, or to put it another way this is getting me nowhere! Maybe I could flick back through the pages and see if there are any clues, seems like a good idea!

There are some smears of red stuff, Claret? As any good cockney would ask, meaning Blood! Well if the red smears are blood they are not mine, and if they are not mine and I have just said they aren't then they must belong to the thief, hopefully he hurt himself stealing the precious pages, at least that would be a consolation for losing the pages!

Wait a minute! Day 57 is covered in the stuff and it is sticky, and what is that? It seems to have little seeds in it, how odd.

Now that isn't right the next page is very thick! Oh dear I think I know what has happened here! I was eating a summer fruit Jam Sandwich a few days ago and I remember it being a little sticky and getting my paws covered in the stuff.

I think we may have found an answer to the mystery. The missing pages are stuck together, let's see if I can open them, carefully does it, what an advantage having claws is sometimes, whoops that has torn it, or to put it another way I have torn them!

All that work ripped to shreds and worse still no one to blame except yours truly, pass the milk, please; well after all it drives one to drink!

Day 62 of My Captivity:

At least the mystery of the missing pages has been solved, mind you, that hasn't brought back the missing pages for you to read and you only have my word for it that those pages were some of the best written in the English language, unless you are reading this in Chinese and then they were obviously some of the best written pages in the Chinese language and you will have to take my word for that because I just can't bring myself to write them again.

Thinking about the Chinese translation and here it might be a good idea to say hello to my Chinese readers. Hello my Chinese readers, there I like to include everyone and let's face it China is a big market. It is great that my Diary is successful enough to be translated into your language but please make sure that you have an authentic copy, it would be dreadful if you were reading a pirate copy, think of all the copyright fees I would be missing out on!

So if you are reading a pirate copy or in the near future watching a pirate copy of the Movie on DVD do stop that and please go out now and buy an authentic copy because it was hard work writing this and I am sure you will agree that hard work deserves the proper reward, in this case barrels loads of cash!

Day 63 of My Captivity:

You know I am worried, in fact I didn't get a lot of sleep last night worrying about what worried me.

Yesterday when I was talking to my Chinese readers I was as you might recall struck by a terrible thought that I maybe losing loads of dosh because of pirate copies of this Diary and soon the movie being enjoyed at bargain basement prices in, let's face it, pretty dreadful quality.

But what can one Cat do about that? My initial reaction was to suggest that the selling price for 'authentic' copies be increased and then for the people being charged too much to go and 'sort out' the pirates and get their money back.

Still thinking about it, that wouldn't work, although of course in my opinion my work is priceless and even with a few extra dollars or pounds added onto the cover price you are still getting a good deal, but I don't suppose anyone else would see it that way.

So I have decided that there is only one thing to do to anyone who illegally copies my work and that is to put the legendary 'Curse of the Cat' on them. After all people who make these illegal copies tend to be in the far east – naming no names as it were, and they do tend to be superstitious so here it is, the dreaded and as I said before legendary 'Curse of the Cat.'

If you copy my stuff illegally then all of the Female Humans in your family will grow whiskers.

Yes I know it doesn't sound much of a curse to us westerners who have to pay the full price for books and movies, but let's face it we are civilised and not superstitious and wouldn't even think of stealing from a poor Cat, would we?

Of course no one thinks that buying a pirate CD or DVD is 'not really' a crime, well buster if you want to know how much of a crime it is, just write a book or make a movie and then see how you feel when you lose money through pirate copiers! Sorry it makes my whiskers twitch just thinking about it!

DAY 64 OF MY CAPTIVITY:

Today I have decided to forget all about curses even the 'Curse of the Cat' and rely on the honesty of my dear readers and home entertainment watchers, naïve? Yes, but let's face it I am just a trusting, cuddly and extremely entertaining Cat, and no one would want to hurt me or steal from me would they? Or should that be would you?

Having said that, that is an end to it, except to say that it is no wonder that Disney bombard the buying public with such a lot of 'junk,' no sorry the word I wanted there is 'merchandising,' after all who can blame them? They have to capitalise on their movies even if they are in the main created, written and made by another company now called Pixar!

Which brings me on to another subject! Who would like to have their very own cuddly toy that looks exactly ME (well as close as a Taiwanese toy manufacturer can make a cuddly toy to look like me)?

Yes? I thought you would, and so soon a cuddly toy which looks more or less like me and thousands of other 'must have' merchandised 'things' will be available in the shops when you read this Diary or watch the Movie.

I urge you strongly to go out and buy as much of it as your credit card or someone else's can afford, while stocks last (about ten years if we are lucky, so I am told).

And there will be other 'must have purchasing opportunities' the Director's cut of the Movie if he doesn't like what the studio release and has an argument with them, and even my own copy of this Diary if I don't like how the publishers edit it, the list is endless, Mugs, beach, bath and tea towels, umbrellas and a mind boggling list of jumble featuring yours truly.

With all of the money spent on these worthy products you must wonder where it all will end up and the answer is simple! It will be donated to a wonderful Charity, a Cat's Home, which will look after this Cat and keep him in the comfort and security that he truly deserves.

The Charity's motto is 'A First Class Home for a First Class Cat,' modesty ensures that I don't need to provide you with the identity of the Cat in question! In fact I am sure that you already know who the First Class Cat is!

DAY 65 OF MY CAPTIVITY:

The day was dark today, dark days make one sleepy and make this Cat very sleepy indeed, it was very hard to get up and write some more of my Diary, but I am nothing if I am not dedicated to entertaining you my dear and rather cuddly reader.

The Radio was on and I was sort of half listening to it in the half-light of the morning. Radios are strange things; they are like Televisions without the pictures and in my opinion without the interesting programmes that one watches on Television all too rarely.

Mostly Radio programmes seem to consist of a pimply person chatting about nothing, in a very authorative way in between tired wastes of Rap or R&B music.

Now Rap music can sometimes be quite entertaining especially if it is by Eminem, but let's be honest here, he is an exception to the rule. And what of R&B? Correct me if I am wrong but isn't R&B Rhythm and Blues? Which was originally popular in the fifties and sixties? Because if that is the case then what on earth is the nonsense that the pimply radio presenter is playing?

Still luckily today, someone must have knocked the dial because the Radio programme that I was listening to was a documentary about Global Dimming!

No not a documentary about how stupid Humans have become, although in my opinion that fact needs to be brought out into the open. This was in fact a programme that announced to a mass audience; well ok probably a few hundred thousand; that the Sun is getting dimmer.

Now let's face it, this is a big problem for everyone on earth and you would have thought that instead of being broadcast on a Radio programme it would have been a headline item on the News, but it wasn't, but then the producers probably didn't want to start a panic.

The gist of the programme was; that the Sun is getting 'dimmer,' well the clue was in the title I have to say.

As far as I can remember and I have to admit that I did fall asleep about halfway through the programme (because it was a little boring and the room was more than a little dark as I mentioned earlier), was that the Sunlight we get on earth has reduced over the last fifty years and that was due to the amount of pollution caused by air travel, well jet airliners to be more precise.

So much for global warming I thought, obviously the planet can't be warming up if the sunlight is less than it used to be!

But that isn't so, according to the programme that was broadcast.

Oddly enough two hours later, on the same radio station there was no mention of Global Dimming when a member of a famous Charity was droning on about the problems that Global Warming had caused the poor half of the world, and that the rich half had to send loads of cash immediately to help them, poor devils!

Well correct me if I am wrong and let's face it I am a Cat and could well be wrong, but in order to pay for the large amounts of cash that we will be sending to the poorer half of the world, won't we have to work harder and produce more Global Warming pollutants because of all of the extra manufacturing we will have to do to earn more cash for such a good cause?

Surely that will mean that the poorer other half of the world will suffer even more, and so we here in the west will have to work even harder and produce even more pollution?

Ok my brain hurts and it is now really too dark to think about anything, and even if I could flick a light switch on I wouldn't because I don't want to cause the other half of the world even more problems, so I am just going to sit here in the dark and worry, about Global Dimming and Global Warming and hope that just thinking about it doesn't cause any pollution, because I wouldn't like that on my conscience, would you?

DAY 66 OF MY CAPTIVITY:

This afternoon instead of having the television on to watch afternoon television programmes (which I think is some sort of code for 'dreadful') about people with all sorts of interesting Human relationship problems, the Female Captor sat down in the front room with a bowl of instant soup and a newspaper.

I felt duty bound to hop up on the Sofa next to her and watch her eat, I personally wasn't hungry, but I think that Humans like to be watched by animals when they eat, it probably helps their digestion knowing that they can make a Cat's or Dog's day when they throw them a scrap.

When she was settled she reached for, and used the flicker thing to fire up the stereo, that is usually a signal for me to go to sleep, I can't say that I am Human music's greatest fan, but this was different.

The music was brilliant a man with a golden voice singing about Suspicion, a concept that Cats understand completely, but this man sounded sad because he was suspicious and sung so wonderfully while in the background a Samba (I could be wrong I am a Cat remember) bounced away as a contrast to this man's angelic voice.

I found out from the CD cover that the Human singer was a King, King Elvis to give him his full title, well I don't know what country King Elvis rules but it must be a happy place to have such a great singer ruling it.

When I started swaying to the music and humming the tune, well 'Cat humming' the tune, which I think is something that Humans find difficult to listen to, 'she' tried to distract me by stroking me in time to the music, which was rather nice, what was nicer was the 'she' had the King on repeat, maybe heaven has places where one can go and listen to the King serenading!

Day 67 of My Captivity:

I wanted to find out more about King Elvis and so today I logged onto the internet and did some surfing, strange term 'surfing' when you think about it cause you don't need to be able to swim and no surfboard is required in fact you don't get wet at all, unless you log onto one of the Pet Food sites and see all of that lovely Cat food and of course the rather dishy Cat supermodels who advertise it.

There is one Cat supermodel in particular who makes my toes curl and me dribble, she is a pure white Cat and I wouldn't mind sharing my dinner with her, I can tell you!

Eventually I managed to tear myself away from her pictures, the one with her playfully licking a fish bone sends me nearly insane, and begin my search for the more information about King Elvis.

The first thing that I discovered was that he is dead, which is a little unsettling when you can hear him almost everyday on the Television or Radio!

The second thing I learned was that he has been dead rather a long time, see above for my reaction to that!

Then I discovered something really bizarre the King, Elvis my singing hero has sold more CD's (although he died before they were invented?) after he died, than he did when he was alive, except that they weren't called CD's then, they were called 45's or LP's and were made of black plastic which warped easily and which people now call Vinyl and think is really cool to own.

Lastly I found out that the King wasn't a real King, it was a name which his fans gave him and I can understand why, even though he is dead and has been for a long time he is still a wonderful singer and performer with more life in him than most performers around today and definitely he can sing in tune which is something that seems to have gone out of fashion now that we are lucky enough to have so many famous Rap artists. (P.S. - This is a Cat's dual attempt at music criticism and irony).

Day 68 of My Captivity:

What a few days the last few days have been, Global Dimming, Global Warming and discovering that King Elvis is dead, talk about information overload! But then apparently this is an information society, not that I have noticed many Humans taking advantage of that fact!

I wonder what this age will be called? We have had, not necessarily in this order, the Bronze Age, the Ice Age, the Iron Age and probably a few more 'Ages' too, which I haven't heard about.

Could this age be called after the Computer? No I don't think so because Computer Age sounds odd, but probably the people who first thought of the Bronze Age thought the same. Maybe we should call our 'Age' the Silicon Age, although I am sure that some would not like that because of the possible relationship to certain plastic surgery procedures?

So what can we call the 'Age' we live in? I think it should be the Plastic Age, after all it seems that everything is made from the stuff and it is a material like Iron and Bronze, so it has a lot going for it already.

Still what do I care, I am only a Cat and therefore according to most Humans my opinions don't count, which is probably just as well really.

Day 69 of My Captivity:

Today is a day off, I have been thinking too much and I am very tired and just want to go back to sleep, happily or unhappily depending upon whether you have children or not Global Dimming has helped here, it is too dark to get out of bed, earlier when I looked at the clock it was Eleven o'clock in the morning I couldn't believe that it was so dark being so late in the morning.

Oh sorry I take that back I have just noticed that the Dog's tail is covering my eyes, still it isn't that bright outside and so I think that I will just snuggle up against the 'Hulk' and do some serious snoozing.

Day 70 of My Captivity:

The word 'bomb' could strike fear into the hearts of most normal right thinking people but obviously not everyone because I found lots of sites on the internet the other day that openly discuss 'bombs' and much more.

Oh yes I forgot to mention I am now a fully 'wired' Cat or Wired Wussy as I like to call myself, and can surf the 'net' if the computer has been left on.

It is a fascinating tool, the internet and never ceases to surprise me with the facts and information that one can find, I typed in the word 'bomb' and was surprised and a little alarmed to find out that there were thousands of sites offering information from – Bomb making to Bomb disposal.

Now immediately I was interested in the bomb making sites and have learned a lot, but just in case I also had a look at the Bomb disposal information, well you never know when you are going to need that ability do you!

You see I plan to make a bomb, Not a very big bomb you understand, just one big enough to blow the back door out into the garden and then, once the smoke and flames clear I will be away, free and happy.

The bomb that I have begun to make is a very simple one indeed, just a large bag of sugar and Weed killer to be honest, but according to the Internet and more specifically the 'Bad Bombers of Baden' it should go up like a 'Bloody Rocket' I suppose that is as good as a big bomb?

Actually assembling all of the ingredients for the bomb has been the most difficult of all, of course sugar was no problem, but for a long while I wondered where I was going to get Weed killer from, well it is not something that one would expect to find in a kitchen?

Well let me rephrase that, it is not something one would expect to find in a kitchen, that is what I would think, but then I am only a Cat and what do Cats know?

I actually know that Weed killer and kitchens shouldn't mix for two reasons because I read, that Weed killer not only makes good bombs, which is one reason not to keep it in the kitchen, but that it is also poisonous and that is the other reason that it shouldn't be in a kitchen I would have thought.

Weed killer is apparently especially bad for animals, but I think that is because they in the main don't read the side of the packets before they use it, but I am an animal and so I was alarmed to discover the Weed killer that I have borrowed had been left next to lots of cleaning materials in the cupboard under the sink in the kitchen.

My paws don't fit into rubber gloves, which is a pity because handling Weed killer is safer if one is wearing them, happily my paws do fit into the fingers of the rubber gloves I found under the sink and played tug of war with the Dog so that he snapped off four fingers so that I could use them on each paw.

You may think that I am a little evil, although a little evil what, I don't know when I tell you that I did take some time out to watch the hairy halfwit chew the gloves, just to make sure that they weren't contaminated with Weed killer or anything else nasty from the cupboard, shame on me tee hee!

You can imagine my shock and fright when I heard him start to be sick, I was out of range, which was a small consolation, I suppose.

After he had stopped being sick and it had gone quiet I forced myself to look at him.

Yes I was expecting the kitchen floor to be covered in stiff Dog, so I looked really slowly expecting a shock at any moment.

Happily, the floor was only covered in pieces of rubber glove and grass; slippery yes, but not fatal by any stretch of the imagination for either the Dog, who was drinking enormous quantities of water or me, who was about to, by the looks of it lose a day's supply of drinking water from his Cat bowl.

I was pleased to see that the Dog was ok and to be honest not too worried about the water, Cats in general don't drink too much and if I get thirsty I can usually find a dripping tap somewhere to drink from.

At this moment I was more interested in collecting everything for the bomb than I was in drinking or even eating, I was excited, this was going to be a big moment in my short career, and later today or at the latest tomorrow I was going to blow a hole in the wall and then disappear through it to freedom and beyond.

After I had collected all of the ingredients and had found a Thermos Flask; that probably wasn't lost to be truthful, but whether it was lost or not it would make a wonderful bomb casing; I had everything I needed and took it all through, one by one to the utility room.

On one of my many mini adventures I discovered that the cupboard at the end of a line of cupboards in the utility room was almost completely empty and best of all it was almost next to the back door and so I knew that one of its walls was the wall to blow a hole in and escape through.

There was something nagging me at the back of my mind while I was opening the cupboard door and it had to do with the utility room and as the nagging voice at the back of my mind droned on and on it seemed to be saying that I had left something in the utility room that was important, but for the life of me I couldn't remember doing anything of the kind.

Really how daft can one get, as if a superior being like me could forget something important! So I told the little nagging voice to stop nagging, goodness it wasn't as if we were married or anything.

Inside the cupboard there was plenty of room to work and even with the door almost closed it was light enough to see exactly what I was doing. I pushed a few tins of nails aside and a packet of sticks that smelt a little like Almonds, who knows what they were or indeed what they were for!

I had managed to borrow a pair of the Female Captors knickers and I tied them around my face so that I didn't breath in the Weed killer and Sugar mixture, then after that was safely inside the Thermos Flask casing I took the knickers off because I know they looked silly on but they might have saved my life and if that was the case then it is ok to look silly.

It took me some time to work out what to do with the now redundant knickers until I had a bright idea I would just blow them up and get rid of the evidence of ever having handled them.

Well I don't know if you can get paw prints from a pair of knickers or not, what I do know was that my breath smelt of the Whiskers Liver Cat food I had been eating earlier and I reasoned if the knickers were found smelling of Cat food then I would be the prime suspect and I didn't want that did I?

So I stuffed them into the Thermos Flask bomb casing and packed them down on top of the Sugar and Weed killer mixture. After all of that was done, I added a few secret ingredients of my own.

Well they aren't that secret but we don't want the readers getting ideas and going off and making Weed killer bombs do we? I'll be responsible and leave them to find that out on the Internet!

It had been hot work because at the back of the cupboard I was working in there were several pipes that led up to and from the Central Heating Boiler which at this moment in time seemed to be working overtime.

Still I was ready and better still Cats don't sweat, unlike a lot of Humans, Ugh horrible!

I applied the fuse but you are not going to hear how I applied the fuse that is more information that you crazed juvenile bomb makers are not going to get from me, and then unravelled it as I crawled out of the cupboard backwards and then backed out into the kitchen.

The Dog was standing in the middle of the kitchen floor and as I payed out the fuse; walking backwards my bottom met his wet sniffy nose and gave me quite a shock!

I get a shock when the filthy Dog does that when I am not handling a fuse connected to an explosive device, but this time I was doing exactly that and I jumped almost out of my skin. Happily this reaction freaked him out and he shot off in the opposite direction leaving me to light the fuse and follow him very quickly.

The Dog was standing in the hall and when he saw me race passed and shoot upstairs like a Rabbit at a Greyhound track, I suppose some hidden Greyhound gene took over and he followed me up the stairs and into the bathroom.

Usually when I am on the run and decide to use the bathroom as a sanctuary, I always remember to jump over the bath mat and then come to a more or less gentle skidding rest somewhere under the window.

Well I remembered to do that now, the first time I didn't know that the bath mat was in my path or in fact that the tiles in the bathroom are of the highly polish variety and are therefore very slippery.

It is obvious that the Dog, who I am sure; enjoys the thrill of danger just a little too much, didn't remember where the bath mat was or more likely just didn't care, and when seconds later several tons of Dog followed me into the bathroom he hit the bath mat and using it like a skateboard on a very steep hill, raced after me.

Some person, I don't know who, had left water in the bath! How do I know that? Well to escape the sliding Dog and I think to an extent carried by the explosion's shockwave I was hurled into the bath.

Cats don't like water and they don't overly enjoy swimming, and getting out of a bath is not easy, but although I was soaked to the sink and probably weighed twice as much as normal I hauled myself out and dived onto the crumpled bath mat,

It goes without saying that the Dog was cowering and whimpering in the corner, but then he didn't know what the cause of the loud bang was.

I left him after I had had a quick shake to get rid of some of the excess water and moved purposefully downstairs.

There was a terrible smell in the air and I guess as I started coughing and my eyes began to sting that the cause of all of that was probably the chemicals in the explosion.

My breathing was what I think they called laboured, by the time I blindly wheezed my way to where the cupboard had stood, no let me change that for the sake of accuracy, my breathing was laboured by the time I got to where the utility room wall with all of the cupboards had stood, because they just weren't there anymore.

The smell was really terrible and there was an awful hissing noise, and the sound of running water.

I hopped as best I could over the rubble and jumped to freedom. Well that was the plan, but the plan had obviously got some rather serious defects, I was in the garage.

It was hard work climbing over bricks, dust and rubble, it was quite a hill, and under the hill of rubble I saw the shiny polished bodywork of the Captor's new Car. I was in trouble, and I wasn't free and worst of all I wasn't feeling at all well, the garage was spinning and I was feeling very sick!

The Fire Brigade had been called, nice men they are too, very kind, caring and considerate, the first I saw of them though were some shadowy, fluid figures with masks and breathing apparatus.

One of the Firemen kindly took a big breath in his mask, took it off and pushed it over my nose; oh the air was beautiful without a trace of the terrible smell that I had smelt ever since I entered the utility room.

He turned and still holding his breath and the mask over my nose took me through the rubble into the kitchen and outside into the front garden, I was free at last.

Unfortunately I was feeling so ill that I wasn't able to enjoy my freedom at all and it didn't seem likely that the Fireman was going to let go of me anyway.

I was passed to another Fireman in a white helmet who stroked me and didn't seem to mind in the slightest when I was sick all over his jacket.

He then passed me up to someone in the Fire Engine who had a warm coat laid on the seat next to him and I just laid there listening to the commotion and tried to stop feeling faint and sick and then sick and faint, but I failed.

As I lay in the Fireman's coat, I think his name was George, nice man anyway, I heard people talking about a gas leak and then an explosion and there was me thinking that my bomb had caused all of the mess!

When I woke up I think it was a lot later because the blue flashing lights were noticeable in the half-light of the afternoon's dusk. Reflecting around the cab of the Fire Engine in a nightclub sort of way.

Funnily enough I felt so much better and rather curious as to what was happening now. There didn't seem to be anyone with me in the Fire Engine now, and so I sat up and looked around, everything seemed quite normal, apart from the crowd and a large number of vehicles in the road.

Unfortunately I couldn't quite see out of the window and so I hopped up onto the dashboard and looked out of the big window.

There was still quite a crowd of worried looking onlookers, several Police cars and some vans from the gas company.

Then I noticed to my horror opposite in the other Fire Engine, which was parked in front of mine, was the Parrot sitting on the steering wheel wearing most of the knickers that I had stuffed into the Thermos Flask, in my opinion and that is not one of a fashion guru, they suited him, I have to say.

So the bomb had worked, excellent, I must have just put it against the wrong wall, well I would remember to check more thoroughly next time!

All in all everything had worked out rather well, I still felt a little tired and decided to get back into George's coat bed and have a snooze, but I was hungry and hoped that someone would remember that Cats who are recovering from Gas poisoning do need feeding as well as warm coats to sleep in.

Day 71 of My Captivity:

I woke up in a strange place! It smelt funny and I didn't like it at all. My vision seemed a little worse than yesterday when I was snooping at the crowd through the Fire Engine's windscreen, it was blurred and dark. To make matters worse I felt weak and for some reason very heavy. This was odd and I was beginning to think that I had been badly injured in yesterday's little escapade and worst of all I was very hungry indeed! My built in clock told me that I had missed at least one dinnertime and the little reminder alarms were working overtime suggesting that I had skipped a few elevenses and lunches too.

That was it, I was confused, maybe I had a bump on the head? But before I was able to collect my thoughts and work out exactly what was going on, the cage door. Hang on I was in a cage! This can't be right? The cage door was opened and I was lifted up by a pair of hands and carried into a bright white room, this was not very nice and not going to plan at all, in the Fire Engine I imagined that I would be carried indoors asleep and left sleeping next to a bowl of food which was left waiting for me to eat when I woke up.

My head hurt and someone had just done something to me that I cannot write about even in this open and frank Diary. Let's just say that they don't take a Cat's temperature the same way that they take Human's. My eyes were watering and my legs were wobbly, and if I wasn't unwell before I got here, wherever 'here' is, I was definitely unwell now.

To make matters worse and it surprised me that they could get any worse after having one's temperature taken in such a manner! I was being pinched and prodded and generally examined.

Oh! No, please no, I have just worked out where I am, it is the place that every Cat is warned about by their Mothers as soon as they can hear, a place that any animal is told to avoid at all costs.

All was lost! I was at the Vets.

Ok I know that you think the Vets is somewhere to take sick animals to get them well, but have you ever been just a little frightened of a trip to the Dentist? You have! Well good, no not good that you have been a little worried about going to the dentist, but 'good' that you will now have some idea of just what an animal, and this animal in particular, feels like when he is at the Vets!

Things happen at the Vets, that are whispered about in the animal world, things that are far worse than having your temperature taken, dark, dreadful dangerous things.

My heart sank and so did I onto the table I was being examined on.

'The Cat has passed out again!' Said the nurse who had been watching over me, I heard that as everything went dark.

What struck me was the word 'again' I had passed out before then? Still I couldn't think, my eyes were tap dancing in my head and my thoughts were jumbled like a dreadful Welsh Male Voice Choir singing in an echo chamber, or even a reasonably good Welsh Choir singing in an echo chamber for that matter!

In such cases oblivion is a blessed relief.

I have no idea whether I have been asleep for an hour, a day or indeed several days, there is no way of telling and so from this Cat's point of view there is not much point in worrying about it.

They took the bandage off my head today, of course that was the reason why I couldn't see all that well!

I have to say it was a bit of a shock when I saw my reflection in my water dish I had lost weight and my eyes were still very red that apparently was due to the gas poisoning.

Another consolation, and at the moment consolations seemed to be coming thick and fast; the Parrot was here at the Vets too.

Apparently from what I overheard the nurses saying, bits of the knickers had been rather warm, meltingly so, when they landed on his head after being launched by my bomb and flying all the way through the house to land on the Parrot's head, I bet that made him squawk.

Being made of Polyester and being on the hot side of warm, the knickers had glued themselves to the feathers right at the top of his head and the rest of the material had draped itself down his back; he looked not unlike a desert Arab with a rather fine head dress.

Apparently getting the 'head dress' off was going to have to involve some very special and highly develop skills of a specialist 'feather man,' who was being brought in for the job especially.

Poor Parrot! Sorry if I keep sniggering. It couldn't have happened to a more deserving cause in my humble opinion.

Day 72 of My Captivity:

The Police were here today, yes I am back at the prison again apparently they found traces of Dynamite in what was left of the garage, mmmh Dynamite, where have I heard that word before?

The Police Inspector who seemed to do most of the talking surrounded by a Sergeant and two Police Officers, asked the Captors if they kept any chemicals in the utility room and in particular in the end cupboard next to the back door? Mmmh I didn't like where this questioning was leading? The Captors looked mystified which seems to be a sort of constant look that they have these days. The Police Inspector went on to say that they think that the source of the explosion could have been either a gas leak or a crude Weed killer and Sugar bomb, oh dear, how did they work that out? Or indeed Dynamite, he then asked the Captors again if they stored dynamite in the cupboard in question.

No! They quickly said, never! This was getting a little worrying, how could anyone tell what was in a cupboard that was now just so many bits of burnt wood mixed in a pile of rubble?

Worse was to come though because the Police Inspector seemed convinced that there had been Dynamite stored in the cupboard, he asked the Captors if they had a licence to store and use Dynamite, as if he hadn't heard or understood that they didn't know anything about any Dynamite in the cupboard.

Hang on, Dynamite, I have a feeling that if they were to ask me about the stuff then I wouldn't look as innocent as the Captors had, in fact I may start sweating and wriggling uncomfortably. Wait, sweating and Dynamite, where have I heard those two words in the same sentence before.

Oops!

A nagging voice in the back of my mind was saying 'I tried to warn you, didn't I!' Then rather triumphantly it said 'what did I say about leaving something in the utility room cupboard?'

Oh Dearie me! I remember now, the sweating dynamite, I had put it in the very cupboard that the Police Inspector was talking about, I had a feeling that I had better confess to my crime.

The best thing to do with a feeling though is to ignore it, especially if it is a feeling that you have to do some confessing, of any sort, not only that it wasn't as though I didn't want to blow a hole in the utility room wall, and the revelation about the Dynamite had answered one question, why the bang had been so big!

Dynamite, yes that would have most definitely done the trick and blown a much bigger than expected hole in the wall, well to be more accurate blown up the utility room itself.

The Police Officer was saying that they, the Police that is, as part of their inquiry would check all purchases of explosives over the last year or so, and that they were conducting house to house inquiries in the neighbourhood and that the villain would be caught.

I decided that I had heard enough and as casually as I could threaded my way through the legs of Police Officers and was just about to leave the front room when a hand grabbed me!

Well my number was up, but let's face it, what could they do to me, I was after all already in prison.

The hand was attached to a uniformed arm and so I prepared myself for the worst as another hand slipped under me and I was lifted up to the very large chest of a remarkably strong Female Police Officer. Who didn't slap on the cuffs as I had expected, but cuddled me and stroked my ear, in exactly the 'right' place!

She asked if I was the poor little Cat found by the Firemen in the wreckage and rubble and when that was confirmed she gave me a kiss on the head, another stroke, put me down and let me walk out of the front room and slip away upstairs.

I decided then and there that they were a clever bunch these Police Officers, and one Female Police Officer in particular was nicer than the rest, with great cuddle bumps too!

DAY 73 OF MY CAPTIVITY:

Today seems to have vanished, I have no idea what happened to it. All I know is that I curled up in the bay window after waking up and ignoring breakfast because it was the same bowlful of what can only be described as 'stuff' that I left uneaten last night, and poof, the daylight vanished.

I woke up and it was dark and quiet. As far as I know the end of the world may have happened, tidal waves may have levelled cities, unfortunately if they have they didn't knock any walls down here, so I won't be going anywhere to boldly explore this brave new world, if as I say, we are now in a post apocalypse.

The trouble is I am not too sure we are survivors and I am a bit sleepy. So I am just going to go back to sleep and the post apocalyptic world will have to wait until I wake up!

I do sincerely hope that there are enough survivors left to make my Diary a best seller, what a shame it would be to have done all of this work only to not have an audience any more.

Worse still, what if I am the only survivor and I am stuck in this prison, I would just waste away, what a shame, a pointless waste of a life, not to say a bit of a drag too!

DAY 74 OF MY CAPTIVITY:

Yesterday is a blur, I think I had a bit of a nightmare I know I had a long sleep, 28 hours – and that is a bit of a lie in even for me.

The trouble is when you have had that amount of rest you feel tired, the Dog is out walk'ee'ing, well I think that is what it is called when one goes walkies! The bird is moulting – ha ha serves the little spy right. So I am going to have a perfectly named Catnap or should that be purrfectly named?

Oh by the way, there wasn't an apocalypse yesterday, as you may or may not know.

It turns out that everyone had gone out to somewhere called 'uptown' and as usual they didn't take the Cat, I mean really, doesn't anyone think that I might be just a little interested in going out? Even if it means that I would have to be put in one of those portable prisons, which Humans call Cat baskets.

No obviously not, and the only 'basket' that I will have anything to do with will be when I become a 'basket case' through boredom! Well just let them turn me into a 'basket case' it will be on their conscience for a very long time hopefully!

DAY 75 OF MY CAPTIVITY:

There are some things a self-respecting Cat will do and some things – Oh! I dread to say this – they shouldn't.

From the first few lines of today's Diary you can tell that this has not been a good day.

I am an innocent in all of this I promise and you have to believe me!

Samantha the Captor's niece (whatever that is) visited today and brought some of her dolls. Now dolls are actually rigid little Humans with fixed expressions, although they are small they seem to come in varying sizes, A glamorous woman doll called Barpee as far as I could make out from what Samantha called her was much smaller than a baby doll for instance, very odd!

All in all Dolls are a little scary, but Samantha seemed to like them and of course I had to see if they could help me escape in any way.

I know I should have known better, I do really. Oh! The trouble a curious Cat can get into sometimes!

Samantha had been left in the middle of the living room floor busy with the dolls while the Female Captor and Samantha's Mother went off for some, I think the word was toffee, but I think I still have bits of the inside of the latest fluffy toy to be left out over night in my ears. It had been once a blue Rabbit with very chewy ears before I duffed it up!

I had been watching Samantha from a safe distance for quite a while; she seemed to be happily playing with her dolls.

Mainly, they seemed to be doing a lot of straight legged marching, kissing, and standing on their heads. On reflection I would say that the child was quite mad but I know now that one can never tell with children just by looking at them. More importantly I now know that children are best avoided altogether.

Although at the time something that I can only describe as 'instinct' told me that Cats and little children don't mix, I walked up to the first child I had ever encountered with what I hope could be described a nonchalant air.

I am sure that my nonchalant air works because I have used it on other visitors and on occasions had some nice little presents like bits of Prawns or Chicken – whole Prawns are best but that is probably because of their enormous rarity value – sorry I digress.

The only reason I am veering off the subject is that it is embarrassing and as a consequence difficult to tell you about, let alone come to terms with emotionally, yes I know – that word digress again.

Deep breath! Sigh! Mmmh that helps. So there I was nonchalantly sidling up to the first toddler I have ever seen, and I have to say that I think I made the right impression because Samantha squealed 'Puddytat' delightedly.

Sensibly she reached out her hand so that I could sidle up some more and sniff it and then when we were both sure that neither of us was going to skin the other she started to stroke my head. Now stroking is nice, stroking the head is fine especially if occasionally the stroker scratches under a Cat's chin too.

Everything seemed to be going well especially as in the distance I heard Samantha's Mummy asking. 'Is she ok with little kids?' And the Female Captor's answer to the effect that I was not an infanticidal maniac and then the words 'Sammy be gentle with the pussy.'

Actually Pussy is not a word I like! But then this is not the place to discuss that. And as for the question 'is SHE ok with little kids,' honestly can't Humans tell the difference between a Male and a Female Cat – really!

We were I thought getting on tremendously well, my head had been well and truly stroked and I couldn't complain about the amount of chin scratching that was going on either.

I know now it is called being lulled into a false sense of security, I know now much to my cost, that a Cat should always be very aware of the Human who is doing so well at stroking them, I am very wise after the humiliating event.

I am not going to dwell on what happened because it is all too embarrassing and painful to recall even now several hours after I have escaped the 'Mothering' clutches of a toddler who takes great pride and no little satisfaction in 'Mothering' a defenceless Cat almost to death.

Suddenly the stroking stopped and it went dark, and almost as soon as it had gone dark I found that I couldn't move. A baby doll's baby grow had been wedged over my head and pulled down my body, gripping my legs as tightly as though they had been bound to my body.

I was getting hot inside this fleecy garment and if I could have freed just one clawed paw I would have ripped the baby grow to shreds, but as I said I was trussed up like a Sunday roast.

I opened my mouth to bite the hand of my attacker only to have a comforter shoved gaggingly down my throat which wedged its self between my tongue and the roof of my mouth, which was not nice, what was worse was that the comforter, which wasn't giving me any comfort what so ever was cutting off my air supply and I was feeling giddy and faint as well as very hot.

How do I manage to get myself into these situations, well honestly with the greatest of ease, I just hoped as I enjoyed the last breath of air in my lungs that I was going to get out of this particular situation as easily as I had slipped into it.

To cut a long and very distressing story short and frankly that is what I want to do, I was taken away from little Samantha, as if I was some sort of toy, by Samantha's Mummy, which was a blessing, but my honour had been slighted and as soon as the baby grow was removed I felt compelled to attempt to regain at least a little of my honour and so I ripped the poor woman's arm to shreds.

Yes alright I know I am not proud and worse still when I felt her grip loosen I raced upstairs to hide, which doesn't put me in line for any medals, but let's face it I had had a bad day and I am sure that you wouldn't have covered yourself in much glory if you had been covered in a baby grow and throttled, would you?

Day 76 of My Captivity:

I have found a way out. That simple statement is like music to my ears, well it would be like music to my ears if someone had said it but I am sure that you know what I mean. I have actually found a way out of here and soon I am going to take it!

There are of course, it almost goes without saying, one or two little difficulties to overcome first, but then that probably doesn't surprise you, I know it didn't surprise me.

I will have to collect together some tools but unlike in the past nothing to elaborate, I need tools that I can easily carry, which is a relief.

Although the Dog is willing to help carry the tools especially when he doesn't realise he is actually carrying the tools, but thinks he is playing some elaborate and ultimately (for him) pointless game, I have decided that he is bringing me bad luck, because every time I have had his 'help' something has gone wrong! I am therefore beginning to think that he is cursed, not that I am superstitious you understand and never have been, touch wood!

So I can do this all on my own, I just need a glasscutter and a rubber sucker, the sort of thing you get on the end of an arrow from a Child's bow and arrow set, although I may have to improvise there because I don't come into contact with that many Children who own bow and arrow sets.

I am fairly certain that I saw a glasscutter in the third drawer down in the utility room it was lying just waiting to come in handy next to some matches, which if I had pockets in this Catsuit I would keep with me all the times! Still I haven't got any pockets so never mind.

I have now got a glasscutter, well it isn't a glasscutter because some selfish person has taken that, but never mind I have the next best thing, it is just a little heavy but I can manage it.

Ok the plans have changed so I can tell you what I was going to do and then let you in on the bigger secret, which is of course what I am actually going to do!

Before someone stole the glasscutter, which is as most of you will know a fairly lightweight tool and reasonably easy to carry and use, even if you only have paws and not hands, I was going to go upstairs to the bathroom and balancing on the top of the tall towel cupboard I was going to cut a Cat sized hole in the bathroom window slide through it, drop down onto a sort of half roof thing and then tiptoe across to the edge, jump onto the lower garage roof and then jump down to freedom.

A perfect escape route in my opinion and I have to say a perfect plan, spoilt only by the selfish person who has taken the lightweight glasscutter and left me with the heavier one.

Well when I say heavier glasscutter I am using my imagination, but I am sure that it will do the job, I will just have to do the job downstairs because it will take me all of my time and most of my strength to lug this heavyweight glasscutter to the dining room window, and I have a suspicion that I would never make it to the bathroom, carry such a heavy glasscutter, or I could use the Dog?

The trouble is with the Dog's help as I explained he tends to jinx me. Oh it is ok for him he can go out almost as often as he wants, in fact he is encouraged to do that, mainly I think because he doesn't have a litter tray, although he shows an abnormal (in my view) interest in my litter tray.

If you have seen just how much of a lake a desperate Dog can make when he can't contain himself any more then you would let him out often too.

Where was I? Oh yes! Should I let the Dog help? No this one I am going to 'handle' myself!

It wasn't easy dragging the heavier glasscutter over to the dining room window and lifting it up on to the window seat was even worse, I would use the term nightmare here, but it was daylight, no Global Dimming today thankfully!

Still after an hour or so of dragging, pulling, puffing and muscle straining everything was in place, except for the Dog who had spotted me in the dining room before I could slam the door in his nosey face and was now sniffing and panting behind me!

Undeterred by his interference and the feeling of hot breath on my back I picked up the glasscutter with all my strength and gave the glass a hefty whack.

Imagine my surprise when instead of the glass being cut and a hole appearing as if by magic as I have seen Humans do with glasscutters, my glasscutter bounced off the window and flew over the room landing with an evil sounding scratching noise on the Rosewood Dining table – oops!

Time to make myself scarce was what I was thinking but unfortunately it was too late, the Humans were in the room milling around and it seemed panicking, really I thought it was a poor show, ok so the table was scratched it wasn't as though it was a priceless antique was it?

Soon after I had asked myself that question it was answered, the Female Captor burst into tears, which is a rare occurrence, and usually something to be enjoyed as a spectator event.

Oh Dearie me! Apparently the Rosewood dining room table was a priceless antique, but in my defence I didn't know it was and I hadn't meant to damage it with a four pound hammer.

Still it all turned out alright in the end, well for me that is, the Male Captor got the blame because the Female Captor quite rightly deduced that neither the Dog nor I could have scratched the table with the hammer, because we wouldn't be able to carry it!

The Male Captor didn't do his cause any good by offering to French polish the scratch out either, I left the room as the yellow pages was being thrown at him while in the background a high pitched voice was screaming something like don't be a bloody cheapskate, get a professional, or words to that effect. To be honest, like the Dog I was heading for safety at that moment, which was anywhere but the dining room, so I might not have heard exactly what she said!

DAY 77 OF MY CAPTIVITY:

After all of the excitement of yesterday you would think that a few days of peace and quiet would be called for, but where there is a tradesman there is the opportunity to escape.

I have found that tradesmen tend to be careless about closing doors, I don't know if they are the same at home, but out in the field as it were they are pretty hopeless at remembering to close doors, especially and I say this with a degree of mounting excitement, front doors.

Quite naturally then, I developed a new interest - French polishing, what a shame that I wasn't allowed to develop my new interest.

As soon as the old aproned and bespectacled French polisher had set up his bottles and cloths he disappeared for a moment and I excitedly followed him like a shadow, hoping that he was on his way to his van for something else and that he would be leaving the front door open.

But to my eternal disappointment he went into the kitchen where the Female Captor was making him tea, which I thought was a bit much considering, he hadn't essentially begun French polishing and therefore hadn't actually earned any tea!

Worse was to come when he, and I presume he thought he was being tactful said that it might be best to lock up the Cat away from the wet polish on account of the fact that its fur might get mixed with the French polish, really!

I was affronted and expected at least a little help in my defence, but, Humans always seem to stick together as tightly as Cat fur in French polish (presumably) and I was locked in solitary confinement in the utility room which was doubly unfair because when the French polisher mentioned that Dog hair could also be a problem, the Dog was put outside. How unfair is that?

Day 78 of My Captivity:

I have to say that the overly fussy (in my opinion) French polisher did do a good job, although I didn't get an opportunity to inspect his craftsmanship until today, which I am sure was ages after the polish had dried.

Amazingly I couldn't really tell where the new polish was because there was no sign that he had done anything, which in French polishing circles must be the highest compliment that can be paid to anyone's work!

I did feel a little sad that I wasn't able to leave a few tufts of fur in the wet polish for posterity, after all I have heard that Humans can't resist marking wet concrete with their initials and dating their graffiti, so it seems rather unfair that people in the future won't know that the table was once the occasional bed of a rather important and good looking Cat, what do you mean, which Cat? Me of course!

Day 79 of My Captivity:

There has been mention of a holiday. Quite frankly I am ready for one and if, and I am keeping my claws crossed that this might be the case, the Humans take only me on holiday and leave the Dog and the Parrot behind, I won't be unhappy, actually I will be delighted.

I could do with a break, especially from the Parrot and the Dog, well more especially from the Parrot. I wonder where we are going?

Last night when I was sitting on the sofa the Female Captor was looking at a vast range of holiday brochures, wonderful looking sunlit places shone out from the glossy pages, palm trees and sandy beaches seemed to be most prominent, which is all right by me!

What was better than alright was a few pictures of bright blue sea with an amazing range of assorted fish, I can't wait to get in amongst them and taste them, of course it would be better if they were caught by some kind person and laid out on the dock for me but, at a pinch, I am prepared to dive in and catch a few.

You sound surprised that I am prepared to go swimming and get wet, well it is a little known fact that Cats sometimes like swimming, but only in tropical waters, which is why they pretend not to like swimming in colder climates, can you blame us?

It is something that we have got away with for years, so much so that Humans catch almost all of the fish that we eat, pretty neat trick don't you think?

Day 80 of My Captivity:

Holiday fever is building you can feel the excitement in the air!

I am happy to say that the Parrot is definitely not coming, unless that is that they have sent him on ahead, because he has vanished, which is just fine by me, my only hope is that the bad tempered old bird has gone for good and not just for the few weeks that we will be away.

This afternoon they were packing and I am happy to report that my few paltry possessions were put into a carrier bag with the Dog's less than modest collection of toys.

I had to laugh they packed him a cuddly toy, really what a joke that is, a grown Dog with a cuddly toy, ha ha!

Imagine my surprise when I was loaded into the Cat basket that I arrived in, still never mind one has to make some sacrifices so that one can spend several weeks basking in the sun and with that in mind after only an hour of chasing I allowed the Captors to load me into the Cat basket, and instead of making the usual racket I curled up and contentedly went to sleep dreaming of climbing Palm trees in the sun and trying to work out what a coconut is for?

I woke up in the car, but the Dog was asleep on the back seat next to me and the Captors were in the front so, I wasn't at all worried and again decided to behave and not make any noise, well I made a little noise and was rewarded with a Cat treat, which disappointingly was one of the fishy smelling variety, packed with deliciously healthy fish oils or so the advertisers say, all I will say on that subject is 'they should try them!'

I had to eat it though because in the past when I have spat them out I have found them sticking to my fur later and they are as difficult to get out as a furball, I can tell you!

When we arrived at the Airport I have to say I was disappointed, it looked more like an Army camp, there was ten foot high Chicken wire topped with barbed wire everywhere, but still I wasn't worried after all I had heard about the Mr. Bin Laden's Turbaned martyrs of Islam, and I have to say I was all for as much Airport security as I could get!

Personally like every sane Cat, Dog and Human when aboard an airliner I have no wish to make a detour into a very high building, if I can help it, I have to say, so 'build the perimeter fences high and use as much barbed wire as you can find' is my motto!

It was odd though, there didn't seem to be many cars in the car park, but still I wasn't worried; air travel had dropped off they had been saying and looking around the empty car park I had to agree with the news reports.

Safe in the knowledge that I was going to be protected by airport security, air marshals and anything else that the western world could muster to keep me safe I dozed off and slept for the rest of the afternoon.

Day 81 of My Captivity:

Unfortunately I am having trouble writing this. But then anyone wedged into a rain gutter down pipe would find it difficult to write.

I am, and this is hard to admit, even to myself, locked in a Dog kennel at an establishment called Mrs. O'Riley's. It's noisy, there is a lot of barking and when the barking stops, pining and whining takes over so the noise is constant.

With deep regret I have had to tear out several pages of my Diary and stuff them into my ears, that helps until the paper springs out when I am concentrating on my writing and scares one of my nine lives out of me as it hits my paw, feeling as it does for a split second like the touch of an Alsatian who has become annoyed at a little Cat's constant sarcasm.

I have to say that I think I was the victim of some confusion, for some reason I was convinced that I was to be taken on holiday, fed on a diet of exotic tropical fish and sunbathed until my paw pads turned brown, but oh no none of that is for me I am stuck here in this palace of nightmares.

It is not even a Cattery for goodness sake! Apparently all of the nice centrally heated Catteries were full and I am confined here in cold damp Dog kennel, everywhere I look there are Dogs most of whom are discussing how best to skin and eat a Cat once they have caught it.

I say most of the Dogs are doing that, happily my next door neighbour is a small Mexican lapdog called Maxwell who is obviously Gay and happily can be bullied.

Apparently little Maxwell is the prized possession of a leading London Architect of the same name, what I want to know is if Maxwell is Maxwell's prized possession what is he doing in this dump? Still I am sure I will find out when little Maxwell gets up the courage to speak again, if I am that interested to listen that is.

All Mexican Maxwell, as I have christened him, does all day is make squeaking noises and shiver, well I know it is cold here but for goodness sake he has got a little curly dark brown coat, so although he looks as though he is wearing a rather badly made hairpiece he is warmer than I am!

There is only one good thing about being in this particular Dog kennel as far as I can see and that is the fact that I am semi-detached, no not mentally, although I have to say it probably won't be long until I am as mental as little gay Maxwell!

What I meant was that I am semi-detached in the architectural sense, my kennel is at the end of the row thank goodness and means that I only have one neighbour which as I have said is the shivering Queen of Mexico!

Even so when I go to sleep I think that it is safest to wedge myself up this drainpipe, it goes without saying that I had decided to use it as an escape tunnel and climb out, but I got stuck fast and had to gently and painfully ease myself back out.

There are many disadvantages to sleeping in a drainpipe, but I am, I have to say, trying to be as optimistic as possible and so I will only mention the very few advantages to sleeping in a drainpipe, the main one being that one is more or less out of the wind, but it is very uncomfortable and nothing like sleeping on the Sofa, I can't think of any other advantages at the moment but that might be because my brain is numb from the cold.

If only they had put me in with the Dog I would have been more comfortable and he might have decided that we were 'family' and protected me from the other Dogs, but he seems to have vanished, I hope that he isn't sitting on a beach somewhere squinting in the tropical sunlight, if he is I hope that he gets sunstroke!

DAY 82 OF MY CAPTIVITY:

Maxwell is a funny little creature, he thinks that he is so very well educated, you know the sort they act like a Professor but lack the proper qualifications. Still at least he is talking now, which is occasionally entertaining although he does drone on about his television appearances.

It turns out that he has indeed appeared on television, but in the background when his owner was being interviewed, I mean really how pathetic is that?

What I do like about Maxwell is his size and his age, both of which make him easy to bully, he is an old, small Dog and after a few strong words from yours truly was ready to share his food with me, well when I say share I mean that he gave me all of his food, which was good because it was specially prepared only for him, oddly it was Crab meat.

Well actually there was nothing odd about his food, it was exceedingly good, it is just odd that the Yappy type little Dog eats Crab meat, still it takes all sorts to make a world I say, or I do now! And they are nice too, 'Allsorts,' that is, poor Maxwell, he prefers to be called Maxwell, has a digestion problem and so after meals he is given Liquorice Allsorts to help him go to the loo, they are black sweets and very good so long as you remember two things, don't eat them all at once and try not to remember what they are for!

When I asked him why he ate only Crab meat he said that he didn't eat only Crab meat, he in fact ate all types of fish, because he was, (wait for this, you will, I am sure find it as bizarre as I did) a vegetarian and didn't eat meat, yes I promise you this deluded little twit actually said that!

It got funnier too because he lives with a larger Dog called Georgie who is also a vegetarian and lives on a diet of fish too, I have a feeling that there is something very wrong here! Still what do I care, I know that I am going to have some excellent fish dishes all the time that Maxwell is here, in fact I have decided to become a Maxwell type vegetarian myself.

DAY 83 OF MY CAPTIVITY:

It isn't fair they let the other inmates out once a day, I watch all of the Dogs, even shivering Maxwell go off for a walk, ok they are on leads but what about letting the Cat out once in a while?

Really there isn't much to do but sit and watch the world go by, and out here in the middle of nowhere not much of the world goes by, or you can go to sleep, so I sleep.

Worryingly I am running out of paper, I have had to stuff so much of it in my ears that I don't have much left to write on which is very frustrating indeed.

Day 84 of My Captivity:

Because of the lack of paper, I am having to limit what I write, which I suppose is just as well because there is nothing much to write about and a Diary that is full of things like, the sky was an amazing blue today and I watched another cloud fly by the bars would become more than a little mundane.

Having said that something did happen today, they took mad Maxwell and his fish diet away, I suppose he has gone home to his friend Georgie so that they can share their odd vegetarian diet of fish meat.

I did ask him about the meat bit in fish meat, well I had to really! You would wouldn't you? And he said that eating fish didn't mean he couldn't be a vegetarian because Fish don't count! Well I ask you, what do the numerical skills of a Trout, Halibut or Salmon have to do with whether you can eat them or not? He was clearly as mad as a Hatter.

Day 85 of My Captivity:

I had a great misfortune last night, I was wedged in the drainpipe as usual, my ears stuffed with paper and the Diary wrapped around me like a blanket when it rained.

Now I thought that the drainpipe was probably a toy, you know the sort of thing that you get in the less adventurous, adventure theme parks!

They have big drainpipes, old telegraph poles nailed together to represent forts and tatty bits of rope dangling here and there to swing on, you know the sort of thing I mean I am sure.

Well I was wrong. To be honest I couldn't have been more wrong even if I had been trying to be as wrong as I could be.

As I said it rained and I was wedged in the drainpipe fast asleep until that is the water which had built up behind me got so heavy that it shot me out of the drainpipe like a Champagne cork, without I hasten to add the celebratory feeling.

I was soaked to the skin and lying in a puddle of water that was growing at an alarming rate, things it could be said couldn't get any worse as far as I was concerned.

The trouble with saying that things couldn't get any worse is that they almost invariably do get worse and unfortunately that happened too.

The puddle, which was cold and annoying wasn't life threatening for about an hour; it just made me miserable and cold for the first hour.

After an hour the water level was of some concern to me, after two hours I was getting very worried and when the rain hadn't stopped after three hours I was beginning to swim.

I am actually quite a good swimmer I discovered and the small note book which I decided would be my holiday diary was acting like a float and so although I was cold and wet I wasn't in the same state as say, Leonardo Di Caprio in the film, Titanic.

Mind you I was getting colder and the water level didn't seem to be showing any signs slowing its rise to the ceiling. It did occur to me that if the water got to the ceiling then where would I go, that was worrying I have to say.

The other thing that was beginning to concern me, just a little, was that as my fur became more and more water logged I was not quite as buoyant as I had been earlier.

Mmmh maybe I was going to get the chance to play Leonardo Di Caprio after all!

Just as my ears began to rub the ceiling of the kennel and I began to wonder just how long I could hold my breath under water there was a very welcome sound, the sound of the roof being lifted off the kennel, which probably was more like a hen house, thinking about it, with a removable roof, but frankly I wasn't thinking about that now.

I had been saved, I discovered from the television as I sat in Mrs. O'Riley's kitchen, close to the cooking range, wrapped in a blanket on top of a hot water bottle, that I had survived one of the worst floods in the south for a generation.

I was lucky, which was true, I had survived and I could be considered lucky, except for the fact that Mrs. O'Riley's daft Golden Labrador had obviously decided that I was one of her sick puppies and needed constant licking, will I never be able to escape Dogs who are completely insane.

Mrs. O'Riley's Golden Labrador was obviously and in her own way as deranged as Maxwell the fish-eating vegetarian Mexican lapdog had been, because Mrs. O'Riley's Golden Labrador didn't have any puppies!

Well there weren't any puppies nearby, I had checked obviously, and I couldn't see any or any sign that any had once been here, but that could have meant that they had possessed the good sense to leave home as soon as they could, because Mrs. O'Riley's Golden Labrador practiced the type of stifling motherly love which could turn any offspring into a raving basket case, albeit a neatly woven raving basket case!

Oh if you are interested, all of the Dogs in the kennels were saved, though you will forgive me for celebrating even if I could get this idiot Dog's tongue out of my face for a moment. In fact they were rescued first – really I ask you. Happily after being rescued they were all sheltered on the second storey of the barn with Mr. O'Riley looking after them I almost pity them, if anyone understands 'tough love' it is Mr. O'Riley!

So there were just the three of us in Mrs. O'Riley's house, or that is what I thought until I met Mrs. O'Riley's Cat, an evil bad tempered Tabby Tom Cat, who had taken an instant dislike to me because I was in his favourite chair next to the cooking range.

I did explain that I had been put in the chair after my ordeal, but he was having none of that as an excuse, apparently nearly drowning was no excuse at all for being in his chair.

What a good job that Mrs. O'Riley's Golden Labrador was deluded enough to not only spread spit across her little tabby and white 'Puppy' but also to spend all night protecting him as he dozed in a sleep full of dreams, which contained mad homicidal Tabby Cats and vast oceans of flood water!

Day 86 of My Captivity:

I woke up today, glad that I was in a kitchen in a house on a hill, when I looked out of the window all I could see for what seemed miles was water and kennel rooftops.

Trying not to be too obvious I did look around for Mrs. O'Riley's Cat, but he must have gone off somewhere for a nap, because as far as I could see there was just the doe eyed Golden Labrador gazing at me lovingly from the floor and sighing contently, so for a moment or two I was safe from being either licked or beaten to death, to say nothing of being drowned outside.

I don't know how long I am going to be here and I am sure that I don't have enough paper for even a few more days, I have dried the pages which got wet and flattened out most of the pages, which I previously used to wear in my ears, but still the paper shortage is dire.

There is one consolation in the midst of all of my despair and that is that the pen I 'borrowed' to write my holiday Diary – yes I know, some holiday this turned out to be, is water proof or is that waterproof?

Well whichever it is, the ink didn't run when it got wet, in fact the paper has begun to rot from being so wet, but the words I wrote on it are still readable, must be a nuclear pen with radioactive ink or something with a very long half life! I wonder if the North Koreans would be interested in buying the technology?

Day 87 of My Captivity:

Has anyone got any paper? No not 'that' sort of paper, writing paper, 'that' sort of paper is useless for writing on!

Day 88 of My Captivity:

Sorry saving paper, so can't write any more today.

Day 89 of My Captivity:

As you know and sorry to be a bit of a bore but I have almost run out of paper, so I can't write much today, the good news is that the floods seem to have vanished and the mud is beginning to dry out because of the gale force winds battering the house and surrounding countryside.

Good job it is still nice and warm in the kitchen, although I have to say that if I am kept here any longer then I think I may have my face licked off by a mad motherly Golden Dog. Worse still I have begun to learn how to bark, so obviously I am getting more than a little concerned for my sanity or at least the shreds of whatever sanity I still possess. Woof! Oops sorry!

Day 90 of My Captivity:

Today I ran out of paper completely, I am using the right hand margin just to squeeze this entry into the Diary.

Day 91 of My Captivity:

Sorry, can't make the words small enough to say more! Except help the Dog is licking my face off!

Day 92 of My Captivity:

Just a smudge on the paper today, oops!

Day 93 of My Captivity:

Yesterday I completely ran out of space on the paper that I had left and I have also completely run out of paper altogether, it is just as well that I was collected by the very tanned (I might say) Human Captors and taken back to what they call home. Actually compared to Mrs. O'Riley's even I would call it home now! Although I am beginning to miss my adopted Mother and found myself pinning for her when I found some golden fur stuck down with spit on the top of my head!

Happily I have a large supply of nice new clean and unmuddied paper and have managed to dry out the paper I was using during the flood, soon I will find out if I can read what I wrote, but at the moment I think I just need to relax a little.

I am safe now, don't get me wrong I still want to escape but I need to rest for a while and get my strength back, the last few days have been a real trial and I think I will need several days of serious washing to remove all traces of spit from my rather matted fur, goodness that mad Golden Labrador of Mrs. O'Riley's could give her puppies a thorough washing, shame she had never discovered shampoo, soap and water, what am I saying shampoo, soap and water would have been worse!

Day 94 of My Captivity:

It is good to see the Dog back too! He hasn't spoken about his experience at Mrs. O'Riley's, probably still in shock.

Judging by the scratching he is doing all the time; I bet that he caught some 'little visitors' from the hay in the barn. I feel sorry for the poor Dog; well only a little sorry for him, because he is certain to be sprayed with flea spray if they catch him scratching and the way he is scratching they are bound to catch him!

Hardly seems fair does it? First they put the poor itchy Dog in a kennel, then the kennel floods and he is nearly washed away, and then after recovering in a barn he, through no fault of his own catches Fleas, well it isn't as though he invited them is it?

Now he is going to get sprayed and of course if he gets sprayed you can guarantee that I will, which is why I feel sorry for the Dog because if I get sprayed with flea spray, because of him, he will pay!

I hate being sprayed, well frankly any animal in their right mind hates being sprayed with that filthy stuff, and not only that after a while one gets used to having a few itchy places here and there, speaking of here and there. Oh! There is an itch just 'there,' I hate it when you itch in a place that is really difficult to scratch.

It is awful to see a reflection of yourself in a window or mirror, lying curled up on your back, with most of your legs in the air trying to reach and scratch somewhere that your paws were never supposed to go!

Day 95 of My Captivity:

On the way back from the dreaded Mrs. R's death camp we drove through some really deep floods, and looking out of the window here, I can see that the wood across the road from the house still has large puddles everywhere, glinting in the cruel cold sunlight.

With this in mind I have decided to continue the suspension of escaping and other clandestine activities until things improve, I have even considered decommissioning my tools, now of course this doesn't mean that I am either giving in or indeed giving up, I am merely trying to follow the climate that prevails at the moment, a bit like the Irish Republican Army in fact.

Mind you I did steal a large number of tools today, but of course I can't admit to that on account of the above, because I would hate you to think that I ever contradict myself, ageing like those brave boys in balaclavas!

Day 96 of My Captivity:

Following on from my decision to cease, albeit temporarily, my efforts to escape, I have been able to really relax. I hadn't realised just how much pressure I was putting on myself to be bad.

I know that my new state of mind probably won't last, but I am going to enjoy it until I decide to begin my campaign again, the trouble with my new good intentions is that they will probably make this Diary a bit boring, but we will see, after all I can't be an 'Action Cat' all the time can I?

Day 97 of My Captivity:

The water outside seems to have almost vanished and even the mud in most places seems to be drying out, thanks to the constant gale force winds, that we have had for several days.

It seems to me that it has been blowing a gale since we got back from Mrs. R's death camp. If this wind carries on blowing then I imagine it will be quite dry under paw soon.

Rather cleverly (well would you expect anything else from me?) I am using the Dog to monitor the conditions outside, over the last three days he has been the only one to go outside, and when he is ready to come inside he first has to be hosed down outside the garage. You can't believe what comes out of his fur, enough silt and mud to mark an Estuary at low tide, if he is not careful we will have an army of Chinese Cocklers descending on the garden! And you know how careless they can be!

Today when he came in he was less like a Mudlark and more like a Dog and I noticed that the Captors didn't reach for the hose, which seemed to spoil the Dog's day, I am sure that the idiot enjoyed being hosed down in the cold.

Recently I have watched him from the kitchen window and if he wasn't chasing the stream of water coming out of the hose, he was running round in circles trying to get muddy again so that he would be hosed down once more. He truly is a Dog biscuit short of a light lunch and no doubt about it, in fact there must be a medical term for his condition probably 'Nutter!'

It is clear though from the improving conditions outside that I will obviously be able to begin 'operations' again soon, which is good because the Parrot is back just to spoil the party and not only that and probably more importantly, I am heartily sick and tired of being good, it is the hardest thing I have ever tried to do.

Day 98 of My Captivity:

I would like to confirm that as of today 'operations' are to be resumed, I plan to put all of my strength and brain power into escaping from this prison, but first I would like to state that the Parrot is going to have to be 'dealt' with, he has only been back here a day and I have had quite enough of him!

Ever since I have been here I am sure that the Parrot has spied on me, watching me from above as I go about my innocent way in life. I really can't stand the idea that I am being watched 24/7 (do you like the 'hip' way to say twenty four hours a day, week in week out, no? Neither do I really but you have got to keep up with the times, haven't you). As you can tell the Parrot is really getting to me.

Dead cold lifeless eyes watch me constantly, the eyes of a group of predatory sharks follow me wherever I go in the front room, well the Goldfish do from their bowl, but now that my tortured imagination has been ignited, I see things watching me all the time.

Am I paranoid? Probably! Do I have good reason to be paranoid? Yes I do. Below is just one example of just how paranoid I have become so far on my journey into obvious insanity.

At first I just used to jump when the doorbell rang, but now a lot of the time I find myself sitting in the hallway in a patch of sunlight, staring at the door, dreading the sound of the doorbell, but knowing that I have to wait for it to ring because it will ring and I have to be there when it does.

After the doorbell rings which is unfortunately all to rare ,and I have seen who is ringing the doorbell and tried and failed to escape, then I can relax just a little for a very short time and go and eat.

It is getting so bad that the only time I can eat is after the doorbell has rung, that sounds like a trick I heard of for conditioning Dogs and not the sort of behaviour that befits a Cat.

It is obvious, I have got to snap out of this madness or I will lose my mind and never be able to find it, because I know that usually I am just not very good at remembering where I have left things and let's face it, if you forget where you have put your mind you are in big trouble.

Come on I'm a Cat after all, not some half witted Parrot who has dropped off his perch!

That's better! Insults help! I may just cheer myself up and go and see what the pretty dumb Polly is doing, it is a while since he and I crossed claws!

Sitting in the kitchen doorway, I was distracted from annoying the Parrot because out of the corner of my eye I spotted the can of dreaded flea spray on the work surface between the cooker and the sink.

In all honesty a can of flea spray isn't hard to miss for an observant Cat, even from somewhere as low down as the floor. Some kind Human packaging designer, obviously in a moment of creative zeal decided that the colour of the can's label should be mainly orange, with a bold white band around the middle so that the name can be easily read, and I suppose, so that Humans in moments of absentmindedness wouldn't spray the stuff on their shoes as shoe polish or on their Strawberries as whipped cream!

Shame on the designer is what I say!

'Give the heartless Human devils some of their own medicine,' is something else I say, but actions speak louder than words and as I can't swap the pretty orange label for a nice whipped cream cans, the next best thing is to do something 'creative' with the can.

So forgetting the Parrot for a while I slunk into the kitchen and sidled up to the kitchen cupboards below the can, looked around to see if anyone was watching and when I decided the coast was clear jumped gracefully up onto the work surface.

Well all I can say is that the earlier paranoia was gone from my mind, driven out by my clear thinking, and in its place were the very beginnings of a very cunning little plan – tee hee!

Most cunning plans are rather sly in nature and this one happily was no different, and most sly plans get adapted as they go along and I hasten to say that this cunningly sly plan was no different, because as I gave the can a little sniff I noticed the heat from the cooker hob on my tail where a stew was gently bubbling away for the Human's dinner.

Somewhere I had read that you don't mix aerosol cans and heat, mmmh I can tell you are reading my mind!

The can was surprisingly light, so light that it wasn't difficult to push it right up against a little slither of flame that escaped from around the bottom of the saucepan with the stew in it.

Flames, explosions and the mayhem that they create have always fascinated me, in fact I just love to sit in the front room and watch logs and coal slowly succumb to the fire.

A tiny flame escaping from a gas cooker is sadly not as hot as the heart of an open log fire and so the explosion, that I dived away from, didn't happen, and I sat on the floor as far away from the cooker as I could get, feeling cheated.

I waited patiently with my paws in my ears, but the anticipated big bang just didn't happen. As the kitchen clock clicked off the seconds, my patience began to evaporate and my impatience simmered like the stew, which by now should have coated the ceiling, windows and walls and been slowly sliding down them.

Imagine just how I felt, abject disappointment rose in me as the second hand of the kitchen clock ticked its way from the thirty second mark up to where a minute would have elapsed.

I dared a little peek from my safe hiding place and nothing seemed to be happening, but I wasn't close enough to see properly, and so I edged closer, but then the kitchen table obscured my view of the can completely, very frustrating.

I wasn't that eager to get much closer or indeed to get in the line of fire of the shrapnel, which I expected to fly over my head at any moment, so I just sat still and listened.

The stew was still bubbling, making the lid of the saucepan rattle gently and outside a few birds were having a heated debate, probably with a few squirrels about the ownership of some berries or nuts, why do birds have to make such a racket?

The waiting was agony, and the suspense tense! My curiosity was like a sharp stick prodding me, insisting that I get a closer look and do something if nothing was happening!

Reason suggested gently that it was best to leave well alone, or let sleeping Dog's lie, but have you ever met a Cat who would let a fat lazy sleeping Dog just lie unmolested at peace and asleep? No I thought not, and this situation was no different, except that the sleeping Dog wasn't lying in the kitchen more's the pity!

Talking about reason, it seemed reasonable to nip up onto a chair and poke my head out above the table and have a quick look to see if anything was about to happen, and so I did just that, after all, a little look couldn't hurt anyone could it?

Sitting on the well-proportioned chair seat I waited for a few moments feeling like a soldier in a trench, then I held my breath and poked my head above the table.

I was astonished to discover that the cooker had vanished! Silly me I was facing in the wrong direction, and so slithering around like a poacher in the village stocks I managed to look right at the cooker hob.

The plastic cap of the flea spray can had melted and a merry little yellow flame with a long trail of black smoke was burning at the base of the can. The dreadful orange label was beginning to burn away too, which was handy because it appeared that the label was made of a rather combustible plastic covered paper.

As I watched admiring the very attractive little fire get bigger and less controlled, I started to hear an odd hissing noise, one thing I was sure of was that it most definitely wasn't gas escaping where the cooker that had gone out, in fact the work surface that surrounded the 'built in' cooker hob was burning too so there wasn't a shortage of flames to burn off any gas escaping so I couldn't really work out why any gas was hissing, but it didn't seem important so I just ignored it.

Mind you, I was sure that things were warming up, and decided to get under cover, 'under cover' being the best place to be in an explosion I have always found in my experience!

When I went to pull my head back down under the table, I couldn't understand why it wouldn't respond. Fate can be such a fickle master they say, but this time fate was having a laugh, somehow and I would like to know 'how' to be perfectly honest, because my head was stuck.

No in fact my head wasn't stuck at all! To be precise my neck was stuck for reasons best known either to the gods, fate or most likely in this case the back of the chair. I had become wedged tight and all I could do was to watch the rapidly growing fire and listen to the hissing, which was drowning out the tick of the clock and the noisy birds outside.

I was in trouble, or to put it another way, my head was in trouble because it was right in the line of fire of the explosion, which I was now confident was about to happen at any moment.

Now to read the last few paragraphs you would think that I was relatively calm and that I was merely noting, with a sort of detached interest, the predicament that I found myself in.

Mmmh! Right as if you would be calm in my situation! I am afraid to say that although I would love to say that was the case and I was a cool as a Cucumber or as calm as a Carrot, Cats are too honest to not tell the truth, (a fact that has for centuries separated us from Humans I might add, and in my opinion put Cats at a distinct disadvantage to them, after all how many Cats are successful in politics for example, apart from the Cat who was elected as a Mayor of a small town in France, none as far as I know! Still that is not as important as my current predicament).

I was in a state, and not a good one, frankly I was in several states, panic was the main state I had the misfortune to be in and stuck fast in the line of fire yet another state.

No amount of wriggling, relaxing or screaming helped in anyway what so ever, which was a source of enormous disappointment.

But disappointment is something, you may have noticed that I can cope with, what I didn't think I could cope with was the impending result of my 'creativity' with the flea spray can.

You know and so did I that the can was almost certainly going to explode, it definitely looked that way every time I gave it a quick look before I started wriggling again.

The little fire was no longer little at all and the plastic cap had melted flowing like fiery lava down the can and out over the work surface, where it was being heated by the flame on the cooker hob, and just for good measure the handle of the saucepan had begun to melt adding fuel to the flames, as if it was needed.

I was convinced that the can was actually glowing too, and I knew that any minute the whole lot was going to explode, hopefully in the opposite direction. In fact preferable towards the window and the songbirds outside, that would shut them up once and for all hopefully.

Unfortunately I have some considerable experience of explosions and have noticed that they tend to do the opposite of what one expects, especially if 'one' is a small Tabby and white Cat, who just happens to be trapped by the neck in the line of fire.

Ho hum! As they say in books by Charles Dickens. Well they say a lot more, but none of what they seem at this moment to be as accurate or as interesting as Ho hum!

I wonder if one can watch something and be detached from what is happening especially if what is happening directly effects the person watching?

Still there wasn't time to explore that philosophical question and there isn't really space in my Diary to do so either, what I can say accurately is that the can exploded.

One moment the orange can looked like an orange can with a reasonable sized flame at the bottom, the next moment I was horrified to see the can just blow apart at the bottom and become a silhouette of itself inside a white hot ball of flame.

The rest of the can shot up into the air like a Saturn five rocket under an Apollo Moon shot, but I am sure noisier. The rocket blasted its self off the work surface and leaving a trail of white smoke smashed into the ceiling.

It is no lie to say that I wanted to look away, but it would be far more accurate to say that I wanted to just get my head under the table and use the table as an air raid shelter, because I was confident I was about to experience something called 'incoming' in some circles.

Alas I wasn't going anywhere; well I wasn't going anywhere 'safe'! More's the pity.

The rocket bounced off the ceiling at a very acute angle, showering sparks and flame everywhere, and I knew that the next place it was going to hit was either my head or somewhere so close that you could call it too close and be alarmingly accurate.

The flaming nose of the rocket was pointed at me as it screeched towards me and I have to say that I was really fed up about that, oh and of course terrified, but I am sure you knew that!

What would you do if you were in the same predicament? No sorry no time to find out!

What I did was just simple, I closed my eyes tight and waved bye-bye to about eight of my nine lives, all of whom seemed to be deserting the sinking ship like Rats. What dreadful appalling behaviour, and I have to say most unfair and I also have to say I considered those eight lives to be absolutely disgraceful and would have disowned them if I could, but obviously I needed them and knew that they wouldn't get far!

First I felt heat, very hot heat to be truthful, and then I felt, smelt and heard an impact followed by a very large explosion.

I knew that my fur was on fire, but I couldn't believe that I was dead, but then I thought about it and opened my eyes just a little to see that the world was slipping away and I was falling, oh dear there is a Heaven, I decided, because it felt as though I was on my way down to the 'other' place and it was as hot as had been promised.

I hit something solid and rolled on to my paws, well that seemed the most natural thing to do, I am, as I have said before a Cat and we like to land on our paws or get onto them as soon as we can after falling, not that we fall over very often you understand.

As I was rolling and getting ready to spring onto all fours something large and loud clattered down next to me. It was no good, no matter where I was, heaven or hell alive or dead I had to open my eyes and see what was happening.

The chair was lying around me in smouldering charcoaled pieces and the rocket was just a glowing collection of hot metal trying unsuccessfully to melt itself into the floor tiles.

The smell of burnt fur was really awful and made even more dreadful by the fact that I was pretty confident that it was 'my' fur that was smouldering.

I did a quick check and decided that I was no longer alight, although I could see that I was smoking from some burnt fur around the back of my neck somewhere.

Patiently I waited for things to cool down and also for my eight lives to sneak back, I glowered at them as they shamefacedly sneaked back. I would deal with them later!

I was confused and couldn't work out exactly what had happened and just how I had managed to avoid becoming a char grilled Cat, although I was extremely happy that I wasn't.

Looking back at what happened now, from the comfort of the Sofa cushion in the front room, well I have been moved out of the kitchen because it is a bit of a disaster zone, as you can imagine!

I don't know exactly what happened, all I can think of is that the rocket like can hit the back of the chair with such a force that it knocked it over or maybe it just knocked it off balance, and my weight made it fall to the ground, whatever happened happily I was knocked to the floor by the force of the explosion.

The rocket must have become entangled with the chair back because it reduced most of the chair to charcoal, which was fortunate because it could have been a trapped Cat who turned black, and not the chair.

Looking on the bright side of today's disaster, and one always has to look on the bright side, we have the decorators in tomorrow to do some much needed decorating in the kitchen, so there is a chance that they might leave the front or back door ajar and that is encouraging!

I did hear that the Female Captor got the blame for leaving the can of flea spray too close to the cooker, the Male Captor was really quite indignant saying that they couldn't claim on the insurance because of 'her' mistake! She in turn said that she wasn't 'that' stupid to leave a can next to the gas, and he replied, 'Oh, so the fairies did it!'

I do enjoy a good argument between Humans and so I stretched out, closed my eyes and listened to the argument heat up, it was just like listening to a radio drama, but I soon got bored and nodded off, just as I do when listening to the radio, whether it is a drama being broadcast or one of those dreadful Radio DJ's chatting for all he is worth between the odd and, I use that word deliberately, record!

Day 99 of My Captivity:

There is nothing like a really good night's sleep on a wonderfully comfortable bed, and I have to say that the cushion on the Sofa in the front room is a very comfortable bed indeed.

I slept an untroubled dreamless sleep; I suppose that I should have had a nightmare or two. After all I had been through a lot yesterday, but then I was probably too tired to dream.

Thankfully I had dropped off early, but the Humans argued until late and they kept waking me up, which was unfair because I was the injured party in all of this, but when Humans start arguing they don't consider the consequences that are inflicted on others!

I just counted my blessings that they hadn't bothered to examine my part in what happened yesterday, still if you are arguing you don't think logically, well unless you are a diplomat or a politician, and these two Humans are neither of those.

All in all though, today was a great disappointment, and not only for me, the decorators, who on the telephone yesterday, had promised faithfully to begin decorating the kitchen today, didn't turn up.

Still every cloud, no matter how smoky, has a silver lining, and today's silver lining was supplied by courtesy of the Female Captor who, while she was on the telephone explaining that she had taken a day off work (whatever that is?) and had waited for the missing decorators to turn up, used more rude words than I have ever heard in my whole life, and they say that education is a wonderful thing, well if that is learning, give me more, right F***king now.

They also say, apparently, that Females are the gentler sex, if that is the case then I hate to think what I might have learned if it had been the Male Captor's day, that had been ruined by waiting in for the decorators?

Day 100 of My Captivity:

Life, they say, is full of surprises and my life is surprisingly full of surprises, on balance most are nice surprises, and only a few surprises involve staring at a fiery rocket speeding towards my nose, happily.

Today was one of those days when life dishes up a delicious surprise as a tender delicacy to enjoy at one's leisure?

What am I on about?

Ok here is the simple, dumbed down version, and at the same time a goodbye to any hope of a literary prize, but then no one can say that I don't know my audience – the masses, and the masses apparently like their life to be like their reading –simple!

Today was great, and I haven't laughed so much for a long while, in fact I haven't laughed so much since the keep fit equipment arrived. Remember that little episode? I do and smile whenever I do! It is a shame that a smiling Cat looks either sinister or stupid!

The Male Captor decided that he had waited long enough for the decorators to appear, I presume he had rubbed all the magic lamps he could find - as if decorators just appear – really? What planet is he on?

Anyway he had the day off and spent most of the day waiting in and making ever more manic phone calls to the decorators at ever-shorter intervals, when the telephone calls got down to every five minutes he gave up, in a furious mood.

I knew that the rest of the day was going to be fun because when he brought in a selection of old paint from the garage, he tripped on the doorstep coming in and began using the same words that the Female Captor had used, I am now convinced that some of those words must just be decorating terms! Decorating must be stern stuff I suppose, and delightedly I reflected I was about to find out.

It was a shame that one of the many tins of paint he brought in had a small leak, which traced his path from the garage to the kitchen.

To my way of thinking the wobbly line of cream paint looked just fine, but the Male Captor didn't seem to think so and raced around using lots of 'decorating terms' and turned the place upside down for something called White Spirit.

White Spirit must be truly mystical stuff because it did a really good job of cleaning away the little stream of paint, especially on the kitchen floor tiles, and probably the job would have been perfect, except that the Dog had walked through the paint, sniffing it and tracing the line of paint with his nose, as I suppose he played 'intelligent tracker Dogs' – yeah right!

The mud stuck to the 'Tracker Dog's paws, mingled with the paint, and the resulting mixture was obviously White Spirit proof, in fact the stains seemed to be unaffected by any cleaning agent known to man, well known to this man!

Luckily as the carpet dried and the sun changed angles the stain hardly seemed to notice and so, he obviously thought that he had finished cleaning up and needed to go onto bigger and better things, and I thought so too.

I followed the Male Captor into the kitchen and sat on the draining board, watching the paint tin with the hole in the bottom drain paint slowly into the sink, while he went off to get something else from the garage.

Of course I should have gone out of the front door with him, but today I decided I was going to stay in the warm and get some excellent home entertainment.

The arrival of the stepladder was announced with a series of bangs and clatters, that probably removed paint from the front door and both walls down the hallway as he carried it in and set it up under the scorch mark on the kitchen ceiling.

The stepladder was one of those 'special' ones, which could be set up in all sorts of different ways to access most places around and indeed outside the home.

It is only a guess, but I suppose the correct set up depends greatly upon how closely the instructions are followed!

In a very short time it became clear that he had lost the instructions before he managed to read them, because the stepladder ended up in a sort of painful, ugly modern sculpture pose, which would be more at home in the Museum of Modern Art than a kitchen.

Still you have to hand it to that man on a mission, he didn't give up, even after pinching every finger on one hand and the thumb of the other. Tears were in his eyes as he looked around for help, trapped, as he was by both hands in the unforgiving jaws of the stepladder.

Help was at hand though! Well help was available I should say to be more accurate, because he didn't use his hands and I wasn't going to help him. He balanced on one foot, carefully lifted part of the stepladder off his crushed hands and quickly pulled them free.

Perfect! Except that the stepladder crashed to the floor and magically missed the foot he was standing on and folded itself neatly into the shape, that he had carried it in half an hour ago.

They say that Humans rose out of the primordial pit because they were tool makers and users, well this Human I was pretty confident had never made a tool in his life and as for using them – well!

My theory is that Humans rose out of the primordial pit because they were persistent and this Human was demonstrating just how persistent Humans can be!

Long after I personally would have got bored with the stepladder and gone off to do something more interesting, like sleep, he continued to bend, twist and shape the stepladder into more and more odd shapes and positions, using a large amount of 'decorating' language as he went.

Personally, I was pretty sure that this was really a lazy stepladder that seemed to be happiest collapsed on the floor, but giving credit where credit is due, he persisted, though one couldn't describe his persistence as 'patient.'

In the end he managed to make a sort of triangular shape out of the stepladder, which even I could see, might possibly be used to reach the ceiling.

I must however, hastily add that personally a pack of wild Dogs armed to their foaming teeth, wouldn't have persuaded me to use the stepladder or indeed get too close to it, I am not that daft!

Still after all of the kafuffle it seemed that he was ready to begin painting the ceiling. He had plenty of paint even after he threw the leaking can away, the stepladder was as ready as it could be, but now he began to look around for something, and I watched fascinatedly.

Even I realised what he was looking for, he had so much paint and no brushes, so leaving an open can of paint on the stepladder he went back to the garage to do twenty minutes or so of rummaging.

There was a triumphant grin on his face, right next to a bruise, where he must have bumped into a cupboard door in the garage as he was looking for the paintbrushes, but I have to say I was only one out of the two of us who seemed to notice the bruise.

With the speed and the enthusiasm of the brainless, he climbed the stepladder, which wobbled precariously with every step, when he was at the top he bent down to dip his brush in the open can, an action that made the stepladder lurch forward.

Gracefully and probably thankfully, he grabbed the tin of paint before it fell to the ground, picked it up, scrapped his brush to avoid drips and began painting, with his tongue taking the air, a perfect picture of Human concentration.

Life has a habit of catching up on people who concentrate on one thing too much, and today was no exception. For reasons best known only to themselves both the Parrot and the Dog decided to enter the kitchen at this critical moment.

I suppose if they had both done it quietly then nothing untoward would have happened, but they were, it seemed, having a race to see who could annoy the Male Captor the most and the Dog won, but only by a short head and that was probably because as he raced the Parrot into the kitchen, his head bumped into the wobbly stepladder.

The stepladder and the Human on it both wobbled, but there was no harm done, it was when the Parrot had flown passed the stepladder and, would you believe landed on the work surface next to me (and frankly I couldn't have that) and I lunged at the Parrot, that things happened.

The dreadful squawk that the Parrot made distracted the Male Captor for a moment and what with the stepladder now rocking a little more violently something, I suppose, had to happen!

Why did he drop the tin of paint? I don't know! How did he manage to drop the tin of paint? Again my answer has to be, I don't know!

Was it messy? I can answer that one, you bet'ya!

Still it is really amazing what can be cleaned up with a supply of the best tea towels, and soon he was making the stepladder rock again and the ceiling was changing colour rapidly, although I was a little surprised when he finished so abruptly, only painting the area that had been scorched and not the whole ceiling!

After the ceiling was 'finished' he quickly 'attacked' (yes that is the right word) the window frame, standing on the work surface next to me.

I have to say, two things surprised me. First, he didn't move me and second, by how much I was being splashed by little specks of gloss paint, begrudgingly I had to get up and move to a safer distance, but even at the other end of the work surface I was still occasionally being splashed.

Happily window frames don't take much effort to paint and in no time at all he was finished and jumped lightly down onto the floor to stand back and admire his handiwork, just as a drip dropped from the ceiling onto his chest.

His handiwork, I have to say, though this might just sound a little picky, was a collection of drips, runs, curtains, finger marks and clothing imprints but most importantly he seemed happy, so happy that for the first time he noticed me and kindly wiped me down with a cloth to get some of the paint out of my fur!

In fact he was so pleased that he kindly opened a celebratory tin of Tuna chunks, drained the brine out of the can and when he gave me the whole can, he remarked that he had saved himself a small fortune on decorators! What could I do but join in the celebrations?

So I was busily eating while he tidied up. Sadly there wasn't any White Spirit for the brushes – he cleaned them in the sink for a while and then when the sink was clogged with quick drying gloss paint he threw the brushes away, a little guiltily I thought!

When I finished the Tuna, and after I had burped contentedly, I looked at his handiwork with a slightly more critical eye, there was, I am sure, more paint on furniture, floor, windows, the Dog, Parrot and me than on the ceiling or the window frames, but on reflection I was rather full up and didn't really mind in the slightest.

Apparently there is a strict rule to decorating; one that is obviously more important to Female Humans than to Males, and that rule is broken at the peril of Male Humans.

The rule is simple and sensible on reflection, and it is, always use the right shade of paint that will actually match exactly the area you are painting, if that is, you are only going to paint a small patch of, say the ceiling!

Sounds sensible as I said, what is probably more sensible would be to repaint the entire area, let's say a ceiling, and then the need to observe the aforementioned rule would not come into force.

Did the Male Captor observe the rule? No of course not, the new shade of white, would, he truly believed, blend in after a while and let's face it, who looks at a ceiling?

The answer to the question who looks at a ceiling is simple, Female Humans look at newly painted ceilings, as soon as they get back from work, and it would seem, their eye is even more critical after a long and arduous day at work, and, it goes without saying, because they invented the rule in the first place!

All in all I had had a wonderful day of entertainment and hadn't planned on there being a finale, but as soon as I saw her face when she entered the kitchen I knew I was in for a rare treat!

Through out the day I had made myself quite comfortable on the work surface, after I had realised that the Male Captor was too busy to shoo me off it and I was prepared to make myself scarce as soon as I heard the front door close and the voice of the Female Captor asking 'what do you mean, you did it yourself?'

But there was no need to move at all, she didn't notice me, she was too busy looking at the 'decorating' and turning red with annoyance and then turning an interesting shade of what can only be described as annoyed puce when she looked at the odd coloured mismatched patch of paint on the ceiling.

The front row of any public entertainment is highly prized and usually really expensive, especially say for instance in New York on Broadway, watching a hit musical let's say will cost you a packet. What I didn't know was that it is also quite a dangerous place if one of the cast begins to throw china and the other ducks.

A cup whistled over my head and smashed the kitchen window and still she didn't stop complaining, she just looked around for something else to throw.

I quickly decided that the 'front stalls' were too dangerous a place to watch this pageant and so slowly I slid like a snake off the work surface and picking my moment very carefully ran through the tangle of Human legs to the safety and protection of the table.

As with everywhere else, I had to be careful of the paint splashes that speckled the floor, some so big that they were still wet.

I sat there watching, as a few of the chairs were thrown aside and the Male Captor made a dash for the hall. I could just see him, without compromising my safety, by leaning around the table leg as he slammed the front door shut and escaped, a jar of Marmalade smashed into the closing door and an odd sort of peace returned to the kitchen.

I now know the meaning of the word 'lull,' and happily I can use that word to describe the all too few seconds of peace that followed.

The silence was abruptly broken by a stream of 'decorating language,' which was frankly not becoming of a lady, as the Female Captor first cleaned and then tidied the kitchen.

After she had spent hours mopping, sweeping and washing, and she was satisfied that the kitchen looked more or less as it did when she had left the house that morning, she found a few dustsheets to cover the newly cleaned furniture and most of the floor.

Once the dustsheet had been arranged to cover everything that needed covering she fished the leaking tin of paint out of the rubbish and poured the contents into a little paint pot, (for reasons best known to decorators the little paint pot is called a 'kettle?' Don't ask; is all I can say!)

Then when she was finally ready and had made the stepladder safe, she painted the ceiling in no time at all, with what looked to me like exactly the right colour of paint, that had been there before the Male Captor had got his hands on a paint brush.

In no time at all she had finished, washed out her brushes, and generally cleaned up, although to be honest she hadn't made much in the way of mess anyway.

With a sigh, she poured herself some of the giggle juice that Humans occasionally drink too much of and sat on the kitchen chair next to where I was hiding under the table and gave yet another sigh.

I heard the giggle juice bottle chink on her glass again, she was having another and so I thought that I would let her drink that one down and then come out of hiding, because surely if she was still in a crockery throwing mood, at least the giggle juice would spoil her aim a little!

I am just guessing, but I think that the giggle juice did more than spoil her aim in the end, after several more glasses, she stood up rather unsteadily and stumbled off to bed, making rather too much noise for those of us, who had fallen asleep earlier.

Day 101 of My Captivity:

The Male Captor returned late in the morning today, looking tired, unshaven and generally furtive, I heard him very gently slide his key into the front door lock and then creep into the hallway calling her name so softly that you would think that he didn't want her to hear him.

Maybe that was the plan, if it was then he was fortunate because she had gone off to work, employing the same 'silent running' techniques, in fact she tried to make no noise what so ever because when she did she groaned piteously, stopped what she was doing and held her head.

The Male Captor didn't bother to come into the kitchen where I was enjoying a daydream about cans of Tuna and cans of 'melt in the mouth' Robins and other Hedgerow birds.

I heard him go straight up stairs and that put me off my daydream annoyingly. Still never mind, there was a possibility that he would be in a celebratory mood and give me another tin of Tuna, or a tin of Robin and other Hedgerow birds if that variety has been invented yet and let's face it, it should be.

All of the money he saved on decorating was spent on an hotel for the night apparently and the cost of repairing the car after hitting the gate at the top of the driveway, life can be hard sometimes and obviously yesterday took no prisoners at all.

Still I have to say that these two dopey Humans seem to love each other more than they hate each other and the evening was filled with soppy 'sorrys' and 'I love yous,' all very yuck making if you ask me, and as usual no one had bothered to do that.

The only up side of this love-in was that the animals; even the dumber ones, got a little feastette (that is a word I have invented for a small feast by the way) I was given some Prawns, well when I say 'some' I mean a bowl full but a bowl full of Prawns always seems never to be enough Prawns.

The Dog got a small mountain of 'Cheeky Chappie' Dog food, which later would turn to the most awful smelling gas and the Parrot, well who cares what the Parrot got? Not me!

Day 102 of My Captivity:

Recently you will notice that I have been being really kind and considerate towards the Parrot, ok in truth I have been completely ignoring the feathered freak, but alas 'his' type always exploit kindness.

Folk like the Parrot don't seem to know what the word 'truce' means, it definitely doesn't mean, perching on the light fitting, waiting for a peace loving, good natured Cat, like say for instance, yours truly to walk passed. Then like several banshees dive down from a great height and attack the good looking Samaritan, I ask you what behaviour is that?

Really what type of behaviour would you call that? If he had a dirty white tea towel head dress on his bonce, then you could say that he was a terrorist, but he just looks like a normal Parrot, well he tries to look 'normal,' but fails, still everyone seems to think that he is harmless, so why, oh why, does he attack me, a peace loving Feline?

Did I retaliate? No, well of course I didn't, I had no idea what was going on, one minute I was minding my own business on a stroll around the house looking for open doors or windows, and the next I was being mugged by a feather Boa with claws and a very sharp beak and why? That is what I would like to know! I thought that I and I alone was the master of the surprise/pre-emptive attack, but obviously not, well if I can't be the master of the surprise attack I can promise you that I will be the master of retaliation, and we all know what happened after Pearl Harbour or 9/11 to surprise attackers, don't we.

I know it is an unpopular idea these days that terrorists and freedom fighters are really not very nice people or Parrots for that matter, but I have thought hard and long about them and honestly they really are not very nice people at all, and their crimes, for that is what they are, seem to be forgiven because they belong to some minority or the other.

Well let me tell you as a fully paid up member of a minority, which was much persecuted over the centuries, there is no smoke without fire!

I discovered that Cats have had a questionable past; thousands of years ago Cats were worshipped as gods, Cats have never forgotten this, but there were problems with that sort of adoration and invariably when the Kings of the time were wrapped up in bandages and buried in Pyramids when they died, Cats were bundled up in their off cuts (and it hasn't been proved that they had given their permission or worse that they were actually as dead as the Kings!) and buried too.

Then, as history often highlights Cats fell from favour and ended up only being looked after by Witches and inherited the odd job title of 'Familiar!'

'Familiars,' apparently are Cats who help witches, and get Club Class seats on their brooms, which I suppose is ok, but when the Witches were persecuted the Witches' Cat got the same treatment, riding up and down in Ducking Stools, until their lunch leaves their stomachs, or being burned at the stake, now that is tough love and no mistake!

Even in more enlightened times Cats have suffered taunts and unkind jibes from nursery rhymes and strange folklore sayings.

We have all heard the expression used when describing a small room, 'not enough room to swing a Cat,' I ask you is that a nice way to treat a Cat? Maybe it would be sufficient to just say simply that you could touch the walls of the small room if you stretched out your arms, why do Humans have to swing the poor old Cat?

There are more too.

'Cat got your tongue?' Now honestly what would we do with anyone's tongue, well apart from a lady Cat's wink wink!

It is difficult for this Cat to admit, but all the same it is obvious that Cats from previous times can't have been all good, still even Humans are not proud of their ancestors, and rarely invite them round to dinner.

Still if my ancestors got their brides by sneaking into a rival village, bashing a Female over the head and then keeping her at his home tied up until she decided that it was pointless to escape, I would be ashamed of them. Especially as the Caveman kept just a small piece of rope tied around one of the fingers of his 'wife's' left hand, over the years the string was replaced by gold and the finger became known as the wedding ring finger, but that is progress for you, and oh yes I forgot, civilisation.

So with that in mind maybe one day in the future when Humans have become even more civilised the freedom fighters will be known for what they are, a bunch of bullies and in some cases just plain evil homicidal maniacs!

Speaking of evil, would you believe that even today some people say that Cats are sneaky, evil, and cruel which is all true, and we have many other fine qualities as well.

Believe it or not I haven't finished putting even a tiny bit of the world to rights, and in addition dealing with the terrorist subject yet, but I am very tired and need to rest for a while, well about fourteen hours to be precise, this thinking business is hard work, so expect more Cat wisdom tomorrow. Then maybe I will feel up to getting my own back on the Parrot too, I hope so!

Day 103 of My Captivity:

IRA! I have been confused, I thought that when I heard the letters IRA most nights on the television they meant 'I'm Really Angry,' well they were always used when reports of shootings of innocents, record breaking bank robberies, bombings, assassinations and other really bad things were happening. I had no idea it was a freedom fighter movement.

Correct me if I am wrong but aren't freedom fighters supposed to be heroes who are trying to liberate an oppressed people? And again correct me if I have completely the wrong end of the stick, but these people are fighting the British? Now if they were fighting some sort of fundamentalist state I could sympathise with them but really the British! I ask you? Just how oppressive are they? They eat scones for goodness sake!

Take a typical British person and then nearly bump into one of them in the street and you will find that even though neither of you made contact the British person will still say 'sorry' and mean it! Doesn't sound like the average Briton is capable of being an oppressor does it? And what is more, any nation that has tea with little 'fairy' cakes and Muffins can hardly be 'fundamentalist' can they?

So what is the IRA fighting for? Well, I have heard that there have been 'troubles' in the island of Ireland for hundreds of years and that everyone and his Dog has just recently renounced violence and yet the IRA keep on keeping on, as they say in parts of New York and Chicago where large amounts of cash has over the years been raised for 'the cause.'

Of course 'the cause' is a sort of shorthand for weapons and explosives, but doesn't it sound better than saying 'give money for weapons and explosives,' to say giving money for the cause,' It is a shame 'the effect' of 'the cause' is so devastating to the people of Ireland and Britain where 'the cause's' effect is shattered buildings and broken people.

So as I mentioned earlier, recently everyone, including the IRA, decided that it would be a jolly good idea to hang up their weapons. The IRA thought that it would be a great moment to do one last large bank robbery then declare peace, which is nice except that the IRA seem to have their weapons super glued to their hands and can't actually put them down, let alone give them up, or is it that they are just a bunch of murderous thugs who should be treated to the same sort of public justice as Nicolai Ceausescu, the hated leader of Romania?

Day 104 of My Captivity:

Other people's Shadows – are you scared of them? They scare me! But then I think that most Humans scare me and their shadows are usually a warning that they are approaching and probably as usual not looking where they are going with their big feet ready, willing and able to step on a little, innocent and very cute Cat. Usually they are heading for the tail of the previously described angelic victim and if it isn't the tail they are headed for, then it is almost always a paw and that hurts too!

But it wasn't a Human shadow that got the better of me today, it was mine, it just crept up on me, as the sun filled the hallway.

As usual I wasn't doing anything wrong, well nothing that I could be arrested for anyway, unless thoughts are a crime these days, but one minute I was daydreaming without a care in the world, except for my constant worry about the mountain of uneaten Prawns in the world, and then bang there it was, a dreadful blackness enveloping me from the tail upwards.

The further I moved away from it, the closer it got, very off putting, it was as though the soulless thin black slither was creeping up on me and no matter what I did it stuck to me like glue, honestly it worried me, I don't like being watched or followed, and that it is not just the way I feel it is true for all Cats.

You must have seen how Cats react if they think they are being watched and if you have seen their reaction you will know that Cats don't like being stared at, at best you will get a look, the sort of look that if it can't kill would delight the owner if it did a little casual maiming.

Then if you are brain dead or something and continue to watch you may get spat at, whiskers back and teeth bared and if by that time you haven't given up and gone off to tidy your collection of thimbles or dust your model railway, then the offended Feline will simply get up and walk away muttering unrepeatable insults about you and your entire family, no Cats don't like being watched at all.

I find that totally acceptable behaviour I might add, what do you think we Cats are, birds?

Now birds are really very thick, you have heard of the term bird brained, well I rest my case, they don't mind being watched, in fact they congregate together in large flocks exactly for that purpose, and droves of very sad, country clad weirdo's who call themselves 'twitchers' (if you ever did, still the word sums them up succinctly), spend hours drooling through binoculars at the pointless swarming black clouds of flocks of birds weaving across the countryside pointlessly. Which is a perfect compliment to the daft idiots in their smelly waterlogged clothing, pointlessly watching and whistling.

The whistling is apparently supposed to resemble the 'call' of the birds that the fools called 'twitchers' are watching, dear me if only they knew the truth, they would die of embarrassment, but of course the 'twitchers' will never know just how awful they are, because like all enthusiasts they are incapable of embarrassment.

Enthusiast, now there is a work to strike horror into the soul! When you become an enthusiast I believe that a spark of, well let's call it Humanity for the sake of a description, disappears and what is left is a numbskull, capable of the most desperately embarrassing actions.

Take for instance the case of 'fans,' these 'fans' could be fans of anything really because the rule of total immunisation to embarrassment applies in all cases.

Consider if you will, young girls who get crushes on spotty brat pop stars, with forced style and real braces, who have a few successful records and then disappear to surface years later working in a MacDonald's fast food restaurant, by the way, MacDonald's do not sell Prawns, which I find difficult to believe, but then maybe Prawns aren't fast enough!

The behaviour of the young girls is mad, collecting more posters than they have bedroom wall space for, and then at concerts they scream and squeal themselves enough to spoil their underclothes.

Then on the other hand, there are young boys who collect the same number of glossy posters, putting some of them on the wall to fall off randomly during the next few months that they are cherished.

The posters that seem to be favoured by most teenage boys are either in a Gothic horror style or of muscular men sitting astride massive chrome heavy motorbikes, which makes you worry for them in later life!

Day 105 of My Captivity:

I have a photographic memory - for photographs, which is very handy and sometimes my photographic memory even extends to faces, and places, the problem is that anyone would remember all the places they have visited if they were like me, held prisoner for any length of time.

I know and can picture the inside of every room in this place, I think that I know every room better than anyone here, who else can slide under the beds or indeed bothers to actually get inside all of the cupboards and investigate and occasionally get 'caught short' in them I am embarrassed to say.

One hint here, never let your Cat go to the loo in your cupboards, especially in the kitchen cupboards, it is not at all nice and ruins the breakfast cereal, soggy Muesli is not at all nice, well let's face it, Muesli is not really nice dry, in fact Muesli... yes, ok I know, you get the picture!

Then there is the smell, no not of the Muesli, of the cupboards, once they have been, let's call it 'used' because it is not really very nice to talk about going to the toilet at the best of times, especially in food cupboards and not only that, we should try to be as polite as possible about toilet things in general!

Where was I, ah yes having a wee, no, not literally, I was merely discussing it but hopefully not in literary sense which is boring like Dickens and not what this Diary is I hope, although some would say it is boring, well I would answer them, it is not meant to be boring, in fact this Diary is not designed to bore anyone and so I will just keep quiet and not be literary at all.

Mind you I am sure that you know the type of literature I am on about surely? And I am sure that you will agree that this Diary is different and appeals to everyone because it is one of those new trendy 'cross-over' books that are very popular now, because we all have the same reading age thanks to modern education methods and of course the small fact that if the masses of people are pretty, now how can I put this, ah yes, 'thick,' then they well be happy to go along with any of a long list of government's harebrained schemes and worst of all not blink when the they ask us to pay taxes.

I am sure that no one reads 'difficult' things nowadays and if you disagree with me, answer these questions for me:

1. When was the last time you read the very small print at the bottom of a contract or on the back of a purchase receipt when you bought something?

2. Better than that, when was the last time you read a political party's manifesto? You know that their manifesto is just the simple version of what they intend to do if anyone is dumb enough to elect them!

I bet that the answer to both of those questions is 'never.' That is exactly what I thought! Now remember that the manifesto of a political party is just the stuff that they think they can let you read, and is not too controversial and usually has nothing to do with their avowed intentions, how else do you think Hitler, Robert Mugabe or Mrs. Thatcher got elected?

So no one reads anything difficult these days, and that means happily a Cat can write a bestseller and at the same time give a few half brained scriptwriters at Pixar or Warner Brothers an idea for a blockbusting movie, which is ok by me of course, but if I was Human I would be reading the print of election manifestos looking for a party which will improve education.

Still the first way to improve education would probably be to sack all the teachers, especially the English teachers! We had one here a little while ago, yes yet another visitor, and frankly Ms. (you have noticed that they are all Ms.'s even if they are married and not only are they Ms.'s, they use the names they had before they got married (maiden names to any educated readers, who am I kidding?).

Anyway back to this advert to avoid the teaching profession who was called Ms., (yes I know I have said that bit already but please be patient, it is not easy to set up a gag!), Ms. Ellen Dreary and wasn't she just what her name advertised, a more dreary soul one could not wish to mention.

She had the appearance of a habitual drinker and the sallow complexion of a regular soft drug user and that package was enhanced by her shifting unease, probably brought on by thousands of uncontrolled, over crowded classes, erupting in violence and mayhem over the years.

Ms. Ellen Dreary wasn't old, or to put it another way, Ms. Ellen Dreary was ageing fast and her haunted gaunt looks only exaggerated her sad featureless features.

In some circles I am sure that her face was considered to be blank canvas that would always look wonderful when made up, like a model's on her way to a photo shoot, but models take time with their appearance and it was clear that Ms. Dreary had long given up that particular campaign.

I felt sorry for her and secretly I wished that I could let her know that they do say a lot can be done with a blank canvas, but one has to remember that another word for blank is bland, and anyone with skin resembling the texture of canvas has had one too many late nights and glasses of white wine!

Still there is one up side, her opinions were so strident and badly thought out that she would be a brilliant guest on one of those dreadful radio programmes that discuss the problems with education and life in general, come to think of it, she would probably look good on radio!

As soon as she arrived it seemed like it was time for me to go to bed, as far away from her twitching insecure person as possible, which is exactly what I did, to say she bored me would be unfair, but oh so truthful, I pity the poor children who were forced to sit in airless classrooms, learning English from her!

Now whether on the way out of the front room I deliberately bit her is something that I think the world will never know, in my defence I have to say that through out all of the time she had been in the room she had made me nervous and jumpy, she was definitely infectious in that respect, but my reaction was natural, or that is what I would say in my defence.

As I slunked out of the room she jerked her legs, obviously surprised that I had slid under her outstretched legs, ok I like to slide along nylon covered legs, well we all have our little 'preferences' don't we?

And anyway it is a Cat thing to rub one's body across Human legs, they are supposed to like it, aren't they? Well whatever I just slid under her legs and felt the shimmer of excitement down my spine, when she flew up into the air screaming, this was a teacher, very tightly sprung indeed.

I thought that she was going to attack me at worst or stand on me at best so I did what any self respecting Cat would do; I lunged at her with my claws out and my teeth bared.

Drawing blood is not nice at all and I am sorry that I did that, especially as Human blood is very salty and really not very tasty at all. All I can say is that it is a good job that I have a good set of knashers though, because the terrified teacher swung and kicked like a rabid footballer on the losing side at a cup final.

If she wanted a fight then she wasn't going to be disappointed and I happily used my claws to shred her stockings and the stubble flesh under the glossy material.

I think I won, because I had to be slowly and painfully unhooked and then pulled off the punctured leg by the Female Captor, who apologised profusely, without my permission I have to say, to the tap dancing teacher.

After I was disentangled and rather firmly I thought, removed from the room I went to bed as planned where I laid awake thinking about Humans and their madnesses.

My thoughts led me to a rather momentous decision, which I know will delight all of the people who have got this far in my bestselling Diary.

I have decided that I am going to write a fourth book, especially if money gets tight at any time, I have thought of a catchy title, see what you think?

'Book Four - a Manual for Surviving in the company of Humans.' The essential guide to a peaceful life among the enemy, which has a working title of 'Dozing with the Enemy'!

Ok, so the working title is a little long, but what the hell, that could possibly be a selling point!

It is a shame that Cats aren't generally seen in bookstores and for that matter rarely admit to being able to read, because my new book will definitely be a 'must have' especially for the Feline world.

Come to think of it Humans would also benefit greatly from reading the book and possibly discovering just how complex Cats are, and then Humans armed with their new found knowledge, they could begin to treat Cats in the appropriate way, or in other words properly pamper them!

So there you are, all of you true fans of my Diary, you will soon have a real treat in store, or should that read, a real treat in stores near you soon?

Day 106 of My Captivity:

As you know I have been using the internet for quite some time now and find it the most amazing tool, it has taught me so much, just as the television taught me to understand spoken English, the internet has taught me to read and write in English, and I have to say I am not very proficient (do you like that word I learned that today!) but improving all the time.

Frankly I like the word and so I thought that I would use it again, 'proficient,' there we are, it looks rather good on the page don't you think?

You know I was so impressed with the word that I decided to look it up in the Dictionary and I was shocked to find out that it has a darker side.

Would you like to hear about its darker side, do you have a choice? Well yes, I supposed, you do have a choice, if you don't want to hear about the darker and mysterious side of 'proficient' then you could always put the book down and declare that you will never read any more of that rubbish, but I think you would regret that impetuous decision and I implore you to read on.

There are lots of reasons why you have to read to the end of my Diary. Firstly because everyone else will be reading and talking about my Diary, just like they do with other doorstop sized volumes like good old Harry Potter and sadly you won't be able to join in the conversation because you only read to this point in the book. I am sure that you wouldn't want to risk being a social outcast would you? No I thought not! Secondly I am sure that there are the clues to untold wealth hidden somewhere between here and the end of my Diary and you couldn't pass up the opportunity to become fabulously wealthy could you?

There are so many reasons to read to the end of my Diary but if I include them here I probably will never get to finish writing it and that would be a crime against humanity in my opinion, Humans deserve to read my book and be enriched by my thoughts!

Where was I? Oh yes the dark side of proficient, according to the Dictionary someone can be described as 'proficient' if they have a high degree of skill in something, well that is the short explanation according to the lightweight 'Microsoft Encarta World English Dictionary,' and as usual the definition did more to pique my curiosity than it did clarify meaning of the word.

As you know there is only one Dictionary I trust (and I am still hoping that they will sponsor my Diary, but that is a side issue) The Collins English Dictionary and so I had a peek inside at the page that had proficient on it, at the top on the left hand side to be precise! For some reason I like spotting words that I am using, when they appear at the top of the page, maybe it is just the Kitten in me!

So imagine my surprise when the description of the word proficient did say what I thought it should, yes it said that it meant someone was good at what they do, and a bit of other stuff, but where was the darker side, where was the association with black magic and the darker arts, like I suppose Charcoal drawing, sorry I don't really know what the 'darker arts' are, I was confused and not a little disappointed, pass me more dictionaries please!

Well that is all of the dictionaries known to man including the online ones which seem to be more interested in selling Toyota cars and hair dryers than telling you what a word actually means, I am stumped, stuck, baffled, foiled, mystified, bewildered, perplexed, confounded, flummoxed, dumbfounded, puzzled, though of course not stymied, but yes you guessed I have found the Thesaurus online and that is a consolation of sorts.

Oops silly me, I take all that back about the word proficient, I meant 'adept,' it is a good job that I am only a Cat and not a teacher isn't it!

Now an adept is… ok, if you insist, I will leave the matter there, now that you have got the picture!

DAY 107 OF MY CAPTIVITY:

Invisibility that is obviously the answer to the question of captivity! Why didn't I see it before!

How do I know that is the answer I have been searching for? Well if I am invisible then I can just slip out of the door with the Captors when they leave the prison.

How did I discover the secret of invisibility? Easy! First I found some invisible mending thread, used by Humans to sew up holes in their clothes in a sewing box that I just happened to have my nose in, and then I stole a knitting pattern. I hear you ask what is it with the knitting pattern? Well with the knitting pattern I will make a cloak and when I wear the cloak I will be completely unseen – I can't wait.

There are just a few little teething problems at the moment actually, so I can't wear the cloak and test it out, but I am confident that I will overcome those little niggling problems and then 'Bob's your Uncle' as they say in the east end of London! Quite why they say that I have no idea, but they say it anyway, they're a strange lot the people in the east end of London, I wonder if all people who live in the east end of cities are odd and have strange sayings that only they understand, mmmh! Probably not!

The biggest 'little problem' is that at the moment what I have managed to make is more like a collection of threads looped together, rather than something that looks like the knitted jumpers that I have unravelled in the wardrobe on occasions, but 'I am working on it,' as they say, probably in the east end of London!

Slowly, slowly catchy Parrot is what Humans say, when they are working on something that requires patience, or is that 'slowly, slowly catchy Monkey, well yes ok it is, but I know they say it when they need a lot of patience and I understand that it is probably said in the east end of a city somewhere, and I have all the patience in the world so I will finish my cloak and become invisible very soon and of course given the choice between catching a Monkey and a Parrot, I'll take the Parrot every time.

If this goes well I could start a company producing invisibility cloaks, but why stop at cloaks? I could produce different types of clothing, for say, parties. Imagine wearing just invisible trousers to a party, now that would be an icebreaker, wouldn't it!

Obviously the best place to set up such a company would be the east end of a city, but what would you call the company, hang on, the brain is working, I love the feeling, yes, I have it, the name of the company could be 'The emperor's New Clothes Company' it has a ring to it, stand back and let me make a fortune.

Well I will make a fortune after I have cut out the teething problems, slowly, slowly – yes I know you get the picture!

Now, let's have another look at this knitting pattern, knit one, purl one, what on Earth does that mean, I have no idea, I am afraid I don't understand rap!

Oops I have dropped a stitch, well ok I know a little of the language. I think it is called rap, because if I manage to knit an invisible cloak I will wrap it around me, and the knitting language seems to be just like Rap, a load of utter incomprehensible nonsense.

Do you know, I had no idea just how difficult knitting was, I have seen visiting old ladies, who in the main, can't open Jam jars, rattle their knitting needles at a rate of knots and produce out of a tempting and sometimes rolling ball of wool a strangely shaped jumper, or a pair of booties for a baby, or indeed one sock and even sometimes a very long and misshapen scarf, in fact almost any woollen item that nobody wants, so why is knitting so difficult? If they can do it, talk and drink gallons of tea all at the same time, while baking a large fruit cake and complaining about their pensions, the rudeness of young people and the fact that 'they' don't make wool like 'they' used to, why can't I knit, I don't want to do the other things, just knit.

The last bit of their conversation always confuses me, how can 'they' not make wool like they used to? Wool comes from Sheep right? So are today's Sheep not so dedicated to making wool, or worse still have they lost the secret of the old ways? Or worse still are Sheep about to revolt and try and take over the world and so at the moment they are making substandard wool?

I don't know either, I was asking you, you are a Human after all, I am just a Cat who until now wasn't really interested in the quality of what was on a Sheep's back, I just like to bash the ball of wool around and get into serious trouble with the old ones and their knitting circle.

Why is it called a kitting circle? Ok I'll stop asking silly questions but you could have at least answered one of them!

Still all of this speculation is not helping my knitting skills at all.

Actually I would be very grateful to you if you would not mention the fact that I am knitting, well it is not very 'cool' is it? And I would hate to be the subject of gossip and ridicule in the school yard and at the country club.

I trust you readers and so I am sure that my secret pastime is safe with you, you all seem to be really nice people, especially the ones who are on holiday and are reading this on the beach or next to the pool and I am sure that the people who are reading this aloud will probably censor that bit before they read it.

Oh dear I see your point you have already read that bit aloud, ok well to the people who heard that bit, could you please just forget about it, or as Al Pacino says 'forget about it,' in an Italian accent in Donny Brasco, there now you are thinking about a great film and not my knitting shame, oops done it again!

Back to the knitting now, mmmh if only it was that simple, I could have knocked this cloak up in no time at all, you couldn't lend me an old lady could you? I seem to be fresh out of them and I really do want to finish my invisible cloak!

Still with this new set of knitting needles and a lot of spitting and under the breath muttering something seems to be growing under my paws. There is, I have discovered, one other problem caused by knitting an invisible cloak and that is that it is very hard to see what you have knitted, even when I hold it up to the light I can't see the full extent of the garment.

Ok so I am just going to have to use my judgement and cast off, that is another bit of knitting rap, which is also used by the Johnnies and Ruperts who go sailing, but that isn't important, the invisible cloak on the other hand is important and I wouldn't want to put it down and not be able to find it would I.

It is a very sheer and snug garment and hardly weighs anything at all, a bit like wearing Nylons. I hasten to say that I would imagine that it is a bit like wearing Nylons compared to Tights before you all get any ideas, it is bad enough people talking about what was supposed to be my secret knitting habit, I don't want any other 'complications' in my life, thank you very much! And no I have NEVER worn either, before you ask!

There are a few threads sticking out here and there and I have bitten one of them off because it was sticking in my ear, but other than that I have done a jolly good job considering I was all dewclaws and pads.

Hang on, you thought that I had fooled myself and knitted something that didn't exist I bet, what do you think I am? Royalty? Come on now I am not that stupid!

Now to test the cloak out on an unsuspecting fool, where is the Dog?

Unfortunately there are a few design problems with the cloak the first one is that I have to wear it over my head obviously and I didn't know whether to cut eye holes out and if I did cut them out so that I could see, would innocent bystanders just see a pair of eyes ghostly floating above the floor?

With this in mind I decided that the best thing to do would be to keep the cloak over my head, not worry about the eye holes and when a door was left open, or anyone was leaving the prison just walk in a straight line, once I was outside I could just pop my head out check where I was and make a dash for freedom.

With this part of the plan carefully and successfully rehearsed and completed a dozen times in my mind I crept to the kitchen door and peeked inside.

As usual His Royal Shagginess, The Fool was snoring, dribbling and making other less savoury noises in his basket. I needed to wake him up and then 'test fly' the cloak to see exactly how well it worked, simple!

It is possible to get around the kitchen without touching the ground, in much the same way as children in the 1950's used to play a great bruising and occasionally bone crunching game called 'Pirates' in the gyms of their schools, before that is, that sort of physical fun was outlawed and children and their parents gained the power to sue teachers and schools for inflicting pain through boisterous accidents, resulting in the children of today becoming overactive and overweight!

My game of 'Pirates' began by springing, gracefully and sure footedly as usual, onto the table, sliding along its over polished surface and sending a vase full of flowers and a few items of china to the floor, before jumping from the slippery table to the work surface next to the sink.

Once there I tiptoed around the line of the work surface to the place above the dead to the world Dog, marvelling at his ability to sleep through such an out burst of shattering crockery and glass, but confident that even the heaviest sleeper could not compete with my next little wakey wakey surprise!

Looking down on the peaceful Dog I almost felt sorry for him, but 'almost' feeling sorry for someone is not enough to protect them from harm, or in this case an alarming awakening.

Imprudently the Human Captors leave most of their kitchen appliances out so that they collect dust, well the ones that were bought in a fervour of noble wishes to have freshly baked bread or towers of carefully steamed food.

Prudently the Human Captors leave most of those more or less redundant kitchen appliances unplugged as well as the two appliances that they use regularly, the Toaster and the Kettle.

The Toaster I knew would be of no use what so ever because although I was confident it could be made to make quite a lot of noise, to say nothing of its ability to get really rather hot, it was on the other side of the kitchen, the Kettle however was altogether more conveniently situated, it was just behind me to be precise.

So with one last look at the serene and oblivious Dog I set about arranging his early morning call.

The Kettle was half full of water, which made it nice and stable, and it wasn't too hot either which was something of a bonus because the only way that I could move it was to edge it forward with my nose and the side of my head, and I didn't want to risk burning either and losing my extremely good looks.

In no time at all I was standing back and admiring my handiwork and just making a few very minor adjustments to the position of the teetering Kettle which now stood more or less balanced above the Dog's basket, and well just above the Dog too, but that should be obvious, just as I suppose what was going to happen next was now pretty obvious even to my more mentally challenged readers, although I have to say I love them as much as all of my other readers, I said I love you just as much as my other readers.

'Bombs away!' Sorry I got excited, but for some reason I have always wanted to say that and it is a little premature here, because before I launched my 'bomb' I slipped my cloak of invisibility on!

'Bombs away!' Yes that is now exactly what happened when I gently nudged the kettle and it toppled over the edge of the work surface and crashed onto the back of the dozing dozy Dog.

Rarely have I ever seen anything or anyone move so quickly, in an instant a surprisingly wet surprised Dog was up and out of his basket, snarling and barking and snapping at his 'attacker.'

The Kettle was reduced to its elements in no time at all and the outraged Pooch didn't stop there he bit and chewed at the Kettle's element until he realised that he was never going to do much in the way of damage to the metal.

That was when I suppose he decided that the Kettle was more in the way of a weapon than an attacker and he cast a malicious look around the room for the real 'attacker!'

I was loving this, sitting on the edge of the work surface watching the extremely annoyed Hound getting even more annoyed because he couldn't see any attacker to leap on and extract a terrible revenge, then something quite unexpected happened, he looked up and did something that he wasn't supposed to do, he saw me and ran straight at me. It is safe to say that even though I was very surprised I just didn't sit there and wait to be bitten and covered in Dog spit, I sprung off the edge of the work surface and crash landed on the table, throwing elegance and the rest of the clutter on the table to the wind.

I could hear the Dog behind me as I fell to the floor, rolled and quickly got onto all four feet. Then in panic I ran, the crazy thought 'what a shame that there weren't any trees in this Prison,' insanely went through my brain as I ran, skidding and sliding on the floor tiles with the heat of a mad Dog's breath on my back.

Not looking back I zoomed out of the kitchen and ran for my life and the stairs across the hallway. I took the stairs four at a time and reached the landing at almost the same time as the Dog did. I was done for, I knew that, but Cats don't give up and wave white flags, mainly because they don't carry white hankies, and also probably because it is well known in Cat circles that Dogs don't accept surrender, I was finished and soon to be an ex-Cat.

With that in mind I did the only thing I could do, I jumped up in the air, spun round and landed neatly if not a little surprised on the

Landing handrail or is that called a Banister, who cares I was safe, well not safe exactly because I had a feeling that the Dog would be able to reach me, if he was angry enough to reach up and put his front paws on the same rail and I knew he was!

There was one last option and it was not one that I would have wanted to use unless there was no other, but as you can see, there wasn't another option, I jumped from the banister aiming for the far wall.

Happily I can tell you, that I hadn't taken leave of all of my senses and I wasn't making a leap of faith, hoping to fall the twenty or so feet to the bottom of the stairs and escape unscathed, oh no!

Well yes I was thinking that it is true, but this oh no is in answer to my previous statement, I wasn't even considering plummeting to the bottom of the stairs, I was aiming for a cute little window that let natural light and my salvation shine on the stairs, and the first floor landing.

I crashed into the window and the strange ornament which fortunately for me, though not for the smashed ornament moved aside and took my place in bits at the bottom of the stair.

Happily I was safe, I turned around and looked straight at the top half of a very annoyed Dog, who was leaning his paws on the Banister and snapping, barking and foaming with anger.

I suppose even you Humans have worked out now that for some unknown reason he could see me, and that was odd because I was still wearing my cloak of invisibility!

As I tried to ignore the angry Hound and get his spit off my tail I wondered what had gone wrong! Can Dogs somehow see invisible things? If the answer to that was yes, it would explain a lot, or was it that the cloak just simply didn't work? I was confused.

It seemed certain that I couldn't risk the cloak after such a dismal failure with a dumb animal, after all Humans are usually slightly more intelligent than Dogs!

So I thought I would just wait until things calmed down a little and the riled Dog got bored or hungry, confident that either of those eventualities wouldn't take long. Then I could have a little peace and quiet and summon up the courage to jump back to the safety of the landing.

One thing was certain after all of that palaver I don't think I am even going to try vanishing cream, unless I get very desperate indeed!

DAY 1008 OF MY CAPTIVITY:

Oops seems to be a problem with the number today – I see what I have done, I was writing the headings for several days in advance and must have got confused somehow – still you know that it is really Day 108 and not the one thousand and eight[th] day don't you?

One hundred and eight days would be bad enough, but if I had been a captive here for one thousand and eight days would have driven me completely mad. Still thinking about it one hundred and eight days of captivity is enough to send you crazy, I wonder if I can get a home self assessment kit to test myself and find out if I am mad, you know like the ones you can use to find out if your Cholesterol is too high, or if you have too much sugar in your blood. I bet the pharmacy sell them, even if they don't work and like the other tests that wouldn't really matter because no one that uses any of these ridiculous tests at home actually understands how to use the kits properly or the results at the end of all of their messing about!

Having said all of that about one hundred and eight days of captivity being bad and acknowledging the awful truth that I might be mad, things are not so bad when you know that you have a fool proof escape plan, now all I have to do is not to meet a fool and prove that my latest plan works between now and the moment I go for broke, without breaking anything hopefully.

Well good news, I have a brilliant plan, as usual, and fortunately I always know where I can lay my paws on a fool!

Day 109 of My Captivity:

For some time I have been keeping my eye on a cupboard door under the stairs! You know, just checking to see where it leads, what is behind it? Do they keep food in 'there'? And is the door ever left open? And if it is left open then can one slip through it and do a little casual exploration, which might be advantageous to a curious Feline? You know the sort of thing I mean I am sure!

Guess what? Today the door to the cupboard under the stairs was left open. Well I was going to say left ajar, which is a small bit of 'open' I think, but ajar sounds like a glass pot for Jam and not the way one should describe an open door and such an interesting opportunity, no matter how 'open' that door maybe!

By the way I like Jam and Hedgerow Jam is very nice, a mingling of four Hedgerow fruits in a delicate jelly, well that is what it says on the bit of the label that was still attached to a rather large splinter of Jam jar from which I was sampling Hedgerow Jam, for the first time. To this day I still have no idea which four fruits were used to make Hedgerow Jam mind you which is a shame because I like to know these things! No I don't know why I like to know these things, does it matter, I am a Cat and all Cats are curious or so the story goes. Thinking about it, it might be a good way of telling if a Cat is alive seeing if it is curious, it is only a thought though and a curious one at that!

Back to Hedgerow jam I have to say the Hedgerows that I have seen from the attic window don't look as though they have any fruits in them at all, just a few piles of Doggy Doo and some odd looking stalks with red berries at the top, I do hope that the Hedgerow jam isn't made from those sort of 'fruits!'

Still back to the Jam (again) or is that Jam jars this time, it is funny how glass jars smash when they are pushed off a work surface, well I don't suppose 'funny' is the right word, but for some of us, arranging an 'accident' for an unsuspecting Jam jar is the only way to open them, and for that matter, in fact, any other sort of glass container.

You know that you can also open many other sorts of packets using the 'oops it has fallen off the work surface method of opening.' Takeaways or as they call them in American takeouts are usually opened in this way, well by me anyway, and thinking about it, old ladies with weak hands probably use that method too after they have set their knitting aside!

I have spent many a happy hour licking the floor, cupboards and walls clean after an entire takeaway meal has hit the ground and exploded all over the kitchen. Delicious!

Where was I? Oh yes, the cupboard under the stairs! So, right in front of me the door to the cupboard under the stairs was open, which was convenient.

Casually I walked passed a couple of times, looking as though I wasn't interested in the very tempting opening.

No one was around; fortunately there wasn't a sign of the Humans at all. They had gone off somewhere I supposed, so I had been left behind yet again, still this time I didn't mind being neglected quite so much, I had a feeling that I was going to be rather busy!

I felt excited and I have to say was in for something of an interesting time, as you will see when you read exactly what happened.

After I had walked to the front door and back a few times appearing nonchalant I sat down at the front door and peered out into the road, the coast as they say, was 'clear!' Although that is a bit of a strange saying when one lives so far in land! The 'coast' being clear, oh! Do please keep up!

So doubling back from the front door and watching my rather elegant shadow stretch out in front of me, I have to tell you here just quickly that I like my shadow; but I am still not too keen on other people's shadows, mind you.

As I strolled, with a very casual air, down the hallway my shadow glided across the polished floor and stretched itself up the wall in an elegant, if insane way.

When I got close to the open cupboard door, I stopped and slowly peered into the interior, it wasn't that dark and I could see quite well, especially with my superior eyesight and so I slipped in.

It is incredible just what Humans will put into cupboards, so one has to be careful when browsing in them. So far I have found all sorts of stiff meat, Ice, Frozen or at the very least very cold, little Prawns (poor things would be better off eaten, by me please), frozen little green bullets, Peas I think they are called (which I would not like to eat thank you), are all kept in cupboards, although those are the ones that can trap and freeze a Cat in.

In other cupboards I have found everything from Engine Oil to Bobbins, whatever they are, Humans are very eccentric and probably will never cease to astound and amaze me, with the things that they keep in cupboards.

This cupboard was no different in the eccentric storage stakes, well there were some differences actually, odd things that were too surreal and subtle to notice straight away.

The first weird fact was that the cupboard was carpeted! The second was that high above my head was a light switch and higher still, I suppose, although I couldn't see it in the gloom, was a light.

Fancy wiring one's cupboard for electric light! Bizarre! That is what Humans are!

But maybe, just maybe they are not so mad on reflection, this was a big cupboard by anyone's standards and I suppose it needed a light.

Still none of the strange habits of Humans scare me now, well none of the ones that I reckoned I would find in this cupboard anyway, so I slipped in.

I tried to close the door behind me very gently so that it looked closed from the outside, but so that I wasn't locked in.

On hearing the sharp metallic click, I knew immediately it meant that I had not achieved my objective, just like a British Olympian, I had done my best! But my best was woefully inadequate when viewed globally.

Still I was warm, dry, fed and fit and could worry about my failure later, again just like a British Olympic Athlete, although it almost goes without saying that I wasn't as rich as a failed British Olympic Athlete, but after this Diary is published, well then ,we will see.

Would it be gauche to mention here that if you have enjoyed what you have read so far you should recommend my Diary to all of your friends?

I have to say this and I really mean it, on no circumstances should you lend your friends this copy though because I would lose out on the royalties and that would be a terrible blow to a poor little Pussy Cat, please imagine that I am purring now and smiling, ok forget about the smiling bit, Cats tend to look a little evil when they are smiling, and that would be more than a little counter productive!

With an inward smile at my own little joke about British Olympic Athletes, well they deserve it don't they, and a building level of curiosity that was just about to burst, I set off exploring.

The first few minutes were unfairly disappointing it was obvious that this was not a place where any food was stored, which made the ominous metallic click just a little more important than it might have been originally.

After all; the way I looked at it was, if I was locked in somewhere with food then I could survive until my rescuers found me, picked me up and stroked me, while looking for the can opener and a tin of Salmon, or Tuna, or any of the 'treat fish' that I get once in a while, though not often enough if you ask me!

Still best to not think about food at the moment, as I said, I am not hungry. No, I said I was not hungry! How could I be hungry? I have only just had breakfast and also a bit of a treat!

I was the first one to get to what was just seconds before a spoonful of boiled egg, before it hit the ground and became a yellow splash.

Honestly I was so pleased to beat the Dog to this bit of stray food, he was still trying to get his fat flabby frame out of the Dog basket as I was licking the floor tiles – Mmmh, two delicious delights in one mouth watering snack, the taste of boiled egg and victory over the dozy shaggy one, whatever happened today it had started well.

Hang on! I think I told myself not to think about food! Mind you have you ever tasted a bit of buttered wholemeal bread dipped in the yellow of a boiled or poached egg, without fluff or much else in the way of dirt from the floor? It is divine!

Still there is not much point in asking my younger readers that question, they all see to be junk food junkies according to the Television news, but that is not important, well it is important but it isn't to this bit of my Diary if you see what I mean!

Now where was I? Yes wholemeal bread dipped in the delicious bright yellow yolk of a boiled or poached egg without a dressing of fluff, well thinking about it for a second, it isn't so bad with a bit of fluff on it actually!

Come on now pull yourself together and stop the food fantasy.

Wait a minute what is that over there?

Now I have seen everything! Who would have thought that a carpet should be rolled up and then placed against a wall? Surely carpets belong on the floor securely nailed down so that they don't roll themselves up and migrate to dark cupboards where they can hibernate.

Not only that it is obvious that the reason they are nailed down on the floor is so that Cats can sharpen their claws on them, anyone knows that! Mind you whoever did help the carpet hibernate in this cupboard probably didn't imagine what a favour they were doing for a Cat, what an excellent scratching post, I might just need that later on it depends how the digging goes, but more of that later.

My wonderful night vision is really an advantage, who needs a light when you have evolved so amazingly? Not this Cat or any other, come to think of it!

It is actually a lot of fun exploring this cupboard, now that I have forgotten that the door is locked and I haven't got any food! Sugar, they were two things that I wasn't going to think about, still my curiosity is piqued as they say, well I suppose they say when it takes over from thinking about everything else.

Now let me see, what do we have on these shelves? Goodness me! Humans and clutter, are they joined at the hip? I like investigating shelves though, in the first place they are easier to potter through than say drawers, it is hard to open drawers with paws and I have to say not enough drawers are ever left open just wide enough for an inquisitive Cat to crawl into.

Would you believe that there are still dozens of drawers in this place that I haven't managed to get into, dreadful! Still shelves are 'another kettle of fish,' as they say when they are talking about making fish tea, I suppose. Now that sounds like a nice beverage, maybe that is what a proper English tea is made of? I have no idea really, except that I would dearly like to try some, and I can't understand why I haven't been given any!

I wonder if one has milk in fish tea, yes I would think so, although in America where they have cream in tea, which I think is a pretty ugh idea, they probably put cream in their fish tea, ok I'm game I'll try that too, if anyone is listening and has the fish kettle on!

Sadly the shelves were a little disappointing, but, but oh but, look what I have spotted from the top of the shelves, I didn't see it when I was on the floor, goodness knows why it is big enough.

Wow one of those, move out of the way and let me at it! Oh I am sorry I forgot you are reading this and I haven't told you yet what got me so very excited.

Well honestly, I don't really know its name, but it goes drrrr, drrrr, drrrr, then ping, zip and occasionally per-ching and plays havelock with concrete, I think it is called a drill or a jackhammer, still who cares what it is called because it goes drrrr, drrrr, drrrr etc?

Should I translate the noises for you? Possibly it might make understanding the last paragraph a little easier, drrrr – well you must have heard workmen in the road at eight am on a Sunday morning, just when you are having a well earned lie in, they always start drilling with a Drrrr noise. Ping, zip and per-ching well that is the noise of concrete and anything else being drilled flying off all over the place, I hope that is clear now.

Where was I, look you can't blame me for that interruption can you? I was just proving what a nice, polite and caring Cat I can be when I choose to be and explaining things for you my lovely and cuddly readers; it is just that I usually choose otherwise but then you would feel the same if you were a prisoner, a fact I think you tend to forget now and again when you are reading this Diary, and don't think that I haven't heard that some people find what I do funny, I have and I don't think that is very kind!

Right, back to the, um let's call it a Jackhammer, because then everyone will know what I am talking about. My sense of excitement was growing, I was convinced that if this was an electric Jackhammer then I was a free Cat; well after a little drilling I was going to be a free Cat to be exact.

I leapt, gracefully as usual, down from the top shelf, knocking a box of screws off as I did, but I would do something about the mess later, probably ignore it as usual, and nosed my way over to the Jackhammer, boy they make them solid don't they!

This was an electric Jackhammer, oh thank you god, but unfortunately it was very heavy, but in my opinion that is something which can be overcome with a little planning and ingenuity and we all know who is the master of planning and ingenuiting – oops just created a new word, but you know what I mean.

Judging by the weight of the Jackhammer and looking at its design, once I get started drilling it will bash its way downwards on its own and I am pretty confident of that, so all I have to do is to prop it up and sit on top of it and let it rattle my teeth for a while.

Well first I have to find the plug and a socket, but let's face it if the Humans have put a light in the cupboard then they are sure to have put an electric socket in too.

There we are! What did I say! As if by magic one electric socket, and would you believe it someone has left the Jackhammer plugged in, how dangerous yet how convenient is that? I knew today was going to be one of those good days when everything went right! Well a Cat's luck has to change now and again don't you think?

Right! Roll the sleeves up and start work, sorry, I am so sorry, I thought that I was talking to you and that you were here in the cupboard with me, obviously it would be better if you were here to use the Jackhammer, but then I just realised unfortunately I am not that lucky; you are not here and I am not talking to you; I am writing this especially for you, I just have to keep reminding myself of that fact and inconvenience and consequently not to say unhappily, I will have to do the hard work myself, but I won't be rolling my sleeves up if you don't mind, that just wouldn't be nice would it!

'Well there is no time like the present' as they say when they really mean, 'come on, get on with it,' and that is what I have to do get on with it, but first I have to get on the Jackhammer, here goes, smooth and nimble as usual.

Some thoughtful soul has padded the handle and that means it isn't uncomfortable to sit on, which is a bonus, all I have to do now is reach down and turn the switch on and bang, drrrr, drrrr, drrrr, then ping, zip and occasionally per-ching, freedom here we come!

Well I can only say that I was prepared to have my teeth rattled, in fact I was quite looking forward to it, but the rattling eyeballs was another matter entirely, however I am happy to announce that in no time at all I was through the carpet and merrily bashing my way through wood.

The wooden floor was a little surprising, but I have encountered it before. When I was a Kitten and I had a bit of an 'accident' and tried to hide the mess in the corner of the room by shredding the carpet and underlay and covering the er, mess, when I encountered the wooden floorboards, they were very wet and not a little smelly.

I blush to say I know why the floorboards were wet and smelly. Still those days are long forgotten and the new carpet that replaced the one I destroyed after the floorboards had been disinfected and sanded thoroughly was a nice shade of red, with a deep pile so it was good to sleep on, which was a bonus.

For your information I think red is my favourite colour and I won't mind at all if you choose to buy me presents that are red, I'll leave the type of present to you, but as a hint, Ferrari red is the best shade of red, so much nicer than say Ford red!

Mmmh! Thinking of marvellous and extravagant presents tends to take one's mind off the terrible vibrations and the big splinters of wood, which are flying around this pretty tight space. Even though goggles hurt when you wear them, I kind of wish I had some squeezing my brain now!

Oh that is ok we are through the wood and now that I have switched off the Jackhammer I can jump down and have a look at my tunnel entrance.

Looks like I have made a big hole, by the way! Big enough almost to wriggle inside, but I have made the mistake on several occasions of wriggling into holes without first checking what is inside them.

Obviously this is the void between the floor and the foundations, so if I make the hole wider I can then get on with some serious tunnelling this looks as though it will be a long job.

Well for your sake I am not going to go into the details of each bit of burrowing that would be very boring (get the Cat joke, tunnelling and boring are the same, well more or less ha ha ha), so I suppose I should just cut a long and eye jarringly painful digging story short and tell you that I was able to dig my way through the foundations and use the void under the floor boards to spread out the spoil from the tunnel.

In the very informative documentary I watched and have mentioned before when the prisoners dug their tunnels they filled their trousers with soil and rubble and cleverly spread it out over an area where they all went for a communal chat first thing in the mornings and then again just before they went to bed at night.

It was handy to be able to use that void because I didn't have any trousers to hide bags of earth in or an exercise yard to spread it out over.

But for the sake of authenticity and also for those readers who are a little odd and actually like tunnelling stories, what follows is a short account of my progress!

Dust, dust and just a little more dust settled all over me, changing the colour of my fur to something not unlike a Russian Grey, comrade!

(This first sentence needs to be read in a Russian accent, if you don't mind.) So pass the Vodka bottle and let's forget about the digging for a while shall we? And talk over the old times, times of bumper Potato harvests and Beetroot mountains, oh dear, sorry I got just a little carried away, maybe the dust has got into my brain, I wouldn't be surprised if it had, it has got into everywhere else.

After enduring the dust from the concrete, the going became surprisingly easy; the Jackhammer was burrowing merrily through compacted soil, which was a shock when one considers that this neighbourhood is supposed to have some of the most expensive real estate in the town in its leafy lanes.

Happily as it dug downwards it threw vast quantities of damp soil behind it, fortunately a Cat of my size, well in fact most Cats don't require a particularly large hole to crawl into and soon I had to stop burrowing downwards and let the Jackhammer angle itself so that it began to tunnel out towards the road.

It goes without saying that I had carefully surveyed the land, checked for underground water sources, utility cables and pipes, and meticulously planned my subterranean route to freedom, yeah right! I had meant to do that but never seemed to get around to it, and now things were going so well it seemed a pity to stop, so I just continued excavating.

I did stop to implement one plan, and that was to start two other tunnels which led in different directions to my first tunnel, this was obviously following the example of the brave chaps in the Great Escape documentary who had inspired me so much.

I called the two new tunnels Tom and Dick in honour of the heroic chaps in the Great Escape documentary and the one I had already made a brilliant start on I called Harry again just as they had, though of course I was tempted to change one of the names of the tunnels to George because that seemed fitting.

But in the end I stayed faithful to history and kept the authentic names, hoping as the chaps hoped that my precious tunnels would not be discovered by the 'goons' that they had been so worried about!

I have to admit I had no clear idea what a 'goon' was and just supposed that it was some sort of subterrestrial (yes I like that word, and found it in the Collins dictionary) being like a sort of Mole with a grudge!

For hours I cheerfully dug away through the soil or more accurately I held on to the Jackhammer's handle for dear life as it dug its way through the soil, and Tom, Dick and Harry grew impressively.

I lost all track of time, down in the relative darkness of each tunnel. My only guide in trying to calculate exactly how far I had dug was to crawl back and count, and then compare the result with the number of seconds I thought it would take me to crawl unseen through the garden and out into the road, the neighbour's garden or the electricity substation which I had barely seen from the attic window, because as with all posh neighbourhoods the equipment was hidden by some dense undergrowth.

I wasn't really clear what an electricity substation was but the dense cover provided by the undergrowth seemed an ideal place to surface.

It became clear that dear Tom which I had concentrated on was probably already under the neighbour's lawn and so I decided to concentrate on Tom's companion tunnels, in order to extend them to an equally satisfactory length.

Harry headed towards the road and Dick was going to emerge inside the electricity substation, but that was ok because I was pretty sure that the fence surrounding the equipment could be easily climbed by a good climber and Cats you may have noticed can climb almost anything, ok they sometimes find it difficult to get down again, but the fence probably wasn't that high anyway and wouldn't present any problem for a Cat prepared to scramble down, especially as freedom was the reward for any nervous scrambling.

As the rest of the day passed Dick and Harry matured and sometime towards evening I was rather pleased with my day's work, not to say hungry, it had been I decided, a long time since breakfast, and was definitely time to eat something.

One or two, no let me be honest, hundreds of worms had wriggled in front of me and dropped down on me from the roof of the tunnel, and I have to say occasionally I had been tempted to have a nibble, but it is quite difficult to eat meat that moves and so I had refrained and contented myself with the knowledge that I was building up a healthy appetite.

Almost at the end of my working day a disaster occurred and poor old Tom's roof collapsed, crushing me flat against the tunnel's floor.

Did I panic? Well just ask yourself, would you have panicked? Of course I panicked, and as we all know and even you know now, panic gives one enormous strength as well as cold shivers though happily I managed to wriggle, shiver and crawl to the safety of the tunnel head, then I sat down and tried to wash off the dirt from my coat, that had so nearly become permanent, and that would have been a grave problem, ha ha ha!

I know I can laugh now, but it was a close shave and one that I didn't really want to repeat.

As I was washing myself I heard the Human Captors arrive home with all the noise, clatter and banging that Humans create as they arrive home with bags of food shopping, I wondered if they had any Prawns, yes it was time to eat, then I heard them let the barking bow wow out and call the Cat, maybe they did have Prawns!

It is a well known fact that Cats don't like to come when they are called, in fact I heard someone on the television, in one of those dreadful programmes about wildlife, which had a minor format change to 'cleverly' imply that Cats were wildlife too, yes honestly they suggested that Cats were not civilised, can you believe it? Anyway the presenter mentioned a quotation from a nice understanding lady called Mary Bly, who apparently said that:

'Dogs come when they're called; Cats take a message and get back to you later.'

How true! Now there is a Human who really understands Cats!

As I was having a very serious wash I noticed that the earth around me was drying out and decided that was a good thing, because tomorrow when I recommenced excavations the earth in the tunnels would be hard and hopefully not prone to collapsing and burying a furry tunneller!

Time for dinner!

With this decision I remembered that I was locked in the cupboard under the stairs and would have to do something clever to get out. I had a look and a sniff at the problem and sure enough the door was closed and it wasn't going to be opened with one or even two paws, which was a little disconcerting.

Rather than sit behind the door and try and persuade it to open with some purring and pleading I decided to be proactive, which I believe works in marketing circles, and so it wouldn't hurt to have a go here.

It occurred to me that if I could balance on one of the rolls of stair carpet which had been left opposite the door I could launch myself at the door and try and bash it open, well anything was worth a try! I was getting hungrier, though not desperate; I was saving desperation for later!

Unfortunately or as it turned out fortunately, the roll of stair carpet wasn't propped up against the wall securely and it easily wobbled and fell over, but I am getting ahead of myself here, I sometimes wish I could dictate this, but speech recognition software is pretty useless or the stuff I have experimented with was!

Once I landed gracefully on the top of the roll of stair carpet it wobbled and together we toppled over and hit the door with considerable force. Which was both convenient and painful.

Convenient because the weight of the carpet and furry passenger broke the door lock which was handy because I could just prop the door closed and get into the cupboard whenever I wished and painful because the unravelled carpet roll landed on top of me and though winded I managed to slide out from under it and limp out of the now open door.

I hooked a paw around the door and closed it, this time without any metallic click thankfully and pushed the rest of the roll of carpet over the rather large hole in the floor, I decided that the roll of carpet could be used tomorrow to deaden the noise of more drilling, if the Humans were at home that would be handy.

As I nudged the door to the cupboard under the stairs and my secret tunnels closed I decided that it was definitely time to eat.

Though looking at my now very dirty white fur I thought that I might get an unwelcome bath first, but one has to suffer for one's art, or tunnels in this case!

DAY 110 OF MY CAPTIVITY:

Last night I slept as contentedly and as deeply as a little Kitten, it must have been all of the hard work and the calming effects of the chamomile and Juniper berry shampoo that the Female Captor had used on a mysteriously muddy Cat before she fed me.

Happily the source of the mud that had caked my fur wasn't discovered and as I keenly watched the dawn exit of the Human Captors I was safe to do some more excavating in my tunnels.

Better still as it was a gloriously sunny morning the Dog had been let out into the garden to run himself ragged and the Parrot was asleep perched on the back of one of the dining room chairs, so that all meant that I could have some peace and quiet to do some noisy digging!

Much of today was taken up by earthmoving as each tunnel expanded and undermined the garden and then burrowed onwards towards their destinations, the work was very hard but I was really enjoying myself, the only distraction, well there were two, one mental and one physical and I will record them in that order, the least threatening being the mental one.

So first things first, the mental distraction was the overriding urge to stop burrowing and dig upwards to see where I was and how far I had managed to expand my tunnels, on reflection it might have been a good idea to give into that almost constant nagging little voice which kept saying 'go on have a peek at the landscape.'

I didn't give into the temptation and kept my resolve and I was pretty pleased with my resolve in the light of such temptation.

The other distraction was, as I said, physical and probably not what is going through your mind, unless you have skipped on ahead and read the next few paragraphs, which will probably spoil the suspense I have to say, and actually makes a writer, or to give me my proper title 'Diarist' just a little angry, so please stop doing that if you are and don't do it if you're tempted.

For those of you who I have read on ahead I just have this to say, really I think it is impolite of you to cheat like that, so get back to this bit and humour me, yes I know that you are probably worried about me, but don't worry too much I am still writing aren't I?

So to the physical distraction, I was cheerfully delving away when I came across or to be more accurate bumped into a spike, which had obviously been driven into the earth from above.

'Mmmh' I said, well I said that after I said 'ouch!' The spike had scraped my head and nearly caught on my collar, which can be dangerous!

Personally I think that it isn't a real collar at all, but it is more likely to be a serious electronic 'offenders' tag so that I can be monitored, but that is beside the point, although happily I will be testing that theory soon!

Thinking about the tag for a moment, it might be just a plain common or garden electronic offenders tag, because I don't remember undertaking any electronic crimes!

I have to say that I didn't want to be distracted and didn't think that the first spike that I encountered was anything more than a little painful, but then I encountered the second and later a third and fourth, and that is when my curiosity got the better of me and I decided to investigate this string of spikes which intruded into my tunnel, well I reasoned I deserved a tea break and as I didn't have any tea in my little packed lunch, that I had had the forethought to pack before beginning today, I thought I would munch a little soil filled Cat food and investigate the spikes.

Of course I hadn't planned to eat soil filled Cat food, but down here almost everything is covered in soil so I had no choice really.

Not only was I surprisingly hungry and oddly enough enjoying the gritty Cat food my ears were ringing and my eyes were still joggling in my head even though I had turned the Jackhammer off and I guessed I really needed a break.

The spikes were intriguing, they were almost in line with the route of my tunnel and I wondered if I traced back to the beginning of the tunnel and looked closely whether I would find more, and what do you know, I found five more, strange!

The five new spikes were almost hidden in the tunnel roof and weren't easy to find, but eventually I uncovered them and decided to excavate one and find out what on earth or to be more precise what 'in' earth they were!

The spikes were quite long and they tapered to a point which was very sharp, but they didn't seem to be hollow, well when I gave one a hefty whack it didn't have a hollow sound, giving one a hefty whack turned out to be not such a good idea, but at the time I didn't know that, but it felt so good to whack the spike that I gave it another couple of right hooks just for good luck!

They were obviously all the same and probably had been mass produced and undoubtedly manmade which didn't auger well, I was torn between leaving them alone and having a more detailed look.

After a detailed inspection, well I didn't say I was 'that' torn between the two options, I found a little white label hanging from the one at the farthest end of the tunnel, I needed some space so I pulled the heavy Jackhammer back to the mouth of the tunnel called Harry, left it there and with another pawful of Cat food I went back to read the little white label.

As I crawled back I tried to guess what the label would say and by the time I had got back to it I had sadly decided that it probably only said 'made in Taiwan' or something similar, and almost decided to give up and finish off digging Harry especially as I was convinced after two days of digging and measuring and then a little more digging just for luck, that I had completed the other tunnels.

I scraped around the spike and dislodged quite a lot of earth, enough to enable me to stand up on my back feet, lean on the spike and get a good look at the little white label.

The little white label said 'Mole mine' and then proudly boasted that it was banned in twenty countries, well I suppose that Moles must be sacred in some countries, and it went on to say as I correctly thought it had been made in Taiwan!

Well that didn't mean anything to me, to be honest, I was just intrigued as to why there were so many spikes in the roof of my tunnel, and why hadn't I noticed them before?

It slowly dawned on me that they definitely weren't there before but it occurred to me that they were probably the base of a fence or some other structure, and didn't concern me, I shrugged and decided to get on with finishing Harry, when I spotted a little red tag hanging down just above the little white label, I gave it a speculative tug and it didn't budge, so I bit it and gave it a very big tug and that, on reflection, was patently unwise.

Cats and most other animals except Humans don't like fireworks, and have in the main as little to do with them as they possibly can, I am no exception to that rule, in fact you can include me in another rule too while you are at it, and that is that if something starts to spark and splutter little jets of fire there is only one thing to do and that is to run away from it as fast as you can.

Fortunately Tom was big enough to run in, mainly because I had dug it under my neighbour's lawn and the earth like the lawn above was their pride and joy and beautifully kept in everyway in which you can 'keep' a lawn, and judging by the number of hours and the amount of labour that they expended upon the lawn there are any number of ways to 'keep' a lawn beautiful, and for that reason the soil was beautifully soft and loamy and easy to dig through.

As I ran down the tunnel I happened to notice that all of the spikes were spluttering sparks, but unlike the first one they were big sparks and looked as though they were intent upon getting bigger until they exploded like a trail of gunpowder heading for a large bomb.

I didn't have time to think or to do anything but run, it seemed to take ages to get back to the tunnel entrance and I an sure that I passed a couple of the spikes twice or on one occasion three times, but there wasn't, I can assure you any time to think about that!

Eventually I reached the Jackhammer and used it as an unyielding springboard to launch myself up into the cupboard under the stairs where I crashed into the stair carpet, which seemed in the darkness and panic to be like a spider's web holding me back at the mouth of the tunnel.

Behind me now the tunnel looked as though it had been lit by fairly lights, but not nice twinkling little cheerful fairy lights, these were the ghostly glowing ones which lure travellers off a safe highway through a dark wood into madness and savage oblivion.

I watched in horror, as the lights got brighter and changed from pure white to fiery yellow and I knew what was going to happen, but had no idea why or what I had done to deserve this end.

I jumped again and dug my claws into the carpet, which slipped down into the tunnel opening, leaving me hanging in mid air, I managed to unhook a paw and swing a little, so that the claws of my free paw now dug into the wood of the floorboard, then I heaved myself up and began coughing as black smoke started to billow from the tunnel and go everywhere.

Then it happened. I have been in several explosions and from past experience I know when something is going to blow up, the air seems to get pulled backwards towards the centre of the explosion and as it does it ruffles your fur and pulls you with it towards the centre of the explosion, which incidentally is not a good place to be!

All of the air in the cupboard was being sucked back and worse still so was I, it was like any typical disaster movie, the hero, (me) being dragged backwards to almost certain death and oblivion, if indeed they are not the same thing!

I couldn't hang on!

There that got you worried!

It is true though I couldn't hang on, indeed I had to get a move on, and get out of the cupboard under the stairs as quickly as possible.

It was such a good job that I had broken the lock on the cupboard under the stairs' door yesterday and could burst out of the door in a shower of mud and heavy black smoke, I clattered and rolled into the kitchen, dived in the Dog's basket and buried myself in his smelly blanket and waited for the bang, and anything else that would follow.

What I hadn't expected was that I had woken the Parrot up with all of the noise of my exit from the cupboard under the stairs and being his usual nosy self he decided to squawk loudly and fly after me to see what I was up to and then later report to the Human Captors.

The explosion seemed to be taking ages to go bang and so I risked a quick peek down the hallway.

The Parrot was just flying through the smoke coming out of the open cupboard door and it was making a terrific racket and I thought to myself, 'you probably shouldn't be there at this moment,' but it was pointless to shout a warning, and to be more than honest, I didn't feel like warning the Parrot! Was that bad of me? Did I care? And I didn't I have the time to do that anyway, when I was more interested in saving myself, especially as the first bright spears of red and yellow flame shot out of the cupboard under the stairs, so I did what any intelligent being or indeed any idiot would do and just burrowed under the blanket, got a mouthful of Dog fur and waited as all hell let itself loose in the hallway.

The bang wasn't as big as I thought it was going to be and if I hadn't been more than a little scared I would have been frankly more than a little disappointed, but all the same the bang was quite big enough, and the awful feeling of the house shaking was rather dreadful.

As the smoke swirled down the hallway and into the kitchen and the dust and clods of mud settled I checked to see if there had been any casualties, no was the answer, I was in one piece and that one piece was complete, which was a relief.

By far the best thing to do after an horrendous explosion and earthquake that you have been responsible for is to get up, dust yourself off and casually stroll down to where all of the action happened and take a close look, obviously watching out for any secondary explosions, after shocks and of course falling debris.

Happily the damage wasn't too bad, the hall floor was not damaged at all and the walls were still standing, though everywhere was covered in soot and mud, but there had just been an explosion so what do you expect?

I looked up to check the ceiling wasn't going to fall on me and saw a bedraggled brightly coloured mass of gaudy feathers clinging to the swaying light fitting, it was the Parrot and it was shaking violently and swearing revenge upon me! Ok so if the Parrot was going to be like that I thought I would ignore him and I trotted upstairs and did just that!

As I mounted the stairs I could feel the malice in his cold dark eye sending evil thoughts at me, but I just didn't give him the pleasure of noticing him, I was more interested in having a look out of the bedroom windows and checking what may or may not have happened outside.

Then if everything seemed ok I thought I might try one or other of the tunnels and get out now, yes that seemed a good idea, and as I heard the 'you wait until I get my claws into you,' type of dialogue coming from the Parrot that idea was getting better and better.

I checked the tunnel which I had dug out under the neighbour's garden first, good old Tom, it isn't very often am I shocked, or surprised or indeed lost for words, but looking out of the window at the neighbour's garden did all of those things to me and with just one quick glimpse out of a window, amazing.

The garden looked as though it had been ploughed and the lawn was something that was going to reduce the neighbours to tears I was confident of that, but there was something worse than that devastation and that was that the neighbour's house looked as though it had spent the night drinking giggle juice and now was slumped in a corner trying to sleep the over indulgence off.

The walls that were left standing were cracked and the roof had caved in spreading bricks and tiles everywhere, what a mess.

Then I noticed that the house beyond the immediate neighbour's house was in a similar state, copying the pose almost exactly, the only real noticeable difference was that there were several Humans emerging from the rubble, one seemed unhurt physically but had obviously gone insane because he was dancing around and shouting.

My eye was led to the opposite side of the street by a tree that had fallen across the road and although it was more difficult to see details from the bedroom window I was looking out of, it seemed that the other side of the street had suffered the same sort of damage.

I moved to the master bedroom at the front of the house with its almost panoramic view of the cul-de-sac and was given a commanding view of the devastation.

Streetlights were sparking and one was on fire, trees were lying on the ground everywhere and the boot of a car was sticking out of a considerable hole where the road led to our drive and gateway, the gate and most of the fence was just missing, as was the house opposite.

Oh dear!

Looking down the road made me decide that the two words of regret 'oh dear!' were just insufficient, dazed Humans were congregating together beyond the flaming streetlight, which was, I found out later burning because the sparks from the broken electric cables at the streetlight's base had ignited a cracked gas main.

Oh Dearie, Dearie me! I know that even adding the 'dearies' to the Oh dear, still wasn't regretful enough, but I had an awful feeling that in some obscure way I might just be responsible for the 'accident' outside, and not only the one that had involved a Range Rover and a Chrysler people carrier which had more or less just happened a little way down the cul-de-sac, probably as a result of 'runner necking'.

I traced the tracks of the tunnel I had called Harry and could see a definite path leading from our garden across to the other side of the road oddly it wasn't the straight line I had imagined it would be, it was a collection of mad curves and double backs which eventually led to the other side of the road.

I ducked back as people seemed to look at our house and disconcertingly and not a little accusingly at me. Still there was no surprise that people were looking, this house was the only one standing in the cul-de-sac as far as I could see.

I heard raised voices and they seemed to be getting closer, and so I decided that I had better jump down and hide.

When I was on the floor and out of sight I got a little, though not much of my confidence back and thought that it might be a good idea to have a look at the last tunnel, surely Dick hadn't done any damage and if it had, I was more than a little worried because it led to the electricity sub station.

As I left the bedroom I couldn't help noticing that the electric alarm clock radio was counting the minutes backwards, not a good sign, in my opinion!

At first when I peered around the bedroom curtain the path that good old Dick had taken seemed hidden.

Good old Dick I thought to myself and was just about to hop downstairs and make a bid for freedom, when the garden and the little wood which hid the electricity substation must have suffered a delayed aftershock, because the entire area subsided and sort of folded itself up, this was definitely not good.

I sat just behind the curtain on the window sill and waited transfixed, for the substation to explode, or for the broken house beyond to turn itself into an even bigger wreck than it was already, but nothing happened, and although I was disappointed, which must be an effect of too much adrenaline pumping around my body, I was nevertheless relieved that the devastation had stopped, devastating the area.

In the distance I could hear the squawk and obscenities of a very annoyed Parrot, further in the distance I was sure I could hear the disgruntled seething of an angry lynch mob, but that might have been my imagination, still thankfully, all of the background noises were quickly drowned out by the sirens of the emergence services, which bought me a little thinking time.

I was convinced that the tunnels would be traced back, passed an abandoned Jackhammer through some broken floorboards to a particular under stairs cupboard, and that worried me. It didn't seem as though I was going to wriggle out of this one and I spent several minutes examining excuses and concocting alibis.

'The Parrot made me do it,' yes that was by far and away the best excuse, well I could hardly blame the Dog, he was outside at the time, mmmh that's a good one, I wish that was my alibi!

'Yes it was the Parrot, he is a fundamentalist Parrot and he has been blackmailing me for ages, ordering me to do terrible things, and I had to do them, because I was so very frightened, and why was I frightened, well it is a long story, and I am ashamed of myself really, but about three months ago I accidentally upset my bowl of milk while I was drinking from it and he said that if I didn't do exactly what he told me to do then he would tell everyone that I had broken the bowl and spilt milk everywhere deliberately.'

Well I was horrified, as you can imagine, being such a good, polite and well behaved Cat and although I pleaded with him he wouldn't listen and I just had to commit ever more terrible deeds for the black hearted avian.

'By the way could I sit on your lap for safety?' I am very cuddly and of course sublimely innocent!

Yes that should do the trick; no one will believe the Parrot especially as he is covered in enough forensics to ensure his guilt.

Now I can relax and enjoy the work of the emergency services with a clear conscience, mmmh I wonder if I will be evacuated?

In no time at all swirling everywhere were well trained professionals accompanied by not only their blue flashing lit vehicles but also other vans and cars belonging to the gas and water companies with yellow flashing lights.

It was all in all a rather good turn out, and I was not only secretly excited but also impressed that I had managed to attract such a mass of busy Humans.

For the rest of the day in between practicing a limp with a glassy eyed dazed expression, I waited for someone to knock on the door, wait, and then realise that I was all alone except for the extremely sooty and guilty Parrot, then in the name of affecting a rescue, break the front door open and scour the house looking for the injured. Sadly no one came to rescue me and I had to be content with just watching the drama unfold from the master bedroom window.

One little piece of comfort and amusement was watching the Dog who had been loose in the garden as he ran around barking at the people outside and generally doing what he does best which is to be a nuisance and getting in the way at every opportunity, until tee hee, he was tied to a tree by a Fireman who had obviously had quite enough of his antics.

Within an hour everyone else in the cul-de-sac had been evacuated and I was feeling rather left out and ignored, because even though I had stood up and paraded up and down the window sill in full view, then, when I thought someone might have noticed me and be watching I collapsed several times, no rescuers appeared at the door.

So if I wasn't going to be rescued, and thereby possibly offered a means of escape by these unobservant Humans I decided that I might as well go and see if there was any more food in the kitchen.

On the way down to the kitchen I noticed that the black Parrot was still hanging from the hallway light fitting, shaking and shivering and I was almost sure that I could hear him muttering bang, bang, but I couldn't be sure, but to cheer him up, well ok, to shock him out of his hysteria I called up to him.

'You have really done it now, just you wait until they come and take you away!' Oddly he didn't answer, but then nothing surprises me about the rudeness of some individuals, especially individual desperados who work alone like the Parrot.

To be honest the day which had begun so 'interestingly' had sort of lost its edge and I found that I was bored and disappointed because I hadn't managed to turn the mayhem completely to my advantage, so I nibbled some food and sidled off for a well earned consolation nap.

Day 112 of My Captivity:

The aftermath of a 'major incident,' to give it the title that the Police like to use, wasn't unlike some of the other 'major incidents' that I have been in. As usual the Police seemed to outnumber all of the other experts and workmen put together and speculation dripped from the mouths of all present.

Well I think that it was speculation, which was rife outside, I can, I have to say, lip read after a fashion and that was the only way I was getting any information.

The Human Captors had got back late last night, long after my nap had turned into a rather long and deep sleep. They had expected I should think, a relaxing evening in front of the television, but instead had been treated to the Parrot caused devastation.

The Parrot had obviously been unglued from his perch and as far as I could tell had been imprisoned in his cage, but I couldn't tell if he had been washed because the cage had been covered with a large cloth, still I knew he was in the cage because it was shaking, the shaking was interesting, for ages as I watched the cloth over the cage just vibrate and then all of a sudden it would shake violently and the violent shaking would be accompanied by a crazed squawking of the word 'bang.'

Other people's suffering has never really interested me that much and try as I might to empathise with the Parrot's distress and pain I just couldn't share it.

Looking out of the bedroom window I noticed a new crop of extremely flashy cars and off road vehicles, each had carried a Police officer to the scene of the 'major incident,' probably so that they could go off and give supplementary interviews to the press and a couple of television news crews who were lurking around and it seemed to me were so obviously awaiting a fresh eruption, in this until now quiet neighbourhood.

Over where my tunnel Tom had undermined the neighbour's garden I saw both of the next door neighbours out in the devastation of their lawn and formal gardens, in between sobs they were already digging up the lawn and restoring it to its former glory.

Looking around our garden I checked for signs first, of the Human Captors doing the same, and when I was sure that they weren't because they were not around I began to notice our garden.

The garden was completely intact, unlike the neighbour's, there weren't any fallen trees, and in general the house wasn't sticking out of a large smoking hole, the garage was, but no one lives in that!

Our garden just looked like the perfect picture of tranquillity in an expanse of other people's rubble, no wonder the Human Captors had cleaned up downstairs and sloped off for the day and ignoring the small amount of destruction to most of our walls. I bet that they probably thought that it was all a little suspicious that we had 'escaped' so lightly and didn't want to be lynched by the angry neighbours who were milling around in the cul-de-sac and casting mistrustful looks at our house!

Day 113 of My Captivity:

After the sad collapse of my tunnel escape plan and indeed my tunnels, poor Tom, Dick and Harry, how I miss them, I have decided to lie low for a while, and definitely not start digging my way out again for a while!

I think that I had dug some considerable distance in all three directions! Yes I now knew that I had taken a few wrong turns and at more than one point had indeed doubled back on myself, but I was almost 'out' when disaster struck.

Still the neighbour's building work won't take long, really, just a few months I understand, certainly the noise that the builders will be making for months will quieten down eventually.

I wouldn't go so far as to say that things were quiet at our next door neighbours and at their neighbour's house, or even at the people's houses across the road, but what I can say about the people across the road is that they will almost certainly have their garden back in one piece, the trouble is that the one piece in question is a rather large pile of rubble, which is currently being bulldozed back into their garden from the road.

Anyway I am sure that I wasn't completely to blame for all of the trouble, in fact I heard the Environmental Health Officers, who carried out the inspection of what some called the 'devastation,' say that it was probably a colony of large moles responsible for the collapse of most of the street or did she say that it was probably a large colony of Moles, I forget now!

The Firemen, I overheard, had a different opinion, they thought that a group of disgruntled Badgers' had tried to get even with the inhabitants of the cul-de-sac that I live in, probably not enough bread soaked in milk had been left out for them and that to my way of thinking is a measured response on the Badger's behalf, if indeed it is true!

Lastly the Police had what I personally thought was the most imaginative reason for the carnage.

A senior Police officer was being interviewed by a shinning eyed news film crew and a Weather Lady who was filling in for a 'proper' News reporter.

Between you and me, I think that the day was obviously the opposite to a slow news day as they say in the trade, and that all of the other seasoned news reporters were off reporting 'proper' news that was possibly more earth shattering, or maybe I should rephrase that, less earth shattering, but more international!

The blonde haired Weather Lady was using her opportunity to underline her 'talent,' that in her opinion was greater than just forecasting the weather in the studio or at strange, usually windy locations throughout the country, which dishevelled her beautiful hair and buffeted her so much that she couldn't read the auto-cue properly.

Using the code that Police Officers seem to use when speaking to the Media or their bosses, the Police officer gave his, soon to be 'official' view of the destruction to the pretty weather lady and the masses of viewers, who were hanging on the every word of his live broadcast. So he took a deep breath and launched into a reading of pre-prepared nonsense Police speak!

'Although it would appear outwardly that this destruction was probably due to a burrowing animal or animals with a grudge, at this moment in time, we are not ruling out foul play and to eliminate people from our investigations we are asking that anyone who knows the residents of what was until today a nice quiet road or was working in the area to hand in their shovels and spades.'

The camera then turned to the weather lady and looked for her bewildered reply at the 'explanation,' offered. She froze and gave one of her enchanting smiles as a soft piece of blond hair fluttered by the wind glued itself to her lipstick.

She broadened her smile and waited, obviously hoping that the immaculately uniformed Senior Police Officer would be adding to his confusing statement; then she thrust the microphone back onto his silver buttoned uniform, which delivered an unexpected and delightful farting raspy noise as it slid across his uniform.

'I am sorry but at this time that is all I can say.' By which I think the Policeman was referring to the previous statement and not the farting noise!

While he was being interviewed, which I was watching through the window and on the TV simultaneously, which was pretty cool, in the background hundreds of officers were combing the road and people's gardens.

I was fairly certain that they were not looking for spades or shovels though, as they were on their hands and knees and in my experience of spades and shovels they are usually left sticking out of the garden to rust in the rain over the winter.

Other Police Officers were erecting white tents all over the place, where gardens, pavements, bits of houses or the road had disappeared into one or other of the tunnel or tunnels, or hole or holes. I personally was convinced that these subterranean caverns were too big to have been made by my tunnels.

Still whether a tunnel or tunnels etc., made by an animal or animals with a grudge, had created the mayhem or indeed a colony of large Moles or a large colony of Moles or lastly a few bad tempered Badgers I have no idea. All I could think about at this moment was actually the three tunnels, which I had dug and the awful fact that they would lead the boys in blue back to the cupboard under the stairs? Mind you I was fairly certain that the Parrot would get fingers for this one and so I wasn't that worried about the investigations outside.

Having said that I did have a vague idea that the fireworks, smoke and rumblings that I had heard and which had encouraged me to leave the tunnel in what would have been world record time, if anyone had been timing it, was followed by a very large subterranean explosion and a large amount of earth and rock falling and bouncing all along my tunnel and out of the entrance under the stairs so there was a chance that I had played some very minor part in all of this, but nothing to get het up about, surely?

Secretly I believe that I was lucky to get out of the tunnel alive and even luckier to be able to watch the great circus that is now still going on outside. This is the first time that there have been cameras and news crews in the cul-de-sac, and I am sure that we have never had so many people in the road at one time, this is after all a nice quiet neighbourhood usually.

It was amazing, even the Army turned out at one point. All very exciting!

Happily for the benefit of very frightened residents of the cul-de-sac the official Police 'line' would be changed later by a government spokesperson with a smattering of a moustache and tweeds.

She said 'candidly' (a number of times) that the whole problem had been the result of ancient sewers collapsing, sewers that in fact were commissioned by a previous government and then neglected for years.

In her 'candid' opinion it was a fact that the whole problem was a time bomb waiting for her government to sort out, not that there would be any public money to repair the road, but the government of the day fully and 'candidly' supported the residents in all other areas.

By the time her interview had finished I was confused, why were the residents in all other areas to be supported and not the poor residents of our cul-de-sac?

Unfortunately I never got to find out the reason. She was a big lady and went off to lunch with the Senior Police Officer early, and was never seen in the cul-de-sac ever again.

DAY 114 OF MY CAPTIVITY:

Crafty is not a word I would readily use to describe myself – 'worldly wise' sounds so much nicer but there are times when one has to be either or both.

When the Police came to the door as part of their 'house to house' enquiries, I decided it was time to make myself scarce.

I have always liked the Captor's master bedroom, and although at the moment one wall is covered in industrial weight plastic sheeting and bangs violently like a sail even in a light breeze, I decided that it might be a good idea to go and use the wonderful expanse of their king size bed for a nap.

Well, to be honest, I decided to sleep on the bit of the bed that is furthest away from the new plastic wall, which I have to say I hope is temporary or at least just a designer fad that has gripped the trendy Captor's imagination, or what passes for imagination for them.

I chose that bit of the bed because the other side is very damp, in fact one of the Humans used the word 'sopping' (which I personally thought was very accurate) to describe the other side of the bed and the carpet, not to say draughty as well.

It is inconvenient not to have a roof, although I have to say in all of the mayhem and confusion of the other day I didn't notice that we didn't have a roof, honestly this is really the first time I have noticed that the house is mainly roofless, but then recently I have had other things on my mind, although I am almost certain that we did have a roof once and therefore I have concluded that this house or prison as I usually refer to it, was rather more seriously affected by the little problem of the other day than I had initially thought.

Still looking on the bright side of all of this and it is difficult not to look on the bright side of life when the sun is shining through the roof and one is lying in a patch of warm sun, the builders are very good and I am sure that the roof will be back on in the not too distant future! Well I hope it will be because looking through the roof now I can see large fluffy clouds beginning to clog together and threaten rain.

All of which made me decide on one course of action, I would find another room to sleep in, but upstairs, well upstairs until the Police had gone!

Day 115 of My Captivity:

Today I began praying, so you can see just how desperate to escape I have become, because in my opinion prayer is the last bastion of the frantic, and churches are the twilight homes of the hysterical, which of course is why I was praying hard, everything else seems to have failed.

Really, who in their right minds would put their hands together, close their eyes and whisper (usually aloud) to someone or something who they have never met, never seen and are unlikely to accomplish either, daft if you ask me, but I guess nobody will ask me.

If you ask me, it is like believing in fairies to 'believe,' but Humans do 'believe' which is funny really, you'll never catch a Cat believing in anything except the meal they have in front of them! Believers also like to let you know that they 'believe' with large demonstrations of their devoutness (if that is a word),

Shame they don't do that sort of thing quietly, like I do when I am going to the toilet somewhere I am pretty sure I shouldn't!

Still enough of that sort of blaspheme, if I am not careful I'll have all the Bible thumpers in the world declaring in their ministries that it is ok to have fur coats especially ones made from 'heathen' Cats and we wouldn't want a witch hunt would we?

Day 116 of My Captivity:

I have not really felt myself today; I ache and think that I must have fallen asleep in a draft because I have a stiff neck. It hurts to write as well, so I won't tell you about falling asleep on the washing machine, or the odd fun of being woken up on a full spin cycle.

Then transferring to the back doormat, which looked so very plummy comfortable and inviting, but is there because it obviously stops the back door letting in a draft. So I am going to find somewhere that is warm, comfortable and welcoming, you wouldn't like to nurse a Cat on your lap for a while would you?

Day 117 of My Captivity:

It goes without saying that I have been up for a while, but I don't feel too tired, my back hurts too much for that, and I have been sneezing as well, not just normal sensible sneezes either, I have been sneezing so violently that my knees go weak and the room spins. I don't feel well at all!

I had a bit of a sleep on the Sofa earlier and now that I have woken up at least I feel a little warmer, but the trouble is I think I have a temperature and to feel a little warmer is not good, is it?

My back still hurts and although it is nowhere near as uncomfortable as it was, it is not something I would wish on many people - that should be, it is not something I would wish on anyone, but hey my back hurts!

I think that I am going to try and go back to sleep, I do wish that someone would light the log fire and then I could curl up in front of it, but I am not that fortunate. The Human Captors are out, with the Dog and the Parrot, who sadly has made a full recovery from his recent trauma, is mimicking my sneezes and laughing.

The only thing I can do is to lie on top of the television, which luckily is still warm after the morning dose of mindless breakfast television.

Actually it is a shame that the television is not still on, I could use some brainlessly excited morning television chatter to ensure that I fell asleep quickly through boredom or even one of those 'in-depth' exposés that even I know are about as original and as toothless a bagpuss Pyjama case, and I am a Cat remember!

Day 118 of My Captivity:

I am still feeling peeky and pale and I decided that it would be a thoroughly good idea to go back to bed and have a lie in upstairs on undeniably the most comfortable bed in the house. Made even more comfortable because the builders have finished doing their, um, building and we are apparently all looking forward with bated breath, and some of us with short tempers to the decorators starting work.

As usual the Male Captor has annoyed the tradesmen, namely in this case, the decorators, who were due to start work yesterday, when they telephoned with, in my opinion, a perfectly reasonable excuse for a minor delay.

After a lot of apologising to the Female Captor they explained that their van had exploded, they didn't go into details and say whether the vehicle had exploded on its own without any help, or whether it had been the subject of a terrorist attack, they did say that they would be delayed by a week, all of which the Female Captor seemed to understand, sympathise and I feel take the reasonable attitude that we were lucky we had a roof over our heads, unlike some neighbours, I might add, but only quickly to brush that 'incident' under the carpet as quickly as possible!

The trouble started when she explained the decorator's problem to the Male Captor over breakfast, he went ballistic, which is when the Dog and I decided to go make ourselves scarce just in case we were implicated in the cause of his outburst!

Even from their bedroom, with the door closed I could hear the ranting and raving about the standard and reliability of tradesmen today, incidentally I imagine that the builders, who were finishing the roof, could also hear the accusations of shiftiness and laziness heaped upon every workman in the world, well I think that is why the hammering noise in the roof grew louder to an annoying brain aching pitch for a while, then it stopped abruptly and shortly afterwards several white vans pulled out of the drive at what could only be described as a 'protest' speed with the Male Captor running after them shouting, 'come back right now!'

Still it was nice to have a bit of peace and quiet lying on their bed, I just wish that I felt better and could enjoy the comfort completely.

I just couldn't settle! I was worried about my health! I am not usually ill, or indeed this pale. I stood up on the bed, poked my tongue out and tried to see in it her dressing table Mirror, I couldn't see anything wrong, but then I couldn't see my tongue properly and so I hopped from the bed to the dressing table for a closer look.

Looking in the small freestanding mirror that sits on the dressing table for a closer inspection, it appeared that my face had swollen terribly, which worried me, the shock I might add nearly made me faint, but then I noticed I was looking at the magnifying side of the double sided mirror, well I was relieved for that small mercy.

I stood on a few tubes of makeup stuff and leaned towards the larger mirror and that confirmed my worse nightmare, I was looking peeky as well as feeling it, sadly I am not a doctor and so I have no idea what illness has 'peeky' as its main symptom, but whatever it was, I had it and by the looks of it, a bad case of 'it.'

Maybe it was some sort of epidemic and I was a carrier, that thought alarmed me and I decided that the last thing I needed was to be responsible of an epidemic or worse a pandemic, whatever one of those is and so I thought I would try and disguise my peekiness.

For a few seconds I slapped my face to try and get some colour into it, and the when that didn't seem to work I bashed it into the mirror, but that was even more useless, there had to be something that I could do I decided and looked around for a solution!

Later after an accident with some bronzing mist belonging to the Female Captor, in my opinion the bronzing mist had been left carelessly where a fool, worried about its pale features could get its paws on, I decided that the bronzing mist had been more of a disaster than a solution, I have now learned an important lesson though, a curious Cat and a full bottle of tanning solution should never be left together unattended!

Having said that for a while every time I looked in the mirror I thought that a Tiger was standing in front of me, now that is off putting, but frankly not as off putting as a Tiger standing behind you in a mirror.

If a Tiger is ever standing behind me, I think that I would prefer not to know, but most of all I think that I would prefer not to be a strange and haunting shade of orange.

Looks are a strange thing, and although I am now orange, apparently it will wear off eventually. I feel so much better and have to say I definitely don't look peeky at all!

DAY 119 OF MY CAPTIVITY:

I am avoiding the Male Captor, for a couple of reasons; firstly he is still annoyed about the disappearance of all the builders and other tradesmen.

Apparently his opinions on tradesmen got around the entire building and decorating community and this house has been blackballed.

Secondly the mess that I made in their bedroom was kindly (in my opinion) put down to a faulty bottle of tanning solution by the Female Captor when she explained to him why we had large orange brown stains all over the place, the new carpet will be laid when the tradesmen's embargo of this household is lifted.

So as you can imagine a small Feline whose new colour matches the stains in the bedroom probably wouldn't be the most popular animal in the town, let alone the house.

Lastly I am in hiding from the Parrot and the Dog both of whom didn't stop laughing until they began making, in my opinion 'silly' comments about the Cheshire Cat and asking me when I was going to make just my body disappear and leave my head floating in mid air.

Well I did more than make my body disappear, I disappeared, up to the attic, where the Female Captor brings me my meals and gives me a nice stroke until the orange brown colour comes off in her hands. I have no idea just how many times I have been washed and shampooed, but for the moment I have given up having a Cat wash because all I can taste is tanning solution and soap, ugh!

DAY 120 OF MY CAPTIVITY:

During my forced asylum in the attic I have been able to think, and good news for all my readers, write more of my Diary, please don't cheer too loud, it looks odd if you are reading this and cheering on public transport or at the beach and I am sure that you wouldn't want to be locked up in a prison for loonies would you?

So here are some of my thoughts, these are about languages, Human of course!

Notes on a foreign language

People in other countries don't speak English, what a shock that was, even the ones that do speak English like America and Australia seem to have a few problems with things like the pronunciation of some words and spelling them, but that is another matter and doesn't concern me here.

Fancy people speaking other languages in other countries! Neatly these other languages seem to be named after the people of that country, like Spain and Spanish, although they seem to have misspelt Spanish by losing an 'I' somewhere!

But then thinking about it, the language being named after the people is a really good idea and I suppose English is the same; well it is probably where the idea came from. It must be very confusing if you are American, Canadian, Australian or New Zealandian (I suppose a group of New Zealanders are New Zealandians) though, because their language is English and not named after the country that they live in, poor things.

Worse still, America seems to be becoming a bi-lingual country, but not like say Belgium where the people speak French and their own brand of nonsense, in America half the people speak Spanish and half don't, I wonder why?

What is wrong with speaking Spanish in America? It isn't as though they have a language of their own to protect is it? Like, say, French, which is slowly dying, except for a hardcore enclave of French speakers in, of all places Canada.

The world is a very funny old place isn't it? But I have decided to learn a language and I am slowly making rather limited progress with Russian and you never know in ten or twenty years time I maybe able to not speak it properly and be misunderstood whenever I speak to any Russians.

In Russia when they want to say goodnight they like to use two words instead of one, but they do that a lot I have heard, and they say Dobroy nochi. Dobroy means Good I think but I am not too sure.

They do the same in Poland, the Poles, yes apparently they have talking poles there, but that is another story, they say Dobry vecher or something similar when they say Good Evening, so Dobroy must be common to both languages, now this started to make me wonder if it was the same in Czech, Ukrainian, and say Romanian, but then I thought to myself do I really care! No I don't!

Day 121 of My Captivity:

Even in the attic I keep losing things and it is getting a little worrying! What have I lost? Well my mind soon, I think, if I don't find my mobile phone! Mobile phone I hear you cry in astonishment! A Cat with a mobile phone, really whatever next, or words to that affect, coupled with no doubt a smattering of questions such as.

What does a Cat want with a mobile phone for goodness sake? And what is the world coming to? No doubt!

Well I have my reasons! And most importantly I have worked out how to use the keypad to make calls, no obviously not to Humans, well not a normal Human anyway!

Indeed I have great hopes for this unusual Human who I found on the web (the internet to all of you Humans who are not as computer literate as me), being as you know a 'Wired Wussy' (which is still a Cat for those of you with memories like mine, and don't remember what on earth I am talking about and worse still keep losing things, but please bear with me, because I am trying to create a few catch phrases in the Diary it is good for sales I understand).

This Human called Mr. John Woodcock is a translator, and not just any normal ordinary translator working from say English into Russian or any of those other strange Human languages, which look as though they contain a series of squashed flies in a line, oh no! This brilliant Human can translate and speak Cat reasonably well (although his accent is a little odd).

Yes that is what I thought, it is odd talent, and really shows that he should have got out more, but who cares about that? I have finally found someone 'with whom' (do you like that, 'with whom,' my translator taught me that!) I can communicate to the outside world with (Oops the grammar slipped badly there, but never mind I am only a Cat you know!).

Not only is Mr. Woodcock a translator, he knows an American lawyer who he thinks maybe able to help me publish my Diary, this doesn't get any better doesn't it?

(Author's Note: The entry above was written before I spent months, which is Human speak for a very long time, and even longer for a Cat I might add, dealing with Mr. Woodcock, who quite frankly I have found to be more of a pedantic curse than a blessing, but I am stuck with him now because there are not any other Cat speakers or translators to choose from, don't worry I have tried to find a replacement, but sadly failed!)

Apparently over the next few days we are going to have a conference call, Mr. Woodcock, the American lawyer and I, and so finding my mobile phone is something of a priority now, wouldn't you agree?

Oh you want to know how I got a mobile phone! What is it with you? Just can't take my word for it? Really dear reader I am surprised, I have told you before Cats don't lie, we can't, mind you Cats do know how to bend the truth until it looks like one of those bows that people wear on their lapels (when they want to demonstrate to everybody that they are supporting a Charity), if the need to bend the truth is great enough.

Day 122 of My Captivity:

At last I am out of solitary confinement and not a moment too soon, it seemed like I had been 'banged up' for at least month! You can't imagine how long a few days seem to a Cat who lives seven of your years in one of his own!

Although my effort to kill the Male Captor by weaving myself around his legs while he was walking failed, I did manage to make him trip and swear a lot and this encouraged me enough to think about trying this at the top of the stairs sometime in the future.

If I could get rid of the Captors then I might be able to at least enjoy my captivity a little more, we will see how successful I am, although just killing them wouldn't actually get me out of here and I imagine after a while a couple of dead Captors would start to go all squidgy and smell, so maybe it wouldn't be such a bright idea after all!

Of course thinking about it, it would be so much better to bag a brace of Humans at the same time at the top of the stairs, in fact that would be just like shooting a pair of Pheasants only using both barrels of a double barrelled shotgun and that is apparently quite a feat, although I have no idea why it is so clever, it is not as though the Pheasants are shooting back is it?

Actually there is a great similarity between Humans and Pheasants, they are both stupid, the unfortunate thing is that the Humans have the shotguns, well, that is unfortunate for the unarmed Pheasants.

Shall we all go upstairs?

Day 123 of My Captivity:

There was great excitement today, the builders, the decorators and the carpet fitters all turned up together, for a mass telling off by the Male Captor, well I don't think that is what they thought that they were turning up for, but it is what they got, and they were none too happy about it I can tell you, and an enormous fight ensued, which was one sided and fascinating to watch.

The Male Captor was outnumbered completely, well the Dog, it has to say, was on the side of his master and I am pretty sure that it was in no small way due to his growling, teeth baring and general snarling that the combined forces of the builders, decorators and carpet fitters didn't end up resorting to a bit of 'knuckle arguing' to settle the dispute in a 'manly' way.

The Dog shocked me, I have to be honest; he was like one of those famous rap stars who are weighted down by several pounds of bling and have an attitude as bad as their breath, or is that his breath – don't know and don't care actually!

The Dog decided that if the builder's, decorator's and carpet fitter's alliance was going to start getting the agreement going with some slapping, then he was going to bite a few of them and counter their points of principle with a few points of his own, namely his Canines.

Things were getting heated with the Dog and the Male Captor miles ahead in the red faced shouting at the top of your voice competition, when suddenly the Dog was left making all of the noise on his own, and took full advantage of the centre of the stage to press his argument home.

Until he realised that no one was taking any notice anymore, because the builders, decorators and Carpet fitters were giving the Male Captor CPR and a chest massage. By the way if you don't know what CPR is and I have to say I didn't until today it is Cardiopulmonary Resuscitation there you did ask didn't you!

The fool had obviously overdone the shouting and had what I believe is called a lard'o heart'o drama or a Heart attack in his case and judging by the amount of fatty food he is constantly munching the former name is more probably more accurate.

You know, I have to say that I was impressed by the builders, decorators and Carpet fitters' knowledge of first aid, dressed in their dusty paint splattered overalls they would have passed as paramedics in most underdeveloped countries!

Personally I think the biggest contribution to the 'event' was provided by one of the Carpet fitters who grabbed the telephone and ordered an Ambulance, but then that is just my opinion and as I said I don't have any knowledge what so ever about first aid, except to say here that a plaster can be very difficult to get off your fur if you happen to break open the first aid box and shred the contents, but I hardly think that bit of information is relevant here or indeed particularly useful!

This simple task of calling an Ambulance was made more difficult by the fact that none of the builders, decorators and Carpet fitters knew the exact address of where they were and the emergency operator decided that she was talking to a bunch of three year olds, making a crank call, and kept, by the sound of it asking the carpet fitter, if his Mummy or Daddy was still breathing and was there an adult with him who she could speak to?

DAY 124 OF MY CAPTIVITY:

We are all really worried here, about the poor Male Captor, but what an exit, you have to hand it to him, if you are going to invent a really neat way to get out of being beaten up by several angry builders, decorators and Carpet fitters then a lard'o heart'o drama is 'the' way to escape serious bruising.

Well actually to be honest with you, I personally am not that worried about the Male Captor, every day people across the world are having lard'o heart'o dramas according to Heart Charities, who are always collecting loads of money for them and because those charities always seem to need to collect ever larger amounts of money for the lard'o heart'o drama sufferers they must all survive lard'o heart'o drama.

And of course it almost goes without saying that the Dog with his attention span, which comes a close second to a backward Goldfish suffering from amnesia, has completely forgotten that there was any such person as the Male Captor.

Come to think of it the Female Captor is probably just a little too busy organising the builders, decorators and Carpet fitters, to miss him just yet either, because while he is away in hospital everyone has agreed that it would be best to get all of the work finished and not have to bump into him again, just in case one of the builders, decorators and Carpet fitters decides to bump into the Male Captor with a right hook followed by several combination punches!

In his condition after a lard'o heart'o drama the Male Captor might just die and that would be a pity all round and mean that the builders, decorators and Carpet fitters probably wouldn't get paid for all of their hard work.

So all in all I am guessing that no one is actually missing the Male Captor, but I am sure that we wish him well, although again I can't say that I am totally committed to that statement because personally I never liked the guy, but that is a personal opinion and I am not, I stress, speaking for anyone else, still I just have to tell you that the Dog has just asked who were are all talking about!

I haven't had time to canvass any other opinions and so I think I will just leave this subject there and not venture into it further because there has to be someone somewhere who misses the Male Captor, maybe his mother? But then again I keep having to ask myself this large and very important question when I consider the above – do I give a damn? And the answer is no!

Day 125 of My Captivity:

I have never seen anything so ridiculous in all my life, well that is not entirely true, because I saw the Male Captor in ski pants once, but this is the second most ridiculous thing I have ever seen.

What are the creators of television cartoons thinking of? Why am I asking that question? Well because these creative 'geniuses' have created Mice who almost always beat Cats! No I wouldn't believe it either unless of course I had seen it with my own eyes.

Tom and Jerry is the most disgusting example, Itchy and Scratchy in the Simpsons are a more violent and just plain awful example of my point, but as they are a copy/homage to the Tom and Jerry original I don't think that they are so important.

What I thought was important was to investigate further this Human horror story of misinformation and to that end I got myself comfortable on the Sofa and watched Children's television till my eyes ached and my brain began to die in an agony of inaneness or is that inanity, I am not sure?

All I knew for certain was that I had seen enough; did you know that there is a Mouse who is 'supposedly' the cutest cartoon character ever, a Mouse?

That dreadfully popular dreadful little squirt with the squeaky voice is called Mickey Mouse, he sounds gay, in fact he sounds as though he needs taking down a peg or two, maybe there should be a spin off television series of this Diary, based on the fact that Mickey Mouse has Films, Television and so much more and he is not even half as good looking or one tenth as interesting as, well me, although to my way of thinking Mickey Mouse would look better on Radio.

Surely an astonishingly good looking Cat like me, with all of the obvious charm and good natured humour that I have, would make a brilliant cartoon character? And I would like to say here and now, I am sure that my face will look better on toothbrush mugs, bedspreads, wallpaper and pyjamas than that a dreadful Mouse's does!

Something has to be done to reverse the idea that Humans seem to have, that Mice are stronger, better and more intelligent than Cats, for goodness sake we are stronger, better, more intelligent, cuddlier, better looking and usually not smelly at all, (although some Cats do let themselves go a little sometimes and let the side down there I have to admit) still I am sure that we all are cleverer.

I say put the Mice back in the laboratories where they belong. Let the Cats eat Prawns and sit in the most comfortable seats in the house; Cats deserve nothing less than the best.

This message was brought to you by 'FARTC, Freedom And Respect for The Cat,' it is just as well it is an organisation for Cats, because if it wasn't, our acronym would be just F.A.R.T., and that would be embarrassing!

F.A.R.T.Cat, is a not for profit organisation, which I have to say may still change its name. It has been set up to protect and promote the interests of Cats all over the planet and so that you Humans don't get left out in the cold, will allow you to send money to support its global good works.

I have to stress as the founder and main beneficiary of the F.A.R.T.Cat fund that it is important that you send money now, because all of your friends have probably sent large sums of money already, but are too modest to say so and you wouldn't want to be left out would you?

You will be supporting a wonderful endeavour and spreading joy and happiness to this Cat and in the future probably many Cats will benefit from your continuing generosity.

DAY 126 OF MY CAPTIVITY:

Today was a momentous day! We had our conference call, between my translator, Mr. Woodcock and an American gentleman.

The gentleman in question, or as we writers say, my Agent, is a Mr. T. A. Leibowitz, 'call me Todd,' who said after reading a few sample pages that he can easily get my Diary published! I am in Cat heaven, which is the same as Hog heaven but much cleaner and a lot nicer in general.

The conference call conversation started well with introductions, Mr. Woodcock was beginning to formally introduce me to Mr. Leibowitz but Mr. Leibowitz's natural enthusiasm took over, and before Mr. Woodcock had got passed, 'this is Mr.'

Mr. Leibowitz announced I am Mr. T. A. Leibowitz, 'call me Todd,' (which you have to admit is a long name, but he is an American Human and they tend to be different to any other Humans I have heard, much friendlier!) then he announced, 'I loved the book when can I have the manuscript, and get the presses rolling?' (That made me panic a little).

Apparently Mr. Woodcock had already sent excerpts from my Diary to Mr. T. A. Leibowitz, 'call me Todd,' and he 'digs' it a lot, and said that he had been doing some 'ball park' figures and we could apparently get a good return with this concept as the gross margin is high with a novelty book with merchandising potential, I honestly couldn't see the novelty value myself but an agent knows about these things and I don't.

The above sentences are the highlights of Mr. T. A. Leibowitz, 'call me Todd, fast-talking and the only bits I can remember!

I began to discover all sorts of things that I didn't know, and my head was spinning with all of the 'agent speak,' so I just started to nod a lot, which during a telephone conversation is not very sensible.

But no one seemed to mind that I was quiet at all and Mr. T. A. Leibowitz, 'call me Todd,' and Mr. Woodcock seemed content to discuss percentages and deadlines without me being involved, except, as I said to nod and they kindly seemed to take my general and constant silence as agreement anyway.

You know I am so happy and I actually feel as though we are really getting somewhere now. Although I did stress that, as this was a Diary maybe it would be a good idea to get to the end of the year and therefore the end of the Diary before we go to print!

Mr. T. A. Leibowitz, 'call me Todd,' reluctantly agreed when he couldn't persuade me to 'go with' what I have written and make the second half of the year a sequel.

DAY 127 OF MY CAPTIVITY:

Today I woke up feeling happy and enthusiastic about the future for the first time in a very long while, soon I would be a rich and successful published author and that was fine by me.

In fact I was so pleased with life that I was up bright and early and doing a bit of Feline nosing around when I noticed that 'their' ensuite bathroom door was open, well to give it its full title I suppose one should call it an ensuite bath and shower room, although it does have a toilet in it too and so I suppose, yes I agree I will stop there and I understand that you have got the picture!

Between you and me, I am always a little careful around the edges of baths, they seem very shiny and not a little slippery, and I think that if you slipped into even an empty bath you wouldn't have much in the way of a hope of getting out again until you were rescued and that would make the sneaking around a lot less fun, knowing that your activities had been discovered.

The risk of being discovered is bad enough when you accidentally knock all of the bottles and cans of lotions and potions off the ensuite bathroom shelf, although when they are lying on the floor it is easier to check them out, I have to say.

I discovered Baby Oil today, nasty smelly greasy stuff, I would like to know just how hard you have to squeeze a baby to get oil out of it?

The trouble with Baby Oil, apart from the pain of manufacture for babies, is that I just for the life of me couldn't work out what it is for, and so I just left the jumble of bottles and cans in the middle of the ensuite bath shower room and slopped off to find something more interesting to investigate!

DAY 128 OF MY CAPTIVITY:

With an agent keen to get my Diary published I thought I would spend today checking out how much I have written and how much I still have to write.

This proved to be a real chore and a little disappointing because to my reckoning I have still quite a lot of writing to do and with that in mind I thought that I would press on with the hard work, after all the sooner I get the Diary written the sooner I can get out of here, unless of course one of my escape plans works and I am able to write my Diary from somewhere other than this prison.

After counting the number of words I found that I have written over 110,000 words give or take a few here and there, and have well over 300 contiguous (think that is the right word, I tried contagious but that looked wrong) pages, which is pretty good because it is always best not to have too many blank pages in a book, I would think that to many blank pages would make the readers lose heart if they keep coming across empty pages when they are reading.

Still having a few empty pages hidden in the book/Diary might be fun and it would also stop those dreadful people who have a habit of reading on ahead.

DAY 129 OF MY CAPTIVITY:

Being someone who possesses both a scientific and inquiring mind I know that nose hair grows in one's nose for a good reason because it has evolved that way.

Noses have to have hair in them so that the dust and muck from everyday life is filtered out when we breathe, unless of course one breathes through ones mouth and pants, like a casual and not very committed nuisance telephone caller.

I have another theory about nose hair though, I think that it grows in one's nose to annoy you, especially when it grows so long that it peeps out of a nostril and tickles it.

If the tickling just stopped at tickling it wouldn't be so bad, but it doesn't, does it? The annoying and wayward hair or hairs can make one's life a misery, constantly irritating one of the most sensitive parts of a Cat or I suppose Human (although I have to say I am not so concerned about Human's comfort).

On and on the tickling goes, the wayward hair touching the end of your nostril until you decide to do the unthinkable (and for Cats almost impossible) and try to pull the hair out, with all of the eye watering pain, that you know is going to be attached to that action, and even if you do resort to that desperate attempt at relief, you know that you are going to disturb other hairs which will start poking out and begin the tickling all over again!

Thinking about this annoying and uncomfortable fact of life for a moment. Maybe we fellows of the scientific community are wrong, and nose hair is not a result of evolution and the creationists, who believe that everything that is, and was for that matter, has been created by God is correct, and God did in fact create us and the hair in our noses, even the unruly ones, hairs that is, not noses, although noses can get unruly but I haven't got the space, time or patience to get into unruly noses at the moment! So we'll go back to God and nose hair.

If it is so and God knocked up the planet and all around and did it in a week and therefore God is responsible for everything in creation and in particular nose hair I would like to pose a question. What sort of God lets nose hair grow the wrong way and what have we done to deserve the constant irritation of tickly hairs growing out of our noses?

And it doesn't stop there the question of what was God doing?

Why did 'He' or indeed 'She,' (because no one really knows what God is), create some famous people?

Imagine if God had not fancied working on the day that he created Adolf Hitler, what a better place the world would have been, or if he 'had' to create Adolf Hitler for some strange concept of balance why didn't he let his chisel slip and create a Female Human, they at least are not as well known for declaring world wars, are they?

Using this train of thought I had endless hours, (well minutes) of fun slightly amending some of God's creations, I recommend it as a game to be played by all of the family, if that is, you want to let God create all of your family in the first place!

Then there is the 'get out clause' if anything that God has created is not very nice, like the pastry around a Profiteroles, you can say, because you believe in God, that whatever you don't like is the work of the devil, who must exist, because if God exists, and he created everything then the Devil exists, (sadly and obviously created by God).

Armed with these examples to be brutal honesty, you can see why Creationists believe in the Theory of Creation, because you can change the truth of just about anything with a little bit of God's (and the Devil's) help and a quick prayer or two, and if it all goes wrong you can blame the guy or girl downstairs in Hell, because God must have had an off day if he/she created something that is not so nice and left it for the Devil to play with!

Frankly and all things being considered, I think that I will stick with Evolution and the fact that what I do, I do because I want to, and that when I do 'it' I know what the consequences are likely to be and therefore that I am responsible for my actions.

At least a part of my conscience is clear and I don't pass the blame onto someone else even if that someone else is God, poor soul he must have the weight of the world on his shoulders with all the naughty wrongdoers around. I am surprised that he doesn't give up and go and get another job or better still go and create another world somewhere else, where he won't make the same mistakes again! Of course that is assuming that God exists, and sadly that is where we came in isn't it!

DAY 130 OF MY CAPTIVITY:

Thank goodness that the both of the Captors were both out this morning because a package arrived for me today; it was enormous, almost too heavy for the Dog to carry it to my study for me.

Happily my sharp claws and teeth made light work of the wrapping, although it took me a long while to get rid of all of the bubble wrap, there was metres of it, and whenever I tried to grab a bit and move it, it just kept popping all over the place in my paws.

A number of times my claws got hooked in the stuff and I fell over making even more popping sounds as I landed.

Just when I thought that I had the infernal stuff under control and was about to finally pull it free from the mountain of paper (which apparently is a contract), I slipped on the slippery bubble wrap and together we flew through the air landing in a crumpled heap with the dreadful bubble warp covering me in a popping shroud.

Because of static electricity the bubble wrap stuck to my fur, when I tried to move, it just popped and popped, I managed a few steps once I had regained my balance and must have looked like a bubble wrapped Mummy because the Dog who had settled down on the carpet next to where I was unwrapping the parcel, well trying to unwrap the parcel to be more precise, began to look terrified and backed away.

Every time I thought that I had the bubble wrap under some sort of control another setback occurred, usually accompanied by a lot of popping, who would have thought that some clown in a brown coat somewhere in a shipping warehouse would have stuck sticky tape to the bubble wrap?

Just when I thought that I had escaped the mummifying bubble wrap and I began to walk away I heard a slithering noise and looked back to see the dreadful stuff following me, it was a bit of a surprise, but not much phases this Cat.

On closer inspection I saw that my back leg was stuck to some tape, which some fool had used to secure the contract to the bubble wrap.

It was easily dealt with, once I had unstuck my front paws and then my nose, and finally removed the tape from my belly losing clumps of fur from wherever the tape had glued itself to me.

So at last I have my contract, and although I don't know much about contracts, I would say that if good ones are measured by weight then this is possibly perfect.

To be honest the covering letter seems to sum up all of the contents of the contract and I don't think that I will either have time to read it or can be bothered. According to the accompanying letter I have to finish the Diary and ensure the publisher has it before the end of the year so that it can 'hit' the holiday season market and Christmas.

I think that means I have to finish my Diary some time in November because of Thanksgiving which is before Christmas, trust the Americans to have two big holidays, still that means those who didn't get my book as a Thanksgiving present (and what a great Thanksgiving present it would make), can have it at Christmas time, I am sure that it would fit in most Christmas stockings, especially the industrial sized bin liner models I have seen parents use on television in commercials that advertise a traditional Yule Tide!

Still the early delivery deadline does seem odd when you think that my Diary (as it is a daily account of my life) won't be finished until the end of the year and that was when we had agreed I would finish, if you don't remember I do, because I am the one who is going to have to 'do' something to comply with the new requirement.

What makes matters worse is that Cat years are, as I thought everyone knew, much longer than Human ones! Still my Agent and Publisher both know the market and both know best, I will just have to hurry up the last few days, if you know what I mean, wink, wink!

Well I will have to 'box clever' as they say, because the contract's covering letter mentions Penalty Clauses for not delivering on time, and I may have a little fur behind my ears but even I know that a Penalty Clause for late delivery is not a healthy thing for a Cat who is a Diarist, and so it is a case of 'needs must as the devil drives.' A saying that although I don't think I fully understand, that doesn't matter, I like!

DAY 131 OF MY CAPTIVITY:

I have decided! I do that a lot have you noticed? Still this recent decision is an important decision and so I thought that I would share it with you! So here goes, I have decided that there is no point in worrying about worrying.

What was I worried about, well apart from the premature delivery of this Diary, I seem to be worried about everything and that in itself is worrying, the word worry is a bit alarming too, but worrying about worrying is desperately concerning and when I am worrying about finishing the Diary, I am too worried to write anything interesting, and that is again, yes you guessed! Worrying!

Still there has to be some way around a spate of unwelcome worrying and that is to write about what happened today, after all that is what a Diary is all about and I promise that I will make it as interesting as I can.

Here goes!

Today the Female Human Captor stayed in and didn't go off to work or wherever she goes when she brings back large carrier bagfuls of shopping, and so my routine was disrupted which is not good, I quite like a routine that does just that and stays routine, and I don't think I am alone in that view, all Cats like routine.

Routine after all is handy, and offers the opportunity to do the important things in life, like sleep and eat at the usual times, but it also lulls others and when saying 'others' I mean Humans into a false sense of security, and that is the exact time when a clever Cat can turn life to his or her advantage.

The reason why the Female Captor stayed at home today was to make sure that the radiator repair man could have a look at some radiators, it strikes me as odd that he would want to do that as he must get to see a fair number of radiators during his working week, but maybe our radiators are special!

I am guessing but there was also another reason for the Female Captor staying home too and that was to make sure that I did too, I have a reputation for charging at the open door when visitors arrive and have to be locked in securely, more's the pity!

The radiator repairman arrived and sauntered around the house with a noisy bag of tools, stopping every so often to do just what his title suggested he would do, which I suppose was handy, though unlike the last radiator repairman, who was called to look at some problem valves. This one 'reseated,' a few valves, and before you ask, no I have no idea what 'reseating' the valve means, the other man just fitted new valves which was better in my opinion, but then what do I know?

I am supposing that 'reseating' a valve means that you have to make the valve sit properly, it is a shame that valves can't get comfortable on their own, but there you go, that is valves for you. Honestly what can we do with the younger generation of valves?

As it turned out in the end it was rather handy that the radiator repairman was here, because after I had got bored watching him I disappeared into the main bathroom and continued a little game that I have been playing with the taps, I know I have done this before a while ago, but it is such a good game that I am hooked, so humour me.

As you also know for sometime I have been trying to work out why water comes out of taps, unfortunately this sort of game makes one more than a little wet, but despite that a dripping tap is a very interesting thing to a curious Cat like say, me!

Sadly the tap in the main bathroom wasn't dripping and so I set about the task of making it drip. I have watched the Humans turn a tap on and if they can do it, then it can't be that difficult can it?

After a while I had to admit that it is a real skill to get a tap to work, but I persevered, well I hadn't got anything else to do today.

In the end I managed to turn the tap on but I was immediately soaked from the top of my head to the tip of my tail! The water was doing the, see if I can create a fountain several feet, high trick. Ok well maybe it is very funny to watch, but it isn't so funny if you are the bedraggled dripping one in the middle of it all, I have to say.

Water was going everywhere and I was trying as hard as I could to stop it, so hard I nearly got my nose stuck in the hole where the water comes out and that hurt.

I was now beyond wet and getting just a little angry with the reluctance of the tap to do what it was being encouraged to do, and I lost my cool, now isn't that rare, especially as I was being drowned in cold water.

When I hit the tap I was shocked to see the top fly off and an even bigger fountain gush out of the bit that was left, but then I suppose I shouldn't have hit the tap with a hammer, still it wasn't my fault the radiator repairman shouldn't have left his bag of tools in the main bathroom, because if he hadn't then I wouldn't have been able to use his hammer would I?

Still at least he had finished reseating the radiator valves when he started work on his new project, which was to save the house from flooding, so you can see what a good job it was he was here, and to think of it, what a good job he left his tool bag in the main bathroom or the leak might not have been discovered until he was on his way home in his little blue van.

I wonder what 'overtime' is, because whatever it is he told the Female Captor that he was going to have to do a lot of it to repair the tap.

It was a shame that I seemed to be the only one who was in a reasonably good mood, judging by the attitude of both Humans, the radiator repairman it seemed, was missing his Wedding anniversary party and the Female Captor was moaning about the cost of all of the repairs that seemed to haunt this household.

Really some people always look on the gloomy side of life! Meanwhile I slipped away to dry out and have a sleep in the master bedroom in the last rays of sunshine, if no one else was happy, I was, dozing in my little patch of bright sunlight.

After I had drip dried on the pillows of the wonderful wide bed I slipped under the covers to get warm and have a serious sleep, it had been after all a rather eventful day and as usual after one of those days I was very sleepy!

Day 132 of My Captivity:

This is embarrassing, I know it is embarrassing because it is happening to me, I have to stress that it is the first time it has happened to me though, I promise, paw on my heart!

I am sure that what is happening is going to make people laugh at my expense and frankly that is never a nice thing to do, is it?

Oh it is all very well to laugh at some other person or Cat or even funnier to laugh at their misfortunes, but when it happens to you as they say, 'the shoe is on the other foot.'

Yes another more or less inexplicable and confusing English saying, which although it sounds reasonably sensible and accurate, unless you happen to have paws or indeed you are very unfortunate and only have one leg and therefore are short of the corresponding number of feet on which to put shoes, it is still incomprehensible at best; or at worst just completely insane!

I suppose that is why there are so many words in the English language, so that they can invent more and more abstract sayings to pour words into!

Another strange saying that I heard on the Radio the other day was, 'A stitch in time saves nine.' Now, again, just as with the saying above, that sounds perfectly sensible doesn't it? Believe it or not a whole twenty minute Radio program was devoted to the saying, you Humans are monumentally weird, from this Cat's point of view.

Thinking about the latest bit of nonsense 'a stitch in time' etc., if one (you or I that is, except it would be you because I can't do what follows), quickly sows up a small hole in a garment then one (you or I, but mainly you because of the aforementioned Cat disability), won't have to sew up a much large hole at some later date, which all sounds sensible enough.

However, have you heard or seen anyone sew up a little hole with one stitch?

How do 'they' know that it will only require nine stitches to repair the bigger hole that will eventually appear if they leave the original hole and don't sew it up in the first place?

This is all making me a little annoyed, but then that could be the constant need to scratch!

Sorry, oh that is better.

I had to completely stop writing and have a good scratch you know the sort; ears at strange angles, eyes almost closed and chin jutting out at an odd angle.

For a couple of days I have felt itchy, nothing serious, but a little more itchy than normal, but then, hey! We all get itchy now and again don't we?

Sorry I had to stop again and scratch around my ears, and then, unfortunately, as soon as that felt better, I had to scratch under my chin and then my ears yet again; I told you this was serious!

Really the need to scratch is getting a little intrusive. I will have to find out what it is that is making me itch. Wait, it is my front leg itching this time, which is of course one of the most difficult place to scratch.

It doesn't matter how you try to scratch your front leg you always fall over, still at least I am alone and there isn't anyone to witness that little pantomime and laugh at me after I end up in an itchy heap on the ground!

I wonder what it is that is making me itch so much? It could be something that I have eaten. I did steal some Dog food on the quiet earlier; well I had to, the dreadful greedy mutt had eaten my food again, no I don't like my food, awful dried stuff, but that doesn't give him license to help himself does it?

Surely it can't be his Dog food though, because all that would do is make me sick, let's face it his food usually does, even if he had done something to it like lick it all over, I don't think I would be itching, would I?

I am sure that the Dog wouldn't do anything too terrible to his food because if he did he wouldn't be able to eat it would he? But just supposing he did something like; say for instance… well I am sure you can imagine what 'he' might do if he wasn't hungry and not planning to eat what was in his bowl later, but I don't have to stoop to his level and graphically describe what he is capable of, although you can imagine it would be disgusting. Dogs are like that!

So we can rule out poisoning then, and other words that begin with 'P'! What else? Maybe I have some terrible skin complaint, after all my skin is itchy enough to complain about!

What could it be? I am more than a little – hang on!

Ooh that is better! Sorry, yes another scratching session, ears again and the bit just at the back of my neck which is yet another place that a poor little Cat can't reach on his own. Where are the Humans when they are needed?

Just like them to be missing!

Hang on! What is that at the end of my nose, ooh it is making me go cross-eyed looking at it!

Something small and black and a little shiny, now where has that come from I wonder?

Wait, now where has it gone?

One minute it was sitting on the end of my nose and the next it did a marvellous impression of a spring, it shot off my nose and vanished somewhere on 'their' bed, well 'my' bed at the moment, it vanished just when I was going to try and gently get down off the bed and carefully walk over to the mirror and try and get a closer look at it.

There it is, on the duvet cover, sitting really still probably resting from what must have been an enormous leapt for such a little 'thing.'

It is a good job that the duvet cover is a cream colour or I would never have spotted the little blighter.

Steady now! It is just out of pouncing range so I will have to use stealth!

Brilliant it didn't seem to notice me shuffle along on my belly to get closer, gently now, let's try to get into a pouncing position so that I can grab it, whatever 'it' is!

Here we go, with Cat like grace, which is only to be expected as I am a Cat, I pounced on the little black thing and all it did was to jump again, but this time not yards away but straight into the fur around my neck.

I can tell you that made me really itch and I sat up and had a jolly good 'riddle!'

When I had finished there were loads of little black specs of crunchy dust spread all over the Duvet cover, I had no idea what they were what so ever!

Anyway the little black shiny bouncy thing had vanished, I had no idea where it had gone, it was lost somewhere in my fur and that is not a nice thought, in fact just thinking about it wandering free amongst my fur made me feel really itchy and I just had to have another long scratch.

More black crunchy dust appeared, this was serious and I had a dreadful feeling in the pit of my stomach that the little black thing and the dust were connected in some way, and of course knowing my luck, not a nice way!

What was I to do? Well there was only one option and it wasn't much of an option when all things were considered!

I would have to go down and ask the Dog if it knew what I was suffering from, now my 'Dog' is not particularly good at talking or thinking for that matter and he has never bothered to learn Cat. But thinking about it, what other choice did I have though? It was chat to his Royal denseness or nothing so I had no choice as far as I could tell!

I found the Dog it didn't take much looking to be frank, he was where he seems to spend much of his life, in his bed, he was snoring and making other noises that may have come from his mouth! Wherever they came from, they began somewhere deep inside.

Waking a snoring and possibly farting Dog is something that one does not do lightly. Dogs are in my experience quite unpredictable, they are limited in their responses by… how can I put this politely so as not to offend Dogs and Dog lovers? Unfortunately after thinking about it, there isn't a way to be polite. Dogs are really rather thick and so their responses are limited.

Hold up food and they will sit, if that doesn't get them anywhere and a mouthful of food, then they will usually as a second to last resort beg, and if still they haven't got the food they will start barking.

Most Dog responses involve barking somewhere along the line I have noticed!

As I have already said though waking a sleeping Dog is tricky, especially when they are as big as this Dog is and if he happens to have been dreaming then almost anything can happen.

It isn't easy to tell if a Dog is asleep, let alone dreaming, yes I will grant you, there are the classic dreaming signs, the weird and wonderful noises, little Woofs, and usually a lot of sniffing, but sometimes it is easier to tell when he is dreaming, I have to say, and that is when he starts the amazingly bizarre dream running and very occasionally begins dream barking.

But a Dog's brain seems to run in subconscious mode quite often and so sometimes Dogs may actually look wide awake and still be asleep and vice versa.

It is easier to tell if Dogs are fast asleep; because their tongues are stuck to the carpet or they look as though they are not breathing at all, then I am sure that they are really fast asleep.

A while ago I thought it would be really amusing to jump down onto the sleeping hound and so I just stood on the work surface and jumped, doing a fair imitation of a skydiver on the way down to a much softer landing than they usually get.

Well the Dozy (literally) Dog didn't see the funny side of it at all and jumped up startled as though he had been attacked and began barking and snapping his enormous jaws together in the middle of barking and then raced around the kitchen wagging his tail and growling.

Very outlandish behaviour if you ask me!

Still this time the Dog was out for the count, so fast asleep that the gentle prodding I gave him with my front paw didn't even make him shuffle to get more comfortable. He hardly seemed to notice at all when I bit his ear either.

This was too much for me and I decided to try later when he was more rested and easier to wake up, so I nimbly jumped into his bed, wrapped his tail around me like a furry feather boa and closed my eyes.

Would you believe it? The Dog woke me up! Really he has no manners at all! I was fast asleep delving in a Prawn mine, worse still I had just hit a very rich vein and was digging for all I was worth, filling barrel loads of pretty plump pink Prawns ready to be taken to a swimming pool!

Well I think you know the rest of that dream, what a shame to have missed out on the most delicious dream I have had in ages.

The mutt was scratching for all he was worth, but had he considered others and politely got out of the bed before doing that? Oh no! He was scratching for all he was worth, worse still it wasn't until he had rolled over to scratch the other side of his body that I woke up. Just in time to see his enormous bottom roll on to me and pin me to the bed, what a terrible way to wake up. I could hardly breathe because the shaggy horror was right on top of me.

I was crushed to the mattress under this great lump of smelly itchy Dog. It was about then that I started to get suspicious. He was scratching, which meant he was itching, that sounded familiar!

Oh dear, I think I had infected the Dog with the same itchy disease as I have.

Immediately I felt sorry for the poor boy, he wasn't really that bad and when he was asleep you could even describe him as 'good,' but then there are very few animals who are bad when they are asleep as well as awake, Grey Squirrels are one variety of animals I can think of who are though. Of course there are Parrots too and I can think of one fine-feathered gaudy greedy gannet in particular!

I looked up at the awful bird sitting on his perch, pretending to mind his own business, as usual he was always watching, probably compiling a report for the Captors, well I have nothing to worry about, today I have been good, well by my standards and they are not very high in that area I have to say if I am honest.

Staring back at the Pious Parrot never does any good, he watches unblinking, I did feel sorry for him, just the once, Mmmh! My guilty conscience is working overtime today. It was when the children were here. Actually looking back on the episode it was funny. The Parrot was employing both beady eyes that day I can tell you; the essence of naughty was thick in the air.

The kids were excitedly playing under his perch when quite by chance one of his technicolour tail feathers detached itself and dropped to the floor to be 'found' by one of the little boys, who immediately put it in his hair and ran round and round making what I discovered later was Red Indian noises, by patting his open mouth and hollering.

That noise was bad enough but when the three other little boys all wanted a Red Indian feather too, and began to try and get one by pulling other tail feathers that were, even I could tell, securely attached to the Parrot, who was quite rightly in no mood to share with them, all hell broke loose.

The commotion was deafening. A very put out Parrot was snapping and biting, children were screaming and crying as they held their hands.

Then just to make matters worse or better, depending upon your point of view, and for good measure, all of the hunting instincts of the Dog came out and he waded into the skirmish barking and biting at anything that moved, which at that moment was everything. Everything that is, except yours truly, I was happily watching from on top of the top cupboard in the kitchen, it is a great vantage point, higher than even the Parrot's perch and somewhere that is safe, well safe until the Captors come in and remove me as they often do.

It took quite a while for the Captors to sort that one out on the day I can tell you, and I think that the Parrot never really recovered, now when the little Red Indians visit he is put in the Captor's bedroom until the little Red Indians go home without any more headdress feathers, but with all of their fingers intact.

The Parrot lost three of his longest feathers that day, I know it is cruel to laugh but, ha, ha, ha.

Now that was very bad of me to laugh I know! Can I say anything in my defence? No not really I concede I can be quite a bad Cat when I want to be, but I didn't ask to be here and indeed if I wasn't here then I wouldn't be laughing at the Parrot's misfortune would I? So at least we know it is not my fault I am laughing is it?

Still today the Parrot was content to mind his and everyone else's business quietly from his perch and no doubt was getting ready to tell his stories to the Captors.

No I haven't forgotten about the itching and judging by the state of the Dog neither had he. While I had been watching the Parrot and laughing quietly to myself, the Dog had been busy standing on three legs and using his back leg to scratch his chest, which I thought was a pretty neat trick, I will have to remember that one.

It was obvious that whatever illness we had got, it was probably beyond us to cure, so itchily I sat waiting for the Captors to come home and see what they could do.

It must be just great being a Human, what with the hands and tools and cans of spray stuff. Don't get me wrong the spray stuff is just about the most awful stuff I have been sprayed with or because that list isn't very long the most awful stuff I have ever encountered, but whatever is locked away in the little orange can, it works.

The Dog, poor mutt was the first to be held and sprayed, It is amazing how such a large animal can struggle, again he impressed me, but it was the whimpering and whining that most awed me, the noise made my teeth rattle in my head, what a performance for the big brave Bow wow.

When they had finished spraying he was brushed, this was hilarious because every time they released their grip on him he was off and several times he managed to get up enough momentum to drag the Captors along with him.

In what seemed like a long while, well he does have a very long coat, he was declared 'done' and the Captors cleaned up the mess of combed out fur and loads of little black shiny things that were no longer jumping around or doing anything at all.

It was my turn now apparently, if I had realised that it was my turn I think I would have legged it, watching the performance with the Dog had quite sapped my courage and not only that I hadn't asked for a 'turn' and now frankly I didn't want one, thank you, if it was all the same to everyone.

Humans don't listen to those sorts of reasonable arguments though and they are as sneaky as the slipperiest snake when they want to be. I was busy sitting on the work surface minding my own business and having a scratch when, with a nod, from one to the other I was grabbed and held tightly as the orange can was wafted everywhere and a fine stream of cold wet grotty stuff was pumped into my fur.

It went everywhere except my eyes thankfully, which I think was deliberate they hadn't aim for them I was almost sure.

Did I make a noise, scream or bite like the soppy Dog, you really want to know, and can't you guess?

Well first I have to say that I was scared, that is my defence! I feel duty bound to also say that the Dog decided to join in and not offer me the same courtesy as I gave him and just watch and smirk.

Honestly at one point (from the beginning to the end) I thought that the Humans and the Dog were attacking me and with one Human holding me tightly and the other wielding the orange can with its choking spray I believed truthfully that I was in desperate danger.

So I believe I did what anyone - Human or Animal would have done in the same circumstances, I, um, how can I put this? I was very frightened and I 'went!'

Yes this is another one of those occasions where I am more than a little embarrassed so please be kind when I tell you that, I went to the loo, but I didn't or more exactly wasn't able to leave the room when I 'went.'

And scream? If our house had been in an area where the neighbours were friendly, I am sure that several would have come around to find out if everything was ok and that no one was being murdered.

A small consolation came when I was turned over to have my belly sprayed and while one paw was free I scratched the Mutt's nose and bit the hand of one of the Humans, so all wasn't lost. But as usual I ended feeling really humiliated.

The number of little black shiny bugs that came out with the old fur, a bit of dandruff and the crunchy black specs was amazing, if there is an Oscar awarded to the number of little black bouncing bugs contained in a fur coat I know I would have won it easily that day!

Today wasn't a total wash out though I did learn something, well when I say learn, I actually mean remember something, the name of the little black bouncing bugs. Dear old Mrs. Riley knew a thing or two about Fleas, I would say, because I remember them bouncing over everywhere after that little adventure from Hell. The Dog may have brought them in after a visit to the garden during the week, or and this makes you want to be just a little sick; they might have come into the house on his coat and then jumped off and spent a few weeks in the carpet waiting for an unsuspecting little Cat to wander passed; minding his own business, and then jump off the carpet and begun living in a good quality Cat fur coat and not an inferior Doggy one.

I admire their taste there but really I hope that they stay outside, I don't want to be sprayed too often. There is one bit of good news in all of this; the stuff that tastes so foul in my fur will keep the little black bouncing bugs away for up to three months apparently or so the writing on the can says, but we all know that when they say three months they mean around 40 days, but at least I won't be scratching for a while, I just wish it was three months, no I wish that it was longer than that.

Believe it or not I heard the Female Human say that the spray would last for three months (but we know the truth don't we) after she read the instructions on the can, now don't trust my word or opinion here because I am only a Cat, but don't you think it would be better to read the instructions first and then use the spray!

So all in all today was a busy day and not one that I would like to repeat in a hurry if it is all the same to everyone!

Now I am really sleepy and just have to put my notebook pencil away before I......................

Day 133 of My Captivity:

When I woke up today I was cuddling the Diary and had been laying on the pencil, not the most comfortable way to get a night's sleep I can tell you! I am really still very tired.

On top of the aches and pains caused by my odd choice of things to cuddle and sleep on, I also had the awful taste of the spray stuff in my mouth, which I managed to get while having a quick lick wash last night before finishing my Diary and going to sleep, well actually I dropped off before finishing my Diary to tell the truth, but you probably know that.

Still I suppose a little spray here and there is better than turning into an itchy nervous wreck, and when I went down for breakfast I was given a little bowl of milk and a couple of Prawns as a peace offering from the Captors, which I graciously ate without too many black and recriminating looks cast in their direction.

It goes without saying I gorged myself on the Prawns and drank some of the milk before the Dog nosed me out of the way and finished it, which was ok, because like most Cats I am not that keen on milk, although most Humans seem to think that Cats like milk, now cream is another matter, but that is probably because of its rarity value, hint, hint!

Right in front of my eyes they let the Dog out into the garden, I couldn't believe it, the cheek of it all, don't they know that Cats like the outdoors and this Cat especially? Not only that, I bet he is off to find some new little shiny black bugs and bring them in for tea!

Still I suppose the Humans are not that stupid and unlike the Dog who is obviously content to sniff around in the garden, this Cat would be off into the distance like a 'Long Dog,' another weird Human expression, well that is what I thought until I watched a Bassett Hound on television run after a Human with a bowl of food and now I think I know what it means!

Until seeing the long Dog in question, suddenly and totally out of character, run around like a Puppy, I didn't have any idea what that saying meant either, and at the moment I am too tired and stiff to do any racing around if that is really what it means, so you will just have to take my word for it, not that I actually care whether you believe me or not at the moment!

It has often puzzled to me why the Dog doesn't try and escape because every night and morning and sometimes around midday he gets taken for a walk or let out in the garden, no matter what the weather is like, really how is it possible that he gets such preferential treatment?

It stands to reason then, that Cats are really second class animals, but we obviously are so good natured that we are not taking part in mass demonstrations with banners and placards demanding a fairer deal for Catkind.

I wish I could negotiate a better life for all Cats; together we could list our grievances with our oppressors and if possible agree a better working relationship with not only Humans but also other household pets.

It would be really excellent if once and for all we could come to some sort of 'arrangement' with all Dogs for instance. The Dog and I have, well to a limited extent and that is probably more to do with his level of intelligence than with him wanting to be my enemy. He no longer chases me and in return I share a portion of whatever I can steal in the way of food, he has on occasions held the fridge door open for me when I have been having a rummage around inside.

Having said that it took an enormous amount of patient explaining in sign language, baby talk and thousands of 'good boys,' or the closest that a Cat can get to sounding like a Human saying that, to get him to grasp the very simple concept of moving his vast bulk so that it was between the door and the fridge and then even more patience to get the idiot to stand still and wait for the food to be thrown out, instead of chasing after the first morsel, that was flung out and onto the floor.

I had a couple of close calls. Let me tell you that it is no fun being locked in a fridge! First it goes quite dark which is not so much of a problem because I have wonderful night vision, but what is a problem is getting the door open from the inside, much more difficult than from the outside for some reason that I can't quite work out.

In spite of all of the problems of communication, dealing with an animal, who couldn't ever be described as an intellectual giant and the constant twittering, insults and barracking of the Parrot, I succeeded in 'training' the Dog and that was just the first cooperative venture of ours, more followed which I can tell you about later.

Although I wouldn't, by any stretch of anyone's imagination, call the Dog a friend we do have a pretty good working relationship. It goes without saying that usually I end up with a better deal, but then that is what happens when one is intelligent, it is in my opinion a just reward, after all left to do things himself, the Dog would not be half as well fed.

Where was I? I have done it again interrupted myself, but then as you have worked out by now, I do have a lot to say. Yes it is ok I have got my train of thought back; I was compiling a list of demands!

Freedom would have to be at the top of the any list of demands I suppose! But that is a bit of a shame because Prawns on demand strikes me as pretty important too. Mmmh this demand business is not as simple as one would first think, no wonder political conflicts go on for so long around the world.

DAY 134 OF MY CAPTIVITY:

Lots of things these days are rated with stars - hotels, websites, beer, Astrologers and so on, although come to think of it, it can't be lots of things, because I have just run out of things on my list, but I was using a figure of speech, and so I hope you know what I mean and I bet right now you are thinking of more things that are rated with stars. Very clever of you, but a little irrelevant, don't you think?

So while patting myself on the back for making you think twice as it were! I will get around to the point of what I was beginning to say.

These days lots of things are rated by 'stars' for excellence; cars, books, TV programmes and films. Yes I have been thinking too!

The more stars that something gets awarded the better it is apparently and so I have been wondering if there shouldn't be a similar rating in reverse, for bad things too, and I have come up with a suggestion.

My suggestion is to award 'Kings,' which will look like playing cards, for things that are:

One King	not very good
Two Kings	pretty dreadful
Three Kings	dreadful
Four Kings	downright terrible

The least 'worst' service or product would be awarded one King and the worst of the worst Four Kings and then it could be referred to as 'Fourking' terrible! Sorry kids this is an idea for adults only, I suppose, and of course I can gauge their reaction and how popular this rating system will be by all of the hate mail and complaints that I will receive from the 'moral majority,' bless them, or you never know there might be some encouragement from consumer organisations to ensure that the King system of mediocrity is adopted worldwide!

So why have I come up with this idea I hear you ask? With some of you probably asking in desperation I imagine! Well it is a bit of a long story, but let's face it that is what we are all here for after all, I thought that it would be a cracking idea to have a laptop to help me when writing my Diary, my paws seem to get covered in ink because my pen (awarded two Kings naturally) keeps leaking and the pages of my Diary are getting covered with paw prints, ink blots and smudges, which is not so good – one King awarded for presentation obviously.

So borrowing a credit card which belonged to one of the Captors who left it carelessly next to their computer, I ordered myself a rather swish Apple PowerBook G4, which for those of you who don't know what an Apple PowerBook G4 might be, it is a very sleek, silver laptop computer which offers and promises all sorts of wonderful things and delivers some of those things, but not all.

In my defence I was young, without a care and as a Cat obviously not aware of the consequences. No silly not the consequences of 'borrowing' someone's credit card, after all they can't send this Cat to prison he is already there (by the way there is a hint here for any Human considering a copycat crime).

No I was naïve about the consequences of buying an Apple PowerBook G4. I had heard from my translator that there was no better invention since they started slicing bread, but as you will see since I have got to know him better I have begun to doubt his judgement!

After ordering the Apple PowerBook G4 on the web it arrived several days later which was nice and initially it was awarded four stars by yours truly (but that was before the king rating was invented), based I have to say on looks alone, but what does a Cat know about computers?

To be honest the Apple laptop worked well too and for thirty-two days I happily bashed away on the keys, achieving a typing speed of thirty letters a minute and that with two paws, of course I had to learn to balance on my bottom and back paws so that my front paws could do the typing and at first that involved quite a bit of mistyping due to a lot of falling over.

But I persevered and was rewarded by a growing number of words on each page, and the spell checker more or less and to a lesser degree the grammar checker helped sort out the jumble of strangely spelt words and heaps of double spaces.

I was rather pleased with my purchase in fact, you could say, indeed you could go so far to say that I was proud of my purchase, but we all know that pride comes before a fall, which is why I pity Lions, who live in 'prides' and must be tripping over each other all the time!

Because I was new to computing and the computer was new to me, I was very careful with it, I had watched one of those BBC television programmes which pretends to educate the masses by talking down to them about serious subjects and so I was becoming an expert computer user. This level of expertise is signified, I believe, by the fact that a computer expert carefully does something called 'backing up,' which is not creeping backwards away from the computer, but copying all of the important files and folders to somewhere safe.

Now I have to admit here that I had made one small error and that was believing that the computer would have a facility to back itself up, it had, so the advertising proudly announced a DVD-RW, which was supposed to mean that I could copy all of my important 'stuff' to a DVD, which sounds really cool.

I found that I couldn't do this though and had to borrow a credit card again to get a proper functioning DVD writer, but hey who cares it is only someone else's money.

So there I was backing up as I was supposed to do as an 'expert' when the screen went black, which is not a colour referred to in the manual.

To cut a long and sorry story short, I was promised by the Apple helpline that my poor little computer's logic board could be replaced and I would be happily clicking away within seven to ten days, great it was according to the helpline the reason for the black screen and the dead computer, fair enough!

Well seven to ten days in Apple speak is in fact over a month and then after Apple speak Apple Drivel takes over and a month becomes a lot longer, but one starts to lose the will to live after not having one's silver sleek Apple PowerBook to bash away on after a couple of months.

I was not a pleased Pussy and complained but was obviously ignored on a daily basis. In the end I was promised a new machine, which according to various people in the Apple organisation would be with me in – oh yes you guessed seven to ten days, well it took forever to arrive.

To try and make things better and to say sorry, the good people at Apple promised to give me something called an iSight, which to all of you non-Apple users is a web camera. I suppose they thought that a web camera could say sorry in a much more sincere way than any Apple employee would, because not one of them apologised for the inconvenience that they put me through.

Well I didn't want a web camera but I said ok, just to make them feel happy, and the two items were booked to arrive together. Of course they didn't and the web camera arrived a long while after the replacement laptop, thought for a time that the web cam was just like Apple's idea of wonderful service, imaginary.

So Apple Computers have the honour of being the first company to be awarded Four Kings for their fourking dreadful service. Nice product Boys and Girls, shame about the service!

Definitely a case of 'buyer beware' which is why I thought that I would share my experience with you all! The shame about all of this is that the people whom you speak to at Apple on the help lines are really nice, it just seems to be the management who are useless, but then what do I know, I am only a Cat, thank goodness!

Day 135 of My Captivity:

Now I have just finished reading a book, well the back cover to be exact which was about Hypnosis! What a marvellous talent to have, and one that I will obviously have to develop.

From what I read, using Hypnotic techniques a Cat (in this case) can impose its will on others.

Whoopee!

I think that I have found a way to get out at last. Basically there are a few things that I need first and I will start collecting them immediately because I don't have a pocket let alone a Gold Pocket Watch and one apparently has to dangle one of those in front of the nose of the 'subject.'

For those of you who don't know who or what the 'subject' is! That is probably just as well because let's face it, it could be you, but for the purposes of my experiment my 'subject' is going to be the Parrot.

I decided on the Parrot because I judged that the Dog is too 'susceptible' to hypnotism.

Sorry for you non-experts! 'Too susceptible' means basically, to easy to hypnotise because they are 'not quite the ticket, or a Dime short of a Dollar,' no still don't get it, they are too stupid and therefore too easy to hypnotise. Maybe I should try it on you first?

Now! I wonder where I can find a Gold Watch and Chain? Hypnotism is really deliriously easy to do, well that is in terms of the amount of equipment that one needs, but unfortunately that is where the only problem may arise!

I have been wondering if the equipment needed is very specific because a Gold Watch and Chain is not something that you can just reach out and grab hold of, whether you have paws or hands! I wonder if I might be able to use something else instead of a Gold Watch on a Chain?

A thought just struck me! I have already, sometime ago to be precise, felt the power of hypnotism. It was when I was watching the washing going round and round in the white machine with the glass door. I spent ages watching multicoloured bits swirl and tumble; my hopes were raised at one point because the Parrot wasn't on his perch! Which is why in the beginning I was watching so intently.

But even when I heard the motley plumed blighter squawk, somewhere off in the distance, I couldn't seem to take my eyes off the swirling tumbling mass of unidentifiable coloured 'things,' sloshing round and round.

Then the sloshing would stop for a moment and the water inside the machine would slop and splash around for a while before the whole process would begin again with the clothes spinning backwards this time.

At the time, when I tore myself away I thought it was captivating, but now with my new knowledge I know it was hypnotising, excellent just what I need.

Now! How do I get the washing machine in front of the Parrot? Because I am pretty sure that the Parrot won't come to the washing machine! Well, unless he was hypnotised that is!

It would take a couple of years to explain what is required to 'Dimbo' the Dog (Translators Note: 'Dimbo is not the Dog's name it is an insult in the Cat language), and even then he isn't tall enough and probably not strong enough to hold the washing machine up in front of the Parrot's face for any length of time!

Not only that, we probably would create a lot of noise and mess, especially if the Dog is involved, and I don't think I need to draw anyone's attention to what I am doing, until I say 'Birdie watch the 'Watch.' Mmmh! I will have to think of a better way of putting that as well, 'watch the 'Watch,' sounds daft!

Right so I think that the washing machine is out unfortunately! I have just tried to lure the Pretty Polly down to the kitchen floor and introduce him to the nice relaxing spinning washing show and the little bas….., (Oops! I hope that Children and Adults will read this so I had better be polite). Um I mean, the awkward Feathered Fiend just ignored me!

Really how can one hope to hypnotise someone if they won't cooperate?

I suppose it was worth a try though! Did I mention a Plan B? No, well that is because as yet there isn't one, which is very frustrating for me and I presume for you too because you are after all expecting a bit of excitement and even worse a lot of entertainment, oh dear, sorry in advance then dear reader.

Could you go off and do something while I have a think? Or should I tell you a Cat joke?

Thinking about it, Cat jokes are a little unkind to Dogs and Humans, to say nothing about how rude they are, which let's face it would alienate my audience just when I want them to put the Diary down and say, 'Wow I can't wait for the movie, that is the most exciting and the funniest book I have ever read! Bridget Jones eat your heart out!' so bearing all of that in mind I think I will pass on the joke and have a think!

Look! Do you think you can give me a few minutes to come up with Plan B! Even someone with as powerful brain as mine needs a minute or two to think.

What do you want me to do, spell it out? I am thinking and really don't want to write, so please stop reading!

If you don't stop interrupting me and ruining my train of thought then I will be forced to leave a large blank space and no one will like that, the publisher will reach for his nerve pills, the reviewers will say that I am a devious Cat and that I am ripping people off because there are large holes in my narrative and worse; in general, the reading public or those being read to, will think I am a little like the Dog because I can't think of anything.

Ok you leave me no choice do you?

Still thinking.

Cats didn't build Rome, and so it took more than a day!

Eureka! As someone said once, accompanied by the sound of bath water spilling on a newly polished floor.

Ladies and Gentlemen, Boys and Girls, or should that be Girls and Boys for consistency? Anyway I am proud to announce and unveil the wonderful, the extravagant, the newly conceptualised Plan B.

Yes I have an idea, and we may as well call it Plan B, B stands for Big and it is always advisable to make one's plans big.

Well I don't suppose the idea is that big but it is a little important part of the overall plan.

Let me explain. A while ago when I was lying on my preferred day bed, the one the Captors sleep in at night, I couldn't get off to sleep for some reason, strange really because like most Cats I can usually sleep for eighteen hours a day and I have to admit that if I don't get at minimum of fourteen hours a day I can get just a little, how can I put this – irritable, yes that is a pretty accurate word!

So there I was, tossing and turning, telling myself to count Sparrows jumping onto the bird table, being dazzled by a slit of sunlight that, no matter where I put my head kept shining directly into my eyes.

Eventually and with a feeling of great regret I gave up the idea of sleep altogether and went for a wander around the dressing table and that is when I found the Jewellery Box, well actually I knocked it onto the floor which you have to admit, is a sure fire way to discover anything.

As I was picking through the bits and pieces that were once inside the Jewellery Box I spotted a very pretty gold necklace with a diamond pendant on the end.

Sadly any detailed search and cataloguing of the contents of the jewellery box was interrupted by the Female Captor rushing upstairs to investigate the noise, I think that she must possess a sort of second sense which lets her know when things of hers are under threat, because I swear that I heard her footsteps on the stairs before the box hit the ground, but then again I might be wrong!

I know it was a gold necklace and a diamond pendant because I heard the Female Captor shout, 'Oh no look at my jewellery box, it 's shattered! Where is my diamond Pendant?'

Then she scrabbled around on all fours for a long while in what could only be described as a blind panic, after the blind panic and a bit of calming down and looking methodically though, she sat up and said the other Captor. 'It is ok I have found it!'

To which he replied, 'thank goodness for that!' and she replied, 'Yes it was my Granny's and although it isn't really valuable it has enormous sentimental value.'

Of course if they had asked me I could have told them where it was because when you are my height you tend to see things that have rolled into the dark areas under furniture!

So I had found the most important 'tool' for my hypnotic purposes when I was ready all I had to do was to slip upstairs to my day bedroom and rifle the jewellery box and 'borrow' (probably indefinitely if this caper works) the Diamond Pendant on the Gold Chain, which in my opinion is far too nice for 'her' anyway!

My reasoning was that although it wasn't a Watch, it was just as good, being sparkly and irresistible to the eye beady or not!

DAY 136 OF MY CAPTIVITY:

I woke up a little while ago and didn't get up, and now I have just noticed that I must have dozed for probably two or three hours (or horus as I typed, but changed because I didn't sleep with two or three Egyptian Gods).

Something occurred to me as I wrote the word 'Gods' and was thinking about Dogs and Gods, well Gods of the Egyptian variety and Dogs of the non-deity variety, and what occurred to me was that 'God' is Dog spelt backwards if you see what I mean, and for that matter the same applies to Dog and God, I wonder if there is any connection there?

You don't suppose that there is a connection do you? Wouldn't that be terrible if all Dogs were Gods, especially if they were looking in a mirror! Now what an off putting thought that is. Just imagine if Dogs ruled Heaven, because they weren't really Dogs but Gods, what on earth (if that is the right expression here) would heaven be like.

My imagination started to run away with me as I explored that thought. There would be a lamp posts every few yards, and thousands of neat heaps of freshly dug soil, each with a bone buried close to the surface to be easily discovered by the casual sniffer.

Worse still, well for Humans at least there would be millions upon millions of Gods on leads, taking endless walks in all weathers, unless heaven is a sunny place all year round that is!

No wonder tail wagging Dogs are so excited and happy all of the time, maybe they already know the secret, and are laughing at all of the other species, because one day, let's call it the Day of reckoning for the sake of a title, the rest of us are going to find out the terrible secret well that's what I reckon any way.

DAY 137 OF MY CAPTIVITY:

I have a gun! There that got your attention and quite rightly, it is one big statement for a very small sentence and it is true, I didn't mean to get a gun, but your attention is welcome! After all you are supposed to be reading this attentively and if you aren't well then, let's face it I am wasting my time!

Back to the gun! I do really have one you know. Curiously it arrived today by courier from the home of the gun, the good old US of A.

How I got a gun was a mystery to me, no let me rephrase that! The parcel that arrived was a nice surprise and at the same time, a mystery. But I like wrapped surprises usually. This surprise turned out to be of the alarming variety as I finally ripped the parcel to pieces, shredded the bubble wrap and started to scratch metal.

There I was sitting on the floor, surrounded by masses of rubbish with the gun resting on some of the litter in front of me, next to the free bonus pack of bullets.

Now that I am concentrating on the events that led up to the delivery of the weapon, I am starting to remember what may have happened, which led to me being sent this awesomely lethal bit of hardware.

The day before yesterday I was casually browsing the Internet, as you do, looking for the correct spelling of the word revolting, someone having put my Collins Dictionary on the top shelf of the bookcase and therefore made it pretty inaccessible to any Cat and especially this one.

I was of course trying to get the right spelling for this Diary so that I could describe the Parrot properly, obviously.

So my inadvertent possession of this elegant and alarming pearl handled firearm was due to the fact that I had not seen the word 'revolting' in my spellchecker when I was checking the spelling, finding other words instead, like 'revoke,' 'revolute,' as you do and I have to say, what a useless word 'revolute' is, nothing Parrotlike at all and finally I found revolution but not 'revolting.'

The Internet, I decided, would be my saviour. Mmmh! I wish! So in a flash, yes I have broadband, I had typed in my spelling of revolting, which I won't confuse you with now and bang (oops not a good choice of words in the circumstances), there it was in front of me on the screen what I thought was the answer to my problem and not, as it turns out the beginning of a whole new one!

I did think at the time that there were several strange things about the site that I was Googled to, but then lots of Human things are strange to me and always will be, so I wasn't unduly bothered by the pictures of firearms and I suppose that has to do with the fact that I had no idea that a 'revolver' was anything to do with guns specifically, or indeed, in general. Not only that I thought that the pictures had something to do with advertising and I know about that, but as I said I know nothing about revolvers, well I do now obviously.

It was odd that the page morphed almost immediately, and asked me for what I thought was some form of registration. The great thing about computers is that they do a lot of work for you and kindly my computer automatically filled in the blank boxes on the webpage and when it had finished doing that, I merely clicked a box with the word ammo on it (I have to say I thought 'ammo' was Latin for 'enter'), at the bottom of the page, which exploded nicely thanking me for visiting the site.

I was impressed by the animation, though a little confused by the explosive nature of this Dictionary website, but I thought nothing of it really and armed (literally as it turns out) with the right spelling, I exited the web.

When I pasted the correct spelling into new Diary manuscript I immediately realised that 'revolver' was not the correct spelling of revolting and found the correct spelling in the reverence tools, which was only a few words away from 'revolver.'

With all of the confusion of success (I do hate misspelling words I have to say), I didn't really think anymore about my visit to the site with the animated exploding boxes.

Now I have two dilemmas the first is sitting in front of me on a bonus box of ammunition, and the second is the nagging worry that I liked the little explosive animations so much that I clicked quite a few and some, oh dear me, were sitting next to Assault Rifles, Hand Grenades and Rocket Launchers, if I am not careful I might be able to start and arm my own insurgency.

No they wouldn't be daft enough to send that sort of armament to someone who filling in the order form stated that their profession is Cat? Would they? Mmmh! Hang on, let's think about this they sent me this handgun without questioning my profession didn't they?

The only thing I can hope is that in some magical way I may have busted the limit of the Male Captor's credit card, it wouldn't be the first time that has happened!

Oh dear I am dreading the doorbell going now, opening the door and finding a budget priced Rocket Launcher and several special offer M16's lying on the threshold with a couple of end of range Tanks parked in the garden.

What should I do? I don't know! I am stuck and worse the silver grey muzzle of the gun is pointing at me, I hope that it isn't loaded; no surely they wouldn't send a loaded gun by FedEx would they? I don't know though, they didn't seem to care about selling it to a Cat in the first place did they? I am really worried and not only about the lack of control of firearms sales on the Internet, I am worried that I will get caught with a gun with my pawprints on it, I wish I hadn't opened this surprise package!

What should I do? I don't know, well I do know something, I should stop repeating myself, that isn't getting us anywhere is it? I could share the problem, did you see that I said that repeating myself wasn't getting 'us' anywhere, so at least you are now involved by implication even if your hand isn't on the gun, smoking or not.

Well that is the first step to some form of resolution because a problem shared is a problem halved and I think that if we share this problem with all of the readers then the number of times the problem is halved will make the problem so small as to be statistically unrecordable, and if those statistics just happen to be crime statistics, I would say that we have got away with this one wouldn't you?

But then who am I kidding? I have been lumbered with this Hot Potato and I know in my heart or somewhere else deep down inside that I will have to sort it out.

First things first, let's get rid of the packaging. I do wish I didn't get so carried away and do such a good job of ripping packages open, just look at the mess, it'll take ages for us to clear this up! Well don't just sit there reading, lend a paw; you can carry the big bits of cardboard.

Wait I am not thinking straight am I! You can't do anything but sit there and read can you? Sorry to shout at you like that, please get comfy and keep reading, or if you want to stretch your legs do go out and buy another copy of this Diary, there must be someone who you know, who deserves it.

Don't worry you are not being subjected to subliminal advertising I promise, this is up front and in your face advertising, this Diary makes a great present I promise you, I would buy another one if I were you – honestly!

If you do that it will make me feel so much better and let's face it I need cheering up now, and if the worst comes to the worst I will need all of the money that this Diary makes to pay for my defence council, so don't even think about it, just get you coat!

There that has made me feel better and I would like to personally thank all of you who have bought several copies of my wonderful Diary, the ones among you who have only bought one copy could do better frankly, but then the shops are still open I think!

Ok while you have been reading the last bit, and now that you have come back from the shops with a couple of very useful spare copies of my Diary, I have managed to clear up the rubbish, and I have thought of a little spot that will be the final resting place of the firearm, so all that I need to do now is to move it! Unfortunately it is too heavy for me to lift, let alone carry. 'Here Doggie!'

I know that sometimes the Dog is as dense as a group of Irish Republicans at a decommissioning ceremony, but he does have his uses and he loves a challenge, so all I had to do was to call him and simply tell him that there was no way he could carry the gun, he defiantly proved me wrong of course, clever Doggie!

Then he did it again and proved that he could carry the gun upstairs, let's face it, he is 'gifted.'

There was a sweaty moment (well twenty minutes to be accurate) when he nearly did prove me wrong, when, he wasn't able to lift the toilet seat and after dropping the gun down the loo flush it with his right paw, but with lots of anti-encouragement (if you see what I mean) he finally did flush the loo seven times. I couldn't believe that it would take that many flushes to get rid of the thing, after all it wasn't floating or anything!

Still it is good to see the back of that little problem, I just hope that there isn't a fleet of courier vans wending their way here at this moment in time, loaded to the gunnels with more guns, one was quite enough of a problem thank you!

DAY 138 OF MY CAPTIVITY:

You would think after yesterday's little misadventure (I like that word for some reason) that I would choose to have a quiet day and that is what I planned, spending most of the morning so far away from the front door that I couldn't hear the doorbell ringing even if it was being rung by an army of deliverymen delivering vast amounts of lethal hardware.

Until lunchtime I slept on the work surface in the utility room, in spite of the fact that my teeth were being rattled by the combined efforts of the washing machine and the tumble dryer, very distracting and very annoying all at the same time.

However I was content to sit it out and hide from the prospect of most of the arms from the next war being delivered here. Imagine then my horror when the doorbell went and I could hear it, even above the noise of an unbalanced load of washing being spun to extinction below me.

The Dog, as usual was doing his 'I'm a foaming at the mouth Guard Dog, make my day and break in' act at the front door, just when I wished that he would choke on his tongue and be quiet frankly. To my way of thinking it meant that the delivery man might just leave the parcel of death on the doorstep for the Captors to find when they came home and that would never do.

In the end and much to my eternal relief the idiot Dog went quiet, but as you will probably know, there is quiet and then there is 'too quiet' and Dimbo the Dog had definitely gone 'too quiet,' yes it may have been my guilty conscience working overtime to jump to the wrong conclusions, but I believed that something was not as it should be, and that made me worry even more.

Oh dear this was going to be what most people describe as 'a bad day.' You know the sort of day I seem to have everyday. I had to slink down and investigate, avoiding the little window in the door if possible.

Because the chief barker had gone unusually quiet there was no telling where he was or what sort of mischief he may or may not be wrapped up in, and more importantly if the mischief he was involved with, was anything to do with me.

Why is it that everything seems to happen in the dinning room, think back to all of those dreadful post First World War English crime novels that you have read and the crime, murder or action in general always happens in the dining room. Today was no different, I felt at any minute Hercule Poirot would be announcing that the murder had happened in the dining room and that the Cat was the murderer, why?

Why? Oh! Yes, why? Sorry I forgot to mention the Dog was lying dead in the middle of the dining room floor, and next to him, and rather unfortunately I thought, was the small box of bonus ammunition that had arrived with the gun and had been missed when I cleared, no I remember now, when 'we' cleared up the mess.

So you are an accomplice, at least I won't get all the blame, after all I am just a Cat, you on the other hand are a responsible Human, um what's the definition, ah yes 'Dog murderer!' Or is that Caninicide? Don't know really, but if a King killer is a Regicide then a Dog murderer has to be a Caninicide, though why the King killer only murdered Kings called Reg I have no idea, I am slipping away from the point aren't I?

Well the point is that one of us has to check to see if the Dog is dead, no I didn't think you would want to do it. I'll do it, but I have to close my eyes.

With my eyes closed I approached the stiff, 'stiff,' something was damp, no, wet under paw, no. The poor Dog, the dampness was warm and sticky, poor, poor Dog and so young!

I opened my eyes when I bumped into the stiff Dog, he didn't move but he was still cuddly and warm and I was beginning to miss the old fella already.

Then I looked down! Really, it was sick! No really, it was sick, or what looked like sick. It definitely wasn't red and I knew the colour of the Dog's blood from scratching him regularly.

On the other side of the rigid Dog and just passed the soaking wet box of ammunition was a clue to what had happened. A chair had been knocked over! Well that is a rare understatement for me! The chair had been shattered, by, I presume, employing in my best Hercule Poirot detective abilities, the looney lump crashing into it, while barking at the doorstep caller and not looking where he was going. Typical actions of a Parrot brained Dog.

He had obviously received a severe blow to the head and so I wasn't worried! The thick skulled idiot would be ok; he just needed the vase full of water (incidentally full of flowers as well), pushed off the table and over him to wake him up.

Always more than willing to oblige, I nipped up onto the slippery polished table and slid down behind the vase, then carefully pushed it to a place just above the unconscious shaggy one.

After a shower and a little wake up bump on the head from the vase, the Dog eventually came round, shook himself to get rid of the water and some of the flowers which had somehow woven themselves rather attractively in a Hawaiian sort of style around his neck, then he ate the remaining flowers much to my gastric horror, so at least there were no signs of any unusual behaviour or madness there then, he was ok!

His full recovery back to the land of the half brained was much to my relief because we had work to do, I needed him to take the box of bullets upstairs and do some flushing.

Still maybe I should be kind to him, after all he had just suffered a substantial blow to the head and had been unconscious for quite a time, I had heard somewhere that patients with similar injuries should be treated gently, maybe I should let him have a rest? Yes there is no reason why he can't use the downstairs loo instead.

Day 139 of My Captivity:

Can I have today off please? Just a quiet day, with no worries, well none over and above the worry that the better part of the Royal Arsenal is going to get delivered to the doorstep any time now.

Still if all of the ominous parcels were being delivered on the next day delivery system, I should be due some compensation, I wonder if I could refuse delivery as well as pocketing a tidy packet?

Day 140 of My Captivity:

Well I seem to have been in this prison a very long time and much longer than I had planned for, but regrettably I have had a few unfortunate setbacks and I have to say I have probably caused a few unfortunate setbacks of my own too, but let's face it what else have I got for enjoyment.

Still I content myself with the belief that I am mentally very strong and can cope with this sort of punishment.

Just like the great Russian Nobel Prize winning writer Alexander Solshencinine (or was it Alexander Solchinskine), did when he was in the Gulag Archipelago, well his name was something like that, no not Gulag Archipelago, Solshencinine!

I know his first name was definitely Alexander, but like all Russians when you ask for their first or Christian name they will immediately and without prompting, give you a selection of names that sound the same, or are fairly closely related, to choose from and then probably some other names too, that they swear they can be called by, but that appear to have been made up on the spot.

For instance I heard a Russian man introduce himself as Yuri, he then said that you could also call him Yan, Yanni, Joe, and John, I called him George just to annoy him, but sadly I failed, he took a shine to his new name and added it to his list of names.

I tend to call most men George now though, it just simplifies things and saves time I think and it isn't really important what Humans call themselves is it, they all look the same after all and so why shouldn't they have the same name?

To my way of thinking it would seem that all Russians are born with the ability to avoid any from of direct questioning as if the entire nation is always 'helping' the Police with their inquiries!

Going back to George, no sorry I mean Alexander Solshencinine! I did look in a Dictionary to get the correct spelling of the great man's name, but the trouble with dictionaries is that one has to know how to spell the word before one looks it up to get the right spelling; almost like the trouble with life sometimes, but in that case nothing to do with spelling if you see what I mean!

More importantly he, (let's call him the great Russian writer), was just like me a great writer and a consummate survivor. He again, like me, spent years imprisoned in terrible conditions and managed to keep all of his marbles, even writing a book, 'The Gulag Archipelago' about his mistreatment, into the bargain, you have to admire us, don't you!

Now if either of us were for the sake of argument, Bridget Jones, we would be coughing our hearts out from smoking too many cigarettes and falling over a lot from drinking too much, because we couldn't cope with the pressure.

You should therefore be thankful that you are reading an interesting Diary for a change, can look forward to a wonderful film and have been touched by the spirit of a true hero, what do you mean who is the hero? Me of course! Now let's have less of your cheek and get back to this wonderful and ground breaking piece of literature! (My Diary, did you really need to ask!)

So Bridget would be blubbing her eyes out in an alcohol fuelled, smoke filled fit of depression, silly bint. But Alexander and I are made from stronger stuff than the Bridgets of this world, who seem to think that life would be better if they were out of their tiny minds all the time. In my opinion all of the Bridgets of this world (and I have to say some of the Helens, but that is another story and not for this Diary), should wake up and get a life.

There, having said that I feel better and more able to get on with the job in paw and get out of here, the great Russian writer escaped and eventually found critical acclaim, fame and fortune, personally I'll settle for the last two on that list!

DAY 141 OF MY CAPTIVITY:

Kippers, boy -- nothing else in the world smells like that! I love the smell of Kippers in the morning!

One time we had Kippers and the smell lingered all day, that oily fishy smell, the whole house smelt of it. It smelt like - breakfast!

And today breakfast was Kippers obviously, I wonder if there are enough Kippers to go round? It is odd that Humans never seem to want to share Kippers, I would be quite happy to eat the bits that they leave, Humans being a wasteful bunch and not eating the skin or the hard to get at bits of fish in between the bones, which is something that is difficult for a Cat to understand. But no, they always mumble about not giving the Cat bones because they will stick in its throat!

Idiots, haven't they heard about the Fishing Cats, who come from somewhere like Asia or even my much bigger, and a little distant cousins Tigers, who will happily wade into a river and hook out a wriggling and thrashing big fish and happily munch through the whole lot leaving only a neat pile of oddments when they have finished munching!

The trouble with Humans is that they know too much about everything, but what they don't realise is that they know a lot about all sorts of things but not everything about everything, if you see what I am getting at.

I think that I will have to take a breather and work out if what I have just said makes sense, so I will just let you imagine the sound of an intake of heavy breath here to make it all seem more real. That bit will be better in the film, when Harrison Ford or Richard Gere or another sex symbol film star does my voice over, I bet, but you probably understand what I am getting at!

Yes it does make sense! Well to me anyway, I am sure I have said before that a little knowledge is a dangerous thing, well Humans prove that constantly they know too much about everything and very little about anything.

Quick, bandage my brain; it hurts from all of this deep thinking.

Let's get back to Kippers, something I personally am not ashamed to say I would like to know more about, especially the taste.

But no, just like the other night when large amounts of Chick Chicken meat were left on the bones and then thrown away because the bones might break and get stuck in a Cat's throat, well let me tell you now, I have never had a bone stuck in my throat and don't intend to start, so just chuck it down on the floor and let me demonstrate, please, or toss me a Kipper now and I can do the same, but do they, no!

Haven't they heard that half the world is starving and one of the starving is here, sitting impatiently under the kitchen table?

Really what a waste, just imagine what someone from the Third World would do with some, or all of the leftovers that the western world throw away, they might even put down their rifles for a while stop fighting and feed their families!

Have you noticed, that most of the starving nations are at war, in the main with each other? Does that mean that bullets and bombs are cheaper or more readily available than food? Bear in mind that I am only a Cat, but this has always confused me.

Or is it, and again remember I am only a Cat and therefore a novice at this game of thinking and international politics, that the starving nations can afford to fight because the West send them so much food and they don't have to buy it themselves so they can spend the money they save on guns and bombs and groovy tanks?

So even though the West send vast quantities of food it is obviously not enough in this case, because we constantly see pictures of starving children and women on television, although have you noticed, never many pictures of starving young men, well obviously they need to eat to keep their strength up so that they can continue to wage war amongst themselves!

Cats will never in a million years understand Humans, although I keep trying, they're a mystery to me and probably will remain one too!

Yes the bandage around my brain had slipped off like a badly fitting baseball cap! I am better now, I have pushed it back in place and will stop thinking such politically improper thoughts.

Sadly I have to report that the poor leftover bits of the Kippers were wrapped up in paper and then dropped into a carrier bag that was in turn, tied up to stop the aroma escaping and driving this little Cat wild, I have to say that this tactic failed. I love the smell of Kippers in the morning, even if that smell is escaping from a plastic cage somewhere at the bottom of a swivel bin!

Day 142 of My Captivity:

In an attempt to be really disgusting and in the hope that the Captors would think twice about keeping a revolting animal such as yours truly in the house, I have just managed to make myself sick and vomit on their favourite chair.

It worked a treat because when I heard the anguished cries I rushed into the front room and saw the Female Captor rising from a pancake of slipperiness.

What an excellent sight it is to watch these tormentors getting some of their own medicine and the look on her face, I wished I'd had a camera to record the event and then I could have added a few illustrations to this Diary, still never mind the mental picture of her horror will live with me for a very long time.

Thinking about it, I must try to do the same on their bed, somewhere under the Duvet would be just perfect or I could do something worse, but that requires a lot of time and concentration, well can you do that sort of thing when you might be discovered at anytime and are not sitting in your litter tray?

No I didn't think so, and so why should you expect me to be able to 'perform' instantly either, I am happily, not a Dog, who it would seem from my observations of the revolting habits of the Looney furry one, can do anything disgusting in just about any place he chooses, immediately, which could be considered in some circles to be something of a gift.

Day 143 of My Captivity:

As part of my studies on the English Language, every day I read one page of the Dictionary, it helps to increase my vocabulary and to discover words that in my opinion need to be kicked back into play in the English Language.

Today my new word is actually two words, that happens in Dictionaries sometimes, one discovers a word that just has to have a bit nailed onto it which changes the meaning of the first word when it is read on its own, if you see what I mean.

The first word is quite boring 'Parthian,' and quite rightly I hear you saying 'so what? It is just an adjective of the word 'Parthia,' you are clever aren't you!

Now should I assume that you are clever enough to know what an adjective is? No ok I thought not! Well I only found out while reading the 'A' section of the Dictionary, here is what the Dictionary says on adjectives:

Ad.jec.tive *n*
A word that qualifies or describes a noun or pronoun

adj
1.Relating to, forming, or functioning as an adjective
2.Relating to court practice and procedure rather than the principles of law

As usual the Dictionary goes on a little, but the most important bit of the definition is the part that says an adjective n - a word that qualifies or describes a noun or pronoun. So the word 'adjective' is a noun that qualifies a noun, huh! Ok you are right, don't go there!

Leading on from that I am assuming that we all know that Parthia was a country in ancient Asia in the second century that expanded into a great empire over a hundred years or so, but was destroyed in the third century, well we would know that if we have all read the same page in the Dictionary!

Yes I know this is all a bit dull so far, but wait for the interesting bit please and then you will see why I like reading Dictionaries, I hope!

'Parthian shot' appears in the Dictionary underneath the boring and some would say deservedly extinct empire and what it means is both funny and odd.

'Parthian shot' is funny because there is, as usual, with a lot of English words, a perfectly good substitute which I will tell you in a minute, unless you think of it yourselves before I get around to telling you the meaning, after all most Human minds think faster than writers can write, especially this writer!

So 'Parthian shot' is a noun and I am sure that you don't want me to insult your intelligence and explain that a noun is a word or group words used as the name of a class of people, places or things, or of a particular person, place or thing. Oops! Sorry I explained it anyway!

Back to what I was saying!

The meaning of 'Parthian shot' is that it is a hostile remark or gesture delivered while departing. Apparently Parthian Archers shot their arrows backwards while retreating! Yes I know! Pathetic!

Well this explanation says a lot about so many things, first the English language which has great piles of close to extinct words stacked up in Dictionaries that really should be dumped for all time, no wonder Dictionaries are not to be dropped on one's paws.

The second thing it says, to me at least, is that the English Language is a minefield of words that mean the same; I would think that 'Parting Shot' has the same definition as 'Parthian shot' and probably sounds better. But if there is a rule that says that Dictionary publishers should just concentrate on explaining words in the Dictionary that are words in use in the English language then it is likely that any Dictionary would be a rather slim volume and as such unable to command the sort of price that publishers of dictionaries can get for very heavy volumes.

And last but by no means least, Archers firing their arrows backwards while retreating tends to suggest that their empire was lucky to stay in business as long as a whole century. In my opinion if the Archers had stood still and faced the enemy they may have won a battle or two.

Having said all of that, 'Parthian shot' is a great couple of words, don't you agree?

Unfortunately the second part of my plan for reading a page of the Dictionary a day is to use what I have read, sometimes that can be a trial, after all Cats in the main don't play Scrabble but, and I am sure that you will agree I have achieved my ambition today.

On the subject of Archers and fast forwarding through History and Geography, but relating that rapid shift in time and scenery to my newly learned words and Sir Winston Churchill, which you have to admit is no mean feat for anyone Human, but a feat of pure genius for a Cat. Did you know that English Archers during the time of the Battle of Agincourt used to wave two fingers at their enemy?

Really you didn't? Well! Their actions were probably responsible for Sir Winston Churchill's V for Victory sign and if you turn your fingers around while showing someone that sign you make a very rude one indeed, which was a fact that I am sure didn't escape Sir Winston Churchill either.

Now, how can simple Archers working for King Henry V be responsible for such amazing inspiration for Sir Winston Churchill and in addition a really very rude gesture?

Simple the English Archers were so good at their job of inflicting casualties on the French armoured Knights in 1415 (the year of the battle of Agincourt I think) that if they were captured they had the two fingers, which they used to draw the bow and consequently fire the arrow, cut off, which let's face it, is a pretty severe punishment but on the whole better than some of the consequences of war!

So the cheeky Archers used to wave at the enemy prior to any battle and I am sure by now you can guess what they waved, V for Victory, exactly.

Which just goes to show that it is a funny old life and that delving into a Dictionary can make it even more amusing!

My favourite Dictionary is the Collins English Dictionary, which is handy for several reasons.

The first reason is that it is in English of course.

The second reason is that we may well be able to get a little sponsorship from the publishers of my favourite Dictionary.

Although I could of course change my choice of favourite if we don't get any sponsorship from Collins, to say the enormous 'Complete Oxford English Dictionary' twenty volume set, even if it is a little big for me to handle.

But if Collins don't shell out with a few crisp notes I may have to change favourites so that you take my recommendation and buy the 'Complete Oxford English Dictionary' instead of the Collins one and that would be inconvenient for me because I am just not big enough to handle or of course 'pawdle' one of the very large Complete Oxford English Dictionaries, let alone all twenty that make up the set!

Dictionary Note:
'Pawdle' means the same as handle does in this context but I noticed that it is not in either Dictionary, such an oversight is lamentable, maybe I should write my own Dictionary? It could be a combination of English and Cat and prove very convenient when Humans and Cats need to speak to each other, hang on what am I saying why would we do that, Humans and Cats have not been on speaking terms for centuries.

Where was I? Oh yes, sponsorship potential. If the Oxford English Dictionary people and Collins keep their hands in their pockets I could always go for the World Encarta Dictionary which would be a serious step because it really is not very good at all, still sponsorship and product placement are more important to a struggling Diarist, trying to struggle to a first million that is than little niggling things like quality!

There is one other reason that I decided to read a page of a Dictionary a day, and that has to do with the famous British Prime Minister Sir Winston Churchill who knew a thing or two about words, and he said the reason for his great command of the English Language in his speeches was that he read a page a day of a Dictionary (though I haven't yet worked out if a particular Dictionary publisher sponsored him) and let's face it if it was good enough for him then who am I to argue?

Unfortunately Sir Winston Churchill neglected to say that his speech writers helped enormously, but then I suppose when one becomes famous for being clever, no one questions what you say and if no one questions what you say, then you can pretty much say what you like without fear of being criticised.

Happily it is also the position of a Cat writing a Diary; who in their right mind would want to bother to correct a Cat? So even though my English is a little wonky here and there and my opinions might be considered anything but mainstream; I am a Cat for goodness sake and I don't know any better, which is I suppose the same as good old Sir Winston Churchill! And if anyone criticises me then I do what he suggested and 'fight them over Peaches,' or something like that!

I have just moved the Dictionary and I have to tell you this because you will laugh and I like to make my readers smile. When I moved the Dictionary it fell open at 'Agglutinate' not a word that brings a smile to your face automatically I know, in fact probably you are like me and can easily say that it is not a word that you have ever seen before I bet, and more than likely not a word that you ever want to see again, but humour me, guess what it means?

Ok you are bored with the game before you start, come on, I like words so please guess, oh go on please, I'll sit on your lap and purr for you and make you think you are adored!

Alright you drive a hard bargain, just guess what the short version means; 'Glue together,' now do you agree with me, that if the English language was actually a person, would it be locked up somewhere very secure for howling at the Moon?

I think it would be!

Day 144 of My Captivity:

Well I have seen it all now! I was at a loss to describe exactly what I had seen and had to ask the Dog for his opinion. There right in front of the window, but happily in the road, was what I thought at first was an Alien on a bit of rope.

As I said I was so intrigued that I called the Dog up to the bedroom to see if he could identify what it was that I was watching.

It took him forever to actually drag his shaggy self upstairs and I had to employ my extra special shrieking call to make sure he heard me. It is the type of call that makes windows wobble and sound like they are shaking themselves to pieces, it is I think, about ten thousand times worse than the annoying noise created by Humans when they run a wet finger around the rim of a glass.

The Hound must have been really fast asleep to have not heard the first five minutes of my special shrieking or deaf, but I now know he isn't deaf because I thought I would give him a little hearing test, so when he sauntered grumpily into the bedroom I let out another cream curdling shriek and he cowered pathetically trying to bury his grubby, slobbery face in their bedclothes to deaden the noise.

It almost goes without saying that when I asked him what was on the end of the rope he said he couldn't hear a word I was saying, because his ears were ringing, I ask you how did he know I was talking?

So I ignored his complaint and the dazed look in his eyes and asked him again, what was on the end of the rope, his answer surprised and annoyed me. 'A Human!'

I pointedly pointed out that it was the 'other' end of the rope that I was talking about!

At first his latest answer threw me, what he said completely confused me because it was totally beyond my terms of reference and understanding.

A Dog? I asked him again, just to make sure that I hadn't misheard him, my ears were ringing too, but he said a Dog again, well I thought to myself it could be! Could it?

I asked the sleepy eyed grumpy one what sort of Dog and he brightened up as I pretended to take an interest in the other members of his race.

'We don't talk about them much, those Dogs!' He said airily with a strange emphasis on 'those!' He did disclose that they apparently, were in his opinion a breeding program too far that had developed some sort of terrible, genetic mistake.

With that information imparted he pushed his front paws off the windowsill, knocking a small vase of wild flowers to the floor and ground the petals into the carpet as he left the room, obviously in an attempt to demonstrate that not all Dogs are Nancy boys!

I thought about what the disgusted Dog had said, 'a Poodle,' even the sound of its name gave the listener an idea of the sort of Dog that would like having its bum shaved.

I wonder if other Dogs think Poodles are members of a weird religious cult or maybe they think that Poodles just have a very highly developed feminine side?

In my opinion all Dogs should be poodles, it would definitely make life a safer place for Cats big and small, not that I am referring to myself as small, although often I do wish that I was the size of a Tiger or even if I can't have such a large wish granted just sort of Lynx size would do! Still that wouldn't be necessary if all Dogs were Poodles, in fact if all Dogs were Poodles Cats would rule the world, well the Canine bit of it at least.

Day 145 of My Captivity:

Recently I have discovered more little Human sayings and expressions that are directly related to Cats, which almost make sense even to Cats.

'Letting the Cat out of the bag,' can only be described as a humane action, while anyone saying that 'the Cat has got 'their' tongue,' is lying, honestly what upstanding Cat in their right mind would bother to grab a tongue and then dangle like a crazed bungee jumper from a Human's mouth?

The last little saying I have discovered is one that is so accurate that I can't imagine any Human being intelligent enough or indeed honest enough to have invented it and therefore I can only imagine that there have been other Cats before me, who have managed to learn a Human language and left an epitaph. 'A Cat thinks it owns everything it sees,' I have to say that is true, although I would go further and say that 'a Cat knows it owns everything it sees.'

I am rather encouraged by these little Human sayings because until now I have only heard ones which malign Cats.

Still I suppose I am guilty of maligning other animals too, I have called the Dog and probably the Humans harebrained, who was it that said Hares are stupid, poor Hares I feel sorry for them, what a way to be immortalised!

I have even been guilty of calling the Dog Bird brained and that is worse than Harebrained because it suggests that the Dog is similar to a Parrot and that is not true, he is so much nicer than that malicious multicoloured maniac.

Really I think that I will have to snap out of this reverie, I am beginning to have some sympathy for my enemies, well except the Parrot of course.

I must be tired, or not feeling myself, not that I feel myself often that is!

Day 146 of My Captivity:

I can assure you that as a Cat I find lap dancing to be an amazingly rewarding and fun pastime, I have gained enormous pleasure from jumping up onto any Male Human's lap and using my claws to scratch a fresh tattoo.

It is incredible just how defensive all Male Humans can be of their laps. In fact I have noticed that Female Humans are far less likely to try and shield their laps with both hands, or hold you at bay with the palm of one hand, while trying to knock you off the Sofa with the other when you have jumped up next to them, with that glint in your eye that says I have jumped up here to tread all over your naughty bits and my claws are out!

In fact I have noticed that Female Humans actually find my actions rather amusing, because they tend to laugh out loud at the defensive actions of Male Humans after I have jumped on to their laps, which usually means that the type of retribution dished out by a startled and defensive Human Male is limited almost to timidity, and of course means that a clever Cat can take full advantage of the situation.

Day 147 of My Captivity:

Today we were treated to a little family gathering; the house was full of a vast assortment of rejects, suspicious characters, shoplifters, pickpockets, crooks and murderously ugly Humans, or to give them their proper name the Human's extended family. In fact the house was so tightly packed with these dreadful people that the whole noisy affair seemed like a political party's convention.

The main event apparently was a celebration of the fact that little Clarence, a distant, though in my opinion not distant enough, cousin, had passed some sort of exam to do with squeezing ear splitting notes out of an Oboe!

I have to say here and now that Clarence and the Oboe did have an affinity, they were uncannily alike, wooden, jaundiced and very tall and skinny, in fact when Clarence stood behind the Oboe it was as if they were one because Clarence was so skinny that he almost disappeared, apart from a pair of skinny legs oddly protruding out of the bottom of the instrument.

It's a shame that the disappearance was just an optical illusion, because he began playing the dreadful instrument while standing behind it, this was very off putting, the noise was awful and the fact, that it appeared to be coming from a wooden instrument with unnaturally skinny legs was bizarre to say the least.

Clarence's Mother clapped her hands with such force that the entire noisy gathering abruptly stopped nattering, arguing, trading punches and shouting and even the young children stopped running around and stealing things that hadn't either been hidden or nailed down.

I clearly heard Clarence's Mother announce that Clarence was going to play some music for us all. The very piece of music, which had secured Clarence and I presume the unmentioned Oboe some sort of obscure Oboe related achievement.

'Music?' Never, she said must have said 'Moosick' well that is what it sounded like to me, and we all know that Moosick is Cow Vomit! And Clarence obviously deserved some sort of prize for creating a noise so surreal, that it made every one think of Cows vomiting.

If the noise that Clarence was making was especially unusual, what was most remarkable was the length of the piece, which seemed to lack all of the important aspects of a musical piece, namely melody, tone and most importantly an ending.

The crowd of some of the most hardened Humans ever to have gathered together in a suburban front room wept openly, which filled Clarence's Mother with misguided and misplaced pride she, one could tell, believed that the tears being shed by one and all, were tears of joy, even the occasional excited squeal Clarence's Mother attributed to awe inspired by Clarence's expertise with his instrument.

Sadly the recital was cut short before several of the silver haired Grandparents had managed to edge close enough to strike Clarence down with their plastic picnic cutlery, a particularly long and shrill note, which climbed beyond most Human hearing shattered the French windows with such force, that a large slither of glass flew through the air and cruelly, some would say, although the word 'thankfully' was probably on most people's lips, buried itself into the Oboe, just above the 'G' key.

Clarence was almost as distraught as his Mother at what had happened, without the 'G' key it was apparently impossible to continue the recital, which devastated little

Clarence who vanished in a flood of artistic tears but not before he threw the stricken instrument to the floor and caused it even more damage.

Later as people huddled together in groups still apparently worried that Clarence and his instrument might recover and cause their hearing even more harm, I overheard Clarence's Mother lament that they didn't own the Oboe, which was obviously beyond repair, it was in fact rented and that the family might have to give up paying for Clarence's Oboe lessons to pay for the damage.

I have a feeling that as Clarence's Mother moved around the crowd speaking loudly at various groups of hearing impaired relations she was expecting some kind soul to say that it was ok, they would save Clarence's musical career and pick up the bill for the repair and future music lessons, happily she was wrong!

Day 148 of My Captivity:

I wonder if you can imagine my surprise when (although I was very busy minding my own business on the Sofa with my eyes closing gently and my mind in that nodding off sleepy state), there in front of me on the television a man appeared.

A man who in a fit of sheer insanity declared that he was fit and sane (yeah right!) He further declared that he was going to spend a month eating only fast food and worse than that, only burgers, which I later discovered were not elderly statesmen, but buns filled with odd bits of beelike meat, rendered from heavily processed naughty bits of animals and red and yellow slime masquerading as ketchup and mustard.

This person was obviously an attention seeking idiot and clearly a liar, because he may have been fit as he stated but he couldn't have been sane to have even considered this monumental act of life threatening stupidity. After all he could have demonstrated that he had all of his marbles and announced that he was going to spend a month eating only Prawns!

Imagine eating only Prawns for a month, I can!

But this act of epic foolishness set me thinking, no not about whether the cretin managed to finish his month of eating fast food alive or not, I am sure that not many people were interested, I wasn't, it made me think about TV Chefs.

Not I hasten to add, a bunch of white overalled cooks, who create menus involving televisions, but the nitwits who invade our homes through television to tell us what we should cook.

Now don't get me wrong, it must be nice to have an interesting afternoon's entertainment, watching someone who is a master of their profession demonstrating just how to cook elaborate Human food that the average person wouldn't dream of cooking. However the types of Chefs who make it onto television and become true TV Chefs are failed entertainers and comics who also cook.

Some of the shows, that they haunt, have game show formats and others are just the sort of endless waffle of chat shows, but whether the TV Chef is cooking or not they are dressed in their Chef's whites and ready willing and able to make puerile jokes and pointless conversation.

What makes the ordeal of TV Chefs even worse is that in between their dreadful dull programmes they 'star' in the commercials for washing up liquid, supermarkets and all sorts of dross, who I ask you has decided that these 'experts' can influence the public?

Indeed who in their right mind would shop at a supermarket just because a second rate celebrity tells you that the profit conscious supermarket is providing value, while relating the delights of the supermarket's own brand ready made meals? Surely a Chef even a TV Chef should know that it is cheaper to cook from fresh ingredients rather than buy this type of highly processed rubbish. And it gets worse because at some stage you know that the dreaded TV Chef is going to launch himself into a campaign to make, say for instance school dinners better, the campaign will obviously have a petition signed by viewers, its own television series and a book, which will go some way to enhancing the TV Chef's image, to say nothing about lining his bulging pockets with hard cash.

Now I am sure that it is laudable of the TV Chef who I watched doing this, to care as much as he does to give up so much of his time and money, oops sorry I forgot he would have made the television programmes with his own production company and been paid a hefty whack for the broadcast.

But all of that aside, it strikes me that if parents wanted to improve their children's school meals, surely they could have dug deeper into their pockets and stumped up more than the few pennies they give to the school meals providers and not expect the government to pay for their children's meals! Or indeed bring the little blighters home for a cooked lunch, thus guaranteeing that they would get exactly the right type of lunch, because we are of course talking about 'School Lunches' and not 'School Dinners,' dinner being something that is served in the evening I believe, although one could argue that I am splitting fur here.

After all, the parents are getting their children's education for nothing, surely they don't expect to get nearly one third of their children's meals almost for free do they, while they are being educated?

Still what do I know, I am just a Cat and I get all of my meals free, but that doesn't stop me saying: TV Chefs don't you just loath them?

Day 149 of My Captivity:

I am afraid that I have been a little lax recently and I have not been trying very hard to escape, I have I am ashamed to say, become addicted to television and the television in the front room in particular and occasionally some of the programmes shown on that television.

As with all addicts I have to first defend my addiction, it is not my fault I am addicted, the television is on all of the time, and I just started using it and before you can say 'over to the local newsrooms for a round up of the news where you are,' I was hooked.

This addiction is both dreadful and disgusting equally I know I have it bad! I even like the weather now and tend to believe all of the nonsense delivered by the frivolous men and women of the weather department.

I have noticed one thing about the weather forecast and that is strangely there is some sort of weird hierarchy, weathermen are just that 'men', but weather women are 'girls,' can anyone tell me why that is, is it that weather forecasting is a young science which has only recently allowed women to talk drivel in front of a weather map?

Then there are the adverts in between the programmes, well it is true to say I know that some programmes are like adverts, but even they have adverts in between parts of their broadcast.

I love the adverts which use 'research' to sell their products, these are usually anti aging face creams and shampoo adverts and say things like 98% of all of our customers recommend our products, what does that mean when it says at the bottom that they only asked a few hundred or at the most a few thousand customers? Is the product only effective on a few people out of the millions watching, is that why they asked so few people, or did several million people refuse to offer an opinion, as they do when general elections come around?

Or worse when questioned about the product did 98% recommend the product and the other 2% die under interrogation?

Who knows the answer to this question? Not me for sure!

And I would like to know what has happened to the silent majority, the great and good people who just get on with life, oh sorry I know the answer to that question, they are the ones who wouldn't answer the question posed by the product manufacturers in the first place simple really, when you think about it.

Having said all of that I do believe that there is one product which has carefully researched its consumers, and that is the wonderful Cat food 'Tiddles®' which is made by those excellent sponsors of mine the Whisker's Corporation of America.

I would like to go on record by saying that 'Tiddles®' Cat food as we all know, is a 'real meal in delicious jelly™' which any Cat in his right mind would cross a busy road (at considerable risk to their person, it has to be said) for. Indeed Whisker's Corporation research has shown that 8 out of 10 Cats do® cross the road for their excellent products and that most Cats make it to the other side of the road.

Well you shouldn't condemn me for mentioning a valued sponsor, thinking about it I wonder if I could get my own series as a TV Chef? I am sure that I can come up with hundreds if not thousands of delicious nutritious recipes for the Whiskers Corporation of America's excellent Cat food and maybe even squeeze some of it into lunches at school and I bet that the little darlings wouldn't notice the difference between a chunky Tiddles burger and a chunky Chicken nugget.

DAY 150 OF MY CAPTIVITY:

How can you carry a grudge? Because, that is what they say when someone harbours a grievance, they carry a grudge, but it is another daft piece of the English Language. Honestly, speaking as a Cat, how did English become the most widely used language in the world when it is so obscure?

There is no way that a Cat would carry a grudge, we just don't have the pockets or the temperament.

Don't get me wrong I have tried to carry a grudge because there are so many things and people who get under my skin, oops another weird saying, as if people could actually get under one's skin, but then that is probably a saying that is slightly less obscure than the grudge business. It probably dates back to when people were not so clean and things actually got under their skin, like me you are probably shuddering at that thought.

Thinking of all of those old itchy people, scratching their way through life, is enough to make your skin crawl. Still society must have been more democratic back, then when all of the population was scratching together.

Just imagine having an audience with a King and coming away with more than you bargained for in the way of skin complaints. Henry the Eighth was big on giving his subjects more than they bargained for in the way of little gifts. In terms of diseases he was definitely a King among men, and more to the point women for that matter.

And goodness me, couldn't he carry a grudge too! If anyone got on the wrong side of him they were in trouble, wives beheaded, entire religions stamped out for what seem very petty and trivial reasons.

Now you are asking yourself what is this mad Cat talking about? I know it is all a little vague, but you have to remember this is a Diary and therefore a collection of my thoughts and experiences and last night I watched a programme on television about the British Royal family, and what a bunch of petty bullies they turned out to be all in all!

Goodness me if I was related to any of the criminals, murderers and mean individuals that the present royal family were related to directly, I think that I would try to hush it up or indeed keep it quiet rather than celebrate my linage!

But the British royal family, not only celebrates their not so humble or honest beginnings but make television programmes about it, oh! Sorry I forgot to mention that this television programme was made by the youngest member of the British royal family, unfortunately I didn't catch his name because although he was the presenter of the programme he didn't make as much of an impression on me as his ancestors did.

Well all I can say is that I will have to watch out for all of the members of the current Royal family if they ever come anywhere near me. You know hide the valuables and lock up the women and nail down anything that could be slipped into an Ermine stole! Because if they're anything like their ancestors described in the television programme that I watched, in horror I might add, then they would happily make off with whatever their light fingers could lay a hand on.

Which neatly brings me back to 'carrying a grudge,' it would seem from how the British people regard their royal family that they not only admire them, but that they have a strange wish to give them presents.

Yes I watched another television programme about gifts that had been given to a couple of members of the current 'family' who had been selling those gifts secretly, something that they apparently shouldn't do!

It seems to me and of course I am only a Cat after all, that this family is not much different to all of the, well let's call them 'swashbuckling' (I have no wish to lose my head after all) ancestors that this young balding royal prince was talking about in the programme before.

So if the British have endured so much from their numerous Kings and Queens over centuries, why don't they carry a grudge? Sometimes being a Cat looking at Humans and trying to understand them is difficult, but obviously not as difficult as being a British subject even in these 'enlightened' times.

Still if the British are that gullible, and the evidence is substantial, then a clever Cat can, will and does get away with anything. Still I don't think that I could go as far as the royal family's relations that went to exploit people, and let's face it if my ancestors had continually caused so many wars, ripped off, raped and murdered so many people I don't think that I would be inclined to make a television programme about them and get paid vast sums of money for the pleasure! But then I don't have any royal blood in me what so ever, thankfully!

It just goes to show how clever the Americans were to get rid of British rule and do all of their own stealing, squabbling and warring instead of being told to do it on behalf of a mad British monarch.

DAY 151 OF MY CAPTIVITY:

Earlier I found a large piece of ugly fluff probably an old furball or something equally awful, although I think it might be an old toy mouse and so as it had some Mouselike characteristics I decided to pretend that it was a mouse and drop it in the lap of the Female Captor in the hope that I could scare her into putting me outside! I mean who in their right mind wants to live with a killer?

I soaked the mangled 'body' in my own special way (no I don't think you need to know how actually), it was really disgusting by the time I had finished with it, I even found some Ketchup to complete the disguise and trotted into the front room and leapt up onto the Sofa dropping my 'gift' into her lap.

I couldn't believe her reaction all she did was to stroke me and pat me on the head and say 'good Cat,' while asking the Male Captor to get rid of the 'body,' they are worse than me in the unpredictable stakes, not that I am really bad, but don't they realise I could be a killer and not just acting like one.

So my plan to warn my Captors and show them just what I am capable of doing back fired, I thought that I would just get them really worried, that they had a being of such power in their midst, but all they did was congratulate me, unbelievable, don't they know they have a killer on the loose in their house? I don't think I will ever understand Humans!

I may have to try this tactic on a real animal, instead of a stuffed one and so I will have to become much more desperate than I am at the moment to carry out such an act of barbarism, where's the Parrot?

DAY 152 OF MY CAPTIVITY:

What sort of person, or for that matter animal, does an Internet search using their own name for goodness sake? I suppose they would have to be very confident or to put that another way, self important, I suppose that they would have to have done something interesting or at least think that they had done something interesting!

Or maybe there is a darker side to their actions, maybe they have some terrible secret hidden away that they don't want discovered and so they are constantly searching for any sign of it to surface, for instance they could be debtors, crooks or merely cross dressers or worse Mormons.

Anyway I wanted to search the web to see if I was on it anywhere and realised that I don't have a name to make a search with or for, I of course tried Cat, but that sent back so many websites that I thought my hard drive would melt.

You know it is a bit of a set back not having a name. Most people have two names, unless they are 'Sting' but not everyone is that perfect.

So based on the idea that one should have two names I have decided to call myself The Cat. 'The' being my forename, and absolutely not a Christian name, because I am not a Christian, if I was a Christian I would have called myself 'Christian Cat.'

Now don't get me wrong 'Christian Cat' has a bit of a ring to it as names go, but in my humble opinion all too obviously demonstrates one's religious convictions!

Not only that, the Christian name 'Christian' sounds a bit, well (how can I put this without hurting the precious feelings of any of the probably millions of people whose Christian names are 'Christian),' I don't know because they are probably very sensitive people, but it sounds a bit camp.

And for my last name, or surname as you Humans like to call it, I have chosen 'Cat,' because like 'Wheelwright,' 'Cooper,' 'Smith,' and 'Bastard,' my surname describes exactly what I am. The most obvious example above being 'Smith' as in 'Blacksmith,' oh that isn't as obvious as I thought, because there are 'Goldsmiths' and 'Silversmiths,' but you see what I am getting at, a 'Wheelwright' made wagon wheels and a 'Cooper' made Barrels although why they didn't get called 'Mr. Wagonwheel' or 'Mr. Barrelmaker' I don't rightly know!

Anyway you can see that I have thought about needing a name a lot, and I have come to the conclusion that I really do need a name, if I don't have a name whose name is going to be on the cover of my Diary? Whose name will all of the cheques get made out to? How will I open a bank account? Worse still how will I find myself on the Internet?

DAY 153 OF MY CAPTIVITY:

I am now in a divine state of mind, which is better than being in Cat heaven as I was a few days ago. Today I really do feel like the Cat that got the cream, and that Cat is me, 'The Cat,' sorry I was just practicing using my new name!

Why am I in such a good mood? Because, I have just been talking to my Agent online, and he has told me that he has already secured a publishing deal, which is wonderful news.

The not so good news is that, my Agent, sorry to use that term again, I am sure that I will get used to talking about Mr. Leibowitz, 'call me Todd' instead of my 'Agent,' but you, I am sure will forgive me at the moment because it is not everyday that a Cat has a Literary Agent, is it?

Still I am sure you will understand and forgive me! Anyway there is also some not so good news and that is that both my Agent and my Publisher think that I should stay here in captivity until I have finished writing the book which is as we all know a Diary, but I didn't fancy mentioning that little fact to my Agent, because I don't want to spoil things and lose my publishing deal, I can always wait and spoil things later after I have signed the contract, like most writers do!

Although I have around 130,000 words which have already been translated from the original Cat I need a lot more than that number to make it appear to the general public, or my readers as I like to think of them, so that they are not being ripped off, or that is what the Publisher said at any rate, I was personally ready to leave this prison now and invent the rest of the Diary, but they said no, that wouldn't be ethical, I mean really what do Cats know about ethics?

In my opinion I can't believe that people could be so inhumane, but then I suppose no one could ever invent what has happened to me while I have been here and I wouldn't want to turn my hard work into fiction would I? I suppose not, but I did fancy being holed up in a penthouse luxury apartment, where I could enjoy my sizable advance and finish the Diary in comfort!

With all of that in mind, it is a little worrying that I will be here for a good while longer, I am not looking forward to that prospect or what might happen to me in the future. Although in the end after I had whined and asked then to reconsider their decision, my publisher said that they would give me a final answer on Wednesday after I had put my case to them in an email.

So I can't wait until Wednesday, which is only a few days away after all.

DAY 154 OF MY CAPTIVITY:

The Male Captor's Mother was here today, she is what I can only describe as a difficult woman, and to be honest difficult to describe too. Her dress sense is sort of hand-me-down; Rocco Woolworth's and her make-up looks as though she has it sprayed on by several unkind Graffiti artists in the dark. She looks like - well I don't know what she looks like; nature can be so unkind sometimes!

Worst of all she will insist on stroking me with her leathery hands and trying to feed me Dolly Mixtures and Jelly Tots, which sadly I am addicted to now, which in turn is awful, not just because I am addicted to them but because they stick to my teeth and take hours of rough licking to remove.

Of course they are never totally removed because I am fed another and another, in the end I start to get a little nervy and ratty because of the overdose of sugar and the fact that I can't remove the sweets from my teeth and I bite her, leaving a couple of sugar encrusted marks on her finger.

It looks like a sweet-toothed vampire has been having a Human snack, not at all attractive.

The last time I bit her she just tasselled the fur on my head and said, 'I wonder why people love you, when you are so terrible to them?' Mmmh, she is so even tempered I could get contaminated and become nice and that would probably mean that I would give up wanting to escape and become content to be a lap Cat, and although that has its upside, obviously, I would never be free or indeed be my own boss!

Am I terrible to the people who love me? Does that mean that the Human Captors... No I can't finish the sentence it is too terrible to think of what I might really feel for them! Having said that if they would leave the door open for an hour or so I would love them and always think fondly of them, but from somewhere else.

There is a Human saying that: 'No amount of time can erase the memory of a good Cat,' and that is true but as it is a Human saying it has a sting in the tail and finishes, 'and no amount of masking tape can ever totally remove his fur from your couch!' It pays to remember things like that at times like this!

Day 155 of My Captivity:

There is one good thing about today, Tuesday, apart from the fact that it is sunny here and that is, as days of the week go it is closest to Wednesday and on Wednesday I am promised the news from my Publisher which may see me released from this prison early, you will remember (I hope) that the Publisher said that I would get my decision on Wednesday and so I am hopeful that I can finish the Diary in comfort somewhere else, as you know I have already made my suggestions as to where I would prefer to finish writing my Diary.

The sad thing about Wednesdays here where I live, is that they are only Tuesdays in America, so maybe Tuesdays aren't so good here after all because I will probably have to wait until Thursday here to get Wednesday's news and that isn't very good is it? Now would you look at that, the sun has gone in and the clouds have clotted together!

So as you can see the only problem with Tuesday is that it isn't Wednesday and I bet when Wednesday actually dawns I will be told that I have to wait until Thursday, does anyone know how frustrating all of this is, it makes a Cat feel like putting on pounds, while eating to occupy the idle moments, although I suppose because of the all of the photographs people will want to take of me when I am famous, maybe I should watch the waistline a bit so I can't eat, although here is a little waistline tip, Prawns are not fattening.

Day 156 of My Captivity:

Ok I am sure that you want to know whether I am packed and waiting to leave this prison in a limousine for the comfort of a New York penthouse where I will finish my Diary in luxury! So I won't disappoint you and string out the suspense, isn't that nice of me?

It was decided by my Agent and my Publisher that I should stay here in prison and finish the Diary, which will apparently give the whole story authenticity, well I am appalled, happily I can be appalled and even say I am appalled because I have signed my contract and have online confirmation from my offshore bank that the book advance for my Diary has been transferred to my account, which is great I hope that it likes being in a tropical paradise, I know I would like to be with it too.

The decision did upset me for a while, but then I got to thinking about it and I came to the conclusion that I should just go on trying to escape and if I managed to escape then all I had to do would be to join my money in the Bahamas and finish the Diary on a sun lounger in the shade of a palm tree or two.

So you will be happy to hear that I am as determined to escape now as I was last week, I am just a lot richer, even after Mr. Leibowitz, 'call me Todd' has had his percentage.

In fact if anything I am even more determined to escape because I want to get my paws on my cash and take the opportunity to look at the world from above, because there is no doubt when I do get my paws on my cash I will be enjoying the very highest 'hi-life.'

There was one little complication in setting up the bank account and that was the small fact that the bank required a signature for the account, obviously there isn't much that a clever Cat can't do, but providing a signature is sadly one of those things that is impossible.

Happily I discovered that offshore banks and offshore bankers are… how can I put this, without offence? Unfortunately I can't think of a way, so here is the truth, offshore bankers and offshore banks are always happy to bend the rules for a wealthy client who requires anonymity, all I had to do was ask!

My bank gladly demonstrated a way of creating a trail of bank accounts and shell companies from Switzerland through to the Bahamas via Luxembourg and Liechtenstein and other shady locations, where money has a loud voice of its own, until I was presented with a bank account which although had my money in it, that fact wasn't immediately apparent and therefore didn't need my signature and better still wasn't sullied by common things like taxation.

Really, financial experts are amazingly clever, and happily announced that I had nothing to worry about as my money was safe with them and they would make sure that I didn't pay tax anywhere, which sounds good to me. When I thanked them they said that it was all in a day's work and what they had done for me was something that they did for all rich people the world over.

Isn't it nice to be rich? Although I do wish that I could have some of the trappings of being rich, but that will come, just as soon as I manage to get out of here, so you will excuse me if I go back to planning my next escape, I won't call it an escape 'attempt' because that suggests failure!

Day 157 of My Captivity:

There is a saying that success is the ability to go from one failure seamlessly to another without losing enthusiasm, I wonder if that is true and if it is, is that why I haven't given up trying my hardest to escape or is it a fact that persistence is the last refuge of the foolish?

Undaunted by what mostly seems to amount to failure I am just about to launch another escape attempt and I use the word 'launch' advisedly here.

As you will know by now, if you have been paying attention and if you haven't been reading ahead most of the inspiration for my escape plans comes from the television and this one is no different, in the afternoon there are some animated public information programmes that I have developed a great liking for and watch avidly.

The hero is an odd looking Wolfie sort of character who to his credit is probably an honorary Cat, because his educational programme is dedicated to the various and very creative ways to exterminate a particularly nasty looking deformed Chicken type bird that definitely has some sort of appalling disease, which has made its legs grow out of proportion to the rest of its body.

This odd looking Chicken individual has as far as I can tell only one advantage over the rather adorable Wolfie looking hero and that advantage is that the Chicken can run like the wind. Oddly he only runs on public highways, which should mean that the advantage belongs to the Wolfie hero, but alas that is not the case because the Chicken always seems to escape any injury.

I have to say I would like to get my paws around his scrawny neck and hold him down while the Wolfie hero finishes off the job of getting rid of the last of his kind.

Life isn't like that sadly, but happily the hero keeps trying and obviously employs the motto 'if at first you don't succeed, try, try again.'

It was a famous King in a Kilt who apparently said that one has to try, try again first, while he kept spoiling a web that the spider was trying to spin by cutting bit of the web with his fingers.

Apparently the Kilted King was hiding from the English after losing a battle or two, and he watched the patient spider as it continued to try and undo his unkindness.

I have to say that the spider must have been rather dim to have kept on trying, while that idiot kept messing up his web building, but he did keep trying, and his efforts inspired the King in a Kilt to keep on trying! Which of course is why Scotland is an independent country today – oops!

Having said all of that I am sure that persistence pays in the end, although I have no idea whether the spider did manage to spin the web that he needed to catch his dinner with or not, history unkindly forgot to mention that fact!

History is not very kind to the King in a Kilt either, let's face it; if the sum of your life's achievement is to be remembered for persistently molesting a Spider and ruining the poor defenceless creature's web, you didn't really achieve much in life did you?

DAY 158 OF MY CAPTIVITY:

It is strange where Humans leave their discarded toe and fingernails; you know the bits that they snip at and that fly off anywhere and all over the place!

Would you believe that they just let them fly off into oblivion would you, how unsavoury, well to be more precise they don't just let them fly off, oh no they let them land on the floor and lie in waiting for some poor unsuspecting, and good looking Cat, to be pricked by the sharp end sticking up out of the carpet, like a tyre shredder that stops cars using the wrong lane when exiting car parks, or stops them pretty soon after they have used the wrong lane, that's for sure!

Now you see, if Humans had claws they wouldn't have to cut them, all they would have to do is sharpen them. Yes getting your claws really sharp is time consuming but really rewarding. When you are able to have a long uninterrupted sharpening session the feeling transports you, until that is, you get a tap from a shoe somewhere 'personal' to remind you not to sharpen your claws on the Sofa.

Honestly Humans just don't understand Cats at all, if they did they wouldn't offer a boot on one's 'booty' as a reward to a Cat innocently sharpening its claws would they?

Still if one's claws still need a little honing after being interrupted while using the Sofa, you can just continue the sharpening on the carpet, though I have to say I prefer the texture of a Sofa, because the carpet tends to burn the tips of one's pads.

I am sure that all Mummies and Daddies know how carpet burns hurt don't you! It is ok I won't say any more on that subject, and hurt the sales of this Diary across both the adult and children's market!

Day 159 of My Captivity:

We have just got a new Sofa and some matching armchairs that seem to just come with the Sofa whether you want them or not, maybe the Sofa gets lonely without matching armchairs, I have noticed this fact from the television, even when a room, is full to bursting with the trendy two Sofa deal you can guarantee that there will be two armchairs lurking in the corners of the room like lonely bachelors at a 'meet the neighbours' cocktail party.

The new Sofa and, of course, the armchairs are leather, and I have to say they are extremely comfortable. I heard an environmentalist on the television say that it takes around ten cows to make a leather Sofa and I am so glad that they bothered.

Do you suppose I watch too much television? Maybe I should use the Internet more! Hang on what am I saying? I should get out more! Well truthfully just once would be enough.

What a 'Great Escape' that would be, oh no I am talking in old film titles now, I think I will go and lie down, or I could have a look through my 'Secret window,' while I eat some 'Chocolat,' I just hope that there isn't a 'Nutty Professor' to 'Analyze This' or 'Analyze That' for that matter, I know I need help I wouldn't like to fall into a 'Matrix' of despair would you? Well there is one comfort to be had, only one of the film titles was of a really bad film, and maybe I will let you decide which one I think it was, needless to say here is a clue – 'The Nutty Professor' was dreadful!

Sorry that wasn't much of a clue! Really what was the studio thinking of? But then thinking about bad films for a moment and there have been a few, just think the Irish guy in Alexander who set a trend for speaking Irish in films about classical Greek myths, made Ronald Reagan look like a classic actor, but then thinking about it again, he would have made Lassie look good!

Day 160 of My Captivity:

After putting on a few pounds here and unfortunately 'there' I have decided that it is time to go on a diet, the major problem is choosing which one is just perfect for me because there are just so many to make a selection from.

Oddly enough I have discovered that I have the same requirements as most Humans have when choosing a diet! I want one that obviously doesn't involve actually not eating or cutting out my favourite little treats and snacks, one that helps me to maintain a balanced healthy and active lifestyle, although I have to say that recently I have not been exercising or eating properly so that might be a novel idea, but all the same not a very appealing idea!

What to eat? That is a definite consideration and much more appealing than considering what not to eat! I have noticed on television and actually in real life from the Human Captors that diets themselves can be rather odd, combining all sorts of unusual and to my way of thinking incompatible foods or worse still only one type of food. Imagine spending a few weeks of your life eating Rice cakes recommended by one diet only to find that they are in the dreaded 'red' or 'avoid' category of another.

Surely doing something like that would be enough to drive a Cat to drink, so long as it is low fat milk that is!

Food itself doesn't seem to want to help the committed dieter, for instance I discovered that the delightfully dainty dish of Prawns wrapped in little jackets of crispy breadcrumb batter, which I believe is called Scampi after the French chef who invented the dish, is not recommended in any of the diets that I have heard of, worse still, it is positively discriminated against by all of the diet experts, who I have discovered don't like food or the people who eat it and express their dislike by inventing diets that firstly never work and secondly are full of the most awful food known to man and Cat for that matter.

These evil fiends write large horror books, full of the do's and don'ts of eating, they are obviously in the pay of several subversive organizations like the Soil Association and the Brassica Growers Co-operative, because the diets in their books are full of alarming lightly steamed Broccoli and Cabbage, how, I ask you, is a Prawn eating carnivore going to lose weight eating sticks of crunchy green things?

I know the answer, don't eat anything, and I believe that I may have suggested that to the health conscious fatties amongst my dear readers before, but what is 'sauce for the goose,' is not necessarily sauce for this Pussy Cat! And this is the problem for all committed dieters as far as I can tell.

We can all read excellent diet books and we can even offer others good advice about not eating, or eating healthily, exercise and all that stuff, which sounds like a lot of pain and hard work, so long as the pain and hard work is specifically for others, but when the pain and hard work is for one's self that is another matter and not to be recommended at all!

Still I have discovered the perfect diet, one that is a masterpiece of carefully balanced nutritional advice, easy to follow and requires very little effort to stick to and no exercise what so ever, so I am as happy as that person who always seems to be very happy, 'larry.'

Sorry? What did you say? You want me to share the secret of my amazingly successful diet and fitness regime! Yes I thought that you would like to know, well I have a real treat for you, and you too can share in this incredible life changing wonder diet!

All you have to do is to buy my book, which explains the diet in full, available as a limited edition 'e-book' only on the Internet.

This valuable 'no effort slimming resource' will only be available to a specially selected and lucky few who I contact with a spam email, so do please have your credit card, or someone else's, close to the computer when the spam email arrives, so that you can take advantage of this never to be repeated opportunity of a lifetime and become the new you!

Now I have to stop writing for a while because I am going into the kitchen to indulge little self, in one of my five daily portions of invigorating meals, after that I will feel like a new Cat, but also very sleepy and won't be able to write anymore of my Diary today!

Don't forget to look out for the spam email though, so that you can share my 'miracle of life diet,' and achieve the new you that is slimmer, better looking and definitely not the one, which is currently popping the buttons on your trousers, or splitting zips on your dresses, and unfortunately just waiting to burst out.

Day 161 of My Captivity:

Today I had a bit of a shock, I was getting to know more about my mobile phone, you know pressing some of the buttons dotted around the phone, which have strange little icons painted on them, when the phone made an odd clicking noise, just like the shutter on an expensive camera.

I quickly checked the display to see if I had done something wrong, not that I have ever managed to work out what most of the information on the display actually means, when right in front of me was a picture of me, it was amazing, and not only that it was an amazingly good picture too and I was very impressed with it and also the phone's ability to take pictures, to be honest it wasn't the sort of thing I had expected from my phone.

I had expected to be able to make calls and read almost unintelligible text messages and even be able to send and receive emails or that is what it said on the box that the phone came in, but I was surprised and delighted by this photographic ability which until now I had not known about.

Yes I suppose that I would have known about the phone's other more or less hidden abilities if I had read the manual, but let's face it, who reads manuals? Only the terminally lonely in my opinion! Surely you have to be pretty sad to do that!

With that in mind, I was in my opinion, and I am sure that you will back me up here, very surprised to see me looking back at me from the phone's screen.

In fact I was so impressed with this useful photographic discovery that I spent the next five hours exploring the phone trying out all of the hidden features that the phone had to offer and that until now I hadn't known about.

I suppose that I could have saved myself an enormous amount of confusion and even more time, to say nothing about my reserves of patience, had I remembered where I had left the manual and read it. But for the life of me I just couldn't think where I had tossed the box which held the manual and all of the other bits and pieces of clutter, that seem to come with every new piece of electronic equipment that one buys these days.

But I wasn't too bothered; surely I reasoned that an intelligent Cat could easily master something as simple as a mobile phone.

Sadly that was not to be the case, because the people who design mobile phones don't have the same type of minds as us mere mortals, and I obviously include myself in that description although I do consider myself to be slightly above 'mere' I have to say.

After spending several hours trying just to get the picture of me off the screen and returning the screen back to what it looked like before it had a picture of me on it, I began to lose heart and think that maybe I had lost the capacity of normal logical thought.

In the end though I managed that simple task and the screen looked perfect, sadly I have to admit that this was not due to me discovering how to do what was required, oh no it was due to the fact that I turned the phone off and then back on. It was about this time that I realised that getting to know all of the features on this phone wasn't going to be easy.

In fact I had concluded that it was going to be as easy as connecting the phone to its charger, which for a Human is probably easy enough but for a Cat without fingers is unbelievably hard.

Cats rarely give up, which is why this Cat will one day escape from this prison, but I have discovered that determination is a double edged sword, because the more perplexing, confusing and just plain difficult the task is the more determined one becomes to complete it successfully and the consequences are not always attractive, especially when one's tongue starts to poke out of one's mouth in a vain attempt to assist one's thought processes.

Yes you guessed it the next thing I managed to do with the phone was to take a less than flattering picture of me concentrating, and I was appalled with the image, I looked like a refugee from an unsuccessful expedition which had been trying to trek across a large desert and had lost its water supply on the third day of a ten day ordeal, very nasty.

I then spent even more time trying to get rid of the offending image, and I had to be really careful that I didn't somehow send it as a text message (yes I know when a picture is a text message, when it is on a mobile phone of course) or an email attachment to all of the people in my address book.

Why, I hear you ask, was I worried about that, well before I took the offending and offensive picture of me with my tongue lolling out of my mouth I had discovered something called 'Bluetooth.'

With this amazing 'connectivity feature,' no I haven't read the manual, I am just guessing that is how it would describe 'Bluetooth,' I found out that I could upload the address book of all other 'Bluetooth' phones nearby.

At the time I was delighted by this facility because I have always been a curious individual and to be able to 'borrow' this type of information intrigued me, in fact the facility excited me because we all know that knowledge is power and knowing who other people talk to is, it struck me, very powerful indeed.

So you can see just how worried I was now to think that any minute all of the people in my bulging address book, who it has to be said I didn't know, might receive a picture of me was a little distressing, firstly because the picture was just so awful, and secondly because it was more than a little incriminating, because they would find out that I had 'borrowed' their contact details.

You can imagine just how careful I was, even if I had known how to delete all of my new contacts I didn't really want to, simply because I was confident that at some time in the future I could use the information, that I had obtained, to my advantage.

I could tell that there was a problem developing and that problem was that I was becoming mesmerised by all of the phone's functions and options, what else could this little spy do? What other information could I glean from the ether or radio waves or wherever the information pops up from?

The prospect of spying on my neighbours and their Bluetooth mobile phones was enticing, but at the same time I was concerned that I would suddenly spoil my fun and betray myself, what a quandary, but at the same time what fun!

After a while I managed to find out how to unlock the phone. I wasn't really trying to do this but as I had somehow managed to lock the phone, unlocking it became something of a priority. Like everything to do with a mobile phone, it is simple when you know how to do it, but that is part of the problem as far as I can tell, because once you have found out how to do something you have to practise doing whatever you have done over and over again because what you achieved is so simple that you forget how you did it all too easily.

Finally after hours of playing with the little black and silver phone I had a fair idea of what I could do with it, sadly that wasn't exactly a lot, but I had learned how to do the basics and that you will have to admit, is more than most Cats know. Most Cats would feign disinterest and purr for some attention, but then, as you will have gathered by now, I am not like most Cats!

DAY 162 OF MY CAPTIVITY:

By now after several days of what seems like a lull in my escape attempts, you probably think that I have gone soft and have given up any thoughts of escape, and frankly all I can say in reply is! 'You are so completely wrong that you should be awarded some sort of prize for achieving such a pinnacle of wrongness.'

After more or less giving up with the deeper workings of my mobile phone I watched some television and as usual was astounded by the quality of the documentaries. The marvel in question was a serious and a little complicated documentary called 'Time Tunnel,' the programme was a little old having been made in the 1960's, but it was, in spite of its age, very interesting.

I have a feeling that it was more of a 'docu drama', which I understand, is a programme which is part fact and part drama, the main drama of this programme being the shape of the presenter's haircut and the style of his clothes, but for all of that interesting statement in taste, it was very inspiring and extremely engaging.

If the desire of this programme's producers was to inspire and educate, then they hit the target with one viewer at least, and judging by the fact that it was only me who drained the National Grid of electricity today, they, I have to say, succeeded in their brief.

That is not to say that other viewers of this incredible documentary didn't try their hand at replicating the experiment for all I know, they just didn't succeed, which with hindsight is probably just as well!

Still, I prefer to think that I was probably the only viewer, who was sufficiently enthused with the desire to repeat the experiment demonstrated in the wonderful programme, but then I have always liked science, especially when science can be put to use and to my personal advantage to boot, and even though I blush when I admit it, I am probably a lot cleverer than most viewers and definitely more dedicated to harnessing science for my personal gain.

It took most of the day to assemble the equipment required by the experiment and I have to say a lot of improvisation, but by lunchtime I had managed to get most of what I needed and had laid it out on the utility room floor.

The choice of the utility room was governed more by the fact that the Male Captor had left an old washing machine in it rather than its suitability.

Personally I would have preferred a proper laboratory with banks of computers with flashing red and green lights along one wall and in a corner large columns of white light pulsating through filmy clouds of smoke, the virgin sparks of light causing reflections in the glass of thistle flasks, filled with primordial liquid, that are being gently heated by roaring Bunsen burners, but sadly that was just wishful thinking.

I was lucky that the old washing machine had just been forgotten about and been left in the utility room because the Male Captor hadn't got around to putting it outside, where it was going to be collected and recycled, mind you I bet I know one of the Captors who hasn't forgotten about the collection of scrap metal and redundant wires, and more than that I also know one other Captor of the Male variety, who will get his ear bent constantly until he shakes a leg and moves the redundant machine.

Of course the reason why the poor old washing machine has been abandoned in the utility room is that as the Male Captor was manhandling the washing machine out of the kitchen, he banged his knuckles on the utility room door frame, scraping off the paintwork and replacing it with some of his skin, then in a fit of temper he dragged and kicked the washing machine into the utility room, losing interest in putting the washing machine outside he went off to bandage his hand and swear some more upstairs in the bathroom, where the Humans keep the first aid kit.

Still as you can tell I wasn't the one complaining, most of the 'parts' that I needed for my experiment were actually components of the washing machine and if they weren't exactly what I needed then I believed, quite rightly as it turned out, they could be easily adapted!

They say that necessity is the mother of invention and as I definitely needed this invention to ensure I escaped, I took quite a while to gather all of the parts that I needed, but wasn't able to find inside the washing machine.

Most of the bits and bobs I needed, that weren't available in the carcase of the washing machine I took from other electrical appliances around the house, the curling tongs from their bedroom, and a pair of headphones from the spare room I knew would come in handy.

Although I have to say I regretted slightly the fact that I wasn't able to carry the mini stereo downstairs, nor could I 'persuade' it to fall off the shelving and burst open so that I could get at the circuits that I thought I might just need, still be thankful for small mercies is what easily contented people say and for a moment I adopted their philosophy.

I also stopped by the bathroom to 'borrow' several reels of the sticking plaster which had been left out by the Male Captor when he bandaged his hand, and a couple of other bits and pieces which I knew I would probably need.

By lunchtime I had the floor of the utility room covered with most of the innards of the washing machine and bits of assorted electrical appliances and was happily taping together all sorts of interesting electrical components around my central core which of course was the middle of the washing machine.

For those of you, who are not so technically minded I will try to explain what I am constructing. At the heart of a washing machine is an electric motor and an electric motor has wound around it miles of copper wire, which was going to be the centre of my apparatus.

The first thing I did was to dismantle the motor casing and drape the copper coil around the washing machine drum, then without much assistance from an electric jigsaw, but just enough to cut a ragged hole at the back of the drum I managed to create my own tunnel, which would be the heart of my mechanism.

All I had to do then was to mount the drum, sadly I couldn't find a couple of bricks in the utility room which would have been perfect, but I did find two very large packs of washing powder that were almost as good, and I pushed them together to form a solid base which would stop the 'tunnel' moving if there were any vibration problems and between you and me, I expected a bit of vibration, nothing terrible, just enough to put a smile on your face if you get my meaning.

Running from the copper coil 'tunnel' I fixed a series of fuses, capacitors and switches, which hopefully will mean that I can switch the machine on and off, deal with any electrical overloads and direct all of the enormous pulsating energy into the copper coil.

The whole construction took just over an hour, which was great although unfortunately it was getting dark outside and obviously meant that the dismantling of the various electrical appliances had taken much longer than I had expected, and it also meant that there was no time for any clearing up.

So with a big smile on my face, which comes from the certain fact that success is just around the corner or in this case going to come from the flick of a switch, I plugged the machine in and switched it on.

I am delighted to say, that almost immediately the whole apparatus began to get hot, wires that were glowing yellow one minute began to turn white hot the next, some of these wires weren't really supposed to turn white hot, but they did all the same, probably because their blue and brown protective plastic coatings melted, but that was a little detail that I didn't really think was particularly important.

What was important was to put on my emergency mask, sadly I hadn't been that fortunate when looking for safety equipment, but as one's face is one's fortune I had found something which I thought would at least protect my fortune.

I had never heard of 'masque rapide éclat pureté,' but I did notice under the almost impenetrable French a few words of clarity, yes they were in English and I have found, if you want to make yourself understood by most of the people of the world, then English is 'just the ticket' as they say, funnily enough in England.

The more comprehensible name for the tube of stuff that I was now liberally smearing all over my face and for good measure all over my body was 'deep cleansing emergency mask' I wasn't too bothered about its deep cleansing powers but the idea of a semi liquid mask for emergencies was alright by me! When I found the tube in the bathroom, after the entire contents of the bathroom cupboard had 'somehow' spontaneously fallen out I was impressed by the one large silver lettered word 'masque' and my intuition told me that it would come in handy and of course I was right, it is nice being right, but nicer being right all the time, like I am!

Now to be honest with you I hadn't planned to actually have any emergencies, but then I never do, and so based on past experiences I decided that the precaution of covering myself in the creamy emergency mask was an exceptionally good idea and would be bound to pay dividends if anything went wrong, which I have to say I considered to be unlikely.

As I slopped the last dollop of emergency mask into my face and smoothed it down as best I could over my back and legs, I noticed that in the middle of my mini Time Tunnel the air was shimmering and wherever you looked an enormous power radiated through and out of the structure, obviously the machine was nearly ready (whatever that means), though I was a little disturbed to find that the metal was very hot and the scorching air billowing from the centre of the machine started to heat up the thick coating of emergency mask all over my body.

In fact the blistering heat that was emanating from the machine began to drive all of the moisture from my emergency mask, which I had prudently smeared from my head to the tip of my tail and that wasn't a nice feeling at all, I knew that I had to act swiftly.

As I strode in what I imagined was true Neil Armstrong style towards the machine, the lights everywhere in the utility room and kitchen began to dim until the only light left anywhere was the fierce blaze of light radiating in cruel rays from the centre of my wonderful mini Time Tunnel and teleportation machine.

The experience of wading closer to the machine through the electric force field was exhilarating, unfortunately I had to squint because the light was so bright that I could feel it burning my eyelashes and so I could see even less of where I was going with each shuffling step forward.

With every smouldering step I found it more and more difficult to stagger to the entrance of my mini Time Tunnel, the emergency mask was drying out very quickly and as it dried out it became extremely stiff, until I was walking like a knight in a rusted suit of armour, most uncomfortable and very inconvenient because if I couldn't bend my knees and that was getting more difficult as each second passed, I didn't know how I was going to climb into the opening of the Time Tunnel, let alone run down into it and vanish to wherever destiny was going to deliver me.

During the whole of the time I had been working on the mini Time Tunnel or I suppose to give it its proper scientific name the Transportation Device I had been fantasising about where the amazing contraption might take me? What strange worlds would I visit, and what would the people be like there? Because I reckoned that even unbelievably odd and ugly green skinned and purple eyed aliens would be nicer to a Cat than the Humans I had encountered on planet Earth.

So finally as I strode (ok stumbled really) with my head held proudly erect (yes you are right I couldn't move my neck at all) towards new worlds, different time continuums (alright or oblivion, keep your hair on won't you), I was prepared for the most amazing experience and indeed experiment of a lifetime (yes ok I was scared shiftless but this is my account so I'll tell my 'braver' side of the story thank you, without any interference from readers, if you can bear that in mind for the rest of the book and the others to follow in the series).

It was a shame that the heat was so ferocious, but I knew I could cope, to a certain extent it was also a shame that I seemed to be completely encased in the sort of plaster that is used to set broken bones.

However I believe that everything has an up side, the porcelain finish on the emergency mask was reflecting heat and also seemed to be acting as an insulation so that the violent bolts of electricity, which showered me as I stumbled to the mouth of the Time Tunnel, didn't turn me into the same sort of smouldering offering that one gets in a traditional roadside restaurant.

Probably looking more like an odd china Robot than a Cat, I stumbled to the mouth of the fiery tunnel, my legs were locked straight and so using the word walking is definitely out of the question, my passage to the tunnel entrance was much more mechanical than that.

Eventually I made it to the outer lip of my fiery machine and the promise of travelling infinity, or at the very least to the end of the cul-de-sac and freedom.

With some difficulty I managed to climb up to tunnel entrance and without any regrets what so ever I took one last look around at the world which I was about to say goodbye to, unfortunately there wasn't a crowd to witness my triumph, I am sure that the Dog and Parrot were too scared of the pyrotechnics, but that was probably just as well because I could hardly move my legs and wouldn't have been able to wave farewell anyway.

Just as I was about to take a small step for Catkind, I tripped and fell, touching the outer edge of the apparatus and must have shorted the machine because I remember hearing all of the light bulbs in the house explode and then the fainter sound of streetlights exploding, in tall infernos outside and in the distance, although of course some of that noise I later found out were light bulbs in neighbours' houses and oh yes, their washing machines, electric cookers, refrigerators and basically anything else that runs on mains electricity.

Having said all of that, those small detonations were brief and insignificant compared to the next explosion, I think when I fell I must have touched a wire or two because I have a suspicion that I caused a little electrical short, come to think of it I am pretty sure that the fire was mainly electrical because of all of the blue flames which raced around and through the Time Tunnel.

Bright nimbuses of sharp stabbing electric blue flame shot everywhere, racing around and through the tunnel turning it into a Catherine wheel of sparks, smoke and searing flame.

The energy right in front of my nose was incredible and as it whizzed and crackled around the tunnel's entrance the bright piercingly blue nimbuses spun together to form an enormous vortex of pure energy. I would say here that I was exhilarated, but that might be obvious and a little frightening too, but that is natural, the atmosphere was electric, but I think that you have probably worked that out for yourself.

The raw energy spinning in the spiralling clouds of blue fire had an odd effect upon me, it very gently picked me up until I was floating inside the entrance to the machine and then drew me closer so that I was suspended between the world I was leaving and the unknown void beyond the machine.

Now in times of panic, and I have to admit sheer terror, I have discovered that one's mind tends to play tricks on even the sanest Cat and so what I saw may have been fright induced and with that in mind, you will have to forgive me a few paragraphs of what might, in the cold light of the next day, (yes it took that long to get the national Grid to function again), sound mad, but what I saw at the end of the tunnel and just a little out of reach was amazing.

They say that as one drowns one's life passes before one's eyes and I have to say that I now fervently believe that to be the truth, but with one or two qualifications.

If it was my life racing in front of me now, then it was unbelievable! Everywhere the blue flame and hissing clouds had been replaced by gold, in the distance I could see graceful golden trees nestling against shores of placid golden water.

Several golden suns delicately and lovingly caressed a glittering landscape, golden weightless beings, who were walking passed the end of the tunnel stopped to smiled fondly at me, one or two even stooped to try and take hold of my paws and pull me to their side of the vortex.

Then the air shimmered and billowed like a sheer curtain in a breath of wind sighing at a window and everything that I had seen changed, there before me now was the beautiful smiling benevolent face of a golden Human looking God. His golden face was dusted with the white fur of wisdom and without moving his mouth he was talking to me, welcoming me to an eternity of peace and tranquillity.

It sounded tempting at first and I began to move towards the divine face and eternal rest, but then I started to think about the offer and realised that I was not the sort of Cat who was desperately interested in peace and tranquillity and that thought made me stop moving towards this placid eternity, as I thought more about the offer and became more certain that what was on offer was just not me, the whispers from the God like being grew louder and more urgent.

I was shown more of what I was missing, comfort, peace, freedom, and then when those temptations failed, eternal life.

Now that was tempting, eternal life has to be tempting and you probably think I was mad to say no thank you very much Mr. God, but I prefer the life I have now, if it is all the same to you, but just think about what life is like when you haven't got something to do, in no time at all you become bored, now magnify a few minutes of inaction to an eternity and you will see why I started to back-pedal as fast as I could.

When it was clear that I wasn't buying into the lifestyle offered, Mr. God disappeared in a huff and puff of golden smoke and I was left hanging in mid air inside my Time Tunnel machine, which was altogether an unusual experience I have to say.

The golden light had been replaced by the blue nimbuses again, I don't know if the emergency mask was failing like the doggy tiles under the Space Shuttle, but I was getting rather warm in my underneath bits, if this was what re-entry was like it was not very comfortable at all, I tried to roll on to my side and attain the same angle of re-entry that I had heard the Space Shuttle used, but two things stopped me!

The first thing to stop me was that there just wasn't the room and the second thing was that I had no idea what the required angle was, then just as I was settling into my new weightless state, I had another little problem.

Without thinking of the consequences, (oops that could be my epitaph), I touched the inside of the washing machine drum with my back paw.

It wasn't a prolonged contact but that was because I pulled my paw back as though I had almost touched a flame and flinched, but all the same it was the beginning of a chain reaction as opposed to all of the other little explosions, which until now had seemed to happen independently.

I could see sparks spewing from my paw, like the sparks from an angle grinder munching metal, except of course, and this should go without saying, but I know that I am writing for Humans here, so I'll say it all the same, the sparks were eye piercingly blue.

Part of my brain was saying 'get out of here now,' another part was saying 'oh look at how pretty that is' and the yet another part of my brain was saying 'how can I get out of here, I'm trapped, I'm going to die,' and all the usual stuff that pops into your head in moments of abject despair.

The pretty little blue sparks, began to clog together until they were just one mass of blue flame, which completely engulfed me as I hung painfully in the air.

It was then that I started to spin and tumble like a 1960's rookie astronaut in training. And then, (although I hate beginning a sentence with 'and' I am sure you will forgive me because I am still a little giddy from all of the spinning), I hit the side of the washing machine drum with a very heavy impact.

Everything shuddered, and I was spat out of the mouth of my amazing machine with a disgusting force, I sped like a rocket across the utility room and bounced twice on the floor before crash landing in a heap in the washing basket, thank goodness for dirty clothing is all I could think as I lay dazed and upside down watching the final volcanic end to my amazing creation.

My supersonic exit from the melting Time Tunnel seemed to have caused it to collapse, detonating a stupendous explosion, which in turn ignited a firework display of pyrotechnic insanity as right before my eyes my wonderful invention almost completely vanished leaving a pile of quivering ash and flaming puddles of melted electric cable.

In a fit of what some may call, just plain selfishness, I had a quick check to see if I had all of my legs attached and that more importantly once I had discovered that they were, that I could move them, my sigh of relief was long and heartfelt, and I quickly discovered that the couple of bounces, that I had made as I sped towards the washing basket, had smashed my emergency mask and I was able to move normally if stiffly is normal of course.

As I made a slightly more detailed inspection of my fur I was concerned to discover that it was going to need a lot of scrubbing to get the remnants of the emergency mask out of my fur, but as I reflected on the whole experience of such a wonderful experiment I considered that fact to be a small price to pay for the event.

I did in a moment's reflection consider that the possible cost of damage to the utility room would be a heavier financial burden, but then of course I managed a weak and broadening smile, that wasn't my problem!

If I timed it correctly I would be able to get upstairs, paddle in a bath, though that was not an inviting prospect, then curl up on their bed and have a sleep so that when the Human Captors returned I would be in the clear.

Later in the darkness and flashlight confusion that seemed to have engulfed the whole world, I could pretend to be oblivious to any of the damage that might be discovered and by the morning when the dreadful truth and daylight dawned, someone or something else would be the suspect for blame and not me, the worst that could happen to me was that I would just get into trouble for sleeping on their bed.

Just how clever am I? No don't answer that question please I haven't got time to listen at the moment and need to get the rest of this emergency mask off and complete my plan.

Day 163 of My Captivity:

It is a great feeling when a plan comes together and although it is sad and true to say that yet another of my plans to escape came crashing around my ears and in this case spat me across the utility room, it is nice to know that my planned alibi worked a treat.

There is an art to creating an alibi and even though it sounds immodest I believe that I have perfected that art, in fact after the money starts rolling in and I get bored with writing best selling Books, Diaries, Travelogues etc., I may go on the lecture circuit and give talks on the 'Art of the Alibi.'

Well I think that even with several millions in the bank and a freezer full of Prawns I would get bored easily if I just gave up work and not only that, it is always good to have several revenue streams I understand.

So unless I finish this Diary and you the wonderfully intelligent, very discerning, and phenomenally generous reading public, buy this Diary in its thousands I won't be able to give my lectures and think what a loss to the world that would be!

Although I have said this before, do please buy this Diary and I promise I won't be offended in anyway what so ever if you buy more than one copy.

Even if you don't like the Diary, just think what an attractive doorstop, for each and every door in the house my Diary would make, every door stop brilliantly decorated with a picture of me on the cover, between you and I, I am pretty sure that if you had such a door stop at every door in your home it would drastically increase the value of your home, so just consider the purchase of this Diary as an investment.

Apart from delighting in my successful alibi and writing this page of the Diary just for you, I have had an easy day, because I still feel a little disorientated, which I have put down to the experience of yesterday's experiment.

I was going to start hunting for some new components and begin building an improved Time Tunnel, but unfortunately there is only one washing machine left in the house now and that seems to be firmly fixed in place near the sink in the utility room which is something of a blow, because this time I know I could iron out many of the little design faults that obviously crept into the prototype Time Tunnel.

I have just heard the last bit of good news for today and that was announced via a large loud speaker on top of a National Grid van, and that bit of good news is that the power will be on by tomorrow evening at the latest, so that is nice isn't it, and I imagine that the Dog and the Parrot might both have come out of hiding by then!

Day 164 of My Captivity:

Today has been interesting so far and I have been intrigued by quite an unexpected event in the kitchen.

The freezer has been crying or that is what it looks like to an uneducated Cat, I have never seen the freezer so sad until today, in fact I was pretty sure that the freezer was incapable of feelings of any kind, but it appears to be crying uncontrollably, poor thing.

I haven't been able to work out what is wrong with the freezer even though I have spent a couple of hours keeping a protective eye on it, obviously I was too busy to actually sit with it, the floor being cold and very wet, but I did keep popping into the kitchen to see if it had cheered up at all.

It's like visiting a sick friend I suppose, one feels one should be there but when one is it is boring just watching someone be ill and worse one might catch something and so one makes the visit as short as possible and then feels guilty for a little while after the flying visit.

On one of my fleeting visits I was a little distressed to see that the fridge, which stands next to the freezer had also started to grizzle, just a few teardrops splashed onto the floor at first, but now on my fourth visit to the kitchen in as many hours, things seem to be going downhill for the fridge as well as the freezer.

Although I have to say, I don't exactly know the correct time because the kitchen clock has decided to stop working too, I am sure that I have been watching the fridge and the freezer for a fair amount of time and that could be a few hours and in that time I have noticed that the fridge is now almost as miserable as the freezer, really what is wrong with the kitchen appliances?

Wondering if there was something going on, that had affected all of the things in the house, with - how can I say this - not much brain power, yes that seems a good way to describe the appliances, I went off to see if the Dog and Parrot were inconsolable, but sadly when I found them they seemed to be in exceedingly good moods. So it is just the simple appliances that are distressed, shame.

The Parrot was jabbering away on his perch and looking out of the window at the mad Dog who was ripping up some newly planted shrubs, so no change there then. The mystery will have to be just that a mystery!

Maybe when the power comes on tomorrow things will get back to normal, well the variety of 'normal' that applies to this household anyway!

DAY 165 OF MY CAPTIVITY:

At around what would usually be 'Coffee morning time' in the cul-de-sac on a normal day, though not being a 'normal' day in what hasn't actually been a 'normal' week and consequently this moment today was probably more likely to be time for a 'Dry Sherry time' instead of Coffee morning time, if you see what I mean, among the neighbourhoods' middle aged ladies, the power came back on.

In our the house there were all sorts of odd little noises, which accompanied the return of the electricity, as it flowed back into the house and whizzed through the wiring.

In the kitchen both the freezer and the fridge clunked and then whirred back to life, oddly the kitchen clock didn't react to the sudden resumption of the power which drove it immediately, and when it did react the thin red second hand started to stutter and then confidently tick off the seconds recording the time since the power had awoken it.

I have to say that I thought that the second hand's confidence was just a little misplaced, because instead of doing what it had done for every second of its former life, now it was ticking backwards.

I decided that it could be forgiven for that little misdemeanour because the minute hand was also having some identity problems of it's own, and it was beginning to move in the right direction but at the speed of the second hand. Which left the poor and obviously completely confused hour hand frozen in the place where it had stopped earlier, I presume that it was just too worried to commit itself to any action which might have made it look as insane as its companions!

The problems of the appliances in the kitchen was nothing compared to the problems that were happening in other parts of the house, the electric door bell was ringing, and that wasn't because some idiot had their finger jammed on the doorbell button, it was just ringing without any explanation and it was very annoying indeed. Still that annoyance was dealt with rather swiftly by the Male Captor standing on a chair, then wrenching the bell off the wall, in his excitement he managed to unbalance the chair and fall off.

I could still hear his moans as the Female Captor drove him off to casualty.

It was a shame that Humans were too preoccupied to deal with the other problems that were occurring around the house, because newly replaced light bulbs were coming on all over the place where switches had been switched on and forgotten about.

I was confident that those lights would burn away brightly until the Humans came back from the local Hospital, which was probably enough provocation to drive a conservationist into a 'Shrek' like fury at the waste of all that non-renewable energy.

As you probably have guessed the utility room was worst hit by the return of power.

Personally I had a feeling it might be, and standing on top of a tea towel which was making a pointlessly brave effort to soak up the puddle in front of the freezer, I peered through the doorway and watched the results of the tortured wiring spark and flame inside the walls, what a good job houses have fuse boxes and I quietly thanked ours because it cut the power in the utility room and the sparks and flames subsided quickly.

Still at least the ladies of the cul-de-sac had been saved from drinking Sherry so early in the day, and as normality returned to the cul-de-sac, they could have their Coffee in the morning and even give some to the large numbers of builders, who were still working on the rebuilding of the nice ladies' homes, rebuilding which as you may remember was urgently needed after most of their homes subsided after the unfortunate and mysterious tunnel incident, which I was pretty confident was still the main topic of most Coffee morning conversations, that and obviously the blighting of real estate prices in the cul-de-sac of course!

DAY 166 OF MY CAPTIVITY:

Electricians are mad! But in their defence they react brilliantly in emergencies and apparently we were having another emergency today.

As you may have gathered, if you are clever enough, the latest emergency was electrical, hence appearance of the mad electricians, but having the mad electricians in the house wasn't the only inconvenience that the Dog and I were suffering from, oh no, the Male Captor was in a foul mood, because this 'man of action' (I am sure the word portly could be inserted into that statement) was reduced to a degree of inaction that he was completely and utterly unsuited to.

In fact the Male Captor sadly was off work, which meant that he was at home for at least the rest of the day, (depending upon how quickly hurt Humans heal), and that wasn't good whichever way you looked at it.

His fall from the chair yesterday was a little more serious than anyone had thought, except I have to say that he had mentioned the fact that he was in agony at the time, but as he is a man and frequently mentions he is in agony, we all more or less ignored him although the Female Captor did ask him what was wrong when he was lying on the floor making 'I'm in agony' noises.

Yesterday when he mumbled through gritted teeth that he was in agony the Female Captor had used her usual 'pull yourself together, it can't be that bad' look and tone and ignored his grunts of pain, and replied 'don't be daft, get up and get on with it.' There may have also been a reference to men never having to experience the pain of child birth, and other exclusively women's pains, there usually is, but honestly I can't be sure that there was this time, I was trying not to listen and also avoid the pool of blood on the hall floor.

Eventually, more as a threat of final embarrassment than an offer of compassion she agreed to drive him to the hospital so that he could be examined, where I suppose she expected him to be exposed as an uninjured fraud. So she went off to start the car leaving him to moan and groan as he hopped unassisted to the car.

It was now obvious that on this occasion his cries were not of 'Wolf,' or if indeed he had been crying 'Wolf,' his cries were of a Wolf with a broken leg, three broken fingers on one hand and two on the other, makes you almost feel sorry for him doesn't it?

Mmmh although all of this information about the Male Captor's broken bits is without doubt interesting, it isn't explaining my comments about electricians is it?

The electricians had to be summoned in a hurry when the full extent of the electrical problems was spotted by the Female Captor when she went into the utility room, switched on the light and the light bulb exploded above her head (like an arsonists' petrol filled balloon (but that is really about something I learned recently and should be saved for another time). She ran out of the utility room like she was being chased by a mob of Kalashnikov waving fundamentalists.

I am sure that the Male Captor would have spotted the problems too, but he is not very mobile at the moment, unfortunately because of his broken fingers he can't use crutches and so he has been forced to lie on a temporary bed in the front room, well the Sofa to be more precise.

I might add that although he can't use crutches he can use the remote control for the television and it is agony to be in the same room as him at the moment.

His foul temper means that he moans at all of the programmes and presenters on every single one of the 150 channels that are piped into the house.

Then when you add that fact to the other annoying fact that he changes channels so often that the television screen looks more like a strobe light than a television screen, the whole experience of being in the same room as him is unbearable, especially as he is lying full stretched on what is, as I thought everyone knew, 'my' Sofa!

Back to the electricians, I decided that it would be more entertaining to watch them while the channel junkie was playing in the front room and so I ambled down to the utility room to watch some 'professionals' at work.

They were in the middle and sleep inducing explanation of what 'they was gonna have to do' which sounded very complicated, but I think I got their drift, it was going to be an 'expensive' job, what with all of floor boards in the room above, that would have to come up and there was going to have to be a lot of something called 'chasing out' in the utility room itself, but, and this was the good news they could have the job done in a day or so, for something called 'cash in hand.'

Well they must have had big hands, that all I can say, because I think I have heard of some Third World countries with less debt than the cost of the electricians' labour alone.

In a twinkling of an eye after the shocked Female Captor had agreed to the smiling electrical extortionists, they both disappeared to their van, one zoomed off up the drive with a large handful of cash which had once belonged to the Captors, and the other came back carrying two heavy bags of tools and began attacking the walls with a chug chug brr tap tap machine, which dug channels in a sort of zigzag pattern, all across the utility room walls.

Every time the electrician, who I am tempted to call George, but I have overcome that confusion, I am happy to say and know now that not all Male Humans are called 'George,' which is sad but never mind about that just now. Every time George, oops old habits die hard, found a wire he grabbed hold of it, got an electric shock and swore, then pulled it out of the wall.

The electrician, who was not called George, found five bits of wire that had been plastered into the utility room walls and each time the same thing happened, bang, he got an electric shock swore and then pulled at the cable like the maniac he obviously was.

By the time his colleague had raced back down the drive on no more than two of the four wheels provided by the van's manufacturer, the electrician who wasn't called George had chased out the wall so much, that it had probably given up, then had attacked the lights in the ceiling, draining them of electricity each time as they gave him an electric shock and then moved upstairs to rip up the carpet and floorboards, and then stopped for the fuel of all workmen, tea, 'milky and two sugars'.

When the other part time getaway driver and electrician had dumped rolls of cable and all sorts of electrical equipment in the forward base camp (or as we know it - kitchen) the electrician not called George was finishing his tea and losing the battle straighten his static filled hair.

So they were ready to start work as far as this untrained observer could tell, but no I was wrong, the electrician not called George washed up his tea cup (a nice touch I thought) and together they left, leaving behind them a kitchen, that looked more like an electrical factors' shop than somewhere that people cook food in.

I was fairly certain that the Female Captor hadn't been informed that they had left for the day because her mood matched the Male Captor's, or would have if he hadn't dozed off in front of the television, which amazingly was still working.

Tools, reels of cable, dustsheets (unused) and more or less everything that an electrician needs to make an untidy mess, was moved into the utility room and stacked neatly, after the utility room itself had been swept, hoovered and polished, by the Female Captor who seemed to have learned a lot of swear words from the electrician not called George!

As I curled up on the broken leg of the Male Captor, which was resting on top of my bit of the Sofa, I thought to myself just how much I was looking forward to the return of the electricians tomorrow, I could say I expected sparks to fly, but that would be a bit obvious wouldn't it, tee hee!

Day 167 of My Captivity:

Today was a bit of an anticlimax to be honest, I had expected a lot more electrical fun, but when the electricians arrived they were ambushed by the Female Captor who gave them a long lecture about site safety (which as far as I can work out consists of a lot of sweeping up and cleaning), and how they might like to think about the consequences of extortion if the tax man got to hear about their original bill.

The two electricians still worked manically but sadly in a quiet and well ordered fashion because they were told that the injured Male Captor was asleep and it would be better for all if he stayed that way!

At the end of a disappointing and anticlimactic day the electricians, who had been forced to recalculate their bill and made to promise to keep their exit speed down to less that 50 mph when they left with a more moderate handful of cash, disappeared quietly, although I had to smile as the electrician, who was definitely not called George, stuck his fingers up in a spirited way at the Female Captor, who had spent all day overseeing and supervising the work.

Whether she saw the final act of defiance I couldn't be sure because she had closed the door on the pair rather abruptly, moaning about tradesmen in general and electricians in particular!

Day 168 of My Captivity:

As well as watching the fascinating documentary about escaping from a prison camp, called 'The Great Escape,' I have found a veritable mine of the most wonderful tips and information buried deep in one of those unwatched satellite television channels that can only be broadcast by a publicly owned broadcaster because they have viewing figures that range from naught to several hundred and the programmes are usually too obscure or more likely contain 'sensitive' information that would cause problems if every Tom, Dick or Harry got hold of it.

Of course these satellite television channels without any viewers are usually funded by governments, taxpayers and religious groups or indeed some sort of fanatical crackpot institutions, well thinking about religious groups and governments usually are fanatical, and crackpot, and should be in institutions!

Anyway I digress, but it is always worth stopping to criticise something, I think, don't you?

The programme I was watching had been watched by one person so far and I know that because I checked the viewing figures for that week just in case I had to amend what I said in this bit of my Diary and it is obvious that the one person, was 'me,' isn't it nice to feel special! Well anyway the one viewer who viewed the programme on the rather forlorn channel enjoyed the program intensely so the broadcaster shouldn't be too downhearted.

The riveting programme was about yet another group of mainly British soldiers in the Second World War escaping from yet another collection of humourless guards, from a desperately bleak and forbidding castle, so usual story, but my goodness me, how interesting.

Now, one particular escape attempt that caught my eye and I have to say my imagination was put together by an Army Captain with no psychiatric training what so ever! I mention the complete lack of psychiatric training for a reason, which I will try to remember to tell you before I finish writing today, but if I don't do please remind me and I will let you have the information later on, or if I forget entirely I'll try to weave the information into one of my books, that will follow this one, and in doing so, make a nice and very collectable set, so please don't forget to buy them will all you? Just in case!

The Captain, a small man, who probably would have only been good at tunnelling had obviously decided that the only way for him to escape from the dreadful prison was going to be by using his brain, and that is the core of his plan, he faked madness, brilliant, what a clever guy!

Can you imagine the number of ways that a 'mad' person can annoy his Captors, I can, what unbridled fun!

At first he just started twitching and walking around getting in the way of people and on the guards nerves and his fellow prisoners, who in the main were not let into the big secret – he wasn't mad, he was just pretending – fantastic, I was caught between being on the edge of my comfy seat on the sofa one minute and rolling around laughing at his antics the next.

I didn't catch the Captain's name but he was a wonderful actor and obviously dedicated to his craft and escaping, because once he had started howling at the moon, making wet patches in his trousers on parade and generally being very annoying and very silly he couldn't stop, mind you I suppose if he had stopped he would have been rumbled and his escape attempt would have been over.

You can tell, can't you? I was very impressed with this Captain's terrific escape attempt and decided to use it immediately, in no time I was convinced I would be out of here once and for all.

So my plan was fool proof, which I don't think means that I needed to find a fool to make it work? But anyway my Captors are just as dumb as the ones on the television and so I was in with a chance, even if I needed a few fools to fool, if you get my drift, ok I'll stop now, but didn't you notice I was faking being mad!

'Whoop, whoop three cents please, move along down inside the Antelope, plenty of room on top.'

There I was doing it again, oddly it seems to come quite naturally to me! I'll have to watch that, it might be addictive or worse, what happened to the Army Captain might happen to me, do remind me to tell you what happened, slap, slap Chocolate Bar!

Sorry!

So I peed on the floor, climbed the curtains, refused to eat my food until the bowl was upside down and I could lick the gravy seeping out from under it. I ran around the house time after time at dizzyingly fast speeds and when I knew that they were watching sprang onto the mantelpiece and had a fight with my reflection in the mirror which hangs above it, knocking several prized ornaments and statuettes off as I was whacking the Cat that looks like me, but just a little more insane!

Nothing!

I couldn't believe it!

Where was I going wrong, I had done all of the things that the mad Army Captain had done and even added a selection of my favourites, and nothing, no reaction what so ever, were the Captors dead? No, they were standing in the middle of the wreckage of the front room, their jaws gaping, just watching me!

But when I stopped being mad, they stopped watching me, as though they weren't that interested, as though this sort of thing happened all the time, oh dear it does, doesn't it?

You know what that could mean don't you? No please don't mention it; you might curse me with the thought!

I'm going to lie down somewhere quiet and dark and have a think about all of this, I hasten to add that I am not going to talk to myself while I am thinking, I promise no words will even form in my mind, I am going to do it all in an abstract sort of way, so that you can't call me mad, no you can't, any of you, so stop that immediately!

DAY 169 OF MY CAPTIVITY:

I have had the most wonderful sleep, although it was only a mere sixteen hours I feel as if I have slept for days and in fact really feel great.

What do you mean? What happened to the Army Captain? I have no idea what you are talking about, oh hang on yes I do, you are talking about yesterday! Well that's kind of you, thanks very much for reminding me!

I was frightened yesterday that people were ignoring me and then worse, that I really was of my trolley, but the little sleep helped and I would prefer it if we closed the subject now, thank you very much.

And by the way, I have forgotten what happened to the Army Captain anyway, and that is probably a form of defence strategy employed by my mind because it doesn't want to lose its grip on reality, which I have to say some unkind people seem to think is pretty slender at times anyway!

What I might be able to do is to remember before the end of the book, if I can't as I said earlier, don't hesitate to buy the follow up books will you, because I am sure I will remember at some stage and I promise I will just drop the comment into the conversation. As long as none of you out there accuse me of being mad for doing it. I am not mad; honestly, I always walk this way!

DAY 170 OF MY CAPTIVITY:

Sssh! We all have to be quiet because the Male Captor is asleep, which is just as well because his temper is healing at a slower rate than his broken bones.

Actually I am reasonably certain that the Female Captor has doubled the dose of painkillers and he is asleep for some other reason than just being tired if you catch my drift.

I checked in on him, well I was checking to see if my sleeping place was available, which it wasn't, and he was lying out full at stretch on the Sofa, dribbling on the cover, which was keeping him warm, and making the most dreadful snoring noise, as though he had a pack of angry Ferrets squatting in his throat, being chased by a bigger pack of Weasels, who were the rightful tenants and none too pleased at the Ferrets for squatting in their home.

But as I said sssh! Mustn't wake the patient.

Day 171 of My Captivity:

I have discovered that just because someone is described as a patient, it doesn't mean that they actually have any patience. All I did was jump up onto my bit of the Sofa and try and get comfortable and I woke the patient up.

You would have thought I had started a war, I am now completely convinced that the Female Captor has drugged the patient, because his reaction was very violent, he kick his plaster covered leg hard and I shot off the Sofa and landed in the hallway.

If the Dog hadn't been outside I would have set him on the drug-crazed madman. So now I am going to find somewhere else to have a sleep. I know, there is a large portion of their bed that hasn't been slept on for a few days and as an added bonus I can get my own back and do a little casual moulting over the pristine area while I have a much needed sleep.

Day 172 of My Captivity:

I am of the opinion that the Male Captor, should be in hospital, not that a few broken fingers and a broken leg are life threatening or anything, it is just that I think that the Female Captor is definitely putting too many painkillers in his food.

Obviously her intentions are good, she, like me, wants nothing more than a quiet life and it is clear that the best way to achieve that is to keep the 'patient' comatose, because when, on the increasingly rare occasions, that he is awake, life is one long round of fetching and carrying, complaints and confrontations.

With all of that exhausting work, coupled to the constant ranting at the television, life in the house when the Male Captor is awake is hell at the moment, and so whenever he is fed I slip into the front room to watch him eat and then take heart when I see his head slump down on his pillows.

Day 173 of My Captivity:

Do you know I think my memory is going or maybe my brain is overheating because of all of the thinking that I have been doing lately and so I can't remember anything that I have done today!

Well that is not completely true, I remember doing the things that one does automatically, like check the windows and doors to see if any are open, and then I remember eating as well, it was an economy Cat food brand, you know the sort that you have to eat while trying not to breath in the aroma of suspicious fish oils!

Why Humans take Fish Oil Capsules I will never know, have you noticed that the Brown Bread Brigade and Earth Huggers Co-operative Alliance, who take all of these vitamins and supplements, look really ill all the time, and worse when they smile and breathe on you, confident that the fish oil capsules and the low aroma garlic pills, that they take, haven't made their breath smell at all! Well good for them and their self-helped wellbeing, to say nothing of their amazing oral hygiene confidence, but I have news for these disgustingly healthy idiots, it is true their breath doesn't smell, it stinks!

Going back to what I have been doing lately though for another moment or at least trying to remember what I have been doing other than walking around the house and eating, I can't remember anything of the day and that is worrying, what if I have lost my memory through sheer boredom, it wouldn't make the rest of the Diary much of a read would it, still I suppose what I have written before today is enough to make this a cracking best seller so if I do have a memory problem, then others can ghost write the last bit and everyone will be happy!

Although thinking about it again for yet another minute, my memory can't be that bad because I was made to be quiet because of the invalid and I remember that and I remember ignoring that command ha, ha, ha!

Day 174 of My Captivity:

The telephone is an unfathomable device, it seems to ring when no one wants it to and never when it is expected to.

After stating the above, Humans, probably because most if not all of whom are insane, use the telephone a lot. I can't pick up the receiver and so it is, as far as I am concerned an all but pointless object d'art.

Tell me what is the difference between a Mobile or Cellphone and a cordless phone? I have no idea really, although I have one clue, when the bill for the Mobile or Cellphones comes, it makes more noise!

What do I mean? Well what do you think I mean? When the Captors open the Cordless telephone bill they just make a sort of resigned sigh when they see the amount that they have to pay at the bottom of the bill. But when they do the same with the Mobile/Cellphone bill the sound is altogether different, it usually starts with a growing groan and turns into a collection of shouted words and insults.

I don't know if the people who own the mobile/Cellphone companies do have parents, but if they do then that would prove the Captors wrong and worse, the poor old people would be desperately offended by the incredibly bad language shouted at, a such a small piece of paper with so many naughts on, before sometimes it is ripped into more shreds than an electronic shredder can achieve, with a triumphant howl from the Captors.

There is only one word for all that behaviour, primeval!

Day 175 of My Captivity:

Happily there is something of an improvement in the Male Captor's condition, no he is still not able to get up very easily, but that problem is most likely caused by the painkiller overdose which keeps him docile, and he is still having most meals through a straw, because he can't hold a knife and fork, which is bizarrely what Humans used to eat with occasionally these days, if they aren't in fast food restaurants.

Of course the straw is important to the Male Captor's well being because the Female Captor has refused to cut up his food and spoon-feed him.

So the improvement is not related to any of those factors, the improvement comes from the fact that he dropped the channel changer flicker thing into the unfinished bowl of soup and the insane channel hopping has stopped completely.

It was fortunate for me that I was waiting for the discarded bowl of soup to cool before helping myself, well let me correct that last statement, if the soup was something like Tomato and Basil then I would have helped myself, because I could have had my head in it at the time that the channel changer dropped out of the sky.

Mind you if the soup was something like Ham and Pea, I would have sniffed it a couple of times, then sneezed in it, and left it so I probably would have escaped any channel changer accidents that way as well.

Some soups are not so nice as Basil and Tomato, especially ones that Pensioners like, such as Chicken, Lentil and finally Mulligatawny, which because it is a curry soup is just too hot for me.

I bet Mulligatawny Soup keeps Pensioners warm though, if they have the strength to get into the can and still have enough in the way of marbles to light the gas without blowing up the neighbourhood and then the most important fact, they remember that the soup is on the gas and needs serving at sometime in the near future after they have started heating it.

Is it a shame that old people become forgetful? That is a question that I have asked myself a lot recently, when I have been sitting on the arm of the Sofa watching the Male Captor do an amazingly accurate impression of a person in the last stages of Dementia.

Of course I keep reminding myself that he has been made to be like that because of the Female Captor's lack of Human kindness and a serious over supply of painkillers from the Doctors, but all the same, the effect is the same as Dementia, he is almost completely out of his tree and therefore in my opinion has replicated the condition perfectly.

But back to my question! Is it a shame that old people become forgetful? Well to answer that you have to look at what sort of life the old grey ones have lived, most of the current mob lived through very difficult times, like the stock market crash, 1920's hunger, 1930's hunger, 1940's hunger and rationing, 1950's rationing and shortages and yes you guessed it a bit of hunger, one or even two World Wars, several entire series of 'I Love Lucy,' on black and white television, some series of 'I Love Lucy' in colour, family meals together around a table and many other homely horrors.

So with that in mind a little respect for the old ones might be something that we should give them freely, still before we get carried away granting the old ones something they refuse to give anyone else, let's hang on a minute, and ask ourselves this question.

Which set of Humans has had its snout in the 'Pork Barrel' for the longest amount of time?

Try another question too!

What group of workers didn't allow their wives (except for the Second World War of course) out to work and therefore earn a living, because a woman's place was to go mental with boredom in the home?

If you have finished thinking about the two questions above, get your teeth into this one, well get your teeth into it if you are under say seventy years of age!

Which group of silvery haired heroes paid almost nothing a week for their pension plans when they worked for next to nothing a week? And now get a pension payment each month which is probably equivalent to their years wages when they earned almost nothing a week?

Now if you have answered those, in my view, reasonably fair questions of the old ones, you may start to see where I am coming from on this issue of fairness.

Are these grey-headed highwaymen and women, (and remember the women weren't employed at all) grateful to the younger generation for being so generous and some would say reckless with their tax payments to stump up such large pensions and other fringe retirement benefits? No of course not, what do the old ones want, well when they are asked they are clear, they want 'more' and when do they want it 'now.'

Oops I seem to have slipped away from the question! Is it a shame that old people become forgetful? Still some of the above is relevant and all of it is truthful and this is a Diary so you have to be prepared for very strong opinions, my opinions.

So, is it a shame that old people become forgetful?

Yes on balance I think it is, if they remembered how lucky they were to be living in a society that picks up their tab, then maybe, just maybe, we would hear less from them, because like any pressure group of narrow thinkers they are uncaring and selfish.

However if I had lived through one or two World Wars I think I would prefer not to have such a good memory, wouldn't you?

DAY 176 OF MY CAPTIVITY:

Having an invalid in the house is something of a drag, which is why I am trying to hypnotise ours. Hypnotising someone who is heavily sedated is almost impossible, but I keep trying and failing but I have an amazing capacity to keep on trying and that single mindedness is worth its weight in gold, diamonds and anything else sparkly I would think.

The idea behind Hypnotising or invalid is to get him to try and stand up and use his leg, maybe then he would go and have a wash and a shave, he is beginning to smell just like the Dog does sometimes before he is hosed down outside.

Maybe I should try and encourage him to have a wash, I could use hypnotism there's an idea, if I could get the 'subject' hypnotised then maybe I could get him to open the back door, I would even hose him down myself before I escaped, just for the fun of it all. Now one more time, 'look into my eyes. No I said look into my eyes!'

Some 'subjects' are so dense that they make even a patient Cat lose its temper; trust me to get one of those subjects. Still I don't think I will give up just yet.

'Yes we know you are feeling sleepy, but wake up a bit, so I can hypnotise you!'

At this rate I would be better off hypnotising myself, now hold on, that is an idea.

All I have to do is to watch the gentle fluttering of the Male Captor's eyes and say to myself that I am feeling sleepy, and when I fall asleep I will imagine that I am incredibly strong, and using that incredible strength I will break open the back door and escape, although I would miss out on the fun of hosing the Male Captor down sadly, but I would be free!

'I am getting sleepy, I am extremely strong, this is working, what's that smell, no, keep focused, I am getting sleepy, I am extremely strong, this is working, what's that smell, yes what is that awful smell!'

Really how can I work in conditions like this, I think I will move a long way away from the Male Captor, until he has had that wash I recommended.

Even in the spare bedroom with the door almost closed I can still smell that smell, have you noticed that smells have a tendency to follow one around, it is no good, I can't concentrate enough to work, I think I'll go and have a mouthful or two of smelly Cat food that should make things better!

DAY 177 OF MY CAPTIVITY:

Today the Male Captor was more like his old self, moaning and calling for a Coffee and sandwiches, which he had no way to hold in his bent plastered hands.

Still if he is better, he might go upstairs and have a wash, let's hope so, I will keep an eye on him and see, but for the moment I am just going to slip around the back of the Sofa and then round to the other side, hopefully unseen and unnoticed. Then when I have got to within biting distance of the sandwich, which had been left just out of reach for him, yes you guessed it, he is still not back in 'her' good books ha, ha, ha, I will see if I can't hook out the Ham, I hope that there isn't any Mustard on it though, I am not very partial to Mustard.

DAY 178 OF MY CAPTIVITY:

A major event has just happened, after the false alarm of yesterday's almost wash, today accompanied by a lot of sighing, a good deal of moaning and far too much groaning the Male Captor managed to climb the stairs and spend some very productive time in the bathroom.

Had it been up to me and I had been the individual with the gammy leg I think I would have used the cloakroom downstairs, it has a serviceable sink and even a spare razor I've noticed, but then Humans are an unfathomable law unto themselves I've noticed too.

I have some other good news as well, while he was making his painful assault on the north face of the staircase, I 'shared' his Tuna sandwich with him, well I ate all of the Tuna, Mayonnaise and licked the butter off the bread, leaving him the bread and salad, well I like to share, don't you?

As I was finishing sharing and rubbing my Mayonnaise covered cheeks on the Sofa to get the worst of it off before having a wash, I was disappointed to hear the clatter of the invalid coming downstairs, either he had been very quick at washing or alternatively he had given up half way through and decided to come back to the bed.

Really I hate quitters don't you? Especially when their scent enters the room before they do, excuse me, I must get out of here!

Day 179 of My Captivity:

You must be wondering now what has happened to the Female Captor, well I was trying to be discreet but as you ask I may as well share the goss (short for gossip – just in case you don't know) with you.

At first she was reasonably helpful and every once in a while she looked in on the invalid and was always around when the painkiller double doses were handed out, but after the first couple of days she said, to no one in particular that she couldn't take anymore of the running around something which I have to say I must have blinked and missed, and she went back to work.

Obviously she comes back in the evening and the Parrot, Dog and I benefit from her presence but I don't think that the Male Captor does, it is almost as though she has washed her hands off him, although personally I wish she would do a little washing of him, if you get my drift, which is always downwind of him.

In her defence, she, like probably millions of people just isn't the sort of person to enjoy nursing or doctoring and who can blame her, nursing that smelly lump, who is polluting my bit of the Sofa, must be a trial, but at least a professional would have given the invalid a bed bath by now.

Yes I know, I am going on about his hygiene a lot. But as you know Cats are fastidious about that sort of thing, although of course unlike some Humans we don't shave our faces or any of our other bits!

Day 180 of My Captivity:

I have decided, come what may, this is the last day I am going to mention the invalid as the main topic of conversation, I seem to have got a little preoccupied by him.

All I have to say then, today is that he hobbled to the downstairs cloakroom (clever move) and had a considerable wash, he may even have changed his underwear, but I can't be sure of that fact, he did indeed change his clothes because before she went to work the Female Captor put some fresh ones out for him, she has attained sainthood as far as I am concerned if she was responsible for encouraging him to wash and change his clothes.

And now after a wash, shave and all the rest he is actually sitting like a normal person on the Sofa, watching television, he looks dazed, but that is probably a reaction to all of the drugs he has been prescribed and the other ones too.

For the moment I am going to let my Sofa seat cushion air a bit and freshen up before I use it again.

Still it is nice to have the Male Captor returning to normal, at least you know where you are with a conscious unpredictable Human and they don't smell too badly at all, unlike a semiconscious one.

Day 181 of My Captivity:

So this is the first day since the 'accident,' that I will more or less be able to ignore the Male Captor, although if I was going to mention him and I have now of course, I could say that he is better today, which is good, The Dog was even brave enough to go into the front room and come out again after having had a bit of a stroke from his master. Well as much of a stroke as someone, who doesn't have the use of many fingers can achieve.

Still all things considered, the Dog seemed happy that he has his master back and that he is reasonably lucid. Mind you I don't think I would like him to drive me anywhere, no not the Dog, he can't drive, obviously, I mean the Male Captor, he is still 'a little out of it,' as they say.

Day 182 of My Captivity:

I have to apologise now don't I? Ok I am sorry I know I promised not to mention the invalid again and that I made that promise on the day before yesterday, but really he is fascinating, well that maybe an over statement, but he is the most interesting 'thing' in the house recently.

I suppose that it is my fault really that he is so interesting, firstly it is me writing about him and that is bound to make him interesting, probably even more interesting than he actually is I expect, and secondly I think that just for the moment I may have run out of any plans of escape.

Now you see what good friends we have become, for me to feel that I can share that little embarrassing secret with you, and I hope that you are flattered, you should be. It is really a good job that this Diary is more in the way of a Diary than a book about escaping, mind you that doesn't mean that I don't wish it was a book about a successful escape, yes just one successful escape, mine!

Day 183 of My Captivity:

Are you familiar with the expression, to have painted yourself into a corner; I think that I may have done that, not in real life, no one seems to trust me with tins of paint or brushes for that matter, quite why I don't know?

No my corner is a literary one, I promised that I wouldn't mention you know who and his leg in the you know what and his gammy thingies on each hand and I want to keep that promise as you can see by the gibberish I have just written here.

And there is my little embarrassing secret which I trusted you with yesterday, no not the one about the sore patches of skin, I haven't decided to tell you about that yet, no this was the confession that I think I was running out of escape plans.

Now that little problem would be all very well I suppose in a normal Diary, of a normal person who went out of the house and actually had a life outside, sadly I don't and to make matters worse I am surrounded by a boring Parrot and a dull Dog and, well not to mention the person who I can't mention, but you know who I mean, he is currently almost as boring and dull as the Parrot and the Dog put together.

All in all that leaves me with not much to say and a lot of white space on the page, unless I can come up with another plan, or if the Parrot does something interesting like take up mountain biking or better still has a heart attack, both of which sadly are unlikely although I am working on the latter of course.

So you can see my problem, I hope you sympathise with it and when you tell your friends about this Diary and how they just have to go out and buy it, maybe you could do us all a favour and gloss over this section of the Diary, it really isn't going anywhere is it, unlike my ability to get my paws on a literary prize, which currently is going south.

The only up side is that what has been written so far is so incredibly good that by this page the decision should be made already to award me a significant literary prize, though I blush to say which one, but having said that I don't want one for children's writers they don't have big enough prizes, I want the big one of course.

I wonder, does anyone know whether you get one of those satin sashes dropped over your head when you win a literary prize, like the winner of the Miss World contest does. Actually I wouldn't mind that, but I think I will draw the line at wearing a bathing suit!

DAY 184 OF MY CAPTIVITY:

Ok so yesterday's Diary entry wasn't too dull in the end, thank goodness, we are all lucky that I am just such an interesting little Cat.

Imagine for a minute if I was a Hamster and I had decided to write a Diary, what a drag that would be.

Day 1

Got up early today to look around my cage. Everything is much bigger than me, except the distance between bars of the cage, I can get my nose between them, but that is it and I nearly had a panic earlier, I thought I had got my nose wedged in the bars.

Day 2

In the middle of the cage sticking down from the ceiling is a big red wheel; I have a feeling that I am supposed to use it, although I am not sure about that or what to do with it.

Day 3

I got up a little later than normal, because I had been lying in my nest thinking about the red wheel and trying to work out if I was supposed to use it or not!

Day 4

I got up at the same time as I did two days ago, early, that red wheel is still worrying me; in fact I think of nothing else, I think I am going to have a go on it and see what happens.

Wow it is very wobbly and doesn't feel very safe. I nearly fell off as soon as I had one foot on the wheel because it just started to move away from me.

Day 5

I spent all day in my nest, working up the courage to have another go on the red wheel and working out exactly how to get into it without falling off immediately.

Then when I did have a go on it after I had decided, that the best way to deal with the wheel would be to jump into it quickly, when I did that I fell out of the other side.

Day 6

I thought I would have a rest today and spend all day in the nest thinking about the red wheel and nursing my sprained front paw.

Day 7

I have been in this cage a week and haven't really achieved a lot, so I have decided even if it does me serious damage I am going to master that red wheel.

Here goes, oops run, run, run faster, wow, this is great I love it, look how fast I can go, I am going to do this every day from now on forever.

The End

There, that is what the diary of a Hamster would be like, now aren't you grateful you have my Diary to read instead?

DAY 185 OF MY CAPTIVITY:

I feel a little better after a couple of days of not thinking about anything in particular or worrying that I was boring.

I know that the last couple of days haven't been up to my normal standard of captivating interest, but today I do feel that I am offering value for money, especially now that I have found out that other books that will be on the same bookshop shelves as my Diary will only be half a long, so I am happy that I am offering unbelievable value for money and can afford to have a few off days, and resist the temptation to invent any action.

Just think if I was the type of individual, who wanted to make a quick buck, I would hack this baby apart and have two volumes on the shelves, that way the sales volume would be double and I would make so much more money.

Don't you just want to stroke me and give me a little hug for being such a nice Cat and ensuring you get excellent value for money!

DAY 186 OF MY CAPTIVITY:

I remember promising that I wouldn't mention the Male Captor, but I just have one question! Did we agree a timescale? No I didn't think we did, which is just as well because he nearly helped me out of here today and I would like to tell you what happened.

No, he obviously didn't know he was helping me in anyway what so ever.

I suppose in his defence the plaster cast is quite heavy and because when you have a broken leg you try to rest it regularly and you probably don't get used to the extra weight that you have to swing around when you walk.

Well be all of that as it may, what happened was brilliant right up to the bit where I failed. Still I am sure that you will find it funny even though I may have slightly spoilt the ending for you!

There was a note stuck to the television screen this morning and I could make out most of what it said, but not all because the handwriting was just so awful.

The Male Captor is probably more familiar with the handwriting of his beloved and so he mumbled all of it aloud and then shuffled around the house getting ready.

I shadowed him because I had no idea what he was up to and obviously was keen to find out.

At ten thirty on the dot a taxi turned into the drive and soon afterwards someone rang the new doorbell, which sounds like more of a chime than a bell if you have a good ear for music, which of course I do. The Male Captor obviously knew who the caller was and shouted out to her (as it turned out) to come in, the front door was not locked.

The Dog attacked the visitor, which is his traditional 'welcome to the house' action and when the invalid hobbled to the front door the Dog was gently strangling the lady taxi driver with her own scarf, you have to hand it to him for style and content and give him a maximum ten don't you.

The invalid wasn't that impressed and with a few words sent the crestfallen Dog packing with just a few bits of scarf hanging from his whimpering mouth.

The Male Captor invited the lady taxi driver to come inside and close the door, shame I thought I hadn't managed to get close enough to the door to make a break for it so I just hung back under the table with the telephone on and waited to see what would develop.

The nice lady taxi driver helped the invalid on with his coat and listened very sympathetically I thought to his tale of broken bones and woe.

After just a few minutes I saw her eyes glaze over and her interest and concern for and in him drain away, she did put her arm around his shoulders, but that was designed to steer him towards the door, as was the reminder that if they didn't get a move on they might not make the appointment.

It was then, as they both turned their backs to me that I saw my chance and very carefully tiptoed up behind the invalid, then I sprung opening my front and back legs so that when I landed on the invalid's plaster cast I spreadeagled it and like a bit of Velcro finding its partner stuck to the cast and held on for all that I was worth.

I managed a few steps towards the door before a strange sound made the lady taxi driver and the invalid stop. The sort of noise that usually comes from dragging your nails down a blackboard, seemed to be coming from somewhere under the invalid's coat he said to the lady taxi driver that he thought his plaster cast was cracking and she kindly suggested if he stayed still she would have a look under his coat and see what was happening.

The lady taxi driver got down on her hands and knees and was fumbling around the cast when our eyes met as we looked at each other face to face. I have to say that neither of us expected either of us to be peering around the same plaster cast under the same coat in the darkness, caused by the aforementioned coat.

I remember screaming loudly and scrabbling to get away, but all that I heard was the sound of the lady taxi driver's scream of sheer terror, in fact the terror was so sheer that if it had been a pair of tights it would have only been about 15 denier.

'It's a Rat and it's running up your leg,' she shouted, 'A Rat!' Rarely have I been so insulted, but things were going to get worse, it was obvious right from the first shout of alarm that the lady taxi driver didn't like Rats.

She scooped backwards and pulled her Mule off her foot and set about bashing the 'Rat' with it, well I can tell you that 'this' Rat wasn't about to be paddled with a Mule, a Brogue, or any other shoe with a strange sounding name and so I pushed backwards off the plaster cast and did a sort of creditable back flip landing on almost all fours and made a run for it.

The lady taxi driver wasn't going to give in that easily and chased after me, but on all fours, maybe she had forgotten that she could walk, I don't know. The only thing I did know was that I was grateful that the stupid, um lady taxi driver had probably forgotten that she could walk and scuttled after me on her hands and knees, which gave me just enough time to rush into the kitchen, spring onto the work surface, upset the kettle and then as I was sliding towards the end of the work surface, launch myself up to the cupboard tops and hide behind a discarded empty box of glass tumblers.

When she came into the kitchen she had murder in her eyes and rather hot water on her hands, luckily she had crawled through a large puddle of very hot water that had spilt out of the kettle after it had fallen on the floor. Happily the invalid was hot on her heels and persuaded her that the Rat had gone and that they both needed to see a doctor now, and as she couldn't drive with badly burned hands, they would have to order a taxi to take them.

I watched them, it was like the blind leading the blind, she dialled the number by punching the telephone keys with the tip of her thumb, which seemed the only part of her hands that wasn't burned, and he held the telephone to her head as she made the call to her boss and arranged another taxi.

The second taxi arrived reasonably quickly after the emergency had been described and I watched the new driver shepherd both of the invalids into his cab and then speed off out of the drive as if he had a blue light flashing on the roof.

I curled up in the warm space under the ceiling; watching little bits of my fur float off in the thermals of warm air that circulate in the kitchen. When fur dances in the sunlight it is fun to watch the little bits of meander through the air to land all over the place.

DAY 187 OF MY CAPTIVITY:

Can Flies read your mind? No before you think that this Cat has completely lost his marbles and will start foaming at the mouth any minute, just think about it for a moment!

I have something in common with most Humans I can't abide Flies, nasty, dirty, buzzing things, that taste dreadful, although the wings are a delicacy in some countries I believe!

Why do I think that Flies can read your mind? Well it is simple really. I have watched them and flies seem to know when they have been spotted and not only by me, but also when Humans who begin to roll up newspapers or knot tea towels ready to start swinging them viciously and to be honest pointlessly through the air.

I have often noticed just as the Humans line up a shot at a Fly who might be aimlessly circling the central light fitting or banging its head on the window pane, the Fly will swerve taking avoiding action as the Humans swings to deliver a death blow, missing the Fly altogether and usually smashing something that was innocently minding its own business like all of the crockery on the draining board or several treasured ornaments in the living room!

And it is no difference when this highly trained and deadly hunter stalks his prey, sneaking up to within pouncing distance, waiting patiently for just the right moment to strike and then striking with the full force aggression of a Special Forces operative, only to find that the Fly has not been impaled on the end of ones claws but has flown off and is buzzing just out of reach around its ears!

How do they do that?

I am sure that there is only one answer, well to be accurate there is only one answer I can think of that makes any sense - they read your mind! Well it can't be that difficult can it? After all what I am thinking is going to be the same as what any Human with a rolled up newspaper and a grimace is thinking, kill the Fly, and Flies must be pretty used to that sort of thinking, because I don't suppose there are many thoughts that they read that say, Ahh look at that pretty little fellow isn't he cute!

So there we have it, almost scientifically proved, Flies can read your mind, and there is an upside to all this and it isn't the fact that we now know that Flies can read our minds, I am sure that you will agree, it is that we aren't Flies!

So before you hunt the next clever Fly with a rolled up newspaper in your hand, take a minute to empty your mind of all conscious thought I have a feeling that will be more difficult for me than it will be for you Humans, but give it a go anyway, you never know we might get our own back on these clever Flies and stop that incessant buzzing and darting about!

One other thing about Flies just quickly, have you noticed that they don't vanish in the winter like they used to do! Now I don't know whether to be worried about that or not, I have a feeling that they used to disappear somewhere to read and improve their minds and now that they don't, does that mean that they are as clever as they think they should be? Worrying, if true.

Mind you I am sure that some tree hugger somewhere will say that the reason that Flies don't vanish in the winter now is due to global warming! If there is so much global warming how come I am cold in the winter, that is what I would like to know?

Have you noticed how tree huggers always have bundles of advice as to what we should be doing to save the planet?

I think that the earth has seen them before, tree huggers that is, they went around for hundreds of thousands of years telling the Dinosaurs what they should be doing, and the Dinosaurs got so fed up with the constant nagging, that they collectively decided to become extinct, which left the tree huggers with no one to offer their incessant advice to and so they died out too, until now that is!

Nowadays it seems there is a tree hugger on television every night telling you and I that doom is upon us and that we should change our ways before it is too late, surely less civilised nations would have these people stoned for being false prophets!

Day 188 of My Captivity:

Over the last few days, well more than a few days I suppose I have started to wonder if I have become a radical, my opinions seem to be very strong and some would probably say that they are almost too strong, but I am pretty sure that I am the type of Cat who is in Cat terms at least very middle of the road in my views.

Under the calm exterior of every purring Cat there is a tyrant waiting to get out and take over if not all of the world then as much as it can grab in five minutes, I know that fact might come as a shock to all you, Humans, but it is never the less true.

And so with that in mind you can see that I am just a victim of my race's natural desires and therefore I hope that you will forgive me any views that, you think, might be extreme and just stroke me with your index finger just under my chin, oh that is good, more please.

See sometimes Cats are just little fun balls of fur, just like you Humans think we should be, no don't stop stroking!

Day 189 of My Captivity:

For a few days now while pretending to be a 'normal' Cat doing normal Cat things I have been observing something very interesting. Every three or four days, the Humans take the rubbish, that they collect in a big black plastic sack, inside a large freestanding swivel top bin, outside, I am not sure what they do with the sack when they are outside, but the bit that interests me is the outside.

Now can you see why, that performance is interesting, no? Don't tell me, I am going to have to spell it out for you, really some Humans are a little slow, but please don't catch up with Cats, that would only make life difficult for you after the Cats take over the world.

So far I have watched the bin emptying, as the Humans call it over the last week or so and the pattern seems to be that the bin needs emptying every three days, unless they have been shopping and then they get other big black plastic sacks out and fill them up with all of the redundant packaging that everything, that comes into this house, seems to need for reasons that are beyond me, unless it is to just fill big black plastic sacks that is!

My plan like all good plans that succeed, paws crossed, is to slip into the bin and snuggle down inside then simply wait to be carried outside, perfect, and by watching the Humans routine and finding out when they change the bin I will make the wait shorter.

All I had to do was to make sure that when I saw a new big black plastic sack get put into the bin was to wait three days then hop in and be carried to freedom, perfect.

Now that I am inside the black sack I have discovered a few minor problems with the plan, but nothing too awful, although it's a bit dark and a bit smelly too, but I am glad I didn't bring a packed lunch because there is plenty to snack on while I wait, even for a choosy Cat.

Actually the waiting was a little boring, especially as I said it is very dark inside a black bag and worse, once or twice I was squashed down into the black sack by more rubbish being pushed down on top of me, but my spirits were high because it was getting quite late on the third day and I knew I would soon be taken outside.

Just as the plan began to work and my freedom began to wave hello to me from the darkness of the garden, things began to go a little awry.

The Male Captor was fumbling with the bin lid with both of his broken hands and couldn't seem to be able to pull the black sack free from the bin, so he asked for a little help which seemed reasonable to me, but obviously not to 'others!'

The Human Captors rarely argue, but often have 'differences of opinion,' well that is what I have heard them tell their friends, but I couldn't believe my ears when I heard them begin a major 'difference of opinion,' at the top of their voices about who should change the bin.

Why did they choose this day of all days to have what sounded more like an argument than a difference of opinion about who should put the rubbish out?

Mind you the Male Captor did have a point, his hands couldn't really cope with the weight of the black sack, which he complained was heavier than usual, I hope he wasn't referring to my added weight!

I waited patiently while they bickered for what seemed ages, as the welcome fresh air from the kitchen seeped into the black sack, until I made up my mind that neither the black sack nor I were going to go anywhere tonight and so I calmly wriggled to the surface of the accumulated rubbish and nonchalantly appeared on top of the rubbish and sat watching their astonished faces register my presence.

Even my sudden appearance didn't stop the argument, all that happened was that they changed the subject slightly and began arguing about who was going to wash the Cat before they put the bin out and went to bed.

After what seemed like ages I had had enough and hopped out of the bin, casually walked passed the astonished pair of Humans, who stopped arguing to watch me disappear upstairs to their bedroom.

When I got to the landing I heard them start another round, but by that time I was snuggled into their duvet and as their raised voices faded into the background I dozed off, wondering why my plans either get affected by bad luck or annoying Humans.

Day 190 of My Captivity:

It must have been late when the Humans came to bed last night because I didn't hear them, in fact I didn't hear them get up this morning either and go their separate ways, consequently I don't know whether they resolved their argument satisfactorily or not.

I do know that I had been moved in my sleep though; because when I woke up this morning I was very disorientated, I was in the kitchen lying next to the debris and rubbish from the black sack, as I opened my eyes I saw that I was surrounded by all of the rubbish from the last few days.

At first I thought that there had been some sort of natural disaster like the ones that you see on television before some faded celebrity asks you to send money for relief, when what is obviously needed is a team of competent cleaners.

Then the reason for the little disaster became apparent as the Dog blindly backed out of the utility room at speed, wearing an empty cereal box on his head.

Which all goes to demonstrate that if you leave a black sack unattended in the kitchen, some dumb animal will rifle it!

I was too tired to help the dumb animal in question, so I just managed to jump up onto the work surface and take a nap, which was continually interrupted by the sound of a Dog wearing a cereal box banging into the cupboards and the table and chairs.

DAY 191 OF MY CAPTIVITY:

The disagreement over the emptying of the bin is almost completely forgotten, in fact as if the old swivel lid bin had got the blame for the argument it was thrown out when the Female Captor cleaned up the kitchen and utility room floor. You have to hand it to the Dog, even when he is impeded by a cereal box, acting as a blindfold, he is very thorough at making a mess.

My guess is that had we not been shut in the kitchen with the 'run' of the utility room for the day he would have managed to spread rubbish all over the house, even though it took him over an hour to wrestle free from the cereal box!

So we have a new bin and that is a shame really because it doesn't have a swivel lid, it has a hinged lid, and what that means is that I can't get into it, and in turn that means that the plan to hide in the black sack has gone out of the window, I just wish I could follow it!

DAY 192 OF MY CAPTIVITY:

Crestfallen is a good word and so much nicer than depressed, which suggests that one is having to take large cocktails of happy pills just to get through the day.

So I have decided to report that I am crestfallen. Why? Well it is nice to know that you care, I have to say and that simple fact might just change my state of mind, I may with the help of your kindness and concern become despondent or if I cheer up just little more, just plain disappointed.

As to why I am on the verge (thanks to your concern and kindness) of disappointment is that I just can't seem to escape and it is now 192 days since I was imprisoned here.

Wouldn't that make you disappointed? I have been here for around 27 weeks, that is six months in old money I think!

DAY 193 OF MY CAPTIVITY:

It is the weekend today and on a weekend the Male Captor likes to get settled on the Sofa and watch motor racing.

To be honest it doesn't seem to matter what sort of brightly coloured cars he watches whiz around a wobbly circle of tarmac, so long as there is the risk of them hitting each other, well as far as I can tell anyway!

After the motor racing, which because it was being broadcast from America was televised in the very early hours of the morning, he usually dozes off while the television continues gaily to broadcast the next programme.

Usually at this time of the early morning the ideas for the programmes broadcast seem to come from either the broadcasters' wastepaper basket in the bargain basement or they throw innovation and creativity completely out of the window and show an old black and white movie, which is usually made during the 'golden age of British cinema production' and is about the Second World War.

Either way the broadcaster seems to believe that what is most important is to have a schedule of programmes which covers 24 hours, and that anyone dumb enough to actually be watching at that time of the day is half asleep and won't notice the dross being beamed to them.

The black and white movies, even if they aren't about the war, are simple and uncomplicated, and use dialogue and storylines that dispense with their credibility after a few minutes.

The 'special effects' that filmmakers use, which must have wowed audiences in the 1940's and 50's don't even fool a Cat these days.

Wobbling aeroplanes hanging by wires in front of still pictures of the sky, while flying out over occupied territory to bomb cardboard models, always makes me smile.

Then there is my favourite film, which shows an almost empty railway station buffet, with a stilted sad couple droning on about how pointless their unrequited love is, which must have jerked floods of tears from stilted sad 1950's couples, who all too easily understood unrequited love and have me rolling around in fits of laughter.

Which all makes me think that the old days were simpler times, which is just as well because the people were simpler in the old days.

DAY 194 OF MY CAPTIVITY:

Today I emailed my Diary to Mr. T. A. Leibowitz, 'call me Todd,' so that he could, as he put it, 'see how things were coming along.'

His automated reply said that he had received my communication and that he would 'get back to me ASAP.'

I wonder if he has persuaded the publisher that I can write the rest of the Diary from somewhere else?

That would be good because I am having a very bad attack of 'cabin fever' and would hate that to develop into writer's block, what makes matters worse is that to write an entertaining Diary the pressure is on me to come up with ever more extravagant plans and I can tell you that isn't easy when one is still feeling a little disconcerted bordering on disheartened I can tell you!

DAY 195 OF MY CAPTIVITY:

My malaise of the last few days has developed into full scale inaction and so in the interests of making this Dairy interesting and action packed, I have a choice, I can try my paw at inventing an escape plan and then carrying it out in my imagination and then when I have carried it out in my head, ask you if you noticed!

Of course there is one draw back with that plan and that is that if my imaginary escape plan actually worked and because it is imaginary it is very likely to succeed then I would have to own up and say that I invented it and really I am still a prisoner.

Now that is the sort of moral dilemma, that on a good day when things are going right I could cope with, but today I think that I will be honest and say that I am about to start planning something special, an escape attempt, so audacious that it is bound to succeed and dazzle you with my brilliance.

DAY 196 OF MY CAPTIVITY:

What would you say if I said that I have a brilliant plan? 'Just like you!' Thank you, that will do nicely and by the way you are very kind, and I am pleased to announce I do have a brilliant plan, which is bound to get me out of here.

Earlier today I managed to 'find' a micro cassette recorder thing, as you know I am rather good at 'finding' things, in particular things that are apparently, usually not lost, but after I have found them, they either get lost somewhere where no one can find them, or they get broken in some pretty disastrous way.

I am not going to tell you my plan just yet, because I know I am going to have to take the rest of the day off to work out how to use this nice little machine, and then when I have done that I'll have to wait for the right moment to record exactly what I need.

So bear with me and maybe we could meet up on the outside, I know you will probably want to come to my book signings or indeed be a spectator at the premiere of the movie where I promise to wave at you.

Well sorry to get your hopes up, I have waited all day with my paw hovering above the red record button, but I just haven't heard the right words, still 'patience,' as they say 'is a virtue,' and I know that because I have heard people, who are tired of waiting say it often.

DAY 197 OF MY CAPTIVITY:

I was up almost before the crack of dawn and the Sparrows could start choking on the fumes from the main road half a mile away and I think that the same people I mentioned yesterday, who talked about patience also said that 'the early bird always catches the worm,' well I'm not after a worm, but I was after something much larger and I wasn't disappointed.

I managed to record a little helpless moment outside the bathroom door, which until today had been left open by the Female Captor for the invalid, whose fingers were still rather weak.

So now after expending a lot of patience I was half way to getting my recording phase of this escape plan finished, and it was still only 6.30 am, brilliant maybe today would be a good one.

The second recording needed to be the voice of the Male Captor as well, but this time instead of a sort of weak my hand hurts' bit of dialogue I needed him to speak to the Dog.

I sneaked down to the kitchen and shadowed the Dog; of course as it was still quite early and the 'Guard Dog' had been on patrol all night (yeah right), he was fast asleep.

In my opinion if a burglar broke into this house and happened to have a couple of Twix bars on him, he could more or less clean the place out before the 'Guard Dog' would make more than a murmur, always assuming that the burglar was noisy enough to wake 'Guard Dog' in the first place.

Well I am disgusted, I waited for ages for the Male Captor to let the Dog out and say the words that I needed to record and he didn't co-operate, I got excited when he eventually hobbled to the back door and called up to the Female Captor to help with the back door handle, but I had already recorded him saying that, still I can wait.

It is the evening now and I am getting sleepy hugging the little recording machine and getting really bored waiting for the Male Captor to say the magic words, but did he? No he didn't, really why don't people do what you want them to?

DAY 198 OF MY CAPTIVITY:

Well it's a new day and I am now confident that I will be able to get the recording I need and then I will be off sometime in the early evening I expect.

Bingo! Everything worked like clockwork, well clockwork that had been wound up properly of course, which is great, all I have to do now is a little bit of editing on the laptop and then email my Diary to Mr. Leibowitz, 'Call me Todd' and then I can escape.

It is a shame that I can't take the laptop with me, but I just can't carry it because it is just too heavy and I will be travelling light, let me rephrase that, I will be travelling light and free, sorry I just thought I would indulge myself a little there, I like that word, 'free,' actually I like the other word too 'travelling,' no not 'light,' although I have nothing against the word 'light' personally, it is just not relevant here at the moment!

Right the Humans have left and I have a while to mess around on the computer and edit my little recording.

The first thing that you notice when you have something new to do on any computer is that it is not as easy to do what you want to do, and the second thing you notice is that what you think is going to take a couple of minutes always takes half a day!

Well editing the recording was no exception to this rule, first I realised I needed a cable to link the recorder and the computer, what a shame the wireless revolution seems to have gone off like a damp Squibb.

Eventually I found a cable, but unfortunately when I pulled on it and then reeled it down to the floor I had the Male Captor's laptop following it, like a fisherman's dream catch. Still I am sure that the laptop isn't damaged and when they notice that the laptop is on the floor, I will be at least several miles away happily.

After that false start I was ready to begin my masterpiece, all I had to do was to create a new recording from the bits that I had recorded, which said. 'Come on then, walkies! Darling I am taking the Dog for a walk, can you open the door for me, I'll be there in a minute!'

Simple, well you would think it was simple when million selling R&B records can be created in DJ's bedrooms, ok so they are not very good and to call most of them music is to stretch the term almost as much as elastic around the shell suit trousers of some Rap stars' bottoms, but I digress!

The first little compilation complication came when I was inserting the word 'walkies,' I thought that the Dog was outside, but I was wrong and that was confirmed when our hero with the acute hearing bounded into their bedroom and ran all over the carpet barking and being annoyingly excited.

I had to stop and wait for the shaggy idiot to calm down, and flop onto the floor in a disappointed heap, then the little devil in me, that forces me to border on evil made me play 'walkies' again.

As I expected the furry fool jumped up and began his noisy performance again, he was so excited at the prospect of a daytime walk that I thought he was going to wet himself.

When I stopped playing the word over and over again, he eventually realised that the Human Captor had stopped inviting him to a nice bracing walk, and again he crashed down on the floor and let the sides of his face which looked as though they were more or less stuck to the carpet, flap and shudder with each sigh.

Eventually I had to stop the fun because my stomach was beginning to ache from laughing too much, so I just let the fed up Fido stew for a while.

I have to say I was feeling a little sorry for him as he sauntered dejectedly downstairs to his basket and I closed the door for some peace and quiet.

After a while I had stopped hiccupping and finished my little masterpiece of editing and sent the digital file back to the little recorder. I was now ready to play my last little trick and the recording. Then freedom, mmmh I like that word most of all!

I decided that the best time to play the recording was after dinner, when the Female Captor would be in the kitchen and the washing up and the Male Captor usually finds something urgent to do out of the way somewhere else in the house, but occasionally when he can't think of anything to do, to avoid the crockery and soap suds, will take the Dog for a walk.

After they had finished eating and the Dog and I had fought over the few scraps, which we get treated to usually, I surreptitiously sneaked into the hall and sat next to where I had hidden the little recording machine.

Things were going brilliantly well, because as I expected the Male Captor limped past me and hobbled upstairs as I heard plates and other crockery being clattered around in the kitchen.

Now all I had to do was to make sure my timing was absolutely perfect and that wasn't going to be difficult, I could hear the Male Captor shuffling down the landing and banging his plaster cast on the study door, well they call it a 'study' it is really a small bedroom, which in a minute I won't ever see again, hooray!

The noise of the crockery had changed and I could hear running water, now was 'the' moment, to strike a blow for all Cats imprisoned everywhere and so I made sure the volume was at max and pressed the play button on the little miracle machine.

'Come on then, walkies! Darling I am taking the Dog for a walk, can you open the door for me, I'll be there in a minute!'

'Yes that was it, perfect, now come on 'darling,' get your bits into gear please!'

The Dog was up and off like an athlete on steroids at the Olympics, he dashed into the hallway and danced and barked ready to let off some of his energy on a nice long walk.

'Do it yourself, I'm busy, doing the washing up, as usual!'

I didn't like the tone of her reply at all, but risked another stab at the pre-recorded question.

'Come on then, walkies! Darling I am taking the Dog for a walk, can you open the door for me, I'll be there in a minute!'

A glass shattered on the floor in the kitchen and the heavy clump of 'annoyed' footsteps came towards me, it was one of the most frightening moments of my life and I shrunk back under the table with the telephone on it, as the clumping feet passed me.

For a moment I thought that the second playing of the recording had worked and the catch on the door might get undone, and then the Female Captor would return to the kitchen, but I probably couldn't have been more wrong!

There was a lot of muttering going on from somewhere above the shapely legs and the hem of the little black work dress, and the small person inside was not the happiest of Bunnies, especially as this unhappy Bunny had come into the hallway to confront the lazy Male Captor and tell the Dog to behave.

The Dog though was behaving like a complete and utter nutter, this was the second time today that he had been promised 'walkies' and this time he was going to get what he had been promised, even if it killed him or anyone who stood in his way, or that is what it seemed to me.

Sadly for the Dog he had met his match in the Female Captor, who although small is more than a match for... well I was going to say more than a match for him, but she is more than a match for anyone or anything when she is annoyed and she was not best pleased at the moment and well on the way to being annoyed.

The Dog over stepped the mark when he jumped up at her and managed to rub his spit and bits of food covered mouth over the little black dress.

He was grabbed by the collar and marched into the kitchen, I have to credit the Dog with possessing more sense today than usual, he didn't resist and was led back into the kitchen like the proverbial Lamb, heading off to become a Moroccan delicacy.

Some of the Dog's good sense obviously rubbed off on me and I stayed exactly where I was, not moving a muscle and hoping that the returning stockinged footsteps were not coming for me. Happily they weren't, they passed me by and on their angry way upstairs and a confrontation with the poor unfortunate and lazy Male Captor.

As soon as I heard the landing shake I sneaked out of my hiding place and headed for the front room, where after jumping onto the Sofa I let a cushion fall on my head and block out some of the high pitched angry words that were being shouted at an innocent Male Captor in the study.

Sometime much later after everyone had gone to separate beds (tee hee) I slipped back into the hall and erased my little recording because I was convinced that was the safest thing to do under the circumstances!

DAY 199 OF MY CAPTIVITY:

I seem to have adopted a sort of routine and that routine is that after one of my little escape plans goes horribly wrong I lie low for a few days and so I am afraid that you can't expect the next few days to be action packed, but I am sure you will understand.

Again after one of my brilliant plans goes wrong, usually I make one or two enemies, but have at least one person where I can get a stroke and a bit of sympathy and always before there has been the Dog to rely on for a cuddle when I get desperate, but this time, all that has changed.

The Male and Female Captors aren't speaking to each other and I don't know if they have found my paw prints on the little recording machine after they found it suspiciously hidden in the hall, but I have the dreadful feeling that they think I have something to do with yesterday's upset, but they obviously can't put their finger on how I was involved, still if they do work it out, I know that that finger will be pointing at me and I don't like that feeling.

The Dog 'knows,' I don't know how he 'knows' he is never usually that perceptive! Thinking about it, the Parrot might have told him I suppose, but that is the only theory I have, he surely couldn't have worked it all out in his head on his own, his brain is too small.

Still he may have a small brain, but until now he was my pal and now he sniffs at me and turns his head away when I go into a room where he is, and then he walks out not looking at me, it isn't fair, I was only using him!

I even tried to apologise, and he pretended to be deaf, but I did notice that after I said 'I am really sorry' for the tenth time he nearly nudged me with his nose to knock me off balance, indicating that I was forgiven.

I think I would give anything to be nudged off balance at the moment!

Of course the Parrot thinks it is very funny and every time I go near his cage, yes he is still imprisoned if the Humans are out, which helps alleviate my misery a little, he says 'Come on then, walkies! Darling I am taking the Dog for a walk, can you open the door for me, I'll be there in a minute!'

Very Funny but the accent is wrong!

DAY 200 OF MY CAPTIVITY:

My campaign to win my way back into the Dog's good books continues, I deliberately didn't even try to compete with him when the breakfast scraps were given out and then after the Humans had gone I tried to snuggle into his basket just like old times, after I had settled down comfortably next to him he got out and went to sit next to the back door in the utility room.

So I too got out of his basket after he left, because it isn't the same in there on your own and that is what I told him as I stood in front of him apologising, again.

He didn't even open his eyes, which is probably just as well because I don't know if I could have looked at him straight in the eyes, for the moment I am just a little ashamed.

This evening the Male Captor brought in what I believe is called a peace offering, I have to say it was pretty impressive, a bunch of Roses, Chocolates, Champagne and an Chinese Takeaway, at first I thought that the presents were for me, but they weren't they were for his someone special and I actually understood why he had bought them. When he dished up the Chinese and promised that he would be doing the washing up for I think eternity, he was forgiven, which is nice.

I hoped that the Dog would follow the Female Captor's example and forgive me, but he was going to extract the ultimate punishment before I was forgiven.

Two of the Chinese dishes had Prawns in them, Prawn balls, and Prawns in Szechuan sauce which is of course is one of the Female Captor's favourites and it goes without saying that there is someone else who likes Prawns, no matter how that have been cooked.

The Dog and I lurked competitively under the table waiting for bits of dinner to make a run for it, so that we could be helpful and catch them before they made a mess on the kitchen floor.

But instead of covering both ends of the table at the same time, as usual and creating a bit of friendly good natured rivalry, the Dog stayed near his master, which is a good spot because he seems to miss his mouth with his forkful of food more often than the Female Captor ever does, which is where I was not enjoying the thin pickings or the nasty looks and growls from the Dog just a few feet away.

I have always been amazed at how long Humans take over eating food, it almost goes without saying that compared to Dogs, Cats are delicate eaters and have been known to chew their food in a thankfully most undoglike manner, but compared to Humans, Cats are fast eaters and so I had to endure the uncomfortable hurtful gaze of the Dog for quite a long while, I was under the table, but I had to stay where I was because Prawns were at stake!

The Humans eventually finished their meal with kisses and Tiramisu generously covered with cream and even Dessert Wine so there was no doubt that they had made up successfully. I wondered what I would have to do to make everything better with the Dog. Personally I didn't fancy a kiss, but I actually found myself considering it because I was that desperate.

Then all of a sudden as the plates were cleared from the table and the scraps distributed into two separate earthenware bowls, one of a medium size and the other lunatic large and marked Cat and Dog respectively.

This was, I realised with horror, my opportunity to make up with the dear old Dog and at least avoid a snog. In seconds he had wolfed down a mouth wateringly delightful mixture of Tiramisu, Cream, Szechuan Prawns, delicately topped with two Prawn Balls, which was a larger version of exactly what I was looking down at in my bowl.

The Szechuan Prawns and their lovely sauce had been gently chilled by the addition of the Tiramisu and Cream, with all of it topped off by the Prawn Balls, which had daintily sunk into the whole delicious runny mixture.

After licking his bowl clean and moving it suspiciously close to mine, he looked up and made that awful sucking and splashing noise that shows just how much he enjoyed eating whatever it was he had eaten and if he ever smelt it again he would eat it again. I knew that he would probably never recognise what he had just eaten if he couldn't smell it though, because he had just eaten it never giving it a second glance, never savouring the delicate batter shell of the Prawn Balls, or the soft piquant sauce of the Szechuan Prawns, there was, in his opinion, no time to do that, which I suppose is a pack thing.

The juicy jaw smacking continued, but slowed as his gaze wandered from my bowlful of delicious treats to me and back again, several times, until he stopped the dreadful sloppy noise and stared at me expectantly.

He knew what I had to do, and I knew what I had to do too, there was no debate, if this was the price of Doggy forgiveness then I was prepared to pay it, I wasn't happy about paying the exorbitant price, but I knew the Dog knew that too and that would make his second dinner all the more enjoyable.

Granting the pack leader his status and humbly offering my sincerest apology I backed away from my bowl a little and watched as the Dog dived nose first into my food.

Little splashes of Cream and other goodies covered the area around the bowl for milliseconds until like the bowl they were licked clean and a triumphant Dog looked at me and smiled an odd satisfied smile.

I edged closer to him and he didn't back away, he lowered his head and nudged me with his greasy nose and knocked me off balance, I was very grateful and also forgiven!

Ah! I hear you say, well in a minute you are going to go ugh! When I picked myself up from the second rather more forceful nudging, the Dog nodded his head to me and opened his mouth and let a spit covered Prawn Ball present whiz through the air and land at my feet.

I had no choice did I? We were friends again and friends sometimes share food! Ugh!

DAY 201 OF MY CAPTIVITY:

I had something odd in my dinner tonight! Actually I seem to remember the dish before, it is called 'leftovers' and really not fit for a Cat, which is why I let the Dog eat it. Well I use the word 'eat' in the loosest sense of the word, it was more like noisily wolfing it, but that only just describes the true horror of watching and for that matter listening to the savage eat.

The hairy mop head seems to take particular pride in eating my food as though he has won some sort of victory over me, which is why the secret delight of knowing that I won't have touched the unwholesome mess with the proverbial 'bargepole' is all the more satisfying.

On this occasion the 'leftovers' were similar to the ones that I have ignored before, cold and covered in a jelly, but unlike last time I noticed before the dish was slopped onto my plate the smell of King Prawns, 'mmmh!' I thought to myself, smells interesting!'

For a while I got excited because of that divine aroma, I know the smell of King Prawns and can identify them at great distances, even when they are sealed in their little cave like plastic bag homes, and have only just arrived in the house in a carrier bag. Experience has taught me that this is the best time to get one's paws on them, ripping through an unguarded carrier bag and then slicing through the little King Prawn cave, raking as many out onto the floor as possible and gnawing at the tasty little blighters until someone discovers what the 'naughty' Cat has done.

Happily Humans don't over enjoy food that has been spread across even a clean kitchen floor or gnawed by a Cat either, would you believe, yes I suppose you would, most readers are more or less Human, I forget that sometimes, and so usually they wash the 'dirty' King Prawns and drop them into my food dish, I am sure that they know that is simpler than dropping them in the waste bin because when their backs are turned I will only mount a full frontal attack on it, and get the King Prawns that way!

So for a while I got excited and began my 'give it to me this instant' Caterwauling and may I say what an excellent and accurate word that is. Happily the Caterwauling didn't last long because the 'leftovers' slopped into my dish, which was put on the floor for me to munch.

Imagine my horror and frustration when I couldn't find any King Prawns, I even got my nose wet nudging the awful mess aside to see if they were hidden at the bottom of the dish.

But my meal wasn't to be King Prawns oh no! All that my dinner consisted of were cold vegetables, mainly strips of red shiny slimy vegetables, I was outraged honestly, fancy feeding a Cat vegetables, I ask you, what is the world coming to?

Sadly all of the King Prawns in what was I discovered called a 'stir fry' had been eaten by the self indulgent and greedy Humans, but still the red vegetable strips intrigued me, what were they and where did they come from? I had no idea, all the same they were very strange and interesting, not I have to say that my curiosity was sufficiently pricked to see what they tasted like of course, they were vegetables after all!

They say that travel broadens the mind and I would happily have my mind broadened, because it would mean that I was out of here, but my ability to travel is sadly on a par with every stiff road killed Hedgehog, but if I was well travelled then maybe I would be sufficiently cosmopolitan to try eating vegetables, well it is just a thought!

So saddened by the fact that I can't travel and broaden my mind in a sort of two for one deal, I have decided to use the good old internet to find out more about these shiny fiery coloured vegetables, well research makes the time pass and does a little of what travel does, namely broadens the mind, trouble is it can also broaden the bottom, have you see pictures of all those awful people who spend day after day selling things on that dreadful auction website, yes thanks it is called eBay, I think that as 'couch potatoes' got their name from lying on sofas watching television, then eBay addicts should be called 'vast ass,' no I know it has nothing to do with eBay and only if you think about it sitting down, but it is a perfect description of their big bums don't you think?

Research on the internet is an interesting endeavour, but like all research if you know most of the answer then it makes the questions, that you have to ask in order to get the exact answers, your require easier, listen to me I sound like a furry Professor!

Search engines are oddly named, but if you ignore the misnomer of 'engine' and just think of them as search thingies then I for one feel more comfortable with them.

I typed in 'red shiny things' and was astonished at some of the results, some of which were not at all nice and in fact totally unsuitable for inclusion in my Diary, I just mention that fact here to demonstrate how difficult it is to find an answer on the Internet.

After the shock of 'red shiny things' I changed my search to 'red vegetable,' which was closer to the mark and indeed happily discovered that these red shiny vegetables were called Red Peppers.

I know a bit about pepper, it makes me sneeze, not in the same way as a Cat nip flavoured mouse does, but in a 'I have got a stinking cold' sort of way. So you can imagine why I began to think that Red Peppers might be called Red Peppers, because they make you sneeze until your nose bleeds, well it was as I found out a simple mistake to make!

It turns out that Red Peppers are not really called Red Peppers at all but Capsicums, and Capsicums are not only red, they come in all sorts of colours including, white, yellow, green, orange and blue, no sorry I made the last one up, there aren't any blue peppers called Capsicums! There are some deep purple ones though, but they are called Aubergines and don't associate with Capsicums, unless they are in a Ratatouille.

The bit about the blue peppers that was a Cat joke! Ok so our sense of humour is different, is that my fault? And if you didn't laugh I did, thinking that you would be wondering to yourself as you read 'blue peppers,' 'what are they, I have never seen them!'

Ok enough hilarity, anyone would think that I was writing a comedy Diary and we don't want that do we?

I found out that Red Peppers are eaten the world over by more or less everyone and like most vegetables are grown from seed.

My first thought was that there must be billions of peppers in the world, hundreds of thousands actually being cut up as I am writing this, others being shipped to the shops, still more being grown in people's gardens and finally ever such a lot being grown on farms, which prompted a question that I can't find an answer to, no not 'why are so many grown when they end up all slimy,' but just 'how many Red Peppers are there in the world?'

Try as I might I just couldn't find an answer to that knotty little problem, and I know exactly what you are going to say now, why would I want to know the answer, because you don't really care and not only that I am wasting your time making you read about Red Peppers, well the answer to that question I'll have you, know, is that one of us wants to broaden out mind!

DAY 202 OF MY CAPTIVITY:

After thinking about Red Peppers for too much of yesterday I have decided to focus on travel, while curled up in the Dog's basket.

I suppose I should mention that the Dog, who has slipped outside for a moment, doesn't need his basket and anyway if I decided to have a snooze in his basket and he was in it, I would still use it. Having said all of that it did occur to me that I would do him a kindness and keep the basket warm anyway, I can be nice like that, sometimes.

Travel, what a nice word that is! It has contained in its six letters real promise. Although I know that it probably means different things to different people, for me and let's face it, it is my opinion that I want to convey to you and not the other way around, travel means freedom and to get freedom I am going to have to escape.

Yes you may have noticed I still haven't done that yet, escape that is, which is all rather depressing, especially for someone who is so basically clever, and inventive, and cunning and clever, oops I have repeated myself but I am sure you get the picture, although you could have stopped me after I had said 'handsome' which was the next word, and not before, surely?

I have to tell you proudly that the latest plan is a cunning one and I am sure that you will offer me a pat on my back for its cleverness as I disappear out of here and into my new life travelling the world, or at least Tunbridge Wells which I understand is what the place is called on the other side of these prison walls.

The world, even the little bit of it that I inhabit, is an interesting and varied place, and as you know by now we have our fair share of its inhabitants visiting here often, rather too often for my liking really.

A lot of those visitors seem to be tradesmen (and the occasional tradeswoman I might add, but I don't think that we have much in the way of 'trade' for them really), who come in, leave tools all over the floor, shake their heads, tut a little, hold their chins, suck air in between their teeth and announce that the repair will be whatever it costs.

I have noticed that the longer they take to do all of the above usually is equal to the scale of the cost for the job (usually a repair) that they invent on the spot.

Almost always on the occasions when one or the other, or both of the Human Captors question the cost of the repair, (occasionally rather vehemently in my opinion) the tradesman or woman will usually point out that the damage was caused by what looks like a wild animal, as though that justifies the enormous bill!

It is usually at that juncture that I disappear to see if anyone has kindly left a door open, or if they haven't, have they left a tool bag lying around which I can sneak into and get literally carried away in. You may have noticed that to date I haven't been successful with either of these escape plans, but I live in hope!

The latest thing to look like 'it has been attacked by a wild animal,' is a wall socket, and a kettle, and a toaster and a food processor and well a few other electrical appliances, including the dishwasher.

Alright quite a few appliances if you want me to spell it out, and as I am in 'owning up' mode, several more electric wall sockets, all as you may have gathered in the kitchen.

In my defence I had run out of explosives! Ok it is a rather weak defence, but there is more. I got confused, the lights definitely went out and last, but by no means least, I panicked.

It had all started so promisingly too, which just adds to the disappointment really, I got confused, yes I know I said that before, but it is the truth! Electricity, I have found out, is very confusing and dangerous stuff, which Humans have made even more dangerous by making it invisible and hiding it inside wires and then sending it everywhere.

The wires that have the electricity trapped in them are confusing too, they are all different colours, but here is the confusing bit, some of the wires you can touch and not get an electric shock from, I must stress here that I don't recommend doing this if my younger and more adventurous readers (for 'adventurous' read 'stupid') have suddenly started to think, mmmh I might stop skateboarding in the traffic today and try that!

I don't even recommend licking the wires that are 'safe' but you actually could if you wanted to and were insane, oh although I forgot to mention that wires that are 'safe' today may well not be 'safe' tomorrow because the electricity (and I am afraid this bit is technical and I don't really understand it), maybe 'off' when you lick them today and 'on' when you lick them tomorrow.

I don't know exactly what happens when the electric is 'off' except that it doesn't give you a shock, it maybe like milk or cream, which has gone off, but as my electric, or I should say the stuff inside the electric socket which I had broken into, didn't smell off, until after it had burned out all of the appliances in the kitchen and taken some of my whiskers and most of my eyebrows off, as you will see in a minute.

It was surprisingly easy to crack open the electric socket; I just hit it with a rather heavy hammer, a four pound one (and for our metricised readers I will translate the weight 'pour vous,' that is 'for you,' in metric language, - the hammer weight a lot - there that should do it, well I didn't say I could speak metric language fluently did I?).

It took two or three heavy whacks and the whole of the face of the plug shattered into convenient bits, which crumbled and dropped away onto the work surface.

Behind the face of the socket was a confusing array of wires, made even more confusing because I had smashed the electric kettle's plug that was in the socket and the three wires from the kettle seemed to be totally different colours to the ones sticking out of the wall.

Still I wasn't that worried; after all I was trying to create an explosion wasn't I? Didn't you know that, what do you mean I didn't tell you? Well I was ok! I told you I had run out of explosives and I thought that you would know what I was up to, I was confident that my clever readers were clever enough to do that, now I am a little disappointed as they obviously aren't! Still there isn't any time to ponder the intelligence of my readers now, back to the explosion.

As I fiddled with the wires I said to myself, 'now let me see, do I join the yellow and green wire to the black or the pretty red one to the brown? If I do that what happens with the blue one? Electricity is confusing because it is invisible but electric cables are no less confusing even though you can see them, ouch that hurt, it bit me!

Eventually after several more little electric shocks that had my fur standing on end, I had joined all of the wires together that I could and then pulled out the last long red wire and balanced the kettle over it at a crazy angle which would allow me to easily spill water onto the red wire and jump clear.

Everything was set and I was, I have to admit, more than ready to escape and by setting off this, more or less, controlled explosion and by blowing the window out I was going to be free, fantastic.

Well there is never ever any time like the present, as they would say if they didn't usually cut what they say down to 'there is no time like the present,' so after practising knocking over the kettle and swamping the red wire with water, with a few dry runs I was ready.

I was also a little nervous, because as I have said electricity is dangerous stuff, but underneath my nervousness I was confident, mind you my confidence was a long way underneath my nervousness, but here goes, sorry every time I get to the point of describing, I have to stop, because of the potential for disaster that was haunting me at the time and still smarts as I write about it.

One big breath and one last time, here goes!

Things went according to plan, at first, the kettle fell over as I expected after the lightest of touches with my right paw and before it fell to the work surface I was diving out of the way and falling down to the kitchen floor.

The first thing that surprised me was that the bolt of blue lightning seared its way past me before the bang that started the series of electric explosions, which did so much damage to the kitchen and all of the kitchen appliances, and burned away my whiskers and most of my eyelashes.

I hit the floor in agony, bolts of electric blue fire whirling around me blurring my vision and doing nothing to make my day!

As soon as I was on my burning feet I hotfooted it out of the kitchen at the speed usually described as 'like a scalded Cat.'

In the shadow of the hall table I cooled down enough to realise that I wasn't going to make my escape today, although I had been in a hurry to get out of the kitchen I had been listening for the crack and clatter of the broken window hitting the garden path outside and it hadn't happened, there hadn't even been the slightest tinkle of glass, how disappointing is that?

I also began to realise that I had just made a bit of a mess, which was confirmed by the black smoke, which crept across the hall floor from the direction of the kitchen.

I peered into the black mess of the kitchen it looked as if we were going to have the electricians in again.

Day 203 of My Captivity:

The electricians turned up and were surprisingly pleased to see all of us despite what had happened on the last occasion that they visited, again they seemed to think that a wild animal had been the major cause of the damage, but this time they didn't mention that fact while the Human Captors were around and only did so when they were talking quietly together.

I also heard them say that work was a little quiet and that it was a good job that this place was haunted by the aforementioned wild animal, then they patted me on the head, gave me a big bit of Ham from a sandwich, finished their tea and happily got on with what they described as a nice little earner!

This Diary is getting very long, in fact much bigger than I ever imagined it would be, and I am convinced that the large file is making the laptop heavier, although I am not completely sure about that!

What I do know is that this Diary is much better value than that one by Bridget Jones, because her Diary can't have had an entry for every day, can it? Or it would have been as big as this one surely? She I think had a lot to say, although most of it was about her silly self, thinking about it, and I can't imagine Bridget Jones getting involved in action, not because she is an awful fat self obsessed creep, but because she doesn't have the imagination to create a bit of action and mayhem that I do.

Day 204 of My Captivity:

Transcendental meditation is a remarkable, um er… thing! I don't quite know how to describe it, and I doubt that most people do, but having said that, I am sure that most people would know what happens if you can achieve a higher mental state and I am not thinking here about jumping from a ledge or anything you understand I am actually talking about an expanded consciousness.

Quite how high that higher state has to be, to do what I wanted to do with transcendental meditation, I had no idea, but I was determined to give it a go.

What was it I wanted to achieve? Well at least that is less complicated than transcendental meditation itself! I wanted to levitate, not much of an ambition for a clever Cat I hear you say, well all I can say is you try it!

Happily I had managed to find some help to achieve my goal, two books, one by a famous Burmese Guru and Holy Man, and the other about his great works and teachings by one of his ex-followers.

I think that the Female Captor had bought them when she was in one of those phases that Humans sometimes go through, 'trying to find herself,' or as some more sensible people call it 'hitting thirty.' It is a time when people with a lot of money, not much sense and too much time on their hands start to question life, the Universe and whatever else they don't understand and begin to delve into the mysteries for answers only to get even more confused and then give up even more disillusioned than they were when they started.

The books were rather dusty, and had started to take on that stale old book smell that also seems to cling to the trousers of old men of pensionable age, but even if they didn't smell too good they were really rather readable.

The one entitled 'Making A Packet Out Of New Age believers' which was an exposé of the Burmese Guru and Holy Man who had managed over three or four decades to get celebrities, entire pop groups and millions of ordinary people to part with millions of dollars, pounds, euros and as far as I could work out any other currency that was offered to him.

Now although this book wasn't going to help me in my quest to levitate, I was absolutely sure that it would become a book that I would refer to time and again in the future!

It was obvious that the Burmese Guru and Holy Man had a lot of brilliant money making schemes and wheezes and if they had worked once then they were bound to work again for a Cat who is confident that a dollar, or pound or euro in his pocket (I use the word 'pocket' loosely) is better than it being in anyone else's.

Still, having said that, it was the other book, 'The Teachings of Sanjit Nee Anel,' which had a lot more colour pictures than the other book, mainly of the Burmese Guru and Holy Man, I feel compelled to say was going to be more helpful to me at the moment.

One colour photograph printed over an entire double page spread showed dozens of his 'converts' in the hall of his mansion located in the English countryside, levitated so far off the ground that one could only describe them as 'flying.' Now that was very encouraging.

Sadly there was no way that I could go on retreat to the Guru and Holy Man's mansion, for two reasons, the first being that travel for a prisoner is a little limited and the second was that the cost of a weekend's retreat had far to many naughts on the end of the figure for comfort.

'Never mind' I thought to myself, I have the next best thing, the teachings of the Guru and Holy Man, and as it said in the foreword, by reading his words I had taken the first step to enlightenment, and I hadn't even noticed that I had gone anywhere, this was powerful stuff indeed!

The foreword droned on a bit I have to say if I am honest about it and at the end of almost all of the paragraphs and then again at the end of the foreword I was promised that I would have a greater understanding of the Guru and Holy Man's teaching if I sent him what I could afford, I made a mental note to send him the Parrot and read on.

For all of the deep mysticism in the book it was a remarkable light and easy read, and I have to say if you ignored the photographs almost 'light' on text, which meant that although the cover price of $70 was a bit steep, I was able to learn the bits of the secret of levitation very quickly.

In fact by lunchtime I was ready to notch up my first flying hour, which was fantastic, this teacher was indeed a Guru and he would get my vote if he ever reformed his colourful alliance political party and stood for election again. Well he would get my vote if they enfranchised Cats and other 'domestic' animals that is, but that is not relevant here really, I just mention it so that you know that some domesticated animals wouldn't mind voting in elections even if a large proportion of Humans can't be bothered or don't want to!

I did have one dilemma and that was, should I have lunch before I took to the air? Although that question was quickly answered, there wasn't any point in adding to my take off weight was there? And once I had landed I would celebrate with a slap up meal, before leaving this place for good.

I dragged the book and a cushion over to the open fireplace, propped the book open at Chapter 6, 'Transcendental Mediation and Levitation,' and hopped up on the cushion.

Now before I tell you what actually happened, I will let you know my plan, which aided by the Burmese Guru and Holy Man's teaching was going to get me out of this prison and onto the roof.

According to the confirmation I got from reading the last but one chapter of the wise man's book, 'There Is No Limit To Your Power,' I was going to slip into a trance and then levitate, but not just a little way off the ground, by focusing all of my internal energies and orientating my subconscious and powerful inner being, I was going to fly. Wow I was impressed with the idea and I was impressed by me, fancy having all of that power pent up inside one!

My flight plan had been easy to work out, up off the cushion, into the fireplace and then zoom and probably a bit of a whoosh straight up the chimney and out through the chimney pot, and onto the roof.

Piece of something beginning with 'P' as they say, well the electricians said anyway, because it wasn't only going to be me flying, oh no I had help, I had the combined mental power of the great Guru and Holy Man himself, and every single one of his disciples through-out the world, or I would have had, had I paid to join his organisation, but then I reasoned 'I could owe it to the big fella and pay him once I was on the outside!'

So I sat in the middle of the cushion feeling the combined power of the great man and all of his disciples flow through me, it was almost like sitting on a sharp stone, then I lost my concentration sadly, stood up to 'centre' myself as the great teacher recommends and noticed that I was sitting on the cushion cover zipper, I must have half folded the cushion over as I entered my trance.

Again I centred myself and breathed deeply, letting life and the majesty of creation flow through my being, (the great man's words not mine!).

Just as I felt the warmth of the rising energy flowing from somewhere underneath me, my peace and quiet was shattered by the Male and Female Captor opening the front door, my mind had been so incredibly concentrated that I hadn't heard their car on the driveway.

I jumped off the cushion and kicked the Guru and Holy Man's book under the Sofa and then sprawled on the cushion trying to look delighted at their homecoming.

It was obvious that the escape would have to wait until the next day.

I didn't mind that my peace and quiet were disturbed again when I heard the fridge door open, which is always a cue to run into the kitchen and see what scraps I can beg for.

Day 205 of My Captivity:

I didn't bother to get up early this morning, in fact I lay in bed, collecting my thoughts and mustering all of the energy that I could gather.

I even rubbed my nose over the crystal that sits on the dresser in their bedroom, which was good for me, but not so good for the crystal because as I took its mystic power, it toppled and crashed to the ground breaking into two almost identical halves.

After the Humans let the Dog out for the day, because the weather forecast promised long periods of sunny weather and then left for work, I slipped into the front room and pulled out the great man's book from its hiding place and opened it as I had yesterday.

Then I nudged one of the cushions onto the floor and drawing energy from the room and all my fellow disciples in the world to say nothing of the Guru and Holy Man himself, I popped up onto the cushion and sat down to begin my final preparations.

Some people like to chant or hum a mantra as they enter a trance, but I couldn't because I had a fragment of a Geri Haliwell's pop song running around in my head and couldn't budge it, even when I called upon my Red Indian Spirit Guide to help me, but then I reasoned that if some people hum a mantra is there any reason why I can't hum a bit of 'Ride it?' It does have a sort of mystic flavour to it, actually I rather like it, but then a Cat's taste in music is often thought to be a little suspect!

Oooo, ooo e ooo, sorry I wish that you could hear the humming, but you will just have to listen to the original Geri Haliwell song, but I am sure that your get the picture I had my eyes closed and I was humming 'Ride It,' well my own sort of mystic remix version anyway!

Again I could feel the wonderful sensation of the power rising up from somewhere between my bottom and the cushion underneath me, in fact I could honestly say that my bottom was getting hot.

I closed my eyes and then screwed the eyelids down tight to increase my concentration and let the power flow through me.

Slowly my consciousness floated up above me and I could see myself below and just out of reach, beginning to float off the cushion and hover above it.

This was simply miraculous, it was just like the great Guru and holy Man had written in his book, I was levitating; I was ready to fly to freedom.

I let my breathing slow and my heart rate drop for the exertion of changing state from hovering to soaring, which according to the great Guru and Holy Man's book required that I reach towards the gates of ecstasy, wherever that is, still I was on my way this time I knew it, I could feel the air under me and from above I could see that I was levitating, the feeling was amazing, my soul was free and soon the rest of me was going to catch up with it.

There seemed to be a small problem, as I told my mind to take me closer to the open fireplace, it seemed to be reluctant to go anywhere and when I commanded it to comply it refused completely, I was confused this bit hadn't been covered in the great Guru and Holy Man's book!

Looking down from my celestial vantage point (as you can tell from the name, that had been covered in the great man's book), I couldn't quite see what was holding me back, so I opened one eye, and then in complete and total disbelief the other, I hadn't travelled anywhere, and I had a suspicion that I hadn't even floated above the cushion, judging by the fact that I was sitting in the same place as when I started.

Still never mind, Cats who live with or have any contact with Humans practise having short memories and so I decided that although I had been taken in by a charlatan I wouldn't let it spoil my lunch.

I merely tipped the book into the hearth and after a couple of strikes managed to set a match to one of the great man's books. The other one as I said earlier would probably come in handy later, especially if I got cold.

DAY 206 OF MY CAPTIVITY:

There was some sort of family gathering today and was I invited? No of course I wasn't. I was thrown into solitary confinement throughout the event like the monstrous family member that no one talks about.

They must be really ashamed of me, just like the poor person I read about on the Internet.

This poor soul might even have been worse off than me as a relative of the Queen Mother, whose family were so ashamed of 'it' because the unwanted family member was apparently so ugly and dribbly that 'it' (I have no idea if it was a he or a she and I wonder if it did, if you get my meaning) was left in a tower at the family home in Glamis Castle, which probably rightly is one of the most haunted castles in the world!

Still even being locked in the kitchen, which is not as bad as a dark and cold tower in a castle I have to admit, I could hear the noise of people enjoying themselves and smell food, but what did I get? I'll tell you, ignored, that is what.

Still I did hear something very interesting, I heard them say that my solitary confinement was due to my ability to give some of the visitors an allergic reaction!

That sounds like quite a power and I will have to use it to my advantage. (Note to self) Must learn what allergies are and how to use it to my advantage.

DAY 207 OF MY CAPTIVITY:

Have you noticed that warning signs don't have any punctuation in them? And no, before you ask I am not talking about the ones that only use pictures, I am not that dumb!

I mean the warning signs that are sown into blankets, duvets, stuck to the back of electrical goods and attached to quilted jackets, made of what is called manmade fibres, you know the sort that melt and catch fire easily.

Indeed if warning signs had punctuation it would give you time to think before you did something silly?

Like say for instance, 'Nylon, keep away from Fire, made in Bulgaria!'

Mind you, maybe if the warning signs were more precise then you wouldn't get into trouble with quilted jackets in the first place, actually I don't mean 'you' in that sentence sadly I mean 'me!'

When I discovered the quilted jacket on the arm of the Sofa with its sleeve carelessly draped over my cushion I obviously didn't read the little warning label which is always sown discreetly into the inside of the jacket, in fact these helpful little labels, or signs, if you will, are sown into jackets too discreetly if you ask my opinion!

As I said the jacket was in my way and so I swiped it off the seat cushion and curled up and went to sleep.

I was totally unaware that the jacket had fallen off the arm of the Sofa and the wayward arm had been propelled into the hearth where a log fire was merrily burning attractively without the benefit or visual intrusion of a fire guard, which I understand is a sort of metal device to stop burning things like logs or sparks rolling out of the fire and setting alight to the carpet, or the pile of logs attractively piled in a rustic way in the hearth, oh by the way I imagine that a fire guard would also be handy if the sleeve of a discarded quilted jacket happened to drop in the hearth too.

Of course a fire guard would prevent Cats and Dogs from getting too close to the fire and getting singed and occasionally burned by sparks which can fly out of the fire from unseasoned logs.

So although a fire guard is a reasonably good idea, I am quite pleased that we don't have one, because on unusually cold days it would mean that some animals couldn't get toasted, and getting toasted in front of a log fire on a very cold day is worth all of the risks of being singed I can tell you.

Not only that if you are reasonably clever and or reasonably small you get to be shielded by the large bulk of a dozing Dog anyway and the sparks usually therefore only land in the Dog's fur, which is handy!

Anyway today the Dog was in the garden with the Male Captor doing what Dogs do in gardens, which is occasionally unsavoury and if it isn't unsavoury then it is naughty like digging up the plants and eating ancient bits of bread that have fallen off the bird table.

So at least by saying where the Dog and the Male Captor are, you can now tell whose small quilted jacket had been on the arm of the chair, which is most unusual because if you were to say who was the untidiest out of the Dog and the Male and Female Captors, the Female Captor wouldn't be the obvious choice!

Still this wasn't what I was thinking about after I had carefully 'moved' the offending jacket and settled down for a sleep. What you could say was that if the Dog had been indoors then I wouldn't be telling you about this little disaster because I would have been competing with the Dog for the closest toasting position, so maybe it is the Dog's fault and not the Female Captor's after all!

Furthermore it can't have been my fault, I was asleep and I was dreaming about soup, yes I know that is a little surreal, but I can't be held responsible for my dreams can I?

Swimming in the soup were dozens of King Prawns, and the soup with the swimming Prawns in was bubbling irresistibly away on the cooker, the smell of the Tomato and Prawn soup suggested that dinner was going to be heavenly and I think that I may have been dribbling in my sleep at the prospect, well we all do, don't we?

It was the dribbling which probably saved my life, come to think of it! You know when you wake up and you have been dreaming and your face is wet from the side of your mouth right up to your cheek and sometimes beyond and the first thing you do is wipe your face with your hand if you are polite and either the bed clothes or your partner's pyjamas if you aren't so polite!

Well with Cats it is a little different, because of all of the fur covering our faces we have to wipe the fur to straighten it and then just wait until the soggy patches dry out, and that was what made me think that there might be a problem close by, because the patch of fur was drying out very quickly, which is when my sleepy eyes started to focus.

I noticed that the heat from the burning jacket was drying my fur out rather quickly, and then my brain, which was still sleepy, registered what I had just seen and felt. The heat from the burning jacket right in front of me was drying my face. Well that would have been enough to put the Cat amongst the Pigeons, had there been any Pigeons in the front room.

I jumped up and hissed at the flames, as though I was expecting them to back away in fear, but when I saw that was not going to be the case, so I jumped onto the back of the Sofa and escaped, squealing with fear, Cats don't like being awoken suddenly, and they don't like being awoken suddenly by a flaming jacket.

I ran through the legs of the Female Captor, got hit on the head by her trailing leg and bounced painfully into the corner of the hall.

She was too busy to stop and see if I was ok which was all right by me because she had a large bucket of water which she calmly placed next to the blazing jacket and then using the hearth tongs lifted the jacket and dropped it into the bucket, where it sizzled and hissed noisily, but thankfully harmlessly. I have to say I was impressed with her coolness and fire fighting abilities.

Happily the burning jacket had not caused any damage to the carpet because it had been burning on the stone floor of the hearth where it had made large puddles of burning dribbly stuff like candles that have almost finished burning, pretty by just a little dangerous all at the same time.

After she had made the front room safe again the Female Captor rushed over to where I was lying, and I have to say feeling a little groggy, she picked me up and stroked my head, checking to see if I was ok before she carried me into the kitchen and opened a tin of Tuna especially for me, and although I have to say I half expected to see a Tomato and Prawn Soup in my bowl I wasn't too disappointed with this impromptu snack, honestly!

Day 208 of My Captivity:

After my 'experience' of yesterday, I am pleased to announce that I am being pampered by a certain guilty Female Captor, which is nice, so nice in fact that I did get a little carried away and went to the back door and tried crying to go out like the Dog does.

I do wish that people wouldn't ignore me when I do that!

Day 209 of My Captivity:

I am still being pampered, and with good reason, it is nice to feel special. Happily I don't think I will ever get bored with the taste of Tuna and Prawns and I understand that eating fish is good for the brain, so I have decided to be good for a while, play on the slightly disturbed, but incredibly brave nearly barbecued Cat and see if I can use my improving brain power to think of an amazing escape plan.

Excuse me I have to go and eat some more tuna!

Day 210 of My Captivity:

It has been a very busy day today, I have found that as my brain power increases in size fuelled by Tuna treat food I have to rest, so you will excuse me, I need to have a snooze.

Day 211 of My Captivity:

Today has been amazing; I know that my brain is getting even more powerful.

I decided to test my new mental abilities and solve a few of the world's unsolved mysteries.

At first I had a go at a few extremely complicated equations and as soon as I had laid out the mathematical problems which had apparently caused head scratching amongst the world's finest brains for centuries, I had the answers immediately, piece of fish as they say, or they should say, but I understand they insert a different word for 'fish' in that sentence. Ok it's 'cake' for those of you who don't eat much fish.

Encouraged by my initial successes I thought that I would have a bash at spelling calmodulin and succeeded, I even managed to come up with a meaning for 'calmodulin', which was pretty close to the one in the dictionary, which if you are at all interested is a protein found in the cells of most living organisms that plays a crucial role in maintaining stable calcium concentration in the cell cytoplasm, relatively neat don't you think?

I was impressed with my new powers and unselfishly decided that I would dedicate my life to helping mankind, by applying my brain to science, well that was before I remembered some rather disturbing pictures of a Cat I had seen in a magazine using his brain to 'help' science and I changed my mind.

Nor did I not like the idea of having electrodes attached all over the place, but I asked myself. 'Did I have time to help mankind if I was going to escape, then have all of my books published and then turned into motion pictures?' 'No I didn't, and anyway my writing was going to be my wonderful contribution to mankind,' Humans love Cat stories written by other Humans and so imagine how they will feel when they have a few books actually written by a Cat!

Day 212 of My Captivity:

I am so pleased that I am so much more intelligent than I was several days ago, because the supply of Tuna brain food is beginning to dry up, much as I thought it would as someone's guilt wore off.

It is amazing just how quickly Humans forget what they have done, it's a gift in my opinion, mind you I am happy that I have recorded what happened to me in my Diary, just think how the Female Captor will feel when she reads that part of my Diary.

But all the same at least I can now say 'thanks for the fish!' Now where have I heard that before? Mmmh! I can't remember.

At least there was Tuna in my bowl this evening after the shock of Cat food this morning.

Day 213 of My Captivity:

One thing I have noticed which is a little sad, is that unlike Humans I don't have a belt that I can let out when my stomach expands, which is a shame because no one told me that all of that amazing Tuna brain food would not only make my brain bigger but also my stomach.

I can see that I will have to do something about the beginnings of a 'sway belly,' that is definitely something I don't want to develop and neither do I want my throat to swell or to get several chins either.

Imagine what I would look like in my promotional publicity photographs, urgh, just like the 'father' of Star Wars, who I saw on the television today, mmmh I would cut out the burgers Mr. Lucas, if I were you!

Day 214 of My Captivity:

'Down to the left and bend for the fish, down to the right and now reach up for the birds, on your toes and hold. Look at that, you are becoming really beautiful!'

Sorry you caught me in the middle of rehearsing my fitness and motivational video, well, celebrities some major, and some unbelievably minor have fitness videos and some have motivational videos, but I haven't seen the two combined, well until now that is!

Let's face it, I don't think that my fame is going to last that long, just long enough for the three books, yes you lucky people I plan to write three books, and I am sure that you can reserve them at your local bookstore now, they will just keep your money for the next three years until the books are all printed.

There will of course be the movies as well but I can't see my celebrity lasting much longer than say a year after the second movie and I would expect the third to get canned to be honest, well sequels are always pretty naff and Disney have proved by producing ever greater numbers of sequels that just get worse and worse with each one.

So I need as much cash out of all this fame in as short a time as possible, hence the Fitness and Motivational Video. Before I retire I intend to have a substantial fortune, after all who wants to be a faded star, reduced to opening supermarkets and cheesy malls. Not this pussy that is for sure!

Can you imagine me of all Cats appearing in 'The Cat's Diary on Ice?' Believe it or not there was a 'Beauty and the Beast On Ice' and even a 'Toy Story 2?' No I thought you couldn't see me being that desperate and I am not going to stoop that low, when I have nothing left to say on the chat shows and the guest spots on quiz panel games runs dry, I won't be trying to resurrect my career in a 'celebrity' jungle show, oh no I will be out of here, and be lounging somewhere very comfortable!

At least that way even if in my own opinion, I am not a legend or a celebrity at least I will have some dignity left, yes stardom is tiring, but trying to be a celebrity forever that sounds like some sort of glittering hell to me, it is a shame that other 'celebrities' don't have the same opinion, because if they did I am sure that the standard of entertainment available would be so much higher and the number of real 'celebrities' would be very small and their rarity would make them very special, or true celebrities!

DAY 215 OF MY CAPTIVITY:

I'm in love, no I don't know my beloved's name yet; together we will overcome the shyness and learn all about each other, but oh, now I know how wonderful it is to be absolutely and completely in love.

It all happened so quickly, as I believe love does indeed happen, one minute I was a bachelor, a free spirit without a care in the world and I suppose it could be said a free heart, an instant later my heart belonged to someone else, and now always will.

From now on I can see our lives interlocked and stretching out for us, together forever. We will be happy and so very much in love for the rest of our lives; Kittens, a cottage in the country, shared bliss, yes now it all makes sense to me, isn't love a peculiar thing? In the past I would have laughed at anyone suggesting I would settle down, I was young free and single, or as some would say immature, feckless and selfish, but now all of that is behind me.

Yes! Sure I still want to escape from this prison, but now I want both of us to get out and begin a new life together forever!

(All the more reason to recommend that your friends buy this Diary, but now maybe because of my new responsibility and commitments you should approach total strangers in the street and ask them if they have bought a copy and if they haven't march them down to the closest bookstore and make sure they do).

Now I am making plans for the two of us and that is a wonderful experience, for someone who until now, thought that they were totally self contained and didn't need anyone else in their life.

I can't tell you how happy I am just to share the simple pleasure of snuggling up together at night on the floor, breathing in the unique perfume of my most treasured love.

We cuddle for hours on end, content in each other's quiet company and that is fine for me because I have discovered that I am not much of a conversationalist myself either really!

Together we have discovered poetry, my beloved wears a delightful poem like a necklace.

'When the wind blows, I will keep you warm
So that at night you come to no harm
Together we will share
The comfort of draft free air
Made in Barnstable UK

Machine washable, underlay.'

I admit I didn't say that we were sharing very highbrow poetry did I? And to be honest like all Cats and most Humans I don't really understand poetry, but surely the important thing is to share common interests, isn't it?

I saw the Captors watching us, we unlike them were just minding our own business, and it is a shame that they couldn't mind their own business, but like all Humans they couldn't resist interfering, barging in on others happiness.

For the whole of the evening they kept getting up from their television viewing and peering over the Sofa back at us, and what may I ask were we doing, nothing just dozing contently together.

Every time I closed my eyes they would disturb us and move us out of the way of the door so that they, the selfish Humans, could go and get snacks, soft drinks and then after my love and I had settled down again the Humans would return from the kitchen and move us back to where we had been in the first place, just inside the front room door, until the next time they decided to disturb us.

On reflection moving us from what Shakespeare described as 'my bower in Fairyland' was not as bad as the almost constant snooping, which I may have mentioned earlier.

I heard them say something insulting about us, 'the Cat is getting a little too attached to the draft excluder,' how insulting is that to call my beloved a 'draft excluder' don't they know that my beloved has feelings? For that matter don't they know that I have feelings!

Day 216 of My Captivity:

Why do people and I mean Animals and Humans when I say 'people,' although of course they are the same thing, only Humans think that they aren't animals, so who are the dumb animals I ask you?

But really why do people have to interfere with the course of true love? Just take the greatest love story ever told, performed, and filmed, 'Romeo and Juliet,' they were split apart because of… well basically because of their own stupidity, but let's face it they didn't have a lot going for them did they, she was only fourteen and that is illegal surely? And even worse than that they were Humans so they were at a disadvantage to start with.

So when Romeo and Juliet got confused and completely misunderstood life around them no one should have been too surprised especially them, it is such a shame that they didn't live though, they would have probably grown out of the infatuation they had for each other, and maybe Juliet would have married a nice Italian pasta maker and Romeo could have lived his dream and become a bus driver, actually it is a little known fact that Romeo wanted to become a bus driver, but I believe it is true.

I know another thing too, and that is that I would never ever have stopped loving my beloved and now I am desolate without my sweet love.

I miss everything that we shared now that they have hidden my beloved.

One minute we were lying next to the door and the next my beloved had vanished, I had only turned my back on my beloved for a minute and my beloved had completely disappeared.

I am convinced that the Humans kidnapped my beloved because the Female Captor was acting suspiciously and walking backwards away from the door as I strolled back to my beloved for a cuddle.

It was the sort of backward walking that you must have seen, on birthdays for instance, Humans like to hide presents behind their backs and very rarely the Male Captor brings a bunch of flowers into the house for the Female Captor, mind you she always knows when he is hiding anything, and not only that he is incapable of walking backwards and hiding anything he has behind his back, most Male Humans are I believe.

Still I know she had my beloved, behind her back and she was going to hide my beloved away somewhere, why, that is what I want to know, what on earth had we done wrong? I don't think I shall ever know!

Day 217 of My Captivity:

Dealing with anyone with a broken heart is not easy, dealing with a Cat with a broken heart is hell, or that is what I plan to make it. I am, I promise, going to pay them back for taking my beloved away, just you wait and see!

Hell hath no fury like a Feline scorned, I can tell you.

Surprisingly enough the Dog has been very understanding, in his Doggy way, and at night I have taken advantage of his good nature and cuddled into his tail to dream of my lost love.

Day 218 of My Captivity:

I'm still mopping about, life is hard without my beloved and today it was made even harder. As if my lonely torture wasn't bad enough, my life has just been made worse by a new set of visitors, this latest batch of visitors is a pair called Grandparents, and apparently they belong in some strange way to the Male Captor.

They call me 'Kitty' and they stroke me with their gnarled wrinkled hands, the first time they did this was when I jumped up onto my seat on the Sofa and found both of them sitting on the Sofa, one of them was right in my place as bold as brass.

All they did was smile at me! They didn't seem to want to move out of 'my' place on the cushion, which I personally thought was very rude!

My first encounter with them was very off putting I can tell you. I am sure that you know the smile that old people give you, the one that says. 'We are completely insane, how are you?'

Then they stroked me, the older one leaning across the other to get closer.

Well I suppose that they are very nice people, but I suggest that you always keep your hands on your wallet when they are around, because I have noticed that they touch, pick up and examine everything that they find in a room and if they are left unattended they have a tendency to wander off and open drawers and cupboards to investigate the contents, really don't any visitors know how to behave properly?

And don't ask their opinion on anything because they are guaranteed to have one and because they seem to have so much time on their wrinkly hands they don't mind taking hours of your precious time to tell you just what is wrong with society, the younger generation and anything and everything else you could possibly imagine!

They say that the old are wise, but for old and wise, please read senile and talkative, and the things that they say! I think that age must dim Human's sensitivity; there isn't a subject, no matter how embarrassing or indeed lavatorial that the oldsters will launch into and offer a bizarre opinion upon.

Now for example, just how controversial would you think that eating could be? Not very I hear you say, and I would agree with you readily. Normally you and for that matter I would be right, it isn't at all controversial unless you have passed your diamond jubilee of years on the planet, seventy five years to be precise for those of you who don't know and I didn't until I spent several hours listening to the old ones.

Where was I, oh yes eating, well first I have to explain that Cats have 'manners' and 'standards,' but they are very different to Human's, simply ours are higher, but if you listen to the old ones you would think that Humankind had degenerated to a level below Horsefly and let's face it they spend most of their life feeding on Horse, well let's call it manure!

And all of this criticism is delivered while they have their mouths full of food, which they spray around the table and the room while they lecture everyone else who are quite rightly shielding their plates from the fall out.

Do they wash their hands before the meal or after, no they don't and you don't have to be told how that turns the stomachs of Cats, we are renowned the world over for our devotion to washing, as far as a Cat is concerned, one can never be too clean.

DAY 219 OF MY CAPTIVITY:

What is the worst thing that could happen to you? Yes I have been thinking about what could be the worst thing that could happen to me and I thought I would ask you before I told you what I think, I am kind like that and of course it shows that I care about my readers to canvass their opinions!

Really! Is that what worries you, wow I didn't know that sort of thing could happen to a Human!

No, no I am not laughing, have you ever seen a Cat laugh? No I thought not, thank you.

What? You want to know what is the worst thing that could happen to me, mmmh there are a few things, but I think that if I went bald I would hate it.

Happily only Human males in the main go bald, and again happily it seems that most bald men are also short and are called Michael and as if their baldness and their names weren't bad enough, they always get their pates tanned, or sometimes in extreme cases grow beards, which are usually grey.

So baldness is the worst thing that could happen to me as you asked so nicely!

DAY 220 OF MY CAPTIVITY:

More thoughts today, well I like to exercise my newly acquired brainpower!

Thoughts on taste: Today I have been thinking! Well to be honest I think every day and it seems as though I think about things every minute of the day and sometimes deep into the night too.

I suppose that is just the consequence of having a very highly developed brain, I am sure that it is the reason why I interrupt myself so often, because sometimes I have hundreds of thoughts at the same time, which can be very confusing and actually occasionally painful!

It is just as well that I do have so many thoughts because if I didn't then this Diary would be more than a little boring, imagine a Diary without any thoughts in it, 'and I'll show you Bridget Jones's Diary!' Who said that although truthful don't you think it is a little cruel on the chubby, bubbly cigarette butt bundle of fun?

Seriously a dull Diary would be one which just described what the writer had done every day, after the fourth or fifth day I am sure that you would want to kill the writer, I would, if all he or she did was to just report what he or she had done.

That sort of Diary would be like listening to the news on the television in the old days before broadcasters started to add little anecdotes and opinions, and speculate about news that hasn't happened yet, like they do now, mind you thinking about that for a moment they do more of that nowadays than actually bring viewers the news and that makes the news programmes just plain boring, and the opinions which news reports actually should have in them rather narrow and dull, making the news nearly as boring as the weather forecast that always follows it like vomit follows heavy drinking, but I didn't mean to mention Bridget Jones again, sorry.

Anyway enough of what sends me to sleep. Today I was lucky really, I was only thinking about one thing, now when you hear Humans say that someone only thinks about one thing, they are being rude about the person that they are talking about (and usually behind their backs I have found), but I am sure that can't be said of me, because I wasn't thinking about the 'obvious,' I was thinking about other people's taste.

I have come to the conclusion, after a lot of thinking (of course) and some of that rather hard and deep, that other people's taste can be so different to one's own. In fact one could say that other people's taste is sometimes totally incomprehensible.

Take as an example what Humans wear, me I am content with a fur coat, which on me I have to say looks rather fine, but on a Human, well all I can say is that it looks odd, and where do they get the fur from? I have a feeling that there is a dark secret there, which I don't think I want to discover.

This example proves I think, that taste is as I said odd, and there are so many examples of odd taste in Human clothing.

I imagine that we all have our various likes and dislikes to be honest, for instance the Dog's literary criticism is harsh but to him fair, he enjoys ripping a book to shreds, I think that he prefers the challenge of hard covered books to paperbacks, which don't seem to offer any resistance! For some odd reason he enjoys books on cookery most of all and I know that because every so often we get a whole new library of cookery books for the kitchen shelf after he has pulled them off the shelf and ripped them to shreds.

Day 221 of My Captivity:

I was listening to the radio earlier and I heard of an institution so terrible in its aims and ambitions that it has the capacity to destroy people's lives and reduce them to beggars, no I am not talking about government, though from what I have heard that is bad enough, I am talking about something far worse with a black agenda so subversive that I feel compelled to issue a health warning to you, my friend the reader.

Please stay away from Libraries, places where apparently they will lend you this Diary and a range of other books and you won't have to pay for any of them, now on the face of it that sounds like a pretty good deal, and until I can do a little more digging and research on libraries even I find it difficult to spot their hidden agenda, although we all know that there is no such thing as getting something for nothing in this life, unless you are in banking or Insurance that is.

As I said I haven't quite found out what 'the angle' is with libraries just yet, but I have discovered that their first step to enslavement is to encourage ordinary citizens to borrow books and then return them after they have read them, and it strikes me once you get on that treadmill you are committed to constant visits, and worse still you are expected to read very quickly because you can only 'borrow' the books for a short period of time.

The worst thing I have found out about libraries so far and I hope that you don't think that I am merely thinking of myself here is that if you borrow books and this Diary in particular, the author won't get paid quite so much for working his paws to the bone writing them in the first place, because authors, and I class myself as one of them, get paid for each book sold and as far as I can tell get nothing for a book borrowed.

I am sure that you will agree that sounds that dreadful and as a Cat lover I am sure that you wouldn't want to see me begging for a living, I personally need all of the money I can get from this Diary, not only to fund my life on the outside once I have escaped, but also to pay back all of the money I have 'borrowed' on other people's credit cards.

The first reason being the more urgent and pressing though, as I am sure you will agree, I think I deserve a little luxury after all of the suffering I have caused, no sorry I mean after all of the pain and suffering I have endured here! I have a nasty feeling that some people might say that Freud would have enjoyed that slip!

Day 222 of My Captivity:

Coming to terms with a death in the family can be almost impossible, but sadly I had to.

The blow was like a knockout punch, and the sadness like a lake of disappointment, mmmh so poetic that, I maybe in the running for a literary prize after all.

It was all so sudden, one day we were laugh joking and scratching around and the next moment darkness, and a void in my life that was bigger than the Grand Canyon, whatever that is!

Frankly Franky was a friend, Franky had become a large part of my life in a very short time, and then instantly and almost without any warning he was gone.

Yes I had been sprayed for Fleas again and little Franky the Flea was one of the causalities. Oh the horror of his little squeaking as he scrambled with the other Fleas to reach the high ground of my nose as they were all being chased by a tidal wave of spray, mowing everything flat in its wake.

There was me smugly thinking that I had got rid of the Flea spray, during a little explosion a while ago, but no, obviously not and sadly I had even told Franky that he was safe.

He had been so happy to find out that he was living in a safe paradise, good clean thick fur, with plenty of warmth and sunshine, but in a cruel instant that was all wiped away forever and Franky and his paradise were lost.

Still there is an upside, I don't itch so much and have almost completely stopped scratching. I do it more now out of habit, oh and to worry the Dog. It is a little consolation to have a good scratch when sitting next to the Dog's basket and whisper to him that he'll be sprayed for Fleas soon.

I try to keep busy and not let the loss of such a good friend and loyal companion as Franky undoubtedly was, get me down, so now I am going to try the Soya milk that the Female Human has left for me.

Yes she is on one of her slimming health kicks again; I have a tip for her and also for anyone else wanting to shed a few extra pounds that they may have gained. STOP EATING YOU FATTIES! There that is the simplest, and most effective way to slim and you have to get the information from a Cat, really!

Mind you there is a market for slimming videos and so I am sure that I will be producing one, so I have to say that the little piece of advice above is the last bit of free advice I can give you, now if you'll excuse me I am going to make a few notes for my forthcoming slimming cook book that will accompany my slimming video, I thought that a chapter devoted to authentic Indian sub-continent cooking and hygiene methods might help westerners slim, after all amoebic dysentery is the ideal way to ensure that the digestive system works effectively and body mass reduces quickly.

DAY 223 OF MY CAPTIVITY:

I have just found out that what I have been writing over the last long months of captivity is called a Diary and that many others have written one too, well they have written one each too, if you see what I mean. Writers of diaries include a man called Samuel Pepys but his Diary was it would seem written mainly in gibberish.

If you are confused now that I have mentioned the fact that I was writing a Diary before today and yet I have just discovered that what I am writing is actually called a Diary, to be frank that is one of the reasons why I am not best pleased. I have just spent several days going back over the last two hundred and twenty two entries to change 'this written thingy' which is of course what I called my Diary before I knew it was called a Diary and I am not happy, no not happy at all, but I care for my readers and have just finished slaving away for them and making their life easier and mine more difficult, but I am used to that!

Another diarist (as we are apparently called, so the Translator told me with a superior air) was someone called Anne Frank; she seems to have lived in an attic and not built a Glider to escape – durr!

There was also some other woman called Bridget Jones who seems to have almost exclusively written about her revolting smoking and drinking habits – no wonder you can't get a man Bridget! She sounded so awful that I 'accidentally' added her to some of the entries before today, well I was changing the name of 'my written thingy' so I thought I would add a bit here and there, so that the shock of not knowing that I didn't know that I was writing a Diary was less embarrassing, it didn't work did it?

And then last, but by the sound of it not least, a small man called Hitler wrote some Diaries (although this might not be the case as far as everyone apart from The Epoch newspaper is concerned, although I have it on good authority that The Epoch Newspaper is a reputable occasional publisher of historic diaries and discoverer of 'lost' Diaries and a fine example of the responsible side of the press, and a jolly good read[R]).

(Furthermore The Epoch newspaper is happy to be associated with, and to serialise my Diary, which their well respected reviewer Mr. Tad Z. Rowlocks said was such an excellent example of the Diary genre and in his opinion a classic).

Now that I know that I am not the first Diary writer I am appalled, although I console myself in the knowledge that I must be the first Cat to write a Diary!

Indeed thinking about it I am the first animal to write a Diary! After all I haven't seen any Diaries by an Aardvark up along side my Diary in the best sellers list recently, or any professorial Diary writing pigs interviewed by Parkinson, have you?

(Translator's note: The reference to Parkinson is a reference to a chat show host in the UK and apparently although most of the world's inhabitants won't know who he is, the Author demanded that this obscure reference be left in the manuscript because he likes to go to sleep listening to his show, apparently after a few minutes of listening to the host, the Author gets a wonderful night's sleep).

This week just to add insult to injury I have also found out that other captives just scratch a mark representing a day of the week on the wall and when they get to six marks strike through them to show that another week has passed. Now I could have done that and saved a lot of effort and ink, especially with my sharp claws – how stupid do you think I feel?

'No please don't answer that!'

'All right! Don't rub it in please!'

Still I suppose there is one compensation, and to my way of thinking it had better be a big compensation at that, apparently I stand to make a lot of money out of this Diary caper as my lawyer Mr. T. A. Leibowitz, 'call me Todd,' has indicated before, although he used the word 'Dough,' if the Diary is a success, and I am sure that a cute though slightly naughty Cat just like me has got to be a winner, liked by all young and old!

Personally I would prefer the cash to dough any day, but according to the Translator (no there is no need for one of your notes here thank you), dough is American for cash, it must be handy to speak American as well as Cat, as they are two of the most important languages in the world!

Let's face it I am better looking and more of an action character than the other Diarists that I heard about for a start!

The amazingly dull and chubby Bridget Jones made a fortune and apparently she wasn't even a real person, (yes another bombshell, they are coming thick and fast at the moment), not like me, well I am not a real person but I am a real Cat.

Then there was that cute poor little girl, Anne Frank, her Diary has never been out of print and they made a film of her hiding in an attic for years on end, couldn't have been much of a film to my way of thinking!

Still it was probably a black and white film for people in the nineteen fifties who had a very low threshold of enjoyment and sophistication. But hang on if Bridget Jones who doesn't exist and Anne Frank who was just plain boring had movies made of their Diaries there is no reason to suggest that I couldn't star in my own movie.

Just think I could do my own stunts and have a whale of a time, mmmh better write some more love interest into this somewhere I wouldn't mind meeting a nice young shapely Cat of the opposite sex.

I wonder who should be allowed to do my voice over in the film? There are a number of people who I could think of and of course it goes without saying that the voice would have to be one of the biggest names in Hollywood at the moment which I suppose rules out that nice small man, Tom Cruise!

In terms of make-up the only thing I want or even need is for the hairdresser who did the MGM's Lion's mane to stay away from me, have you seen that poor old Lion who roars at the beginning of every MGM movie while trying, it would appear to keep his quiff in place?

Mangy is a word that is used rarely and advisedly so in the Animal Kingdom, because we know just how uncomfortable that condition is, but for goodness sake who hired that tired old Lion?

Apparently he didn't even have his own teeth! If you ask me he was just one shuffling step away from being a rug, the only explanation I can think of for him being employed at all is that the guy worked cheap!

Yes I definitely think that my Diary should be turned into a movie, we owe it to the viewing public, move over Lord of the Rings here comes the, I haven't thought of a title yet, well one that I am completely comfortable with, but I can get the advertising guys to do that, or should I say I shall get my people to talk to their people.

Day 224 of My Captivity:

I have been reading some history books, and have been rather taken with the notion that there have been events in history that are so significant that they have days named after them, like Trafalgar Day, when in 1805 the English fleet led (in a ship I think) by Admiral Nelson, who was almost as famous an adulterer as he was an Admiral, completely ruined the day of the combined and much bigger fleets of the French and the Spanish navies.

Of course since 1805 the English celebrated the victory of Nelson in his ship, The Victory (yes the ship was called The Victory, I know it is a little confusing isn't it, but true) until eventually a few years ago the petulant French politicians' whining got on the nerves of the English so much that they decided that they had better stop celebrating Trafalgar Day, which is a bit sad really.

There are so many days that are famous because 'things' happened on them, or even better in my view, there are days named after people, like Martin Luther King Day, which is a holiday in the US, although everywhere else it is unlikely that people will have heard of this most Human of Humans.

With the above in mind today is a day that will go down in the history books, because I have decided that today is 'Parrot Attack Day.'

That Parrot must have been patiently waiting for its comeuppance, surely he didn't think that he was going to get away with all that he has done to me ever since I have been here did he?

And the day for revenge has arrived; that Pretty Polly is about to get more than it ever bargained for.

I have to admit that it is a little difficult to get at the Parrot these days, since he was put in a cage and only let out when the Humans are around because as you will remember he proved to be so unreliable, or to put it another way, truthfully for example, someone else was unreliable and he got the blame.

Still I have a plan and after I have implemented it, I hope that you will agree with me that Parrot Attack Day should be a public holiday, because if it isn't, we just won't have enough time to celebrate it properly.

It is pointless to annoy the Parrot while he is in his cage, after all he is sufficiently annoyed already, and the only way one could annoy him any more would be to poke him with a stick through the bars, now don't think that I didn't consider this method, but even though I practised using the stick I just couldn't hold it properly and poke at the same time.

Sometimes it is so cruelly obvious just how handy it would be to have hands, you monkey descendants are very lucky that the great Earth Mother Mrs. Evolution, let you grow those, and dispense with the prehensile tails which I don't think would have caught on, mind you saying that they would have been a real novelty at Foam or Pool parties.

Happily today was one of those days when the Parrot was locked in his cage and so I was able to sneak up on him without him noticing me, and rather cleverly I think I have come up with a plan to really ruin his day which is not reliant on a stick or the uses of fingers and thumbs.

There were only few little teething problems with the plan, I had trouble getting the small gas tank into the dining room and then to get it to stand on its end, oh and then there was the little problem of unscrewing the gas tap at the top, and of course attaching the pipe, but apart from all of those little problems things didn't go too badly at all.

Luckily the Dog is being really rather helpful at the moment, I don't quite know why he is being helpful, but one thing I can guarantee is that he isn't planning anything, he just hasn't got the mental capacity to do that sort of thing, but all the same it is handy to have a willing helper.

So very quickly I managed to get everything assembled, it was hilarious to watch the Parrot getting all flustered and bothered because I was 'lurking' around his precious cage.

I don't know where he learned his language but it must have been somewhere very common, the complete sentences of swear words in several languages would have made anyone blanche at the insults that he threw at me.

Still there was nothing he could do to stop me pushing the pipe through the bars and even though he danced around on the cage floor and reached up to the pipe to take large lumps out of it, still more pipe was available to push into the cage.

When I thought that the Parrot patient was ready I carefully turned on the gas tap and stood back, in such a surprisingly short time the Laughing Gas took effect, the Parrot's screamed abuse was delivered in a squeaky little almost metallic voice, and at the end of each sentence he couldn't resist the urge to giggle.

I turned the tape recorder on and rattled the cage to knock him off balance and get the most amazing high-pitched, whiny tirade of abuse on tape.

After several minutes of insane laughter I switched the tape machine off, to let the giggles subside and then started to whisper, 'Come on then, walkies! Darling I am taking the Dog for a walk, can you open the door for me, I'll be there in a minute!' After repeating myself a few times the Parrot's addled brain took over and remembered the phrase from the past, and started to shout it at the top of his shrill, squeaky voice, straight into the microphone.

Oh I was going to have such fun playing and replaying the tape machine over and over again in the future just for the Parrot of course, I especially liked the high-pitched sound of the Parrot saying, 'Come on then, walkies! Darling I am taking the Dog for a walk, can you open the door for me, I'll be there in a minute!' because of course he had taunted me with a version of it and now I had the perfect recording of our clever old bird.

DAY 225 OF MY CAPTIVITY:

Just one little entry in the Diary today, because I am still suffering, the after effect from yesterday nausea and vomiting and that is only when I look at the Parrot.

Regarding special days, between you and me I know it is only a matter of time until this Cat has his day, after all Cats should have their days as well as Dogs, I think someone really wise said that, oh it was me a long while ago, still as usual I was right...................Tee Hee

DAY 226 OF MY CAPTIVITY:

Recently I have started to say things like, 'Oh I wouldn't do that, no, not at my age!' Which is a little worrying, why, well because it suggests that I have begun to think that I am getting old and that is never a good thing is it, getting old that is!

But there is something even worse about saying things like, 'Oh I wouldn't do that, no, not at my age!' And it is the awfully, terrible and really dreadful fact that I was talking to myself, now I can cope with the trips to the litter tray in the middle of the night, I can even accommodate the thinning of my fur and my joints aching, but I have to face the hard reality that I am talking to myself and there are only three (as far as I know) reasons why you would talk to yourself, loneliness, craziness or worst of all - age.

Have you noticed how oldsters talk to themselves all the time, explaining over and again to themselves what they are doing, what they are about to do and when they have done whatever it was they were going to do they congratulate themselves with a discussion about what they achieved, even though what they achieved was so insignificant that it wasn't worth talking about in the first place.

That is what worries me about old age; I will become boring and delight in my own petty achievements, 'oh would you look at that I have spilt the milk!' No please no I have started reporting what I have just done, when I could be licking my paws too!

Help me before it is too late!

DAY 227 OF MY CAPTIVITY:

I am not well today, my broken heart is not beating properly, yes I still miss my beloved, I know I hide it well, but the clue to how I feel is in the word 'hide' in this sentence.

I don't want to seem boring, whining on about my broken heart, but I do suffer and mostly in silence, although just mentioning how I feel has brought it all to the surface, no, no I am inconsolable, but if you are going to the kitchen, can you have a look and see if there are any Prawns in the freezer or better still, fresh ones in the refrigerator, if there are could you peel me a few and bring them through.

Yes I will still be here, having a broken heart means that exercise is out of the question, and so I will do what the Doctor would advise and just rest.

By the way, and sorry to bother you, as you are on the way to the kitchen, if there is any milk that might help!

DAY 228 OF MY CAPTIVITY:

Today I feel better, not so old and full of aches, which is good, although of course what is not so good is that I am talking about how I feel and as I have already said, that is a sure sign of age or marbles lost, as is repeating oneself oops!

Still there is only one thing to do and that is to ignore it all, no that would be a definite give away, old people ignore everything but themselves and their needs and don't pay attention to anybody else's problems, still that is also what people do if they are in the army and the oldsters now think that they belong to something comically called the 'Grey Army.'

Still I suppose that they call themselves the 'Grey Army' because they are all so close to being ghosts!

Having said all of that, I must be getting old because sometimes when I am talking to myself, even I think I am talking rubbish!

DAY 229 OF MY CAPTIVITY:

I thought that I was seeing things! I was taking my everyday (Translator's Note: the idiot means daily.) early morning walk around the prison, looking for open windows, doors half closed, skylights partly open you know the usual, when after covering all of the other floors and rooms I entered the front room and as I said above, I thought I was seeing things!

(Author's Note: The Translator is being rested at present, which is code for the fact that he has walked out and refuses to work with me. I have annoyed him, yes little cuddly, furry me, I wanted him fired, but apparently, and I have no idea why this is, there are very few people who can speak Cat and to make matters worse, 'it is a very highly developed skill achieved by only very intelligent and talented Humans,' as you can tell they are not my words but part of the written apology I was 'encouraged' to send to the idiot Translator – Oops! I mean the intelligent and talented Translator. Yes it was like being 'encouraged' at gunpoint!)

Changing the subject for a minute, to something more interesting. Someone had left a large Palm tree standing in the corner of the room, and when I saw it I at once dropped down on to my belly and crawled behind the Sofa, well it is sensible to be on one's guard when something as peculiar as that happens. Palm trees don't just appear in your living room usually do they?

It didn't move for ages and neither did I, to be honest I didn't expect it to move really, trees as far as I know don't move much normally, a little light swaying in a gentle breeze, with bending and snapping in Hurricanes, but walking no never, except that is in the imagination of Mr. J.R.R. Tolkien, but then he was mental as far as I know.

Naturally they tried to explain the illness away by saying that he had a very powerful imagination, yeah right! Talking, walking trees and the middle of the Earth populated by noble Elves and a ring that makes the owner disappear, sit down Mr. T and have another tranquiliser.

So reason soon grabbed hold of me, the palm tree wasn't going to move, so it would be safe to have a look at it? That seemed a reasonable idea.

I stayed where I was for a little while longer though just in case of, well just in case, watching the Palm tree from behind the sofa, nothing moved and nothing was either out of place or in a place that it hadn't occupied since I arrived here.

When I made my move it was with stealth and caution, I slipped from the edge of the sofa back to the door, then down the side of the wall furthest away from the Palm tree.

Still nothing moved and there was no sound apart from a clock ticking somewhere and the occasional faint squawk and bird sounds from the Parrot, who seemed to be happily minding his own business for a change.

I have no idea where the Dog is, probably snoring and passing wind somewhere, or he could be out with the Humans, still it is too late to worry about him now, although I do wish that the Door to the front room was closed, covert operations are best undertaken in privacy.

Reaching the other end of the sofa I stopped for a look around, still nothing was moving and there wasn't anyone around to spoil my investigation of the tree.

Occasionally when I am up to no good, I wish that I had hands like Humans, I thought as I sneaked passed the fireplace full of logs that it must be great to be able to feel the weight of one of those babies in your hand as you crawl towards your quarry.

But then claws are useful too, by now I had completely circled the room and was very close to the tree, it seemed very large from where I was crouching as my eyes travelled up it. This was no time for thinking though and I moved underneath it and stood next to the very large pot that it was standing in.

The Palm tree was very big and made the corner of the room dark and I could smell something, which I suppose was the tree itself, but I was unsure because I had never been that close to a Palm tree before.

Very slowly I lifted my front paws and like an Otter sat up until I was tall enough to just let both paws balance on the edge of the pot and feel the soil in the pot. It was wet and not very nice and it made me jump with surprise.

So far so good was actually what I was thinking when the tree stopped shaking in the pot, which had been caused by my surprised reaction.

Still happily nothing happened and I was thankful for that, it was just then that the tree attacked me, to my surprise and horror a shower of water rained down on me.

I sprang up in the air, turning like any sensible Cat can do when attacked and used my back legs against the pot to propel myself away from the attack, now I was glad that the front room door was open and dashed through it as fast as my wobbly worried legs would carry me. And I didn't stop in the hallway I was up the stairs as quickly as you could say Boo!

Shaking with fear and almost glued flat to the landing at the top of the stairs, I waited for the next phase of the Palm tree attack to come and my awful fate.

It was dark when I woke up, horrified to think that I had after so many hours fallen asleep when I could have been, well I don't know what an annoyed Palm tree does to little Cats! Let's just say 'Treed to death.'

Much later and after a very long period of waiting in the growing dark I went downstairs it wasn't something that I planned but let's just say that I had little choice in the matter.

As I was carried passed the front room door I expected to see the tree sitting on my bit of the sofa all comfortable and gloating, but it wasn't. To my surprise it was still standing where I had left it in the corner of the room.

I noticed that there were unfortunately, and not for the first time, a lot of black dried paw prints over the front room carpet.

When I was placed gently in front of my food I began eating; yes I was hungry, but I was more relieved that the tree hadn't got me and that I wasn't at this moment in the bathroom having my paws washed.

After a while and quite a bit of food and strangely a few Prawns thrown to me so that I could catch them in my mouth to the apparent delight of the Male Captor, I relaxed a little, just enough to seek out the dozy Dog and slip unnoticed into his basket for a cuddle and some smelly Dog warmth, well after all I had had a bad day and needed to forget about it with some sleep!

As I dropped off I pondered what the Male Captor had said to the Female Captor when she had asked what he was doing throwing me Prawns, he had said that I looked as though I had a bad day, how true!

Mmmh! I wish this Dog would keep still, and just be what I want him to be, a nice warm comfortable bed, after all I am the one who has had the bad day you know.

Oh no! What is that smell, he hasn't has he, well I am just too tired to move now, this just hasn't been my day, I will have to have a very serious wash in the morning.

Day 230 of My Captivity:

I didn't bother to go into the front room today and probably will give it a miss for a few more days, I am missing my sofa place already, but I think that it is better this way, there is something lurking in the front room and I don't want to encounter it again, it is sinister and evil Palm tree.

Day 231 of My Captivity:

I peered into the front room today through the crack between the door and the doorframe; nothing was happening but all the same the front room has a few bad memories at the moment.

Luckily I have a new project!

Day 232 of My Captivity:

Something odd is happening in the front room today, yes the front room and the large Palm tree are playing on my mind, but it isn't them today that are making me feel uneasy, well I don't think it is them anyway.

The Captors were in the front room together almost all morning and they were making a lot of noise and rushing around a lot. I couldn't really see what they were doing, the door was almost closed and I don't like to get too close to the threshold and because the door was almost closed, even the view from the fifth step up on the staircase wasn't any good today.

And then they closed the door completely, something is going on and I think I should be told! And if I am not going to be informed then I should at least find out, now of course that means that I will have to do something dreadful, enter the front room. Still time they say is a great healer and Cats are blessed with selective memories, which is very convenient.

Humans don't think we have long memories at all, but it is the opposite I can remember exactly what I want to remember, some safe guard don't you think? And frankly handy in all sorts of other ways, in fact I remember everything bad that had happened to me and who did it, so they had better watch out, hadn't they!

Day 233 of My Captivity:

Thanks once again to the wonders of the world wide web and a 'borrowed' credit card I now have a very handy cellphone, I use the word cellphone because I ordered this one from an American website, so obviously I will have to be careful charging it or I will blow it up.

It is always a good idea to use an American website if the credit card you are using is not 'completely' yours! The Americans, bless them, are a lot more relaxed about people who think they are allowed to use a credit cards, when that might not always be the case.

Anyway my cellphone is great and allows me the freedom to make calls from anywhere in the house and one day I will be able to use it from anywhere outside and what a treat that will be!

Day 234 of My Captivity:

It is time to set the record straight, or as straight as I can, I have, I know, made a few little errors here and there since I started writing this Diary and so they need to be corrected where possible.

Although of course it is possible that I won't be able to correct all of the little errors, but that will probably be for two reasons, I am a Cat and know no better; or I just don't know that I am in the wrong. Are they the same thing? Well I don't really know whether they are the same thing or not, but I have written it down now and I don't feel like changing it.

As I said there are a few things that I have to 'own' up to. The first is my recent discovery that not all Male Humans are called George, which is odd because I thought that they were, as a consequence of that discovery it has occurred to me that all of the Georges who have made an appearance in this Diary so far may not have been called George in the first place.

That is a bit of a pity really because it is a nice name and I think rather suited Mr. Fat Face and George the H'pprentice, just think the poor things could be called something terrible, 'Harry' for example!

I may also have led you astray with my 'illnesses' as well, still we all know now that I get to finish the Diary and therefore don't suffer from any life threatening diseases or run out of lives and have to sign off in general.

This is good news, not only because you get to read a completed Diary but also as you can imagine from my point of view because 'popping my clogs' was never in my game plan at all.

Having said all of that I do have to announce that I do have one disease and it is unfortunately incurable, though happily not life (or clogs) threatening! Because I am often ill or as my Pet Psychiatrist says, 'feeling ill,' I have been diagnosed as a hypochondriac, which though not nice for some, is really rather reassuring for me, because as I have said often I am not well, and now that has been proved!

Please don't worry about me; I will be ok, really, although the Pet Psychiatrist bills are high, so if you could buy an extra copy of this Diary then I can ensure that I can afford to keep up the treatment. In fact if you can buy two extra copies I will be able to afford to go to the Caribbean for a complete rest and that would be nice wouldn't it? You would like that wouldn't you? They say the Caribbean is nice this time of year!

Day 235 of My Captivity:

When I am talking or thinking I often change the subject in mid sentence and never manage to get back to what I was talking about, now I know I change the subject when I am writing my Diary and sometimes I even do that in the middle of what I am writing, but have you noticed that luckily, by the end of the page or at least the end of the day's entry, you always know all of what I have been talking about because I always go back to what I was writing before I interrupted myself aren't you lucky! Ok you maybe confused occasionally but that doesn't mean you aren't lucky!

Today is going to be an exception to the above rule because I have had a quiet day and quiet days seem to calm my brain cells and almost hinder original thought, take the Parrot for instance, actually you can take him as far as you like, sorry old joke, but sometimes it is difficult to disguise old jokes and make them sound new, just ask any modern comedian, on second thoughts please don't bother to ask a modern comedian because they talk so fast and so much and frankly they are boring, it is just that no one has told them that they are boring, until now that is!

Oops I interrupted myself sorry I promised I wouldn't to. Where was I, oh yes, we were talking about the dumb Parrot. Well I was talking and you were listening (you have to use your imagination there because it almost goes without saying that I am 'writing' and you are 'reading' but you know what I mean, I hope! Don't you?) That as far as I am concerned is an idea arrangement.

The Parrot has an easy life really, there isn't much to trouble him and if I didn't exist, and that must be one of the Parrot's greatest wishes, his life would also be completely free from stress and disruption.

But has that almost Monastic existence done him any good? No I don't think so. He doesn't seem to have any original thoughts and his opinions, comments and conversation are all things that he has heard that he just repeats, and worse he doesn't seem to know that if he repeats something once then it might be considered novel or even bordering on clever for a bird to repeat back what you have said, but to then keep doing it until even the previously impressed and almost enchanted Humans put the Parrot cage cover over the Parrot in the cage to shut him up is not only annoying it is cretinous.

Just repeating words or sentences over and over again doesn't demonstrate cleverness does it? And so proves my point about brain cells, the less exciting and active your life is the more stupid you are or become. If you don't get up in the morning and do things for yourself and if your life is almost one long holiday then the dumber you become. And to prove my point, just look at the Royal family now they are dumb on a grand scale!

Actually that leads me on to something else, no not really about the Royal family although they are a bit like expensive ornaments, they cost a lot and although they are very nice etc., they take a lot of one's time and energy to look after and keep clean, and when one gets damaged the mess is very difficult to clean up.

No this is not about the Royal Family, it is still about the Parrot, have you noticed that with his gaudy coloured feathers and his lack of intelligence, I imagine that he would have been a Royalist in the English Civil war, although why they call this sort of war 'civil' I have no idea, it is usually the last thing it is, look at the American Civil War, it makes the recent Iraq conflict (have you noticed that we have conflicts now and not wars) look like a picnic, not once has a town or city been burnt down by the Americans, what a shame they didn't have that same sense of conservation when they captured Atlanta.

There that has probably opened old wounds for my American readers but all I can say is sorry and please wait for the news crews to arrive here, because as you know you cannot start a war any more unless you have a camera crew getting in the firing line, oh that is unless you are in Uzbekistan of course and there you can do almost anything you want to if you happen to be lucky enough to be in charge.

Oops I had better put down my bandana and roll up the red pictures of the revolutionary heroes, I would hate to be described as subversive.

Sorry I interrupted myself big time today, but you get the picture, the Parrot has a lot in common with the Royal family and indeed is almost as thick as them and wears the same sort of gaudy uniform that they do on ceremonial occasions.

DAY 236 OF MY CAPTIVITY:

The Congressional Hearings for something or the other are on the television today, no happily not the whole thing but sort of edited highlights, well I don't know if they are the highlights because when you watch something as opinionated as the BBC's 24 hour news broadcast, which has managed the near impossible of dumbing news down to a level where even I find it dull and uninteresting and I am a Cat.

Let's face it you have to hand it to the BBC news team (for my American readers the BBC is the British Broadcasting Corporation, who sell you excellent programmes that the British taxpayer, well actually the English tax payer pays for, not the Scottish or Welsh ones, because they have their own programmes which they pay for, but they are not very good or in some cases in Welsh and don't sell well.

So anyway where was I, ah yes the BBC, they get a massive amount of money every year from a tax, and then they make television programmes which they sell around the world, seems like they should pay back some of the revenue to their investors, to me, well believe it or not I pay tax and it is not somethinmg that I would reccommend.

Anyway with all of the cash that is sloshing around in the BBC they have done useful things like created a whole load of new and uninteresting digital channels, which no one watches.

Worst of all the BBC have set up a 24 hours news channel, which if you think CNN is dumb, then you should watch this cookie, it is dreadful and desperately bias especially against America and the Iraq conflict, still that might be because the beloved hero and architect of all of the wonderful changes I have just mentioned lost his job because he was against the war and didn't mind what he said in order to demonstrate that opposition because he thought that he had some freedom to critcise others when not in possession of the full fact, oops sounds familiar ha, ha, ha. What a good job I am a Cat!

So what does all of that mean and what is the relevance and also while we are asking, what has that all got to do with a Cat? Well I watch a lot of television and most of it insults my intelligence and surely Humans have a greater intellect than a Cat and must be feeling even more insulted by this sort of behaviour? Surely?

Anyway the dreadful BBC were broadcasting some sort of congressional hearing about all of the crooks who plunged their noses into the Iraq oil for food crisis trough, and please don't get me started on those greedy idiots in the UN, although I would say that to a Cat it seems that this planet is ready for world government, you have perfected the corrupt bureaucracy.

Still there was a Congressional Hearing and it was amazing, I have no idea what the two people who opposed each other were saying but it was an amazing battle of wits, like two superior brains locked in mortal combat, it was like a complex and challenging game of chess when neither player knows what they are doing!

Yes I think I will stop now too, I am a little tired and if I am finding Congressional Hearings interesting I must be deranged, so I am off to bed, you can do whatever you like now, but I am going to sleep, goodnight!

DAY 237 OF MY CAPTIVITY:

Speaking of Gliders, can you feel the pride in my writing, I was going to say voice, but I am writing this and you wouldn't therefore hear my voice, but rest assured I am proud of my Glider; it is very nearly finished – hooray.

Now, I haven't mentioned my Glider before because it has had to remain a complete and total secret, as you know both the bird and the idiot Dog are definitely informers and I have a feeling that if either of them had got to hear about my Glider then it would be just so much matchwood by now.

Well I suppose it is just so much matchwood at the moment having been made mainly from so many matches, but you probably know what I mean!

It hasn't been easy to slip up to the attic and work on the Glider on the quiet, but getting the materials to make it has been even worse I can assure. Still I have been very clever and very, very secretive, just how successful I have been at being so secretive can easily be proved too by just one simple question: 'Did you know I was working on a Glider in the attic?' No I thought not, I rest my case, well if I had a case I would rest it, in fact I would have packed it and by now rested in the bucket seat of the Glider ready for take off,' so it is quite sad that I don't have a case don't you think?

DAY 238 OF MY CAPTIVITY:

Glue – now there is a simple word that has all sorts of dangerous and embarrassing implications attached to it, especially when one becomes attached to the glue, or as happened to me the tube of glue becomes attached to one's tail.

It seemed to take forever to chase my tail and then at last to corner it and keep whacking it, even when the pain made my eyes water. The pain of course grew worse when I began to chew off the glue that had stuck the tube so successfully to my tail. A note of caution whatever you do in life, please don't chew glue. Arrgh I can still taste the stuff.

Glue was just the first of my problems when I was working on my Glider in the attic, another of the problems that I encountered was design; my knowledge of aerodynamics is that I can just about spell the word, so as you can imagine that is not the best start for designing a Glider that has to be aerodynamically sound, or to put it another way - fly.

Having said that I have heard the expression used by Humans 'that one has to start somewhere' and that 'the most difficult part of the journey is the first step,' someone called Little Red Mao said that I believe. Anyway he was right even if he wasn't that tall and had a very red skin colour because my first step was unfortunately to step onto a drawing pin.

It hurt but there wasn't much blood because Cats in the main, no matter what, I have heard some Captors call us, are not 'bleeders,' Well I think that they were referring to our ability to bleed, and honestly I can't think of any other use of the word and so that must be the case, don't you think so too!

Even though my paw wasn't bleeding a lot, I had to go and rest it for the rest of today because it throbbed like mad, and so I took the time to use the 'wonderful' facilities of the software I am using to write this Diary with, it is called Word, I may have mentioned it before, it is indeed a strange name for a word processing software, because the last thing it does is produce one word, it helps to produce a few hundred or in the case of books a few hundred thousand, but not just one word, so the name is a misnomer, which would be another disastrous name for the software.

Words might be a better name for the software and if the mighty Microsoft Corporation, who create Word, want to change the name of their product they will find it a little expensive because I have already registered the name and they will have to buy it from a Cat, who has never been afraid of large sums of money especially if they are about to drop into his numbered Swiss bank account.

DAY 239 OF MY CAPTIVITY:

Unfortunately, I do seem to say that word a lot don't I? Well never mind this happens occasionally unfortunately. Unfortunately the building work on the Glider was delayed because of my bad paw which was a blow really because I wanted to get up early so that I could take advantage of the early dawn light of the dying summer; gosh that sounded poetic, fancy that.

There was another reason for using the word 'unfortunately' when referring to my little accident with the drawing pin and that was that the whole project was nearly scuppered before it got going.

Today I put some weight on my paw and the pad seemed fine and so I went up to the loft to check that everything was ok and then slipped back downstairs to rest my paw, unfortunately I didn't know that I had blood on my paw pad and that it had spread out over the pad so perfectly that when I walked it was like stamping my paw print everywhere.

The Male Captor found the trail that I had left from the white Sofa where I was taking a well earned and pain filled rest and followed it across the front room carpet, out across the hall and was beginning to climb the stairs when I dived in front of him raced up the stairs, turned half way and because we were on the same eye level looked him in the eye as he was following me.

I gave him one of my most perfect smiles and breathed fishy breath as hard as I could into his face, which was very close to mine and although I felt a little hurt by my nice gesture being rejected, he backed away, then happily the phone rang and he shuffled off to answer it wiping his nose as though it itched.

I seized the opportunity and dashed upstairs and began erasing the paw prints from the landing. Happily the phone call was from somewhere called 'work' and he spent hours talking about some nonsense or the other so that by the time I heard him put the phone down he had forgotten all about red paw prints, but it was a close call.

For a moment or two I thought about cleaning the other paw prints up but only for a moment, I had gone back to my place on the Sofa and unless a tin of fish (unlikely), or a tin of food (a possibility) was to be opened, that was where I was going to stay for the night and if I could get away with it until morning.

Usually I have to say I am forcibly removed from the Sofa at night and locked away in the kitchen, it has to do with several misunderstandings when I was a Kitten.

Day 240 of My Captivity:

As you can imagine it was a slow process building the Glider from matches, in fact everything took forever, first I had to find all of the matches to build my Glider and then to carry them up into the Attic. Cats are very clever, and some Cats are cleverer than others and other Cats believe that, they are cleverer than they are but even a very clever Cat like me found it hard to find the matches and then carry them all upstairs, while wrestling with the problems of flight, flying and aerodynamics!

Personally I believe no matter how controversial the belief that Cats are the most intelligent species on the planet, Cats do have their limitations, but only in a very few areas. One of those limitations is that us Cats don't have hands and feet, now in my opinion I could quite happily do without feet, Human feet are big and remarkably ugly, really most of them look as though it wasn't long ago they were peeling fruit.

Cat's paws are perfect, they are soft, nicely shaped and elegant, but gosh couldn't we do with a pair of hands? What would I give for a pair of hands? That is a good question! What would I give for a pair of hands? My most precious possession at the moment is a nail file, but if I gave that away and got a pair of hands I could actually have yet another use for the nail file, filing my new nails, and so I would regret having given it away in the first place.

Having said that, if I had a pair of hands after trading them for a nail file, then I could go and probably easily steal back my old nail file or get a new nail file. I know; I would give my most treasured possession for a pair of hands, it is a nail file!

But I don't know where I could do the trade which is a shame; a big shame so without a pair of really useful hands I have had to carry the matches up to the Attic in my mouth, well that was until I managed to find a little shoulder bag, and a very nice accessory too! Well I think so anyway. I will definitely take it with me when I fly out of here soon, in my wonderful Glider!

Day 241 of My Captivity:

It has taken me months to build my Glider and I am so impressed with the result and I know you will be, that I decided to polish and sand it, well I had to sand it and then polish it actually.

First I tried to sand it with my precious nail file but I couldn't reach into all of the crevices so I sat and thought about it for a while because I really wanted the Glider to be as streamlined as possible so that it streaks through the air.

Then it suddenly occurred to me, I could use my tongue, Cat's tongues are great for all sorts of things from being magnificent combs for untangling matted fur, to making Humans feel just a little uncomfortable when you lick them, especially if you lick them on the face after eating fish.

Licking a Human's face, particularly if they are asleep; is one of my favourite ways to make me chuckle and smile secretly, well it is difficult to chuckle and smile when you are actually licking someone, but afterwards I usually roll around and howl with laughter, which usually means that I have to wash myself over again because invariably one rolls in something that one wishes one hadn't if you see what I mean! See above about the comb.

Sanding and polishing would have taken a few hours with a power tool but I didn't manage to find the ones that the Male Captor got for Christmas; which was a shame because polishing and sanding with my tongue took weeks.

Have you ever had to lick thousands of postage stamps or envelopes? No let me ask that question again. Have you ever had to lick more than five postage stamps or envelopes? Your tongue goes very dry and leathery after the third, after the fourth you need a drink. After the fifth you need a break. Well just imagine that you had to lick a thousand postage stamps or envelopes and that they were made of splintery wood!

After the first few hours my poor tongue felt numb it was hanging out of my mouth and I had difficulty getting it to go back in. I needed a drink, but a drink was one of the things that I didn't bring with me to the Attic, well water is heavy and I had plenty of other things to carry and I might add, no help from you, yes you, all you have ever done is sit there and read and occasionally laugh at my misfortunes, is that fair? Well yes ok you did buy the Diary, so I will let you off this time, but I am going to keep my eye on you!

I was so thirsty and I knew that I had to do something before my tongue finally shrivelled up and fell out of my mouth. I looked around for inspiration and a drink and that was when I noticed that it was misty outside and I couldn't see much through the windows.

The warmth of the Attic had condensed on the windowpanes and so I staggered over to the window, with my tongue lolling and wobbling to and fro as I walked over to the window.

Cats are in the main conservative animals, they are well mannered, polite, and enjoy refined conversation, well in comparison to Dogs at least and so it took a lot, (I can tell you) to overcome my delicate sensibilities and to lick the window, lapping up the condensation, but once I started, the wonderful cool liquid was just divine and I couldn't stop licking the glass, I wanted more and more of this heavenly drink.

Even though I had licked every window in the Attic, I still wanted more and went downstairs to lick the bedroom windows, then the bathroom ones, I even licked the one on the upstairs landing and that is really difficult to get at, I was hooked and had turned into a crazed glass licking junkie!

It was not good I had to stop and regain my self-respect and so I went down to one of my favourite places in the house, the kitchen to get some cold Turkey and have a rest while I nibbled it. Happily the windows in the kitchen were not covered in tantalising droplets of cool water, I suppose it was too warm in there and the heat had dried them out.

I was a little sad that I couldn't feed my new and disgusting 'habit,' but at the same time relieved too. Still I consoled myself with the thought of a little cold Turkey, which I had spotted earlier in the day while I was watching the fridge being opened, one of my other daily chores.

Still although it is often all work and no play being a Cat, it is good to know what there is to eat, and what is in general going on. I had learned to open the fridge door ages ago and often while away an afternoon in amongst the Human food when the Captors are out.

In seconds I had the door open and the attention of the sniffing Dog behind me as I wandered through the middle shelf, where the pieces of Turkey had been stored. I picked up a couple of pieces in my mouth, bits of leg I think and tossed them out of the fridge as far as I could throw them, as I knew with a 'huh' and a scuffle the idiot Dog would run after the Turkey on its last flight. Now I had to be quick before he had finished wolfing down the bits of leg meat I tossed two more pieces in opposite directions, picked up a few choice cuts of white meat and made a run for it to the work surface and safety.

I settled down at the back of the work surface with my nice pieces of Turkey and listened to the dozy Dog sniff around the kitchen floor for any other bits of errant Turkey, then back track looking for any crumbs and other specks that may have parted company with the Turkey in flight.

As I expected the sniffing stopped all too quickly and first two very large black and tan paws landed on the edge of the work surface, followed by a black wet nose that had begun sniffing again.

Watching in amusement I waited for the head to peer over the edge of the work surface, as I knew it would and looked straight into the imploring dark eyes of the idiot Alsatian.

It was a big sacrifice, but worth it really, I stood up with the last piece of Turkey in my mouth, walked almost to the edge of the work surface where an excited Dog was wagging his tail, then jumped across the room onto the top of the top cupboards opposite.

Once I had my balance I looked down at the Dog who was tracking me with his eager eyes as I walked to the end of the cupboards he followed. When I got to the end cupboard I sat down with the Turkey still in my mouth and waited.

He got the message and sat too, and then following my lead again the 'good' Dog sat up and begged for the meat, rivers of drool flowing from the edges of his hungry mouth.

After he had begged like a 'good' boy for a while I dropped the meat into his open and scarily large mouth, sat down, curled up and went to sleep, thinking to myself that I must remember to close the fridge door at some point today, but it was nice to be able to treat the Dog after making him look like an idiot, this is probably the last day I will spend with him because tomorrow I will be flying high, literally!

DAY 242 OF MY CAPTIVITY:

I have to say that I did have a feeling that the Glider's wingspan was a little larger than the width of the window and consider myself rather unlucky that I didn't have a tape measure to paw (translator's note 'to hand' should be used here but the 'Author' apparently has power of veto over the Translator), but then as I have explained tools were at a premium.

You have to admit bearing that piece of information in mind; and the fact that my Glider was built mainly with a nail file and a pair of kitchen scissors and a lot of glue, oh gallons of glue, I don't think I did too bad a job do you?

In fact I am proud of my Glider, it was big and I think that Gliders should have big as their first design criteria. My reasoning is that if a Glider is big it is strong.

Strong being the second design criteria, then even if it is aerodynamically challenged at least it will hold up well under impact.

Elegance is important in Glider design too, especially to a Cat, but an elegant design that is on the tough side of robust, if you see what I mean is to be desired.

Early on, I regrettably, had to discard the machine gun, which I had mounted behind me just like the World War One aircraft I had seen in books and on TV, for two reasons really, the first was weight, with the gun mounted the Glider tilted so much I couldn't see over the nose.

The second reason was arrived at after a little thought, which is always welcome when working on projects like building one's own Glider, the reason was that if I was looking forward flying the Glider and I wanted to shoot at someone, well if I wanted to shoot at anyone, let's not be too specific here. I would have to turn around.

Suddenly I realised that if I turned around to fire the machine gun then without any doubt I would be heading down in a dive probably too difficult to get out of and for again two reasons really; first I could keep hold of the joystick if I was firing the gun and secondly and probably as importantly I could see where we were going, or is that where I was going, either way I couldn't see forwards.

When the Glider or as some Royal Air force types say in old black and white movies of the Second World War, when the 'Kite' was nearly finished I tried the controls and to this day think that I had glued the flap pedals in the up position.

Have you noticed that every time there is a black and white World War Two, war film on the Television we win it, when I say we I am including myself in the Allied effort. We must have been very good because our record in World wars is two – nil.

Two – nil is a great score, well for the winners at least, but I have to say I find it difficult to understand how 'chaps' called 'Ginger' and 'Nobby' managed to win the war for us. The first thing I noticed was that they appear to be speaking a totally foreign language.

Well let me try to explain what I mean, as you know English is my second (and last as far as I am concerned) language and I think that I now know it rather well and I have to say with some authority that I have never heard anyone speaking it like the 'chaps' in these black and white war films.

'Gosh I don't think Ginger is going to make it,' says one man in a dark uniform with a large and stupid moustache. 'Nobby don't worry, if our number is up we'll give the Bosh one in the eye.' Replies a man with an oily hair problem.

That is an example of what I have heard in these films and I am totally confused.

They also seem to want to get 'Jerry' at all costs, I have no idea what Jerry has done to them, but all I can say is that I am happy I am not Jerry and I think that Jerry ought to really watch out, there are some obvious nutters after him and worse the truly bad news for Jerry is that some idiot has given those nutters a pair of very heavily armed Spitfire warplanes to come after him in! Duck Jerry that is all the advice I have for you!

With amazing forethought I built the Glider on a ramp so that when I cut the string holding the Glider in place it would slide down the ramp picking up speed almost to take off speed before it shot through the attic window, of course this is where it would have been crucial to have had a tape measure for any number of technical reasons! But what can I say? I just couldn't find one and that was that!

Still I proudly believe that I have a good 'eye' for measuring and judging distances most of the time and figured that I could 'busk it.' They say pride comes before a fall and so I was very careful indeed, checking everything I had done at least twice, the trouble is I suppose that my critics would say not careful enough but eventually the Glider in all of its smooth majestic glory was ready for its test, inaugural and final flight all wrapped up into one successful escape.

I thought to myself, 'well here goes,' as I adjusted my goggles, straightened my flying hat, threw my white scarf over the left shoulder of my flying jacket and settled myself into a comfortable seating position inside the cockpit, just like all of the famous, Douglases, Gingers and Nobbys had done before me, and then pulled the rope that held the Glider in place and shot forward into the wide blue yonder.

The crash site was littered with pieces of broken Glider, broken matches, empty toilet roll holders, and glass from the window; in fact I should rephrase that, most of the attic window and frame and large ugly chunks of the Human's bird bath lay everywhere covered in bits of the Glider.

Lying in the middle of this devastation was a stunned Sparrow, which was a shame, and to my way of thinking a waste of a good Sparrow; they make an excellent Brunch you understand. As far as I was concerned the Sparrow wasn't just out of reach of a paw or to put it another way out of harms way, he was completely off the menu.

Why? Do I hear you ask, well the reason that I was able to survey the damage that my Glider had done to the bird bath, the Sparrow and the garden in general was that I was suspended above it all, in mid air.

As the Glider had crashed though the window and taken most of the window frame with it as it headed for the ground, I had been scooped out of the cockpit, quite by chance by the window stay, hence the dangling. Unfortunately there wasn't only dangling going on, I could hear my flying jacket beginning to make discreet tearing sounds. Now discreet tearing sounds generally are something that one should be concerned about, but in my experience they are no reason to panic. One should however panic when distinct tearing sounds can be heard and as a rule I would say that if one can hear ripping sounds one should really panic and completely stop any pretence at beginning to panic.

I have no recollection as to whether the ripping sounds were getting louder or not, I may have passed out for a while, if I did when I came round I was swaying and now instead of dangling I was definitely hanging and no longer by my flying jacket, oh no, now I was hanging by just a small piece of leather that had split away from the collar.

Personally I feel that panic, if controlled, is a powerful ally to anyone in a difficult situation, more powerful than say for instance, rational thought. Though of course I would have to try rational thought whilst cornered to be absolutely certain of this fact and unfortunately I have never remembered to do so when I am in a difficult situation.

Most of the difficult situations I have been in the middle of, or may indeed have caused, have just created blind panic in me, but that is probably just the way I am, a bit of a panicker which is ok, it is important to know one's limitations and then of course ignore them completely.

Luckily I still had my white silk scarf jauntily tossed over my left shoulder, and although panicking, I thought that if I knotted one end I could probably hook the guttering, then pull on the scarf to make sure it was safe and then slip out of my flying jacket and holding tightly onto the end of the scarf, employ some sort of Harrison Ford/Indiana Jones stunt and land standing up on the roof tiles.

It was, I was sure, going to be an excellent stunt and one that I could use to increase my fame and renown, although I think those two things are the same.

Yes it would have been an excellent stunt and I was just doing some deep breathing whilst hanging and spinning a little getting ready for 'the' moment when I heard a rip that sounded so final that I just had to open my eyes.

Yes they had been closed almost all the time. I ask you, would you have your eyes open if you were dangling by a few threads of a flying jacket from where an attic window used to be, no I thought not.

Yes I did see the last shreds of leather snap and I really did feel the dropping sensation, that expression 'my heart in my mouth' it is true I promise you, but my heart wasn't in my mouth for long because I stopped with such force that my bottom seemed to be on my paws.

For a long while I have no idea what had happened first to my heart and then to my bottom and more importantly there were two things I couldn't work out; the first was why wasn't I standing on all four paws on the roof tiles expecting applause? And the second conundrum was if I wasn't standing on four paws on the roof tiles, why wasn't I lying crumpled and dazed on top of the Sparrow and the bird bath? I was confused, worse I was trapped.

The answer to those questions was appallingly simple and no I didn't believe it at first and it 'happened' to me, I was there sort of thing, and so you will have to take my word for what happened. The wings snapped on the window frame and I take the blame for that one, I should have thought to cut a large hole out of the roof, but you think of these little things afterwards don't you. Worse than the wings snapping I had been grabbed by the window frame and left to dangle and then fall to my almost certain death, but fate or something with the same sense of humour as fate had intervened.

Whatever was holding me in mid air snapped and I am pretty sure that was my nice flying jacket, which seems to have disappeared I might add and if anyone 'finds' it in a guilty moment, can they please return it, no questions asked. When I dropped expecting death at the worse or the cold roof tiles at best, I actually fell inside the attic window, probably because a breeze had freshened among the dormer windows.

I suppose I should be grateful that I didn't fall onto the roof tiles and then roll hideously to my death, but I fell onto the broken battered window frame and now have a splinter in my bottom, not only does it hurt, but it is going to be embarrassing to persuade someone to pull that out.

So another escape attempt goes down in flames metaphorically speaking, one day I will get out of here and I am content with the fact that even if I can't manage to complete successfully an escape attempt, then at least I will get out when my Agent and

Publisher send a limo for me, actually it might be worth waiting just for that moment, can you imagine the look on the assembled faces as I am shielded from the crowd of neighbours and curtain twitchers, by a couple of heavies from a support car and guided into the limo and off to stardom.

Thinking about it I will need the heavies to guide me because I have practised wearing sunglasses, and I find it very difficult to see out of them, and at night it just gets worse, it must be something to do with the way Cat's eyes see things or not as the case maybe when they are wearing dark glasses. But in spite of the fact that I can't see out of sunglasses, I have to wear them and especially at night because all cool people wear 'shades' day or night, I don't know why all cool people wear 'shades' and I have a feeling that they don't know why either, we just do!

I wonder if the Parrot, the Human Captors and the Dogs will miss me, I sometimes imagine saying goodbye to them and there being tearful eyes all round, I would tell them just how much I will miss them, of course that overt demonstration of how much I care maybe accompanied by an aerial display by a squadron of pink pigs and a Blue Moon after sunset.

Seriously if you were headed for a comfortable and rich life, would you miss the dull one you were leaving behind or the people that populated it, or maybe that is a little difficult for you to imagine dear reader because you know you are stuck in your life, I was going to say stuck at university, or with a mortgage and three kids, but the research guys haven't managed to provide a definite picture of the demographic who will be reading this Diary and so I am sorry I just had to generalise.

And to think that some publishers thought that this was just a children's book and that is probably only because there isn't a lot of swearing and there most definitely isn't any sex, sadly!

DAY 243 OF MY CAPTIVITY:

Apparently there is such a thing called 'having a grip on reality.' If there is indeed such a thing as having a grip on reality then I truly believe that I have not exactly lost mine, but my grip on reality may well be loosening.

Everything I do seems to be just a little surreal and I have to say that sometimes I feel less like a Cat and more like a Human and that is not right at all, surely I am far too good looking for that affliction.

I believe that my uneasy feeling probably comes from mastering the English language which seems to be an instrument of the most sublime madness sometimes, but then I could be wrong, I am after all paying a translator to translate my Diary from Cat into Human, when I now think that I could do a better job myself, is that surreal or what?

Having said that! I don't think that the above is the whole problem, maybe I am a Human trapped inside the body of a Cat? No surely life couldn't be that diabolical could it? Still there is something wrong with reality and I intend to find out what it is and fix it as soon as I can and have assembled the tools to do a proper job!

In the meantime I will just have to be content with the situation as it is, every week I email the most recent Diary entries to my translator and he translates what I have written (in Cat obviously but sometimes in English) and I read it back in the English version he has produced.

At the beginning I had lots of corrections and subsequent arguments over almost everything I had written and that was probably because I wasn't fluent in English, but now I am and have decided that maybe my translator is not so fluent in Cat.

Still we have less to argue about these days and usually I agree with his little criticisms and deletions. Actually I suppose that it would be a good idea to retain his services until the Cat language is taught in schools across the world and I can be published in my own language.

Day 244 of My Captivity:

It is about time that we had some action isn't it? Or you may not feel compelled to finish reading the book.

Having said that, it isn't easy to write a Diary which has an entry for every day of my life that is interesting all of the time, because if I it was like that, the continuous action would obviously be false, and not a true account of my captivity and on top of that I would be too worn out most days to write about what I have done don't you think that is true?

Which neatly leads me on to some of the other Diaries that I have read snippets of on the web, they have large blanks of inaction and so you should be grateful that my Diaries don't obviously follow the same pattern as Diaries from not necessarily more famous people, just people who are older than me.

Take that nice man who was beaten to the South Pole, Captain Robert F. Scott (and the 'F' stands for, wait for it 'Falcon' goodness his parents didn't like him much did they), his Diary wasn't even finished, but then I suppose he had a good reason for that, and so we can forgive him that small oversight, he was dead, but there are large chunks of his Diary where he didn't write in it at all, then again if all you can say is, Monday – 'it was cold today and it snowed in the afternoon.' I don't suppose there is much point in writing an entry every day.

Having said that I thought I would help the good Captain and fill in some of the blank days for him, like this:

Tuesday – We fed the Penguins today and the ungrateful little devils came back later and stole a whole tin of Chocolate Digestive biscuits, we laughed so much that from now we are going to hide the last tin of what we have christened 'Penguins.'

Wednesday – We are on our way back from the Pole now and in good spirits.

Captain Oakes is a right character, this morning he went off for his 'constitutional' and was missing for quite some time, when we went out to look for him we found him standing behind the tents finishing off a little sign in yellow writing that said 'Oatsie was 'ere!' Although he is a great laugh, he's his own worst enemy and will get lost if he tries that again in a blizzard and we told him as much, but you can't stay mad at someone with such a good sense of humour!

There are lots of other examples of Diaries, which have large blank bits and not all of them because the writers hadn't imagined that they would not be around to finish them. The great explorer Dr. Livingstone is one example of that I presume!

I read a bit of his Diary online and was fascinated to see that more or less seven years was missing from its pages, below is what I remember reading, but as my memory is not brilliant all the time bits of it might be wrong and other bits quite frankly I may have made up because I can't remember what was actually written, enjoy anyway.

Extracts from the Diary of Dr. David Livingstone.

Thursday June 2 1859 – I am so excited, we have just set out in native canoes up the River Nile, in search of its source.

It isn't a particularly wide river, in comparison with say, the Zambezi and therefore I have concluded that this will be a rather brief trip and so our limited provisions should be sufficient for the short excursion to the Nile's source.

Friday July 19, 1866 – Mmmh I couldn't have been more wrong about this damn river, we are in dire straits, as you can imagine, having paddled up stream for seven years, to make matters worse we have lived, poorly off the land for the last seven years.

As well as being constantly hungry I am also in need of a good tailor, not only because I am now so thin that my clothes don't fit, but also they have all but worn out and I look extremely ragged.

On the brighter side I bumped into a journalist today called Mr. Stanley who said that he wanted to write about me, he suggested that this would make me a household name and if we were lucky we might get a movie deal. Mr. Stanley is a nice man, but I presume he is insane, after all movies haven't been invented yet.

It is a lot of fun reading other people's Diaries (yes this is me again, The Cat and until I say otherwise you are back reading my Diary), unless they are written by politicians where the effort of sifting out the truth from the self aggrandisement just isn't worth the effort, I would draw your attention to two examples here, one time British Prime Minister, Mrs. Thatcher, her Diaries are in biographical form similar to the writings of the prophets in the bible, who I believe were just as potty as she is.

And then there are the Diaries of Mr. Richard Milhous Nixon, the almost impeached President of the United States of America, only read them if you have a strong will and are not easily brainwashed or bamboozled, sorry to use the word bamboozled, but I had a small wager with the Dog that I couldn't use the word bamboozled three times in my writings (he is not aware I am writing a Diary and am destined for literary fame and fortune).

So I think I won that wager.

DAY 245 OF MY CAPTIVITY:

I was so impressed with the fun and games I had with other people's Diaries yesterday that I was tempted to play the same games today, yes you are right not much is going on today either, but I have decided that it wouldn't be fair to play with the memories of famous people who are unable to defend themselves and not only that, this is my Diary and should be about me, which is a shame because as I said it was a lot of more or less harmless fun.

However I do think that it is a good idea and I may well produce a little book devoted to extracts from other people's Diaries, I think they are called 'spoofs,' but you have to be careful who you call a 'spoof' these days, oops sorry I think I may have misunderstood that word and got it a little confused with another slightly different word with fewer 's's' in it!

Mind you the little book idea is a cracker and as they say in the publishing game, a nice little earner.

As for what is going on in the real world, if you can call my imprisonment the 'real' world there is a big fat zero going on and that is the sad truth.

As I was on my daily tour of the windows and doors this morning I did wonder how anyone could be so careful that they could ensure that all of the windows and doors were securely locked and bolted, doesn't anyone understand that I would just like one little tiny window to be left open?

Hold on, I am turning into a 'sad'o' aren't I?

DAY 246 OF MY CAPTIVITY:

I suppose one has to have quiet periods in one's life doesn't one? I know that is an odd way to talk, but let's face it I could easily make the Diary almost completely incomprehensible, I could revert to my native language for example and who understands Cat, apart from Cats that is?

Or worse I could speak like a member of the British Royal family, have you ever heard any of them chatting? No probably not and I have to say that because they are on almost permanent vacation few people do, but every so often like for instance, woodworm they appear for no reason at all and make a little speech well the woodworm don't make speeches and so at least we have found some organism with less mental abilities than the Royal family.

The two biggest offenders nowadays are the Queen of England and Prince Charles, Prince Charles having taken over the former role of the Duke of Edinburgh, which is to talk utter nonsense and see if he can offend and annoy most of the people all of the time.

The Queen of England on the other hand is an ever more remote and confused figure who on the odd occasion when she is allowed near a microphone, or more accurately her minders haven't noticed that she is near one, will chat away for hours, talking about 'we' when she is referring to herself!

Bless her, she is obviously getting old and confused, because the term 'we' is the Royal 'we' that was used by absolute monarchs when they chatted about themselves and thought that they were divine, and it is worth remembering that the most famous absolute monarch, and some would say the last in England, was Charles the first and we all know what happened to him!

Still to prove that the monarch does have a relevant function in modern Great Britain, a little while ago the Queen and her family provided bed and breakfast to a visiting President, and at what I believe was a pretty good rate too!

In my opinion to encourage good relations with other countries more such mini breaks should be organised for world leaders and maybe the Royal family should look at providing evening meals, and even cream teas during the afternoon.

It would be really nice if they could earn a crust instead of getting handouts from the state; that sets a bad example for the populace at large.

Day 247 of My Captivity:

What is Packet wisdom? Well have you ever read the side of a packet of food and seen just how much information is available to anyone curious enough, or bored enough to read it?

The amount of information actually on the side of anything that contains things we eat these days could actually, honestly and accurately be called a confusion of information, and would definitely be informative, if it wasn't so confusing.

An intelligent Cat can get mentally trapped between the RDA's, (Required Daily Amount) the GDA's, (Guideline Daily Amounts) and the very detailed Nutritional Information on the side of any container of food, because there is just too much information and no commonsense statements, like say for instance, 'the food in this packet won't do you any harm if you eat it and may actually be good for you, after all we would prefer to keep you alive, fit and well, so that we can sell you more food.'

So why is there so much information available in very small print on the sides of packets of food? Is it there to inform the consumer or to confuse them? I am sure that we all know don't we!

Indeed would the manufacturer of a cheap bag of 'delicious Golden Chicken Nuggets' want you to know what had gone into the mincing machine before it was turned on? No probably not!

Food is a big issue, well they call it food, but what they really mean is over processed mechanically recovered bits of stuff that are teased, flavoured and generally messed about with before being shaped, covered in breadcrumbs or batter and frozen individually, ready to be part defrosted and fried by people who profess not to have enough time on their hands to cook proper food, properly.

Which is all awful, but I have to ask, what do you really expect food to be like if it doesn't bear any resemblance to what food really is?

Real food is less of an issue than bad food, which means that bland food must be generally acknowledged by most people as good food, if you see what I mean and that is a shame really because I don't want to worry you, but until recently that juicy lump of steak might have been winking at the moon and singing Arias for a nuclear family of disinterested but glowing sheep.

Still I put some of the blame on supermarkets, they are responsible for injecting water and other slime into food and selling it to the dim-witted British public as good food, oh and of course there is one TV Chef in Britain who allegedly wants British school children to eat better less processed food, who advertises for a supermarket known to sell over developed Chicken and bacon and ham that has been injected with brine, which until now I thought was something to do with the sea.

Day 248 of My Captivity:

As you know I have been taking things easy recently and some might just say that I have become just a little lazy, and although I don't like that suggestion, after all who likes to be called lazy, I am inclined to agree with them.

The trouble is that the best friend of lazy, is fat, and they are such good friends that they are rarely seen apart. I am getting, let's call it, 'well-upholstered' shall we, and I have decided that I have to do something about the bigger me and quickly, although, like everyone I am rather keen not to actually reduce the amount I eat. I am sure that if you saw what I eat you would agree with me, it is hardly enough to keep a Mouse alive. So I am going to start taking exercise and watching what I eat, in fact I promise to keep my eyes glued to every morsel of food in my bowl until it is completely gone, sorry that was a Cat joke, I try to keep them to a minimum because Humans tend not to appreciate them.

Day 249 of My Captivity:

I have not been very truthful with you recently and I am sorry, but I have a very good reason for my secretiveness I have been busy, but needed the smoke screen of a few 'boring' days of nothing to do, recorded in my Diary just in case anyone here is reading it, but now it is ok I have managed to get all of the material together and I am ready to begin the construction phase of my latest and hopefully most successful means of escape.

I know that my Rocket failed in every way possible a while ago, but the building of a rocket sled seems like sensible idea to me in spite of the failures of my Rocket after all I learned a lot from building the Rocket because although I wasn't launched to freedom the technology was more or less successful.

So with all of that in mind I have been secretly building my second version or V2, to give it a short catchy name.

The V2 is, as I mentioned, a Rocket sled, and I know you will say Rocket Sleds need things like rails and plenty of space to work properly but I tend to disagree and my opposing viewpoint is based on sound research and like all clever scientists on my ability to innovate. Or as some would say not to listen to opposing arguments or sound facts, but then if we all listened to and agreed with proven research and sound facts, there would never be any innovation, would there?

I got the inspiration for a Rocket Sled from yes you guessed it, the television, are you trying to suggest something there? The other day there was a brilliant programme about the work of scientists' years ago, when life was just in black and white and to see how much the scientists could try the patience and durability of prospective Astronauts and Cosmonauts, employing all sorts of strange and painful experiments culminating on a ride on a Rocket Sled, I have to say that I don't know if the Rocket Sled ride was a reward for the Guinea Pigs after all of the painful experiments or a final attempt to despatch them beyond the stars!

My design, like all good designs is based on readily available components, which have been tried and tested and indeed work perfectly doing what they have been designed for, and my genius for adapting these technologies to my own design has allowed me to create something so elegant, efficient and effective that I am assured of success this time!

I did have a bit of luck too and that was with the engine. And before you decided that I am insane when I explain my propulsion system let me tell you that I had decided that the best way to power the Rocket Sled was to copy the idea behind NASA's Space Shuttles propulsion system, which is effectively to have a couple of massive tanks of gas strapped to the Space Shuttle! Although I thought that I would leave out the bits of loose foam that tend to fall off occasionally and make heartbeats rise at mission control.

Obviously the first things to scour the house for were a couple of large tanks of combustible gas, but sadly I couldn't lay my paws on any and concluded that it is likely that the Captors don't keep that type of explosive in the house, more's the pity.

But happily I found a pair of Butane gas cylinders, which are used to refill the thing-a-me-jig that lights the gas cooker, and not to refill gas cigarette lighters this being a place where there aren't any smokers, but Humans who like to keep stocks of things.

At first it crossed my mind to follow the example of the scientists at NASA and use both gas tanks, but then after thinking about it for a while I came up with a clever idea. I wasn't after all trying to launch myself into space, I was just going to crash through the glass of the dining room window and therefore I would most likely only need one tank of gas to power the Rocket Sled.

Now the clever bit! If I only needed one tank of gas I would be able to do a couple of things, the first, actually test the Rocket Sled, not that I doubted that it would work, and the second thing I could accomplish by a test firing was that I would be able to actually break the glass and then when I was securely strapped into the Rocket Sled it would be easy to launch myself through the hole.

Perfection is simplicity and this was a simple plan and we all know that simple plans work, so I was delighted by the prospect of landing somewhere in the garden later during the following day!

With that thought in mind, I went to sleep and dreamed of a fiery escape.

DAY 250 OF MY CAPTIVITY:

Weather conditions are always an important factor for any escape and also for any Rocket testing or launching, I have noticed that NASA watches the weather very closely, even if the equipment is a bit doggy they will have a go at getting a Rocket into the air, but if the weather is bad then they always postpone any launch.

So what is good enough for NASA is good enough for me, and following their prudent course of action, when I discovered it was raining and just a little too blustery outside I decided to wait and see if the weather improved. I waited patiently all day, with my nose pressed up against the very window pane that I was going to smash through, for the weather to change and annoyingly it didn't.

By the end of the day I was so tired and tense from waiting that I just curled up on the window sill and fell asleep, waking up after it was dark and cursing today's lost opportunity.

DAY 251 OF MY CAPTIVITY:

Happily today when it dawned was brighter and better altogether than yesterday, and one has to say looking out of the dining room window, where I had woken up, was perfect.

The minutes dragged by waiting for the house to become quiet, but after what seemed an eternity I watched the Male and Female Captor drive off up the drive and confirm that I now had some peace and quiet to shatter.

Everything was in place and set up on the dining room table very quickly, I tutted at my inability to be able to turn the table around and use the length of the ancient mahogany table as a launch surface but that couldn't be helped and meant that I was able to arrange the two rows of books, which would act as channel down which I would travel along (instead of rails, clever don't you think), and then at the end of the channel I would take off momentarily flying across the gap between the table and the window before flying through the hole in the window rather quickly too, but that couldn't be helped.

So in no time at all I had everything in place and was just making a few minor technical adjustments to the Rocket Sled with my hammer, before finally aiming it at the window.

The table proved to be quite an asset because it was a treasured Human possession and consequently very highly polished which meant that the runners of my sled slid over it beautifully.

For the test run I had propped up a couple of large volumes at the end of the run of books so that I could use them to duck behind once the Rocket Sled's engine was fired up and the long flame started to roar out of the back of the Butane gas cylinder and when I was happy with the Rocket Sled I practised ducking back and then quickly peering over the top of the books so that I could watch the impact, once I was happy with everything, I reached for the box of matches and pulled out a paw full.

Lighting the nozzle on the end of a cylinder of Butane gas is not really something that one should attempt unless you are like me a proficient scientist, because it is dangerous and as I quickly found out it is not easy to get the red plastic nozzle to actually catch alight and so one could have a little accident, which could very quickly turn into a nasty accident.

First I burned my paws holding the burning matches under the nozzle and the shock of that made me drop the matches onto the table, happily they stayed burning in a little pile on the table, eventually drops of melting plastic were dripping from the nozzle and adding to the heat from the pile of matches so that in a short time there was a nice little blaze under the nozzle, and now things were beginning to really happen.

There is a moment just before the valve gives way and the Butane in a gas cylinder bursts out and catches alight when everything seems to go quiet, it is the most amazing thing to experience, you are hyped up with expectation and then all of a sudden silence, a pure silver (I don't know about you but I have always thought of silence as silver and not golden) silence, which was almost instantly replaced by a roar and whoosh of flame and then blast off.

I wasn't disappointed in any way. My chosen viewing point was excellent and I was able to watch the immensely powerful Rocket Sled go from naught to wow that is fast, in much less time than it takes to write about it.

And then there was a more than satisfying crash of the Rocket Sled colliding with the window, sadly at this point the trail of smoke and flames which led across the surface of the table and then off to the point of impact obscured my vision, but I knew that it would only be a short while before a light breeze of fresh air cleared that away as it blew gently through the hole in the window, so I waited patiently for that to happen.

The smoke twirled and billowed in the fresh air then it did exactly what I expected it to, it cleared away. I was impressed with my accurate prediction, but not half as impressed with the sizable jagged hole that my Rocket Sled had punched through the window, 'result' as Humans say sometimes when they are pleased and something good has happened!

I ran down the channel of books and jumped from the table to the windowsill for a closer look at the result or damage depending upon your opinion of these things.

The edges of the hole were very jagged and one bit in the centre seemed to have broken off as a point and this point stabbed its way to the heart of the hole, but on the whole, (Cat joke, sorry) the hole looked to me as if it was big enough to fly through, so I started searching for the bits of my Rocket Sled which weren't readily apparent on the carpet.

Several bits of the Rocket Sled had disappeared under the table, but in no time at all I had collected all the bits together, carried them up to the table and reassembled my Rocket Sled with the second Butane gas cylinder sitting proudly in place.

That was it then, I was I think, more or less ready, I had a pile of matches sitting on the table underneath the red nozzle of the cylinder, ready to be lit and I had arranged the string safety belt carefully so that I could grab both ends and rope myself in quickly while the nozzle burned its way up to the valve.

Carefully I lit the matches with a smile and then dashed down to the seat of the Rocket Sled and tied myself in, all I had to do was wait, is it always true that 'the waiting is the hardest part,' or is that just a Tom Petty song? Who knows? Who cares? This waiting business is hard whether it is a song title or the truth or indeed both.

I could just about hear the sound of the nozzle burning, but I couldn't see anything because I was so tightly strapped in.

Then there was a whoosh and a bang, and I was pressed into the back of the seat and my head was thrown up over the seat, I was travelling at an incredible speed and although I was screaming this was the best rollercoaster ride anyone could imagine.

When I managed to pull my head down and look out of my watery eyes which were bulging forward as the rest of my fur and skin was swept back by the G force, all I could see in front of me was the nasty looking jagged piece of glass which now it seemed to me filled most of the hole.

If I had had time I could have asked myself how could I have been so wrong about the size of the hole and the size of the jagged piece of glass that almost blocked it, but I didn't, because there just wasn't the time.

Have you noticed there is never enough time to answer questions when you are short of time? At this moment in time I had a feeling that I was very short of time and had to act, well maybe act is too strong a word and implies some sort of rational thought and this was definitely no time to be rational or to be thinking, even if I wanted to be doing either, I just had to react.

Indecision takes a lot of time and what little time I had left was stolen by pure refined and unadulterated indecision.

Sorry you can tell now surely that I am stalling for time, trying to actually work out clearly in my mind exactly what I did, or more correctly what happened, I didn't actually do much, I was not only a passenger on the Rocket Sled, for the next five or six seconds I was a passenger in real life, yes it is obvious I survived, this is a Diary and one tends to write it after the 'event,' But I have to try and remember what happened so that I can tell you.

Personally I wish that this was a work of fiction and then I could have just invented something and say that is what happened, well I suppose I could do that, but I am as you know too honest a Cat to do that sort of thing.

In less time than it has taken you to read the last paragraph or so I faced death (that statement depends largely on you not having any reading disability I hasten to add), and that is not a life experience that I would recommend, no matter how spiritual you are or indeed think that you maybe!

So there I was hurtling towards the sharpest of the jagged edges, that surrounded the hole in the window, to say nothing of the bit of sharp glass that jutted out into the hole itself, any sort of reaction or plan or clever wheeze had deserted me, and at this rate the next thing to desert me was going to be my lunch, sorry to get lavatorial but I am sure you know what I mean.

There was only one thing to do, because optional extras like steering, safety cages and all of the sensible things that one should build into a Rocket powered vehicle, I hadn't even considered building into this stripped down Rocket powered Sled, still too late to worry about little incidentals like that now.

I just closed my eyes and held my breath and panicked. Well what would you have done under the same circumstances?

Even now sitting in relative comfort bashing away at my keyboard writing this I can't really 'hand on my heart' say what happened next, mainly because I had my eyes closed, but I think that something happened, no I can say with absolute certainty that 'something' happened.

If you want me to take a guess and judging by the damage to the window I would say that because I was wriggling, sorry I forgot to mention I was doing a bit of that while my eyes were closed and I was panicking, well you would do wouldn't you? I managed to ever so slightly change the course of the Rocket Sled and hit the dinning room window a little to the right of where the test firing had hit previously.

Of course I didn't really know much about where I had actually hit the window, until I realised that the carpet was alight and I opened my eyes as I was scampering away from the Rocket Sled wreckage, even then I only caught a quick glimpse of the latest jagged hole in the dinning room window.

When I was at what I considered to be a safe distance from the fire, the kitchen, I took a few deep breaths and tried to draw on my reserves of courage, sadly I didn't have any reserves of anything left let alone courage and so I just stood there dazed and panting, not a pretty sight really.

Happily Cats can quickly regain their curiosity and as soon as my curiosity level had reached the 'I wonder if the dining room is on fire and is it therefore time to evacuate the house level?' I sneaked back to look at the damage expecting to be confronted by a wall of flame at any moment as I edged through the hall towards the dining room.

The fire in the corner of the dining room had happily burnt itself out, I am just guessing, but it may have just been the remains of the gas from the cylinder that had been burning and so fortunately the carpet wasn't even scorched.

The window was a sorry state with two quite large, and as I mentioned before, jagged holes in it, but as there was nothing I could do about it I decided that the best course of action was to ignore it.

The charred remnants of the Rocket Sled were another matter, there were I suppose you could say incriminating forensic evidence and I had to hide them as my paw prints, also known as 'dabs' in the Feline world were all over the odd twisted bit of metal, so I definitely had to get rid of the evidence somewhere.

Fortunately every room in this house has a fireplace, the one in the dining room is rarely used and so instead having a decorative pile of logs getting dusty in the hearth, the Humans have placed a decorative dried flower arrangement that is as dusty as the logs would have been if they were used, still the dried flower arrangement has one advantage over the logs in my opinion, behind it is a large void which easily accommodated the unrecognizable remains of the Rocket Sled.

I had another little bit of good luck too because as I tossed the odd bits of the Rocket Sled over the dried flower arrangement it brought down a shower of soot, giving the impression to the casual observer that it had been there for some time, happily in my experience Humans tend to be very casual observers and will probably be fooled into thinking that the odd metal bits had fallen down the chimney because of the soot fall or the other way round, but both scenarios mean that the bits of metal and now the soot have nothing what so ever to do with me, excellent.

It was getting dark and I decided that if I pulled the dining room door too when I left there was a chance that the Humans wouldn't notice the damage until they were here in daylight, as they didn't really use the room often, and if that was the case I could check for more damage tomorrow and see if I could do any more tidying up, or hiding of 'evidence,' or better still get some of the Parrots feathers and drop them around the place, like Red Herrings.

Unless that is I could get my paws on some Red Herrings, not that I know what they are, I have just heard that they are handy for leading people off the scent, so I imagine that they are some sort of old fish, although not the seven foot variety that I once imagined when I was younger, more's the pity!

DAY 252 OF MY CAPTIVITY:

I finished off yesterday's entry in the Diary this morning and sort of laid low just in case the Human Captors went into the dining room before they went off to work, happily they had over laid and so they went off in a great hurried panic, not wanting to be late, someone should tell them to calm down, they were late already!

Now it is time to get up and have a snout about and see what, if anything, I can do in the dining room.

On first inspection if you sort of ignored the window and the breeze blowing in through two jagged holes there wasn't any damage, but then my viewpoint is rather low down only being a few inches off the ground, and so I decided to jump up onto the table and get a better view of the room.

At first I wished that I hadn't been so diligent, there wasn't any extra damage to the room, but the table well that was a different matter.

The table had a long scorch mark right across its width, which in my opinion was going to take a lot of sighing and tutting from a French Polisher to repair, if indeed it could ever be repaired. Oh dear, the words haunted their way through my thoughts and quite rightly too, the Humans were or is that 'are' rather attached to their antique mahogany table.

What was I to do? Save my skin, well yes that is the first priority of all Cats and I have noticed all Humans too, but how? That was the niggling little problem to consider today, and currently I was like the last British mass-market car manufacturer, bankrupt of ideas.

I could sleep on it! But that would only delay sorting out the problem and that wasn't a solution, but then it was the best idea I had come up with so far and would work for me!

As I left the dining room I pulled the door to and hoped that in the darkness and bustle of the house at night no one would go in there.

In fact I do have one plan and that is not really a plan to sort out the problem of the dining room table, but at least it will keep the Captors busy, and the plan matched the way I felt, I was going to be sick all over the place tonight, well all over the place except for the dining room that is, that should keep them occupied all evening, excuse me I need to go and be sick somewhere now and as far away from where I am going to sleep tonight as possible, but where? I know their bed; that is always a good place for that sort of thing!

Day 253 of My Captivity:

I still don't really know why I was sick last night. Worry? Yes! Red Herring? No still haven't found one of those to eat!

What I can tell you is that 'the balloon went up' as they say when trouble is discovered or someone is alerted by something. The Female Captor found the scorch mark on the dining room table; well to be honest it wasn't going to be that difficult was it?

After she screamed at the vandalism, she then did a sort of flash audit, looking around the room and really looking, which is the way we actually see things isn't it, have you noticed when you walk into a room normally and do something like sit down, you don't really take in what the room is like or what is going on, like say for instance what colour is the ceiling, or indeed does the room have a ceiling?

Well for the first time for a long time the Female Captor looked around the dining room and saw the damage, belatedly accompanied by the Male Captor, though why she would want his help I have no idea, because he is pretty useless at the best of times and it was obvious that this moment was not the best of times!

Happily if that is the word, but it is a good word and so it will do, happily the Male Captor who found the 'contraption' at the back of the fireplace behind the dried flowers decided that the window had been smashed by thugs, hoodies and vandals, which to me sounds like quite a criminal gang.

He looked at the holes in the window, the burn across the table and the 'thing,' behind the dried flowers, (now that he had examined it, he had obviously down graded the 'contraption' to a 'thing,') and decided that the gang had thrown 'missiles' at the window and the remnants of one of those missiles had scorched the table and landed harmlessly 'thank goodness' (his words although I share the sentiment) in the hearth.

Well I don't know about you, but I was pleased to hear his explanation, and was rather looking forward to two things, the first was to stop being sick and I have to say I felt better that I was not a hoodie suspect and the second thing that I was looking forward to was the visit of the glaziers.

Imagine, the whole of the dining room window needs to be replaced, and that is a big wide-open space in anyone's book.

Do excuse me while I plan an escape, won't you!

Day 254 of My Captivity:

It was a long night, partly due to my excitement; well it isn't every day that you know that half of the wall is going to be taken out of the dining room; that is how big the window is, wall sized.

I am pretty sure that it is going to be a big job, lots of workers, some of whom might be called George and yes I know now, some not called George. There will be a couple of vans and at least one lorry, perfect!

Well I was up early and I am now ready for the invasion and I am looking forward to a quick run, hop and a jump to freedom.

Because there might be glass around I have taken a sensible precaution and wrapped my paws in a towel that I got the Dog to rip up for me, it is a shame that the only towel we could get our or is that his teeth into was a very bright pink, but never mind I won't be wearing these little pink booties for long will I?

Well the glaziers have arrived and what a disappointment they are so far, just the one vehicle and that is not big enough to be called a proper lorry and only two men in neat green overalls, all I can say is that so far glaziers are something of a disappointment.

Obviously I am in hiding, a pink pawed (I don't want to use the 'bootie' word too often if it is ok with you) Cat is a little noticeable and to be seen now would be a bit of a disaster, and wreck the escape attempt completely.

These glaziers are quick workers, they took out the old glass, from the outside of the house and so they didn't go into the dining room, then they did something rather unusual for workmen, they swept and tidied up.

I was surprised they hadn't been at the house for more than half an hour and they were well on their way to being finished and the tricky glaziers hadn't once left any door open, and in fact had only been in the dining room once, what were they playing at?

Time for the big sheet of glass to go in, here goes, the dining room door will surely be left open.

Would you believe it, not once was a door opened while the glass was being replaced, not once did I get a chance of freedom, what a bunch of spoilsports glaziers are!

Mind you I knew they were going to be trouble because they refused tea, and that is not natural for a tradesman is it?

Well I was desolate, so desolate that I slunked out of my hiding place and passed the two glaziers who were just cleaning the dining room door knob, one had touched it with a puttied hand (how about that, they were cleaning up everything after themselves at this rate there wouldn't be a trace of their visit, told you they weren't normal tradesmen).

As I walked down the hallway, I heard them laughing and looked round to see what was so funny and they were both laughing their heads off and pointing at my feet, one even said 'hello poofy Cat!' Really some people have an odd sense of humour I can tell you!

DAY 255 OF MY CAPTIVITY:

It would appear that my plan to auction the Queen and the rest of the Royal family on eBay hasn't worked, which is a shame because I really think that if they had gone to new owners then it would be best. Because you see the current owners, the British Public are tired of meeting the cost of maintaining them and frankly are, it seems to me, just bored with them, after all they have owned a Royal family in one form or another for almost a couple of thousand years and they must have got through a mountain of Royal Cat litter!

(I was going to use the word millennia, but I wondered if you would understand what it meant, but then I found out I couldn't spell it, so that made me decide to say a couple of thousand years).

I pity the British Public, it must be a trial having to be responsible for something as time consuming as a pet Royal family and for nearly two thousand years, the British Public need a medal just for looking after their Royal pets, but there is more to owning a pet Royal family there is the cost, although the cost of maintaining a pet Royal family has reduced in recent years, apparently because they have weeded out the less attractive Royal family members.

Still even looking after the new smaller 'handbag' size Royal family of recent times, the expense is still quite enough, although nowadays most of their very expensive and pretty useless toys, that were once everyday items in the life of a Royal family member, like the Royal Yacht, the Royal Train and several Royal Aeroplanes and Helicopters have been confiscated.

But sadly the pint sized Royal family still have too many homes, houses and castles to look after, and clean which they only rarely use and it would be so sad to take them away from the Royal family too and leave them with nothing and so I thought that the best thing to do would be to give the Royal family a new home, in a new country, preferably together, but if they have to be split up then I suppose what must be, must be!

One thing is certain and that is that the poor under valued Royal family would have a new lease of life in a new country and surely we have to give them that chance, hence my eBay offering.

There were a few minor problems, proving ownership was one, but because I said I was acting as an agent for the British Public everything was ok, well eBay are not that fussy about what they are selling and who actually 'owns' it are they? They just want the commission from a sale after all and are prepared to do a Lord Nelson now and again, for a bit of a profit.

Just imagine how happy a revitalised Royal family would be with new challenges in a new country, it would have done them so much good to be loved, needed and even occasionally useful, then they wouldn't be described as a lethargic bunch of wasters who don't seem to be very good value for money at all. Still we don't want to dwell on the Royal family's lack of marketability or is that merchantability (I don't know) before an auction.

Sadly there were no bidders and I don't understand why, although maybe I shouldn't have put a reserve on my sale items. Anyway never mind the fact that I will be putting the Royal family back into stock, because I have just noticed that the bidding for a highly polished antique government opposition party is at long last beginning to attract some modest bids and there is still plenty of time before the auction ends and of course no reserve, so I can be thankful for small mercies, as 'they' say when 'they' are disappointed, but not desolate.

Still it is something of a surprise auction success because I had always been led to understand that the ordinary general public across the world had little or no interest in politics, I will have to have a ferret around and see what else I can auction on eBay. Well I suppose that there is an entire 'upper chamber,' The House of Lords.

The Lords wouldn't be missed by anyone would they? It doesn't seem to me that they do much and there are definite signs of Woodworm on an almost epidemic scale in some of the dowdy creatures that haunt the Lords chamber.

Even if they are completely useless you couldn't just throw them away could you, and so you never know there might just be a few buyers out there discerning enough to want to buy the Lords, or is that dumb enough, who cares?

It has just occurred to me that if I can get away with selling off some of the major British political institutions, maybe I can get people to part with hard cash for things that are really useful as well.

First I need to think of a list of things to sell and then I can go through it and weed out the things that even I think won't sell, because of a complete lack of appeal like say for instance the Welsh.

Well now I have finished my list of items for sale on eBay and it seems to have grown bigger than even I could have imagined. I was very careful to only list things that no one would really miss, well until it is too late anyway.

At the top of my list is the country, Great Britain, which is a great name don't you think and manages to hide the truth just like any great product name should because any real interest in Great Britain is going to be in England, that is where all of the money is after all, and so it will probably be more profitable to sell England separately from the rest of the Union, as they call the United Kingdom or Great Britain, and from the different titles it has you can see that someone has probably tried to sell it in the past!

Having said that, I should split the country of Great Britain I don't really want to be stuck with the other three countries which complete the set and so I will have to come up with some sort of gimmick to move them, 'buy part of Great Britain and get one bonus country free' I suppose would work, although who in their right mind would want Northern Ireland, hang on though I know, the other Irish population, no not the New York Irish the Eire Irish, they won't be able to afford a big price tag, but just think I will have solved a major political crises and pocketed a few grand too.

Mmmh! I wonder if I will get a Nobel Prize and offered a job at the United Nations? Probably!

So that leaves Scotland and Wales and as I said they are going to be difficult to sell, even empty, it is a shame that we can't move the Welsh and Scottish to Ireland before we sell it, but that has been done before and it didn't work then. I suppose that we will have to make them 'lost leaders.'

I'll use the slogan 'buy England and get a bonus country and very special secret bonus,' and then only tell the poor devil what they have bought after the check has cleared!

So that is the land, but I think I should sell the major towns and cities separately, that way I can flog the more interesting cities as boxed sets.

London would attract a good price if we can clean it up and get rid of some of the congestion on the roads, and to make a positive start there we will have to get rid of the Mayor, but I don't think I will worry too much about the fine detail at this stage or I won't ever be able to start listing all of the details on eBay.

Right, time to stop typing the Diary for a moment and go onto the internet, you will excuse me as I go off and make some real dough won't you!

DAY 256 OF MY CAPTIVITY:

The problem with eBay apart from all of the crooks who use it, is the time it takes to sell anything, and for an impatient Cat that is something of a nightmare, still I suppose that I can spare a few hours keeping an eye on the bidding, and to pass the time I could do a bit of casual daydreaming about what I am going to buy with all of the money from my neat little scam.

Today I waited and watched the screen with the avariciousness of a city trader watching the millions mount up as most of the world goes hungry.

All day the bids grew in size, this was like having a Birthday early, if indeed I knew when my birthday was, still never mind about that now I am just going to use the calculator and pat myself on the back for having had such a brilliant idea and being as the marketers say 'first in the field.'

At this rate I might need someone to help me do a little financial engineering and creative accounting, if you know what I mean. Now who is above suspicion and could help with that. How about the Secretary General of the United Nations, I know he is no longer above suspicion but I bet he could help tidy up the columns of figures and brush some of the minor financial irregularities under the carpet or if he can't get too involved directly I am sure his relations can.

DAY 257 OF MY CAPTIVITY:

Well today has been a bit of a shock, I logged onto eBay to discover that I couldn't log on and instead I was redirected to a page which basically informed me that I was undertaking a fraudulent sale, me? I ask you, would I do something like that? Um! You don't have to anwser that question.

What a good job that I took the precaution of entering false contact details or we would have had Mr. Plod with his blue flashing lights all over this place like a rash.

So the money making scheme has come crashing around my ears like a, well like a… well, you know like a noisy thing that comes crashing down around your ears of course, really do I have to spell it out for you all the time?

No I am sorry it isn't your fault that the neat little scheme failed, and I am sorry to snap at you, you are only minding your own business and reading this Diary, let's face it even the biggest scams fail eventually, like a certain UN Oil for Food programme, need I say more, the shame of that is that the people involved are so rich and so powerful that they won't see the inside of a prison, unlike some of us.

Anyway none of that matters now, something is going on here, something strange, this morning bright and early the Male Captor went out into the garden and dug up a Fir tree, popped it into a pot, and then brought it in doors and put in the corner of the front room. Very odd behaviour even for him wouldn't you say?

The oddness didn't stop there though, because the Female Captor, wait for this you won't believe it, wrapped the pot that the Fir tree was standing in covering it in bright red metallic paper, very eccentric, when the pot was a perfectly nice red colour in the first place, and in my opinion was ok as it was, if that is, you have to have a potted Fir tree in the front room.

Still the bizarre behaviour didn't stop there though, and all morning the mad pair have been hanging shiny decorations first over the Fir tree and then all over the place, draping them across entire rooms.

You know I have to say that the Fir tree is rather tempting and I am sure that I will have a go at climbing it later, there is a small space round the back that isn't covered in Tinsel and decorations so I can go in there, the North Face, then climb up to a base camp about half way up and have a rest because from there to the summit it is very steep and will have to be climbed in one session.

No I don't think I will need Oxygen and as usual I don't have a support team not even one toothless grinning Sherpa, but I don't need any of that, I just have to pray that the Fir tree doesn't topple over when I am at the top, but it looks like it is a pretty strong Fir tree, and that is good enough for me!

I laughed like a drain when the Male Captor then, under the instruction and guidance of the Female Captor sprayed the windows with some white fluffy spray, which eventually looked as though snow had laid up against the window panes. The effect was quite good, though possibly more than a little eccentric, but of course it was spoilt by the obvious nature of all Humans, when they added enormous stencilled snowflakes above the snowdrifts, Humans are like that, no sense of scale or style they just can't keep things in proportion.

The pair of Humans are also managing to be even more annoying than usual and keep humming some old tunes and smiling at each other, most off putting.

To crown the madness that has seized the pair, they have erected a peculiar wooden structure with an assortment of carved wooden people dotted around it and in the centre there is a couple of mini Human statues gazing down lovingly at a baby in a very shoddily made crib, while what I can only describe as an angel (the clue was the golden wings that have been glued on to his back) interferes with the proud Mum and Dad by swaying between them and kicking them on the head with his bare feet.

Weird and wonderful that is what it is, still at least everyone is in a good mood, well everyone except me that is, I was happy enough earlier and even joined in a little when the Humans grabbed the Dog and threaded what they called 'Tinsel' around his collar, and gazed at him with odd approval, as the idiot just stood there looking at them, with those, 'if I don't rip this off will I get a chocolate drop eyes.'

As I said that was mildly amusing, the Dog looks like two complete idiots, which of course is a look twice as dumb as his normal one, but as every so often he is slipped another chocolate drop he doesn't seem to mind and the Tinsel is still in one piece around his neck.

But after the fun and games accompanied by singing the day began to cloud over, they called me and I decided to see what they wanted me for after a little wait, just to demonstrate that I don't come running when called obviously, actually I thought that there might be a chocolate drop or two going spare, but oh no, no such luck for a much maligned Cat.

They grabbed me as soon as I was within arms length and began wrapping more Tinsel, a strange pink colour I might add, around my collar and when they had finished they giggled like a pair of kids and seemed very pleased with their handiwork.

Well I erupted, I shook my head and I backed away from the manacle of pink Tinsel, I tried to bite it, I bit the Dog, I scratched the Male Captor, but I didn't manage to get rid of the awful humiliating pink Tinsel noose and had to just give up, exhausted.

All the time the Humans watched and after I had calmed down they patted me on the head and cleared up the little strands of Tinsel I had managed to pull out of the dreadful neck ornament.

No chocolate drops came my way, so I bit the silver tinselled neck of the Dog and went off for a sulk and a sleep. All I can tell you now as I am writing this Diary in the dark, is that I am plotting my revenge for making me look like some sort of gay furry Christmas fairy, they will pay for that and pay dearly!

Day 258 of My Captivity:

I stayed out of the way today, there were all sorts of comings and goings, people, delivery vans and worst of all visitors, in fact I was going to stay hidden all day and all night, mainly because of the visitors and this dreadful and now very wet pink Tinsel collar thing. Yes I have been trying to chew my way out of it, but I have discovered that Tinsel is deceptively strong stuff!

As it began to get dark I had to get up because the outside suddenly lit up, trees seemed to be glowing, an odd light radiated from the front of the house, it was as if the house was on fire and it had set most of the garden alight.

I got a shock when I looked out of the window too, in the garden were strange shimmering and shining shapes, one was what at one time might have been a Human, but now was very white and had a large black hat on his head.

In the other corner of the garden was an entire herd of lustrous Reindeer looking slightly menacing, which if you know what Reindeer look like is an achievement.

Out of the ethereal glow from the house appeared the Male Captor with what can only be described as a mob of Humans, although some might also call them a family, and together they were guided by the Male Captor around the garden to look at the odd illuminated figures.

When the family mob got up to the gate they were all instructed to turn around and look at the roof of the house I think, judging by the hand signals from the Male Captor, obviously something very disturbing was on the roof, because they all appeared to be overcome by the sight.

I ducked back down out of the window just in case it was actually me that they were looking at and were shocked at the pink Tinsel collar shimmering in the garden illuminations. I jumped down from the window sill and decided to hide again and went to sleep, so long as the house wasn't on fire and that didn't seem to be the case, I thought I would stay away from all of the Humans tonight and whatever madness had gripped them!

Day 259 of My Captivity:

It apparently is Christmas Day. The Male Captor got power tools, (now they might come in handy if this plan fails) and the Female Captor got a new car (shame I can't drive). I got a toy mouse that someone had dipped in catnip, it smells like a teenager on a first date, I have to say I don't like it, but somehow I am strangely drawn to it.

There seem to be literally hundreds of Humans here at the moment, some are in the front room watching Christmas Morning Television, which is a new low in the annals of broadcasting history, there is some idiot in a dreadful jumper with a 'wonderful' sense of humour and equally 'wonderful' sense of his own importance scuffing around a hospital reminding people that they are not at home for Christmas, as if they didn't know or something!

There is a big team of people in the kitchen bumping into each other with hot saucepans and generally getting on each other's nerves, and finally everywhere there is a posse of loud children, who it seems took several seconds to open their Christmas presents, break them and then move on to taking the house apart.

Of course the Dog is in his element with all of the little hooligans and is running around with them and after them at full steam barking and adding to the mayhem by knocking over the heavier objects that the children couldn't manage on their own!

Is it me, or do people change on Christmas Day? Everyone seems to be nicer and more ready to have fun, things that would normally make people angry seem to just wash over them, I wonder why?

Maybe it is the fact that the house is festooned with decorations, or maybe it is the fact that the recycling sack is already filled with a number of empty bottles of giggle juice, whatever is making the Humans so happy it is something of a mystery to me!

The smell from the kitchen is alluring and I am dying to know and taste what is being cooked up for the massive assembly who will sit down in the dinning room at the newly repolished antique Mahogany table.

I slipped into the deserted dinning room earlier to see if any food had been put out already, and was astonished that the table was brimming with the best china, cutlery, serving dishes, and a massive centre piece that looked like a log from the fire with several candles glued to and covered in bright red berried Holly, what a bizarre thing to have on the table, no forget that statement, what a bizarre thing to have in the house anywhere, Humans are weird.

The Holly, candle log thing looked to me like a fire hazard waiting to happen, but it is just one of the many confusing things that abounds today.

I had to jump down from the table, where I had been snooping, and make a hurried exit when one of the 'helpers' from the kitchen came in with a large tray of what Humans call 'starters,' which in fact were little Salmon Mousse parcels wrapped in slithers of Smoked Salmon and tied with strands of Chives, now I can take or leave Chives but I was looking forward to getting my Paws on my parcel, surely today of all days (an expression I have heard a lot today), I will get given a Salmon parcel, won't I?

Unfortunately I was spotted, and after the little parcels were lovingly placed on the sparkling plates next to long bulging cheerful Christmas Crackers, I was picked up and carried out of the dining room and the door was close pointedly behind me, which was disappointing, I was sure that I could have accounted for quite a large number of parcels before the 'guests' were even invited to sit down at the table and that way I wouldn't have had to rely on the inconsistent generosity of Humans, still I was pretty sure that there would be a parcel for me somewhere today.

Quite unexpectedly the 'helper' who I didn't recognise, but I think was probably Big Auntie Susan, well if it was Big Auntie Susan, her weight problem is glandular so I have heard, anyway she opened the front door and deposited me on the door step, patted me on the head and closed the door.

I was staggered sitting on the front door step in the bright sunlight thinking I am free, I have escaped, I don't believe it, on the other side of the front door in the dining room someone is about to eat my Smoked Salmon parcel.

Then it hit me, Big Auntie Susan had a plan, with me out of the way she was going to eat my Smoked Salmon parcel, the heartless, well the last word rhymes with 'itch.' Right I wasn't having that, this was Christmas day and I was determined that I was going to get my Smoked Salmon parcel, no one gets one over on me like that.

I nipped down the front steps of the house and through the flowerbed then I jumped up onto the dining room window ledge and stared pointedly through the window.

People of all sorts of shapes and sizes (though none as big as Big Auntie Susan I have to say), were thronging the dining room, trying to sort out where they were to sit, the children were trying to ignore the adults, and being told off for pulling the hefty Christmas Crackers and arguing over the little expensive presents that had tumbled out when the Christmas Crackers had snapped.

Then the Female Captor waltzed into the dining room smiling, until our eyes met and I heard her shout that the Cat was out!

I had forgotten that I was on the right side (in my opinion) of the window and so I thought quickly, did I want a bigger taste of freedom or did I want more than a mouthful of Smoked Salmon parcel?

It was the delay and indecision that caught me out and as I turned my back on the Smoked Salmon parcels forever I jumped right into the hands of Big Auntie Susan's husband, thin Uncle Dick, (Dick by name and Dick by nature, was how the children described him behind his back and he was being a 'dick' again), I'll give him this, he was good at catching!

Unceremoniously I was carried into the house, bypassing the dining room, where, I was sure, my Smoked Salmon parcel was waiting for me, and straight into the kitchen, dropped on the floor and left there to find my Salmon Mousse filled Smoked Salmon parcel as the kitchen door was closed, none too gently behind me!

So now I was alone, everyone else was enjoying an enormous Christmas Lunch and I was in the kitchen, and although the smell of delicious food haunted the kitchen there wasn't so much as a scrap of Smoked Salmon Moose left in the Cat's bowl, let alone a delicately wrapped parcel!

No doubt I will get cold leftovers again, I am surprised they didn't have done with it and just call me Oliver!

Well they can stick Christmas where the sun doesn't shine as far as I am concerned, sometimes I surprise myself with my command of the English language, but never at the cruelty of Human beings.

Day 260 of My Captivity:

I want to know whose idea it was to get me a Cat coat for Christmas? Of course they didn't get round to giving it to me until today, the day after Christmas Day, but that is just typical of what Humans are like, they were too busy

As everyone in the house found somewhere to nod off in front of the television, or secretly drink more giggle juice like Grandma after another enormous Boxing Day lunch that would have kept most of the population of one of the medium sized starving African countries fed for a few weeks, if they had stopped their civil war for long enough to catch a bite. I was 'found,' picked up and taken up into their bedroom!

I had no idea what I had done wrong, I hadn't stolen any Smoked Salmon parcels, not for the wont of trying I might add, I had searched the kitchen high and low and not even found a scrap of a Smoked Salmon parcel or the delicate pink Mousse that legend has it was contained inside them!

Still I decided that I wasn't in hot water because I was placed on the bed cover, which is always unusual and confusing because I am not normally allowed in the bedroom let alone on the bed, now of course you know that I pay no attention to that rule, but the Humans don't know that.

When the two Captors had settled next to me on the big comfy bed, I was astonished to be sitting uneasily in between them, maybe I was in trouble after all, this had the feel of an inquisition and with every minute that passed I expected specially adapted thumbscrews to appear, but you could have knocked me over with a multicoloured Parrot feather, when something 'nice' happened, well the Captors must have thought they were being nice!

First they placed a gaudily wrapped parcel in front of me and unwrapped it for me, the disappointing result being one Cat coat, and after that they produced several other presents, one wasn't wrapped, it was on a plate and was carefully placed on top of the used wrapping paper, it was a Smoked Salmon parcel, now we were talking, Christmas at last, mmmh!

Day 261 of My Captivity:

The goggles are so tight they are making my eyes bulge, but I have managed to light the blowtorch and now I can set about cutting my way out of this dungeon.

Yes I know it isn't a dungeon, it is in fact a living room, don't you appreciate drama?

The fool of a Dog is fast asleep in front of the log fire, the Christmas lights are twinkling on the Fir tree and reflected on a few unclaimed and unopened presents, suggesting that even though the visitors have gone there maybe more arriving.

More visitors, that is like one threat to many and I have to get out of here, I can't stand the idea of more children oohing and ahing at my Cat coat and worse being inspired by the Cat coat to find more things to 'dress' me in!

Still I can just about handle the blowtorch, it is a little heavy but I don't think I will have to hold it long once we get going and so here goes!

Wow the flame blows back rather fiercely and very feels very hot, it is a good job that I have the goggles on and I suppose the Cat coat is helping to deflect the heat; even so it is very hot in the corner behind the Fir tree.

Well the paint on the wall has melted and now let's see just how strong plaster and brick is, I just wish that the flame wouldn't blow back quite so strongly, it is heating up the handle of the blowtorch and that isn't very comfortable.

What is that noise? What is that wet nose? Just when you don't need help you get it, get off me, you idiot Dog. No please don't nibble my neck, you fool this handle is hot, and haven't you heard about the dangers of fire?

All I did was to turn round to shoo the manic mongrel away, that is all I swear!

How was I to know that the Dog was expecting a Cat to turn around and not a glowing goggled fiend, no wonder the pedigree cretin took fright I suppose I would too if I had been looking in a mirror at that moment, but the only reflection I saw was in one of the bright Christmas baubles and that showed the behind of a frightened Dog running out of the front room.

Sadly I held the blowtorch in one place for just a moment or two too long, but the daft Dog had unnerved me too!

Don't Christmas Trees burn well! It must be all of the sap in the little pine needles, to say nothing of all of the flammable bits of Tinsel and Angel hair. I was sad; I would never get to climb the Christmas tree now as it was ablaze.

There are some consolations for having a house that seems to be constantly plagued by little disasters and more than its fair share of fires and that consolation appeared in the form of the Male Captor and one of the fire extinguishers, which are now dotted about his home.

Although the Christmas tree was a complete right off, the damage to the front room was happily minimal, and because both Captors were busily employed taking the charred remains of the Christmas tree out into the garden there weren't any recriminations for the fire raising 'culprit.' In fact later when, as I expected, a new crop of visitors arrived, the whole thing was passed off as a bit of a Christmas joke.

The blowtorch had been found by them and its presence blamed on one or other of the children who had been visiting previously, obviously one or other of them had been busy with something else rather than vomiting after consuming too much chocolate and other sweets.

Needless to say that I didn't therefore have to keep a low profile and snoozed on the Sofa breathing in only a hint of smoky air that lingered in the front room and to the uninformed might be blamed on the large roaring open fire.

Tonight at least there was peace on Earth to all Men and Cats.

Day 262 of My Captivity:

It is another of those slow days, which will I am sure add up to a slow week, sorry about that, it doesn't exactly make for interesting reading does it?

I decided to add the writing I have done today to the previous day because there wasn't anything of interest on the page above, but having done that I now feel uncomfortable about having a blank page in my Diary, yes I know it is probably a Cat thing, but there you go, I had to fill it with this.

Call me old fashioned, but I am not like other Diarists, say for instance Bridget Jones, who skipped not only a few pages in the Diary, but entire weeks on occasion, not that I am jealous of her initial success, and the subsequent second book and two films, oh no I am not envious at all, because I know that my audience won't let me down, and my Diary probably will become a better seller than any of the dreadful Jones's Diaries, you won't let me down will you! Will you?

Day 263 of My Captivity:

See above, and please accept this Cat's apologise, there just isn't much happening, which is worrying, because if there was something happening it would mean that I was beginning to enact an escape plan, but as a loyal reader you will just have to bare with me here, you know that something will come up and in the interlude you know that I will provide you with some of my interesting observations of life in general!

Day 264 of My Captivity:

The National Accident Helpline, mmmh the first time I heard that advertised on daytime television, yes I know I am sad, I am watching a lot of television again though because being cooped up in here all day would drive you insane unless you have some light relief and frankly daytime television is very light relief.

The first time I heard the advert for The National Accident Helpline I wasn't really listening, daytime television does that to you, you end up after twenty minutes of watching glazing over, first your eyes go glassy and then your mind starts to do an impression of a Tropical Fish tank and life just begins to flow over you as though you are there, but not there.

Strangely enough you do hear and see things though and what I was seeing and hearing for the first time was the advert for The National Accident Helpline, but in my confused state I thought that it was a sort of national company, which helped you to have an accident.

Of course when I realised the truth I found out that I was right, here is a company, which helps the clumsy and plain stupid to make financial claims against others when they fall over or hurt themselves because they were not looking, where they were going. And better still these idiots who have accidents then get paid for the privilege minus the costs incurred by the aforementioned helpline obviously.

Seems like a way that even an idiot could make money doesn't it, using this service, mmmh wish I was an idiot and a Human, no I won't say what you are thinking, 'same thing really,' now look at that you made me say it anyway!

All one has to do is just fall over if you aren't looking where you are going or trip up in the street and claim against the people whatever you tripped over and are heavily insured and bang, you get a check as extorted by the helpful helpline.

It wasn't only the immorality of the hidden meaning of the advert that offended this occasionally honest and upright Cat, it was also the whiney people who offered 'case histories,' they were as awful as the advert itself.

One woman said something along the lines of this; I was walking along the street and I fell over on a wet, wobbly paving slab, I broke my wrist, The National Accident helpline handled my claim after I had contacted them on the free phone number and I got a cheque for several thousands, yeah right, maybe you should look where you are going and avoid wet wobbly paving stones Mrs.!

Not only is what she said a very short version of what must have happened it doesn't seem to ring true does it? Surely even an idiot would take more care when walking on a wet pavement and keep an eye on where they were going if the pavement looked even a little wobbly.

Not only that, there was no mention of the court battle that must have followed any claim, I can't imagine that anyone who is responsible and can therefore be claimed against would just agree to pay clumsy people large sums of money for being clumsy, would you?

DAY 265 OF MY CAPTIVITY:

Hang on, don't look now, no, I said don't look now! Is that what I think it is? Over there, no, not down, over there, up over there, yes all the way up there. It is isn't it? You're right, it is exactly what I need isn't it! This is brilliant, and you can tell, I am excited.

It is a little high up, no let me rephrase that, it is very high up, but I think I can climb up there, not you are right it won't be easy, in fact you are right again, it will be difficult, but I don't agree with you that it is impossible, it has to be done, and it has to be done this instant!

I am sorry I got carried away! What am I talking about? Yes you have a right to ask! Well it is the small window in the bathroom and it is open, just waiting for a Cat of similar size to climb through and be free, fancy that, how very convenient!

The little window is only open a little way, but I am pretty sure that I can get through it and we all know what is on the outside don't we! Freedom and it is waiting patiently outside just for me!

Actually I am not at all sure what is actually immediately outside, but there will probably be a window ledge or even a bit of roof, better still there might just be a ladder, but one could say that is wishful thinking, still as an optimist I am used to a bit of wishful thinking.

Now if I jump onto the back of the toilet I think it is called a cistern, and then make a scrabbling leap I am sure that I can end up or should that be 'land' on the window frame.

Well that bit wasn't difficult although I do wish Humans would put the lid down on the toilet and not just the seat, when they have finished using their watery Cat litter machine.

Mmmh this toilet cistern lid thing is cold on the paws. Ok here goes, one big leap to freedom and then we are well, free!

It was a lot higher than I thought, but happily not too high a jump for an agile Cat with a spring in its step.

Balancing on the window frame was a little more challenging than I had expected though, but if a Cat can't keep its balance then who can?

I managed to get and keep my balance, with a little paw shuffling and by readjusting my balance once I had got it I was surprisingly comfortable.

Things started to change though when I was just about to climb out of the toilet window and I don't really know what happened, my paw may have slipped, the glass was slippery and the window frame was narrow I remember that, worse than the fact that my paw may have slipped was the other fact, my confidence was shaken just a little when I looked out of the window at the dizzying drop on the other side.

As views go it was rather impressive, the back garden in all of its wintry floral glory, and of course the mad Woolly Brat of a Dog charging round and round the house like some sort of mad animal, being chased by a large pack of imaginary and equally mad animals.

The Canine crank must have caught sight of me out of the corner of his eye, because he skidded to a halt and looked first over his shoulder to make sure that his imaginary pack of followers had also stopped, then he looked up at me and began barking at me.

I tried to shut him up, this was a covert operation, didn't he understand that, and the last thing I needed was him to draw attention to my escape attempt, but when he starts barking there isn't much that can shut him up unless you have a treat or two and that was the last thing I had thought to pack, I have to admit.

There were one or two other problems on my mind as well as the shaggy alarm that was waking up the sleepy neighbourhood, the major problem being the sheer drop from the window that I was perched on, personally I think that in the light of that problem the other problems don't warrant mentioning.

Obviously I could go back, but at least at this moment in time my head was free and the rest of me wanted to follow its excellent example, but quite how? For the moment I wasn't sure exactly how I was going to achieve that.

When the Dog made a particularly loud bark, which was followed by a mouthful of grassy vomit I was so disgusted that I shuddered, lost my hold on the window frame and must have nudged the window bar, which jerked up and closed the window on me, I was wedged half way in the bathroom and half out.

If I had a choice at that moment I think I would have preferred to have had all of my body on the outside, but sadly I didn't have a choice in the matter and thinking about it, I was too high up just to wriggle and then dive out of the window, even if I could lure the Dog closer and drop on top of him.

Mind you in his current wild state if I had managed to lure him closer and used him to break my fall and then made a break for freedom I have a feeling that he would have chased after me leading his snarling, barking pack of imaginary wild animals.

There was nothing for it, I was going to have to go back, but that wasn't going to be easy, because I couldn't exactly see where I was going to land, although of course like you I had a pretty good idea, and I am sure you will agree the idea of dropping back and landing in the toilet bowl wasn't exactly enticing.

Sometimes life seems to laugh at those who live it, and this was one of those times obviously, I rehearsed my retreat time and again in my mind and each time all I could hear was the splash as I plunged into the toilet, and so I suppose I was resigned to the watery end to yet another escape attempt.

I presume because I was resigned to the drop and then the revolting splash, it wasn't so bad when I fell and hit the little pond inside the toilet, at least it broke my fall, and for your information the modern toilet is not that difficult to climb out of, if you ever want to try this at home!

In the time honoured tradition of story telling there is good news and bad news here, would you like the good news first? Well I didn't hurt myself, the bad news is I got very wet, but you know by now that my Diary is not just an ordinary story, oh no, and so as you would expect there is worse news to come and then there is the really terrible news following that.

The even worse news is that I fell into the water with such force that I went under and swallowed gallons and the really terrible news, I fell into the toilet, but you know that anyway!

That is all I want to say on the matter though, apart from the fact that as you know Cats use their tongues to wash and I never want to have to wash myself again!

Day 266 of My Captivity:

'I am sailing, I am sailing, over water, over sea, I am sailing tee tweedly tee, tee,' sorry I was singing and couldn't remember any more words, but what a song and what a singer, the singer is Rod Stewart and the song is 'Sailing,' there who said that a Cat doesn't know anything about popular music, I am a veritable mine field of information, or should that be mine, still never mind now.

'I am sailing, I am sailing, over water, over sea, I am sailing,' sorry singing yet again, you can't help it can you, it is just so catchy and I have to say, it is sung brilliantly, by the peroxided gravelled voiced old gentleman of rock.

Personally I can't understand why that nice elder statesman of rock isn't more popular these days with a voice like that! And the song, I am sailing, no I wasn't singing there are no quotation marks, please pay attention! Where was I oh yes the song, it is just wonderful and I think it should be re-released, I am sure that it would top the charts, mind you I suppose I should keep my opinions and preferences about songs and singing to myself, because we all know that a Cat is completely and outstandingly tone deaf, but never mind about that 'I am sailing, I am sailing, over water, over sea, I am sailing tee tweedly tee, tee.' It sort of carries you away and lets all of your worries stay behind doesn't it.

While we are on the subject of sailing, one thing puzzles me in particular about sailing, although a lot of things in general puzzle me about sailing, like why do it? It seems such a drag to rely on the wind and ocean currents when you can strap an enormous engine or five onto a boat and get where you want to go in no time at all, and not have to think about the wind, well not the wind and the weather sort of wind anyway.

There is one thing that has always intrigued me when I have seen sailors on television, they set out from land and in no time at all they are in the middle of vast oceans or is that in the middle of a vast ocean, because they presumable can only be in one ocean at a time, where everything is the colour of sea, looks like sea and basically is sea, where all they can see is sea, how do they know where they are going and how to get there? I have no idea at all, do you?

Day 267 of My Captivity:

Today is a Saturday, I may have mentioned them before, Saturdays that is, it is sadly one of two days of the week when Humans don't go out to work, although usually on most Saturdays Male and Female Humans go to shopping centres to have arguments and buy a range of useless fashion items and then usually fit in an hour or so of all important Cat food shopping.

Sorry, the information in most of the last paragraph is something that Humans would know all about, unless they have been living in a box, and as I heard a radio station playing a song called 'Living in a box' the other day I suppose Humans do live in them, but not around here.

No the notes about the habits of Humans on a Saturday are for any Cats, who might be reading the untranslated version of my Diary.

Anyway, today is Saturday, well it was a Saturday, because it is quite late in the evening now and I am writing this on my own in the study, why the study? Because it is where the computer is, and where all of the serious paperwork is all too rarely undertaken, and so the study is hardly ever used and therefore it is the quietest room in the house.

Still I know that some people would say that where I am actually writing this Diary is not really too important and I should get on with this Diary entry. Ok, well calm down and take another Valium and I will begin doing just that.

By the way: 'Calm down and take another Valium,' is a sentence that has now replaced the: 'Once upon a time,' beginning to most children's stories, on the assumption that it is easier to deal with hyperactive children if they are addicted to the tranquilisers that they will be taking in adult life.

Yes I noticed too, I have digressed, so I will immediately go back to my entry for today and the fact that it is Saturday!

On some Saturdays, if they can, and for reasons best known to themselves, Male Humans disappear into the front room, stretch out on the Sofa armed with Potato Chips and cans of frothy brown giggle juice with the television switched on.

After several cans of frothy brown giggle juice to warm up with and the television providing a series of odd and especially boring reports from a football stadium, from both 'ordinary' (which I think is a shorthand for 'brainless') fans, and then from celebrity ones (I have covered the definition of celebrity before and therefore I don't need to cover these nonentities a second time. In fact to give them a mention at all probably would encourage them and that is the last thing I would want to do), a football match begins.

So today the scene was set and as the Male Captor obviously had no intention of moving off my Sofa, it was apparent that we were going to watch 'the match,' which implies that we were about to witness some sort of exciting contest between worthy opponents, it is amazing just how wrong implications can be, isn't it!

Where does one start when talking about a football match, well I suppose I have started, I was sitting on the Sofa and being made to share it, and I was not best pleased, however the Male Human obviously viewed all of this nonsense 'as a clash titans,' yes someone actually said that in the match build up, in fact there were so many clichés used in the match build up and then later in the match commentary that my cliché monitor broke.

After what seems like several hours of in depth clichés and pointless reports the 'match' began, and we had ninety whole minutes to enjoy the 'spectacle;' I made a mental note to watch out for the 'spectacle' because so far after thirty minutes had slowly ticked by nothing spectacular had happen.

The game continued proceed to in much the same way with one side running up the pitch only to fail to kick the ball into the back of the other side's net and that would be followed by the opposition doing exactly the same, little breaks were made for leg breaking fouls and instantaneous miracles recoveries and I have to say an inordinate amount of spitting by the players on both sides.

There were things to break the boredom of this sad exhibition of the mundane, the commentators, who both had very squeaky voices, do you know the sort of voice I am talking about? They both had the sort of voices one imagines a train spotter to have, and the train spotter analogy doesn't just end with their voices, both of these men had Honours Degrees in drivel and PhD's in incomprehensible English Grammar.

Probably the most annoying thing about the commentators I noticed was that they seemed to be watching completely different football matches to each other, and also different football matches from the one that I was watching judging by their constant contradictions of each other and the strange fact that they kept getting very excited when the 'action' on the pitch was almost nonexistent.

In fact the inaction on the pitch made me think that all of the young men had been drinking giggle juice all night or were dreadfully despondent because they were anticipating a spell in prison for dangerous driving and I have heard since watching this 'clash of titans' that this may well have been the case for some of the 'athletes' on the pitch!

It is obvious to me that the main qualifications for a football commentator are to be able to recognise all of the players on the pitch and ignore all of the professional fouls which happen almost continuously, and to beat a drum that stirs up animosity between the opposing fans, while trying to impart as many odd and frankly irritating historical facts, concerning past encounters between the teams as they possibly can during the ninety minutes that the match drags on for.

Odd little facts like, the date of the last time that a loose Dog managed to get onto the pitch and widdle over the one of the team's goalposts, seemed to abound in the lulls between inactivity on the pitch and there were plenty of those!

All very odd, I have to say!

Worst of all were the blatant professional fouls and dreadful hammy playacting which offended my Cat's sense of honesty and fairplay, and by now you will have probably known that my standards of honesty and fairplay are probably not the highest standards in the world either, so this doesn't say much for theirs does it!

Every four or five minutes the game would be stopped because there was a lot of players kicking each other all over the field, although mainly in a place called 'the edge of the box' and if that is the same 'box' that they use in Cricket, it must be very painful to be kicked there, but still these hair gelled jessies kept doing it.

I was so bored that I fell asleep for a little while and awoke at halftime, which you would think would signal a welcome break from the astoundingly inept escapades of the idiots on the pitch and that is the case, but for this fifteen minute interval you, the viewer are then subjected to a panel of 'experts' and eloquent ex-footballers (no sorry I am lying, the two ex-footballers were fluent, but only in the same sort of cliché driven rubbish that was the 'stock in trade' of the commentators) and their opinions, which amount to a grand total of zero in the interesting stakes.

As the experts agreed with each other and droned on and on I almost lost the will to live, but happily by covering my ears and closing my eyes I was saved having to self harm myself just to make sure I was still alive and hadn't been sent to Hades.

When I looked up, the match had just trundled into the beginning of the second half. One commentator said something which I think is worth reporting here word of word, I am sorry about this, I don't like quoting other people in my Diary but when you read this drivel you will, I am sure, agree with me, it was worth including it just to hear what these highly paid idiots are actually saying.

'Manchester United have started the second half the way they had finished the first half.'

Does that mean that they were playing football in both halves, by any chance?

At one point during this titanic contest between the best English football teams I almost completely lost the will to live and I was so bored that I began counting the hairs on my right leg.

Imagine my despair when one of the commentators announced with relish that the rather useless teams would be playing an extra thirty minutes because neither side had managed to score, and if the score was still level after that, then we would be 'treated' (his word not mine) to a penalty shoot out, what unalloyed joy spread over me, no sorry it wasn't that, I have just noticed that I have been sitting in the taco dip!

You know I almost stopped writing today's diary page just then, but there is one thing that I forgot to mention, the outcome of the 'game' a term I use in the loosest sense of the word.

The result of one hundred and twenty minutes of football, was that neither side won, and they had to have the aforementioned penalty shoot out, and when one of the members of one of the teams missed, the other side won, I won't bother you with the name of the winning team because they don't deserved, to grace the pages of this Diary, yes they were that bad!

Still there is one thing that is worse than one terrible result in a football match, yes you have guessed it, a whole season of football matches, and they seriously expect the Americans to start watching English football, dream on, the Americans like to be entertained, still I have heard that the English fans get drunk before and after the matches and so how would they know just how bad English football is? They don't!

Day 268 of My Captivity:

I like Jam, but I try not to eat it often because I end up with jam everywhere and there is nothing worse than being in a jam! Have I written this before? Am I repeating myself, I don't know! And if I don't know, do you the reader know either? Can you remember if I have mentioned this before? Come to that have I asked if I am repeating myself before, I don't remember doing that either, but just because I don't remember it doesn't mean I haven't.

What is interesting is that if say 12 of you reading this Diary had listened to me saying what I have just written instead of writing it and then some time later none of us remembered whether I had said it or not, and then were to say in court that none of us could say beyond reasonable doubt that I had said anything about Jam before, then I would be innocent and the court would have to say that, because it couldn't be proved.

That little fact demonstrates just how powerful the written word is and goes to prove why I think that politicians invented the paper shredder and secretly hate microphones!

Day 269 of My Captivity:

I haven't been able until now, to let you into another big secret, and I am sorry for that and will make it up to you later when I come and sit on your lap and not dig my claws into your legs as you stroke me, no matter how much I enjoy it, I promise.

Look, I know I may have said some time ago that I wasn't going to keep anymore secrets from you, but this was a very important secret which I thought might be best kept from you, for your own safety!

Yes I may go in politics after I retire from writing, why, do you ask?

Back to the secret, well happily I think I can tell you now; I managed to get my paws on some plastic explosive, what a delight, it was so very simple really, the internet and a FedEx delivery and I am ready to get freed with a bang.

Sadly the bang won't be that big, because of the cost of shipping, really FedEx ought to look at their shipping costs, do you know it was almost as expensive to ship the 'plastic,' as the experts call it, as it was to actually buy the 'plastic,' with as it turns out more plastic, or as we know it, a credit card, the credit card is probably the best invention of the 20th century, especially if it is someone else's!

But enough of that, I know I have mentioned my little 'habit' for 'employing' other people's credit cards, all very wrong etc., yeah, yeah, but exciting all the same!

Plastic explosive is wonderful stuff, so much like chewing gum that I was almost tempted to chew some, after I had open my small shrink wrapped parcel, but I resisted the temptation because I had other plans for the two small sticks.

I took my parcel into the kitchen and carefully put it next the back door and then laid out the all of the bits and pieces, I carefully separated the detonators from the other things in the parcel, then I unravelled the wires and then tried to stop them ravelling back up.

When I bought the plastic explosive I chose the oddly named 'Executive Pack' of plastic explosive, which had been two hundred dollars extra, but came with a radio controlled detonation system, which had impressed me when I had been browsing the website, and it wasn't as though it had actually cost me two hundred dollars more was it?

In no time at all I got the hang of what I needed to do and didn't bother reading the instructions, I was in a hurry and too excited to be slowed down by details and I was sure I knew what to do.

The first thing to do was to sort out the detonator and the little black box that was the 'trigger,' it was quite impressive really and had a bright red firing button sticking out of it, which I couldn't wait to press.

Sorting everything out carefully took a lot of concentration but I didn't want to make a mistake although I suppose I should have been more observant and noticed that I had a 'helper' sniffing around behind me as usual.

It was too late when I noticed what the Dog was doing, and I have to say that it was only the slurpy chewing noise that made me look around. I couldn't believe my eyes. The reason for the chewing was that the complete and utter shaggy clown had eaten the plastic explosive! No I didn't believe it either! How could he do it, why did he always have to interfere?

The Dog stopped chewing when he realised that I was looking at him, and all he did was slurp a smile at me and then swallow, content in the knowledge I presume that he had finally beaten me to an unattended tasty morsel.

Obviously I was very tempted to press the red button and see if the plastic explosive detonated. Well I was annoyed, but I am not that evil, no really I am not all that bad, and anyway if I had detonated the Dog the mess would have probably covered me as well as the walls and ceiling, but in my view I did have just cause to press the little red button, surely anyone would be tempted after what the idiot had done, but I just cleared away all of the bits that the fool hadn't eaten and snuggled into his basket with him as he fidgeted with indigestion next to me.

I think it was then that I decided that in spite of everything I quite liked the Dog, think of it this way, if he had done what he did to anyone else I would have laughed, wouldn't you?

Day 270 of My Captivity:

I had a food scare earlier, but it is ok now, it was a close call though, and even though as I said it is ok now, it took ages to resolve.

Believe it or not when the Human Captors left this morning they forgot to put any food out for either the Dog or Me and that was terribly thoughtless.

We had no idea what we were going to do without food all day, I more or less decided to sit in the Dog's basket and go to sleep and hopefully get woken up with a plate of Prawns or something later in the day.

But the Dog took what I think they call 'direct' action, he decided that he was so hungry that he ate the plastic Electric Kettle, then the plastic bits on the Sandwich Toaster, followed by the ordinary Toaster, well only the wire of the ordinary Toaster because the Toaster itself is metal, then for dessert he chewed on the edges of the cupboard doors and along a little bookshelf, and I have to say some of the cookery books on the bookshelf too.

Trouble was he didn't seem very full up when he finished, but he had caused a terrible mess, but then it is the sort of thing that all animal rights activists do so it doesn't matter that much does it?

DAY 271 OF MY CAPTIVITY:

No one told me that the Dog had been sick, no one told me that the Dog had been sick over my little pile of rubbish, which contained a couple of detonators, no one even told me that plastic explosive is so waterproof that it works even after it has been somewhere as disgusting as the inside of the aforementioned shaggy idiot.

I did know that when Dogs are sick they tend to back away from what they, how can I put this delicately? Produce, yes that will do nicely, and that every time Dogs are sick they back even further away from the previous 'production.' In fact I even, if I didn't know that little gem of a fact, I would have been able to learn it pretty quickly because the Dog had almost finished vomiting a long straight line of 'stuff' as he backed out of the kitchen door and started creating a slime trail across the hallway.

But to be honest what the Dog was doing hardly seems important now, although his actions did set in motion a series of reactions that I guess proves the chaos theory, a theory which if not devised to explain the actions of a Dog with wits so dim, that they have almost been turned off then can be easily adapted to describe his daily life.

So the Dog was sick, nothing special in that I hear you say apart from a bit of revulsion and some squeamishness in the description, which I have tried to limit, yes I do love my readers, at last you believe me! But what is so special about the Dogs technicolour yawn it happens almost everyday. Well today was different, so different that it was painful.

A couple of days ago you will remember that the hungry Hound had wolfed my little pack of plastic explosive, ok I was annoyed, who wouldn't be, it was a disaster on the scale of the Titanic as far as I was concerned, the only difference being that none of us got wet and that was probably because today the Dog had kindly today go out of his basket to flood the floor.

After eating the plastic explosive and spoiling my escape plan you may recall that I graciously forgave the Dog and resigned to spending more days here behind bars, I got into the Dog's basket with him and had a snooze, what I forgot to do was to tidy up after my disappointment and that oversight had meant that I had left a few bits and bobs of rubbish on the kitchen floor, still never mind I would have said to myself when I remembered the next day and tidied them away then or indeed more likely hid them somewhere.

But I didn't remember the next day, because as you will also recall we had a food scare and some missing Humans, who were late back last night, did an amount of tidying and swearing at the mess, this time none of which was caused by yours truly and I have to say that I felt quite pleased about that, some might even say smug, but before I get into too much self criticism I will go back to the point.

My little pile of rubbish and obviously the target for the Dog's first mouthful of vomit had again been missed in the rapid clear up last night and had even gone unnoticed this morning while we all had a rather leisurely breakfast, before the Humans went off to work.

Personally I imagine that my little pile of rubbish, which was very small and I hasten to add all neatly secured in a plastic bag, which I presume had those holes which help babies and other animals breath when they wear the plastic bags on their heads, so it wasn't as though it was a large pile of rubbish or even an untidy one, but it was obviously a little porous and indeed porous enough to allow some liquid plastic explosive to slosh over the detonators.

The detonation process was obviously slow because of the strange nature of the explosive, not many are liquid I believe except Nitro, but I digress and this is a long enough Diary entry already without going off too far at a tangent to the story.

Cutting back to the chase or in this case the very loud and painful bang, which blew me from the middle of the Dog's basket to the middle of the kitchen floor via a hefty whack on the head from the ceiling and near strangulation from the light fitting I landed on all fours, dazed, deafened, dazzled and frightened, sorry I couldn't think of another word beginning with 'd.' Well there is 'dead' but I was only nearly dead so that would be accurate.

When the smoke had stopped swirling and the dust had settled I began to count, legs? Four, good! Eyes? Two, thank goodness! Ears? Two, handy! Fur? Well too many strands to count individually but general coverage? Excellent! Everything seemed to be in order, everything that is, except my sense of awe and wonder.

How did I survive that? I have no idea! Is the all too terrifyingly honest answer, in truth after, being at 'ground zero' of an explosion of that ferocity, I most definitely should be a post Pussy, or just so much dust and mist settling onto the place where the floor used to be.

Mmmh! The day is full of alarming surprises, I looked down at where the dust that should have been me would have settled and guess what? The floor wasn't there at all; I was standing on a metal beam used as part of the foundations or something, but who cares about that?

Under the beam it was dark. You know the sort of darkness, which definitely has no end. The type of darkness that if you fall into it, you tumble endlessly as an ever decreasing scream. It was the sort of darkness that easily swallows entire planets and never even chews them.

Well I was feeling wobbly and looking down wasn't doing anything for my balance, but I was determined to continue being saved.

I knew that there had to be a reason why I was saved, and not only that it was fine by me, but I was going to take full advantage of the reason and do something very important something really good and charitable for either Man or Feline kind.

Now what could I do for Humanity, something which is worthy and very important, I need to find something that will truly benefit Mankind and be not only uplifting, but also add knowledge?

Yes, I know what I can do for Mankind! I will write another book, but this time not a Diary, I will commend my thoughts to the pages of a Journal, yes what a jolly good idea! A Journal is not that far away from a Diary so I won't have to do any research or any real hard work. Or maybe my memoirs, well I have plenty of time to decide which, don't I!

Better still I have noticed that Humans like to buy things that are similar to other successful things, Disney makes oodles of money bring out more and more films with the same titles, but a larger number tagged on the end, which (unless they pick up the film option of my Diary) is pretty cynical and disgustingly uncreative, (mind you if they do pick up the film option for my Diary, then do watch out for the Diary series 2 through to 5 after the first series of course).

Still back to the beam and a feeling of wobbliness, which was getting worse somewhere down in my stomach and creating tingling, furball like feelings in my throat, I was, I knew, going to be as sick if not sicker than a Dog, strange expression that, but so true, I had to get off the beam before all of the heaving and rocking began, burp! Oops pardon me!

Edging back to safety from the middle and I have to ask why is it that I always find myself in the middle of dangerous places and situations? Anyway edging back from the middle of the beam to solid if not rubble strewn ground I was struck by the feeling that I was really going to puke, I felt sicker than a Dog, maybe as sick as a Hamster, not that is not the same as feeling as sick as a Dog, it is the result of eating a Hamster, dreadful tasting little things they are too, oh no, Burp, pardon me.

Look I am afraid that I am just going to have to stop writing for a little while and deal with this discomfort, it is not nice and I am sure that it is awful to read about and like copying people who you see, Urp! (Sorry) yawning, you might be feeling a little, Ugh! No please not the bits of Carrot too, sick as well!

What do you mean is the Dog ok? Really that takes the biscuit! Yes he is ok thank you and was as usual about as much help as a spoon.

DAY 272 OF MY CAPTIVITY:

Desperate times require desperate measures, and that is so true, and I need to escape from this prison desperately and am prepared to go to any measures to get out no matter how desperate they maybe!

First off I am going to ignore the extensive renovations going on in the kitchen, well why shouldn't I, everybody else seems to have ignored them and concentrate on getting out before the take away food cartons and dirty washing takes over the house, yes life is difficult without a you know what, no you know what, look I said I wasn't going to mention the kitchen, there now look what you made me do!

Changing the subject and to be honest I think that on occasions recently I have started to get 'comfortable' and even briefly 'contented' and that will never do if I am serious about escaping!

If I get settled here I will be a prisoner forever and even our slowest readers must have gathered that is definitely not part of my master plan, which if my slower readers need to be reminded is to be free and rich, or alternatively rich and free, I am not fussy about the order!

Bearing all of that in mind I will say that playing dead is not easy, and it is made even more difficult by the idiots (or Humans you can choose the description you prefer), who surround me and hamper every escape attempt.

So from the last few paragraphs you will understand that I am becoming more and more desperate to get out of here, and this last plan was it has to be said, desperate and not a little risky, but Cats are used to risk, just look at the way they cross roads, though desperation is usually a stranger to Felines.

The plan, like all of the better quality plans, was deadly simple, sorry about the pun! But because the plan was simple I was convinced that I was, at long last, going to be granted my wish, however just like 'the results of blowing out the candles on a Birthday cake, wishes rarely come true, and plans, well we all know about plans, especially this Cat's plans, sadly.

It was early, but the day was, a bright and sunny and so I decided to 'die' in a patch of dappled sunlight which was playing and shimmering on the Sofa seat cushion, well in my opinion if you are going to 'pop your clogs' then you may as well do it in comfort to say nothing of style!

The noise of the workmen putting a new floor down in the kitchen and shoring up the walls only marginally spoilt the tranquil and poignant affect that I was after, damn I mention the kitchen didn't I, too late now.

As luck would have it and just as I took my 'last' breath the radio started to play some of that very old sad church music sung by young choir boys, who may have had the same operation as the one that I had, but the less said about that the better, except that it all added to the ambience of my passing and my sense of theatre.

The type of music that was playing by the way for the uneducated amongst you and I imagine that is most of my dear readers, is called 'Sacred Music' and it really gets the tear ducts working overtime, happily.

I sighed (which I thought was a nice touch) and then gave a little shudder, to see if anyone had noticed my last breath!

Well I am pleased to say that I was noticed eventually, I am very disappointed to tell you that I had to lay very still, hardly taking a breath for over ten minutes before anyone actually noticed that I had slipped away to the 'land of milk and honey.' Hopefully there will be a gallon or two of cream to go with the milk and honey, in the 'land of milk and honey,' but that is just a side issue!

When I was noticed there was a shriek of despair from of all people the Male Captor, which may, I have to say, have initially been more to do with shock than sorrow, because he almost sat on me, I mean, I ask you, here I am dead and a great big bottom was about to crush me, not the decorum I had anticipated, but of course it almost goes without saying that worse was to come! Having said that I am by now though totally resigned to the indignity of my life, and I have come to terms with my luck and never expect to be treated half decently by Humans, even in death!

The Female Captor was a little kinder and rather flustered, which might have been actually real grieve at the loss of such a good looking lap warmer and companion, but for all I know the tears in her eyes might have come from the Male Captor standing on her toe as he stood transfixed and wide eyed pointing at my lifeless body.

I was still warm, but they put that down to the patch of sunlight I was resting in, and rather convincingly I had made myself stiff, which I had heard was what they called dead people on television and so I thought it would be a good idea to go rigid and actually 'be' a stiff, 'stiff!'

Neither Human wanted to touch me, but the Male Captor poked me in the stomach which I thought was unkind and after this brief medical examination, pronounced that I was dead, while moving cowardly away from my poor earthly remains, as though he might catch something from me.

So much for Human compassion, I thought, but I knew that they weren't finished yet and consequently I was waiting for the next indignity that they would heap on me even in death.

Then believe it or not, he just disappeared, saying that he was going to get the car because they were, (now wait for this, because I hope that you are like me and can't believe he really said this) late, I was feeling so sorry that I had inconvenienced him!

The Female Captor sniffed, but I think it was a sniff of disgust at what he had said rather than any out pouring of sorrow at my demise, and barked after him, 'ok I'll deal with this then!' It was good to hear that her sarcasm hadn't been diminished by grieve, but then again neither had mine!

While the Female Captor was out of the room rummaging somewhere in the hallway, I took a few delightfully restoring deep breaths, and moved my aching legs, and decided that this dying business was a lot harder work than I had imagined!

I gently placed my head back down on the seat cushion and because there was no time for even a quick wash I pushed my head along the fabric to make sure that all of my fur was in place and to ensure that I looked my best, even in Death.

After a lot of rummaging, some crashing cupboard interior noises and the slamming the hall cupboard door she came back accompanied by the rustling of a large roll of redundant Christmas wrapping paper, which had become unravelled.

I sneaked another look because I couldn't believe what I had seen through my almost closed eyes, and yes it was Christmas wrapping paper! In her other hand she was carrying a shoebox and a ball of string!

I know that the workings of the Human mind has always confused me, but I couldn't for the life of me fathom out what she was up to!

The shoebox, well that could be an improvised coffin, and fair do's it was a reasonable idea, although I imagined that I might get wrapped in a towel or a blanket, but the redundant Christmas wrapping paper and string confused me and I began to get a little worried, still the prospect of escape from all of the loonies here made me keep quiet and very still, just like a dead Cat should be.

Very gently I was lifted into the shoebox and carefully arranged to fit in the small space, which was not uncomfortable I have to say because I am used to sleeping curled up.

It went dark when the lid of the shoebox was placed on top but I was pleased to see a little shaft of sunlight piercing the lid and illuminating the tip of my tail, so I was going to be able to breath and although that probably isn't too important for a dead Cat it was really very important to me!

Just when I thought that I could relax and wait until it had gone quiet and hopefully I had been left outside, the box began to shake and wobble as the Female Captor shook it first end to end and then from side to side.

The small hole in the lid went dark and I got a little worried and took a few deep breaths but happily I didn't run out of air, then she started shaking the box again and it dawned on me as I was sliding first to one end of the box then the next, and then from side to side, just what she was doing.

It worried me that she had obviously wrapped the shoebox in the Christmas wrapping paper and then tied the string round it. I had become the filling of some sort of obscene Christmas present; this was not a good sign at all! I heard a muffled shout and the car's engine revving, the Male Captor was getting impatient!

Suddenly I experienced the sensation of flying and as I sailed through the air I heard the Female Captor shout a reply, that she was going to put the Cat in the dining room and then she would be ready.

My short flight ended and I assumed that I was in the dining room, which was not exactly the place I had wanted to end up, all I could hope for was that the Dog had been left in the garden or I had been left on a table out of his way.

Isn't it funny that no matter how hard one hopes for something or how much one eventually desperately prays for something, it never happens!

I could tell that the Dog was not outside or judging by where the sniffing noise was coming from that I had been left on the table, I was on the dining room floor, with a nosy Dog sniffing my little parcel. I thought I would start thinking of the wrapped shoebox as a parcel in the hope that it didn't become a coffin because nothing else had gone right so far and I didn't want to tempt fate any more than I had to from now on.

It didn't take long for the Dog to lose interest in the odd looking parcel, confirming my believe that the size of a brain is directly related to the size of one's attention span and the Dog's attention span was happily very short!

Soon after quiet descended on the dining room and I heard the sound of the Dog getting back in his basket, the Captors had obviously thought about his comfort as the kitchen was out of action and moved the basket into the dining room, lucky him, oops I mentioned the kitchen again didn't I!

Well I decided that there was only one thing to do for the present, not to panic and so I didn't, I dozed off instead, well what else was there to do?

I must have been asleep for good few hours and would have spent longer asleep if the noise of the Dog whimpering and scratching at the front door hadn't awoken me from a rather pleasant dream about open spaces, blue sky, rivers of milk with islands of honey and oddly little rock pools of cream.

Unfortunately I knew exactly why the Dog was whimpering at the front door, in the confusion of finding me dead earlier this morning I presumed that the Humans had forgotten to let the Dog out for his morning, how can I say this, 'constitutional,' yes that is a good word, for what he wanted to do and by the sound of the growing desperation in his whimpering he needed a constitutional quite urgently and now he was whining to go out of the front door because the back door in the kitchen was off limits, there is that word again, sorry!

While I listened to the Dog's pleading I felt sorry for him, but when I heard the sniffing above the shoebox I started to feel less and less sorry for him as it dawned on me what he was getting ready to do!

There is no real way of communicating with a Dog who is distracted by two things, let's face it a Dog rarely has more than one thing on his mind at any one time and so all of the hairy idiot's brain cells were currently fully occupied, so no matter how loudly I shouted at the fool there was no way that he was going to hear me, and that was bad, oh that was so very bad indeed!

The sniffing stopped abruptly and I hoped, wished and prayed that the Dog had found something to distract him, but no, my luck just isn't that good and I have mentioned just how useful wishes are!

I felt the shoebox shake, which I put down to an ill judged back leg being cocked over it, and I was right because the next thing that happened was it started to rain, but we all know that it doesn't rain in a dining room, well not unless some idiot Human has been dumb enough to sell someone like me explosives!

The shoebox lid got very wet, but I am sure you will forgive me for not watching it get wet, then soggy and sag, let's call it 'liquid' shall we, was everywhere, torrents of the stuff filled the shoebox which because of the stupid wrapping paper didn't drain very easily.

I was soaked, no, that is not entirely true, I was swimming in 'liquid' and it was a good job that some primeval instinct had kicked in and I discovered that I could swim, because by swimming I managed to keep my head above the 'liquid' and not get too much down my nose. Yes dear reader that description might well make you feel a little sick, but just for a moment, think about poor me, and how I felt.

Soggy was not the only feeling, I felt sicker than I had ever felt in my life, happily I was also sinking as the 'liquid' level started to drop, slowly the 'liquid' vanished but as the 'liquid' seeped out of the very soggy shoebox, the sides and the lid slumped down on me and like an evil smelling Clingfilm parcel I was wrapped tightly in it.

To say that I was annoyed was probably the biggest understatement ever said, and I was shouting at the Dog at the top of my voice, being rewarded now and again by getting a mouthful of soggy cardboard from the box that seemed to have had enough mistreatment and was breaking apart.

Using my claws I ripped through the lid, which sounds a tough thing to do, but it wasn't really much of a contest between the soggy shoebox and me, because the shoebox was breaking apart, but to be honest the shoebox could have been made of the finest steel, stainless and I would still have ripped my way out because after I dragged myself out I was going to sink my claws into the Dog, and after that I was going to have some totally unprintable words with him!

It was obvious that the Dog had realised that the shoebox was alive because he had backed away all the way to the front door and was whimpering to get out again. But this time it was for a newer and more urgent reason, there was a very wet and ultra annoyed Cat after him.

There is an expression in English, which comes from the sport of Boxing, 'saved by the bell,' which I am sure that you all should be familiar with, and now there is a new expression that should enter Dog language and you never know even English and that is 'saved by the door,' because just as I was going to show the Dog exactly just how peed off, literally, I was.

The Humans came in through the front door and rescued the Dog from a fate worse than death, well they actually did that after the Male Captor had slipped on a mixture of the soggy dining room carpet and bits of shoe box still wrapped with sodden Christmas wrapping paper, and had plashed into a puddle of 'liquid' then screamed a bit at the shock of seeing me as the Female Captor was dragged me screaming, spitting and swinging punches, away from the Dog.

She didn't let go of me, and instead of hugging me and thanking providence that I was still alive, even after I had died, she sniffed me and then swung me by the scruff of the neck as she carried me upstairs to the bathroom where I landed in the sink for another soaking while shouting orders down to the Male Captor to go and get the medicated Cat shampoo and then disinfect the dining room carpet.

I had had enough for one day by the time I had been rinsed under the tap for a few minutes I just gave up and patiently waited for the shampoo to arrive.

The Dog wouldn't get away with this, but he was not the person with the biggest blame, oh no that was the Female Captor, after all it was she who had wrapped me up and left me on the dining room floor.

To be honest I was going to hold a grudge against her for a long time, but I sort of relented when she carried me into the front room where she lit the log fire and then sat with me on her lap, wrapped in a towel, and from our comfy place shouted to the Male Captor that she was going to be busy for the rest of the evening looking after the poor Cat and he could bring the take away into the front room and fish out some Prawns for the poor little soul, who I automatically took to be yours truly!

Which just goes to show that sometimes there is a heaven on earth for poor little souls!

Day 273 of My Captivity:

I am happy to announce that I have recovered from my death and as one famous author once said, reports of my death were greatly exaggerated, which when you think about it proves beautifully how alive he was!

Same here, last night I was treated in a way to which I am determined to become accustomed, Prawns flowed like, well Prawns that couldn't swim in a flooded river, and other treats were showered on me.

I can also happily announce that we have our kitchen back which is good, it has a new floor and stronger walls, but I was quite getting used to take away food and I think I am going to miss it, which is a shame, on both counts. Mind you now that the kitchen is back to its operational status I have been on an expedition to explore the nearly new room, which is very sparkly and new as is everything inside it and guess what I have just made a discovery.

Have you ever eaten Ice Cream, yes, well you are just a lucky Human, us Cats don't get Ice Cream often enough to my way of thinking!

The Ice Cream I was fed off the Female Captor's finger was called Cookie Dough, which is unbelievable, it is wonderful creamy Ice Cream with big lumps of chewy Cookie Dough, I was amazed at the taste, which lingers on the tongue for almost as long as the Cookie Dough clings immovable to ones teeth – did I say I was in Heaven, probably!

There is however one really bad problem with Cookie Dough Ice Cream and that is that the tubs that the divine stuff comes in are just not big enough!

It is my considered and some would say, greedy opinion that the manufacturers should do buckets of the stuff, not the small variety that they obviously sell here.

I understand in that wonderfully civilised country called America they actually do sell buckets of the stuff, all I can say is get me there as quickly as possible!

When I got up today, 'the spoil the Cat programme,' of which I thoroughly approve, continued and large amounts of Tuna mixed with Chicken were generously available on demand and this Cat can demand a lot. Until, I have to say, that I spoilt things and cooked the Golden Goose as they say, by eating enough to explode, well to be honest I did explode, from both ends at the same time, burping and farting in unison.

After that rather awkward and uncomfortable episode, I was given an enforced rest from eating sadly and carried, yes you read it right the first time, 'carried' to the Sofa for a well deserved and occasionally explosive snooze.

All in all looking back on my death and the aftermath, it has been rather a good thing and although I don't recommend 'dying' to anyone, if I could get away with it, like this time, I would do it all over again.

Well I would prefer that the Dog didn't um, let's call it 'liquidise' me if you see what I mean, which reminds me the Dog has given me a rather wide berth since the 'episode' although the Parrot has been extremely rude, with lots of squawks and rude jokes, but then as you have noticed I have learned to more or less ignore the ignorant erratic avian.

Day 274 of My Captivity:

One thing I do know like last time is that the pampering is not going to last and I am 'making hay while the sun shines,' which is an expression that farmers used originally to let people know that they would do whatever they were doing while the conditions were optimal, which of course is to make lots of noise when making hay and spraying enormous quantities of harmful chemicals at other times from equally noisy enormous tractor driven spray machines.

Thinking about 'making hay while the sun shines,' is a daft expression, if you ask me, you are hardly likely to make hay when it is dark are you, but then no one said that farming needed much in the way of intelligence did they? There are only two things that farmers need, raw brute strength and a red face, well as far as I can tell.

Happily the expression has sort of migrated from being used to describing the actions of noisy, polluting farmers and now really means that anyone who makes hay while the sun shines, is going to take advantage of the moment or as the Romans used to say in Latin, Carpe Diem, which roughly translated means seize the day and I followed the Romans advice and did.

So at least with my new motto Carpe Diem I am ready for the time when the pampering stops, and I am sure, knowing my luck that it will be soon, I also know that I am going to have to be very careful with the next stunt, or should we call it an escape attempt, I don't fancy being buried alive next time, and let's face it I haven't been very far away from being buried alive recently.

I am sure that being buried alive isn't something that everyone could handle, still I am reasonably confident that if it happens again and I am actually buried alive I could cope, because I came very close the other day, and not only that I have watched late night television and survived.

There I think that circular argument has managed to put the dreadful incident behind me, well the pampering helped obviously, now for some beauty sleep, what do you mean, sounds like I am back to my old cocky self? I have to say that sounds rude!

Day 275 of My Captivity:

10th (tragedy), cigarettes 27, alcohol units 14, (am I drunk? Probably, and bloated? Probably, after all I drunk probably the best lager in the world,) calories 3400 (blame the glands), big Susan would, Instants 0 (no idea what they are.)

Sorry to use italics it is not that professional for a diarist, but I have just read a page, yes I could only stand the one page, of the dreaded Bridget Jones's Diary. I found it open in the toilet (best place for it as far as I am concerned); the Female Captor must have been reading it, in a moment of weakness I suppose.

I don't get it, are we supposed to feel sorry for this woman. Obviously for copyright and other legal reasons I have been advised to alter what I actually read, but the italics at the top are a reasonably faithful version of the drivel that comes from that woman's pen, and they made two films of it, wow you Humans have a pretty low threshold of entertainment.

Still it is encouraging to think that when my Diary is published and you all get some real entertainment from the true story of the life of a poor little Cat, you will all clamour for it.

I can't wait for the fame and fortune, though I would settle just for the fortune!

Day 276 of My Captivity:

On this bright Sunday morning my brother, I have developed a taste for Gospel Music I just wish they wouldn't sing about Jesus all the time! But having said that, have you listened to Gospel Music or as I have, seen it on television, incredible? There is an extra dimension to watching the massed Choirs of Humans singing Gospel Music and that is their costumes.

Obviously most Human endeavour makes me smile, and very occasionally that smile turns to laughter, and why was I laughing at these very devout people singing, well it was what they were wearing, great big cloaks in the brightest colours imaginable, all very colourful, but having said that there is a joy and sense of marvel that comes from the big choirs of big brightly dressed people that is just a little wonderful, no really I promise you there is.

The spectacle of the choir is amazing but then there is the conductor, who throws his arms around and waves at the massed ranks of the brightly clad choir like a man drowning in a sea of jelly (or Jell-O if you are American), what a virtuoso performance.

Day 277 of My Captivity:

I was listening to the radio today and waiting rather excitedly to see if any Gospel Choirs' music was being played when I heard something that I think can only be described as a racket, but was described by the DJ as R&B music.

Music? Never, the DJ said Moosick I was certain of that and he was right there, that is what it sounded like to me and we all know that Moosick is Cow Vomit don't we.

Not only has this R&B 'Moosick' got a quality to make you want to join the cows vomiting, it also has the wrong name, according to the History Channel documentary on Black music that I watched a while ago about R&B Music, which I understand is short for rhythm and blues music and doesn't sound anything like the rubbish that assaulted my furry ears today.

Or maybe what I heard today was RnB and the DJ was about to be sick himself and was making a dreadful racket in the background which I heard and thought that both sounds were coming from the same track, well that is just possible I suppose but likely? I don't think so! Well whatever noise or noises were responsible for the insult to the original R&B music it was dreadful but a worse insult was to suggest that it was the same sort of music as that classic stuff.

Unfortunately and as yet no one will allow me to put a sample of the Moosick that I heard today inside this Diary, which I have to say I personally think would be a pretty cool idea, like one of those Birthday or Christmas cards that play music when you open them, not I hasten to add that anyone has ever sent me a card for my Birthday or Christmas, no I am apparently not worth the postage, but I have seem them when others have opened them.

There just doesn't seem to be anything original about this new R&B Moosick, most of the songs are actually old ones borrowed from any genre though mainly pop that were so much better by the original artists, there are also strange electronic little noises and voices that suggest music for toddlers, and then following the music for toddlers theme I heard something really dreadful called the revolting little Frog, well it wasn't called that, they had missed out the word 'revolting' but it was revolting.

I have to say I thought at first the revolting little Frog was a reference to the French President, but instead turned out to be a ring tone for mobile or cellphones, and that sums up today's R&B music, in the main it is perfect for mobile or cellphone ring tones, but surely not for the mainstream, and so maybe it should be called 'RT' music.

All I can say is that this new R&B will, I am sure, have Count Basie, Bull Moose Jackson, and at some time in the not to distant future The Rolling Stones, spinning in their graves, but obviously in a cool R&B, melodic and soulful way!

Still there is one upside judging by one thing that I have noticed about this 'RT' (Ring Tone music for the slow ones amongst us), sorry this modern R&B music and that is that it makes loads of cash and so you can of course, expect some of the same from me, well if a little Frog can make music and loads of money so can a cute little Cat, who let's face it is better looking than a Frog with or without a crash helmet on (the frog wears a crash helmet for those of you who didn't know that).

DAY 278 OF MY CAPTIVITY:

If you are a Cat and you sneeze three times you are guaranteed a trip to the Veterinarian or as they say in parts of the world, which aren't American, the Vets.

Sneeze four times, especially when you are at the Vets and they will say one more sneeze and we will have to put the Cat to sleep. Cat Flu!

Do you know what they mean when they say put the Cat to sleep? I'll let you into the dark secret of putting Cats to sleep, first it is a very long sleep and as far as I know not full of dreams, unless you believe the second part of the Bible and let's face it not a very large proportion of the world's people believe that any more and that isn't because they just believe the first bit of the Bible because that is just as bad as far as I have heard and jam packed with nonsense.

I was sneezing, well so would you if you had your nose covered in Pepper, yes I know that having my nose covered in Pepper was my own stupid fault, but I was hungry and I was just browsing a cupboard to see if I could find something to eat when I knocked over a Pepper shaker Human thingy. Well in all honesty I didn't really knock it over, there was as there usually is more to it than that, I knocked over and turfed out most of the cupboard contents on to the floor.

The Pepper cloud sort of rose up from the floor after the container had hit the floor tiles, which was quite impressive when you consider that I was rooting around in a cupboard high up on the wall.

It wasn't actually the only cloud of 'ingredients,' there was a lot of flour (self raising and plain and probably oh and more than likely some corn flour too, for those interested in the fine details), but it was only the Pepper that managed to float up to where I was leaning out of the cupboard looking down, and without knowing at the time, obviously, waiting to breathe in the Pepper dust.

So I was sneezing, but it was ok I knew that I wasn't ill and I also knew that I was more or less alone. The Dog was outside playing his latest game of 'frighten the children who were passing in their parent's 4x4 vehicles on their way to the local school.' This is his favourite game at the moment and apparently beats tear bits off the postman, actually I have noticed that he can play his latest game in the early morning and then have a breather while he lies in wait for the postman, which is handy!

The Parrot was in the dining room practicing his diction and failing miserably and the Captors were at work and so there wasn't anyone to say 'the Cat is sneezing, we should take the Cat to the Vets, so I hoped to get off lightly.

It was when I was looking down at the powdery mess on the floor that I saw what looked like little tiny footprints in the white powder.

At first I thought that the sneezing, there had been a lot of that, had made me see things, well my eyes were watering and I was feeling a little dizzy from all of the sneezing, but in between sneezes, when my head and eyes cleared momentarily I knew that my eyesight wasn't playing tricks on me, there were definitely little footprints in the white powder.

My hunter's instincts took over and between sneezes, they just wouldn't go away, I crouched down and 'assumed the pose' as they say.

My whiskers were twitching which I think was part of the hunter's instinct, although it could have been the Pepper and all of my muscles began to tense ready to spring on the owner of the little footprints, if I got half a chance to pounce on it.

After a bit of wriggling and some more whisker twitching I was ready and sprung from the cupboard, yes, ok, completely forgetting just how high up I was, the impact was amazing and I have to say very effective and I got the little blighter.

Well when I say I got him, what I mean was that I ended up lying on the floor staring straight into the eyes of a little mouse covered in most of the contents of what had been spilled on the floor. Flour, icing sugar, and stuff that turns icing on cakes pink.

As I looked at the little fellow he sort of smiled weakly back at me, it was a very odd and embarrassing situation, neither the Mouse nor I knew what to do next really, never having been in this situation before.

The other thing that was a little out of the ordinary was that the Mouse who as I said was covered in flour, and the pink icing stuff and other bits and pieces looked as though he was wearing make-up, and it suited him, in fact I thought that he looked like a Glamamouse, which I believe is a word I have just invented for an attractive mouse, with, and how can I put this politely, maybe a few too many female genes.

I was rather shocked when the Mouse calmly said, 'you're sitting on me,' and I have to say he was right, although I also have to say that for the moment I was going to continue to sit on him and try and work out what I was supposed to do next! I managed to say sorry, but my politeness didn't disguise the fact that I obviously wasn't going to do anything about the fact that I was sitting on the little chap.

What I wanted to do was to sneeze though and to do that I knew I would have to move and let the Mouse go, and when I said as much he surprised me with his answer which was that he very much doubted that he could move at the moment because he couldn't feel his legs, so with his agreement and a promise not to move even if he could I shuffled off the Mouse and sneezed.

'Bless you, bad cold you've got there!' The Mouse kindly said. I explained about the Pepper and he answered that he wondered what the interesting aroma was, and that he rather liked Pepper, though sadly as a garden dweller he didn't come across it much.

He did say something else that I totally agreed with and that was, in his experience animals should avoid sneezing in front of Humans because some of the other Cats that he had talked to said that if they sneezed in front of Humans they went to the Vets and whatever the Vets actually was, it was not a place for sneezing Cats.

I had to agree with him, it was one of those sort of legends that spreads even amongst Cats whose only contact with the world outside is a dumb, but noisy and generally unreliable Dog, who I might add, judging by the shouts and screams somewhere in the background and coming I think from the garden, the Dog had 'got' the postman.

Still the noise outside stopped abruptly and was replaced by the sound of a car, and that could only mean that one of both of the Captors had popped back to the house, not something that happens often and never before while I have been having an interesting conversation with a very civilised but all the same wild animal.

I casually mentioned the fact that the Humans were arriving home and that the little Glamamouse should leave, but he said that there was probably nothing else in the world that he would rather do than disappear at that moment, but his legs were so numb that he thought that he wouldn't be able to make a run for it, all the same if he stayed he thought that it might be curtains for him, was there anything I could do to help?

I made a suggestion and although he shuddered he agreed, so just as the key turned in the front door I picked the little chap up in my mouth and carried him into the utility room where he assured me there was a little hole next to the wastewater pipe that he would wriggle out of later.

Sadly I had only made it to the open door of the utility room when the Female Captor screamed and in between screams shouted the obvious, 'a Mouse,' over and over again and pointed in my direction although I have no idea why, she knew it was a Mouse she had said as much at the top of her voice and I definitely knew it was a Mouse, because I was carrying it.

With a mouthful of Mouse I wasn't able to agree with the Female Captor and tell her to calm down and that things were under control so I dropped the Mouse as gently as I could and watched as he limped away to freedom, lucky thing.

Happily before the Female Captor, now armed with a broom, could do him any damage he had limped out of sight, I turned around, ducked to avoid the broom and sneezed.

As my watery eyes cleared I felt a hand on my neck and one under my belly and I was picked up and carried away from the Mouse as though he had been infectious and heard the Female Captor say to the Male one, 'the Cat caught a Mouse and it has given it Cat flu, we have to take him to the Vets!' Humans, they are mad!

Well I have just got back from the Vets and happily although I sneezed all the way to the Vets, by the time I got there the Pepper and its affects had worn off, so I was given a medical and the threat of being put to sleep was withdrawn, but it is always there waiting for the next time I sneeze more than once I am sure.

Which all leads me to the conclusion that animal medicine and in particular Cat medicine when compared to Human Medicine could be described as 'tough medicine' and should, like the Vets, be avoided whenever possible.

I wonder what happened to the Glamamouse, I haven't seen him since our chat, which is a shame. Actually I am beginning to wonder if I might have just imagined the mouse, after all I had been doing a lot of sneezing and that always has an odd effect, it makes my ears pop and I shudder after every heavy sneeze.

DAY 279 OF MY CAPTIVITY:

Today I woke up and my nose was sore, it isn't the only thing that is sore but I think I have mentioned elsewhere in this Diary where Vets seem to like to take Cat's temperatures from, well that is sore too, but that is all I am saying about that particular place thank you very much.

So I have decided to have a rest, no let me rephrase that, I am not well, and need to rest, I am going to take a day off and frankly it might end up as a couple of days rest, but I will get back to you on that, the most important thing is not to appear ill to the Humans or I will be dragged back to the Vets and we don't want that do we?

DAY 280 OF MY CAPTIVITY:

This afternoon I thought I would do a bit of slow moving, and then another bit of slow moving after that, and then have a rest and then if I feel up to it I'll do some more and after all of that exercise I hope that I might feel better, so now at least I am hoping to feel a little better any time now, although even after a little tiny exercise like breathing for instance I feel an improvement and don't feel like a total invalid which is a relief.

DAY 281 OF MY CAPTIVITY:

It is amazing what a few days rest does to you isn't it, I feel like a spring Chicken which is probably why we had Turkey today for lunch for some obscure reason because it wasn't Christmas Day and even I knew that, and so why did we have Turkey and why did visitors have to arrive? It must be some sort of special occasion, but what it is and why is beyond me frankly.

I have no idea how long the visitors will stay but I can probably roughly guess, mmmh too long, there that is an accurate guess. So as visitors were lurking on the horizon, the day started with the usual minor spring clean that of course announces that guests are on their way here to make a mess of the newly cleaned and tidied house, which in itself is an insult to the animals who live here, because the Dog, the Parrot and I can do a more than satisfactory job of making the house untidy and dirty without any outside help thank you!

The motley crew of visitors arrived and incredibly the Dog behaved himself or to be more exact, the Dog was made to behave and achieved at least a seven out of ten score for being good for what turned out to be close to an hour, still I don't think that the Dog was particularly pleased at being good for around an hour because he spent almost an hour whining in the kitchen to be let out and meet the guests, in his own special and unique way.

So on this side of the kitchen door, the visitors side, it was rather pleasant, there were even some late Christmas presents distributed among the guests that had not been given on Christmas Day, I suppose that was because this crop of guests were somewhere else at the time.

There was a nice collection of tunes playing on the CD player and apart from the dribbly whining which occasionally reached fever pitch somewhere in the background, it was a rather nice morning, spoilt only by the fact that I was shut in the utility room when the Dog was moved there and dinner was served.

So I missed the Turkey, which was something of a disappointment because apart from never having nibbled a Turkey, I have never actually set eyes on one of these mythical and apparently tasty birds.

Still there was time and as it happened an opportunity after the main course had been gobbled up in the dining room. By some accident, someone knocked the utility room door open as they hurried from the fridge to the kitchen door and the Dog and I discovered that we had the run of the utility room and the kitchen, which I have to say we were pretty pleased about.

Well after sniffing around every bit of the utility room and only smelling washing powder, the kitchen was a completely different matter, and we spent quite a while tiptoeing around the kitchen sniffing the delicious aromas flowing from the work surfaces.

After a while I remembered that I didn't need to copy the Dog and wander around with my nose in the air, I could jump up onto the work surface and have a closer look, a talent which is highly valued among Cats I can tell you.

Every surface was coated in dishes, plates and containers full of tempting leftovers, it was like an Aladdin's cave of goodies, and right in the middle of this field of plenty was a large lump of a thing, part of it had been cut away and the other side was golden brown and looked succulently delicious.

It was the Turkey, I was sure of that and I said as much to the Dog, who was still sniffing the air and debating whether he should commit the cardinal sin of jumping up and leaning his front paws on the work surface to get a better look and then begin stealing large amounts of scrum.

I should have kept my big mouth shut really, but I was excited and so after guiding him to where the Turkey was sitting, waiting to be nibbled, with a series of 'no left a bit, not too far now, right a bit,' which proved to be a little counter productive because 'mastermind' doesn't know his left from his right, it is just a good job that the fool isn't a Guide Dog for the Blind, that is all I can say!

Anyway to cut a story that is getting longer, short, the greedy growler jumped up next on his back legs to get at the Turkey and then leaned closer with his nose between his paws so that he could get as close as possible to the tasty looking bird.

It was just about then that we both heard someone coming down the hall, still talking to the assembled dinners in the dining room.

Like the Dog I decided that being where we were was just a little compromising, and with a hop, a couple of skips and a little jump I was on the floor heading for the utility room door, when I heard the clatter of a few knives and a plate, although I am sure somewhere hidden in the din of the clatter there must have been the noise of some forks hitting the floor to say nothing of the moist slap of a few carrots, a bit of onion and some bacon.

I froze, because it was one of those noises that forces you to freeze and I turned around slowly again driven by the dreadful noise and stared straight at the oddest, funniest thing I have ever seen.

Unfortunately the Dog had not been as clever or as selfless as me and had obviously decided to make a desperate sharp toothed lunge at the Turkey, he must have upset the plate it was standing on, which in turn slid to the floor and broke, leaving the Turkey stuck on his nose, well maybe wedged or jammed on his nose would be more accurate, but there was no mistake that it was stuck fast on his nose as if it was coated in Superglue.

The Dog, quite rightly in my opinion was a little perturbed, well probably more than a little perturbed, but I was too busy laughing to notice to be honest.

For some reason best known to himself he was backing away from the turkey, which of course had no choice in the matter and was following him, not something that I believe he was enjoying.

And so their backward dance was in full balletic flow as the Female Captor came into the kitchen and screamed, she does a lot of that, and I hope it wasn't because she thought that the Turkey they had selfishly eaten earlier had suddenly grown legs and was attacking the Dog, because that is what it may have looked like.

By the way the Dog had now gone into that pointless sort of head shaking that Dogs do when they are stuck, it almost goes without saying that his resistance was ineffectual at best and utterly pointless at worst.

The Female Captor, who I am guessing must have had more than her fair share of giggle juice stopped screaming and started laughing, but then who wouldn't?

The lucky Dog was rescued and then got even luckier; he was put outside and allowed to eat the rest of the Turkey after having been freed. I was just beginning to sulk at the back door alone again when I realised that my Cat bowl was brimming with Turkey, some little sausages and a bit of bacon and not a Brussels Sprout in sight, result!

It was just like Christmas day and I wasn't complaining anymore, just pleased that the Dog had put on such a brilliant floorshow, and you know what, I couldn't wait for his encore.

DAY 282 OF MY CAPTIVITY:

The guests are still here, but as yet no food has attacked the Dog, although I am happy to report that he is keeping well away from the edges of the work surfaces above his head, I am guessing, but I think he is worried that another large bit of food maybe waiting to ambush him and jump on him.

One of the guests I think his name is Phil, looks just like someone called Boy George, now is there anyone who doesn't know who Boy George is? No good, Boy George is odd, not because he wears rather flamboyant clothes and has a wicked sense of humour, oh no, Boy George is odd for another reason, and that is that he is definitely not a 'boy.'

Obviously he was a boy once, but now he is mature and really should drop the 'boy' part of his name bless him, mind you he is a great singer with an amazingly strong voice that strangely appeals to my Feline nature. If you haven't heard him singing with another odd looking person called Antony, you just haven't lived yet I promise you, still having said all of that, the song they sing to each other is 'You Are My Sister' which when you think about it is confusing because neither of them are girls or as far as I can tell 'sisters'? This sort of thing confuses a Cat and I do wish that people wouldn't confuse me like that, I am only Feline you know!

I am sure that someone will explain it all to me one day though, but for the moment I just ignore the peculiar words to the song and enjoy the music.

Have you noticed just how 'hip,' this 'Hip Cat' is becoming? I have decided that I like Human music, of course I would go so far as to say I understand either Human music or indeed Musicians like Boy George and Antony and the Johnsons but do you have to understand everything in the world, no I think not, now music taught me that, isn't it amazing!

Hip Cat Note:

Yes I know I have tried to do away with 'notes,' but sometimes some things need a bit of explaining and unlike some other notes this isn't a long one, well it won't be long if I get to the point quickly of course.

I am relying on the fact that Antony and the Johnsons will become popular before this Diary is published, then you will be able to see what excellent musical taste I have developed. If in the unlikely event that they don't 'make it big,' then do go out and buy their records, your ears will reward you and you never know that nice man Antony might reward me for making his records a success!

There that wasn't a big note was it?

PS

Well a postscript isn't a note in my defence, but I forgot to mention that the CD you might have to order if it isn't the success I am predicting, is called 'I Am Bird Girl' and please don't get put off by the title, you have to buy it!

Day 283 of My Captivity:

What a busy week it has been for a no smaller than average (I am sure) Cat, we have had wonderful music and a shed load of guests, you might have noticed that I have kept out of their way and they happily have returned the compliment, I like guests like that I have to say, but the best type of guest, in my occasionally humble opinion are the guests that are saying goodbye, especially the guests that were saying goodbye earlier, with the front door open and a pile of suitcases in the hallway.

I decided that a frontal attack would be best and managed to slide and sneak all the way to the front door hidden by various wheelie suitcases, discarded overcoats and a large mess of other Human possessions, at one point I thought that I had been spotted, but I laid down and kept very still and was probably mistaken for a fur collar belonging to one of the discarded overcoats which for some reason is a rather off putting thought, fancy being turned into a collar? I don't.

So far so good, was what I was thinking as I took a bit of a breather and waited for the confusion to begin again after a lull, while someone went to fetch mad Auntie Alice from the loo where it seemed she had barricaded herself inside, for reasons best known to the addled brain of the aforementioned Auntie.

Actually out of all the visitors we have had here ever I like mad Auntie Alice the best, she hates Cats and won't have anything to do with them what so ever and that I have to say suits this Cat down to the ground! We both know exactly where we stand, which is actually as far away from each other as possible and although it wouldn't be true to say our paths never cross, when they do we never acknowledge each other.

Although having said that we did have a little bit of a confrontation over a Prawn sandwich the other afternoon, but that was more of a misunderstanding on my part, I was sure that because she hadn't pecked at it for half an hour that she didn't want it any longer and was going to let it go to waste.

It is a shame that she lashed out at me, because that sort of behaviour is hardly becoming of a pensioner, but having said that the silly old bird missed, so there are no hard feelings, and I think that the sentiment is a common one and she doesn't bear a grudge either, mind you if she had 'gone' for the sandwich and not the fleet footed Cat then she might have got to eat the neglected sandwich and not had to make such a fuss and make do with a Cheese and Pickle sandwich replacement as the Prawns had run out because most of them had been 'interfered' with earlier by some Cat or other, yes me of course ha ha ha!

I have to say that no one present wanted or needed to share in the knowledge that Cheese and Pickle sandwiches made mad Auntie Alice fart, but all the same she seemed intent on making sure that everyone knew about that very personal little fact, in between mouthfuls of the soon to be offending article.

Oh sorry you want to know if I managed to escape during the latest mad Auntie Alice episode, no I didn't I was apprehended, by one of the Eagle-eyed children looking to impress the adults and some form of reward too I imagine, it was such a shame that I was caught because I was very close to being free, but I was collected up in a bundle of overcoats and fell out and pounced upon by the dreadful brat, who screamed the house down when I scratched, well what did she expect? When she dropped me I have myself to blame for the fact that instead of running through the open door I ran into the kitchen, yes sometime even I can be stupid. Obviously that sort of experience of being grabbed without warning makes one a little flustered and I just made a mistake, but it was a big one wasn't it, because I will spend another night behind bars just because of a wrong turn!

DAY 284 OF MY CAPTIVITY:

The Good Samaritan, I heard about him on Sunday, (it is the day that follows Saturday in the Human week, Humans like to name the twenty fours of daylight and darkness but weren't imaginative enough to think of more than seven names so they repeat them every seven days, yes I know but what can you do, they are only Human after all!)

Sorry that bit of information is for my Feline readers, I would be even more impressed with Samaritanism, if I knew exactly what a Good Samaritan was and where they come from, all the same it got me thinking, can Samaritans actually practice Samaritanism, I doubt it, because I don't think that their country exists any longer and so there aren't any good or indeed bad Samaritans left in the world, in fact the news gets worse, well for Samaritans at least and those who they might have helped I suppose there aren't potential good Samaritans either, well not ones born in Samaria. That is because nowadays Samaria is called the West Bank and there doesn't seem to be a lot of Samaritanism going on there towards their neighbours or indeed from their neighbours.

Still there is one good thing about being a Good Samaritan today and that is you get a capital letter applied automatically at the beginning of the word 'good' when it is applied to a Good Samaritan, I have no idea why, but even the American spell checker (which would not have a capital 'g' even if it was a good spell checker) built into Microsoft Word said that a Good Samaritan should have a capital 'g' at the beginning of good when used in conjunction with Samaritan, still after writing ninety-nine thousand nine hundred and ninety-nine words in your Diary the spell checker goes a bit wobbly which is sadly yet another of its limitations.

However what this all proves is of course just how dotty the English language is if it proves anything at all that is.

In fact the English language has been used to bamboozle people and occasionally entire nations almost constantly since the English decided that they would invent, steal and generally construct their own almost grammarless language and deliberately make it one that could cope with constructing sentences that can mean anything to anyone at any time.

So there you have it that is exactly why English was invented to bamboozle people and I have been using it a lot recently to do the very same.

DAY 285 OF MY CAPTIVITY:

There has been a terrible and most unfortunate accident and I suppose that it was as a result of 'things' getting out of control if that is, flames are 'things,' and the way they have just raced over a large bit of my stomach and shoulders to say nothing of parts of my face I would say that were almost alive.

One minute I was gently tipping a can of petrol so that it would pour a trickle of liquid over the back door step, just enough to make it damp you understand and not wet enough to blow the kitchen up.

Now obviously there is a fine line between pouring enough petrol over the floor and allowing it to soak a little into the wooden surround of the door and too much, and I am guessing here, I may have erred on the side of pouring too much!

I am pretty sure that what happened, happened in spite of all of my precautions and safety measures, although have you noticed just how hard it is to control your enthusiasm when splashing petrol around the home, but I am sure that I did, well I know I did because this time apart from a few light, hardly noticeable scorch marks around the kitchen there wasn't any damage, well that isn't exactly truthful, there wasn't a lot of damage caused by the explosion and subsequent flash fire, but, and I still don't understand how or indeed why I was the only one seriously damaged. And of course we are not only talking about the physical damage here, to my fur, I am talking about the emotional scarring and mental hurt caused by being balder than I was minutes ago.

As I have indicated, it wasn't as though I didn't take the all the right precautions once I poured a drop or two of petrol around a little and then carefully moved the petrol can well away from what I thought was going to be the heart of the fire, and then I tossed a match at the back door. Unbelievably the match didn't even have to touch the back door step or floor, fire just happened with a small woof of an explosion.

Somehow and I still don't have any ideas on how it happened, the modest ball of flame licked at me and the next thing I knew I was hopping up and down and looking for a fire extinguisher, I panicked, you will have noticed I do that sometimes, but actually I didn't have time to have a full panic attack, because it seemed that no sooner I was alight and a bit of a flaming ball than I was out, if you see what I mean. Obviously I didn't have much of in the way of petrol on my fur thankfully, but in these circumstances even a little petrol is actually too much.

I knew I was smouldering and in a few places I was actually smoking but I didn't think that I had been burnt badly, and as it turned out I hadn't been burnt badly, sadly my fur had.

The air in the kitchen was too hot and so I thought to myself 'Best get out of the kitchen, it is too hot in here,' and trundled off to find a mirror, as I turned around and began walking something awful, sick making and really rather disgusting happened, large charred, charcoaled bits of fur crackled and snapped and fell off me as I walked, that wasn't nice on any level and I felt my self esteem sink as I walked out of the kitchen leaving a trail of crisp black fur.

It took me most of the morning to clean myself up in their ensuite bathroom, I chose that one because it has a lever handled tap on the shower unit and I can use it easily. At first as I doused my fur, more alarmingly large clumps of blackened fur fell off my nice coat, but as the morning wore on and I thought that I couldn't get any soggier the steady stream of black water and blackened bits slowed and stopped and I was able to hop out of the bath and dry myself on one of the Captor's nice thick white dressing gowns which had been carelessly left on the floor.

They say that it is uncomfortable without eyebrows, well I can assure you that life without half the fur on one's body is very chilly, especially as winter has set in.

Still I imagine that no one will take any photographs of a Cat with half its fur missing and so when I escape and they put up the wanted posters that say LOST TABBY AND WHITE (WITH SILVER HIGHLIGHTS) CAT I should go unnoticed. Still it is cold just curling up on the Sofa let alone being out on a windy day like today. So I think, just for today I will shelve any escaping plans and have a snooze.

DAY 286 OF MY CAPTIVITY:

It honestly hadn't occurred to me just how long it takes for fur to grow, I woke up this morning expecting to not necessarily be covered in the stuff, but to have some growing back, but no I look like a Christmas Turkey, well not exactly like a Christmas Turkey because they don't seem to have heads, or much in the way of legs, or wings come to think of it, but I think you know what I mean.

Bear with me for a moment, I am just going to veer off the point for a moment because what I said about Christmas Turkeys made me think about them for the first time as animals in the wild or wherever they come from. They don't have legs and so the can't run, they don't have much in the way of wings, so they can't fly and they lose their heads easily, they are weird aren't they?

You know I have had fur for such a long time that I didn't really think anything of it, after all it is just there every morning when you wake up, most of it is fixed to you, but some of it has wriggled free in the night and covered whatever you are sleeping on, which proves I think that fur does grow, because if it didn't most Cats would look more or less like I do now, so I hope that it starts growing soon.

DAY 287 OF MY CAPTIVITY:

No fur has grown today, oh dear I think I am going to be bald, but not nicely bald in a sort of bald and mysterious way, like what happened to your fur if you are in a bad accident which is sort of bald! I am going to be, 'oh my god, did you see that Cat, part fur and ugh!' Part bald, it's hideous, they should put it out of its misery.

And maybe they would be right to put me out of my misery too because I would be very upset to be like this forever, a Cat that is part fur and part bald is not a pretty sight. I know you can get away with being a bald Cat I have seen pictures of those ugly wrinkly pink monsters that Humans go 'Oh look at that Cat isn't it sweet,' over. But like this, I look like a tired rug, and all they are good for is being thrown away.

DAY 288 OF MY CAPTIVITY:

Have you noticed that nutters and idiots continually dog my life? I thought you might have!

Yes I thought I would change the subject, I will get back to you on the fur problem if and when it begins to grow back. But as you asked, there is no news yet on the fur front or back for that matter!

Where was I? Oh yes, nutters and idiots, the usual cast to a life of misery, welcome to my life, well to be honest it isn't that bad and I have finally agreed in principle without currently having signed heads of agreement (whatever they are) with my lawyer, the publisher and all of the others involved in the global publishing behemoth who are going to publish my Diary, that I will be released soon, though when exactly 'soon' is, was apparently subject to more negotiation.

Goodness anyone would think we were negotiating a Federal Europe or something really hard by all of the hot air being generated between the 'interested' parties, well the main interest of this 'party' is to get out of here and the quicker the better, and that is why I have suggested that I leave, or better still am collected, (that way we can ensure success) at the end of a Cat year.

I don't suppose you Humans know how long a Cat year is, do you?

Well it is pretty close to the length of the Gregorian Calendar, plus the Chinese Calendar, divided by the amount of tax paid by the Whiskers Corporation of America, (who are now the major sponsor of our Feline year), or to put it another way, briefly, yes that will do, 381 days.

As you might have noticed I have been using the Feline Calendar out of habit and because of a very restrictive sponsorship deal with the Whiskers Corporation of America I have ninety-three days to wait until I will be collected, and released from this prison, if everyone sticks to their agreements and they don't do what some pimply bright spark in the marketing department of the Whiskers Corporation of America suggested and 'go for a second year, because he had a feeling in his water' (apparently), that this one was a go'er and would run and run.

Well I hope that the feeling in his water is not his instinct for a winner and is instead some nasty pond fever or something more or less terminal, honestly do they think that I can last another year here? I would go mad, and I don't mean hilariously mad like the Dog with his one brain cell, I mean out of my tree mad.

DAY 289 OF MY CAPTIVITY:

I honestly thought that after yesterday's conference call the matter of how long I was going to be locked up here was decided, one Cat year as I explained to you yesterday after hearing the news myself, but the pimply idiot has been stirring the pot again and called me today to tell me that his brilliant idea had been approved by the board of the Whiskers Corporation of America.

Then he began to explain exactly what this Einstein of an idea actually was. I was going to stay in this prison for another year, so that the Diary I am writing can be published, 'have its 'bits' hyped off,' to quote him directly and even in quoting him and seeing it in black and white on a page I have no idea what he means.

But that wasn't the end of the brilliant plan, oh no just wait for the rest of it, they will install cameras everywhere and turn my imprisonment into an interactive reality television show, where the public will vote people and animals into the prison, really!

I had to do some fast talking to dissuade this ego maniac who blithely was about to condemn me to another year of hell or should that read another year of a worse hell, yes that sounds about right, with, by the sound of it, an assortment of rejects and idiots, so the fast talking seemed to be failing and I had to go to plan B and do something of rather out of the ordinary.

First I discovered that he was quite prepared to roll his sleeves up and slug 'this' out until we got an agreement, I really didn't believe that real people talked this sort of

1980's business language, if they ever did, but he continued with the hyperbole, I was convinced that he would never be afraid to call a spade - a spade, or to be accused of being a tool for doing that. No one would call him a 'tool' was what I thought to myself; they are useful after all and nothing like this idiot.

Still unlike him I was pacing myself in this argument and when he drew a breath, to (I presume) deliver yet another tirade of idiocy I struck with just a few simple questions.

Did he know that I had used explosives on a number of occasions? Yes he did! Did he have a family? Yes he replied he did. Did he want to ever see them again? But sadly the subtly was lost on him and I had to spell my little plan for getting out at the end of the Cat year and not becoming part of a bizarre or is that even more bizarre than normal, reality show.

So very gently and in the kindest way I could I suggested that if he forced me to do what he wanted, his family would meet an explosive end, eventually he took the point and said he would 'get back to me,' but I am guessing that is just a little more nonsense. I don't think we will be seeing him around here again; in my opinion his ego collided with his talent!

DAY 290 OF MY CAPTIVITY:

After yesterday's argument I had to have a lie in, goodness what was the idiot thinking of? More importantly what was his name, because if he ignores my persuasive argument to not take part in his ridiculous reality show, then I will have to find out where he lives won't I.

After some lunch I had a wander about the Prison and am happy to say that when I was looking in the mirror in the third bathroom I think I spotted some little shoots (if that is the right word, well it is better than stubble don't you think) of hair

DAY 291 OF MY CAPTIVITY:

At last I have stubble where I was bald! I think that this is an encouraging sign and that eventually my fur will grow back, I hope so, it is very windy around the bottomly area even when there isn't a wind, if you know what I mean!

So at least the appearance of some stubble is a start and quite a good one at that! Let's hope that from such an excellent start my fur grows back beautifully, it won't be long until I have to do some publicity photographs and I want to look my best for those, although I have an idea for the cover shot on my Diary, I thought that we could fake some sort of action shot, with me very high up looking just a little worried.

Yes I know it will require a lot of acting skill as well as some posing skill but I think I am up to it, don't you? I thought you would, so if I get my way that is the picture for the cover of my Diary, do you agree? That is nice of you thanks, I thought you would agree because you are so very nice, well you must be to have bought this Diary with the excellent posed and acted picture on the cover. There I told you I would win the cover picture argument didn't I.

Day 292 of My Captivity:

Do you know what, publishers, sponsors, agents and lawyers are such hard work, I haven't had a chance to make a plan to escape recently, in fact I haven't even had time to tour the house recently to check on the windows and doors, not that they have ever been open before, but then you never know do you?

So I thought that I would take a break from the email and conference call arguments, oops sorry, negotiations and indulge myself with a little wander around the house.

Have you noticed that I now call this place a house, I have to stress to you that I don't consider it a home, but that awful pain in the posterior Mr. Woodcock, you must remember him, he has a minor part to play in my Diary, the translator, or that is what he calls himself without any embarrassment what so ever I believe, which in my opinion I think is a bit of a cheek because I think he should have the job title of 'superfluous.'

Mind you happily I don't have much to do with him, just the daily exchange of emails and insults and now my almost automatic responses to his constant nitpicking over something obscure called English Grammar, as if anyone cared about that these days! I am sure that he is only being pedantic so that he can get his fat percentage at the end of the day when we start to rake in the spondulixs, (another word he suggested we change for 'money,' what sort of limp prose would that be I ask you? Still that sort of attitude sums him up,) ok that is it I will stop there, he isn't worth it you are right and I am stuck with the fool because of something annoyingly called 'a signed watertight contract.'

Day 293 of My Captivity:

Fur! Yes you read it right, new fur is growing nicely now and amazingly my nice new fur is growing exactly on the bits of me that were balder than a Badger. Mind you I haven't ever seen a bald Badger have you? But then it is an old saying 'as bald as a Badger and so probably refers to Victorian farmed badgers, they were the ones grown for their lush fur which was used in every shaving brush once upon a time.

Presumably the fur once harvested for the shaving brush trade never grew back, mmmh I wonder what happened to the massive ranks of bald Badgers? They must have survived alive, unlike most animals that Humans keep on farms, but what do you suppose they did all day? Hid probably, but then I suppose that depends upon the extent of their baldness.

I wonder why Badgers were singled out for such kind treatment by the Victorians, because they weren't noted for their kindness were they, even to their own children, as far as I can tell from that rather morose author Mr. Charles Dickens.

Still can you trust the word of someone like Charles Dickens or indeed the words of someone who moved around so much and so often that he had to be moving to avoid paying rent and other pressing financial demands. Wherever you look in England that guy has apparently lived and I think that he was either on the run or he wanted to out do Queen Elizabeth I, who seems to have slept in most beds in England, if you believe the guide books to every old half timbered town in England.

The guidebooks only record that she, the Queen slept in the beds, they never say who she slept with, no wonder she has the legendary reputation of being a virgin

Queen, silly cow! Oops sorry about the sentiments, behead me now and let's get it over and done with; I am a Republican to the core and always will be, ha, ha, ha! But honestly can you really believe that Queen Elizabeth I wasn't tempted just once, I can't!

Mind you I am not saying that all Republicans are perfect, you only have to look at a few past Presidents to prove that Nixon and Reagan come to mind, and then there is Ben Franklin, he was as mad as a hatter, if what they show on cable television is anything to go by, what was that business with the Kite and the thunderstorm?

DAY 294 OF MY CAPTIVITY:

I ordered some Pencils today from an American website, it is better to get things shipped from the states if you can, because you almost always pay less tax than in Europe and around half the price of whatever you are buying. Still that little tip is not really that relevant but I thought I would mention it anyway.

Having told you about that little tip and while we are on the subject if you 'borrow' an American friend's address and Credit Card you can download most software at half the price you would pay in Europe, well that is unless you download software that is illegal and then of course you are saving much more than half price heh, heh, heh!

I would like to say here and now though that I couldn't possibly condone that sort of theft because it leads to illegally downloading things like books, movies and other recordings and that sort of thing will obviously adversely affect my income, so please don't do it ever, well don't ever do it to cuddly little me that is!

Anyway back to pencils which is after all what I was talking about, I noticed that the graphite (pencil lead) grading system is different in the UK to the US, we use the letter 'B' to identify 'soft' and 'H' for 'hard' then we add numbers and letters like '6B' which indicates a very soft, very black pencil and 4H which tells you that this pencil will rip paper to shreds and I think some South American native tribes use to tip their arrows when hunting thick skinned prey, actually I made the last bit up, but you know what I am getting at I hope.

It is odd how things are different and the same when comparing America and England, someone cleverer than me, (but not much) said that we the English and Americans were one people separated by a common language and I think that is true, although the person who said that should have noticed the big Ocean as well, which is why I don't think that they were 'that' clever!

DAY 295 OF MY CAPTIVITY:

Have you noticed just how odd Dogs are? They don't have any of the social graces that are so abundant in Cats and can also be occasionally observed in Humans too!

After what happened today here is a warning to all Dog lovers who wear aftershave or perfume, mmmh maybe I should rephrase that in the light of what I am about to tell you! Here is a warning for everyone who likes Dogs and wears aftershave or perfume, yes that sounds better.

Today one of our visitors was a rather shy Human called Larry, who is the Male Captor's third cousin on his Mother's side of the family.

Larry was standing chatting to the Male Captor in the hall and as well as chatting to the Male Captor, Larry was I have to say, smelling rather good, whether that was deliberate or not I don't really know.

However when the Dog got a tiny whiff of Larry's aftershave he lost all control, sniffed the air that carried Larry's aftershave into the kitchen then the mad furry one raced down this wonderful smelling airwave and bounded up to Larry and without any warning started trying to make love to Larry's leg. It was Larry's left leg that got all of the attention, I don't know if that has any significance or indeed if Larry's right leg got jealous.

Apparently Dogs do this sort of thing quite often bless them, usually in the most noisy and attention attracting way possible, to the shyest person in a largish crowd, people like Larry just aren't safe it would seem, but maybe they should favour their right leg when they are standing near Dogs or indeed not wear aftershave in order to try and protect themselves.

We don't see Larry that often and I wonder if the Dog is the reason, I am also wondering if all Dogs are similarly attracted to Larry, if so it must make life hard for him, or is that make the Dogs in his life very hard, ha, ha , ha!

I suppose you could call the Dog's actions a form of 'happy slapping.'

DAY 296 OF MY CAPTIVITY:

Thinking of Larry as I was yesterday the word 'mince' came to mind, now there is a word to play with especially in the light of the Dog's display yesterday.

It is odd though that a word which originally described meat that has been finely chopped can also be used to described the way that some men walk, though whether Larry minces or not I didn't notice, he was too busy running away from the Dog the last time I saw him!

I wonder if the Dog has 'tendencies' too, probably not, he is far too earthy and let's face it he would look ridiculous in tight jeans and a cravat. But then wouldn't we all look a little ridiculous wearing that type of outfit.

Having said all of that I remember the Dog's cruel comments about a certain 'Poofy Cat' when the poor unfortunate Cat in question was made to wear Tinsel around his collar, to say nothing of the just plain nastiness that was attached to similar comments about the Cat coat that I was given for Christmas, so the Dog isn't innocent is he.

Maybe he was just being 'friendly' to Larry who knows the truth, but one thing is certain and that is that since his little escapade the embarrassed Dog has been frequently reminded of his 'happy slapping display' by the 'Poofy Cat' as they say, revenge is definitely a dish best served cold.

DAY 297 OF MY CAPTIVITY:

Bullying is not a subject that I have covered so far, but I think that it is time to have a look at bullying and indeed bullies, especially as today I have not really been doing anything of interest, well nothing of interest that I would like the world to know about and so write about it in my Diary.

Over the months that I have been occasionally glued to the television I have seen various programmes about bullying and thousands of instances of it. I am very fortunate though because I can't think of an occasion when I have been bullied, unless of course one thinks of the times when I have woken up underneath the Dog, but on every occasion I am sure that the reason for the Dog being on top is because we have been sharing a basket that was really only designed for a Dog and not a Dog and a Cat to sleep in.

Having said that, it does put a whole new meaning to the term 'underdog' I can tell you.

If an underdog is something that has crawled out from under a Dog then it is a truly unfortunate individual and must have been subjected to an awful experience because the smell is really not nice at all, honestly. Still the dreadful smell does wash off eventually and is really not so bad when balanced with the lovely warm cuddly feeling one has on cold nights, when one is actually under the Dog.

Back to bullying, obviously I feel sorry for the bullied, because it isn't nice to be singled out in the many and variously creative ways that Humans, and especially but not exclusively, their darling little children think up to bully others, but and this is a big but and one that might not be a very popular 'but,' I feel sorry for the bullies, who feel that they are so dreadfully inadequate that they have to find someone less fortunate than themselves to pick on.

So I have a plan for them. Bullies rely on secrecy and trust, yes really trust, they believe that the person that they are bullying can be trusted to keep a secret, just how stupid are these bullies?

My plan is as usual a simple one and some may say rather neat, I promise that everyone, who writes or emails me in the first year after my Diary is published will have their story published, on a special part of my website, called something like 'get your own back' and then we will all be able to share in the escapades of these heroes, when you write in or email me. I promise that you will be ok, tell me about any bullying that you are suffering because remember you are letting a Cat know what is happening, and how could a bully be threatened by a Cat, imagine what his friends in his gang would say if they heard that he, the big bad bully was frightened because a Cat knew about what he was doing.

I am not expecting you to name names, that would not be very sensible or so my lawyer tells me, but I am expecting you to be truthful and not a 'truth dazzler,' so get writing, because as you may have noticed I like my readers and indeed like talking to them so if there is anything that I can do to make their lives just a little more bearable then they only have to ask.

But as I said don't write and tell me a pack of lies because there is one thing I dislike more than bullies and that is truth dazzlers and if I find out that you have been dazzling the truth I will publish your story and your name on my website, there that is only fair isn't it?

If we get this right and you keep your side of the bargain and I keep mine we might just be able to do some good and that would be nice, especially as unlike a charity I am not going to ever ask any of you for any money to do this, because as I have said I like my readers and worry about them, especially as they will be buying my next book and that is good enough for me, obviously if they buy two books or more then I just get to like them even more too, it is a sort of sliding scale of purchase vs. affection, well what do you expect, I am a capitalist after all.

Day 298 of My Captivity:

Some people are born lucky, others become lucky and a few Cats and Dogs are unfortunately called 'Lucky,' but are they lucky? After all what sort of name is that? And more importantly is anyone born lucky? They say black Cats are lucky or is it that they have just an excellent understanding of rhythm and can dance brilliantly I wonder, but don't know?

Thinking about being lucky for a moment, and I think about a lot of things you may have noticed, what is in a name? I am proud to announce that I don't have a name, other than the fact that I am referred to as 'The Cat' and I would stress that is what should appear on any cheques, bankers drafts or any letters crammed with cash that you may feel you want to send me!

Obviously cash is best because I don't have to declare it as income and will escape being taxed, yes even a Cat without a name gets taxed, still don't worry if you want to send cheques or as the Americans say 'checks' because I have some amazing accountants who can hide money from the tax authorities and anyone else, sometimes even their own clients so you have to keep a close eye on them, having said that they are a little, how can I put this, larcenous, it doesn't matter because they are just incredible at financial hocus pocus, I visited their offices the other day and had to count the number of claws I had when I left just in case they had sent several 'offshore' to hedge my fiscal return.

Day 299 of My Captivity:

I am an Alien, that is the only explanation, it has to be, I am confident that I just do not belong here on this strange little blue and green planet, with its pretty little fluffy white clouds and I definitely do not belong in a posh housing development (if it wasn't posh it would be an estate) on the outskirts of Tunbridge Wells I promise you.

Something must have gone wrong somewhere and I arrived here by mistake, because I belong on a planet where there is intelligent life not like here, and I am not only talking about the dim Humans who inhabit this backward little backwater of the Universe, the Dogs are mad and the parrots, well just don't get me started on the parrots that's all I can say!

Day 300 of My Captivity:

It came as quite a shock, but I have heard that some people think that I am cruel or even god forbid, a bully! Yes me? Worse still, some people seem to think that I am not civilised; I'll repeat myself here! Yes me! I may well have to report myself to my website if this continues.

I will concede that I do have a wicked sense of humour; well I think it is good, and have been known to do one or two things that on reflection I might have regretted, but as yet haven't. I have, I concede been a little harsh on the Parrot, but it is for his 'own' good I assure you.

But then what have I really done to the Parrot, yes I tried to give him away because I didn't want him around, I did indeed blow him up, and I believe that I was responsible for him being pronounced missing, presumed dead on the partial collapse of the house, that may or may not have been as a result of a tunnel that I did indeed have a little to do with now and again!

Unfortunately if all of those charges are lumped together it sounds as though I may have been a little unkind to the Parrot I'll grant you, but in my defence I have to ask you one thing! Have I done anything that Humans don't do to each other almost on a daily basis and thinking about it not only to themselves?

And not only have Humans been rather awful to each other, the Dodo and several thousands of species of feathered, furred, finned, scaled and bald animals are testament to that fact and probably would like a 'word' with Humans when and if there is a final reckoning?

Taking all of that into consideration I am not that bad am I? No! I thought not, and it is good of you to agree with me!

So if this is about being civilised then let's for a moment consider who is just a little more advanced in the evolutionary stakes shall we! Who exactly crawled out of the jungle more recently and began to walk upright? Cat or Man?

No Cat actually, we evolved some time before Humans lost most of their fur and stopped scratching under their armpits in public.

Actually that isn't completely true! So let me rephrase that statement for the sake of accuracy. Cats evolved before Humans lost most of their fur, some Humans still scratch under their armpits in public, especially the males I have noticed!

However I will grant you the point that if height is anything to go by then Humans should be considered more civilised, but Dinosaurs were much bigger than Humans and were in fact Lords of the Earth for longer than Humans think they have been and Dinosaurs were most definitely not the sort of animals who knew the proper cutlery to use at a dinner table, so size is not a guide to being civilised is it?

DAY 301 OF MY CAPTIVITY:

When I got up this morning I realised that although I haven't managed to escape yet, I had done some significant things, I have made a friend, the shaggy one snoring and drooling delicately in the Dog basket next to me.

And also I have achieved a lot although some things are better not mentioned, you know what they are because if you have got this far in my Diary you will have noticed one or two of my little achievements on the way.

Then I realised that I am more or less on the last lap, if you see what I mean, I have eighty days left and if I had thought to chalk the days up on a wall somewhere, I would I am sure have run out of space, so all in all the Diary was a good idea and I am confident it will be a good little earner for all concerned happily and I have to say that I am concerned that it is a good little earner.

So all in all, when all of the, 'all' in all of the things that make up everything that one considers when one says 'all in all' I am rather pleased with the way things have turned out, sorry I hope that you are still with me, and if I am boring you now, by patting myself on my back metaphorically then look at it this way, together my dear readers and I are on the last lap, I will be out very soon and you will have finished reading this Diary in the not too distant future too, I hope you are still enjoying it, really, I do!

DAY 302 OF MY CAPTIVITY:

Yesterday I will admit I was patting myself on the back, but you do have to hand it to me, how many Cats do you know have written a Diary, and from the ones that you might know, how many have written such a complete and comprehensive Diary, a work of pure genius, and any reviewers can quote me there!

It has suddenly occurred to me just how big this book is going to be when it is published and a dreadful thought hit me, just imagine what the large print version is going to be like!

The nearsighted and short sighted will be able to use it to see over fences if they need to, now how many books do you know can be that useful? Well yes there is War and Peace I suppose, and a few histories of the Napoleonic wars, but not many others.

No I am not frightened to mention Lord of the Rings or the wizard books by Ms J. K. Rowling here, which seem to get bigger with every new volume in the set, but even if you add those to the list it still isn't a long list of very thick books, and I have to ask you how many were written by a Cat and if any were written by a Cat surely this book is the thickest, mmmh I think I am going to stop there, I have started to be a little concerned about the use of the word thick in the same sentence as any reference to me and indeed my Diary!

DAY 303 OF MY CAPTIVITY:

What do you mean I have given up on the idea of escaping? That is a downright lie if you are suggesting what I think you are suggesting and you should be ashamed of yourselves for suggesting such a thing.

There is nothing I would like more in the world (apart from obscene amounts of cash of course) than to feel the fresh dew covered grass on my paw pads, but to be fair I have been taking a bit of a breather I suppose.

Please don't for a moment believe that I have the cash advance from the publisher yet though, and therefore have become three chins worth of fat and lazy Cat, not that I won't give that a try for a while after I get the cash well the lazy bit, I don't fancy the three chins, but for the moment I am thinking and planning my next escape attempt, no honestly I am.

Actually I am glad that you brought up the subject of the cash advance from the publisher, the agreed amount is a long time in coming isn't it!

Actually you prompted me to have a look back at when the first tranche, yes that is what the posh people call a large wad of readies, was paid into my offshore bank account and all of the complicated little tributaries which will help me avoid tax and other little complications, or so the bank manager said, it was paid over one hundred days ago, so someone is earning a little extra interest somewhere and that should be me, shouldn't it!

All I can say is that they better not think that just because I am a Cat they can get away with not coughing up the rest of the large wad I am owed because we all know that this Cat isn't a normal Cat who would be content with half a ton of Prawns as payment instead of all the ready cash he can squeeze out of the deal.

Damn I should have asked for the half a ton of Prawns as well as the balance of the cash, next time I will remember that when I arrange an auction for the next publishing event.

But anyway I am a sophisticated Cat and no one will pull the wool over my eyes and get away with it, but all the same I will be a happier Feline when the rest of my money is in my offshore bank account which I may have mentioned before.

DAY 304 OF MY CAPTIVITY:

Who is up for an escape attempt? Well me for one, I meant you though, coming?

In fact this is a novel escape attempt and I thought that it might be fun if you came along, but that is stretching the suspension of disbelief just a little too far I suppose isn't it.

A while ago the Captors were the dead weight in a charity event, but then these events need dozens of the mindless to do the fetching and carrying and get told what to do by the dreadfully bossy people who seem to organise such events.

The upshot of the charity event was that the Captors ended up with a large pack of balloons and a cylinder of Helium, which in a fit of tight fistedness they never bothered to give back to the charity people.

Now before I go on and get carried away, oh a little joke, which will become funny later, I suppose, I think that I should tell you that the charity event was. It was a Balloon Race.

By all accounts the lame 'event' became an even more of a limp episode when there were problems and lots of red faces because the mass launch of balloons went wrong and hundreds of balloons didn't fly off into the wide blue yonder, but bounced lethargically along the ground, landing in Dog's poo and later causing something of a road hazard to local traffic, but that, as they say, is another story.

Mind you I quite like a bit of gossip and at the time the neighbourhood tongues were just dripping with it, needless to say it was my Captors who had not pumped enough of the floaty air stuff, also known as Helium, into the balloons so that the mass launch was actually a mass launch and not a mass bobble across the ground.

Still enough of embarrassment and gossip, it is fun when it is about something or someone else, but so funny when it is about oneself and anyway I have something important to tell you, I want to let you know what my big escape plan is.

I have in my possession as I said a number, (the pack says five hundred and I don't intend to count them) of balloons, and a cylinder of Helium, and the will to try anything to escape.

By now you probably have a good idea of what I am going to try tomorrow (so I won't spell it out as if I was talking to dummies), weather permitting that is exactly what I am going to do, around three o'clock in the afternoon!

Why such a precise time, well to be honest I am going to have to fill a lot of balloons if I am not going to repeat the disaster of the last mass launch. So I will be busy tomorrow not only filling balloons and tying string on them very tightly, but I will be checking the weather. Still if I have all of the balloons filled and the weather turns nasty I will go anyway wouldn't you? It isn't as if I have to travel very far is it.

And if you ask me that sounds like the sort of planning that the British scientists responsible for the ill fated Beagle Space Explorer, who were described as reckless with the one hundred plus million dollars they spent so that they could completely lose the little space craft somewhere on the planet Mars, so I am in good aeronautical company.

Day 305 of My Captivity:

This morning I am happy to announce that the weather is cold but glorious; the sun is shining like a happy smiley maniac so it is all systems go for the balloon launch, once I have filled enough balloons for take off that is!

The balloon filling process is rather time consuming, and in addition to that, once the balloons are filled they seem to develop a mind of their own, even when tethered.

The Parrot thought it was his birthday I think and after I had spent a couple of hours filling around a hundred balloons the mental Macaw decided that it would be ever such a lot of fun to fly through the crowd of balloons and burst as many as he could with his beak.

Actually although the Parrot managed to achieve his aim, which obviously was to annoy me, the escapade backfired, after bursting the first dozen balloons his voice began to sound like a gas filled squeak, and in the end he sounded like the ridiculous cartoon character that his multicoloured feathers always remind me of.

When he realised that the joke was not working as planned he flew off and settled on his perch trying out his new squeaky voice and looked increasingly worried, as the squeakiness would go away.

'Who's a pretty squeaky boy then?'

Sometime after lunch I knotted the strings of the massive array of balloons together and then climbed up the knotted rope that I had woven together.

Halfway up the rope the balloons were pulled down from the ceiling where they had been nestling and I had a wobbly lift off, excellent all I needed to do now was to tidy up a bit and then float away to freedom.

It was at this moment when I looked down at the floor and the debris of bits of string; popped balloons and general rubbish that I started to see just a small hitch with my wonderful plan.

Yes I could fly, in a manner of speaking, I was indeed airborne, but steering would be difficult and worse, in order for this brilliant plan to work I needed to be outside.

'Sugar' let's agree that 'sugar' is the word that I used here, how was I going to get out?

Well I suppose the answer to that big question could wait, until I had manoeuvred the balloons to the hallway, because I had worked out in my head that I was going to need the wind behind me, and judging by the way the trees and bushes were swaying the wind was coming from the back of the house and if I went out of the back door

I would probably end up crashing into the back of the house or worse being blown back inside after expending so much effort to get out in the first place that would be very disappointing.

For the moment I had another problem and that problem was how was I going to drag the large bundle of balloons through the kitchen door, but that is what servants are for and happily the Dog wandered into the kitchen just when he was needed.

I slowly explained and then repeated that this was a marvellous and very enjoyable game and that he would really like the sense of achievement in pulling the bundle through the door, he said 'huh!' I remember, and so I went through the idiot version of what I had just explained two or three times.

'Rope. Dog. Pull!'

At last he grasped what was needed for him to have such a lot of 'fun,' and then he grasped the rope, and yanked it through the doorway with such force that the balloons at first squeezed tightly together, so tightly I thought that they were going to burst, but instead of bursting when they got to a point when they couldn't resist anymore they simply burst through the door frame, instead of popping, which was handy, although probably not for the Dog who flew backwards and rolled down the hallway landing with a thump at the front door.

Happily the Dog didn't at any time let go of the rope and so when I grabbed the soggy end to tie it around my waist I didn't even have to stretch, which was handy, but on reflection I think I should have not told the Dog to let go, because when I did, he let go immediately and shuffled off a little downcast because the game hadn't really been much of a game and I suppose he felt cheated.

It was actually a little bit of a shame that the Dog had slopped away because I could have really used his help again and quickly.

The balloons were ok, there wasn't any problem with them, they were doing exactly what they were supposed to do, the problem was with the 'ballast' and the 'ballast' was me, I wasn't heavy enough and sadly I only found that fact out now that the balloons had space to do what they do best which was rise!

So up we went, I watched the ground with a mixture of interest and fear as it got further away, which of course was an illusion and not a very nice one, because it was yours truly who was getting further away from the ground.

As we rose, we soon passed the banister on the first floor landing and in no time at all I was looking down on that elegant carved safety feature of most neo-classical homes wishing that I was peering through the elegant uprights down at the ground floor and not doing what I was doing now which was been treated to a panoramic view of the landing and the first floor.

'Sugar' came to mind again but I don't like to repeat myself and so I won't labour mention what words were actually coming to mind, I realised that I was in 'a very bad place' and that was without any expensive psychotherapy.

Eventually I rose as high as I could do and the balloons above me came to a rest under the ceiling and then I did just a few feet below them, with my back legs dangling, 'my back legs were dangling,' that little point had escaped me until now, what also struck me was that in all of the excitement I hadn't managed to tie the rope around my waist and I was hanging on, and the bit about that statement, that I didn't like was the 'hanging' bit.

This was serious, and I didn't have a clue just how I was going to get down, which I am sure you will agree with me is definitely serious, and worse, yes there is worse, isn't there always in my life!

I knew that if I was going to hang onto the end of the rope successfully, and I can tell you that the incentive to do so was enormous, then I was going to need the help of my back legs, which were not helping at all currently, in fact it is true to say that they were positively hindering my attempt to cling on to the rope, because they were twitching with concern if not outright fear and making me sway, not nice, not nice at all, and I still hate repeating myself.

The solution, I had resolved was to try and haul myself up and dig the claws on my back paws into the rope, and then think about a plan to get down, because let's face it, getting down would be nice, really nice.

'Nice' being a much maligned and misrepresented word these days, in my opinion but I am sorry there is no time for the English language lecture, I must do some scrabbling and then some climbing and quickly.

You may have tried climbing a rope fixed to the ceiling in a gym when at school and I am sure that you found it rather hard, unless you have more muscles in your arms than say for instance in your head, but I can assure you the effort and difficulty is much greater when you are dangling, but if you are dangling and swaying and then the balloons that are holding you up decided to go for a little walk about and you start travelling and swaying, climbing a dangling swaying rope becomes almost impossible.

Happily the impossible can be achieved, well Robbie Williams continues to get number ones, and Russell Crowe is still employed as a part time movie star, but that isn't important right now. I eventually managed to achieve the impossible, I got high enough up the rope to dig first one set of back claws into it and then the other pawful, excellent, a tiny Angel's touch of optimism caressed me, now if the balloons would just stop swaying because it is like being on the ocean up here at the moment and this Cat is no Ship's Cat!

The last thing I needed was to be sick and so because I have a habit of always pushing my luck to the limit, it was the next thing to happen, Rats or to be more exact, Urrrgghh! Sorry that is the closest I want to get to describing aerial vomiting, what a shame the Dog had stopped sulking and come back into the hall to see what I was up to, in fact he was looking up at what I was up to as I managed the old technicolour yawn, and got a face full.

Dogs are quite disgusting and after an initial yelp of surprise and a bark of annoyance he took a tentative lick of his chops and then began imitating a Cat, cleaning his face and oh this is too awful to write, he ate up everything, there that is the most delicate way I can describe what the filthy furry fiend did then!

It is strange just how much better you feel after being sick and I did, after shutting out the display that I had just witnessed down below me because I knew thinking about that would make me heave again.

There was no point in taking stock of the situation, I knew exactly where I was and what I was doing and I had to do something about it quickly, the muscles in my legs were beginning to burn with tiredness.

Then it struck me, I knew in an instant exactly what I was going to do and I was rather relieved, all I needed was the co-operation of the Dog and, oh dear my instant elation was beginning to wane rather, the additional co-operation of the Parrot, some chance of that happening, still desperate situations require desperate measures and I was a desperate Cat in a desperate situation.

I heard myself say the most dreadful things to the expectant Dog who was gazing up at me, 'was that nice,' just the thought of what I was referring to made me ill.

After the Dog had busily licked himself clean he looked up and I said in my most fun filled, encouraging way, 'go and get the Parrot,' only much, much slower than that, so that the brain cell that bounces around in the void inside the dim Dog's head had time to process what it had heard.

'Go on, go and get the Parrot,' I said again and he looked up excitedly, well there was the possibility of 'food' on offer.

I said the same simple sentence over and over again and even at one point made those sort of snappy, stilted movements I had seen the Male Captor use to make it look as though he was playing with mastermind down there.

Eventually he actually got the message and raced off in the opposite direction to the dining room where the Parrot was hiccupping on his perch, as I was thinking that the Dog was an idiot and did the Parrot have gas poisoning? The Dog returned with a rope tug, his current favourite toy.

'No, go and get the Parrot,' just when I was beginning to give up the will to live and seriously considering dropping on the idiot lump, he got the message and disappeared again, but this time in more or less the right direction, except that he went into the front room, so I shouted to his disappearing tail 'go and get the Parrot.'

When he came back he was really excited with a large cushion from the Sofa in his dribbly mouth. 'Give me strength,' went through my mind as I said again, 'no, please go and get the Parrot,'

As he sat down and stared up at me, I started to wonder if he was doing this deliberately?

'Go on, go and get the Parrot,' I pleaded with a 'good boy' added for luck and good measure. Well it worked and as the tail disappeared this time it went in exactly the right direction, whoopee!

I hung on patiently, well it is obvious that I was hanging on, but it occurred to me that it was better to be patient and calm because that would use less energy and I was running out of energy and my hold on the rope was slipping, still looking down I sort of guessed that if I fell I might just be able to land on the Sofa cushion, if I aimed for the wet mouth imprint.

At long last after some terrible fighting noises and a lot of breaking glass, although why there was breaking glass noises I was too exasperated to even dare to wonder about, clever clogs came back, really, really pleased with himself and with the Parrot exactly where the cushion had been on his last trip back to the middle of the hall floor.

'Drop it, now,' the furious writhing Parrot bit the Dog on the nose just before he did what I had asked and then without pressing home his attack, he flew up to where I was dangling and attacked me, as if I was the brains behind his recent uncomfortable damp humiliation.

Still luckily his wings were very wet making his flight path erratic and therefore spoiling his aim. The Parrot crashed into the bundle of balloons, the ones that he didn't strip out of the bundle he popped in his frenzied revenge filled attack.

Balloons were going off all over the place; it was like the sound of a thousand Kalashnikovs at Birthday party in Baghdad, and with every sharp report I began to sink lower, towards the ground and safety, which was let's face it pretty handy.

The Parrot's frenzy was in full flight now and I was pretty glad that I wasn't a balloon, although I did feel a little exposed, dangling as I was somewhere just above the landing banister I had passed on the way up.

I was still too high to jump but we were going in the right direction, which was encouraging, and then the frightful fury grabbed hold of the rope and climbed aboard, looking just like a Pirate Parrot must have done when Pirates who cruised the Caribbean had Parrots and wooden galleons and not the ones nowadays, who terrorise the South China sea and have motor patrol boats and the consent of some governments in the area.

The added weight of the pecking Parrot was just too much for the remaining balloons and our descent began to pick up speed, in fact one could say that we began to pick up too much speed.

We landed like a couple of badly trained paratroops on their first jump, in a mangle of rope, string, feathers, balloons still being attacked and me, happily unlike the badly trained paratroops we landed on the Sofa cushion, which though still remarkably wet was at least a soft wet, landing and broke our fall.

Well I was prepared to call it a day, I was shattered after all and probably traumatised too, but I don't think that the Parrot was at all interested in my physical or mental condition and he untangled himself rather too quickly for me or my liking and began attacking me, why me? What had I done?

Happily the Dog stepped in, no not in my defence, it is just that he can't resist a 'bundle' and happily pranced about snapping into thin air and barking at the top end of his considerable gas effected voice, it was deafening.

Very quickly the Parrot decided that he was outnumbered by the Dog alone I shouldn't wonder and he wisely retreated to his perch, in what can only be described as a drunken flight.

I was rolling on the floor now laughing a squeaky little silly sort of laugh; wow the stuff in these balloons was powerful. All evening my meow was seriously affected as was the Dog's bark, I can't say what the Parrot sounded like because he stayed in the dining room as though someone had nailed him to his perch, now there is a good idea, I wonder if I can get my paws on some nails.

After things had calmed down, I slowly explained to the Dog in an unrecognisable voice that he had to 'put the cushion back in the front room,' and although the command contained eight words he eventually got the hang of what was required, and happily sauntered off with the cushion in his mouth to the front room, I had a feeling that he only went straight to the front room with his burden because I blocked the way into the kitchen and he didn't fancy either climbing the stairs or going into the dining room for obvious reasons!

I made a reasonable fist of tidying up the popped balloons and other debris and so when they Captors came home there was just the usual mess skilfully created by two maladjusted pets, and myself!

Day 306 of My Captivity:

Can't move much, took all day to type this. Back hurts, all four legs hurt; if I were a doctor I would prescribe bed rest and lots of it!

Day 307 of My Captivity:

No Diary entry today, I am too stiff to type, it feels as though every muscle I have has been stretched on a rack, and I have a terrible headache, forgive me please I am going back to bed!

Day 308 of My Captivity:

I am feeling bad about feeling bad and will try to write some more of the Diary, but at the moment I am feeling very 'Bridget Jones' or as we Cats say useless, or is that the other way around? I don't know, and for once I don't actually care, work it out for yourselves!

Day 309 of My Captivity:

It was raining today, I actually didn't see the rain, but I heard it splashing, I was to well wrapped up in my little pit to actually get up and look out of the window at something as mundane as rain, I'm ill you know.

Still thinking about it, the waterfall noise might have been someone in the shower, still who cares? Not me I am sleepy and I am still ill.

Day 310 of My Captivity:

My poor aching body still aches and I may have lost a little weight, but as I can't be bothered to look in the mirror I couldn't say for certain if I have slimmed down or not, I know one thing for sure, because that knowledge didn't require much effort to discover and that is that my legs have gone numb.

What I don't know is whether my numb legs are some sort of by product from the wrenching and twisting one experiences when one dangles twenty or so feet above the hall, or if it is from not moving for a few days, while taking a well earned breather.

What I do know about the problem of numb legs is that it feels like someone has sprayed your legs with industrial strength hair spray, not nice.

I tried to move earlier and failed, maybe later I will try again, or maybe I will just have a sleep and see if the numbness wears off on its own.

Day 311 of My Captivity:

I managed a few hours sleep today, twenty three hours to be precise and since I woke up I have been deliberating whether to go and get something to eat or to have a lie in?

I can't decide really, having something to eat would involve getting up and that is not a very nice prospect when you are as snug as a bug in a rug, which incidentally is where I prefer bugs to be rather than snug in Cat fur.

One bit of good news is that either my legs are so incredibly numb now that I can't even feel the numbness or it has worn off, if I could be bothered to find out I would tell you, but that would require a considerable effort on my part and frankly I think that I will pass on that one, if it is all the same to you!

Day 312 of My Captivity:

Now of course I have got used to the all day lie-ins and am just being lazy, but would you begrudge a cute little Cat a bit of self-indulgence? No I thought not!

Day 313 of My Captivity:

What do you mean I am play acting; I will have you know that I am ill I tell you, ill!

Day 314 of My Captivity:

Mmmh sorry about yesterday's snappiness, but I am in pain now after such a good night's sleep, so for a moment imagine how I felt yesterday and how you would feel!

No it is too late for grapes, and please don't send flowers although, if you want to make me feel better, then send money, as much of it as you can afford to my favourite charity, Me! Care of me at the publisher's address.

There that should make the chubby secretary in the red dress work, she might even run off a few pounds, who knows, she could do with it.

Day 315 of My Captivity:

Ok, send grapes if you aren't going to send money, no one has yet, but I might be being a little impatient, I wonder what grapes taste like? Do you think I will like them?

My translator, Mr. Woodcock, I may have mentioned him before, told me on the telephone the other day in a moment of unusual impoliteness in our relationship that he is allergic to fresh fruit, that must be tough.

He went on to say that Apples make him sick and most other fresh fruit like Strawberries for example make the inside of his mouth swell up. Weird, but then I guessed a long time ago he was an oddball, and the fact that he bothered to learn to speak Cat sort of sums him up, a bit of a loner.

He is just the sort of person in my view who would be a prime suspect if anything untoward were to happen in his neighbourhood, need I say more?

Having said that I wonder what fresh fruit is like? I don't suppose I would be allergic to it, as far as I understand normal Humans aren't allergic to fruit and although I am not a Human I am normal, well more 'normal' than Mr. Woodcock and that's the truth!

Day 316 of My Captivity:

Good news, I am feeling much better and in a few days I may well be up and around, having said that, being ill has been like having a holiday or indeed better still like being a member of the royal family, meals have been brought up to me, and almost my every whim has been catered for and a sick Cat can have a lot of 'whims' I can tell you!

But it is time to get up and do some light work, the windows and doors haven't been checked for quite a while and the security may have relaxed a little, so there might just be an opportunity for a stiff muscled Cat to escape, you never know, we all live in hope unless we are manic depressives I suppose!

Do I feel guilty for neglecting my readers with shorter entries than usual in my Diary, no I don't and I didn't, not even for one minute, what you have to remember is that this is an honest account of my incarceration and so you, the reader have to take 'the rough with the smooth' as they say, would you want it any other way?

No I thought not, because by now we sort of know each other you and I, and I have to say I hope that you like the Diary and also yours truly, I like you but then you have good taste don't you, you bought this Diary and that is proof enough for me about your good taste that is!

Maybe after this is all over we could get together, there will be little Diary launch events and you are most welcome to them, they won't be anything fancy, you know just a Coffee, and the opportunity to purchase merchandise, but I look forward to you being there, but please don't stroke me when we meet, because we should get to know each other a little better before we get into any form of petting!

Day 317 of My Captivity:

After the failed fun and games of the balloon escape I have had time to recuperate a little and reflect, and out of all the things that have happened recently the one thing I have noticed is that the weather forecasts are pretty useless!

From the beginning of the balloon escape through the planning stage and beyond I kept more than a weather eye on the weather and there wasn't one day's weather that followed what the forecasters had forecasted.

It is a shame that in a days television there are so many repeats of the dreadfully inaccurate weather forecasts, but to be honest the boredom generated by the repeated weather forecasts pales into insignificance when you see what happens on the News itself.

Which nicely leads me onto yet another moan, before the weather on television there is usually the News and more often than not I had to watch it.

The News seems to not only repeat itself during the day but also on a monthly basis, I won't bore you with details but what I am thinking about was a report from the government that said that they would be doing something to the way car drivers pay for driving their cars, and there is nothing wrong with that except that the same report was broadcast about two weeks ago.

So I wondered, do the television companies and the government think that Humans are so stupid that they need to be told at least twice, well 'I suppose so' has to be the answer.

Day 318 of My Captivity:

Aging Pop stars have begun lecturing governments and the general public, again about poverty, the thickness of yellow no parking lines in the cities and anything and everything that they think will be popular!

Does anyone take a look at why they are complaining so much, and doing their 'good works,' after coming back from their exotic holiday breaks or finishing their world tours? Both of which incidentally use vast quantities of the world's resources that they would by the way, very much like you to save, probably because they will soon need to use your fair share I don't doubt.

Really should we believe the middle aged long grey haired pop stars? What motivates them to tell us and our governments what we should and shouldn't do, well a clue might come from watching a graph of their CD sales after doing something wonderful like a mass charity concert, the sales graph rockets skywards, what a shame that the production of CD's and music DVD's requires such a large amount of the very resources that they are banging on about conserving.

As soon as you hear someone say 'it's for charity' you know that a succession of fools will be dressing up as women, go jogging in fun runs, bathe in vats of cold Baked Beans or want to be just really annoying in the street with a big red nose and a bucket. Just proving that you can do exactly what you like and make others pay for you to enjoy yourself, because it's for charity, ah!

Well the best thing you can do for the world at the moment you can apparently do at home and it won't cost you a penny, how about that, what is it I hear you ask and how many red noses will I have to wear? Wonderfully the answer is you don't have to wear a red nose, or dress up or do anything else demeaning and that includes watching televised comedy marathon phone-in programmes, oh no nothing like that at all.

All you have to do is to turn of a light, or more if you have left them switched on around the house, that will save power stations having to consume more fuel, reduce carbon emissions and generally give the world a bit of a breather, well literally give the world a breather, but I am sorry to say that turning off a light is mundane and ordinary and not glamorous, it is merely effective and will save you money and may give the world a chance, so I hardly think that anyone will do it, what do you think?.

Day 319 of My Captivity:

There are times when my life cooped up here in this prison lurches from miserable and boring to total desolation, and one of those times is as you will know very well is when we have visitors.

There is no collection of visitors worse than the Female Captor's, or as the Male Captor calls them 'her' family! They are an awful bunch of part time thugs and petty criminals as far as I can tell, from as safe a distance as possible and that is only the four, yes four children, really some animals don't know when to stop breeding, still the good news is that sweet smelling Lonely Larry isn't among the guests and so the Dog was forced to behave himself, well at least for a while as the visitors arrived, but later he excelled himself I am proud to say, well we all did our bit to make the guests feel at home, yeah right.

I have often wondered, after a visit by 'her' family, if it wouldn't be a good idea to have some sort of test for people considering having children, before they are allowed to actually have them!

To be fair to the children though, they do occasionally calm down and stroke a bewildered and part terrified Cat, which I think maybe something to do with not consuming so many sugary drinks when they visit here, but having said that, mostly they like to run riot and therefore are to be avoided whenever possible!

The only consolation in all of the misery that these visitors create when they arrive is that when they all line up for a 'family' photograph or drape themselves over the Sofa for one of the same type of pictures I can usually cause a bit of a rumpus.

The 'rumpus,' I like the idea that the word has 'pus' on the end; short for Pussy Cat, obviously, although I have no idea why 'Rum' is attached at the beginning, maybe the first Cat to cause a Rumpus had been sniffing the Rum bottle?

Anyway I digress, the 'rumpus' can take the form of jumping on the arm of the Sofa just as everyone is settled for a family portrait and then running with claws out across every lap just as the camera clicks and the flash blinds them.

The 'sitters' all jump up in a Mexican wave fashion as if electrocuted and manage to look terrified, horrified and annoyed all at the same time when they review the picture, or should we call it a digital image, on the computer later.

Another little trick I have perfected is when the family are standing by the Patio doors waiting patiently for the camera to be set up and smiling that fixed, 'I am being photographed and get on with it' type of smile, and their face muscles are beginning to ache and they are getting more and more bored, because the 'brilliant' photographer is delicately balancing the camera on a wobbly pile of books on top of a chair dragged across the carpet especially for the occasion, because he wants to use the remote shutter release and be 'in' the picture.

This disruption of the family group shot takes a lot of patience, but it is worth it! Patience, because you can guarantee that when the photographer joins the group and whispers 'smile everyone,' Why whisper I aks you? Then presses the remote button, and nothing happens usually because he has forgotten to set the camera to take that sort of picture or it has taken so long to line the 'shot' up that the camera has automatically turned itself off!

So while everyone groans, shuffles about and moans and the children run off and have to be shepherded back to the family group and told sternly to stand still while they voice the opinion of all of the models, that it is boring and taking too long.

The hapless photographer will then go back to the wobbly pile and set up the camera, sometimes properly, he will always fumble with it and drop it.

When he looks at the camera to make sure no damage has been done, he will press the shutter release in his hap handed confusion so that the flash blinds him for a few seconds and he can't see what he is doing when he replaces the camera on the wobbly pile and it falls to the floor. Occasionally he will repeat this process and really test the patience of the 'models' who have been known to just give up in desperation.

Inside half an hour he will have successfully set the camera up and moved back smiling to the family group. By that time the idea of a family murder would be on most of the models' minds, rather than a picture of them all hugging and forcing a collective smile!

But invariably they patiently persist because to almost everyone a family portrait is for some reason worth waiting for, and if the smaller children refuse to wait patiently the adults threaten them with considerable violence, which I can only say is well deserved, though that sort of violence is not something I generally approve of!

Finally everything is ready and after the photographer has rejoined the 'happy band' he whispers 'smile' yet again, but strangely few follow his instructions.

The flash flickers, which is, as we all know to stop something called 'red eye' which makes the family resemble Satan's when it appears in pictures, although it doesn't seem to work with pictures of this family because I am convinced that they are actually Satan's family, I might add!

Just as the flash flickers it is time for me to act and I jump from the bookcase down through the shot, occasionally knocking the camera down, but more often, just putting my body in between the camera lens and the family group, what fun!

DAY 320 OF MY CAPTIVITY:

This 'family' get together is, I heard, set to go on for a few days, because the Female Captor's niece is having her extremely ugly baby baptised.

I know that the baby is called Jane, but I don't have much of an idea of exactly what a baptism is, but then neither do most of the Humans who are occupying all of the spare bedrooms and emptying the refrigerator, it maybe that a baptism is something that all Humans have to have in the vain hope from the parents that it will make their children more attractive, well I have a tip here for Humans, in the main it doesn't work and is not worth the effort or the family rows.

The sinister baby Jane, mmmh sounds like a film title, is the absolute centre of attention and as a curious Cat I thought that I would risk a closer look at the little bundle of joy and pink baby clothes. To my horror I got a close look, but there was a bigger horror frankly and that was every time I sneaked over to the rather elaborately muslin draped baby container I was shooed away. Me of all people who usually has the run of the house, was shooed away, how dare they do that.

Well I don't know if you have been shooed away from something that you had a casual interest in, like say Area 51 for instance, it just makes you even more curious and the more that the security is stepped up to shoo you away, the more curious you become, until you have migrated to a state that can only be described as insanely curious.

Needless to say the long explanation above was written to describe exactly how I was feeling about snatching a peek at the ugly little one.

Sadly I spent the rest of the day getting closer to the little ugly bundle of joy only to be rebuffed, and as the hours dripped by so the security increased until there was a Human stationed next to the baby container constantly and this guard was only stepped down to condition red from black when I got bored and retired to write my Diary.

Though of course not to write it in peace, because there is no peace in this house at the moment, it is like London, there are just too many people to have a minute's peace and quiet.

Day 321 of My Captivity:

The plan for today was to get a look at the baby, but that was put on ice because another happy family joined the bulging ranks today. Great Auntie Mary led this ragged bunch, she is great by name and grate by nature frankly and without being too harsh she is like a giant fingernail and the world is her blackboard, do you know the expression 'putting the Cat amongst the Pigeons?' Well Great Auntie Mary is the Cat and everyone else, and for some unknown reason this Cat especially, would be the Pigeons!

Great Auntie Mary is an aggressive woman and has the incredible belief that everyone except her is an idiot and that is the reason why most traffic signs don't have words on them.

She arrived with her very thin parents Bob and Angela, who looked as though they had both given up eating a decade or so ago.

Apparently it isn't fair to say that people are slow, because it is considered an insult, so I will just say that both of them move with the urgency of a legless spider, just not as quickly, well when they are moving that is, Bob and Angela don't do much moving though, in fact they don't do much of anything, apart from Championship level moaning, the Dog, the Cold, the Cat (if you ever did!), the Sofa, the heat (after it has been turned on especially for them) and so on.

In short Bob and Angela are not happy people, but I guess when you know that you are standing on the precipice of life and are just a shuffling step away from where death awaits you, you would get a little grouchy too I expect.

Day 322 of My Captivity:

So all the guests have assembled, like a large flock of noisy Turkeys getting ready for Christmas, they have had their pictures taken, then reminisced, argued, eaten lots of large meals and cooed at the dreadfully ugly child whose Baptism has brought them together, strange how few if any of the visitors wanted to actually hold the little bundle of joy after they had looked it in the eyes!

Instead of picking the little bundle of joy up they have nodded at the ugly little thing's parents or patted them on the shoulder in a sort of comforting way, suggesting that looks are not everything and that even if they are, then the poor parents couldn't be entirely responsible for the dreadful result lying in the baby container, heavily shrouded by what looks like, but probably isn't, Mosquito netting.

I am pretty sure that the netting isn't Mosquito netting because there hasn't been a Mosquito found in the Tunbridge Wells area since the Stone Age, when I suppose pre-historic Elephants used to visit the Wells to drink the awful water for the same reasons that the looney Victorians did when they made Tunbridge Wells so fashionable.

For days now these guests have been doing the exact opposite of what I wanted them to do and that is leave, but I over heard one clique gossiping earlier and discovered some great news, the Baptism is tomorrow and then they are all going home, roll on tomorrow that is all I have to say.

Still after they had eventually got into their cars they have all disappeared on some sort of family trip to a Theme Park, so that they can eat lots of disgusting fast food and vomit on larger than life fairground rides, and better still the parents can complain about the long drive while they stand in long queues for the Go-karts.

DAY 323 OF MY CAPTIVITY:

Well today is the day that the baby will get its Baptism, and good luck to it, I have a feeling that child is going to need all of the advantages that it can get given, still it maybe like an ugly duckling and one day grow into a Swan, stranger things have happened at sea.

Sorry I got distracted and the last paragraph began to be just a little meaningless and you will see why in the next paragraph.

The visitors were busy being harassed by the Dog, while bickering amongst themselves, filling up cars full of spotty, noisy children and shuffling old ones.

They didn't know and I hadn't realised that they had left the front door wide open. As I said it took me a while to realise they had left the front door open, yes unbelievably the front door was open and my slow brain was trying to tell me something, you know when there is something important that you should remember and you can't and your brain is screaming at you, 'come on look at the clues, and try and concentrate, this is important,' but it was no good I couldn't think of what it was that I should do, then it hit me, but not before I had to go over what was and had happened, 'the front door was open and no one was looking and no one had noticed me sitting watching the fun of the Humans getting ready.'

'That was it,' yes it must have been a slow day for my brain, the front door was open and just as I had seen the English Prisoners all those months ago, I could just walk out of the front door, although they had walked out of a couple of barbed wire covered gates. They were in grey uniform and I wasn't but I reckoned that fact didn't matter, and stood up and walked forward towards freedom.

At first I walked tall and proud, but as the noise of the Humans organising each other in the driveway inside and outside of their cars got louder as I approached the front door I started to stoop and become more wary, but still no one had noticed me.

By the time I had crossed the threshold I was almost crawling and probably looked like some sort of furry slug sliding down towards and then across the path but I didn't care.

The first thing to do was to find some cover and so I picked up my pace and crossed the neat front lawn, and disappeared into the longer grass under the trees, then I slunk down onto my belly and waited, watching while the last car was loaded up with Humans, the front door was closed tightly to deter burglars and keep the animals in and then the long procession of cars began to drive up the driveway and out of the garden.

Well this animal wasn't locked 'in', this animal was 'in' seventh heaven, this animal was free, If I could dance then I imagine I would have danced for 'Joy,' whoever she is, but this was no time for idiot displays in front of strangers so I watched the last car drive away and waited to make sure that no one came back for a hat, or whatever might have been forgotten. No one came back, and so I left the long grass and headed for the road.

I made my way out of the garden through a hole in the fence and then stepped onto the pavement or because I am a bilingual Cat 'the sidewalk' and stopped just as blue car steamed passed very close on the black road, 'that was close' I thought to myself from the alleged safety of the pavement, another inch or so and I would have been doing an impression of a Hedgehog.

That encounter was really too close for comfort, and I could now see the point of the television companies showing all of those public information films about road safety.

I looked left, then right and then left again and ran like a nutter to the other side of the road, thankfully not meeting any other cars, because if the last one was an example of how fast they go, then all I can say is that cars go far too quickly for my liking.

On the other side of the road was a small wood which I knew from long days spent gazing wistfully out of the bedroom windows, had two houses bordering it, but was quite big enough for me to rest up in while I had a think about what to do next.

Have you noticed, that on special occasions like Weddings and Baptisms it starts to rain, well I guessed that I had been in the little sun dappled wood for about an hour, just getting used to the smell of freedom which I reckoned was enough time for the Baptism to be over and the photographers to start taking pictures of the great assembly of bickering relations outside the church when the rain began.

As it started to get really heavy almost immediately I imagined that there wouldn't have been any time for anyone to have made it into the dry before all of the happy campers were soaked to the skin, whether they had headed back into the church and made lots of noise to accompany the next Baptism and annoy the next congregation, or been more polite and tried to make it to their cars.

So I suppose, as the Humans would have been soaked too that was some consolation to me as I began to get very soggy, I think one could describe my fur as uncomfortably waterlogged, but I was free, although I was wet.

Still there isn't much more I could do today while it is raining so very hard, apart from trying to find somewhere warm to curl up in and go to sleep.

DAY 324 OF MY CAPTIVITY:

Even though it was only early in the evening when I decided to go to sleep last night it was rather dark and finding shelter was not easy, finding shelter that was dry proved impossible and I fell asleep inside a hollow log, like the ones that wild animals live in, in Disney cartoons and I suppose real life too.

Now I am not complaining although I ache and my fur is still very damp, I would like to make this observation, sleeping in a real hollow log is a smelly and rather unpleasant experience and not at all like the dry logs where Bambi's friends live, amongst pretty dry flowers and twittering brightly coloured little birds.

Talking of twittering brightly coloured little birds I am hungry and there doesn't seem to be anything around here to eat apart from wet leaves and tree bark, which is not my cup of tea even if Tree Bark Teas are considered health giving in parts of China, this is Tunbridge Wells and not China for a start and the other thing is that I am not thirsty either.

Anyway never mind, as they say when 'they' are trying to take your mind of something and change the subject, the sky is a lighter shade of grey now and I am free, the ground isn't drying out, but then tonight I have plans that involve sleeping somewhere dry, all I have to do is to find the village and a shop or two, and then worry about the somewhere dry to sleep.

Well you know how I like to cut long stories short; well you can pat me on the back because I haven't even bothered to describe the long march that I undertook, although I will tell you that every branch I brushed against produced a shower of very cold water droplets that had spent the morning getting colder and waiting patiently for me to pass.

I couldn't understand it, where was the village that I had heard the Captors refer to when they used to shout out to each other, 'I'm just off to the village, I won't be long.'

Maybe cars get people to and from far away places quickly? It was beginning to look like they did, and that cars were quite important to people if they weren't going to spend all day trudging through mud and getting wet even when it wasn't raining.

All of the squelching through mud was very tiring and I was, so my stomach rumblings told me, really very hungry now, I had to find somewhere warm soon, preferably with something to eat, wouldn't it be nice to find a little cottage in the woods with a merry fire and a mad old lady who couldn't believe her luck to have some company and therefore kept giving the visitor brimming platefuls of food. That would be nice too I imagine, but imaginings and reality are rarely similar, or that is what I was discovering.

Then I cheered myself up a little. Still at least it wasn't raining!

Then it began to rain, life couldn't get any worse, could it? I knew one thing; the next time it wasn't raining I wouldn't say to myself, still it isn't raining!

Happily, I did have one bit of luck and that was that I found a Rabbit hole which was surprisingly dry and so I settled down to a dry nap after I had had a rather serious chat with the previous owner about a little bit of temporary ownership, but a Rabbit is no match for a clever Cat, he was frightened not only with my well constructed argument but also the fact that I began to show my claws meant that I settled in nicely.

You know, I have to say that there is a direct correlation between the tastiness of tree bark and just how hungry you happen to be, I munched on some and saved the rest for an early breakfast, I was going to need it if I was to find the elusive village.

DAY 325 OF MY CAPTIVITY:

I don't think I slept, but then that is the problem of being in a wood full of nocturnal animals, all over the place there were noises, creaks and rumblings, mind you the rumblings were mine, well I was hungry and my stomach had decided that it wasn't going to let me forget that.

In what was probably the middle of the night the cheeky Rabbit came back, personally I think it had taken him that long to think of a counter argument to my peerless logic, but I was in no mood for rhetoric and so I chased him away. As far as the rest of his shivering family of soft furry little ones were concerned, sadly it didn't occur to me to introduce myself to the smaller ones and let them know how hungry I was, so as they disappeared in all directions I went back to the burrow and some food filled dreams.

The burrow was so warm and snuggly that I was reluctant to leave and that was what saved me from being recaptured I think, because above ground I heard two voices that I knew very well indeed, the Captors were searching for me and as usual arguing, which was lucky because if they hadn't been shouting at each other I probably would have surfaced and bumped right into them.

I was without doubt now on the run and even if I could have grown stubble on chin I couldn't have been more a desperate fugitive.

When I heard the aggressive shouts fading I slipped out of the burrow and headed off in the opposite direction.

At least I wasn't cold, I said to myself, and I had dried out, but hold on, I hadn't congratulated myself because it wasn't raining so why had it started? That just wasn't fair!

As luck would have it, and I don't really want to do much bragging here just in case my luck changes, I found the edge of the village and better still I had found an open back door, now all I needed was to find an old lady with a big heart and larger platefuls of food.

Very carefully I broke into the little cottage, ok admittedly through an open back door, but I was now a Cat burglar because nowhere in sight was a sign saying 'welcome all hungry little Cats, come in and have something to eat for free.'

The interior of the cottage was lovely, just the sort of place you want to be when you are cold, tired, hungry and wet. There was a large cooking range, that yuppies have in their kitchens, but this smelt like it was burning wood like they were designed to do, and on the draining board was a pair of Kippers, and I can vouch for just how good they were, they were so good that even if you weren't hungry you would have had to have eaten the pair.

In front of the cooking range was a homemade woven rag rug, that was thick, inviting and had been gently warmed by the heat of the delightfully hot range, I jumped down, and throwing caution to the wind or wherever else one throws caution, I curled up and in seconds I was contently burping up fish oil and beginning to doze.

Sadly, I can't say how long I was asleep, long enough to get dry and forget where I was I suppose, because when I was chased out of the kitchen by an angry broom wielding pensioner in a vest and braces, it was dark outside.

Fearing for my life I didn't stop running until I had darted around the house doubled back several times and found myself in the only road that the village possessed.

I was quite out of breath and had stitch where I obviously hadn't completely digested my Kippers before I was forced to imitate an Olympic fifteen hundred metres runner.

Still all in all things weren't too bad, there would be somewhere dry to sleep tonight I was sure, I was dry, I was pantingly hot and it wasn't raining, wow, would you believe it I managed to say it wasn't raining without it beginning a Monsoon.

My optimism concerning a bed for the night wasn't unfounded, and although I hadn't planned on sleeping in a garden shed, this one was easy to break into (for a now practiced Cat burglar) and better still it was dry, although it still hadn't rained.

So after a much better day of freedom I settled down on a mattress of dry sacking for a very good night's sleep.

Day 326 of My Captivity:

No I don't believe it either, it is raining, but before I share a moan with you about that, I will tell you what else I don't believe, I was woken up by yet another angry pensioner, who threw a seed tray at me, just as I was opening my eyes and trying to work out what the noise was as he opened the shed door.

'Martha 'es after me onions,' followed me as the angry pensioner lunged at me with a garden Hoe and missed thankfully because it looked shiningly sharp.

What is it with pensioners these days, what happened to the War spirit of sharing everything you possessed (though not that 'we' had much, you'll hear them moan) with your neighbour or any stranger who might have fallen on hard times through no fault of their own?

Well I didn't start pondering the above until I had been run out of the old scrot's garden, without, I might add, any of the grumpy old git's onions, why on earth would I want his onions for goodness sake?

The village turned out to be a little gold mine in terms of places to eat, there was an excellent Old Tea Shop that had dyslexic owners', well they must have been dyslexic, because they had added and extra 'e' to 'Old' and a worse a completely superfluous 'pe' to the word 'shop' on the sign that said. 'Olde tea Shoppe,' but was I worried about the owners dyslexia, not in the slightest, because once I had followed even more pensioners into the olde shoppe, I started to sample the wares on display.

I can unreservedly recommend the Cornish Pasties, even though they were homemade in Kent and not Cornwall, they were amazing, the soft crust melted to reveal a juicy meat and vegetable filling that would have tempted even the most devout Vegetarian to break their solemn Vegetarian vows.

After two pasties, yes ok I burped, but I wasn't going to say that, so please don't interrupt, after two pasties I started on a plate covered with a mountain of little cream cakes, although I just removed the cream from them, most of which I ate and some of which I have to say seemed to go all over my face.

I was just about to find a table with a tablecloth that rather conveniently swept the floor when I was spotted by the half wit waitress who until she had spotted me had passed me in both directions to and from the kitchen and not noticed that the plates of food were beginning to empty.

Unfortunately the shop front door wasn't open and just when I needed someone to come into the olde shoppe no one did, and so I began the first of several circuits of the olde shoppe, which included the kitchen and upstairs through the dyslexic owners' accommodation.

On the circuits of the olde shoppe and the owners' accommodation I was only chased by the slightly disabled myopic waitress, but when I took a left at the back of the tea room and entered the kitchen I had an almost full posse pursuing me, the owner and his wife (although wife might have two 'e's' here), the washer up person and a Parrot, well there would be a Parrot wouldn't there, just to add some noise.

I hope that the authorities go and look at that Olde Tea Shoppe because it can't be healthy to have a Parrot in the kitchen can it?

Anyway no time to deliberate over the hygiene practices of the shoppe's owners, I had to get out, as I ran over the work surface and swerved to avoid a particularly vicious peck from the Parrot while at the same time changing direction to avoid being hit by a flying rolling pin, I spotted my escape route.

I made a cross between a dive and a lunge for an open window, if I had had time I might have even made the sign of the cross like footballers do before they go onto the pitch for good luck, but I didn't have time and anyway as I looked back a Kentish made Cornish Pasty, which had obviously been thrown at me in desperation, was gaining one me.

I hit the ground on the outside of the kitchen happily, and the Pasty whistled over my head, so as I passed it I made a grab for it and came away with a sizeable chunk, as I speed off in the direction of my escape.

I'll tell you something, all of this running on a full stomach is bad for you, it is lucky that I didn't have to run far, on the left of the Olde Tea Shoppe was a sort of barn type place, probably used by people in the Olde days, fortunately it was not particularly difficult to get into and in the darkness I dropped the bit of the Pasty to the floor and then slunk down next to it panting desperately like at least a pair of pants.

DAY 327 OF MY CAPTIVITY:

Sometimes it is a good idea for a fugitive to lay low, and today seemed to be a good day for laying low, although it was wet and cold outside I had my nice warm piece of Cornish Pasty, happily it was still warm because I had cuddled into it all night, and although it was no substitute for the old Dog it was a little cuddly.

Unfortunately during the day the Barn leaked and the piece of Cornish Pasty and I moved several times trying to stay dry, with mixed results, I was a little wet and cold and so I ate the piece of Pasty. All day I heard voices, but I stayed hidden hoping that their owners would go away or find the Rat that they kept shouting about.

As night fell I could see the glare from searchlights on cars flood their way over the walls of the barn, I was beginning to think that whoever it was who was looking for the 'Rat' were closing in and so if they didn't find the Rat they would find me and that wasn't very helpful.

There were a couple of occasions when it crossed my mind that the Rat that the Olde Tea Shoppe owners were looking for might actually be me, but I dismissed that thought because no one is that stupid, but still the thought came back to me again and again. Maybe they were that stupid, they couldn't spell properly and they kept a Parrot.

I thought to myself 'I suppose that it is time to move on, well it will be time to move on tomorrow,' which was sad I liked this little village, but I have to say in the main I didn't like the people, too old and too angry, well aren't most pensioners like that? The ones I have encountered seem to be like that, it also crossed my mind that it was strange that the whole village population was so old!

After weighing everything up I decided that I could hide out in the barn for another night, because although it was wet and I was hungry, the searchers, if indeed there were still some looking for me, hadn't found me last night and probably wouldn't find me tonight either, I was fairly confident that it was a risk worth taking.

Day 328 of My Captivity:

I was quite sad to leave the barn, and even sadder that I had out stayed my welcome at the Olde Tea Shoppe, but only because of the Kentish made Cornish Pasties, so I decided to explore the village some more and to see if I could get something to eat, in fact eating was top of my list of things to do today!

What I needed was a Butcher's shop and although a lot of English villages have become little ghost towns, this one, because the villagers had obviously and resolutely refused to die had become pensioners' paradise and so luckily the village Butchers was still a thriving concern.

The sign outside the Butcher's shop was a little off putting, Johnson and Son, Family Butchers, I decided that it was probably a family run business rather than a local drop off point for those people who were tired of their relations.

There was a little access problem, in the form of an old guard, the door way was filled by an orderly queue of gossiping oldies, which meant that I was just going to have to do my stealing very quickly, sort of like a ram raid, but sadly a ram raid without a car, however hunger had driven me to the point of desperation, well to be honest hunger had driven me just a little beyond desperation and into the stark landscape of hopelessness.

I kept telling myself over and over again as I walked briskly towards the entrance that good wonderful things had been created out of desperation and that sometimes in history the Forlorn Hope made it through breach and captured the castle, sometimes.

Once among the Ecco soft shoe shod pensioners in the queue, I was safe, they were too busy discussing noisily a family who had just moved into Glebe Cottage several years ago and were to their way of thinking still strangers in the village, I wasn't really listening, but it was hard not to hear the old ones pouring scorn on this unfortunate family who had probably thought that the country would be a better place to bring up their children.

No wonder the inhabitants of Glebe Cottage were considered strangers and hadn't integrated into village life because the assembly collectively agreed that they would never talk to them, but even so they also collectively hoped that the head of the family would be footing the bill for the May Fayre, once again this year.

I knew that the 'Fayre,' bit of the 'May Fayre' was spelt with another of those erratic 'e's' because there was a giant banner on the village green, announcing the May Fayre and it had obviously been written by the same people who had produced the sign at the Olde Tea Shoppe.

Still this wasn't the time to be distracted by the prejudices of pensioners, and indeed wandering 'e's' looking for a home among innocent pieces of advertising, this was the time to grab something tasty and leg it. I had managed to wheedle my way through the legs of the old ones and had slipped around the back of the Butcher's counter, happily the Butcher was too preoccupied catering to the particular needs of the pensioners, trimming fat off meat, scoring Pork for roasting and dicing Lamb for casseroles, I was surprised that he hadn't been asked to chew the meat for them as well.

Just above me was the end of a link of sausages that would do rather nicely, and I had no trouble reaching up on my back legs and grabbing them, as soon as they were in my mouth I was off like a long Dog, back through the queue of legs and out into the street, not stopping to pass the time of day or enquire whether the sausages I had in my mouth were Organic Pork or Low fat, Low Cholesterol.

The link of sausages was very long and dragged somewhat as I escaped, but in spite of getting caught up around several of the wrinklie's legs I was soon so far across the village green that the old ones chasing me had given up and were heading to the Doctor's surgery for some Oxygen.

The sausages were really very good and tasted better because I knew that I had probably stolen the entire supply, depriving several old ones of a nice light evening meal.

Sitting on a big flat stone in the village's graveyard I ate as much as I could and then hid the rest, saving them for later on today, while I had a look around for somewhere warm and comfortable to spend the night!

My search for a warm bed was fruitless, all of the doors and windows of the little village had been locked and barred as the terrible rumours of a large Feral Cat spread, and so I returned to the graveyard and in the rain had a cold sausage supper, because that sounds better than a raw sausage supper.

Feeling very full, but very wet, I slept under a pew in the windy Church porch, the stone was as cold as I was, but it was safe.

DAY 329 OF MY CAPTIVITY:

I hadn't imagined that my little adventure yesterday would have attracted so much attention, but the tale of a large Panther like Cat loose in the village had attracted quite a number of camera crews from the local and national television news, who were now spreading out through the village and being stopped every few feet by an old villager wanting to give an 'exclusive' interview and demanding cash for the privilege.

I was quite pleased, apparently according to the reporters standing in front of their cameras I was the size of a Panther, really I hadn't realised that I had grown that much!

Better still I was news and television news to boot! Still I was the sort of news that didn't feel like being interviewed, especially as I had heard that Police and Army marksmen had been drafted in to 'deal' with the vicious sausage stealing 'Panther.'

Having said that I had to stick around just to watch the circus of news hounds sniffing out the 'truth,' well I had to stick around for as long as it was safe and no shots were being potted at me.

I was hungry, but there wasn't much to eat in the churchyard since the link of sausages had gone, so I nibbled on a few Dandelions as I had seen Rabbits do and all I can say is that Rabbits don't have any taste for the finer things in life, the Dandelions were awful and I could only manage one or two, my Dandelion meal was also cut short because I had noticed over the Churchyard wall a line of Police, Army and television news reporters, their cameramen and sound recordists combing the area and heading my way, I had to leave.

I'll tell you this, being a fugitive is as exhausting as being a 'large Panther' is complimentary, but I hadn't time to improve the legend that I was creating, well not yet, I had to leave because some of the Police and all of the Soldiers had guns and the mistakes that the Police and Army make at shooting indiscriminately or at 'friends' is well known, I was going to say legendary but then that would devalue the legend that I have become recently.

It is a shame that there weren't any hills around because in Western Movies the 'baddies', who I have noticed are usually really the 'goodies' head for the hills, still this baddie who is really a goody would have to think of something else, while preferably getting a move on, because the line of uniforms and sheepskin coats was getting closer.

As the line approached the southern wall of the Churchyard, well that is where the weather vane on top of the Church tower was pointing, I leapt over the northern wall and began running through a large green field of what was probably Winter Wheat, although I didn't really notice what the tall crop actually was because I was running for my life and was just happy that I was lost to view in it.

In fact I was more than lost to view in the tall sharp green stalks I was lost, and had to stop and try and figure out where I was, still as I didn't have a map or know the area that was a little pointless. Then I heard Human voices and knew that I was still in front of the hunters but only just.

After the Human voices I heard a sound that chilled my blood, Dogs choking on their leads, and fearfully I knew that these were not Dogs like the Dog at home, that is stupid and cuddly, these were Police Dogs and anyone who wears a uniform and has a little authority can be both spiteful and officious, and I had a fair idea that Police Dogs would probably have the same characteristics as their handlers.

The little breather had helped, and I ran on, but because recently I hadn't had much to eat and my daily dose of a minimum of ten hours sleep had been reduced drastically, I knew that I couldn't go on forever and I had to think of something soon, or I might be transformed from a legend into history.

At the edge of the field was a thick hedge and with some difficulty I managed to get through it and found that I was sitting on a bank that led down to a road that had at some time in the past been cut through the fields that bordered the road.

To be honest I didn't fancy trudging through another muddy field and so for a while I jogged along the bank, until I heard a noise coming around a bend in the road. The noise wasn't Human, or it didn't sound Human, in fact it wasn't just one noise it was a combination of singing and mechanical noises all twisted together into the most awful clatter.

Luckily I didn't need to look for somewhere to hide I just slid behind a gatepost and waited for whatever the noise was to appear. Happily it turned out to be a singing farm worker driving a tractor and the tractor was pulling a massive road blocking trailer loaded to a toppling height with bales of straw.

With only a little thought I decided to risk the awful singing and hitch a lift. Even at the dreadfully slow rate that the tractor was moving, it was probably going faster than I could manage and not only that it was going in the opposite direction to my armed pursuers. Stealthily I jumped aboard and climbed up to the top of the straw bales and enjoyed a rocking view of the long line of traffic, obviously trapped behind the heavily loaded tractor and over to the right in the distance beyond the hedge, I could just make out a line of uniforms trampling the Winter Wheat.

Some avarice farmer somewhere was probably rubbing his calloused hands with glee as he watched the Wheat get mangled, thinking of the compensation that would be coming his way soon.

The tractor and the snake of honking cars with their annoyed occupants slowly trundled away from the village and into the deepest country I had seen so far.

Occasionally near a passing place the tractor would slow down as if tempting the drivers from behind to have a desperate stab at overtaking before the driver ramped up the engine and we pressed on while he changed from one old song to the next, with hardly a break for breath.

Eventually at a crossroads the tractor came to a sliding halt, the heavy load competing with the tractor's brakes until the brakes just won, but only just.

Desperate motorists sped passed as the tractor driver treated them to probably his most out of tune song, to which he added the strangest chorus of whistling.

When all of the cars, that had been following the procession's slow leader, had sped away, the driver dropped the tractor into probably one of the gears that he was aiming for and we began to trundle along the right hand lane that followed the gentle contours of the countryside, but it seemed almost too much of a climb for the tractor as it revved manically and edged very gingerly up the lane.

I have to say that although my ears hurt and the dangerous swaying of the load of straw bales had made me feel just a little ill, the view was very picturesque, an unending vista of green, although in the distance I could see what I thought was rain and that spoilt the view slightly.

Tonight I was determined not to sleep in the open and get wet if I could possibly help it, but the realist in me reminded me that there wasn't much I could do about it all, except take advantage of whatever opportunity came my way.

I was so busy thinking that I hadn't realised that we had stopped, well the tractor and the farmer were still making their respective dreadful noises so it was an easy mistake to make, made easier by the fact that the trailer load was still rocking.

There was another voice beyond the edge of the bales and I sneaked over to the edge to have a good look at voice's owner. It was probably the farmer's wife, but they breed them tough around here obviously and a very manly looking Wellington boot clad person was calling over the noise of the engine and the singer, who had been busy retying the rope around his trousers, after he had added to a puddle in the farmyard by the looks of it.

'I told you about that David, my dear!' The (let's call her the farmer's wife, I like to think they were married because they definitely were a 'pair') farmer's wife waved a struggling Chicken at the farmer and then added, 'tea's ready so come in and have that, and don't forget to take your boots off and wash your hands this time, 'cos I've just cleaned the floor.'

I was curious to see what washing one's hands had to do with clean floors and more than that I was keen to see what was for tea, and so at a safe distance I tracked the farmer as he squelched across the muddy farmyard and headed for the attractive farmhouse.

The farmhouse kitchen was wonderful and unlike the farmer or his wife was spotlessly clean, from the doorway I could see that a farmhouse tea was a joy to behold, especially for a very hungry Cat.

The view of the kitchen was also delightfully warm and cosy and just too inviting not to enter and so taking my courage in all four paws and relying on my recently acquired burglary skills, I slipped in after the farmer, but didn't tread in the muddy pools left on the glossy tiled floor by the entrance of the farmer.

'David, I told you to take them boots off. Really, you don't care about the work you make, do you!' The farmer's wife attacked the muddy pools with a cloth, as the farmer delivered his defence, 'no my love, that 'aint my boots, I took them off at the door, that's my socks, I better get a new pair of wellies.'

The farmer's wife obviously used to years of this sort of behaviour just cleaned the floor. As she swept the cloth across the floor she looked straight into my shining eyes as I watched her from under the table.

'Would you look at that David, what a poor, scrawny looking little thing it is!' Well that killed the legend of the Panther, 'poor love, come here Puss, you hungry, look David a stray Cat and 'her's' on 'his' last legs by the looks of 'him."

What a perceptive woman the farmer's wife proved to be and better still her perception was totally eclipsed by her generosity and so we won't mention the fact that she had just strangled the English language with her strange dialect will we?

I allowed her to pick me up in her gentle hands that were well used to picking up Cats by the feel of them and then I accepted the mountains of food that she swept off the table and placed in front of me. I decided there and then that I like farmer's wives and farmer's food.

In no time I had helped the couple eat their way through the mountain of food that had been on the table and as I began to blink and doze on my feet, my new friends talked about the activity in the village, apparently there was a Panther loose in the village, and wouldn't it be really funny if the villagers had spotted the scrawny Cat that was now under the table and thought that it was a Panther!

Yes wouldn't that be hilarious I thought to myself as I began to drop off standing up. I felt those same gentle hands pick me up and carry me to a barn, as we left the kitchen together I didn't even register what the farmer's wife said, 'I'll put the stray in the barn 'cos 'es a little smelly and dirtee and you never know what 'e might 'ave!'

I was too tired to be insulted, but as the couple gazed at me, in my straw bed from the door I did catch the last thing they said, 'as the Vet was comin' out t'morrow to have a look at the Heifers they would get 'im to give the Cat the once over too.'

So I knew I had an early start in the morning and sadly I wasn't going to find out what a farmhouse breakfast was like, never mind I had an incentive to travel, Vets after all must be avoided whenever possible.

DAY 330 OF MY CAPTIVITY:

It was still dark when my alarm clock woke me up and if I could have found that damn Cockerel I would have happily strangled it, but there was no time to be lost, as they say in adventure books, I needed to put some distance between me and the Vet.

The farmhouse kitchen door was open and there was the smell of breakfast cooking straying through the early morning swirling mist, but sadly I said goodbye to the warm delights of the kitchen and made my squidgy, squelching way through the farmyard and out into a field.

At the far end of the field were a couple of horses that barely noticed my passing because they were heading for the dry shelter of their stable, yes guess what! It had begun to rain as the early morning mist cleared.

There is an old saying that country folk like to use and then nod sagely to each other, 'rain before seven, fine before eleven,' so with that in mind I calculated that according to my body clock it was about six in the morning, which meant that I was going to be treated to about five hours of rain, wonderful.

With the exception of the wonderful kindly people in the farmhouse I was rather sick of the countryside and its inhabitants, to say nothing of the wet, muddy countryside itself, and I have to say I was beginning to get a little tired of fending for myself, there is a lot to be said for room service and so I was I suppose a little homesick, this escape hadn't been what I thought it would be all in all, and I rather felt that I would be better off going home and waiting for Mr. Leibowitz, 'call me Todd' and my publisher to spring me and deliver me to somewhere cosmopolitan and unbelievably comfortable!

Day 331 of My Captivity:

I tell you what I am shattered, wet and very cold, this life of being on the run in the open air is definitely not for me, I feel I know what it is like to be a Gypsy now and I can appreciate their plight, even if I don't agree with their lifestyle, by the way anyone want to buy some clothes pegs or have their knives sharpened?

Last night was almost unbearable, the 'rain before seven, fine before eleven,' country saying that the Fred, Ned or Ted's have for generations said with such conviction is obviously wrong.

Who are these Fred's, Ned's or Ted's, well they are the country equivalent of the Tom, Dick or Harry's who live in the towns and cities of course, you always hear people saying that it could be any Tom, Dick or Harry who did whatever it was that had been done, and Fred, Ned or Ted's sounds more country folkish, no it wasn't that important, but I have noticed that if you say something and then say that it wasn't important, people tend to think that you are hiding something and I didn't want you to think that I was hiding anything, honestly.

Something else I won't hide from you now is that I have made a decision, I am going home, all I have to do is to work out the way, and happily I have a fair idea of the direction, I am just lucky that I have such a good sense of direction, some would call it a blessing, I call it talent.

Day 332 of My Captivity:

It took me all of yesterday to get here, and I mean all of yesterday because I didn't go to sleep, I just kept walking through the darkness.

Yes I have been wandering around in circles, and I know that for a fact because this is where I live, and that must mean that I have completed a circle of sorts. I just am too tired and cold to believe it, I am standing in my garden, and oh no please not that! Here comes the Dog and judging by the flapping of his big wet pink tongue I am going to get a wet welcome home.

Well the Dog was very pleased to see me and in one way he actually did me a little favour probably without knowing it though. To get away from the constant licking welcome I ran off down the side of the house and jumped up on to one of the many bin bags sitting next to the back door awaiting collection by the happy refuse crew, who like to collect the rubbish that is left in the bags once the Foxes have ripped the bottoms of the bags and the refuse men themselves have spread bits of rubbish across the garden and driveway.

The black sack that I jumped onto toppled over and I was able to gorge on some of the tasty leftovers, while hiding from the Dog, who using his renown tracking skills had gone off in the opposite direction and was now busy piddling over some young saplings at the top of the garden. Nothing much had changed then, but all the same it was good to be home and at least one member of the family had obviously missed me.

Unfortunately my dinner, breakfast and about a dozen meals besides were interrupted by the dustmen who arrived to collect and redistribute the garbage and I had to hide, well my newly acquired fugitive habits were going to be hard to suppress, and anyway those sorts of skills might come in handy again one day knowing my luck, so I wasn't going to suppress them too deeply, was I?

Day 333 of My Captivity:

This morning I was quite touched, the Captors searched the garden before they went off to work and although I hid from them, I knew that soon I was going to be back in the warm.

As I waited for them to leave I watched them from the garage roof as they searched in vain and made themselves late, ahh, how touching. After the Captors left I continued to wait for the Dog to bring the promised food, well if the Dog remembered to bring some food that is, and I hoped that he would remember because I was on the starving end of famished.

I may have to give myself up soon though because the Dog had remembered to bring food, but turned up, eventually, with a bone, of all things, what good is a bone to me?

Day 334 of My Captivity:

Last night in the open, well in my little dug out covered in last Autumn's leaves I decided that I didn't need this sort of punishment, it was worse than being inside and so I made up my mind to get 'caught' today, especially as I had seen that I had actually been missed and therefore I would probably get a few treats as well as the unavoidable bath, sadly I knew I needed a bath when I turned around earlier and mistakenly got briefly down wind of myself, it wasn't at all nice.

Day 335 of My Captivity:

I would be lying if I said that I didn't lay low today, and by the same token I would be lying if I didn't say that I hadn't been laid low, by my recent little adventure, I was beginning to get tired of the great shivering out doors, this wasn't the freedom that I wanted, actually let me rephrase that, this wasn't the type of freedom I wanted or had expected.

The type of freedom I had expected involved comfort, good food and most of all pampering, with me being the most pampered, and not sitting under a bush somewhere wet and shivering, no the 'somewhere' isn't wet and shivering, I am, and I don't like it!

So without warning as the Captors stepped out of the car I appeared, it was not unlike a sort of resurrection I have to say and I was greeted with open arms, which stayed outstretched I have to say as I was carried at arms length in the house. I didn't struggle; I was banged to rights as they say! I was also rather relieved that my adventure was over and if the last few days is what adventures are like I don't want any more of that variety for a long while, thank you very much.

The bath was no more or less embarrassing or generally awful than I had expected, and the treat Mexican Prawn leftovers and as much Cat food as I could eat before being sick was simply divine. Then I got a pat from the Male captor and a cuddle from the Female, life was looking up already and I had only been in the house for around an hour.

The sixteen hour nap next to my warm, cuddly furry canine friend was also a much missed treat, yes I was definitely home for a while, but I didn't lose sight of the fact that I had to catch up with my Diary and also my agent and find out just when I could get out of here for some real luxury and comfort, to say nothing of the small fortune that I was going to earn from the hardship that I have suffered since being imprisoned.

Day 336 of My Captivity:

I am happy to say that I am back in prison and I am warm, full up and ready to go to sleep, no wonder ex-cons reoffend just to get warm and well fed, my time outside without any support, food, shelter or most importantly cash was awful.

Next time when I leave here I will have to make sure that I have planned my escape better.

Sorry I am still busy writing up the Diary too I missed a few days and need to crack on here.

Day 337 of My Captivity:

You have to forgive me for the short entries to the Diary over the next few days and obviously yesterday and today, at first, while I was out I kept a mental note of what I had done and on which day, ready to write it up after I had sent for my laptop, but I think all of the shivering I did, shook the words out of my head, and so I only was able to write the bits that I remembered as they came to me and so writing the Diary for the last few days has and is proving almost as difficult as being out in all weathers.

I know I suffered which wasn't nice, doing a lot of shivering and shaking with cold, and being very very wet for long periods and I would like you to suffer with me, oh that doesn't sound very nice, but I mean I want to make the record of what happened as authentic as possible and so I am trying to remember as many details as I can.

Day 338 of My Captivity:

Well this account of my time on the outside is quite painful, bringing back memories that I would rather not be reminded of, to be honest. I know that I was not acting perfectly by any stretch of the imagination, but really the actions of the pensioners who seem to haunt both the village and me is terrible really, you would think that they were old enough to know better, wouldn't you!

Mind you there were some kind people too, surprisingly the farmer and his wife were wonderful, and you usually hear just how dreadful farmers are don't you! Usually farmers are like pensioners, always moaning that they don't get enough money, that they are funding the nation's food, I mean get real, until recently they could afford all of the enormously expensive kit and livestock required to hunt poor little foxes, to say nothing of footing the bill for their horsey looking children to compete in gymkhanas.

So somewhere along the line there is a discrepancy, although I suppose that if some people don't change their 4x4's every year they think that they are poor, yes that sounds more like it.

But the farming couple I met were nice, although they seemed a bit too ready to consult Vets and that is not a good trait in people who spend most of their lives dealing with animals, well not in my book.

Day 339 of My Captivity:

The Dog has been shadowing me for the last couple of days since I have been back, at night he has slept with his front paw over me, as if at sometime during the night I am going to slip away again without telling him, as if I will do that. I fully intend to tell him when the car arrives and Mr. Leibowitz's 'call me Todd' henchmen call for me.

Really the Dog's behaviour has been strange and I do wish that he would believe me when I say that I neither like bones or Doggy clean teeth chews, whether they have been pre-chewed or not, if he did believe me, not only would he be able to chew the bone and chews that he has presented me, but he wouldn't have to gaze longingly at them when I refuse to eat them and he doesn't want to seem rude and offend me, goodness that furry brained Bow wow is a real idiot, but a kind hearted one at that.

I will miss him when I go and I will have to see if he can come and visit me from time to time, on a sort of holiday if you like.

Still I shouldn't be too bothered about being missed, after a couple of weeks I am pretty sure that he will forget me, especially if my leaving coincides with him getting a large Marrow bone, they always make him forget everything for days, while he chews, licks and generally is absolutely disgusting with it. Still as I said I will miss the fool!

Day 340 of My Captivity:

Well did I learn anything from my days on the run? I should say so, I realised that I will have to have a computer game created of this Diary so that you readers can experience just what it is like to outwit Humans, go on the run, be chased by aggressive pensioners, suffer from mistaken identity problems and be pursued by the Police and the Army most of whom were 'tooled' up and trigger happy and also to have paws so that you can see what a handicap they can be on occasions.

Of course I see no reason why the game can't have the same title as the book so that everyone knows it is going to be extremely exciting. I almost envy you having the opportunity to play the game, because of all of those fingers and thumbs you have, but I am content in the knowledge that I 'lived' the experience, although I am sure that the programmers will probably enhance the action and make the puzzles that I have had to solve, like how to knit string into rope, easier, because not all Humans are that clever.

Still the game of the Diary is just another item in a vast range of merchandise that you lucky Humans can invest in, but I promise you that my integrity is such that I won't make the last few days until I am collected deliberately 'action packed.' Just because I have decided to create a computer game, oh no, that is why I am not sitting on the edge of a precipice while flames and volcanic explosions whistle passed my whiskers, oh no, not at all, but then again if the programmers want to use that scenario, at least they can now say it is in the book! Can't they!

Day 341 of My Captivity:

It is colder today and looking out at the sky it seems as though the dark grey clouds were deliberately pressing down on the earth. I am pretty confident that the country folk will have a saying for that sort of cloud behaviour and probably one that sounds perfectly reasonable, and if you sort of half hear it, sensible too, there will only be one problem with the saying and that is that it will be complete untrue.

I wonder if country people have deliberately invented sayings, which are completely meaningless so that when city dwellers or indeed more sophisticated people hear their rural wisdom they are in awe of it and the sages who spout it.

Well this more sophisticated Cat has come up with a little saying of his own which, he hopes, describes perfectly most country people, 'as advanced as mud,' don't you just love it? And happily it can be applied to everything and anything from the Dog and country people in general, right the way through to the British Rail Network, now how many country sayings have that type of utility? Not many!

Day 342 of My Captivity:

If anything today is much colder than yesterday and it is definitely the sort of day to wrap yourself up in your finest Dog fur coat and stay indoors preferably in the toasty Dog basket, if the Dog would only lie still.

The trouble with the Dog, no we haven't got space to write the full list, but the trouble with the Dog today is that he wants to go out and prove that he is the hardy outdoor type, yeah right, I will remind him of that the next time he is twitching, dreaming and scorching in front of the roaring log fire.

You know it is log fire weather and I just wish that the Captors were home because they only light the log fire when they are, which I suppose is sensible when you consider and may even remember that both the Dog and I have on occasions been smouldering while asleep in front of it.

If we hadn't been moved away from the roasting fire we probably would have spontaneously combusted and the only thing we would have to show for that would be a Roman Catholic Shrine, because I know they like to knock them up when something spiritual and mysterious happens, especially if there is some form of smoky apparition too, and I bet if pushed we would have been able to provide one of them too as we barbecued ourselves.

Still there is nothing better than toasting your toes in front of an open fire, especially when you are fairly confident that you won't end up as a warped bit of charcoal.

DAY 343 OF MY CAPTIVITY:

Most of today was spent expensively trying to track down and speak to my Agent Mr. T. A. Leibowitz, 'call me Todd,' on the telephone, which was like trying to chase an aeroplane's shadow, I would imagine not ever having chased one, but having experience of chasing all sorts of other shadows.

The elusive Mr. T. A. Leibowitz, 'call me Todd,' was truly elusive and at a time when the annoying dawn Chorus of birds outside was beginning to be drowned out by the noise of commuter traffic I gave up and went off to bed in a disappointed huff, annoyed at the world and more or less everything in it, which was unfair because the rest of the world and most of the things in it hadn't done me any harm, but I was very tired and had to blame something!

DAY 344 OF MY CAPTIVITY:

Success, in the middle of the night when your mouth can't make your mouth function, no sorry I am writing this when really I am too tired to think properly, what I meant to say was in the middle of the night when your brain can't make your mouth function properly, you manage to get hold of people in America and start doing business with them!

I should also explain that I am trying to write this entry after my telephone conversation with Mr. T. A. Leibowitz, 'call me Todd,' because if I don't then I may forget what was said, and I also feel I should add that in the middle of the night when your brain can't make your mouth work, it also fails with telling your fingers what to type.

It is the time difference and it is not very convenient, but staying up almost all night was worth it because I managed to speak to Mr. T. A. Leibowitz, 'call me Todd,' and apparently ' the last bit of the deal is so very close that if it was Ice Cream you could lick it.

Well that is good enough for me, he also added that he was off to Hollywood on the red eye, which sounded painful and I almost suggested that he should use a jet airliner, but decided to hold my tongue (metaphorically before you ask) because I didn't really know what he was on about!

Day 345 of My Captivity:

Have you met my lawyer? Mr. T. A. Leibowitz, 'call me Todd,' – most people call him Toddler and I can see why, if someone gets him mad, he could well throw all of his toys out of the pram, if you know what I mean!

Still now that all the publishing and other deals have been done and according to Mr. Leibowitz, 'call me Todd' a few Movie studios are getting 'hot' for the Film Rights, he says that there is no reason why I shouldn't move out of this Prison and into his Penthouse.

I was so emotional, nearly in tears, I was leaving the Prison at last and moving to a Penthouse, that is a place with five walls if my Greek is correct, but then what do I know I am just a Cat, well that is true, but I am just a Cat with a Penthouse, a book deal, and a Movie deal almost in the bag, though now, there is no Cat in the bag he is out of the bag, free, good looking and very wealthy.

'This could be the jackpot,' was how Mr. Leibowitz, 'call me Todd,' explained the scope of the opportunity, we apparently are set for blast off and it will all go ballistic.

Sounds like one of my Rockets to me, but then I am looking forward to leaving here and enjoying what Mr. Leibowitz, 'call me Todd' described as the Red Carpet treatment, I hope that doesn't mean I will get hung on a washing line and beaten, no it can't be that surely?

Mr. Leibowitz, 'call me Todd,' said that I had some sponsors now too, independently minded business proprietors who wanted to see a Cat get to the top of the tree.

Well if it is ok with Mr. Leibowitz, 'call me Todd' and the independently minded business proprietors I would like to stay either on the Red Carpet at ground level or curled up on a sofa I don't really do trees, unless there is a Fire Brigade who need their patience testing locally that is.

Day 346 of My Captivity:

This morning has been very busy, I had another of my conference calls booked between my Agent and the Publisher and a couple of people who apparently represented major movie studios.

By all accounts Mr. T. A. Leibowitz, 'call me Todd,' had flown down to Hollywood and was actually in Tinsel Town, mmmh I didn't like the idea of Tinsel Town because it brought up memories of that awful Tinsel covered collar at Christmas, still never mind I imagine that just because somewhere is called Tinsel Town it is probably only the residents who have to wear Tinsel and visitors aren't required to imitate them, well that is what I hoped, just in case I ever have to visit.

Of course I can't divulge the names of the two movie studios at this delicate stage of our negotiations, but I can say that this negotiating business is just that a lot of negotiating and that is hard work, both representatives of the movie studios were on the line at the same time, but because of some very sophisticated piece of electronic equipment originally devised for the Spy industry, we could hear them, but they couldn't hear each other when they talked, very impressive.

Maybe foolishly I imagined that any movie mogul worth his salt would have read my Diary and reached for a telephone and begun throwing large bundles of cash at me, so that they could secure the rights of the movie, before the book becomes a blockbuster, 'think again' is all I would say to that idea.

After some probing I discovered that one couldn't really describe these studio representatives as movie Moguls and not even Magnates either, because although they were negotiating on the telephone right now neither had read my Diary' but when I suggested that would be a good idea they both said that they would read the synopsis if I emailed it to them.

I was incensed and was just about to let them both have a large chunk of my mind when I think Mr. T. A. Leibowitz, 'call me Todd,' said that my line was breaking up and I got cut off, which was a real shame, because I was furious.

Over the next half an hour I blistered the pad on my paw continually pushing the speed dial button, trying and failing to get Mr. T. A. Leibowitz, 'call me Todd,' back on the phone, so that I could rejoin the conference call, but to no avail.

Even though my paw was more or less glued to the phone I nearly jumped out of my skin when the telephone rang, it was Mr. T. A. Leibowitz, 'call me Todd,' apparently he had finished the conference call and was just about to go out to lunch with the lady from one of the movie studios, I asked if Mr. T. A. Leibowitz, 'call me Todd,' would like me to email a synopsis of my Diary because I had just realised that I hadn't written one yet!

Mr. T. A. Leibowitz, 'call me Todd,' said that wouldn't be necessary because of all of the good reviews and excellent feed back from focus groups, he was very close to making a very big deal and one of the animated movie studios was ready to move with a very generous offer for the film rights and so beat their competition and therefore no one had time to read my Diary or even the synopsis.

Talk about sold sight unseen, it is just a good job that the movie studio are buying something really very good, although it makes you wonder whether you should put yourself out and write something brilliant when it isn't even read, before it is bought!

Day 347 of My Captivity:

Well allowing for time differences and everything else that complicates transatlantic calls especially when they are to the West Coast of America, I managed to get hold of Mr. T. A. Leibowitz, 'call me Todd,' hours after he had gone off to lunch with one of the movie studio executives, he explained that he had turned his phone off after lunch as they had gone down to the studio to sign the paperwork and then they had hit Tinsel Town afterwards to celebrate, well I don't know what sort of fight the Studio Executive and Mr. T. A. Leibowitz, 'call me Todd,' had got into, but it seems a strange way to celebrate to me and he sounded very ill and openly complained of a stabbing pain in his head, although he didn't say and I was too polite to ask how he had come to be stabbed in the head, but whatever happened he didn't sound as though he was badly injured thank goodness.

Mind you it did sound as though he doubled over in pain when I shouted 'tell me how much we sold the film rights for,' well I was getting tired of hearing about the celebrations without knowing what we were all celebrating.

'Two million dollars,' was the answer that was accompanied by a lot of fizzing as though Mr. T. A. Leibowitz, 'call me Todd,' was still drinking celebratory Champagne.

Mr. T. A. Leibowitz, 'call me Todd,' had worked out that after his fifteen per cent, and expenses I was one million seven hundred thousand dollars better off, and not to worry about tax, because his company would deal with all of that. I was amazed, no I was more than amazed, I was speechless and Mr. T. A. Leibowitz, 'call me Todd,' said as much, 'you still there?'

Yes I was I just couldn't say anything, I was just shocked, imagining just how many Prawns a Cat could get for just a small portion of that sort of cash, wow, clever me.

Eventually I thanked Mr. T. A. Leibowitz, 'call me Todd,' and said that I just had to go and lie down and recover from the shock, and bless him if he didn't say, 'you deserve it buddy you've worked your nuts off on this one,' I decided that I liked being Mr. T. A. Leibowitz, 'call me Todd's buddy and at some stage I was going to find out just what working one's nuts off meant, but that could wait, I put the phone down and I did exactly what I said I was going to do, recover from the shock, horizontally!

DAY 348 OF MY CAPTIVITY:

If anything it is colder today and why do I bother giving you a weather report, apart from the fact that mine are more accurate than the ones that you get on television, because they are forecasts and mine is an observation, well why I bother to tell you about the weather is an easy question to answer, millionaires don't care about the cold, well this one doesn't and so it doesn't matter if it is rainy or nippy outside because in my world it is warm and dry!

So far just like a lottery winner with a limited imagination it hasn't changed my life, but that is because I haven't got my paws on the loot, you just wait until I do, break out the Caviar and Prawns and let's have a party!

Well there it isn't much of a party so far though, the guests are a thread bare old Parrot and a phenomenally furry Dog, who only eats fish to stop me getting it.

But none of that matters does it? Soon I will be out of this prison with its peculiar inmates and I will be enjoying a life in the lap of luxury, hey; that's a point, I wonder if one can hire a luxurious lap? They say that in America you can buy or rent whatever you want and I want one of them, a nice soft lap of my own to snuggle into!

I am inspired at the moment as you can tell, after the incredible and very pleasant surprise of yesterday, wouldn't you like to be in my paws at this moment? Well of course you can be, all you have to do is to write a best seller and get a movie deal and it can't be that difficult because even a Cat can do it!

DAY 349 OF MY CAPTIVITY:

It snowed today, I only know what was falling out of the sky and settling in ever greater piles on the ground outside was called 'snow' because the Human Captors both raced to the window like a pair of excited children and blurted out loudly 'snow' together!

Happily all of this nonsense and idiot behaviour was explained shortly after all of the rushing to the window when the Male Captor said. 'Look at that, it is snowing heavily!' Which just goes to show that sometimes stating the obvious is helpful.

In a short while the snow, which was apparently 'laying' (another snow related word that I learned today) had reached armpit height, well where the armpits of a Cat would be of course, if a Cat had armpits that is, or even arms if you see what I mean! It didn't stop there and was soon up to a level that would have been over my head even if I stood up on my back legs.

More and more snow fell, covering everything and just piling higher and higher.

Maybe it would be easier to say that the snow was getting deeper and deeper at an alarming quick rate to someone as tall as me. At this rate I was convinced it would cover the house in a few hours.

That sobering thought made me decide that I would postpone any future escape attempts until the stuff went away or at least stopped falling out of the sky and mounting up in such an alarming fashion.

Then I began to notice how cold it had got outside by the way my breath on the window was making 'huff' marks on the cold glass, if you see what I mean. It was then that it occurred to me that if I did escape I might get lost in the Arctic wasteland that had replaced the garden, so my idea to postpone any escape attempts and just to wait a while might be a good idea.

I also got a shock when I got too close to the window and bumped my nose on the glass, it was very cold, well the glass was, and soon so was my nose too and that also confirmed that the cold was coming from the snow and this was definitely no time to be caught out in the open, and not only that inside the house it was nice and warm and rather toasty.

The Human Captors displayed their normal short attention span and went off to do whatever occupies them when they are not at work and so I just sat on the window sill and watched the snow fall from the sky in little dancing pirouettes and mount up in gentle folds, while the wind blew the tops of the folds of snow into what I found out later were called 'drifts' and very attractive the drifts were too.

It was all rather pretty actually, especially when a fat red Robin landed on the window ledge outside to complete the picture. Imagine his surprise when I launched myself at him.

And I suppose you can also imagine my surprise when I bashed my head on the glass, which I forgot was in between us, well the smug little 'chap' fluttered off and landed on the bird table to eat some bacon rind, it is a shame that there is never a Sparrow Hawk around when you need one, isn't it?

Just as I was getting a bit bored with watching the snow fall, well to be honest it is very pretty and picturesque and everything, but it doesn't do much after a while does it, snow it just mounts up, like credit card bills, I was rescued from boredom by the Male Captor, whose antics never cease to make me smile!

Dressed to kill in the Arctic the Male Captor came into my view as he was bundled up with what around ten layers of clothing on, and looked like someone who says they have 'glandular' problems, if you know what I mean!

So there was fatty battling against the blizzard to get to the garage, I couldn't believe what my eyes were seeing, surely he wasn't going to go driving in this weather, at the best of times and in perfect conditions he is a abysmal driver, well that is what the Female Captor always says, and correct me if I am wrong, and do bear in mind I am a Cat who doesn't drive, but I can't imagine that this was the best driving weather!

I needn't have worried, or actually got too excited expecting him to launch the car out of the garage, slide in the snow and take out the ornamental fruit trees which grow close to the drive, and roll a few times coming to rest in the icy water of the fishpond, oh no I needn't have worried at all, something much better was about to happen.

Out came the clothing inflated man, with a ridiculously large shovel, it was I discovered later a snow clearing shovel and because we actually very rarely get snow here it was brand new. The black shovel wasn't a bit scratched or marked from moving large quantities of snow and the handle still beautifully varnished, I was hooked, absolutely fascinated and couldn't wait to see what the idiot was going to do next.

'Fall over,' was the answer, to 'what will he do next?'

That was mildly funny, although because of the padding effect of all of the clothing he didn't hurt himself at all, he just slid along the driveway like a Human toboggan and came to an abrupt stop, buried in a snowdrift.

Judging by the big smile on his face he had enjoyed the adventure and I fully expected him to launch himself down the drive and bash into another snowdrift or do what the Dog was doing, which was acting like even more of a kid than the Human!

Yes they had let the Dog out, but in my opinion he was welcome to the weather.

The Dog was bounding in and out of snowdrifts that often were so deep, that he disappeared jumping around the large front garden like a Deer on steroids, one minute he would be on his back legs rearing up like a frightened horse and the next he would be bouncing up and down the area where the lawn had been.

He was covered in snow and where it had melted he had icicles dangling off his coat, but the funniest and strangest thing was his face, well I suppose it always is funny and strange, but now he had a white beard of frozen snow which made him look like a cross between Scott of the Antarctic and a looney scientist in a B movie from the 1950's.

Then the Male Captor started making balls of snow and lobbing them at the Dog, who instead of getting annoyed started to try and catch them in his mouth or chase after the ones that went wide.

Several snowballs were well aimed and landed with a thump on the Dog, who thought that the whole game was just magic and went scurrying around the garden using up more energy than I think I have ever possessed.

The Dog got his own back for being pelted by snowballs in the end, by running up to the Male Captor, and launching himself at him and pushing him into another and as yet unspoilt snowdrift.

During the time that they were playing in the snow the day became darker and darker and the snow lavishly covered everything, getting thicker, turning the entire garden into even softer curves.

Long after I would have got bored and too cold to play, they continued messing around, the Dog to his credit discovered a marvellous trick, luring the Male Captor to the tree lined edge of the garden, then running along the line of trees crashing into the low lying branches which were heavy with snow and showering the Human until he looked like a fat snowman on a Christmas card, his nose looked so cold that it resembled closely a large carrot, which to my way of thinking just completed the seasonal picture!

To his credit the Male Captor took it all in good part and played for what seemed like hours in the garden with the now almost pure white Snowdog, until it was time to do what he actually went out of the house in the first place to do and that was to use the shovel. Yes I had nearly forgotten that he had taken that with him too! It took the Male Captor a while to find the shovel and then persuade the Snowdog to let go of the handle because the Snowdog had decided to offer him his own special Snowdog brand of help, which in some circles is also called 'hindrance.'

For another hour and a half the Male Captor, with what only can be described as the impediment of the Snowdog, shovelled, for all he was worth, piling shovelfuls of snow on top of the drifts at the side of the drive.

This hard work I later found out was called 'clearing the drive' and seemed to be extraordinarily hard work, similar in a way to what he does in the summer when he mows the grass, only to see it grow back very quickly, which I personally think is as pointless as clearing the snow.

The Dog had a 'Polar Bear' of a time, well I should have said 'a whale of a time,' but 'Polar Bear' seemed to me more accurate. He was running up and down the newly cleared drive, slipping and then sliding heavily into the even taller snowdrifts.

Then when he was bored with that game he started to bite the metal blade of the shovel, which just goes to show his idiot credentials, because the Male Captor was busy using it at the time!

Twice all of the Dog's paws left the ground as he was swung around in the air, hanging onto the shovel with his teeth, letting go when he was pointing into the deepest bit of the snow nearby.

By the time the Male Captor reached the gate at the top of the driveway I could hardly see him, the air was so thick with snow. The same was not true for the Dog, who was still running around the garden, wading in and out of the deep snow like a mental Arctic Hare.

The Human had been so engrossed in his labour that he hadn't noticed that all of his hard work was a complete waste of time because the drive was covered with snow when he walked back down the driveway, red faced and panting white clouds of breath in the cold air.

Still he seemed pleased with himself and that counts for a lot sometimes, because when he is pleased with himself the Prawns come out, so as he disappeared into the garage to put the shovel away before coming back into the warm house I made a dash for the kitchen, scaring the Parrot half out of his feathered mind, serves him right, he was snooping on me again and obviously hadn't expected me to move so quickly!

When the backdoor opened and the overdressed Snowgiant came in, stamping his boots and clapping his gloved hands together, I sat in the middle of the floor with my 'I have been really good, oh and by the way I missed you' expectant look.

All he did was flick snow over me, which I understand he thought was very funny, I had an alternative opinion I can tell you and ran out of his way, back through to the living room and the warmth of the log fire and the squawking of the Parrot, who sadly didn't get the snow shower treatment.

Sitting in the warm room drying out and looking at the fire and occasionally glancing out at the very white garden through the snow covered windows, there didn't seem to be any trace of the driveway; I tried to work out what the Male Captor had been doing all day.

In fact I still haven't worked out what he was doing by wasting his time outside clearing the snow from the driveway. All I can think is that he did it so that there is room for more snow to land tomorrow!

Day 350 of My Captivity:

The snow has either stopped falling and then started again and I didn't notice, or it has been falling for nearly two days, which surely means that by now we have more than enough snow.

The Male Captor was out again clearing the drive so that the snow had even more room, and also rather strangely he went around knocking large icicles off the over hanging bit of the house, maybe he was starting a collection? It probably goes without saying that the Snowdog was out with him, playing fetch with the smaller icicles which the Male Captor obviously didn't think were worthy of his collection.

Does that hairy idiot Dog have any feeling in his mouth, just imagine carrying a large icicle around the garden in your mouth, it is surely enough to freeze you tongue off.

This time the Human wasn't the only one shovelling, the Dog decided to dig lots of holes, eventually choosing one to bury a few icicles in, and then he set about digging the largest hole he possibly could and as he did he resembled a manic Eskimo, showering clouds of snow dust all over the garden.

But not content with all of that madness, he decided that he would be staggeringly revolting and paint the snow yellow, wow does he carry a lot of 'paint!'

Day 351 of My Captivity:

This is the third day of being cut off from the outside world, well it isn't as bad as it sounds, the television and internet still work so we aren't exactly marooned, but I am worried about food stocks, I hope that there is enough Cat food and Prawns for me, the cold weather makes you hungry I have noticed.

I did think about rationing my food, but all that did was make me even hungrier and I ate more, so I have just got to hope that supplies last, or I may have to try Parrot food, I know in a famine I wouldn't be able to eat the Dog's food he would guard it with all of those nasty sharp teeth he hides in his mouth so there isn't much point in even thinking about that idea, I have to say that at this moment eating the Parrot's food isn't a nice prospect, nasty dry nut like stuff, but as we get hungrier we will be less and less choosy about what we eat.

Still I'm not stupid I have taken a few precautions and this morning when everyone was upstairs except the Parrot I broke into the food cupboard where they keep his food and hid a packet of Parrot Muesli right at the back of the cupboard behind a bag of flour.

The Parrot was not pleased, but there wasn't much he could do, just make a racket and dive bomb me, and I can tell you it isn't easy to dive bomb a Cat who is in an air raid shelter like cupboard.

Day 352 of My Captivity:

I have it on good authority (Mr. Woodcock no less, you may remember he is my translator and general know-it-all) that if I was to tell you about my likes and dislikes such as my favourite music, or say for instance my favourite book, that would 'date' the book, because you might think that I had written this Diary in the year that the song or book was released or published.

So I have decided to tell you anyway, I like the 'Scottish Play' as Actors and other luvvies in the theatre call 'Macbeth,' by Shakespeare for those of you who may have not heard of it, and I quite like Handel's Messiah, although in truth only the big numbers in the performance because the rest drags a bit.

Now Shakespeare was breaking quills writing 'Macbeth' in the year 1622 give or take a year and it was first published in 1623, which is a while ago.

Handel on the other hand, whose Christian name was George, which is nice, wrote his 'Messiah,' yes there was at least one other bit of music at the time called the 'Messiah' and obviously written by someone else, which is odd don't you think, but anyway George Handel wrote his 'Messiah' around 1740 and that is the year 1740 and not twenty to six in the evening. Mind you the recording I heard of the 'Messiah' was made in 1988, which means that he might have been the oldest living composer ever, but I maybe wrong about that!

Now if we follow Mr. Woodcock's odd logic and wonky reasoning this Diary could have been written at a time between 1623 and the present day, which would make me a very old Cat indeed.

I say this because I have just heard a really good track by a new artist called James Blunt called 'No Bravery' and I didn't want to date the Diary really I just wanted to share that fact with you, James Blunt is very good, you should try to listen to this track and then get the album 'Back to Bedlam' I hasten to add that I am not being paid to advertise this record, but if it sells a few after my recommendation I don't mind being paid commission on the extra sales, well a Cat has got to make a living hasn't he!

Day 353 of My Captivity:

You may have noticed that this Diary is occasionally a little inconsistent I have to admit I have, and that could be thought of as a little worrying!

My grammar is a tiny bit shabby in places, I freely admit. Definitely on occasions the 'tense' of my writing has problems, but I do, in my defence, occasionally take my Diary with me and I begin writing in the 'present tense' usually when the Humans are not around so that I can make notes first hand (I have told that idiot Translator the phrase is first paw), mmmh! Humans!

So as I said I have my Diary with me reporting things as they happen then something 'happens' like a building catching fire or exploding, you know the normal daily stuff that happens around a cooped up Cat; well this cooped up Cat anyway, and then I get confused and use the wrong tense or I have to put my Diary away and make a run for it and finish the page later sometime minus one of my nine lives so it all gets a little complicated you know, to say nothing about the fact that losing a life is, how can I put it - disturbing!

In addition I have noticed that sometimes I am writing in 'reported speech' I think they call it, and then other times in the first person or as we would probably call it 'First Feline,' consequently I hope that you will understand that the concept of 'tense' to a Cat is totally different to Human's, although we do understand the use of the word for; getting edgy.

Having said all of that in my defence I know that my readers are just plain lovely and I am sure that you will forgive me, I am only a Cat after all and when this inconsistency was pointed out to me by Mr. John Woodcock, the Human who translates and translated my Diary, he 'eventually' was persuaded that I wanted my audience to hear the voice of the Cat, because let's face it at the end of the day; I am a one of them.

Between you and me, I would have got rid of him, Mr. John Woodcock sometime ago if I could have. Oh don't get me wrong, he is nice enough as a person, if you like people who 'know best' and continually try to rewrite vast tracts of one's precious Diary.

In fact I was warned that my Publisher would be a pain in the tail but let me tell you; this Translator takes the biscuit, in comparison to the dreaded and dreadful Mr. John Woodcock my Publisher is a Pussycat if you pardon my little Joke. Honestly all the Publisher ever did at the very beginning was to take me out to dinner a few times. Actually I haven't seen him since, but they do sign the cheques for the royalties every six months and that makes them close to wonderful in my humble opinion.

Consequently I like my Publisher a lot and they reserve their arguments for my agent and apparently continue pressing him for the more instalments of my Diary, but that is understandable I agree with the Publisher, we have to milk this cash cow for every pound, dollar and euro we can squeeze out of the readers while we can, just like they did with the Harry Potter books!

As I told my Agent and Attorney Mr. T. A. Leibowitz, 'call me Todd, I can't write the Movie script and a follow up at the same time, and to be honest the writers that he and the Publisher have brought in to 'ghost' write for me are worse than I am at writing, I don't know much about writing in English because I am a Cat, shame these bozo Humans don't have the same excuse, which means that the job of writing any sequels falls to me, but I don't mind in the slightest, because it means I earn more cash with every new piece of writing!

Lastly I believe that you, the reader will forgive me my little problems with English because English is after all my second language, and as I have said before it is very difficult to learn, which is why it has taken me so long to master it.

Day 354 of My Captivity:

Well the plan seems to have gone wrong before it begun as far as I can work out.

At the time when I thought of it, the plan seemed perfect, have you noticed that, before a plan gets put into action, it always seems to be better than it turns out to be, I suppose you just have to ask the Russians about that, all of those excellent five year plans that crashed and burned over the years from one revolution to the next. Still this wasn't a complicated plan and it definitely didn't involve any tractor plants in Minsk, so you would have thought that it would have worked or as they say, 'gone according to the plan.'

When I dreamed up this particular plan it seemed brilliant and I have to say it has been done before, so I had a sort of template for what I wanted to achieve, although some bits of the plan hadn't worked in the past!

Let me explain, and please don't accuse me of being cynical, please.

The plan actually takes about a minute to explain, but the hidden plan is a little more complicated and will take longer, but here goes and I suppose I will have to tell you all about my 'inspiration' too.

Here is the inspiration 'bit' first then, a while ago after several successful films and some incredibly successful books that preceded the films, a particular book was about to be published which was to be the last opportunity to make mega bucks out of the series.

Unusually the book had been advertised for nearly six months in the shops inviting people to pre-order it, which is I have to stress very unusual, but then again this was to be a very unusual publishing event as they say in publishing circles.

So all over the world people had been parting with cash and putting their names down to reserve the long awaited book, even before it was finished by an author, who had already made so much of the folding stuff out of the previous books in the series.

As the weeks passed it seemed, to me at least, that there were a few problems beginning to turn up, just as the launch of the latest 'blockbuster' was due, and so the launch date was put back several times, which may have meant that the author wasn't as prolific as she had been, or was it the fact that she was wealthy beyond even my dreams and that she was not quite as dedicated as she had once been? Was it that she was running out of ideas and plot lines? Or was it that she was just knackered? Probably the last suggestion is the most accurate; let me tell you it is no picnic writing I promise you!

There was another little problem and that was that the latest film was flagging a bit at the box office and hadn't made the mega bucks that were expected, it had made just big bucks and in a greedy world big bucks just aren't big enough.

So as you can tell the darlings at the publishers were beginning to get a little edgy about their investment and probably said to their PR people that they were getting worried that the latest blockbuster might not quite be the record breaker that they originally thought it would be.

Now people in publishing are lovely and wouldn't come up with the dastardly plan that I am suggesting someone came up with and so one would have to cast about lower down the evolutionary tree to find the person or people who came up with this little wheeze, if you go down the evolutionary tree far enough you get down to a habitat that is full of PR or Advertising people, which as we all know is pretty close to the bottom of the evolutionary tree.

I think that some bright spark, and let's call her Jessica, just because she was probably called Jessica or definitely had a name that was similar, decided that it would be a great idea to get a significant amount of publicity, but how to do that, the series of books had all been so very popular that just to mention that something was happening to the author or the publishing company had an adverse affect on the stock market.

So whatever PR announcement Jessica was about to invent had to relate to the latest book, which once its title had been announced, couldn't really be mentioned because no one would thank her for giving away the plot. Consequently Jessica had a bit of a problem and only a wizard solution would work, to 'life interest' (as they say in PR circles) the latest book and its launch.

But what to do, Jessica suffered for weeks, spending long hours watching candles burn away in dozens of fashionable wine bars through-out London until she realised in one of those flashes of inspiration that happen when bath water spills on the floor or an Apple hits you on the head or indeed when an Apple hits you on the head when you are in the bath, not that that happens all that often and when it does no one bothers to record it.

Still Jessica had her shining inspirational moment and set about slowly leaking the plot to the latest blockbuster.

The clever part of the idea being that although hundreds of people allegedly started betting on a character dying, they were all provided with their crisp £50 notes by Jessica and told to use the same betting shop, ensuring that the 'book' (what they call a record kept by a bookmaker of the bets made and of the money paid out) was closed because the 'authorities' thought that there might be a conspiracy to use privileged information and that of course is not allowed in betting circles, it is well know that only the betting shop owners, Jockeys and race horse owners are allowed to use privileged information to win.

Then when the front pages and column inches started to disappear, Jessica came up with her master plan, to sell a copy of the book, which was actually an authentic cover bound around blank pages to a couple of dozy tabloid newspapers, who have been known to buy all sorts of rubbish, although of course I am not making any reference to one of my sponsors The Epoch Newspaper Group, who when they bought the rights to Hitler's Diaries knew what they were doing, which was to buy Hitler's Diaries and then expose them as fakes, which is exactly what they did.

Strangely enough, history, some say, has a habit of repeating itself and one of the tabloid newspaper reporters who 'faking' interest in the latest blockbuster, said that he was going to buy the book and then return it to the publishers without first reading it or using any of the story inside.

Jessica had done so well that she was celebrating in a very fashionable wine bar for almost a week, the story had gone global, being splashed across every television news bulletin and front page in the world, well apart from some Islamic countries where any book that isn't the Koran is frowned upon and they don't actually report news that isn't related to the Koran in the first place.

Interest for the forthcoming blockbuster publishing event shot up and pre-orders reached the expected level and the first edition sold out in a matter of hours, just in time to line the empty shelves with the already printed second edition!

So bearing all of that in mind naturally I decided to copy Jessica's idea, well wouldn't any author in their right mind? I sent a coded message to the same tabloid newspaper reporter offering an advanced copy of my soon to be published Diary and sadly got a short and extremely rude rebuffal, so I have to stop writing today's entry now and find Jessica's phone number, I have a feeling I have a job for her!

Day 355 of My Captivity:

It is strange what you get up to when you are bored, when you are for instance waiting in a departure lounge to board an airplane, and when the call for boarding is announced you feel as though you have accomplished something, but sadly when you sit down in the airplane you suddenly realise that your waiting has just begun and you have the flight to get through and then the transit after you land and only then you can truly say that you have arrived.

Well that is what these last few days in Prison are like for me, I suppose a better analogy would be to say it is like waiting for a Birthday or for Christmas, but as Cats don't celebrate Christmas, mainly I personally believe because they are made to wear ridiculous Pink Tinsel collar adornments, and secondly as you know I have no idea when my Birthday is and can't celebrate it so both of those occasions are meaningless to me.

I am sure that this Cat could be persuaded to celebrate Christmas if treated with more respect, and so I have decided to accept any Christmas presents that my dear readers might like to send me to help me get a better understanding of the Christmas experience. Now although my wrist is probably too small for the average Rolex watch I am sure that one could be made especially for me and then I would always know what time it is, instead of relying on my body clock, which recently, because of all of the late nights keeps setting off its alarm at all sorts of odd times of the day and night when I am either trying to concentrate and write my Diary or worse when I am fast asleep.

So at least you have an idea of the type of Christmas present that I have in mind, and please no Tinsel not even to adorn any presents that you send, because I have, quite reasonably, an aversion to Tinsel.

Happily that does leave a very long list of potential Christmas gifts for the discerning Cat, from his discerning friends and fans, and I was more than happy to present it here, but the dreadfully bossy Mr. John Woodcock seemed to think that inserting my Christmas list here was not 'seemly,' whatever that means, so after sneaking behind my back to Mr. T. A. Leibowitz, 'call me Todd,' who if you ever did, agreed with the tittle-tattling translator, the list was removed and as yet I haven't been able to reinstate it.

If I don't manage to give you my Christmas present list and you are stuck for a present idea for your best friend, no that is me, the Cat, then I would never be offended, like some people I have heard of, if you send money, now just how good of me is that?

Day 356 of My Captivity:

Thinking of presents, and nice things like that, I had a chat with the publisher's representative today and she agreed with my suggestion that we should give my lovely readers a gift, and so I am pleased to announce that with every hard back copy of this Diary there will be a free dust jacket, isn't that wonderful?

I further suggested that if we needed to, when or should I say in the unlikely event of hardback sales ever dipping, we should use this free gift as part of our advertising, because as far as I understand no other hard back book published has ever advertised the dust jacket as a free gift, usually they oddly include the cost of the dust jacket in the sale price.

Which led my thinking in the direction of actually charging for dust jackets on single copies of the Diary sold, but if readers bought multiples of the Diary, say ten copies and above we would give them the jacket as a free gift.

The publisher's representative thought that although this sounded like a cracking idea she wondered if I had ever considered starting a double glazing company, instead of becoming a writer, I have to say I didn't really understand what she was talking about and I am still trying to work out if she was being polite or not, maybe if any reader has a comment they could write to me and let me know if I have been insulted!

DAY 357 OF MY CAPTIVITY:

I had something of a surprise today and although generally one could describe it as a pleasant surprise, there was an underlying tone to it that suggested hard work and long hours, not something that a Cat, well this Cat is really used to.

The emailed surprise was from my publisher's publicity department, well when I say 'department' I am using the word in the most general sense, I think judging by the harassed tone that this lady seems to add to every communication, I presume that she is first of all too busy to cope and worse she works alone, because everything is just rushed.

The surprise took the form of a long list of engagements, chat show appearances, book launches, book signings and press interviews that had been booked especially for me, well I wrote back saying that surely we could reduce the travelling and work load by combining the book launches with book signings, but I didn't get a reply.

With the horror of the headline in mind 'Month One The Cat's Diary Launch' I realised that I was going to be rather busy and therefore over the next few days I thought that I would have a go at getting fit and do some simple exercises because I have a feeling that I am going to have to be at the top of my game, so to speak, in the coming weeks and months, with all of the publicity and whatnot described in the 'first month,' I didn't want to think what the second month of publicity might have to offer and so I didn't bother to read the hundreds of pages which at a glance suggested even more work of the 'hard' variety.

So exercise, just an hour a day, and it goes without saying that I have a 'friend' helping me, well hindering me is probably more accurate.

I did some simple cardio-vascular exercises and every time I stuck my back paws out to stretch the muscles and get the blood pumping around my veins a bit faster, the Dog bit my feet, not hard just playfully, or annoyingly to be more accurate, after ten minutes of that treatment the blood is beginning to pump around your body I can tell you, and it pumps even faster when, after you slap the Dog in the face he chases you around several laps of the house, upstairs and down.

By the time I had finished fifteen minutes of my exercise programme I was gasping for breath and had to call it a day, however if I can find a place on my own to exercise without the 'assistance' of my 'helper' I think I will continue the new regime because after I had got my breath back and my muscles had stopped aching I felt stronger, and that will help won't it?

Day 358 of My Captivity:

Day two of the exercise regime, or is it a programme, I don't know really, but never mind, let's start again. This is day two of my exercises.

It took almost all day to lose the Dog, who wanted to play the chasing game of yesterday and couldn't get it into his head that I wanted to exercise and that didn't involve the need to be bitten or chased.

Still now I am on my own and have been for nearly an hour and what can I say, I need a bath, yes, but there is more, the exercises have gone really well and I am beginning to feel on top of the world, I can feel my muscles beginning to bulge here and there and happily some of them are even bulging in the right places.

Will I be doing more exercises tomorrow? Yes definitely, if I can give the Dog the slip, but now I have to go and give him some time because he is looking all put out hurt and miserable, what an idiot.

Day 359 of My Captivity:

Today is amazing, first of all I managed to get just over an hour to myself before the Dog barged into the bathroom where I was exercising, and without realising I turned round and gave him a hefty whack which sent him yelping off downstairs.

To be honest I didn't mean to hurt the Dog, but I obviously don't know my own strength now that I am beginning to tone up my muscles, I feel like a Horse of a Cat. But now I have to go and soothe the miserable mongrel, who I think is more shocked at my new strength than being injured in the physical sense.

I'll tell you what, oh don't worry about the Dog he is ok, where was I, oh yes, I was going to tell you something, this exercise business makes you hungry, I don't think I have ever eaten so much in all my life. What a good job I am so strong now that no cupboard door is a barrier to food, I can just hook them open and then with a flick of my wrist swing them wide open, incredible, yes I am, aren't I!

The other benefit from working-out, I like that term more than exercising, it sounds more sort of testosterone filled doesn't it? I would guess that girls exercise, but serious body builders work out so that they don't get pushed around, and how many Females do you know who are that daft?

As if to prove my point there is an old 1950's Charles Atlas advert, have you seen it? Well if you haven't it sort of goes like this - a big bully of body builder kicks sand in the face of a little guy and so the little guy goes home and instead of hiding under the bed he orders some bit of cheap, but expensively packaged gym equipment and works out with it. In just seven days, the little Guy tones all of his muscles and is now bigger in every muscle department. With his new found strength and the confidence that has given him he goes back to the beach and kicks sand in the face of the body builder who picked on him originally, which just goes to prove if you work out you will probably become a bully too!

Anyway the advertising slogan for the muscle building bit of equipment sold by Charles Atlas, who himself was a Champion body builder, although I don't know if he was a bully or not, was 'In Just Seven Days I Can Make You A Man.'

My take on it is that I used to be a one stone weakling but now I am two separate Gorillas!

All of that was in just three days, amazing; just think what I could achieve in seven days with the bit of gym equipment.

DAY 360 OF MY CAPTIVITY:

There appear to be what I can only describe as 'preparations' going on today, the Humans are doing really rather authentic impressions of Bees, busily buzzing in and out of rooms around the house being generally annoying and more annoyingly multi-tasking, which I think, if you want my opinion is a rather pointless and stupid thing to do, because in my experience and let's face it that is all I have to go on multi-tasking means that you do several things at once and all badly because you can't give your dedicated best by concentrating on one thing.

And please don't think I am just saying this, I have tried it, I was eating some Cat food earlier and trying to drink a bowl of rather creamy milk at the same time, well the result of this multi-tasking experiment was that I was covered by a muddy mixture of Cat food and milk and so was the floor and if it hadn't been for a tidy minded Dog, someone might have slipped up on the mess that I made, happily that wasn't the case because the Dog made sure that the floor was sparkling with his tongue.

Other experiments in multi-tasking have also ended in frustration and messiness, although I am pleased to say that I can read and go to the loo like any Male Human, who often seem to disappear for hours into the bathroom with the Sunday newspapers, but then one constantly hears, usually on competitive media like the television and Radio, that the standard of the printed media has gone well below the gutter, where presumably they usually aspire to be.

DAY 361 OF MY CAPTIVITY:

Just my luck! It would be a Leap Year, what a stupid name for a year that contains things like an extra day and the soppy summer Olympics? I ask you who is interested in seeing a lot of over developed muscular Humans messing about in various states of undress.

Still having said that in the summer I watched the ladies' Marathon on the television and had to smile at the competitors, they looked very hot and bothered and were dropping like flies.

It goes almost without saying, the great white hope belonging to the British team gave up and retired not more than half way around, how embarrassing is that, but you have to remember that they don't give you any large cash prizes for winning an Olympic event, just a gold medal and that is probably plated, so I quite understood why the 'wonderful' British lady athlete gave up, she could save her strength and make a pile of cash at the next paying Marathon and what is more the press and PR interest for a 'come back' Marathon would be vast, probably upping her 'appearance' money, she couldn't miss could she?

My working out is still working and I have an idea to register to compete in one of those Marathons with the cash prizes, after all I have one advantage against all of the other competitors already don't I, I have an extra pair of legs and that must shorten my odds of winning some serious dosh!

Day 362 of My Captivity:

I slept on the idea of competing in the Marathon, and I think that I will leave that idea for a while because I have just received the updated and amended second month's personal appearances etc., from the publisher's PR 'department.' Busy is an understatement, and the schedule prompted me to give the dear lady at the PR department a call on the telephone and find out if this sort of activity was 'normal,' or was there a degree of desperation creeping in.

Well the answer was frank if not a little off putting and that was that even the most popular writers have the same schedule for a new book launch, because basically the public are so 'bloody' (her word, not mine) fickle that you couldn't rely on the 'B***ards' (again her word not mine) to buy an author's latest book even if the last one was a block buster, Saint JK, not withstanding that is, oddly I got the impression that when she mentioned St. JK, that the PR lady actually genuflected to the newly canonised patron saint of book publishing.

There were other reasons too and that was that my Diary was one of those new genre types of book, a 'cross-over' book that it was hoped would appeal to adult children and childish adults and so it was important to really 'get out there with it!'

Wow talk about knowing your market, I just listened in fascination, this lady was good, although I was a little put off by the idea of my readership falling into just two categories, and sorry dear readers, not very flattering ones either.

Always remember that after having completed this book launch, it is likely that I probably will have met you personally and that means we are even firmer friends, where as the publisher is only an acquaintance of ours, and firm friends are forever, of course I would give you one of my winning smiles now, but previously I have mentioned how awfully off putting that would be.

Day 363 of My Captivity:

More working out today, I am worried that I will be worn to a frazzle by the two months work that I can now review right in front of me, in their latest incarnation, the updating is constant and it occurs to me that I will have absolutely no idea where I am at any time over the next few months because everything will be just a blur, I am surprised that the PR schedule isn't written in red, the colour of blood, goodness know the publishers seem to want every other bit of me?

Still this afternoon, I put my feet up and spent the rest of the day surfing the Internet, I haven't done that for a while and it was rather restful. I was looking at property as you ask, yes I am looking for a little bolt hole, somewhere to put my feet up in comfort and invest some of my hard earned cash in, well actually your hard earned cash, because you are the dear, wonderful, lovely and very generous people who will buy the book.

And don't forget to buy the merchandise too, we are all relying on you, in fact thousands of people are counting on you, including youngsters in the Far East who will earn a dollar a day making special Cat Marathon trainers, yes we have just signed a fantastic deal with, well I can't say who with, because they were rather coy about how much their 'Far East Operatives' earn a day, as if they were over paying them.

It all happened after the publishers mentioned my 'desire' to run in a Marathon and then N, no sorry I can't use the company's name can I, decided that a Cat running a Marathon would fit well with a demographic whom they find hard to address with advertising. It wasn't until later when I saw the dummy product that I realised I was going to be promoting baby trainers, but still hey a buck is still a buck isn't it, and to some people around the world it is a day's wages.

Still isn't it wonderful that I will have somewhere in the sun to recover after my trials, which have been many and various, tell you what, at some stage you will have to visit me! There as you can tell I am preparing myself of stalkers, well you have to find me first and then you can stalk me all you like!

Day 364 of My Captivity:

Well I am keeping myself busy as everything begins to get more and more complicated and involved at the publishers and at the offices of my agent, 'finessing' is what it is called apparently, although I think I might have another word for it.

An email arrived after dozens of telephone calls, some of which were conference and some were individual and guess what, all of the first two months engagements for the book launch seem to have been shuffled and changed yet again, compressing some book signings and book launches into the same day, I wonder what clever individual thought of that brilliant idea, yes I am blushing.

The problem is that reading the new mile long email with the list of the engagements there seem to be more engagements, which I don't think was in my original plan when I suggested combining some events.

There is also a very strange event pencilled in at the moment, I am going to unveil a monument at NASA to Felix who was apparently the first Cat in space (reading Felix's biography which was kindly attached with the dummy press release), a rather off putting fact is that Felix, if that was indeed his name, was the only Cat ever to go into space and survive, although of course others were sent and I wonder whether they were asked if they actually wanted to go before they were blasted to oblivion.

So, some would say 'lucky' Felix was sent into space by the French on October 18, 1963, he was a black and white stray from the streets of Paris, which is a novel and very French way to deal with stray animals loose on the streets isn't it.

Mind you it is a testament to just how much the French like Cats that no other nation thought that Cats would make good astronauts and that there is no actual record of whether Felix was actually called Felicette, which is a little off putting, mind you not as off putting as being blasted into space at hundreds of miles an hour from a test range in Algeria.

I read all this about poor Cat Felix in the PR blurb and I thought that I would share it with you:

'The capsule in the rocket's nose cone separated at 120 miles altitude and descended by parachute. Electrodes in the Cat's brain transmitted neurological impulses to a ground station. The Cat was recovered.'

Wow the French really treated that poor Feline to it all didn't they; imagine being the first Cat in space and the first animal to have vivisection in space too. Still the French are just nice marvellous people who like to have a lot of world 'firsts' because it helps with their nation's prestige. Of course it took the Americans and those nice people at NASA to actually erect a memorial to the brave stray didn't it!

DAY 365 OF MY CAPTIVITY:

I emailed the publishers back and said that if I didn't do anything else on the whistle stop tour (actually I wish I could think of another term for the tour and not whistle stop, because the way it is panning out whistle stop just doesn't sound fast enough), then I had to do the unveiling of the statue to let's call him, Felix.

I considered it to be my civic duty, me a successful, or soon to be Feline writer paying homage to a brave and unsung Feline hero. Not only that, the PR and photo - op would be too good to miss, and maybe with all of the world's press in attendance the French might want to honour the little guy too!

If they do they might ask me to unveil a statue to him in France and if I could get assurances that I wouldn't be harmed in France I would jump at the chance of all the extra publicity, but I don't fancy getting mugged by a few Garlic crunchers and used for any odd and cruel experiments and so the assurances for my personal safety would have to cast iron! I don't want to be used for any experiments or what have you, and they currently have a great big plane that has only flown twice and both times rather worryingly without passengers!

I can just imagine being bundled into a sack, with tens (metric dozens, you understand) of Cats all with electrodes sticking out of their ears, and then that sack being added to thousands of sacks stuffed into the passenger compartments of the airliner so that the new behemoth can take off with dispensable Cats for its first flight with a full compliment of passengers, that is not the way I like to fly at all!

DAY 366 OF MY CAPTIVITY:

I overheard them saying it was New Year's Day today, that can only mean I have been here for a whole year, apart from the little mistake when I spent a week at Mrs. O'Riley's Dog Kennels and Death Camp and a few days as a fugitive on the run.

Mrs. R's was a place of undisguised horror and to make it worse I was stuck there with the idiot Dog, but I can't bring myself to think about that torrid experience again. No this is a new year and I have a secret which was emailed to me today of all days!

Can I trust you to keep the secret if I tell you? Let me think about that for a minute because to trust any Human is a big step for a Cat and I suppose vice versa!

DAY 367 OF MY CAPTIVITY:

I have sent some pretty stern emails today I can tell you! Where is my Limousine? It is about time that I was 'extracted,' don't you just love that word.

The Defense Department uses the word when they do a number of things, from pulling troops back from behind enemy lines to big withdrawals, not that I am saying the Army get involved in many of them, because if I did I might be in hot water considering most soldiers are much bigger than me, so to suggest that they retreat a lot would not be very sensible would it?

(I am using the American spelling of Defense here because the British Defence Department don't seem to use the term 'extracted' as often as the Americans do, as far as I know, well that is what it said on the back of the cereal packet that I read).

Have you noticed just how much information is available to the curious eye on the side, back, tops and even bottoms of packets of food and that phenomenon is not restricted to Human food either, tins of Cat food are covered with idiot looking Cats, yes but that isn't what I meant, there is so much information on them you just wouldn't believe it.

But as any Politician or State Department Official should but won't tell you, information, no matter how much you may have of it, is pretty useless if it is written in code and I am thinking here about simple word substitutions, where everyday words or phrases like, 'poison, for God's sake don't drink this,' may get changed for something less dramatic like, 'seek medical help if swallowed.'

There are legions of words that have been substituted for more normal ones too so that the ingredients of a product can either be made to sound grander or even disguised completely.

For instance there is a lot of water in Shampoo, well you would expect that it is after all rather runny, but look on the label of all Shampoo bottles and you will find something called 'Aqua,' which is as we all know (although the sly manufacturers think we don't), 'Aqua' is 'Water' in Latin and probably the same in some other non-English languages too. So why when does the list of ingredients have one Latin word and the rest in English I would love to know? Would it be that the manufacturer doesn't want the consumer to know there is water in Shampoo, and if so why. Just think how confusing it might be if more people read the small print on containers of stuff, again using the 'Aqua' example because they would expect to see 'Aqua' in Shampoos, but not on Italian bottled water like 'Aqua Minerale,' why do people complicate life, I wonder?

Another example I saw was in the bathroom when I was having a smooch around the shelves the other day and that was on the back of a tube of toothpaste, the toothpaste was one of those new wonder ones that promises to make your teeth whiter and shinier although they use the present tense and stick an 'n' in between their version of whiter and shinier.

Now reading the back of a tube of toothpaste is a little like reading a short recipe for Dr. Jekyll's refreshing and smoking elixir that turned him into Mr. Hyde, there are things like Disodium Phosphate, which you would expect after all this is a chemical formulation and you have to have chemicals in it don't you and it goes without saying that they have water in the formulation too, disguised as 'Aqua' (of course you would expect that wouldn't you!), but hidden in all of the complicated chemical sounding words is one that I recognised and thought 'oh look they are at it again,' there is 'Mica' in the toothpaste that buffs your teeth and helps to make and keep them white.

'Mica' of course is a type of 'Sand' and sand is used to do all sorts of things as well as keep kids happy in pits, although I would like to stress that the pits should be open and never filled in.

You maybe familiar with some of the uses of sand, but if you aren't, let me give you some hints, Sandblasting. Sand, sorry 'Mica' is really abrasive and great for shining things, so remember that when you are cleaning your teeth in the mornings and evenings. Happily Cats don't have to clean their teeth everyday, we chew things to keep them clean still, each to his own as they say.

Day 368 of My Captivity:

Well I am feeling reflective today, I suppose that working out might do that to you, I definitely seem to have more blood rushing more easily to my brain so that might be the reason.

I was thinking of all of the things that we have shared over this Cat year, we really have been through it, well that is if you have 'lived' what you have read. If not then I guess I have been busy and you have been bored stiff and that wouldn't be any good because you will have to wade through another two, possibly three books in the series.

Then it struck me if you don't like this Diary, how are we going to get you to buy the others in the series, they will be after all a set, and that is good because that will ensure that the 'collectors' among you buy all of the books, but what about the rest of you, mmmh!

Well that turned out to be a problem that was bigger than my brain could deal with, and so I made another call to the publishers and was delighted with the answer, it was simple, innovative and very, very clever.

Apparently according to Steve in the art department, who by the sound of it plays computer games all day long and sub-contracts the book jacket (free to everyone who buys ten books) design out to people he called 'designers' the design for the series had been incorporated into the realisation of the initial concept, I nodded off here, until Steve woke me up shouting, 'got you, you Evil Elven Half Lord from the Planet Zucos.' But apparently that was an Evil Elven Half Lord from a game he was playing and not a reference to any title that I may have been awarded without my knowledge.

Anyway like me, Steve got back to the point eventually, if 'a punter' as he called my precious readers bought just the one book and placed it on his or her bookshelf then the spine design of my Diary was such that it would look really awful, if however the 'punter' (still his word and not mine) bought the second book then the spine design looked a little better and so on until the 'punter' had 'shelled out' (his words again) for the whole set and then the appearance of the spines together on the shelf would look brilliant.

What a clever man don't you think? No not Steve although apparently killing the Evil Elven Half Lord is no mean feat, I meant the designer though, he is the clever one.

So there is yet another reason to invest in the complete set of my books.

Day 369 of My Captivity:

So everything is ready, I have packed, unpacked, repacked, unpacked the repacking and finally packed everything again until I am literally dizzy, but have managed to fit everything into my suitcase neatly.

I have also begun the torture of trying to explain to the Dog that I have to go somewhere and that I maybe gone a long time.

He is now convinced that I am dying and won't leave my side, except to find things to give me to make my journey to the after life more comfortable, so far I will be able to gnaw on three bones of varying ages, a rope Dog tug thing that is almost too heavy for me to carry, although I was made to pick it up and carry it until the daft Dog remembered that I was dying, and if I have room in my pockets I am welcome to take the Dog basket because he knows I have always liked sleeping in it.

What can you do with someone who is both kind and so incredibly stupid at the same time, well I did what I thought was best and thanked him very much and told him that it would be best if he looked after all of the things he wanted me to have and although they would still be 'mine' because he had given them to me, he could have full use of them.

He brightened up then and said that what he was going to miss most of all was the fact that I did all of his thinking for him and he liked that a lot.

I have probably said this before, I am going to miss the fool, but fame and fortune beckon, and I have a greater responsibility now, than just one Dog to look after, I have an enormous readership to entertain, and like the Dog I will always treasure all of my readers, even if they are Human, and I know it would be best if I did the thinking for them too, which although it is a big responsibility, I know I can cope with it, and will give my Dog and Humans time to enjoy their lives unburdened by too much conscious thought!

DAY 370 OF MY CAPTIVITY:

Have you seen the size of this Diary? I must have written enough words now to finish the Diary soon, and I am sure that for you to get here on this page that you have read quite enough, we should finished the hard work now shouldn't we! But it has been fun.

Let me try that paragraph again, I should have finished this hard work now and you have done very well to read to the end of my Diary, it just proves that you like it, doesn't it, you are not some kind of weirdo who hasn't liked the Diary from the beginning but stuck at it because you are mad and like inflicting pain on yourself are you?

No my readers aren't like that, they are cuddly, confident readers who like um, er well like Cats for one, and there aren't many Cats like me are there, what do you mean thank goodness!

I will always be grateful to you dear readers for buying this book and starting your collection of my books, just please don't ever stop collecting them will you?

DAY 371 OF MY CAPTIVITY:

Well I have finally done it, I have escaped, or I will have escaped in a few days time when the limo arrives to whisk me away to America thanks to Mr. Leibowitz, 'call me Todd' who secured the publishing deal and a deal with a Movie studio who want to immortalise me, sounds both painful and lucrative at the same time, bring it on is what I say!

When I got the confirming email I was smiling like a C list star at a photo op I can tell you, but then the excitement subsided, I couldn't tell anyone because to tell anyone would be to endanger my escape, let's face it if I had mentioned it to the Dog, he would have only talked to the Parrot and no secret is safe with that brightly coloured blabber beak. Not only that I do actually like the Dog and I was feeling a little sad that I would never see him again, after all the paths of a Feline literary and movie star and a common Canine are hardly likely to cross once I have left are they?

DAY 372 OF MY CAPTIVITY:

Not long to go now and I am as excited as a Bungee jumper before the trouser filling experience of jumping. My heart is in my mouth and my stomach is just churning like a Bungee jumpers would be if they have any sense.

Still there is one difference and that is that I am not daft enough to jump off somewhere high up, or indeed to eventually get pushed when the people you are with get bored of listening to you saying, 'oh I don't think I can do this!'

Oh no this is one Cat who likes to keep his paws firmly on the ground if possible, although of course occasionally all Cats have to climb incredibly high wobbly swaying things and usually have to be rescued just because they are 'there,' well we wouldn't be Cats if we didn't would we and I am sure that the Mountaineers among my readers will identify with that sentiment.

Having said all of that the pain of waiting to be freed is, how can I describe it? Painful, yes that is the right word, have you noticed how the tension and painfulness of a situation makes one babble nonsense, it is almost as though I am turning into a Dog, I am going to miss him, but not the Parrot or the Humans.

Ok, ok I will stop babbling and go and do some last minute packing, although I will be travelling light because I expect to get everything that I need when I get to the states and of course I have already packed the meagre possessions that I possess.

No you are right I am babbling again I will stop, take a rest and maybe even have a sleep, although I have been that excited recently that sleep is the last thing on my mind, but I had better stop rambling or this work of genius will start to take a nose dive.

DAY 373 OF MY CAPTIVITY:

Oh dear! Apparently across the world there are enormous unsold stacks of my Diary towering over bookshop shoppers.

Why? Well because of the enormous hype, television advertising and PR coverage of the launch of my Diary, billions of copies were ordered by confident booksellers expecting to make the killing of the season, it used to be the killing of the year, but let's face it a blockbuster comes along like a number thirty eight bus nowadays, not exactly regularly but as if it is pretending to work to some sort of timetable.

The Diary sales are a disaster, recriminations are being passed around in one direction as the buck goes around in the other, but I have a feeling that the buck is going to stop in the same place as the recriminations, here with me, oh dear what could have gone so wrong. I have everything going for me don't I? Literary genius, good looks, style, and I am house trained, I can't believe that such a disaster could befall me.

At the moment no one is talking to me, apart from newspaper reporters and television news crews who want my side of the story and to know who was responsible for the whole disaster.

I could describe my state of mind as unbalanced at the moment if I had time to actually consider my situation, Mr. T. A. Leibowitz, 'call me Todd,' has already been on the line and when he announced himself he said Mr. T. A. Leibowitz, ominously there was no 'call me Todd,' today.

He seemed to take ages to say what he wanted to say, slowly choosing his words and spitting them out through gritted teeth, finally after he had described his disappointment in me, and how much he was out of pocket, he told me that he had some very powerful but ill mannered friends, who he lovingly referred to as 'the boys,' and I could expect a visit from them, although I wouldn't have to make an appointment with them as they liked to spring surprises on people who Mr. T. A. Leibowitz considered had wronged him.

Mmmh! My situation was beyond dire, I had to do something, but I was all out of ideas and I was biting the Dog blanket hard expecting any minute a large group of Mr. T. A. Leibowitz's 'boys' to turn up and begin bouncing this Cat around a room, which wasn't big enough to swing it in.

The taste of the Dog's blanket was foul, hang on if I am biting the Dog's blanket then I am probably asleep and that means I am probably having a dream, no not a dream, a nightmare.

Well they say you should reverse your dreams and I suppose that applies to your nightmares as well, now that is handy, because what had so frightened me was only a nightmare!

I suppose that I am worried and excited and my sub-conscious was playing tricks on me, reality is going to be the opposite of my dream/nightmare, surely? I do hope so because I have a feeling that Mr. T. A. Leibowitz, 'call me Todd,' probably does have some 'boys' in Monkey suits somewhere who sort out little problems and inconveniences!

DAY 374 OF MY CAPTIVITY:

The flight wasn't quite what I expected, indeed I had expected to be sitting in the comfort of a first class cabin snuggly dozing in between meals in a large leather first class seat which as evening fell outside at 35,000 feet would convert into a bed, but oh no not for me the individual attention of a smartly dressed cabin attendant, no sadly not, I was in the baggage hold in a cage marked in large red letter 'livestock,' now correct me if I am wrong, but 'livestock' is a term for farm animals isn't it?

DAY 375 OF MY CAPTIVITY:

My dear friends I am now settling into the penthouse nicely thank you, I have even got over the phase of pressing all the buttons on the handheld computer console which remotely controls the curtains, the television and a catalogue of other equipment which appears at the flick of a button from the wall, or the floor or even the ceiling, but as I said I have had enough of pressing a button to see what happens, especially the green button because that one summons the butler and I keep forgetting and have summoned him nine times already, he says it is ok and not to worry 'sir,' but I have a feeling he is the sort of person who wouldn't keep forgetting being summoned and may even bear a grudge.

So I have my feet up and I am going to some serious jet-lag unlagging, good night and good day to the world, I am in Cat heaven and intend now to have a little sleep and some dreams, which I plan to realise tomorrow.

Day 376 of My Captivity:

In a need to finish this Diary quickly for the publishers I have developed a new and revolutionary typing technique, four pawed typing, it is alarmingly fast, and if one is careful can be reasonably accurate, letting the spell checker mop up the little problems and suggest lots of American words that don't really resemble the original English ones.

There is a drawback, well there are several drawbacks apart from the spelling issue, the major one is falling over onto the keyboard and typing several paragraphs of total gibberish, mind you I bet that there are some people who will think that I fell over on the keyboard at the beginning of this Diary and only regained my balance and composure at the end, so that I could type just two words properly, 'the end.'

Still I have had some fun writing this, even though it hasn't all been plain sailing, as they say when at sea, or on a lake as long as you are in a boat, I suppose.

If you ask me if I would do it all again? I would say 'not likely, thank you,' after the books and the films, I know I will just want to take the money and leg it.

Yes I have ideas for the next two books as I think I have mentioned, travelling the world in considerable comfort and style for a Travelogue and then sitting somewhere warm, comfortable and Prawn rich to write my Memoirs. Then after a few attempts at beating the World Record for eating Prawns, I plan to slip into luxurious obscurity and not the 'C' list variety, oh no I will retire and become a celebrity United Nations ambassador so you can tell that I plan total obscurity.

Day 377 of My Captivity:

More visitors today, but these are visitors with a difference, they are my visitors even so I have to say that I view them in the same way as I viewed the Captor's visitors, I do wish that they would go away.

The first set arrived before I had finished breakfast, which at least shows that they were keen I suppose and they were also odd and that was annoying, I had specifically asked the security people not to allow odd Humans any access to my penthouse peace.

This 'happy' couple apparently had got passed security by proving that they were to be my personal assistant and road manager and as they proudly explained they were the best in the business, at one time running a 'family' business dedicated to fulfilling the needs of all of their celebrity clients because at one time they had been married, well that was the gist of what they said because the both talked at the same time as well as managing to contradict each other and argue, my head was reeling.

Apparently they had started their unique business and then things had just snowballed as had the arguments, they agreed to split up, but they decided to get married first, yes it was that sort of relationship.

He was not so bad as personal assistants go, I have to say, and as they were both about to 'go' when I could edge my way to a phone and get my agent to sack them, I tried to smile and listen to them, but they were too wrapped up in themselves to notice my most grimacing Cat smile.

For a road manager she was unique, so she said and had a problem with maps, though like most Female Humans she couldn't read a map, she would just borrow other people's maps and forget to give them back.

In fact it wasn't only maps she had a problem with, she would do the same with map books too.

Apparently sometimes her conscience would get the better of her collecting instincts and she would return a map or a map book, only to find that the gesture was rebuffed, usually with a note saying that she should return the map she had given back to the rightful owner and oh by the way could she also return the map she had borrowed several years ago as she probably had a good selection of maps and probably didn't need all of them.

At last I managed to call my agent and my visitors were ushered away almost immediately by security.

Well I had learned my first lesson in America if this was the type of staff who others appointed for you, there was only one thing to do and that was to interview and appoint staff oneself and I knew I could look forward to even more visitors and my heart sank, but I don't see why we all have to be disconsolate and so I am not going to bore you with those details, yes I am nice, that is what I have been telling you for ages now!

DAY 378 OF MY CAPTIVITY:

I hope that throughout this Diary you have noticed that I have maintained my integrity and because of that you have grown to respect me. Unlike some Diaries and other books you will not find me placing products in the narrative just because I have been paid large amounts of money by a multinational corporations to do so, oh no! I believe that Diaries or any other literature is no place for product placement!

No I have not been paid to mention any products in this way, contrary to the rumours which have been circulating in the, and I use this word advisedly, 'gutter' press.

However I do feel that there is a need for me to put the record straight. Some organisations have been keen to sponsor my lavish expenses and in return I have mentioned them, as I have eaten their delicious food, made calls on their mobile phones or sat on top of their running shoe boxes for a better view.

Obviously some of the companies who have offered cash and product sponsorship might be more interested in communication with you the reader through me, than with my well being and I do take the point that Dr. Schultz corn plasters are not a product that I would use regularly, however I believe that is because my paws don't suffer from corns more than it is to do with 'greed' as some critics have suggested.

I know that if I did ever get a corn then I have several thousand plasters to use on it and a healthy five figure sponsorship deal over two years into the bargain.

I am sure that most of the bad publicity surrounding my lifestyle and enormous earnings from this Diary before it is even published as some critics have mentioned is unfounded and unfair, you have to remember that like many famous writers I have suffered greatly to bring this Diary to you and surely now I deserve a few of the home comforts that most enjoy as a right?

Happily if this controversy does begin to get me down and I feel depressed as a result, we are just about to sign an enormous deal with a large pharmaceutical company who make anti-depressants and so I will probably be ok, although as an artist I beg you to keep your criticism to a minimum please, there is only so much a gentle soul like me can take!

DAY 379 OF MY CAPTIVITY:

Someone told me that a Diary should be for one year and that one year was 365 days long, no one told me that fact when I was writing this Diary, so this is a big Diary with at least 379 days in it, you have to laugh, as they say, 'they' being Humans I suppose. I have to stress that I am writing a Cat's Diary and a Cat's year is a minimum of 379 days and a maximum of exactly then number of days it decides a year should be, still I suppose now that I have been told that my readers may find this fact a little odd maybe I should feel just a little embarrassed and I might well feel like some time in the future, but not at this moment.

Still I have had a few embarrassing moments recently in my new apartment, like when I found out that one didn't have to sit in a dark room all night because there are things called lights controlled by light switches, not that they are much good to me of course, this world seems just to be designed for the benefit of Humans, really!

Sadly I have also discovered more about Human's years apparently a Human year is from January 1st through to December 31st, with all sorts of strangely numbered days in between called dates, in fact some days not only have a numbered date they are special and get given names like New Year's Day and Good Friday.

Well I don't know who has decided that some days need names as well as numbers but I think it is very confusing, let's take Good Friday for a moment, who decided that this Friday, which wait for it actually is a different Friday in April most years, was any better than any other Fridays in April or indeed any other Friday during the rest of the year and why did they decide it was, no one seems to know?

Some days that have been given names are special because they are days before other special days, Christmas Eve for example, but let's face it Christmas Eve is a bit of a dead loss really, it doesn't finish quickly enough in most people's opinion, especially in Children's opinions they want Christmas day to dawn as early as possible.

Another 'Eve' sort of day, that I heard about which is special is Halloween.

Now have you spotted something odd already, the name for this day (which is always the 30th of October so at least it is less erratic and mobile than Good Friday), is not hallow Eve or even Halloween Eve it is Halloween although technically it is the day before All Hallows Day or All Saint's Day and therefore should be an Eve.

Yes I am sorry to say, Hallows Day or all Saint's Day also has two names just to confuse you.

That is not that important though well not as important as following the Christmas Eve example. You would have thought that Halloween (we'll use that spelling I think) would have been an Eve and not an 'En, why an 'En anyway you may ask you? Well to answer my own question here is the answer.

Just to add a little extra confusion Halloween can also be spelt Hallowe'en! Really the people who invented this language were off their heads although as yet I haven't worked out what they were taking.

And another thing! Who do you know, who goes round saying 'Happy All Hallow's day?'

When was the last time you got a card with 'Have a Wonderful All Hallows day, to You and All the Family,' you didn't did you? Why, because it is a very unimportant day, these days!

Now you think I am wrong about Halloween being what I have just said it is! Don't you? The reason you think I am wrong is because I am a Cat and also that Humans couldn't possibly be that dense and that is after reading almost all of my Diary, well you Humans never learn and so I am not surprised.

However I am right, I promise, Halloween is really the night before All Saint's Day or wait for it even more obscure All Hallows Day, but as I said who has ever heard of that, so is it really important in the scheme of things, no it isn't especially if you have some Prawns to share with a peckish Cat!

I had heard of Christmas day it was only the other day in fact, and to be honest it wasn't that special! I got a present or two and some nice Cat Choc drops, which were rather tasty.

One of the rather tatty presents had what I now know is called Cat Nip in it, I understand that Cat Nip is used a lot in Cat toys to make them seem special, when they are really cheap poorly made rubbish.

So what the people were saying about the length of a year, well apart from Leap Years and I don't think we have time to cover those now because they are reasonably rare, is that people who keep Diaries usually begin Jan 1st and then stop on the last day of the year only to begin again on another Jan 1st, sounds mad if you ask me. So if you buy this Diary you will automatically get better value than most people who buy and have bought Diaries in the past, which is good news isn't?

If you think it is good news then you have probably read all the way to this point in my Diary, the majestic day numbered 379, I actually don't know why I like the number 379 it is much bigger than anything I can imagine but all the same it seems a nice sort of number. If it was a Human they may say of it that it had a good home. It is just that sort of number, well it is to my way of thinking and I know that my way of thinking is very different to a Human's.

Day 380 of My Captivity:

I was thinking, I have done a lot of that recently, probably because I have given up trying to escape and taken up thinking instead, although I have to say with hindsight if with some of the escape attempts I had done more thinking then I might have (A)

Escaped and (B) Not caused so much damage here and there, still anyone can be clever with hindsight can't they!

I have to say even now when I am settled in this penthouse that belongs to Mr. Leibowitz, 'call me Todd' which I think is a very strange and rather wonderful name. I still want my freedom.

If Mr. Leibowitz, 'call me Todd' is right, then with the 'loot' I think is the word he used (must be some sort of lawyer terminology) I am getting I will be 'free and clear.' Which I took to mean that I can be completely free and I hope sooner rather than later.

Being free would suit me right down to the ground, although Mr. Leibowitz, 'call me Todd' said that if demand is strong for this 'cookie' (more lawyer terminology this time for my Diary), we will have to think of a sequel and a prequel and more movies, but he did say that I would get help with those, 'Ghosts' were the people he was thinking of getting to help me. I think I would have to have help with all of that too, but I don't know if Ghosts would be much help!

Mr. Leibowitz, 'call me Todd' that is a silly name you know! Being a Cat, and of course you must know that we Cats don't have names, well apart from the ones that you Humans give us and they are just plain puerile, in fact I find Human's names fascinating, I heard of a lady called Florence Foster-Jenkins, what a way to enter a room, 'I am Florence Foster-Jenkins,' people would have to look at anyone called that just to see if she was real, or being serious.

Actually I believe that if there was one person in the world who was serious it would have been Ms. Foster-Jenkins because she was famous for her complete lack of singing ability, and yet she truly and seriously believed that she was a wonderful singer and entertainer. Despite her patent lack of ability, she was firmly convinced of her greatness and that is important in a performer after all.

She compared herself to the great sopranos of her day and dismissed the laughter which often came from the audience during her performances as coming from her rivals consumed by 'professional jealousy.' Although she was aware of her critics, and apparently once said 'People may say I can't sing, but no one can ever say I didn't sing.'

It goes without saying that the lady was probably slightly mad and I have a feeling it was the stress of having that name, still it could be worse, her accompanist and partner in musical crime was none other than a lady called Cosme McMoon, poor soul!

One of their famous recordings is called Murder on the High C's, you have to laugh don't you? Well you do if you understand anything about music, unlike either Florence Foster-Jenkins or Cosme McMoon, and me, obviously.

DAY 381 OF MY CAPTIVITY:

Well this is the last page well it might not be the last page of my Diary because I don't actually know how long the entry for today will be, so let's call it the last day of my Diary which will be the first instalment of a series of diaries once I have finished concluding a mega million deal for the 'prequel' film rights, I think I might just have to write the sequel's sequel, well it is the done thing isn't it after all where would we be without lots of sequels?

I am free now and that is nice, actually luxury is wonderful and I recommend that you try it sometime. I have to say that I am so very pleased to be 'out,' but only in the sense that I have escaped and not in any other way at all.

Obviously getting out is my biggest success, but I am quite proud of the fact that I have written a book that is just a little heavier than my favourite Dictionary, the Collins English Dictionary, which though not the catchiest title for a book it is one of the very few books that you will ever really need in life apart from this Diary of course, which probably goes without saying but oops I have said it now.

Just a word to the guys at Collins though, I caught sight of the latest cover, well what can I say? What were you thinking of, please don't make this wonderful Dictionary look too jazzy, like say the Encarta Dictionary because it will lose its credibility, how did you guess that the Encarta Dictionary people weren't interested in sponsoring me?

So things seem to have worked out rather well really, the Diary is set to sell well, the critics who had review copies a while ago raved about it, the sponsorship deals are getting bigger and more lucrative and Mr. Leibowitz, 'call me Todd' has just told me that new movie offers are beginning to 'firm up', 'Hollywood is Hungry' is how he described the frantic Mogul feeding frenzy that has broken out for the movie rights to books that I didn't even know I was going to write, apparently five million dollars is a record for a first novel by a Cat or more accurately for a first book by a novel Cat.

Mr. Leibowitz, 'call me Todd' has already asked me if I would be prepared to write a sequel to a novel I didn't even know I was going to be writing? Well that is premature if you ask me.

So I have finished my Diary, or I will have soon, actually the reason why you are reading the entry for today, now is that I had the opportunity to do some corrections before the final print run, it goes without saying that the Translator Panicked when he was told that there was a little more work to do, I don't think he likes work, or is it that he just doesn't like working with me!

I do hope that we can get a different translator for the next book and all of the blockbusters to follow.

Thinking about a sequel to my unwritten novel for a moment, yes is the answer, especially if the gelt is good (as Mr. Leibowitz, 'call me Todd' would say, meaning if we got paid well).

Mind you writing a sequel to this Diary would mean going back into captivity though, and I can't say I fancy that to be honest, still I have an idea and it is, as Mr. Leibowitz, 'call me Todd' would say a bit of a doozie, a Peach (something that is really good for those of you who maybe just a little thicker than the door).

I am definitely going to write a Travelogue! A Travelogue is a record of a journey to those who are short of a clue. Just think it would be like an all expenses paid holiday, that would be great! It goes without saying, first class all the way the kind of life a Cat deserves.

Of course you can imagine that it is going to probably take a year or two of total comfort and enjoyment to complete the 'research,' yes I am really beginning to warm to the idea!

The End, thank goodness and please don't show me another keyboard for a long while!

LaVergne, TN USA
12 November 2010
204604LV00004B/103/P